IFRS: A Quick Reference Guide

D1325190

Dedicated to the memory of my father

IFRS: A Quick Reference Guide

Robert J. Kirk

ELSEVIER

Amsterdam • Boston • Heidelberg • London • New York • Oxford
Paris • San Diego • San Francisco • Singapore • Sydney • Tokyo
CIMA Publishing is an imprint of Elsevier

CIMA

PUBLISHING

CIMA Publishing is an imprint of Elsevier
The Boulevard, Langford Lane, Kidlington, Oxford OX5 1GB, UK
Linacre House, Jordan Hill, Oxford OX2 8DP, UK
30 Corporate Drive, Suite 400, Burlington, MA 01803, USA

Notice
No responsibility is assumed by the publisher for any injury and/or damage to persons
or property as a matter of products liability, negligence or otherwise, or from any use
or operation of any methods, products, instructions or ideas contained in the material
herein.

British Library Cataloguing in Publication Data
A catalogue record for this book is available from the British Library

ISBN: 978-1-85617-545-6

For information on all CIMA publications visit
our website at www.elsevierdirect.com

Typeset by Charon Tec Ltd., A Macmillan Company. (www.macmillansolutions.com)

Printed and bound in Great Britain

Working together to grow
libraries in developing countries
www.elsevier.com | www.bookaid.org | www.sabre.org

ELSEVIER   BOOK AID
International   Sabre Foundation

Contents

About the author

Robert Kirk BSc (Econ), FCA, CPA qualified as a chartered accountant in 1976. He was trained in Belfast with Price Waterhouse & Co., and subsequently spent two years in industry in a subsidiary of Shell (UK) and four further years in practice. In 1980, he was appointed as a director of a private teaching college in Dublin where he specialised in the teaching of professional accounting subjects. He later moved into the university sector, and is currently Professor of Financial Reporting in the Department of Accounting at the University of Ulster.

He has been lecturing on the CIMA Mastercourses presentations *Recent Accounting Standards* and *Accounting Standards in Depth* since 1985. He has also presented continuing professional education courses for the Institute of Chartered Accountants in Ireland over the same period specialising in the delivery of programmes on both national and international accounting standards.

His publications to date, in addition to numerous professional journal articles, include two books on company law in Northern Ireland, co-authorship with University College Dublin of the first Survey of Irish Published Accounts, a joint publication with Coopers & Lybrand on the legislation enacting the 7th European Directive into UK legislation, four editions of *Accounting Standards in Depth*, *UK Financial Reporting Standards: A Quick Reference Guide*, *International Reporting Standards in Depth Volume 1 Theory and Practice* and *Volume 2 Solutions*, and two Financial Reporting publications for the CIMA Study Packs.

Preface

The pace of development in financial reporting has accelerated sharply during the last few years, especially since the decision of the European Commission to force the consolidated financial statements of listed companies to be prepared under the auspices of the International Accounting Standards Board (IASB) from 2005 onwards. The pace of progress shows no sign of abating and it has become increasingly difficult for the professionally qualified accountant to keep abreast of the changes.

IFRS: A Quick Reference Guide examines the standards in a unique and detailed way and it has been written with a broad readership in mind. Each chapter includes a brief summary of the relevant accounting standards in force together with the proposed changes contained within outstanding exposure drafts. The standards are illustrated by incorporating live examples of companies applying the standards. These are largely taken from published accounts in the United Kingdom but a number of European companies are also included, where appropriate.

The book commences with an introduction to the standard-setting process. As well as briefly looking at the standard-setting process it covers brief resumes of the role of the main bodies in the process. Chapter 1 briefly examines the *Framework for the Preparation and Presentation of Financial Statements* which underpins the practice of financial accounting and later how those ideas are incorporated in IAS 1 *Presentation of financial information*. The second chapter covers the standards which apply to non-current assets. Chapters 3 and 4 take asset valuation further and investigate inventories, intangible assets, leases and construction contracts.

Chapter 5 is devoted entirely to the coverage of liabilities. Taxation is covered in Chapter 15. Performance measurement is covered in Chapter 6 and encompasses coverage of revenue, earnings per share, the presentation of discontinued operations and changes in accounting policies. Although part of performance measurement, employee costs have been treated separately as they include not only employee benefits in general but also share-based payment. In addition the disclosure required by pension schemes is also included in the chapter.

Foreign trading is examined in Chapter 8 and includes the general standard on transacting and translating from foreign currencies but also the specialist standard on how to account for entities in hyperinflationary economies. Cash flow statements as one of the primary documents is covered separately in its own right in Chapter 9.

One of the longest chapters covers all the four group accounting standards – on associates, joint ventures, goodwill and business combinations. A number of disclosure standards, including related parties and segment reporting are examined in Chapter 10. Chapter 11 covers the thorny issue of financial instruments including the latest standard, IFRS 7, on disclosure.

The penultimate chapter is used to pick up various sundry standards which are devoted to unique industries such as agriculture, mineral resources and insurance as well as the one-off standard that covers the content and disclosure required in interim reports. The final chapter concludes by briefly discussing the output of the International Financial Reporting Interpretations Committee (IFRIC).

The intention of the book is that the reader will have a broad knowledge of both the content and the application of IFRS, in practice.

Introduction

Introduction to the Standard-setting Process

The first Statement of Standard Accounting Practice (SSAP) was published in 1970 in the United Kingdom. Prior to this, there were relatively few financial reporting requirements for companies. It was the highly publicised scandals of the late 1960s, such as the GEC takeover of AEI, that brought the need for more extensive regulations and the setting up of a standards setting body.

The International Accounting Standards Committee (IASC) was set up in 1973. Between 1973 and its demise in April 2001 it published 41 International Accounting Standards (IASs). These were largely drafted by part-time volunteer boards from a wide background of experience and countries. It resulted in a rather slow and protracted process of developing standards. Many of these offered a number of options and thus were largely ignored by the major standard-setting countries. However, problems started to emerge with multinationals having to prepare a number of different sets of financial statements for different jurisdictions. It, therefore, became difficult to make comparisons across countries. For example, when Daimler Benz were first quoted in New York the same set of financial statements disclosed a profit of 630DM in Germany but a loss of 1,300DM using US rules. The International Organisation for Securities and Exchange Commissions (IOSCO), a loose federation of all the major stock exchanges in the world, therefore offered a challenge to the IASC to carry out a review of existing standards to ensure that many of the options be removed and the standards strengthened. If that was satisfactorily achieved then IASs would become acceptable for cross-border listings. That challenge was taken up by the Secretary General of the IASC, Sir Bryan Carsberg, and he largely achieved his objectives by the end of 2000.

The big push, however, for the development of international standards was the need to solve the problem of financial instruments. This could only be solved on an international basis and a group of standard setters (known as G4 + 1) attempted to get agreement. In addition, they also started to investigate leasing and reporting financial performance. They were well on their way to producing some very interesting international agreements on future standards. However, the European Commission (EC) forced the G4 + 1 group to dissolve when it announced that all listed companies in the EC must comply, for their consolidated financial statements, with international standards. The G4 + 1 group (basically the United Kindgdom/Ireland, United States of America, New Zealand, Australia and the IASC as observer) agreed to put their support behind the development of a new Board to further improve existing international standards and to develop new standards. A new structure was finally set up in April 2001.

The principal body under the new structure is the IASB which has sole responsibility for establishing International Financial Reporting Standards (IFRSs). Other components of the structure are the Trustees of the IASC Foundation, the IFRIC and the Standards Advisory Council (SAC). The IASB held its first official meeting in London in April 2001, at which meeting it was resolved that all Standards and Interpretations issued by the IASC should continue to be applicable unless and until they are amended or withdrawn. It was agreed that new IASB standards would be called IFRSs.

When the term IFRS is used it includes standards and interpretations approved by the IASB, and IAS and interpretations issued by the IFRIC.

The revised structure of the IASC is illustrated below:

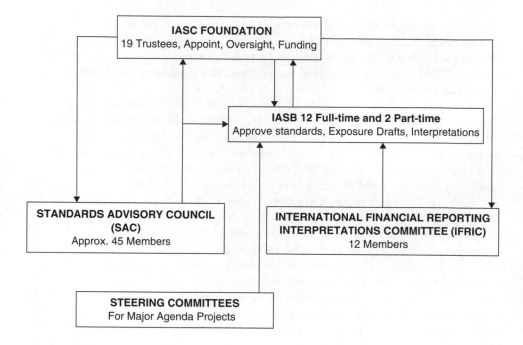

The IASC Foundation

The governance of the IASC Foundation rests with the Trustees. The initial 19 Trustees include six from North America, seven from Europe, four from Asia Pacific and one each from Africa and South America. They come from diverse functional backgrounds.

The Trustees have responsibility to:

- appoint the members of the Board, including those that will serve in liaison capacities with national standard setters, and establish their contracts of service and performance criteria;
- appoint the members of the IFRIC and the SAC;
- review annually the strategy of the IASC and its effectiveness;
- approve annually the budget of the IASC and its effectiveness;
- review broad strategic issues affecting accounting standards, promote the IASC and its work, and promote the objective of rigorous application of IFRS, provided that the

Trustees shall be excluded from involvement in technical matters relating to accounting standards; and

- establish and amend operating procedures for the Board, the IFRIC and the SAC.

The Trustees act by simple majority vote, except for amendments to the constitution, which require a 75% majority.

The International Accounting Standards Board

The IASB is the principal body under the new structure. The Board has 14 members, of whom 12 serve full-time and two part-time. The Board's principal responsibilities are to:

- develop and issue IFRSs and Exposure Drafts and
- approve Interpretations developed by the IFRIC.

The key qualification for Board membership is technical expertise. The Trustees also must ensure that the Board is not dominated by any particular constituency or regional interest. To achieve a balance of perspectives and experience, at least five members must have backgrounds as practising auditors, at least three as financial statement preparers, at least three as users of financial statements and at least one as an academic.

Seven of the 14 board members have direct liaison responsibility with one or more national standard setters. The Board has full discretion over its technical agenda. It may outsource detailed research or other work to national standard setters or other organisations. The Board will normally form Steering Committees or other types of specialist advisory groups to give advice on major projects. The Board is required to consult the SAC on major projects, agenda decisions and work priorities.

Before issuing a final Standard, the Board must publish an Exposure Draft for public comment. Normally, it will also publish a Draft Statement of Principles or other discussion document for public comment on major projects.

The Board will normally issue bases for conclusions within IFRS and Exposure Drafts. Although there is no requirement to hold public hearings or to conduct field tests for every project, the Board must, in each case, consider the need to do so.

The publication of an Exposure Draft, IFRS or final Interpretation of the IFRIC requires approval by 8 of the 14 members of the Board. Other decisions of the Board, including the publication of a Draft Statement of Principles or discussion paper, requires a simple majority of the members of the Board present at a meeting.

The IASB generally meets monthly (except August) for three to five days. It holds several meetings each year with representatives of its liaison standard-setting bodies, and generally three meetings each year with SAC.

International Financial Reporting Interpretations Committee

The IFRIC, until 2002 known as the Standing Interpretations Committee, has 12 members appointed by the Trustees for terms of three years. IFRIC members are not salaried but their expenses are reimbursed. The IFRIC is chaired by a non-voting chair who can be one of the members of the IASB, the Director of Technical Activities, or a member of the IASB's senior technical staff. (In fact, the Director of Technical Activities was appointed the chair of the IFRIC.) The IFRIC's responsibilities are to:

- interpret the application of IFRS and provide timely guidance on financial reporting issues not specifically addressed in IFRS in the context of the IASB's Framework, and undertake other tasks at the request of the Board;
- publish Draft Interpretations for public comment and consider comments made within a reasonable period before finalising an Interpretation; and
- report to the Board and obtain Board approval for final Interpretations.

A Draft or final Interpretation is approved by the IFRIC when not more than three voting members of the IFRIC vote against the Draft or final Interpretation. By allowing the IFRIC to develop Interpretations on financial reporting issues not specifically addressed in an IFRS, the new IASB constitution has broadened the IFRIC's mandate beyond that of the former Standing Interpretations Committee.

The Standards Advisory Council

The SAC currently has 49 members and provides a forum for organisations and individuals with an interest in international financial reporting to participate in the standard-setting process. Members are appointed for a renewable term of three years and have diverse geographical and functional backgrounds. The Chairman of the IASB is also the Chairman of the SAC.

The SAC will normally meet three times each year at meetings open to the public to:

- advise the Board on priorities in the Board's work;
- inform the Board of the implications of proposed standards for users and preparers of financial statements; and
- give other advice to the Board or to the Trustees.

Process of Standard Setting

The process of development of an IFRS will generally include the following:

- IASB staff work to identify and review all the issues related to a topic and study other national. Accounting standards and practices.
- A Steering Committee or advisory group may be formed to give advice on major projects.
- A Draft Statement of Principles or similar discussion document will be developed and published on major projects.
- Following receipt of comments on the initial discussion document, if any, the IASB will develop and publish an Exposure Draft.
- Following receipt of comments on the Exposure Draft, the IASB will approve all IFRSs.

List of Extant International Financial Reporting Standards and Financial Reporting Standards

International Accounting Standards IFRSs and IASs	UK Accounting Standards SSAPs and FRSs
IAS 1 Presentation of Financial Statements	No equivalent, FRS 3 Reporting Financial Performance
IAS 2 Inventories	SSAP 9 Stocks and Long-Term Contracts
IAS 3, 4, 5 and 6	Withdrawn
IAS 7 Cash Flow Statements	FRS 1 Cash Flow Statements
IAS 8 Accounting Policies, Changes in Accounding Estimates and Errors	FRS 18 Accounting Policies FRS 3 Reporting Financial Performance
IAS 9	Withdrawn
IAS 10 Events After the Balance Sheet Date	FRS 21 Events After the Balance Sheet Date
IAS 11 Construction and Service Contracts	SSAP 9 Stocks and Long Term Contracts
IAS 12 Income Taxes	FRS 16 Current Tax FRS 19 Deferred Tax
IAS 13	Withdrawn
IAS 14 Segment Reporting	SSAP 25 Segmental Reporting
IAS 15	Withdrawn
IAS 16 Property, Plant and Equipment	FRS 15 Tangible Fixed Assets
IAS 17 Leases	SSAP 21 Accounting for Leases and Hire Purchase Contracts
IAS 18 Revenue Recognition	FRS 5 Reporting the Substance of Transactions (Application Note G)
IAS 19 Employee Benefits	FRS 17 Retirement Benefits
IAS 20 Accounting for Government Grants and Disclosure of Government Assistance	SSAP 4 Accounting for Government Grants
IAS 21 The Effect of Changes in Foreign Exchange Rates	SSAP 20 Foreign Currency Translation
IAS 22	Withdrawn
IAS 23 Borrowing Costs	FRS 15 Property, plant and equipment
IAS 24 Related Party Disclosures	FRS 8 Related Party Disclosures
IAS 25	Withdrawn
IAS 26 Accounting and Reporting by Retirement Benefit Plans	SORP Retirement Benefit Plans
IAS 27 Consolidated and Separate Financial Statements	FRS 2 Accounting for Subsidiary Undertakings
IAS 28 Investments in Associates	FRS 9 Accounting for Associates and Joint Ventures

(continued)

International Accounting Standards IFRSs and IASs	UK Accounting Standards SSAPs and FRSs
IAS 29 Financial Reporting in Hyperinflationary Economies	UITF 29
IAS 30	Withdrawn
IAS 31 Financial Reporting of Interests in Joint Ventures	FRS 9 Accounting for Associates and Joint Ventures
IAS 32 Financial Instruments: Presentation	FRS 4 Capital Instruments FRS 25 Financial Instruments: Disclosures and Presentation
IAS 33 Earnings Per Share	FRS 22 Earnings Per Share
IAS 34 Interim Financial Reporting	SBP Interim Accounts
IAS 35	Withdrawn
IAS 36 Impairment of Assets	FRS 11 Impairment of Fixed Assets and Goodwill
IAS 37 Provisions, Contingent Liabilities and Contingent Assets	FRS 12 Provisions, Contingent Liabilities and Contingent Assets
IAS 38 Intangible Assets	SSAP 13 Accounting for Research and Development FRS 10 Goodwill and Intangible Assets
IAS 39 Financial Instruments: Recognition and Measurement	FRS 26 Financial Instruments: Measurement
IAS 40 Investment Property	SSAP 19 Investment Properties
IAS 41 Agriculture	No equivalent
IFRS 1 First time adoption of IFRSs	No equivalent
IFRS 2 Share-Based Payment	FRS 20 Share-Based Payment
IFRS 3 Business Combinations	FRS 6 Acquisitions and Mergers FRS 7 Fair Values in Acquisition Accounting FRS 9 Associates and Joint Ventures FRS 10 Goodwill and Intangible Assets
IFRS 4 Insurance Contracts	No equivalent
IFRS 5 Non Current Assets held for Sale and Presentation of Discontinued Operations	FRS 3 Reporting Financial Performance
IFRS 6 Exploration and Evaluation of Mineral Resources	No equivalent but industry SORP
IFRS 7 Financial Instruments: Disclosures	FRS 29 Financial Instruments: Disclosures
IFRS 8 Operating Segments	SSAP 25 Segment Reporting
No equivalent	SSAP 5 Accounting for Value-Added Tax
No equivalent	FRS 5 Reporting the Substance of Transactions
No equivalent	FRS 4 Life Assurance

The regulatory framework and presentation of financial statements

1.1 *Framework for the preparation and presentation of financial statements* (1989)

Background

One of the main problems the standard-setting bodies in their quest to develop authoritative accounting standards have faced was their failure to publish standards which are consistent with each other. There has been no firm foundation on which they could be built. As a result, the actual standards have been produced in an *ad hoc* manner with very little logical thought behind their publication. The Framework is an attempt to put this right by introducing the core principles that should govern financial reporting. It is broken down into a number of key sections.

Objective of financial statements

This section argues that there are several users of financial reporting and that the Annual Report is the main vehicle for communication with users. The information should largely be directed towards meeting their needs. These needs are twofold – to ensure that the reporting entity has performed adequately (the stewardship function) and to ensure that the user has sufficient information on which to make decisions about the future (i.e. the decision-making function). In order to provide information which would be helpful to users, it is recommended that the entity provide information about the *financial position*, *performance* and *changes in financial position* of the organisation. The financial statements should be prepared under both the accruals and the going concern bases. The International Accounting Standards Board (IASB) published a Exposure draft in March 2008 which relegates stewardship into a secondary role and also widens the user group to include both potential shareholders and creditors as key users as well as existing shareholders.

Qualitative characteristics

This section of the Framework identifies the key primary qualitative characteristics that should make the information in the Annual Report useful to users. There are four principal characteristics, two relating to the content of the Report and two in relation to its presentation.

Relevance

The information must be relevant, i.e. be up to date and current and be actually used by the reader. Included within this characteristic is the concept of materiality. It provides a threshold or cut-off judgement rather than a primary qualitative characteristic.

Reliability

The reader must have faith in the information provided and it must be free from material errors and represent faithfully what it is supposed to represent. It must be free from bias and the information must be complete within the bounds of materiality. The IASB in its Exposure draft has proposed replacing this characteristic with the term 'faithful representation' which also appears to put fair-value reporting as more useful than historic cost accounting.

These two characteristics tend to come into conflict since relevance would favour the adoption of current subjective values, whereas reliability would gravitate towards the adoption of historic and more objective costs. Where the two do clash, IASB favours relevance.

Transactions should also be accounted for in accordance with their substance and not merely their legal form. A degree of caution (prudence) must also be exercised in making estimates under the conditions of uncertainty.

Comparability

This is really the former consistency concept and it insists that information must be comparable from period to period as well as within like items in the same period. However, it also requires sufficient disclosure for a user to appreciate the significance of transactions. However, it does not mean uniformity, and accounting policies must be reviewed when more relevant and reliable alternatives exist.

Understandability

This concept insists that the information being provided by the reporting entity be presented in such a way that it is as understandable as possible to the user. However, this does not mean that it is so simple that the information being provided becomes meaningless.

The elements of financial statements

This chapter contains the key elements in a set of financial statements. It defines the balance sheet elements first and then argues that the income statement should pick up any residuals, e.g. a gain is either an increase in an asset or a decrease in a liability. The main definitions are as follows:

Financial position

- *Asset.* Resource controlled by the enterprise as a result of past events and from which future economic benefits are expected to flow to the enterprise.
- *Liability.* A present obligation of the enterprise arising from past events, the settlement of which is expected to result in an outflow from the enterprise of resources embodying economic benefits.
- *Equity.* The residual interest in the assets of the enterprise after deducting all of its liabilities.

Financial performance

- *Incomes.* Increases in economic benefits during the accounting period in the form of inflows or enhancements of assets or decreases in liabilities that result in increases in equity, other than contributions from equity participants.
- *Expenses.* Decreases in economic benefits during the accounting period in the form of outflows or depletions of assets that result in decreases in equity, other than distributions to equity participants.

Clearly, this section of the Framework puts the balance sheet on a pedestal with its concentration on getting the assets and the liabilities right first, before looking at the income statement. This represents a cultural swing for the United Kingdom from its former profit and loss and accruals-based preference. The accruals concept is now clearly downgraded in importance in that expenditure cannot be matched against future income unless it can meet the definition of an asset in the first place. Similarly the prudence concept has been given a 'knock', as a liability can only be created if there is either a legal or a constructive obligation in place. A mere intention to expend monies in the future is not sufficient on its own.

Recognition of the elements of financial statements

Even if a transaction meets the definition of an asset or a liability it will not be recorded on the balance sheet unless it meets the following two recognition criteria:

(1)   Is there sufficient evidence that a change in assets or liabilities has occurred?
(2)   Can it be measured at cost or value with sufficient reliability?

If these cannot be passed initially then the transactions must be written off directly to income. If one of these criteria has subsequently failed, then the asset/liability must be removed or derecognised from the balance sheet. It is possible that the asset/liability will need to be remeasured where there is sufficient evidence that the amount has changed and the new amount measured with sufficient reliability.

Measurement of the elements of financial statements

Measurement is a process of determining the monetary amounts at which the elements are to be recognised in the balance sheet and the income statement.

A number of different measurement bases are employed to different degrees and in various combinations in financial statements. They include the following:

(a) *Historic cost.* Assets recorded at cash paid at the date of acquisition. Liabilities are recorded at the amount of proceeds received in exchange for the obligation or the amount of cash expected to be paid to satisfy the liability, e.g. taxation.

(b) *Current cost.* Assets recorded at cash that would have to be paid to acquire the same or equivalent asset. Liabilities are carried at the undiscounted amount of cash required to settle the obligation.

(c) *Realisable value.* Assets recorded at cash that would be obtained by selling the asset in an orderly disposal. Liabilities are carried at their settlement values, i.e. the undiscounted amounts of cash expected to be paid to satisfy the liabilities in normal course of business.

(d) *Present value.* Assets recorded at the present discounted value of future net cash inflows that the item is expected to generate in the normal course of business. Liabilities are carried at the present discounted value of the future net cash outflows that are expected to be required to settle the liabilities in the normal course of business.

The most popular basis is historic cost but it is usually combined with other bases e.g. inventories at the lower of cost and net realisable value, marketable securities at market value and pension liabilities at present value.

Some entities adopt current cost accounting to cope with the inability of historic cost accounting to deal with the effects of changing prices.

Concepts of capital and capital maintenance

The following concepts exist:

(a) *Financial capital maintenance.* Profit is earned only if the financial amount of net assets at the end of the period exceeds the financial amount of net assets at the start of the period after excluding distributions to and contributions from owners during the period. It can be measured either in nominal or in purchasing power units.

(b) *Physical capital maintenance.* Profit is earned only if the physical productive capacity of the entity at the end of the period exceeds the physical productive capacity at the start of the period after excluding distributions to and contributions from owners during the period.

Capital maintenance links the concepts of capital and the concepts of profit as it provides a reference by which profit is measured. Only inflows of assets in excess of amounts needed to maintain capital may be regarded as profit. Profit is the residual amount that remains after expenses have been deducted from income. If expenses exceed income the residual amount is a net loss.

Physical capital maintenance requires the adoption of the current cost basis of measurement. The financial capital maintenance concept does not require the use of a particular basis of measurement. Selection of appropriate basis is dependent on the type of financial capital that the entity is seeking to maintain.

The main difference between the two types of capital maintenance is on the effects of changes in the prices of assets and liabilities of the entity. Generally capital is maintained if an entity has as much capital at the end of the period as at the start. Any amount over and above that is a profit.

Under financial capital maintenance, where capital is defined in nominal terms, profit is the increase in nominal money capital over the period. Holding gains are therefore included in profit, but only when disposed. Under the current purchasing power approach, profit represents the increase in purchasing power over the period. Thus only that part of the increase in prices of assets that exceeds the increase in the general level of prices is regarded as profit. The rest is a capital maintenance adjustment and therefore part of equity.

Under physical capital maintenance, where capital is defined in terms of productive capacity, profit represents the increase in that capital over the period. All price changes are viewed as changes in the measurement of the physical productive capacity of the entity, and thus are treated as capital maintenance adjustments that are part of equity.

The choice of model will depend on the different degrees of relevance and reliability available and management must seek an appropriate balance between the two. The Framework is applicable to a range of accounting models and provides guidance on preparing and presenting the financial statements constructed under the chosen model. The IASB at present does not intend to prescribe a particular model other than in exceptional circumstances, e.g. hyperinflationary economies (IAS 29) but its intention will be reviewed in the light of world developments.

Summary

The Framework was published in late 1989 in the form of a statement of best practice which will form the cornerstone of all future standard-setting procedures.

The Framework has set out the concepts that underlie the preparation and presentation of financial statements for external users. The purpose of the Framework is to:

(a)   assist the IASB in developing future IFRSs and reviewing existing IFRSs;
(b)   assist the IASB to promote harmonisation;
(c)   assist national standard setters develop national standards;
(d)   assist preparers to apply IFRSs and in dealing with topics not covered by an IFRS; and
(e)   assist auditors in forming an opinion as to whether or not financial statements conform with IFRSs;
(f)   assist users in interpreting information in financial statements;
(g)   provide those with an interest in the work of the IASB about its approach to formulating IFRSs.

It is not an IFRS itself but where an IFRS conflicts with the Framework, the IFRS prevails. However, this is likely to be rare and diminish over time. The Framework will be revised from time to time, with experience.

The financial statements should include a balance sheet, an income statement, a statement of changes in financial position and backup notes. Supplementary information, e.g. segment reporting, is also included but not Directors Reports, Discussion and Analysis Statements or Chairman's Reports. The Framework should be applied to all commercial reporting entities.

Users and their needs are specifically covered in the Framework:

(a)   *Investors.* Concerned about risk and return provided by their investments. Need information to determine buy, hold or sell decisions and to assess the entity's ability to pay dividends.
(b)   *Employees.* Concerned about the stability and profitability of their employers and assessing the ability of the entity to provide remuneration, retirement benefits, etc. to employees.

(c) *Lenders.* Concerned about whether or not their loans and interest can be repaid.

(d) *Suppliers and other trade creditors.* Concerned about whether or not they will be paid when due.

(e) *Customers.* Concerned about the continuance of the business especially if they have a long-term involvement with the entity.

(f) *Governments and their agencies.* Interested in the allocation of resources and information on taxation policies, national statistics, etc.

(g) *Public.* Can provide information about the local economy, numbers employed, environmental issues, etc.

There are common needs of users, and financial statements should meet most of those needs. Information for management purposes is specialised although published statements may be used by them in assessing financial performance, position and changes in financial position of the entity.

1.2   IAS 1 *Presentation of financial information* (revised December 2003)

Key points

The objective of IAS 1 is to prescribe the basis for the presentation of general purpose financial statements. It sets out the overall Framework and responsibilities for the presentation of financial statements, guidelines for their structure and minimum requirements for the content of financial statements. IAS 1 applies to all general-purpose financial statements prepared in accordance with IFRS. General-purpose financial statements are defined as those intended to serve users who do not have the authority to demand financial reports tailored for their own needs.

Content of financial statements

The financial statements should comprise the following:

* Balance sheet.
* Income statement.
* Statement of changes in equity or statement of non-owner changes in equity.
* Cash flow statement.
* Explanatory notes including a summary of significant accounting policies.

There is no prescribed standard format although examples are provided in the appendix of the minimum headings. It does, however, set out minimum disclosures to be made on the face of the financial statements as well as in the notes. For example, an analysis of income and expenditure using a classification based on their nature or function must be disclosed. The standard also requires comparatives to be provided for all items unless a particular accounting standard specifically exempts that requirement.

The reporting currency should generally be that of the country in which the enterprise is domiciled. If a different reporting currency is adopted or a change in reporting currency made, then the reasons must be disclosed.

A reporting enterprise complying with the requirements of IFRSs is considered as providing a fair presentation of the financial statements. A statement that the financial statements comply with IFRSs and IFRIC/SIC interpretations is required. No statement is now permitted stating that compliance with IFRSs has been undertaken with certain specified exemptions. Full compliance is essential.

Overall considerations

Fair presentation and compliance with IFRSs

Financial statements should present fairly the financial position, performance and cash flows of the entity, and the entity should provide an explicit and unreserved statement that the statements are in compliance with IFRSs.

A typical example of that statement is provided by BAE Systems Plc which not only includes a statement of compliance, but also details of the basis of preparation and basis of consolidation as part of their accounting policies note:

BAe Systems Plc   Year Ended 31 December 2005

Notes to the Group Accounts

1. Accounting Policies (Extract)

Statement of compliance

The Group has adopted IFRS for use in the EU in its consolidated accounts for accounting periods from 1 January 2005. The financial statements for the year ended 31 December 2005 have been prepared in accordance with all IFRSs, including Standing Interpretations Committee and International Financial Reporting Interpretations Committee interpretations issued by the IASB.

In preparing this financial information, the Group has decided to adopt early the amendment issued in December 2004 to IAS 19 Employee Benefits – Actuarial Gains and Losses, Group Plans and Disclosures.

With effect from 1 January 2005 the Group has adopted IAS 39 Financial Instruments: Recognition and Measurement (IAS 39). The effect of adopting IAS 39 at 1 January 2005 is presented as a movement in the Group's consolidated statement of recognised income and expense for 2005.

The financial information for the year 31 December 2004 has been prepared on the same basis with the exception of IAS 32 Financial Instruments: Disclosure and Presentation (IAS 32) and IAS 39 that have been applied from 1 January 2006. The comparative financial information for financial assets and financial liabilities is accounted for on the basis of UK Generally Accepted Accounting Practices (UK GAAP).

In general for the first-time adoption of IFRS, the standards are applied retrospectively. However, there are a number of exceptions available under IFRS 1. First-time adoption of IFRS 1 and details of the exceptions that the Group has applied are shown in Note 36.

Basis of preparation

The consolidated financial statements are presented in pounds sterling, and unless stated otherwise rounded to the nearest million. They have been prepared under the historical cost convention, as modified by the revaluation of available-for-sale financial assets and financial liabilities (including derivative instruments) at fair value through profit or loss.

Basis of consolidation

The financial statements of the Group consolidate the results of the company and its subsidiary entities and include the share of its joint ventures' and associates' results accounted for under the equity method, all of which are prepared to 31 December.

A subsidiary is an entity controlled by the Group. Control is the power to govern the financial and operating policies of the entity so as to obtain benefits from its activities. Subsidiaries include the special purpose entities that the Group transacted through for the provision of guarantees in respect of residual values and head lease and finance payments on certain regional aircraft sold.

The purchase method of accounting is used to account for the acquisition of subsidiaries by the Group. The cost of the acquisition is measured as the fair value of the assets given, equity instruments issued and liabilities incurred or assumed at the date of exchange, plus costs directly attributable to the acquisition. Identifiable assets acquired and liabilities and contingent liabilities assumed in a business combination are measured initially at their fair values at the acquisition date. The excess of the cost of acquisition over the fair value of the Group's share of the identifiable net assets acquired is recorded as goodwill. The results of such subsidiaries are included in the consolidated income statement from the date of acquisition up to the date of disposal or closure.

Where the Group contributes a business, or other non-monetary assets for an interest in a subsidiary, joint venture or associate, such transactions are recorded so that the reduction in the ownership of the business being contributed is accounted for as a disposal, whereas the increased interest in the enlarged Group or new interest in the business contributed by other parties to the transaction are accounted for as an acquisition. Fair values are applied to those operations which are subject to the exchange and which have not previously been held within the Group. Any loss or realised gain resulting from the transaction is recorded in the income statement while any unrealised gain is eliminated against the investment.

Goodwill

Goodwill on acquisitions of subsidiaries is included in intangible assets. Goodwill on acquisitions of joint ventures and associates is included in the carrying value of equity accounted investments. Goodwill is tested annually for impairment and carried at cost less accumulated impairment losses. Gains and losses on the disposal of an entity include the carrying amount of goodwill relating to the entity sold.

Goodwill is allocated to cash-generating units for the purpose of impairment testing.

Inappropriate policies are not rectified either by disclosure or by notes.

Entities can depart, in rare circumstances, from an IFRS, if it is regarded as misleading but the following must be disclosed in those cases:

(a) Management has concluded that the financial statements give a fair presentation.
(b) That it has complied with IFRSs, etc. except from a particular requirement to achieve fair presentation.
(c) The title of the IFRS, nature of departure and why the normal treatment was not adopted.
(d) The financial impact for each period of the departure.

If departure is not permitted the entity should reduce the perceived misleading aspects by disclosing:

(a) the title of the standard, the nature of issue and the reason why it was misleading and
(b) the adjustments management has concluded would be appropriate.

Going concern

Management must assess the ability of an entity to continue as a going concern. If there are doubts over that concept, disclosure should be made of the underlying uncertainties but if it is more serious, the financial statements should be prepared on a break-up basis but that fact must be disclosed.

Offsetting

Assets and liabilities as well as income and expenses should not be offset unless required or permitted by a standard or IFRIC/SIC statement.

Comparative information

Should be disclosed for the previous period for all amounts disclosed in the financial statements. If the current period has been reclassified so should the comparatives be, unless that is impracticable. If practical the following should be disclosed:

(a) The nature of the reclassification.
(b) The amount of each item or class of items reclassified.
(c) The reason for the reclassification.

Where it is found to be impractical, the following should be disclosed:

(a) The reason for not reclassifying.
(b) The nature of the adjustments that would have been made.

Structure and content

Identification of the financial statements

The financial statements should be clearly identified and distinguished from other information in the same published document.

Each component should be clearly identified. In addition, the following information should be displayed prominently:

(a) Name of the reporting entity and any change from the preceding year.
(b) Whether the statements cover an individual or group of entities.
(c) The balance sheet date or period covered.
(d) The presentation currency.
(e) The level of rounding adopted.

Reporting period

There is a presumption that financial statements will be prepared annually, at a minimum. If the annual reporting period changes and financial statements are prepared for a different period, the entity should disclose the reason for the change and a warning that the corresponding amounts shown may not be comparable.

Balance sheet

The standard specifies minimum headings to be presented on the face of the balance sheet and guidance is provided for the identification of additional line items.

Entities should present the balance sheet by separating current from non-current assets and liabilities unless a presentation based on liquidity provides information that is more reliable and relevant. In the latter, assets and liabilities must be presented broadly in order of their liquidity (or reverse order), without a current/non-current distinction.

In either case, if an asset or a liability category combines amounts that will be received/settled after 12 months with assets/liabilities that will be received/settled within 12 months, note that disclosure is required which separates the longer term amounts from the amounts due to be received/settled within 12 months.

Current assets

An asset is classified as current when it satisfies any of the following criteria:

(a) It is expected to be realised in the entity's normal operating cycle.
(b) It is held primarily for trade.
(c) It is expected to be realised within 12 months.
(d) It is cash or a cash equivalent.

Non-current assets incorporate tangible, intangible and financial assets of a long-term nature.

Current liabilities

A liability is classified as current when it satisfies any of the following criteria:

(a) it is expected to be settled in the entity's normal operating cycle;
(b) it is held primarily for trade;
(c) it is due to be settled within 12 months; and
(d) the entity does not have an unconditional right to defer settlement for at least 12 months.

Information to be presented on the face of the balance sheet

As a minimum the following should be disclosed on the face of the balance sheet:

(a) Property, plant and equipment.
(b) Investment property.
(c) Intangible assets.
(d) Financial assets.
(e) Investments accounted under the equity method.
(f) Biological assets.
(g) Inventories.
(h) Trade and other receivables.
(i) Cash and cash equivalents.
(j) Trade and other payables.
(k) Provisions.
(l) Financial liabilities.
(m) Current tax.
(n) Deferred tax.
(o) Minority interest.
(p) Capital and reserves.

Additional items may be presented, if relevant to an understanding of the entity's financial position. Deferred tax may not be reclassified as a current asset/liability if an entity adopts the current/non-current approach.

The standard does not prescribe the order or format of the balance sheet – it is merely a list of items warranting separate disclosure. Below are two different examples of preparing a balance sheet – one which totals up all the assets separately from the liabilities and equity (Irish Continental Group Plc) and the other (Vislink Group Plc) which follows the more traditional approach of netting up liabilities against assets to provide a net asset balance, equity representing the second half of the document:

Irish Continental Group Plc   Year Ended 31 December 2005

Consolidated Balance Sheet at 31 December 2005

	Notes	2005 bm	2004 €m
Assets			
Non-current assets			
Property, plant and equipment	14	287.8	295.1
Intangible assets	15	3.3	2.5
Long-term receivable		4.9	3.6
Retirement benefit surplus	34	8.0	2.8
		304.0	304.0
Current assets			
Inventories	16	0.6	0.6
Trade and cash equivalents	17	37.6	42.5
Cash and cash equivalents		14.0	9.2
		52.2	52.3
Total assets		356.2	356.3

Equity and liabilities

Capital and reserves

Share capital	18	**15.8**	15.8
Share premium	19	**39.6**	39.6
Capital reserves	20	**2.2**	2.2
Share options reserve	21	**0.1**	–
Hedging reserve	22	**(0.1)**	–
Translation reserve	22	**3.6**	(2.2)
Retained earnings	23	**77.7**	95.7
Equity attributable to equity holders of the parent		**138.9**	151.1

Non-current liabilities

Bank loans	24	**99.4**	92.3
Obligations under finance leases	27	**5.3**	8.5
Trade and other payables	28	**3.7**	–
Provisions	29	**2.1**	1.8
Deferred tax liabilities	26	**4.9**	5.1
Derivative financial instruments	25	**0.1**	–
Retirement benefit obligation	34	**0.6**	4.7
		116.1	112.4

Current liabilities

Bank overdrafts and loans	24	**11.7**	22.0
Obligations under finance leases	27	**3.5**	4.3
Trade and other payables	28	**47.5**	54.2
Current tax liabilities	28	**4.8**	5.5
Provisions	29	**33.7**	6.8
		101.2	92.8
Total liabilities		**217.3**	205.2
Total equity and liabilities		**356.2**	356.3

Vislink Group Plc   Year Ended 31 December 2005

Consolidated Group Balance Sheet as at 31 December 2005

	Notes	2005 £'000	2004 £'000
Assets			
Non-current assets			
Goodwill	10	23,393	16,922
Intangible assets	11	6,854	1,062
Property, plant and equipment	12	4,547	4,314
Financial assets	13	43	–
Deferred tax assets	24	835	1,602
		35,672	23,900

Current assets			
Inventories	14	13,345	8,936
Trade and other receivables	16	17,032	15,386
Cash and cash equivalents	17	7,122	3,219
		37,499	27,541
Liabilities			
Current liabilities			
Financial liabilities – borrowings	20	3,794	2,190
Trade and other payables	18	22,206	18,363
Current tax liabilities	19	816	206
Provisions	23	732	757
		27,548	21,516
Net current assets		9,951	6,025
Non-current liabilities			
Financial liabilities – borrowings	20	1,169	3,378
Deferred tax liabilities	24	2,608	1,255
Other non-current liabilities	21	3,873	–
Provisions	23	153	291
		7,808	4,924
Net assets		37,815	25,001
Shareholders' equity			
Ordinary shares	25	3,412	2,552
Share premium account	27	4,362	205
Investment in own shares	28	(109)	(160)
Merger reserve	28	30,565	27,895
Translation reserve	28	(1,288)	(3,053)
Retained earnings	29	873	(2,438)
Total shareholders' equity		37,815	25,001

The financial statements on pages 30 to 60 were approved by the Board of Directors on 29 March 2006 and were signed on its behalf by:

I H Scott-Gall Director
J R Trumper Director

Information to be presented either on the face of the balance sheet or in the notes

Further subclassifications may be provided in the notes or on the face of the balance sheet:

(a) For each class of share capital:

number of authorised shares, number of issued shares, par value per share, reconciliation of number outstanding over the year, any rights or restrictions, any treasury shares held and any shares reserved for options including terms and conditions.

(b) A description of the nature and purpose of each reserve.

Any entity without share capital or a trust should provide equivalent information to the above.

Income statement

All items of income and expense recognised in a period should be included in the income statement unless a standard or IFRIC/SIC statement requires otherwise (e.g. IAS 8, 16, 21).

IAS 1 specifies the minimum headings that must be presented on the face of the income statement and provides guidance for the identification of additional line items. There is no particular format or order of presentation mandated.

Information to be presented on the face of the income statement

As a minimum, the following should be disclosed on the face of the income statement for the period:

(a)   Revenue.
(b)   Finance costs.
(c)   Share of profit/loss of associates and joint ventures.
(d)   Pre-tax gain or loss recognised on the disposal of assets or settlement of liabilities attributable to discontinued operations.
(e)   Tax expense.
(f)   Profit or loss.

The following items should be disclosed on the face of the income statement as allocations of profit:

(a)   minority interest;
(b)   profit/loss attributable to equity holders of the parent.

Additional items should be presented when such presentation is relevant to understanding the entity's financial performance. However, extraordinary items are no longer permitted to be disclosed in the statement or in the notes.

Information to be presented either on the face of the income statement or in the notes

Where material, nature and amount of income and expenses should be disclosed separately.

Examples include inventory write-downs, restructurings, disposals of plant, discontinued operations, litigation settlements.

Income and expenses should not be offset unless another IAS requires or permits such offset, or the amounts to be offset arise from the same events and are not material.

Expenses should be analysed either by nature (raw materials, staff costs, depreciation, etc.) or by function (cost of sales, selling, administration, etc.) either on the face of the income statement or in the notes. If an entity categorises by function, additional information on the nature of expenses, including depreciation, amortisation and employee benefit expense should be disclosed. The choice of method should be the one which provides the most reliable and relevant information to the entity.

An example of a company complying with the nature of expense approach is the Glanbia Group Plc but it also introduces multi-column reporting to highlight exceptional items separately:

Glanbia Group Plc   Year Ended 31 December 2005

Consolidated Income Statement for the Year Ended 31 December 2005

	Notes	Pre-exceptional 2005 €'000	Exceptional 2005 €'000	Total 2005 €'000	Pre-exceptional 2004 €'000	Exceptional 2004 €'000	Total 2004 €'000
Revenue	6	1,830,012	–	1,830,012	1,753,645	–	1,753,645
Cost of sales		(1,590,049)	–	(1,590,049)	(1,529,413)	–	(1,529,413)
Gross profit		239,963	–	239,963	224,232	–	224,232
Distribution expenses		(94,743)	–	(94,743)	(77,857)	–	(77,857)
Administration expenses	8	(64,651)	(1,110)	(65,761)	(60,118)	2,895	(57,223)
Operating profit	7	80,569	(1,110)	79,459	86,257	2,895	89,152
Finance income	11	4,209	–	4,209	3,033	–	3,033
Finance costs (note)	11	(16,995)	(5,304)	(22,299)	(8,756)	–	(8,756)
Share of results of joint ventures and associates		932	–	932	(1,523)	–	(1,523)
Profit before taxation (note)	12	68,715	(6,414)	62,301	79,011	2,895	81,906
Income taxes		(7,592)	6,935	(657)	(8,386)	–	(8,386)
Profit after taxation (note)	13	61,123	521	61,644	70,625	2,895	73,520
Loss for the year from discontinued operations		–	–	–	–	(1,601)	(1,601)
Profit for the year (note)		61,123	521	61,644	70,625	1,294	71,919
Attributable to:							
Equity holders of the Parent				61,327			61,119
Non-equity minority interest				317			10,387
Equity minority interest				–			413
				61,644			71,919
Basic earnings per share (cent)							
– Continuing operations	14			21.04			21.58
– Discontinued operations				–			(0.55)
				21.04			21.03
Diluted earnings per share (cent)							
– Continuing operations				20.96			21.47
– Discontinued operations	14			–			(0.55)
				20.96			20.92

Note: The prior year's comparative figures have been restated in line with the Group's transition to IFRS on 4 January 2004, with the exception of IAS 32 and 39, which were implemented from 2 January 2005. Accordingly, interest on preferred securities and preference shares as shown in the income statement as part of finance cost for 2005 and as non-equity minority interest for 2004. When adjusted for this item, the profit after taxation, pre-exceptional items for 2005 and was €61.1 million compared to €60.2 million for 2004.

On behalf of the Board
MJ Walsh JJ Moloney GJ Meaher
Directors

An entity should disclose either on the face of the income statement or the statement of changes in equity, or in the notes, the amount of dividends recognised as distributions to equity holders during the period and the related amount per share.

Statement of changes in equity

IAS 1 also requires the presentation of a Statement of Changes in Equity as a separate component of the financial statements, showing:

- the profit or loss for the period;
- each item of income or expense, and gain or loss, that is recognised directly in equity and the total of those items; and
- the effects of changes in accounting policies or material errors in accordance with IAS 8.

Either within this statement, or separately in the notes, the entity is required to disclose:

- capital transactions;
- the balance of accumulated profits at the beginning and at the end of the period, and the movements for the period; and
- reconciliation between the carrying amount of each class of equity capital, share premium and each reserve at the beginning and end of the period, disclosing each movement.

The more popular of the two approaches in Great Britain is the latter approach and this can be seen in the Annual Report for Benckiser Reckitt. They also include both performance statements on the same page giving equal respect to both:

Reckitt Benckiser Plc   Year Ended 31 December 2005

Group Income Statement for the Year Ended 31 December 2005

	Notes	2005 (£m)	2004 (£m)
Net revenues	1	**4,179**	3,871
Cost of sales	2	**(1,886)**	(1,750)
Gross profit		**2,293**	2,121
Net operating expenses	2	**(1,453)**	(1,372)
Operating profit	1	**840**	749
Finance income		**50**	38
Finance expense		**(14)**	(29)
Net finance income	5	**36**	9
Profit on ordinary activities before taxation		**876**	758
Tax on profit on ordinary activities	6	**(207)**	(181)
Profit for the year		**669**	577
Attributable to equity minority interest		**–**	–
Attributable to ordinary equity holders of the parent		**669**	577
Profit for the year		**669**	577

Earnings per ordinary share			
On profit for the year, basic	7	**92.0p**	80.7p
On profit for the year, diluted	7	**90.0p**	77.1p
Dividend per ordinary share	8	**36.0p**	30.0p
Total dividends for the year	8	**262**	216

Group Statement of Recognised Income and Expense

For the Year Ended 31 December 2005

	Notes	2005 (£m)	2004 (£m)
Profit for the year		669	577
Net exchange adjustment on foreign currency translation		85	(43)
Actuarial gains and losses	4	(14)	(76)
Movement of deferred tax on pension liability		(3)	22
Net hedged gains and losses taken to reserves		(1)	–
Net gains/(losses) not recognised in income statement		67	(97)
Total recognised Income/(expense) relating to the year		736	480
Attributable to equity minority interests		–	–
Attributable to ordinary shareholders of the parent		736	480
		736	480

The full movement in reserves, however, is incorporated in the notes at the back of the Annual Report.

21. Statement of Changes in Shareholders Equity

	Share capital	Share premium	Merger reserve	Equity element of Convertible Bonds	Hedging reserve	Capital redemption reserve	Foreign currency translation reserve	Retained earnings	Minority interest	Total
					Attributable to equity holders of the Company					
	(£m)	(£m)	(£m)	(£m)	(£m)	(£m)	(£m)	(£m)	(£m)	(£m)
Balance at 1 January 2004	**74**	**227**	**142**	**45**	**0**	**0**	**0**	**921**	**4**	**1,413**
Shares allotted under Share schemes:		30								30
Shares allotted on conversion of CCBs:	4	148								152
Reduction in equity component of CCB upon conversion				(36)						(36)
Unvested share awards:								32		32
Deferred tax on share awards:								9		9
Profit for the year:								577		577
Dividends:								(216)		(216)
Own shares repurchased:	(2)							(281)		(283)
Actuarial gains and losses:								(76)		(76)
Movement of deferred tax on pensions liability:								22		22
Transfer to capital redemption reserve:						2		(2)		–
Net exchange adjustments on foreign currency translation:							(43)			(43)
Reduction in minority interest									(1)	(1)
Balance at 31 December 2004	**76**	**405**	**142**	**9**	**0**	**2**	**(43)**	**986**	**3**	**1,580**
Shares allotted under share schemes:	1	35								36
Shares allotted on conversion of CCBs:	1	39								40
Reduction in equity component of CCB upon conversion:				(9)						(9)
Unvested share awards:								36		36

Statement of comprehensive income

An entity should present all components of income and expense recognised in a period:

(a)   in a single statement of comprehensive income; or
(b)   in two statements:
   • a statement displaying components of profit or loss (separate income statement); and
   • a statement beginning with profit/loss and displaying components of other comprehensive income (statement of comprehensive income).

Statement of changes in equity

The following should be disclosed on the face of the statement:

(a)   Total comprehensive income for the period showing separately the total amount due to parent and to the minority.
(b)   For each component of equity, the effect of changes in accounting policies and corrections of errors.
(c)   The amounts of transactions with equity holders in their capacity as equity holders showing separately contributions and distributions.
(d)   For each component of equity a reconciliation between the carrying amount at end and start of the period.

Dividends recognised as distributions should be disclosed on the face of the statement or in the notes as well as the related amounts per share.

Changes in equity reflect the increase/decrease in its net assets during the period. The overall change in equity during a period represents the total amount of income and expenses, including gains and losses, generated by the entity's activities during that period.

IAS 8 requires retrospective adjustments to effect changes in accounting policies to the extent practicable as well as to restatements to correct errors. These are made to retained earnings and should be disclosed for each prior period and at the beginning of the period.

Statement of cash flows

Should provide users with a basis to assess the ability of the entity to generate cash and cash equivalents and the needs of the entity to utilise those cash flows. IAS 7, however, sets out the requirements and disclosures required.

Notes

Structure
The notes should include:

(a)   The basis of preparation of the financial statements and specific accounting policies used.
(b)   Disclose information required by IFRSs that is not presented on the face of the statements of financial position, statement of comprehensive income, changes in equity or cash flows.
(c)   Provide information that is not presented on the face of those documents but is relevant to their understanding.

The notes should be presented in a systematic way and cross referenced to the primary statements. Normally the following is the order:

(a)   a statement of compliance with IFRSs;
(b)   a summary of significant accounting policies applied;
(c)   supporting information for primary statements in the order in which each statement and each line item is presented;
(d)   Other disclosures including contingent liabilities (see IAS 37) and non-financial disclosures e.g. (see IFRS 7 risk management objectives).

However, the order may be altered, if desirable.

Effective date

The new standard will become effective for accounting periods beginning on or after 1 January 2009 and will supersede IAS 1 revised in 2003.

Part 1: Illustrative Presentation of Financial Statements

XYZ Group – Statement of Financial Position as at 31 December 20X7

(in thousands of currency units)

	31 December 20X7	31 December 20X6
ASSETS		
Non-current assets		
Property, plant and equipment	350,700	360,020
Goodwill	80,800	91,200
Other intangible assets	227,470	227,470
Investments in associates	100,150	110,770
Available-for-sale financial assets	142,500	156,000
	901,620	945,460
Current assets		
Inventories	135,230	132,500
Trade receivables	91,600	110,800
Other current assets	25,650	12,540
Cash and cash equivalents	312,400	322,900
	564,880	573,740
Total assets	1,466,500	1,524,200
EQUITY AND LIABILITIES		
Equity attributable to owners of the parent		
Share capital	650,000	600,000
Retained earnings	243,500	161,700
Other components of equity	10,200	21,200
	903,700	782,900
Minority interest	70,050	48,600
Total equity	973,750	831,500

Non-current liabilities		
Long-term borrowings	120,000	160,000
Deferred tax	28,800	26,040
Long-term provisions	28,850	52,240
Total non-current liabilities	177,650	238,280
Current liabilities		
Trade and other payables	115,100	187,620
Short-term borrowings	150,000	200,000
Current portion of long-term borrowings	10,000	20,000
Current tax payable	35,000	42,000
Short-term provisions	5,000	4,800
Total current liabilities	315,100	454,420
Total liabilities	492,750	692,700
Total equity and liabilities	1,466,500	1,524,200

XYZ Group – Statement of Comprehensive Income for the 31 December 20X7 Year Ended

(illustrating the presentation of comprehensive income in one statement and the classification of expenses within profit by function)

(in thousands of currency units)

	20X7	20X6
Revenue	390,000	355,000
Cost of sales	(245,000)	(230,000)
Gross profit	145,000	125,000
Other income	20,667	11,300
Distribution costs	(9,000)	(8,700)
Administrative expenses	(20,000)	(21,000)
Other expenses	(2,100)	(1,200)
Finance costs	(8,000)	(7,500)
Share of profit of associates[a]	35,100	30,100
Profit before tax	161,667	128,000
Income tax expense	(40,417)	(32,000)
Profit for the year from continuing operations	121,250	96,000
Loss for the year from discontinued operations	–	(30,500)
PROFIT FOR THE YEAR	121,250	65,500
Other comprehensive income:		
Exchange differences on translating foreign operations[a]	5,334	10,667
Available-for-sale financial assets[b]	(24,000)	26,667
Cash flow hedges[b]	(667)	(4,000)
Gains on property revaluation	933	3,367
Actuarial gains (losses) on defined benefit pension plans	(667)	1,333
Share of other comprehensive income of associates[c]	400	(700)
Income tax relating to components of other comprehensive income[d]	4,667	(9,334)
Other comprehensive income for the year, net of tax	(14,000)	28,000
TOTAL COMPREHENSIVE INCOME FOR THE YEAR	107,250	93,500

Profit attributable to:		
Owners of the parent	97,000	52,400
Minority interest	24,250	13,100
	121,250	65,500
Total comprehensive income attributable to:		
Owners of the parent	85,800	74,800
Minority interest	21,450	18,700
	107,250	93,500
Earnings per share (in currency units):		
Basic and diluted	0.46	0.30

Alternatively, components of other comprehensive income could be presented in the statement of comprehensive income net of tax:

	20X7	20X6
Other comprehensive income for the year, after tax:		
Exchange differences on translating foreign operations	4,000	8,000
Avail able-for-sale financial assets	(18,000)	20,000
Cash flow hedges	(500)	(3,000)
Gains on property revaluation	600	2,700
Actuarial gains (losses) on defined benefit pension plans	(500)	1,000
Share of other comprehensive income of associates	400	(700)
Other comprehensive income for the year, net of tax[d]	(14,000)	28,000

(a) This means the share of associates' profit attributable to owners of the associates, i.e. it is after tax and minority interests in the associates.

(b) This illustrates the aggregated presentation, with disclosure of the current year gain or loss and reclassification adjustment presented in the notes. Alternatively, a gross presentation can be used.

(c) This means the share of associates' other comprehensive income attributable to owners of the associates, i.e. it is after tax and minority interests in the associates.

(d) The income tax relating to each component of other comprehensive income is disclosed in the notes.

XYZ Group – Income Statement for the Year Ended 31 December 20X7

(illustrating the presentation of comprehensive income in two statements and classification of expenses within profit by nature)

(in thousands of currency units)

	20X7	20X6
Revenue	390,000	355,000
Other income	20,667	11,300
Changes in inventories of finished goods and work in progress	(115,100)	(107,900)
Work performed by the entity and capitalised	16,000	15,000
Raw material and consumables used	(96,000)	(92,000)
Employee benefits expense	(45,000)	(43,000)
Depreciation and amortisation expense	(19,000)	(17,000)
Impairment of property, plant and equipment	(4,000)	–
Other expenses	(6,000)	(5,500)
Finance costs	(15,000)	(18,000)
Share of profit of associates[e]	35,100	30,100
Profit before tax	161,667	128,000
Income tax expense	(40,417)	(32,000)

Profit for the year from continuing operations	121,250	96,000
Loss for the year from discontinued operations	–	(30,500)
PROFIT FOR THE YEAR	121,250	65,500
Profit attributable to:		
Owners of the parent	97,000	52,400
Minority interest	24,250	13,100
	121,250	65,500
Earnings per share (in currency units):		
Basic and diluted	0.46	0.30

[e] This means the share of associates' profit attributable to owners of the associates, i.e. it is after tax and minority interests in the associates.

XYZ Group – Statement of Comprehensive Income for the Year Ended 31 December 20X7

(illustrating the presentation of comprehensive income in two statements)

(in thousands of currency units)

	20X7	20X6
Profit for the year	121,250	65,500
Other comprehensive income:		
Exchange differences on translating foreign operations	5,334	10,667
Available-for-sale financial assets	(24,000)	26,667
Cash flow hedges	(667)	(4,000)
Gains on property revaluation	933	3,367
Actuarial gains (losses) on defined benefit pension plans	(667)	1,333
Share of other comprehensive income of associates[f]	400	(700)
Income tax relating to components of other comprehensive income[g]	4,667	(9,334)
Other comprehensive income for the year, net of tax	(14,000)	28,000
TOTAL COMPREHENSIVE INCOME FOR THE YEAR	107,250	93,500
Total comprehensive income attributable to:		
Owners of the parent	35,800	74,800
Minority interest	21,450	18,700
	107,250	93,500

Alternatively, components of other comprehensive income could be presented, net of tax. Refer to the statement of comprehensive income illustrating the presentation of income and expenses in one statement.

[f] This means the share of associates' other comprehensive income attributable to owners of the associates, i.e. it is after tax and minority interests in associates.

[g] The income tax relating to each component of other comprehensive income is disclosed in the notes.

XYZ Group – Statement of Changes in Equity for the Year Ended 31 December 20X7

(in thousands of currency units)

	Share capital	Retained earnings	Translation of foreign operations	Available for sale financial assets	Cash flow hedges	Revaluation surplus	Total	Minority interest	Total equity
Balance at 1 January 20X6	600,000	118,100	(4,000)	1,600	2,000	–	717,700	29,300	747,500
Changes in accounting policy	–	400	–	–	–	–	400	100	500
Restated balance	600,000	118,500	(4,000)	1,600	2,000	–	718,100	29,900	748,000
Changes in equity for 20X6									
Dividends	–	(10,000)	–	–	–	–	(10,000)	–	(10,000)
Total comprehensive income for the year(f)	–	53,200	6,400	16,000	(2,400)	1,600	74,800	18,700	93,500
Balance at 31 December 20X6	600,000	161,700	2,400	17,600	(400)	1,600	782,900	48,600	831,500
Changes in equity for 20X7									
Issue of share capital	50,000	–	–	–	–	–	50,000	–	50,000
Dividends	–	(15,000)	–	–	–	–	(15,000)	–	(15,000)
Total comprehensive income for the year(g)	–	96,600	3,200	(14,400)	(400)	800	85,800	21,450	107,250
Transfer to retained earnings	–	200	–	–	–	200	–	–	–
Balance at 31 December 20X7	650,000	243,500	5,600	3,200	(800)	2,200	903,700	70,050	973,750

Asset valuation: Non-current assets

2.1 IAS 16 *Property, Plant and Equipment* (revised December 2003)

Background

IAS 16 prescribes the accounting treatment for property, plant and equipment. Key issues include the initial recognition of cost, the determination of their carrying amounts and their related depreciation and impairment charges.

Definitions

- *Property, plant and equipment.* Tangible assets that are held by an entity for use in the production or supply of goods or services, or for rental to others, for administrative purposes and are expected to be used during more than one period.
- *Depreciation.* The systematic allocation of the depreciable amount of an asset over its useful life.

Accounting treatment

Initial measurement

Whether acquired or self-constructed, property, plant and equipment. should initially be recorded at cost. Only those costs that are directly attributable to bringing an asset into *working condition* for its *intended use* are permitted to be capitalised. Capitalisation of costs is also permitted only for the period in which activities are in progress (see IAS 23 *Borrowing costs*).

Capitalisation of interest on construction of a property must now be capitalised and all finance costs directly attributable to the construction of a tangible fixed asset should be capitalised, provided that they do not exceed the total finance costs incurred during the period. A revised standard (IAS 23 March 2007) has now made capitalisation of finance costs compulsory for activities in progress as part of the IASB/FASB convergence project.

Example – Dunloy Plc (Initial Measurement)

Dunloy Plc has recently purchased plant from Annoy plc, the details of which are as follows:

	£	£
Basic list price of plant		240,000
trade discount applicable to Dunloy plc		12.5% on list price
Ancillary costs		
shipping and handling costs		2,750
estimated pre-production testing		12,500
maintenance contract for three years		24,000
site preparation costs		
electrical cable installation	14,000	
concrete reinforcement	4,500	
own labour costs	7,500	26,000

Dunloy Plc paid for the plant (excluding the ancillary costs) within four weeks of order, thereby obtaining an early settlement discount of 3%.

Dunloy Plc had incorrectly specified the power loading of the original electrical cable to be installed by the contractor. In the above table the cost of correcting this error of £6,000 is included in the above figure of £14,000.

The plant is expected to last for 10 years. At the end of this period there will be compulsory costs of £15,000 to dismantle the plant and £3,000 to restore the site to its original useable condition.

Suggested solution – Dunloy Plc

Initial cost of plant purchased from Armoy plc

	£	£
Basic list price of plant	240,000	
Less trade discount (12.5%)	(30,000)	210,000
Shipping and handling costs	2,750	
Pre-production testing	12,500	
Site preparation costs		
Electrical cable installation (14,000–6,000 abnormal)	8,000	
Concrete reinforcement	4,500	
Own labour costs	7,500	35,250
Dismantling and restoration costs (15,000 + 3,000)		18,000
Initial cost plant		263,250

Note: Abnormal costs of rectifying the power loading cannot be included as it would not normally be incurred in getting the asset to its intended location and working condition. Cash discounts of 3% should be treated as administration or selling costs and may not be included as part of property, etc. Maintenance costs are revenue costs although a case may be made for deferring two-thirds as advance payments on account – as a prepayment but not as part of property, etc.

The amount recognised should not exceed an asset's recoverable amount.

Subsequent expenditure should normally be expensed (maintenance) but may be capitalised if either:

(i) a component of an asset has been treated as a separate asset and is now replaced or restored, e.g. Ryanair's splitting up of aircraft into different components and BAA's policy of separating runway surfaces from runway beds; or

BAA Plc   Year Ended 31 March 2006

Accounting Policies (Extract)

Asset lives

Airfields

Runway surfaces	10–15 years
Runway bases	100 years

Ryanair Plc   Year Ended 31 March 2006

Accounting Policies (Extract)

Property, Plant and Equipment (Extract)

An element of the cost of an acquired aircraft is attributed on acquisition to its service potential reflecting the maintenance condition of its engines and airframe. This cost, which can equate to a substantial element of the total aircraft cost, is amortised over the shorter of the period to the next check (usually between 8 and 12 years for Boeing 737–800 'next generation' aircraft) or the remaining life of the aircraft.

The costs of subsequent major airframe and engine maintenance checks are capitalised and amortised over the shorter of the period to the next check or the remaining life of the aircraft.

Irish Continental Group Plc   Year Ended 31 December 2005

Accounting Policies (Extract)

Property, Plant and Equipment

Passenger Ships

Passenger ships are stated at cost, with the exception of the fast ferry *Jonathan Swift* which is stated at deemed cost. Upon transition to IFRS, the amount initially recognised in respect of an item of property, plant and equipment is allocated to its significant parts and each such part is depreciated separately. In respect of passenger ships cost is allocated between hull and machinery and between hotel and catering areas.

For passenger ships, hotel and catering components with intensive wear are depreciated over 10 years. Hull and machinery components with minor wear are depreciated over the useful lives of the ships of 15 years for fast ferries and 30 years to residual value for conventional ferries. Residual values are reviewed on an annual basis.

(ii) where the expenditure enhances the economic benefits of the asset in excess of the original assessed standard of performance; or

(iii) it relates to a major overhaul or inspection whose benefits have already been consumed in the depreciation charge.

In 2004, British Airways Plc charged costs relating to the overhaul of aircraft and engines to the income statement as incurred. In 2005/2006, British Airways Plc followed IAS 16 and treated major engine overhauls as a separate asset component, capitalised them and depreciated them over the period to the next overhaul. However, it does not disclose the overhauls as a separate class of assets in the property schedule.

British Airways Plc   Year Ended 31 December 2005

Property, Plant and Equipment

Property, plant and equipment are held at cost. The Group has a policy of not revaluing tangible fixed assets. Depreciation is calculated to write off the cost less estimated residual value, on a straight-line basis over the useful life of the asset. Residual values, where applicable, are reviewed annually against prevailing market values for equivalently aged assets and depreciation rates adjusted accordingly on a prospective basis.

The carrying value is reviewed for impairment when events or changes in circumstances indicate the carrying value may not be recoverable and the cumulative impairment losses are shown as a reduction in the carrying value of tangible fixed assets.

The Group has taken advantage of the exemption in IFRS 1 that allows it to carry forward properly at deemed cost after taking account of revaluations carried out at 31 March 1995.

(a)   Capitalisation of interest on progress payments:

Interest attributed to progress payments, and related exchange movements on foreign currency amounts, made on account of the aircraft and other significant assets under construction is capitalised and added to the cost of the asset concerned.

(b)   Fleet:

All aircraft are stated at the fair value of the consideration given after taking account of manufacturers' credits. Fleet assets owned, or held on finance lease or hire-purchase arrangements, are depreciated at rates calculated to write-down the cost to the estimated residual value at the end of their planned operational lives on a straight-line basis.

Cabin interior modifications, including those required for brand changes and relaunches, are depreciated over the shorter period of five years and the remaining life of the aircraft.

Aircraft and engine spares acquired on the introduction or expansion of a fleet, as well as notable spares purchased separately, are carried as tangible fixed assets and generally depreciated in line with the fleet to which they relate.

Major overhaul expenditure, including replacement spares and labour costs, is capitalised and amortised over the average expected life between major overhauls. All other replacement spares and other costs relating to maintenance of fleet assets (including maintenance provided under 'power-by-the-hour' contracts) are charged to the income statement on consumption or as incurred respectively.

(c)   Property and equipment:

Prevision is made for the depreciation of all property and equipment, apart from freehold land, based upon expected useful lives, or in the case of leasehold properties over the duration of the leases if shorter, on a straight-line basis.

(d)   Leased and hire purchase assets:

Where assets are financed through finance leases or hire purchase arrangements, under which substantially all the risks and rewards of ownership are transferred to the Group, the assets are treated as if they had been purchased outright. The amount included in the cost of tangible fixed assets represents the aggregate of the capital elements payable during the lease or hire-purchase term. The corresponding obligation, reduced by the appropriate proportion of lease or hire purchase payments made, is included in creditors. The amount included in the cost of tangible fixed assets is depreciated on the basis described in the preceding paragraphs and the interest element of lease or hire purchase payments made is included in interest payable in the income statement. Total minimum payments, measured at inception, under all other lease arrangements, known as operating leases, are charged to the income statement in equal annual amounts over the period of the lease. In respect of aircraft, certain operating lease arrangements allow the Group to terminate the leases after a limited initial period of normally five to seven years without further material financial obligations. In certain cases, the Group is entitled to extend the initial lease period on pre determined terms; such leases are described as extendible operating leases.

Subsequent cost or valuation

An entity should choose either the cost model or revaluation model and apply that policy to the entire class of property, plant and equipment.

Cost model

Property, etc. should be carried at cost less any accumulated depreciation and impairment losses to date.

One company which has switched back to the cost model is Greene King Plc. Previously, Greene King revalued its licensed properties at least every five years on an existing use basis. Surpluses had been taken to a revaluation reserve, which stood at £278 million in 2004.

In 2005/2006, the company adopted the cost model under IAS 16 and valued property at cost or deemed cost. Accordingly, no revaluation reserve was recognised and the effects of historical revaluations were included in retained earnings. The company moved to the cost model in the light of uncertainty in the sector as to an appropriate policy and following a consensus in informal industry discussions to opt, at present, for the cost model. In addition, revaluation is expensive and, as recent valuations are carried over, there is a relatively small difference at present between cost and revaluation.

Greene King Plc   Year Ended 30 April 2006

Property, Plant and Equipment

The group has adopted the transitional provisions of IFRS 1 to use previous revaluations as deemed cost at the transition date. From 3 May 2004, all property, plant and equipment will be stated at cost or deemed cost on transition, less accumulated depreciation and any impairment in value.

Depreciation is calculated on a straight-line basis over the estimated useful life of the asset.

Freehold land is not depreciated. Residual values and useful lives are reviewed annually by management and depreciation adjusted, as applicable. Residual values are those assessed in the annual review. Freehold buildings are depreciated to their estimated residual values over periods up to 50 years. Whereas long leasehold properties are depreciated to their estimated residual values over periods up to 50 years, short leasehold improvements are depreciated to their estimated residual values over the remaining term of the lease. Plant and equipment assets are depreciated over their estimated lives, which range from three to twenty years.

At each balance sheet date, the carrying values of property, plant and equipment are reviewed for indicators of impairment. For the purposes of the impairment testing, a cash generating unit (CGU) is taken as the lowest level (either individual asset or group of assets) where cash inflows are separately identifiable. Where the carrying value of assets may not be recoverable, an impairment in the value of fixed assets is charged to the income statement. The recoverable amount is the greater of the fair value less costs to sell and value in use is determined by discounting the future estimated cash flows to their present value.

Revaluation model

Should be carried at a fair value at the date of revaluation less any subsequent accumulated depreciation and impairment losses. Revaluations should occur sufficiently regularly so that the amount does not differ materially from the fair value at the balance sheet date.

Revaluations

The fair value of land and buildings is usually its market value, normally appraised by professionally qualified valuers. The fair value of plant is usually its market value. If there is no evidence of market values due to its specialised nature or if it is rarely sold, then plant should be valued at depreciated replacement cost.

The frequency of revaluations depends upon their movements. Some items of property may experience significant and volatile movements in fair value, thus necessitating annual revaluation. For those assets with insignificant movements then a revaluation every three or five years may be sufficient.

When an item of property is revalued, any accumulated depreciation at the date of the revaluation is either:

(a)   restated proportionately with the change in the gross carrying value or
(b)   eliminated against the gross carrying amount of the asset and the net amount restated to the revalued amount of the asset (often adopted for buildings).

When an item of property is revalued, the entire class of property must be revalued. A class of property is a grouping of assets of a similar nature and use in an entity's operations. Examples include land, land and buildings, machinery, ships, aircraft, motor vehicles, furniture and fixtures and office equipment.

A class of assets may be revalued on a rolling basis provided the revaluation is completed within a short period of time and the revaluations are kept up to date.

Any increase in valuation must be recognised directly in equity except to the extent that it reverses a revaluation decrease of the same asset previously recognised as an expense. In that case, it should be recognised in the income statement. A decrease shall be recognised in equity until the carrying amount reaches its depreciated historical cost and thereafter in the income statement.

The revaluation surplus may be transferred directly to retained earnings when the asset is derecognised, i.e. disposed of or the asset used up. Transfers are not made through the income statement.

The effects of taxes on income revaluation should be recognised in accordance with IAS 12.

Depreciation

Each part of an item of property, plant and equipment with a significant cost in relation to total cost should be depreciated separately e.g. airframe, engines (component accounting).

The depreciable amount of property, etc., should be allocated on a systematic basis over its useful life and the method adopted should reflect the pattern in which the asset's future economic benefits are expected to be consumed. Depreciation should normally be recognised as an expense.

The useful life and residual value should be reviewed at each year end and adjusted as a change in the accounting estimate as per IAS 8.

Depreciation is recognised even if the value of the asset exceeds its carrying amount. The charge for depreciation should be reflected in the income statement unless included in the carrying amount of the asset. Depreciation usually begins when an asset is ready for use but does not cease when idle or retired from active use. However, if classified as held for sale under IFRS 5 and transferred to current assets it should not be depreciated. The residual value and the useful life of an asset should be reviewed at least at each year end and, if expectations of previous estimates are judged incorrect, the adjustment should be accounted for as a change in an accounting estimate in accordance with IAS 8. Depreciation could be zero under some methods if based on nil production units.

Future economic benefits are principally consumed through the use of an asset but other factors such as technical or commercial obsolescence and wear and tear must be considered.

All the following factors must be considered in determining the useful life of an asset:

(a)   the expected usage of the asset's capacity/output;
(b)   the expected physical wear and tear;
(c)   technical or commercial obsolescence;
(d)   legal limits on the use of the asset such as expiry dates of related leases.

The useful life is defined in terms of the asset's expected utility to the entity. The asset management policy may involve the disposal of assets after a specified time or after consumption of a proportion of future benefits. It can be shorter than its economic life.

Land and buildings must be treated as separable assets. With certain exceptions, such as quarries and landfill sites, land has an unlimited useful life and is therefore not depreciated. Buildings are depreciable assets. If the cost of land includes site dismantling/restoration costs these may be depreciated over the period of benefits obtained by incurring these costs.

The depreciable amount of an asset is after deducting its residual value. In practice, the value is often insignificant and immaterial. If it is material, its value should be reviewed at each balance sheet date. Any change should be accounted for prospectively as an adjustment to future depreciation. An estimate of an asset's residual value is based on the amount recoverable from disposal, at the date of the estimate of similar assets that have reached the end of their useful lives and under similar operating conditions. This could lead to the reintroduction of 'nil' depreciation, particularly in relation to buildings which have very high residual values.

Subsequent developments

*   *Revision of useful economic life.* This should be reviewed on a regular basis and, if necessary, the life of the property, etc., adjusted to recognise depreciation over the asset's remaining economic useful life.

Whilst continuing to depreciate on a straight-line basis, Danish company Rockwool International A/S disclosed that it reassessed the useful economic lives of its fixed assets in 2001. Previously, buildings were depreciated at 5%, plant and machinery at 15% and 20% and other operating equipment at 25%. From 2002, the accounting policies note discloses that buildings are depreciated over 20–40 years, plant and machinery over 5–15 years and other operating equipment and fixtures and fittings over 3–10 years. Rockwool disclosed that the effect of this change was to reduce depreciation by some DKK254 million. The depreciation charge for current and future periods was adjusted.

- *Change in method of depreciation.* The method of depreciation can be changed if it would present a truer and fairer view of the financial statements. The net book value should be written off over an asset's estimated remaining useful life. This is not a change in accounting policy but merely a change in estimate and therefore no prior year adjustment is required. IAS 16 encourages the use of methods based on the expected pattern of consumption of future economic benefits.

A variety of depreciation methods can be used including straight line, diminishing balance and sum of the units. This last method results in a charge based on the expected use or output of the asset. Previously, Dutch company, EADS, disclosed that the costs of specialised tooling for commercial production were capitalised and amortised over five years on a straight-line basis. From 2002, the accounting policies note disclosed that, as an alternative to the straight-line method, the sum-of-the-units method may be more appropriate and identified, in particular, the Airbus 380 production programme that required specialised tools as one such programme where depreciation of tooling is allocated across the number of units produced.

European Aeronautical   Eads NV (2002) Holland Defence and Space Company

Accounting Policies (Extract)

Property, Plant and Equipment

Property, plant and equipment are valued at acquisition or manufacturing costs less accumulated depreciation. Depreciation expense is recognised by principally using the straight-line method. The costs of internally produced equipment and facilities include direct material and labour costs and applicable manufacturing overheads, including depreciation charges. Borrowing costs are not capitalised. The following useful lives are assumed: buildings 6–50 years; site improvements 6–20 years, technical equipment and machinery 3–20 years; and other equipment factory and office equipment 2–10 years. The cost of specialised tooling for commercial production is capitalised and generally depreciated using the straight-line method over 5 years or, if more appropriate, using the number of production or similar units expected to be obtained from the tools (sum-of-the-units method). Especially for aircraft production programmes such as the Airbus A380 with an estimated number of aircraft to be produced using such tools, the sum-of-the-units method effectively allocates the diminution of value of specialised tools to the units produced.

- *Policy of non-depreciation.* All property, etc., with the exception of land, should be depreciated, per IAS 16, with the exception of land. Even buildings are expected to be depreciated over their economic useful lives with the exception of investment properties. There has grown up a practice, however, of non-depreciation of certain buildings which interface with the public, e.g. supermarkets, hotels, public houses, etc. This policy was confirmed in the United Kingdom by the Financial Reporting Review Panel in the test case of Forte plc. However, it was subsequently rejected, for industrial buildings, by the Panel in the case of SEP Industrial Holdings plc. IAS 16, however, still permits this policy but insists that an annual impairment review be carried out (under IAS 36) on such assets to ensure that they are not recorded above their recoverable amount.

Specific disclosures are required with regard to depreciation policies and changes in those policies and, in particular, a property, etc., schedule should be published giving details of the full movement for the year in cost/value and in accumulated depreciation.

Disclosure requirements

For each class of property, etc.

(a)   the measurement bases adopted. Where more than one basis is used, the gross carrying value for each basis adopted shall be disclosed;
(b)   the depreciation methods used;
(c)   the useful lives or depreciation rates used;
(d)   the gross carrying amount and accumulated depreciation at start and end of the year;
(e)   a reconciliation of the carrying amount at start and end of the period showing the following:
- additions
- disposals
- acquisitions through business combinations
- revaluations
- impairment losses
- impairment losses reversed
- depreciation
- net exchange differences on translation of functional currency into a different presentation currency
- other changes.

In addition, the following should also be disclosed:

(a)   the existence and the amounts of restrictions on title and property, etc., pledged as securities;
(b)   the amount of expenditures capitalised in course of construction;
(c)   the amount of contractual commitments for the acquisition of property etc; and
(d)   if not disclosed separately on the face of the income statement, the amount and compensation from third parties included in the income statement.

The selection of the depreciation method and estimate of useful life are matters of judgement. Disclosure of the methods adopted is useful information to users and to allow users to review the policies selected. For similar reasons, it is necessary to disclose:

(a)   depreciation during the period;
(b)   accumulated depreciation at the end of the period.

An entity should disclose the nature and effect of a change in the accounting estimate with respect to residual values, estimated costs of dismantling or restoring property, etc., useful lives and depreciation method in accordance with IAS 8.

When items of property, etc., are revalued the following should be disclosed:

(a) the effective date of the revaluation;
(b) whether an independent valuer was involved;
(c) the methods and significant assumptions applied in estimating the assets' fair values;
(d) the extent to which the assets' fair values were determinable to observable prices in an active market or recent market transactions on arms length or estimated market transaction using other valuation techniques;
(e) for each revalued class of property, the carrying amount at historic cost;
(f) the revaluation surplus, indicating the movement for the period and any restrictions on distribution.

A typical accounting policy note and property schedule has been provided by the Irish quoted company, the Grafton Group Plc. Note the additional disclosure at the foot of the property schedule indicating the amount of finance leases (to accord with IAS 17 *Leases*) that are included within the property total:

Grafton Group Plc   Year Ended 31 December 2005

Property, Plant and Equipment

Property, plant and equipment are stated at cost or deemed cost less accumulated depreciation and impairment losses. The Group's Irish properties were revalued to fair value in 1998 and are measured on the basis of deemed cost being the revalued amount at the date of that revaluation less accumulated depreciation.

Property, plant and equipment are depreciated over their useful economic life on a straight-line basis at the following rates:

Freehold buildings	50–100 years
Freehold land	Not depreciated
Leasehold buildings	Lease term or up to 100 years
Plant and machinery	5–20 years
Motor vehicles	5 years
Plant hire equipment	4–8 years

The residual value and useful lives of property, plant and equipment are reviewed and adjusted if appropriate at each balance sheet date.

On disposal of property, plant and equipment, the cost and related accumulated depreciation and impairments are removed from the financial statements and the net amount, less any proceeds, is taken to the income statement.

The carrying amounts of the Group's property, plant and equipment are reviewed at each balance sheet date to determine whether there is any indication of impairment. An impairment loss is recognised whenever the carrying amount of an asset or its cash generation unit exceeds its recoverable amount. Impairment losses are recognised in the income statement unless the asset is recorded at a revalued amount in which case it is first dealt with through the revaluation reserve relating to that asset with any residual amount being transferred to the income statement.

Subsequent costs are included in an assets carrying amount or recognised as a separate asset, as appropriate, only when it is probable that future economic benefits associated with the item will flow to the Group and the cost of the replaced item can be measured reliably. All other repair and maintenance costs are charged to the income statement during the financial period in which they are incurred.

12. Property, Plant and Equipment

	Freehold Land and Buildings (€'000)	Leasehold Land and Buildings (€'000)	Plant Machinery and Motor Vehicles (€'000)	Total (€'000)
Group cost				
At 1 January 2004	208,928	51,446	180,676	441,050
Additions	26,908	10,590	51,419	88,917
Acquisitions	11,638	2,255	3,868	17,761
Disposals	(12,132)	(596)	(19,707)	(32,435)
Exchange adjustment	(600)	(104)	(526)	(1,230)
At 1 January 2005	234,742	63,591	215,730	514,063
Additions	24,620	8,096	67,843	100,569
Acquisitions	138,774	400	37,537	176,711
Disposals	(9,620)	(850)	(27,892)	(38,162)
Exchange adjustment	5,243	2,156	4,988	12,387
At 31 December 2005	393,759	73,593	298,206	765,553
Depreciation				
At 1 January 2004	7,114	4,960	72,414	84,488
Charge for year	2,917	2,641	29,068	34,626
Disposals	(126)	(186)	(9,657)	(9,969)
Exchange adjustment	(94)	(85)	(1,110)	(1,289)
At 1 January 2005	9,811	7,330	90,715	107,856
Charge for year	5,068	3,176	40,004	48,248
Disposals	(648)	(288)	(16,635)	(17,571)
Exchange adjustment	348	245	3,206	3,797
At 31 December 2005	14,577	10,463	117,290	142,330
Net book amount				
At 31 December 2005	379,182	63,130	180,916	623,228
At 31 December 2004	224,931	55,281	125,015	406,207
At 31 December 2003	201,814	46,486	103,262	356,562

The Group's freehold and long leasehold properties located in the Republic of Ireland were professionally valued as at December 1998 by professional valuers in accordance with the Appraisal and Valuation Manual of the Society of Chartered Surveyors. The valuations, which were made on an open market for existing use basis, amounted to €58.0 million which at the date of transition 1 January 2004, were deemed to be cost for the purpose of the transition to IFRS. The remaining properties, which are located in the United Kingdom, are included at cost less depreciation.

The Property, Plant and Equipment of the Group Includes Leased Assets As Follows:

	Plant, Machinery & Motor Vehicles		Leasehold Properties	
	2005 (€'000)	2004 (€'000)	2005 (€'000)	2004 (€'000)
Cost	13,483	3,618	13,936	9,750
Accumulated depreciation	(4,561)	(2,364)	(1,040)	(429)
Net book amount	8,922	1,234	12,896	9,321
Depreciation charge for year	1,073	1,051	611	429

During the year the Group repaid finance leases amounting to €2.1 million (2004; €23.8 million).

2.2   IAS 40 *Investment Property* (revised December 2003)

IAS 40 prescribes the accounting treatment for investment properties and their related disclosure. It is effective for accounting periods starting on or after 1 January 2005.

Investment property is defined as property held to earn rentals or for capital appreciation or both rather than for use in production, administration or sale in the ordinary course of business.

IAS 40 permits entities to choose between either

(a)   fair value reporting with changes recognised in the income statement or
(b)   cost.

Whichever model is chosen must be to all investment properties. A change from one model to another is only permitted if it gives a fairer presentation which is highly unlikely. If an entity adopts the fair value model but cannot get clear evidence of the fair value of an investment property, then cost must be used until the asset is disposed.

Definition

Investment property

Property held to earn rentals or for capital appreciation or both, rather than for:

(a)   use in the production or supply of goods or services or for administration purposes or
(b)   sale in the ordinary course of business.

Investment properties are acquired to earn rentals or for capital appreciation or both and thus their cash flows are largely independent of those from other assets held by the enterprise. The following are examples:

(a)   land held for long-term capital appreciation;
(b)   land held for a currently undetermined future use;

(c)   a building owned and leased out under an operating lease;

(d)   a vacant building which is to be leased under operating lease.

However, the following are NOT investment properties:

(a)   property held for sale in the ordinary course of business or in the course of construction for such sale (see IAS 2);

(b)   property being constructed for third parties (see IAS 11);

(c)   owner-occupied properties (see IAS 16);

(d)   property that is being constructed or developed for future use as an investment property (see IAS 16); and

(e)   property that is leased to another entity under a finance lease (see IAS 17).

Mixed properties, if sold separately, should be accounted for separately. If not, the property is only classified as investment if an insignificant portion is held for use for production or for administrative purposes. Similarly properties providing ancillary services should be treated as investment properties if the services are a relatively insignificant portion of the whole. Judgement is needed to determine whether a property qualifies or not.

Example – Carrick Plc (Investment Property)

Carrick plc owns three identical properties, North, South and East. North is used as the head office of Carrick Plc. South is let to, and is occupied by, a subsidiary. East is let to, and is occupied by, an associate company. A fourth property, West, is leased by Carrick Plc and the unexpired term on the lease is 15 years. West is let to, and is occupied by, a company outside the group.

Which, if any, of these properties is likely to be an investment property of Carrick plc and what additional information may be necessary for a final decision?

Suggested solution – Carrick Plc

IAS 40 defines an investment property as an interest in land and/or buildings:

(1)   in respect of which construction work and development has been completed and

(2)   which is held for its investment potential, with any rental income being negotiated at arm's length.

However, excluded from the definition are:

(1)   properties owned and occupied by a company for its own purposes and not for investment purposes;

(2)   properties let to and occupied by another member of the group.

These criteria can be applied to the individual properties of Carrick Plc.

(1)   North is used as the head office of the group, therefore under exclusion (1), it would not be an investment property and would be accounted for under the rules of IAS 16.

(2) South is let to and occupied by a subsidiary, therefore under exclusion (2), it would not be an investment property.

(3) East is let to an associated company, but not part of the group. The property would appear to meet the definition of an investment property. Additional information required would include details of market rent to ensure that the asset is held for its investment potential.

(4) West is let to an outside company at an arm's-length rental over a period of 15 years, being the unexpired period of the lease. This would appear to be an investment property.

(5) IAS 16 requires that all property, etc., including buildings but not land, should be depreciated over their estimated useful economic life. This is regardless of the market value of those assets, which may well be increasing.

IAS 40, however, emphasises the concept of current values in determining the balance sheet valuation of investment properties. Changes in the value of investment properties should go through the income statement but it may also be treated at cost in the normal way under IAS 16. IAS 16 is not applicable if the properties are revalued and IAS 40 states that investment properties should not be subject to periodic depreciation charges in that case.

The application of these principles would have the following effect:

(1) North and South are not investment properties, therefore they should both be depreciated as per IAS 16. The value of land and buildings should be separated because no depreciation is charged on land. The cost or revalued amounts for buildings should be depreciated over their estimated useful lives.

(2) East is an investment property, therefore no depreciation should be charged if revaluation option is adopted. The asset should be shown at open market value in the balance sheet.

(3) West is an investment property and again should be revalued with gain being recorded in income or else treated as a normal property and kept at cost less accumulated depreciation.

Recognition

Investment property should be recognised as an asset when, and only when:

(a) it is probable that the future economic benefits associated with the asset will flow to the entity;

(b) the cost of the investment property can be measured reliably.

The former requires an assessment of the degree of certainty attaching to the flows based on available evidence and the second should normally be satisfied at the time of acquisition. Costs of day-to-day servicing should be expensed immediately, as repairs and maintenance. Replacement costs should be capitalised only if they meet the recognition criteria.

Measurement at recognition

Investment properties should be initially measured at cost with transaction costs included. That includes their purchase price and any directly attributable expenditure such as legal and professional fees and property taxes.

Cost is cost when construction is complete. Until that date, IAS 16 applies. Normally start up costs, initial operating losses, abnormal wastage of materials or labour, etc. would not be included.

If payment is deferred, the cost is the cash price equivalent and any difference treated as an interest expense over the period of credit.

Measurement after recognition

Accounting policy

Should choose either the fair value model or the cost model and apply the same model to all of its investment properties. If it opts for fair value, an entity is encouraged, but not required, to determine fair value on the basis of a valuation by an independently qualified valuer.

It is highly unlikely that a change from one model to another could result in a more appropriate policy under IAS 8.

Fair value model

After initial recognition, if adopt fair value, entities must measure all investment properties at that value with any gains/losses being included in net profit/loss for the period in which it arises.

Fair value is usually its market value but excluding any special terms. Any selling costs must not be deducted in arriving at fair value.

When a property interest held by a lessee under an operating lease is classified as an investment property, the fair value model should be applied.

The fair value should reflect the actual market state at the balance sheet date, not of the past or the future. It also assumes simultaneous exchange and completion of the contract between knowledgeable and willing parties.

Fair value should reflect any rental income from current leases and be based on reasonable and supportable assumptions about the market's view on rental income from future leases in the light of current market conditions. Both parties are assumed to be able to buy and sell at the best price possible and are not eager or forced to buy or sell.

The best evidence of fair value is normally provided by current prices on an active market for similar property in the same location and condition. In the absence of this, an entity should consider information from a variety of sources including:

(a)   current prices on an active market for properties of different nature, condition or location, adjusted to reflect those differences;
(b)   recent prices on less active markets, with adjustments to reflect any changes in economic conditions since the date of the transactions that occurred at those prices; and
(c)   discounted cash-flow projections based on reliable estimates of future cash flows supported by external evidence and adopting discount rates reflecting current market assessments of the uncertainty in the amount and timing of the cash flows.

In some cases, a different conclusion as to the fair value of an investment property may be suggested using the above. The reasons for those differences must be considered to arrive at the most reliable estimate of fair value. Where the variability in the range of fair values is great and probabilities so difficult to assess then the fair value may not be determined reliably on a continuing basis.

Fair value is not the same as value in use. It does not reflect any:

(a)   additional value derived from the creation of a portfolio of properties in different locations;
(b)   synergies between investment property and other assets;
(c)   legal rights or restrictions that are specific to the current owner; and
(d)   tax benefits or tax burdens specific to the current owner.

Care must also be taken not to double count assets or liabilities that are recognised separately. For example:

(a)   equipment such as elevators or air conditioning;
(b)   furniture in a furnished lease;
(c)   prepaid or accrued rental income; and
(d)   the fair value of investment property held under a lease reflects expected cash flows and thus need to add back any recognised lease liability to arrive at the fair value of the investment property.

Fair value should also not reflect future capital expenditure that will enhance or improve the property. Also any expected excess expenditure over receipts should be accounted for under IAS 37.

In exceptional cases, where there is clear evidence that the entity will not be able to determine the fair value of an investment property reliably on a continuing basis, an entity should measure the property according to the benchmark treatment in IAS 16 with an assumed residual value of zero. The entity must continue to apply IAS 16 until the property is disposed. However, all other investment properties should be measured at fair value.

If an entity has measured investment properties at fair value, it must continue to do so until disposal or unless the property becomes owner occupied even if comparable market transactions become less frequent or market prices less readily available.

Fair value would appear to be the more popular option, as until recently, property prices have been rising and thus the surpluses on revaluation have a major impact on profitability. One company that has adopted this approach is the British Land Company Plc:

British Land Company Plc   Year Ended 31 March 2006

In 2004, British Land Plc, recognised its investment properties at market value in accordance with SSAP 19 'Accounting for investment properties' with changes in fair value recognised in reserves. In 2005/2006, as permitted by IAS 40 'Investment property', the company applied the fair value model and in the income statement recognised £1.2 billion gains from the revaluation of property.

Properties

Properties are externally valued on an open market basis at the balance sheet date. Investment and development properties are recorded at valuation: trading properties at the lower of cost and valuation.

Any surplus or deficit arising on revaluing investment properties is recognised in the income statement for the year, where an investment property is being redeveloped. Any movement in valuation is recognised in the income statement

Valuation surpluses arising on other development properties, those not previously investment properties, are reflected in the revaluation reserve, unless a deficit reduces the value below cost. In which case the deficit is charged to the income statement.

The cost of properties in the course of development includes attributable interest and other associated outgoings; interest is calculated on the development expenditure by reference to specific borrowings where relevant and otherwise on the average rate applicable to short-term loans. Interest is not capitalised where no development activity is taking place. A property ceases to be treated as a development property on practical completion.

Disposals are recognised on completion: profits and losses arising are recognised through the income statement, the profit on disposal is determined as the difference between the sales proceeds and the carrying amount of the asset at the commencement of the accounting period plus additions in the period.

In determining whether leases and related properties represent operating or finance leases, consideration is given to whether the tenant or landlord bears the risks and rewards of ownership.

Properties acquired in corporate vehicles are generally treated as business acquisition and not asset acquisitions resulting in any contingent capital gains liabilities assumed being reflected in the acquisition balance sheet rather than recorded as contingencies. In adopting this policy the directors place value on transparency and consistency, even though the liabilities are recorded under IFRS on a full provision basis, significantly above their fair value.

11. Investment, Development and Trading Properties (continued)

Current year	Investment (€m)	Development (€m)	Trading (€m)	Total (€m)
Carrying value at 1 April 2005	10,877	212	36	11,125
Additions: – corporate acquisitions	495			495
– property purchases	34	134		168
– other capital expenditure	196	114		310
	725	248		973
Disposals	(1,722)			(1,722)
Property transfer	7	(7)		
Exchange fluctuations	1			1
Revaluations:				
included in income statement	1,159	42		1,201
included in consolidated statement				
of changes in equity		102		102
increase in tenant incentives and				
guaranteed rent uplift balances	34			34
Carrying value of properties on balance sheet 31 March 2006	11,081	597	36	11,714
External valuation surplus on trading properties				67
Head lease liabilities (Note 18)				(28)
Total Group property portfolio valuation 31 March 2006				11,753

At 31 March 2006, the Group book value of properties of £11,714 million (2005: £11,125m) comprises freeholds of £11,017 million (2005: £10,402m), virtual freeholds of £109 million (2005: £96m); long leaseholds of £577 million (2006: £618m) and short, leaseholds of £11 million (2005: £9m).

Investment, development and trading properties were valued by external valuers other than where stated on the basis of open market in accordance with the Appraisal and Valuation Manual published by The Royal Institute of Chartered Surveyors:

	2005 (€m)	2005 (€m)
Knight Frank	11,750	
Atisreal weatheralls		10,802
FPD Savills	2	282
Jones Lang LaSalle (Republic of Ireland)		69
CB Richard Ellis B.V. (Netherlands)	1	1
Total Group property portfolio valuation	11,753	11,154

Properties valued at £7,709 million (2005: £7,052m) were subject to a security interest and other properties of non-recourse companies amounted to £196 million (2005:£42m).

Cumulative interest capitalised in investment and development properties amounts to £40 million and £13 million (2005: £37m and £4m), respectively. Included in leasehold properties is an amount of £32 million (2005: £33m) in respect of property occupied by the Group. The historical cost of properties was £7,698 million (2005: £8,149m).

Cost model

If an entity adopts the cost model, it should measure all of its investment properties in accordance with IAS 16, i.e. at cost less accumulated depreciation and impairment losses. One company which has adopted this model is Tesco Plc:

Tesco Plc   Year Ended 25 February 2006

In 2005, Tesco included its investment properties within tangible fixed assets, measured at cost less accumulated depreciation. In 2006, the company recognised separately, on the face of the balance sheet, £745 million of investment property. In a note, the company disclosed that these assets are buildings held to earn rental income and for capital appreciation rather than being utilised in its operating activities and thus fall under IAS 40 'Investment property'. The company applied the cost model and indicated that it used the diminishing balance method for depreciation. It added that the fair value of these properties was £1.4 billion.

Investment Property

Investment property is property held to earn rental income and/or for capital appreciation rather than for the purpose of Group operating activities. Investment property assets are carried at cost less accumulated depreciation and any recognised impairment in value. The depreciation policies for investment property are consistent with those described for owner-occupied property.

Note 12 Investment property

	£m
Cost	
At 26 February 2005	595
Foreign currency translation	36
Addition	21
Transfers	194
Classified as held for sale	(58)
Disposals	(3)
At 25 February 2006	785

Accumulated depreciation and impairment losses	
At 26 February 2005	30
Foreign currency translation	2
Charge for the period	9
Classified as held for sale	(1)
At 25 February 2006	(1)
Net carrying value	
At 25 February 2006	745
At 26 February 2005	565

The estimated fair value of the Group's Investment property is £1,373 million (2005: £899m). This value has been determined by applying an appropriate rental yield to the rentals earned by the Investment property. The valuation has not been performed by an independent valuer.

Transfers

Transfers to, or from, investment property should be made when, and only when, there is a change in use, evidenced by:

(a)   commencement of owner occupation;
(b)   commencement of development with a view to resale through inventories;
(c)   end of owner occupation and transfer to investment property;
(d)   commencement of an operating lease, for a transfer from inventories to investment property; or
(e)   end of construction for a transfer to investment property.

When an entity adopts the cost model, transfers do not change the carrying amounts of those assets or the cost of that property for disclosure purposes.

When an entity transfers a fair value investment property to owner-occupied property or inventories, the property's cost for subsequent periods should be its fair value at the date of change in use.

If an owner-occupied property becomes an investment property an entity should apply IAS 16 up to the date of change in use. Any difference between the carrying amount of the property under IAS 16 and its fair value should be accounted for as a revaluation as per IAS 16 i.e.:

(1)   Any decrease should be recognised in net profit or loss for the period but, to the extent that a revaluation surplus exists on that asset, the decrease should first be charged against that surplus
(2)   Any resulting increase in the carrying amount should:
    (a)   to the extent it reverses a previous impairment loss, in profit and loss but restored to amount that would have been determined had no impairment been recognised and

(b)   any remaining part of the increase is credited directly to equity – revaluation surplus. On disposal, the surplus may be transferred to retained earnings but not through profit and loss.

For transfers between inventories and investment properties (fair value), any difference between the fair value of the property at that date and its previous carrying value should be recognised in profit or loss for the period i.e. same as sale of inventories.

For transfers from construction to investment properties at fair value, any difference between fair value at that date and its previous carrying amount should be recognised in profit and loss.

Disposals

An investment property should be derecognised on disposal or when the property is permanently withdrawn from use and no future economic benefits are expected to be derived from its disposal. The creation of a finance lease would be one example.

Gains or losses, arising from retirement or disposal, represent the difference between the net disposal proceeds and the carrying amount of the asset and should be recognised as profits or losses in the income statement in the period of that retirement or disposal.

Consideration initially should be at fair value and, if deferred, at the cash price equivalent with any difference in the latter being treated as interest revenue, as per IAS 18, using the effective interest method.

Compensation from third parties for investment properties that have been impaired, lost or given up should be recognised in profit or loss when the compensation becomes receivable. The following should be separately disclosed:

(a)   impairments recognised in accordance with IAS 36;
(b)   retirements/disposals recognised in accordance with IAS 40;
(c)   compensation from third parties recognised in profit and loss when it becomes receivable; and
(d)   the cost of assets restored, purchased or constructed as replacements in accordance with IAS 40.

Disclosure

Fair value and cost models

(a)   whether it applies the fair value or the cost model;
(b)   if it applies to the fair value model, where, and in what circumstances, property interests held under operating leases are classified and accounted for as investment property;
(c)   the criteria to distinguish investment property from owner-occupied property and from property held for normal resale;
(d)   the methods and significant assumptions applied in determining fair value, including a statement supported by market evidence or based on other factors;
(e)   the extent to which the fair value of an investment property is based on a valuation by an independent valuer holding a recognised qualification with recent experience in the location and category of the investment property being valued. If none, that fact should be disclosed;

(f)   The amounts included within income for:
- rental income;
- direct operating expenses arising from investment properties generating rental income; and
- direct operating expenses arising from investment properties not generating rental income.

(g)   the existence and amounts of restrictions on realisability or remittance;

(h)   contractual obligations to purchase, construct or develop investment properties or for repairs, maintenance or enhancements.

Fair value model

In addition to the above, a reconciliation of the carrying amount of investment property from the start to the end of the period is required to show the following:

(a)   additions, disclosing acquisitions separately from capitalised subsequent expenditure;

(b)   additions from business combinations;

(c)   disposals;

(d)   net gains/losses from fair value adjustments;

(e)   the net exchange differences on translation of a foreign entity;

(f)   transfers to/from inventories and owner-occupied property; and

(g)   other movements.

When a valuation obtained for investment property is adjusted significantly e.g. to avoid double counting of assets/liabilities, the entity should disclose a reconciliation between the valuation obtained and the adjusted valuation included in the financial statements, showing separately the aggregate amount of any recognised lease obligations that have been added back, and any other significant adjustments.

In exceptional cases, when using the cost model, the reconciliation shown above in (a) to (g) should be provided separately for that investment property from any others. In addition the following should also be disclosed:

(a)   a description of the investment property;

(b)   an explanation of why fair value cannot be reliably measured;

(c)   if possible, the range of estimates within which fair value is highly likely to lie;

(d)   on disposal of an investment property not carried at fair value:
- the fact that it has disposed of such a property;
- the carrying amount of the investment property at the date of sale; and
- the amount of the gain or loss recognised.

Cost model

In addition to the disclosure required in the joint section above, an entity should also disclose:

(a)   the depreciation methods used;

(b)   the useful lives or depreciation rates adopted;

(c)   the gross carrying amount and accumulated depreciation and impairment at start and end of period;

(d)   a reconciliation of the carrying amount of the investment property at start and end of the period showing:
- additions separately from capitalised subsequent expenditure;
- additions from business combinations;
- disposals;
- depreciation;
- impairment losses recognised in the period;
- net exchange differences;
- transfers to/from inventories and owner-occupied property; and
- other movements;

(e)   the fair value of investment property but when it cannot be reliably determined, the following should be disclosed:
- a description of the investment property;
- an explanation of why fair value cannot be determined reliably; and
- if possible, the range of estimates within which fair value is highly likely to lie.

2.3   IAS 20 *Accounting for Government Grants and Disclosure of Government Assistance* (1994)

The objective of IAS 20 is to prescribe the accounting for, and disclosure of, government grants and other forms of government assistance but the following are exempt:

(a)   special problems where changing prices affect government grants;
(b)   income tax holidays, accelerated depreciation allowances, i.e. tax benefits;
(c)   government participation in the ownership of the enterprise; and
(d)   government grants covered by IAS 41.

Definitions

Government assistance. Action by government to provide an economic benefit specific to an enterprise or range of enterprises qualifying under certain criteria. It does not include provision of infrastructure development or imposition of trading constraints.

Government grants. Assistance by government in the form of transfers of resources to an enterprise in return for past or future compliance with certain conditions relating to the operating activities of the enterprise.

Government Grants

Government grants, including non-monetary grants at fair value, should not be recognised until there is reasonable assurance that:

(a)   the enterprise will comply with the conditions attached to them and
(b)   the grants will be received.

The receipt of grant, by itself, does not provide evidence that the conditions attaching to the grant have been or will be fulfilled. Also the accounting treatment is the same whether the grant is in the form or cash or a non-monetary form.

Once the grant is recognised any related contingent liability or asset should be treated in accordance with IAS 37.

Government grants should be recognised as income over the periods necessary to match them with the related costs which they are intended to compensate on a systematic basis. They should not be credited directly to reserves.

In most cases the periods over which the enterprise recognises the costs related to a government grant are readily ascertainable and thus grants in recognition of specific expenses are recognised as income in the same period as the relevant expense, e.g. capital grants are released to income as the assets are depreciated.

A government grant that becomes receivable for expenses already incurred should be recognised as income in the period it becomes receivable.

Non-monetary government grants

A grant could be the transfer of land or other resources for the use of the enterprise. Should assess the fair value of the non-monetary asset and account for both the grant and the asset at that fair value. An alternative would be to record both asset and grant at a nominal amount.

Presentation of grants related to assets

These should be presented either by setting up a deferred income reserve or by deducting the grant in arriving at the carrying amount of the asset. The former requires the income to be recognised as income on a systematic and rational basis over the useful life of the asset whilst the latter automatically achieves that by reducing the depreciation charge.

A good example of a company following the deferred credit method is CRH Plc:

CRH Plc   Year Ended 31 December 2005

Capital Grants

Capital grants are recognised at their fair value where there is reasonable assurance that the grant will be received and all attaching conditions have been complied with. When the grant relates to an expense item, it is recognised as income over the periods necessary to match the grant on a systematic basis to the costs that it is intended to compensate. When the grant relates to an asset the fair value is treated as a deferred credit and is released to the income statement over the expected useful life of the relevant asset through equal annual instalments.

28. Capital Grants

	2005 (€m)	2004 (€m)
At 1st January	12.4	12.7
Translation adjustment	–	–
Arising on acquisition (Note 33)	0.2	2.2
Received	1.5	0.2
Repayments		0.5
	14.1	14.6
Released to Group Income Statement	(2.0)	(2.2)
At 31st December	12.1	12.4

There are no unfulfilled conditions or other contingencies attaching to capital grants received.

Cypriot company, SFS Group, however, adopts a net of cost approach:

SFS Group   Year Ended 31 December 2005

Government Grants

Amounts receivable from government grants are presented in the financial statements only when there is reasonable assurance that the Group fulfils the necessary conditions and that the grants will be received.

Government grants in relation to income are credited in the income statement for the year

Government grants in relation to new machinery are deducted from the acquisition cost of the asset. The depreciation of machinery is calculated on the adjusted cost of the asset after deducting the government grant.

Presentation of grants related to income

These are sometimes presented as a credit in the income statement, either separately or under the general heading of 'other income'. Alternatively they may be deducted in reporting the related expense. The former method enables better comparison with other expenses not affected by a grant but it could be argued that the expense would not have been incurred unless the grant was available.

Both methods are therefore acceptable but disclosure of the grant may be necessary for a proper understanding of the financial statements.

Repayment of government grants

A government grant that becomes repayable should be accounted for as a revision of an accounting estimate (see IAS 8). Repayment of a revenue grant should be applied first against any unamortised deferred credit balance and any excess recorded as an expense. Repayment of a capital-based grant should be recorded by increasing the carrying amount of the asset or reducing the deferred income reserve by the amount payable. The cumulative additional depreciation that would have to be recognised to date as an expense in the absence of the grant should be recognised as an expense immediately.

Consideration should also be given to a possible impairment review of the asset.

Government assistance

Excluded from the definition of government grants are certain forms of government assistance, which cannot reasonably have a value placed upon them and also transactions with government, which cannot be distinguished from normal trading transactions.

Examples of the former include free technical advice and the provision of guarantees. An example of the latter would be a government procurement policy that is responsible for a portion of the enterprise's sales. Any attempt to segregate the trading activities from government assistance would be purely arbitrary.

Disclosure of the benefit, however, may be necessary in order that the financial statements may not be misleading. Loans at nil or low interest are a form of government assistance but the benefit is not quantified by the imputation of interest.

Government assistance does not include the provision of infrastructure, such as transport facilities, communications network, water or irrigation systems as these benefit the whole community.

Disclosure

The following should be disclosed:

(a)   the accounting policy adopted;
(b)   the nature and extent of government grants recognised in the financial statements and an indication of other forms of government assistance from which the enterprise has directly benefited;
(c)   unfulfilled conditions and other contingencies attached to government assistance that has been recognised.

Application

(1)   Job creation grant

£100,000 to create 100 jobs in four years. The jobs have been created as follows:

Year		Income Statement (grant released)
		£
1	20	20,000
2	30	30,000
3	20	20,000
4	10	10,000
	80	80,000

The £20,000 in the deferred grants reserve is now effectively a liability, as it will have to be paid back to government. It should therefore be transferred from the deferred grants reserve to current liabilities.

(2)   Purchase of equipment £80,000 with attached grant of 20% and estimated useful life of four years

Net of cost method		Deferred income reserve method	
Cost	£80,000	Cost	£80,000
Grant (20%)	£16,000	Capital grants reserve*	£16,000
	£64,000		
Depreciation straight line over 4 years	£16,000 p.a.		£20,000 p.a.
Release of grant to profit and loss			£(4,000) p.a.

*Recorded on the balance sheet outside shareholders' funds.

It is likely that IAS 20 will be changed in order to bring it closer to the IASB's conceptual framework. New Zealand is currently preparing an international draft standard which will probably require all capital-based grants to be recorded immediately in income and not spread over the useful life of the fixed assets.

2.4   IAS 36 *Impairment of Assets* (revised 2003)

The objective of IAS 36 is to prescribe the procedures an entity should apply to ensure that its assets are carried at no more than their recoverable amount. If the asset value is above its future use or sale value it is said to be impaired and an impairment loss should be recognised immediately. IAS 36 also covers situations when impairment should be reversed as well as disclosures.

IAS 36 applies to the impairment of all assets other than:

(a)   inventories – see IAS 2
(b)   deferred tax assets – see IAS 12
(c)   employee benefit assets – see IAS 19
(d)   financial assets – see IAS 39

(e)   investment properties – see IAS 40
(f)   biological assets – see IAS 41.

However, it does apply to subsidiaries as defined in IAS 27, associates as defined in IAS 28 and joint ventures as defined in IAS 31. It also applies to revalued assets governed by IAS 16. In the latter case if the fair value is its market value, the only difference is the direct incremental costs of disposal and if these are negligible then no impairment has occurred. If the disposal costs are substantial, then IAS 36 applies. If the asset is valued at other than market value, then IAS 36 only should be applied after the revaluation adjustments have been applied to determine whether or not it has been impaired.

Definitions

Recoverable amount. The higher of an asset's net selling price and its value in use
Value in use. The present value of future cash flows expected to be derived from the asset or CGU.
Net selling price. The amount obtainable from the sale of an asset or CGU in an arms length transaction less costs of disposal.
Costs of disposal. Incremental costs directly attributable to the disposal of an asset but excluding finance costs and income tax.
Impairment loss. The amount by which the carrying amount of an asset or CGU exceeds its recoverable amount.
Cash generating unit. The smallest identifiable group of assets that generates cash flows that are largely independent of cash inflows from other assets or groups of assets.

Identifying an asset that may be impaired

IAS 36 is structured in four stages as follows:

(a)   Measuring recoverable amount;
(b)   Recognising and measuring impairment losses;
(c)   Reversing impairment losses; and
(d)   Information to be disclosed.

An asset is impaired when the carrying amount of an asset exceeds its recoverable amount. Except for intangible assets with indefinite lives and goodwill, a formal estimate of recoverable amount does not occur annually unless there is an indication of a potential impairment loss. At each balance sheet date, however, an entity should assess whether or not there are indications of impairment losses.

In making an assessment of whether or not there are indications of impairment an entity, as a minimum, should consider the following:
    External sources:

(a)   a significant decline in an asset's market value;
(b)   significant changes with an adverse effect on the entity that have taken place during the period or in the near future – in the technological, economic or legal environments;
(c)   market interest rates have increased during the period, which have effected the discount rate;
(d)   the carrying amount of the net assets in the entity is more than its market capitalisation.

Internal sources:

(e)   evidence of obsolescence or physical damage;
(f)   plans to discontinue or restructure the operation to which the asset belongs or plans to dispose of the asset or reassessing its useful life;
(g)   evidence that economic performance is worse than expected.

The list is not intended to be exhaustive and there may be other indications that are equally important.

Evidence from internal reporting of impairment includes the existence of:

(a)   cash flows for operating and maintaining the asset are considerably higher than budgeted;
(b)   actual cash flows are worse than budgeted;
(c)   a significant decline in budgeted cash flows or operating profit; or
(d)   operating losses.

Intangible assets with infinite lives or not yet in use, as well as goodwill, should be tested for impairment on an annual basis. Materiality, however, applies and if interest rates have increased during the period an asset's recoverable amount need not be formally estimated if the discount rate is unlikely to be affected or if previous sensitivity analysis makes it unlikely that a material decrease has occurred or has resulted in a material impairment loss.

If an asset is impaired depreciation should also be reviewed and adjusted as the remaining useful life may be considerably shorter.

(a) *Measuring Recoverable Amount*

Recoverable amount is the higher of net selling price and value in use. Both need not necessarily be determined if either exceeds the NBV then the asset is not impaired.

If it is not possible to determine net selling price as there is no reliable estimate then value in use should be adopted instead. Also if there is no reason to believe that an asset's value in use is materially different from its net selling price then the asset's recoverable amount will be its net selling price.

Recoverable amount is determined for individual assets unless the asset does not generate cash flows that are largely independent of those from a group of assets. If the latter, then the recoverable amount is determined for the CGU to which the asset belongs unless either:

(a)   the assets net selling price is higher than its NBV or
(b)   the assets value in use can be determined to be close to its net selling price.

In some cases averages may provide a reasonable approximation of the detailed computations.

Measuring the recoverable amount of an intangible asset with an indefinite useful life

This must be measured at the end of each reporting period but a previous detailed calculation in a preceding period may be adopted, provided all of the following criteria are met:

(a)   if the intangible asset does not generate cash inflows largely independent from other assets and is therefore tested as part of an CGU whose assets and liabilities have largely remain unchanged since the last calculation.
(b)   the most recent recoverable amount resulted in an amount that exceeded the asset's NBV by a considerable amount.

(c)   based on an analysis of events since the last valuation, the likelihood that a current recoverable amount would be less than the asset's NBV is remote.

Net selling price

Best evidence is a binding sale agreement at arm's length, adjusted for incremental costs directly attributable to disposal of the asset.

If there is no binding sale agreement but it is traded on an active market, net selling price is the asset's market price less costs of disposal. The price should be the current bid price or the price of the most recent transaction. If none exists, it should be based on the best information available to reflect what would be received between willing parties at arms length but it should not be based on a forced sale. Costs of disposal include legal costs, stamp duty and other direct incremental costs but not reorganisation or termination benefits.

Value in use

The following elements should be reflected in the calculation of value in use:

(a)   an estimate of future cash flows to be derived from the asset;
(b)   expectations about possible variations in the amount or timing of such flows;
(c)   the time value of money;
(d)   the price for bearing the uncertainty inherent in the asset; and
(e)   other factors, including poor liquidity, that market participants would reflect in pricing expected future cash flows.

This requires estimating the future cash flows to be derived from continuing use of the asset and from its ultimate disposal as well as applying the appropriate discount rate to those flows. Either cash flows or the discount rate can be adjusted to reflect (a) to (e).

Basis for estimates of future cash flows

Cash flows should be based on reasonable and supportable assumptions that represent management's best estimate of a range of economic conditions that exist over the life of the asset and take into account the past ability of the management to accurately forecast cash flows.

Greater weight should be given to external evidence and cash flows should be based on the most recent financial forecasts approved by management covering a normal maximum period of five years. If a longer period is justified, budgets/forecasts should be extrapolated using a steady or declining growth rate that should not exceed the long-term average growth rate for the products, industries or countries in which the entity operates, unless a higher rate is justified. If appropriate, the growth rate should be zero or negative.

Composition of estimates of future cash flows

These shall include:

(a)   projections of cash inflows from continuing use of the asset;
(b)   projections of cash outflows necessarily incurred to generate the cash inflows and can be directly attributed to the asset;
(c)   net cash flows to be received for the disposal of the asset at the end of its useful life.

Estimates should reflect consistent assumptions about price increases due to general inflation and should include future overheads that can be directly attributed or allocated to the asset. If the asset is not in use yet, all expected future costs to get it ready should be included within future cash outflows.

Cash flows do not include either cash inflows from assets that generate cash inflows largely independent of the cash inflows from the asset nor cash outflows related to obligations already recognised as liabilities.

Future cash flows should be estimated for the asset in its current condition and should not include cash inflows from restructuring (under IAS 37) or from future capital expenditure that will enhance or improve the asset's performance.

Estimates of future cash flows shall not include:

(a)   cash inflows from financing activities or
(b)   income tax receipts or payments.

This will avoid double counting of the interest cost and ensure that the discount rate is determined on a pre tax-rate basis.

Estimates of net cash flows to be received from disposal are those expected to be obtained on an arms length basis after deducting disposal costs. It should be based on prices prevailing at the date of the estimate for assets operating under similar conditions and should reflect the effect of future price increases (general and specific).

Discount rate

Should be a pre-tax rate that reflects both the time value of money and the specific risks attached to the asset. The latter is the return that investors would require if they were to choose an investment that would generate cash flows equivalent to those expected to be derived from the asset. Where an asset specific rate is not directly available then surrogates may be adopted.

(b)   *Recognition and measurement of an impairment loss:*

Assets other than goodwill

Only if the recoverable amount of an asset is less than its NBV, should the asset be reduced to its recoverable amount and an impairment loss created. That should then be expensed in the income statement unless the asset has been carried at a revalued amount under IAS 16, in which case it is treated as a revaluation decrease.

A revalued asset is charged to profit and loss to the extent that the loss exceeds the amount held in the revaluation reserve for the same asset. Where the impairment loss is greater than the NBV a liability should be recognised only if required by another standard. After recognition of the impairment loss, depreciation must be adjusted in future periods to allocate the asset's revised book value to be spread over the asset's remaining useful life. Any related deferred tax assets or liabilities are determined under IAS 12 by comparing the revised NBV of the asset with its tax base.

Cash generating units and goodwill

Identification of the CGU to which an asset belongs

If there is any indication that an asset may be impaired, the recoverable amount shall be estimated for that individual asset. If it is not possible to estimate the recoverable amount of the individual asset then the entity should determine the recoverable amount of the CGU to which the asset belongs (the CGU).

This occurs when an asset's value in use cannot be estimated to be close to net selling price and the asset does not generate cash inflows from continuing use that are largely independent of those from other assets. In such cases, the value in use and thus the recoverable amount must be determined only for the asset's CGU. IAS 36 offers a few examples:

EXAMPLE
A mine owns a private railway to support its mining activities. It could only be sold for scrap and does not generate independent cash flows from those of the mine.

The CGU, in this case, is therefore the mine as a whole, including the railway as the railway's value in use cannot be independently determined and would be very different from its scrap value.

Identification of an asset's CGU involves judgement and should be the lowest aggregation of assets that generate largely independent cash inflows from continuing use.

EXAMPLE
A bus company has a contract to provide a minimum service on five separate routes. Cash flows can be separately identified for each route.

Even if one route is operating at a loss, the entity has no option to curtail any one route and the lowest independent level is the group of five routes together. The CGU is the bus company itself.

Cash inflows should be from outside parties only and should consider various factors including how management monitors the entity's operations.

If an active market exists for the asset's or group of assets output then they should be identified as a CGU, even if some of the output is used internally. If this is the case, management's best estimate of future market prices shall be used:

(a)   in determining the value in use of the CGU when estimating the future cash inflows relating to internal use; and
(b)   in determining the value in use of other CGUs of the entity, when estimating future cash outflows that relate to internal use of the output.

CGUs must be identified consistently from period to period unless a change is justified.

Recoverable amount and carrying amount of a CGU

The recoverable amount of a CGU is the higher of its net selling price and value in use. The carrying amount shall be determined consistently with the way the recoverable amount is determined.

The carrying amount of a CGU includes the carrying amount of only those assets that can be attributed directly or allocated on a reasonable and consistent basis to the CGU and does not include the carrying amount of any recognised liability unless the recoverable amount of the CGU cannot be determined without its consideration.

The CGU should exclude cash flows relating to assets that are not part of a CGU. However, all assets that generate cash flows for the CGU should be included. In some cases, e.g. goodwill and head office assets, future cash flows cannot be allocated to the CGU on a reasonable and consistent basis. This is covered later. Also certain liabilities may have to be considered e.g. on disposal of a CGU, if a buyer is forced to take over a liability. In that case the liability must be included as per the example provided in IAS 36 below:

EXAMPLE

A company must restore a mine by law and have provided for the cost of restoration of 500 which is equal to the present value of restoration costs. The CGU is the mine as a whole. Offers of 800 have been received to buy the mine and disposal costs are negligible. The value in use is 1,200 excluding restoration costs and the carrying amount 1,000.

Net selling price	800	
Value in use	700	(1,200 less 500)
Carrying amount of CGU	500	(1,000 less 500)

The recoverable amount of 800 exceeds its carrying amount of 500 by 300 and there is no impairment

Example – Mourne Group (Calculation of Impairment Loss (1))

Mourne Group prepares financial statements to 31 December each year. On 31 December 2005 assets of Binian Ltd at that date were £1.8 million and Mourne paid £2 million to acquire the entity. It is the policy of the Mourne Group to amortise goodwill over 20 years. The amortisation of the goodwill of Binian Ltd commenced in 2006. Binian Ltd made a loss in 2006 and at 31 December 2006 the net assets of Binian Ltd – based on fair values at 1 January 2006 – were as follows:

	£'000
Capitalised development expenditure	200
Tangible fixed assets	1,300
Net current assets	250
	1,750

An impairment review at 31 December 2006 indicated that the value in use of Binian Ltd at that date was £1.5 million. The capitalised development expenditure has no ascertainable external market value.

Suggested solution – Mourne Group

Calculation of the impairment review loss of Binian Ltd on 31 December 2005

Fair value of purchase consideration		£2.0m
Fair value of net assets acquired		1.8m
Goodwill on acquisition		0.2m
On 31 December 2006		
Net book value	(£1.75m + £0.19 goodwill)	£1.94m
Net present value	(given)	1.50m
Impairment		0.44m

Allocation of impairment review loss

	Net book value	Impairment loss	Net present value
Goodwill	£0.19m	£(0.19)m	Nil
Capitalised development expenditure	0.20m	(0.20)m	Nil
Tangible fixed assets	1.30m	(0.05)m	£1.25m
Net current assets	0.25m		0.25m
	£1.94m	£(0.44)m	£1.50m

The journal entry should be as follows:

			£m	£m
Dr		Income statement	0.44	
	Cr	Goodwill		0.19
		Development expenditure		0.20
		Property, etc.		0.05

The charge is to the income statement as it is due to operation problems and not to external factors.

Example – Ahoghill Ltd (Calculation of Impairment Loss (2))

Ahoghill Ltd has a CGU comprising the following assets at net book value at 31 May 2007:

	£
Goodwill	80
Intangible assets	70
Property etc.	180

The net realisable value and value in use of the unit at the same date are £240 million and £230 million respectively. The intangible asset has a readily ascertainable net realisable value of £60m.

Suggested solution – Ahoghill Ltd

Ahoghill Ltd – Cash generating unit

	£m	£m
Net book value		330
Net realisable value	240	
Value in use	230	
Higher of NRV and NPV		240
Impairment loss		(90)

Allocation of loss

	Total (£m)	Goodwill (£m)	Intangible assets (£m)	Property etc (£m)
Net book value	330	80	70	180
Recoverable amount	240			
Impairment	(90)	(80)	(10)	Nil

The balance sheet will now be restated showing intangible assets valued at £60 million and property, etc. at £180 million, i.e. a total of £240 million.

Example – Gracehill Ltd (Calculation of Impairment Loss (3))

Gracehill Ltd has been profitably manufacturing 'Bingos' for some years but technology developments suggest that the machinery involved will become obsolete in the foreseeable future in its present use. The directors of the company estimate that the present manufacturing process can continue for another four years after 30 June 2007. For the record the net book value of the machinery at 30 June 2007 may not be fully recoverable.

The following information relating to the machinery is available at 30 June 2007:

(a) Net book value £5.9 million (accumulated depreciation £2.8 million). Depreciation for the year ended 30 June 2007 was £0.5 million.
(b) Saleable value on the open market – £2.5 million with associated selling costs of £100,000.
(c) Projections prepared by management show that net cash inflows of £1.6 million per annum for the next four years should be obtained as a result of the machinery's continued use while its net realisable value at the end of four years would be immaterial. The discount rate implicit in market transactions of similar assets is 7%. The appropriate present value factor is 0.8468.

Suggested solution – Gracehill Ltd

Gracehill Ltd	£m	£m
Net book value (NBV)		5.9
Net realisable value		
Saleable value	2.5	
Associated selling costs	(0.1)	
	2.4	
Net present value		
Present value of future cash flows		
(£1.6m × 4years = £6.4m × 0.8468)	5.42	
Higher of NRV and NPV		5.42
Impairment loss		(0.48)

Because the impairment is caused by operating problems, the full loss must be charged to income and the net assets reduced by £0.48 million.

Dr	Income Statement	£0.48m
Cr	Property, etc.	£0.48m

The impairment should be included within the accumulated depreciation part of the property schedule as a separate depreciation charge. Thus the cost will remain at £8.7 million and the accumulated depreciation increased from £2.8 million to £3.28 million, leaving the book value at £5.42 million. If the asset had been revalued, then the movement would have been recorded at the top of the property schedule as part of the cost/revalued movement.

Goodwill

Allocating goodwill to CGUs

Goodwill should be allocated to one or more CGUs and the CGUs should represent the smallest CGU to which a portion of the carrying amount of goodwill can be allocated on a reasonable and consistent basis. It is capable of being allocated only when a CGU represents the lowest level at which the management monitors the return on investment in assets that include the goodwill. The CGU should not be larger than a segment based on IAS 14 (now IFRS 8).

Goodwill does not generate cash flows independently, the benefits are not capable of being individually identified and separately recognised and they often contribute to multiple CGUs. If the initial allocation of goodwill cannot be completed before the end of the first annual reporting period in which the business combination occurs, it must be completed before the end of the first annual reporting date beginning after the acquisition date.

If provisional values are adopted the acquiror must initially adopt those provisional figures and then adjust within 12 months to final values. Additional information must be disclosed about the adjustments.

If a CGU is disposed, which includes goodwill previously allocated, the goodwill associated with the disposal shall be:

(a)   included in the NBV of the operation when determining gain or loss on disposal and
(b)   measured on the basis of relative values of the operation disposed of and the portion of the CGU retained.

EXAMPLE
An entity sells for 100, an operation that was part of a CGU to which goodwill was allocated. The recoverable amount of part of CGU retained is 300; 25% of goodwill allocated is included in the NBV of operation that is sold.

If an entity reorganises so that changes in composition of one or more CGUs (to which goodwill has been allocated) the goodwill shall be reallocated to units affected by adopting a relative value approach similar to that used when an entity disposes of an operation within a CGU.

EXAMPLE
Goodwill previously allocated to CGU A but A will now have to be divided into three other CGUs.

Goodwill allocated to A is reallocated to B, C and D are based on the relative values of the three portions of A before those portions are integrated with B, C and D.

Testing CGUs with goodwill for impairment

When goodwill cannot be allocated on a reasonable and consistent basis, the unit should be tested for impairment whenever there is an indication of impairment by comparing its NBV excluding goodwill with its recoverable amount.

If a CGU includes an intangible asset that has an indefinite useful life or is not yet in use, then the asset can be tested for impairment only as part of the CGU.

A CGU to which goodwill has been allocated shall be tested for impairment annually and whenever there is an indication that it may be impaired, its NBV including goodwill should be compared with its recoverable amount. If the NBV exceeds its recoverable amount, the entity shall:

(a)   Determine whether goodwill allocated to CGU is impaired by comparing the implied value of goodwill with its carrying amount.
(b)   Recognise any excess of the carrying value of goodwill immediately in profit and loss as an impairment loss.
(c)   Recognise any remaining excess as an impairment loss on a pro rata basis over all other assets.

Implied value of goodwill

Should be measured as the excess of:

(a)   the recoverable amount of the CGU to which goodwill is allocated, over;
(b)   the net fair value of identifiable assets, liabilities and contingent liabilities the entity would recognise if it acquired the CGU in a business combination on the date of the impairment test.

Minority interest

Under IAS 36 goodwill is based on parent's ownership interest and thus goodwill attributable to minority interest is not recognised. If there is a minority interest in a CGU to which goodwill has been allocated, the carrying amount of that CGU comprises:

(a) both the parent's interest and the minority interest in the identifiable net assets of the CGU; and

(b) the parent's interest in goodwill.

However, part of the recoverable amount of the CGU will be attributable to the minority interest in goodwill. For impairment testing the carrying amount of the CGU should be notionally adjusted by grossing up goodwill to include that attributable to minority interest. This is then compared with the recoverable amount to determine whether the CGU is impaired. If it is, the entity must allocate the impairment loss as per (a) to (c) above.

The implied value of goodwill allocated to a CGU with a minority interest includes goodwill attributable to both the parent and minority interest. This implied value is then compared with the notionally grossed up carrying value of goodwill to determine whether goodwill is impaired. Any impairment loss is apportioned between parent and minority but only the parent's share is recognised.

If the total impairment loss relating to goodwill is less than the amount by which the notionally adjusted carrying amount of the CGU exceeds its recoverable amount, any excess must be accounted for as an impairment loss.

EXAMPLE
Impairment Testing CGUs with Goodwill and Minority Interests

BACKGROUND
Entity X acquires 80% of Entity Y for 1,600 on 1.1.20X3. Y's identifiable net assets at that date have a fair value of 1,500. X recognises:

(a) Goodwill $1,600 – 80\% \times 1500 = 400$
(b) Y's identifiable net assets at fair value of 1,500
(c) Minority interest of $20\% \times 1500 = 300$

The assets of Y are the smallest group of independent assets thus it is a CGU. Because it includes goodwill it must be tested for impairment annually or more frequently if there is an indication of impairment.

At the end of 20X3, X determines that the recoverable amount of Y is 1,000. Assume X adopts straight-line depreciation with a life of 10 years.

Testing Y for impairment

End of 2003	Goodwill	Identifiable net assets	Total
Gross carrying amount	400	1,500	1,900
Accumulated depreciation	—	(150) 10%	(150)
Carrying amount	400	1,350	1,750
Unrecognised minority interest	100 (400 × 20/80)	—	100
Notionally adjusted carrying amount	500	1,350	1,850
Recoverable amount (800 + 200)			1,000
Impairment loss			850

The impairment loss of 850 is allocated by first examining whether goodwill is impaired. That occurs if its carrying amount exceeds its implied value. If X determines that the fair value of the identifiable assets, it would recognise if it had acquired Y at the date of the test is 800, the implied value of goodwill is 200. This implied value includes goodwill attributable to both X and minority interest.

Thus, 300 of the 850 impairment loss is attributable to goodwill (i.e. 500–200). However, because goodwill is only recognised to the extent of X's 80% ownership in Y, X only recognises 80% of the loss (i.e. 240).

The remaining loss of 550 is used to reduce the carrying amount of Y's identifiable assets

End of 20 × 3	Goodwill	Identifiable net assets	Total
Gross carrying value	400	1500	1900
Accumulated depreciation	–	(150)	(150)
Carrying amount	400	1350	1750
Impairment loss	(240)	(550)	(790)
Carrying amount after impairment loss	160	800	960

Timing of impairment tests

The test can be carried out at any time during the year provided it is at the same time every year. Different CGUs may be tested for impairment at different times. However, if some of the goodwill was acquired in a business combination during the year that CGU shall be tested for impairment before the end of the current reporting period.

If other assets or smaller CGUs are tested at the same time as the larger unit they shall be tested for impairment before the larger unit.

The most recent detailed calculation made in a preceding reporting period may be adopted for the test provided all of the following criteria are met:

(a)   The assets and liabilities have not changed significantly since the most recent recoverable amount calculation.
(b)   The most recent recoverable amount calculation resulted in an amount substantially in excess of the CGU's carrying amount.
(c)   Based on an analysis of events and changed circumstances, the likelihood that a current recoverable amount would be less than the current carrying amount of the CGU is remote.

If the carrying amount of a CGU exceeds its recoverable amount but the entity has not completed its determination of whether goodwill is impaired or not it may use its best estimate of any probable impairment loss. Any adjustment shall be recognised in the succeeding reporting period.

Corporate assets

Includes headquarters buildings, research centres, etc. Their key characteristics are that they do not generate independent cash flows, thus their recoverable amount cannot be determined. Thus, if there is an indication that a corporate asset may be impaired, recoverable amount is determined for the CGU to which the corporate asset belongs compared with the carrying amount of this CGU and any impairment loss recognised.

If a portion of the carrying amount of a corporate asset:

(a) Can be allocated on a reasonable and consistent basis then the entity shall compare the carrying amount of the CGU (including corporate asset) with its recoverable amount and any losses recognised.

(b) Cannot be allocated on a reasonable and consistent basis then the entity shall:
  – compare the carrying amount of the CGU, excluding the corporate asset, with its recoverable amount and recognise any impairment loss;
  – identify the smallest CGU to which a portion of the corporate asset can be allocated on a reasonable and consistent basis
  – compare the carrying amount of the larger CGU including a portion of the corporate asset with its recoverable amount. Any impairment loss shall be recognised.

EXAMPLE

Allocation of corporate assets

Background

Entity M has three CGUs – A, B and C. They do not include goodwill. At the end of 20 × 0 the carrying amounts are 100, 150 and 200.

Corporate assets have a carrying amount of 200 (buildings 150, research centre 50). The remaining useful life of CGU's A is 10 years and CGU's B and C 20 years. The entity adopts a straight-line basis for depreciation.

There is no basis to calculate net selling price for each CGU thus recoverable value is based on value in use using a 15% pre-tax discount rate.

Identification of Corporate assets

The carrying amount of headquarters building can be allocated on a reasonable and consistent basis.

The research centre cannot be allocated on such a manner.

Allocation of Corporate Assets

End of 20 × 0	A	B	C	Total
Carrying amount	100	150	200	450
Useful life	10 years	20 years	20 years	
Weighting based on useful life	1	2	2	
Carrying amount after weighting	100	300	400	000
Pro-rata allocation of building	12%	38%	50%	100%
Allocation of carrying amount of building	19	56	75	(150)
Carrying amount after allocation	119	206	275	600

Determination of Recoverable Amount and Calculation of Impairment Losses

The recoverable amount of each individual CGU must be compared with its carrying amount, including the portion of the headquarters, and any impairment loss recognised. IAS 36 then requires the recoverable amount of M as a whole to be compared with its carrying amount, including the headquarters and the research centre.

Calculation of A, B, C and M's value in use at the end of 20 X 0

A	Future cash flows for 10 years discounted at 15%	199
B	Future cash flows for 20 years discounted at 15%	164
C	Future cash flows for 20 years discounted at 15%	271
M	Future cash flows for 20 years discounted at 15%	720

Impairment testing A, B and C

End of 2020	A	B	C
Carrying amount after allocation of building	119	206	275
Recoverable amount	199	164	271
Impairment loss	0	(42)	(4)

Allocation of impairment losses for CGU's B and C

		B	C	
To headquarters building	(42 × 56/206)	(12)	(1)	(4 × 75/275)
To assets in CGU	(42 × 150/206)	(30)	(3)	(4 × 200/275)
		(42)	(4)	

Because the research centre could not be allocated on a reasonable and consistent basis to A, B and C's CGUs, M compares the carrying amount of the smallest CGU to which the carrying amount of the research centre can be allocated (i.e. M as a whole) to its recoverable amount.

Impairment testing the 'larger' CGU (i.e. M as a whole)

End of 2020	A	B	C	Building	Research Centre	M
Carrying amount after allocation of building	100	150	200	150	50	650
Impairment loss (first step)	–	(30)	(3)	(13)	–	(46)
Carrying amount (after first step)	100	120	197	137	50	(604)
Recoverable amount						720
Impairment loss for the larger CGU						0

Thus, no additional impairment loss results from the application of the impairment test to the 'larger' CGU. Only 46 uncovered in step one is recognised.

Impairment loss for a CGU

An impairment loss should be recognised only if its recoverable amount is less than its carrying amount. The carrying amount of the assets are allocated to reduce the carrying amount of the assets carrying amount:

(a)   first, against goodwill to its implied value; and
(b)   then, to other assets on a pro-rata basis based on the carrying amount of each asset in the unit.

These are treated as impairment losses on individual assets. In allocating the loss, an asset should not be reduced below the highest of

(a)   its net selling price (if determinable);
(b)   its value in use (if determinable); and
(c)   zero

The amount of the loss that would otherwise have been allocated to the asset shall be allocated to the other assets on a pro-rata basis.

If the recoverable amount of each individual asset in a CGU cannot be estimated without undue cost or effort, IAS 36 requires an arbitrary allocation between assets of the CGU other than goodwill.

If the recoverable amount of an individual asset cannot be determined:

(a)   An impairment loss is recognised for the asset if its carrying value is greater than the higher of its net selling price and the results of procedures described above.
(b)   No impairment loss is recognised if the related CGU is not impaired even if its net selling price is less than its carrying amount.

(c) Reversing impairment losses

An entity shall assess at each balance sheet date whether there is any indication that an impairment loss recognised in prior periods, other than goodwill, may no longer exist. If such exists the entity shall estimate the recoverable amount of that asset.

In assessing whether or not there is a reversal, the entity should consider the following indications, as a minimum:

External Sources of Information

(a)   the asset's market value has increased significantly during the period;
(b)   significant changes with a favourable impact in the technological, market, economic or legal environment in which the entity operates;
(c)   market interest rates have decreased and are likely to affect the discount rate and the recoverable amount.

Internal Sources of Information

(d)   Significant changes with a favourable effect during the period or in the near future. It includes capital expenditure that enhances an asset's standard of performance.
(e)   Evidence indicates that economic performance is better than expected.

An impairment loss in prior periods, for assets other than goodwill, shall be reversed only if there is a change in estimate used to determine the asset's recoverable amount since the loss was recognised.

Examples of changes in estimate include:

(a)   a change in the basis for recoverable amount;
(b)   if recoverable amount was based on value in use – a change in amount or timing of cash flows or in the discount rate;
(c)   if recoverable amount was based on net selling price – a change in components of net selling price.

An impairment loss, however, is not reversed merely because of the passage of time.

Reversal of an impairment loss for an individual asset
The increased carrying value of an asset, other than goodwill, due to a reversal shall not exceed the carrying amount that would have existed had the asset not been impaired in prior years.

Any increase in the carrying amount above carrying amount, had no impairment taken place, would have been a revaluation.

A reversal shall be recognised immediately in profit and loss unless the asset is carried at a revalued amount under another standard. Any reversal of an impairment loss on a revalued asset shall be treated as a revaluation reserve increase and credited directly to equity. However, to the extent a loss was previously recognised in profit and loss, a reversal is also recognised in profit and loss.

After a reversal, the depreciation charge should be adjusted in future periods to allocate its revised carrying amount over its remaining useful life.

Reversal of an impairment loss for a CGU
A reversal of an impairment loss for a CGU should be allocated to the assets in the unit, except for goodwill, on a pro-rata basis with the carrying amount of those assets.

In allocating a reversal for a CGU, the carrying amount of an asset should not be increased above the lower of:

(a)   its recoverable amount (if determinable) and
(b)   the carrying amount that would be determined had no impairment taken place.

The amount of the reversal of the impairment loss that would otherwise have been allocated to the asset shall be allocated on a pro-rata basis to the other assets of the CGU, except for goodwill.

Reversal of an impairment loss for goodwill
An impairment loss recognised for goodwill shall not be reversed in subsequent periods as IAS 38 expressly forbids the creation of internally generated goodwill.

(d) Disclosure
An entity should disclose the following for each class of assets:

(a)   The amount of impairment losses recognised in profit or loss during the period.
(b)   The amount of reversals of impairment losses recognised in profit and loss during the period.

(c)   the amount of impairment losses recognised directly in equity during the period.

(d)   the amount of reversals of impairment losses recognised directly in equity during the period.

The information may be included in a reconciliation of the carrying amount of property, plant and equipment as required by IAS 16.

The following should be disclosed for each material impairment loss recognised or reversed during the period for an individual asset, including goodwill, or a CGU:

(a)   The events and circumstances that led to the recognition or reversal of the impairment loss.

(b)   The amount of the impairment loss recognised or reversed.

(c)   For an individual asset:
   –   the nature of the asset;
   –   the reportable segment to which the asset belongs, if applicable.

(d)   for a CGU:
   –   a description of the CGU
   –   the amount of the impairment loss recognised or reversed by class of asset and, if applicable, by reportable segment under IAS 14 (IFRS 8).
   –   If the aggregation of assets for identifying the CGU has changed since the previous estimate of the CGU's recoverable amount, a description of the current and former way of aggregating assets and the reasons for changing the way the CGU is identified.

(e)   Whether the recoverable amount of the asset (CGU) is its net selling price or its value in use.

(f)   If recoverable amount is net selling price, the basis used to determine net selling price.

(g)   If recoverable amount is value in use, the discount rate used in the current and previous estimates of value in use.

An entity shall disclose the following information for the aggregate impairment losses and the aggregate reversals of impairment losses recognised during the period for which no information is disclosed above.

(a)   the main classes of assets affected by impairment losses and the main classes of assets affected by reversals of impairment losses.

(b)   the main events and circumstances that led to the recognition of these impairment losses and reversals of impairment losses.

An entity is encouraged to disclose key assumptions used to determine the recoverable amount of assets (CGUs) during the period but required to do so when goodwill or intangible assets with indefinite useful lives are included in a CGU.

If goodwill has not been allocated to a CGU, the amount shall be disclosed together with reasons for non-allocation.

If an entity recognises the best estimate of a probable impairment loss for goodwill the following should be disclosed:

(a)   the fact that the impairment loss recognised for goodwill is an estimate, not yet finalised and

(b)   the reasons why the impairment loss has not been finalised

In the immediate succeeding period, the nature and amount of any adjustments must be disclosed.

There are also considerable additional disclosures for segments.

The amount of diclosure required by IAS 36 has increased substantially from that required by the national standard, FRS 11, and two examples should illustrate this. The first is Ulster Television Plc who provide disclosure of their impairment accounting policy for the first time and in their notes considerable detail on how the impairment exercise has operated during the year on their prior year acquisitions. Goodwill and licences having an infinite useful life are tested annually for impairment and Ulster Television have set up three CGUs to test – Radio GB, Radio Ireland and Internet:

Ulster Television Plc   Year Ended 31 December 2005

Impairment of assets

The Group assesses at each reporting date whether there is an indication that an asset may be impaired. If any such indication exists, or when annual impairment testing for an asset is required, the Croup makes an estimate of the asset's recoverable amount. An asset's recoverable amount is the higher of an asset's or CGU's fair value less costs to sell and its value in use and is determined for an individual asset unless the asset does not generate cash inflows that are largely independent of those from other assets or groups of assets.

When the carrying value of an asset exceeds its recoverable amount, the asset is considered impaired and is written down to its recoverable amount. In assessing value in use, the estimated future cash flows are discounted to their present value using a pre-tax discount rate that reflects current marker assessments of the time value of money and the risks specific to the asset. Impairment losses of continuing operations are recognized in the income statement in those expense categories consistent with the function of the impaired asset.

An assessment is made at each reporting date as to whether there is any indication that previously recognised impairment losses may no longer exist or may have decreased. If such indications exist, the recoverable amount is estimated. A previously recognised impairment loss is only reversed if there has been a change in the estimates used to determine the asset's recoverable amount since the last impairment loss was recognised. If that is the case, the carrying amount of the asset is increased to its recoverable amount. That increased amount cannot exceed the carrying amount that would have been determined, net of depreciation, had no impairment loss been recognised for the asset in prior years. Such reversal is recognised in profit or loss unless the asset is carried at revalued amount, in which case the reversal is treated as a revaluation increase. After such a reversal, the depreciation charge is adjusted in future periods to allocate the asset's revised carrying amount, less any residual value, on a systematic basis over its remaining useful life.

15. Impairment of goodwill and intangible assets with indefinite lives

Goodwill acquired through business combinations and intangible assets identified through business combinations as licences are attributable to individual licence agreements. The CGU for goodwill is the business required and that for intangible assets is individual licence.

The recoverable amount of each CGU has been determined on the basis of a value in use calculation using five years' cash-flow projections approved by the Board. The growth rate used beyond the five years is 2.25% (2004: 2.25%) being representative of the long-term average growth rate for the industry. A discount rate applied to cash-flow projections for the United Kingdom is 12.8% (2004: 12.8%) and for ROI is 10% (2004: 10%).

Carrying amount of goodwill, patents and licences allocated to CGUs:

| | New Media | | Radio GB | | Radio Ireland | | Total | |
| | 2005 | 2004 | 2005 | 2004 | 2005 | 2004 | 2005 | 2004 |
	£'000	£'000	£'000	£'000	£'000	£'000	£'000	£'000
Goodwill	2,667	2,667	7,412	976	44,718	45,184	54,797	48,827
Licences	–	–	142,507	–	7,861	–	150,368	–
	2,667	2,667	149,919	976	52,579	45,184	205,165	48,827

talkSPORT is included in Radio GE at a value of £48,024,000.

Key assumptions used in value in use calculations.

The calculation of value in use is most sensitive to the following assumptions:

* revenue growth;
* discount rates

Revenue growth is based on published industry information but adjusted in the earlier years to reflect budgeted results.

Discount rates reflect management's estimate of the Working Average Cost of Capital (WACC) required to assess operating performance in each business unit and to evaluate future capital investment proposals. The rate used in the calculations of the value in use was a range for Republic of Ireland and United Kingdom of between 10% and 12.8% pre tax. This was calculated based on an appropriate risk-free return, beta factor, market risk premium and cost of debt appropriate to the industry.

Sensitivity to changes in assumptions

With regard to the assessment of value in use of the CGUs, management believes that no reasonably possible change in any of the above key assumptions would cause the carrying value of the unit to exceed its recoverable amount.

The second example taken from Unilever Plc reveals an actual impairment for the year on their Slim Fast line. Again substantial details are provided in the notes about how the calculations were derived:

Unilever Group Plc   Year Ended 31 December 2004

Notes to the Accounts

Note 10 Goodwill and Intangible Assets (Extract)

10 Goodwill and intangible assets (continued)

Movements during 2004	€ million Goodwill	€ million indefinite-lived intangible assets	€ million finte-lived intangible Assets	€ million Software	€ million Total
Cost					
1 January 2004	13,451	4,505	603	110	18,679
Acquisitions of group companies	7	1	2	–	10
Disposals of group companies	(3)	(20)	–	–	(23)
Additions	–	1	1	87	89
Currency retranslation	(445)	(176)	(9)	(4)	(634)
31 December 2004	13,020	4,311	597	193	18,121
Amortisation and impairment					
1 January 2004	–	–	(103)	(7)	(110)
Amortisation for the year	–	–	(45)	(21)	(66)
Impairment losses	(1,003)	–	–	–	(1,003)
Currency retranslation	66	–	(2)	1	65
31 December 2004	(937)	–	(150)	(27)	(1,114)
Net book value 31 December 2004	12,083	431	447	166	17,007

(b)   Includes €(2) million relating to discontinued operations.

There are no significant carrying amounts of goodwill and intangible assets that are allocated across multiple CGUs.

Impairments in the year

During 2005, *Slim-Fast* maintained its leadership of the weight management sector by refreshing its product range and offering a more personalised diet plan. However, the 2005 impairment review of the global *Slim-Fast* business resulted in an impairment charge of €363 million due to the continued decline of the weight management sector. This charge has been reflected in operating profit for The Americas Region.

Value in use of the business was calculated using the present values of projected future cash flows, adjusted to reflect the risk present in the markets in which the business operates. The pre-tax discount rate applied to the business was 11%. As a result of the impairment review, the carrying value of the business was determined to be in excess of the value in use, thereby requiring an impairment loss to be recognised.

The 2004 impairment charge of €791 million in relation to the *Slim-Fast* business was calculated using value in use and applied a pre-tax discount rate of 11%. This charge was also reflected in operating profit for The Americas Region.

The remainder of the impairment loss charged in 2005 of €19 million includes (€2 million representing write-downs in respect of planned business disposals that will complete during 2006, and €10 million in respect of impairment of goodwill and indefinite-lived intangible assets in Colombia and India. In 2004, the remaining balance of €212 million included €156 million in respect of planned business disposals in 2005 Other smaller impairments were recognised during the course of 2004 for tea plantations and a bakery business in India, and a home and personal care business in North Africa.

Significant cash generating units

The goodwill and indefinite-lived intangible assets held in the global savoury and dressings CGU, comprising €11.9 billion and €3.6 billion, respectively, are considered significant in comparison to the total carrying amounts of goodwill and indefinite-lived intangible assets at 31 December 2005.

During 2005, we conducted an impairment review of the carrying value of these assets. Value in use of the global savoury and dressings CGU has been calculated as the present value of projected future cash flows. A pre-tax discount rate of 10% was used.

The following key assumptions were used in the discounted cash flow projections for the savoury and dressings CGU:
- a longer-term sustainable growth rate of 2%, adjusted for market fade, used to determine an appropriate terminal value multiple;
- average near-term nominal growth for the major product groups within the CGU of 4%; and
- average operating margins for the major product groups within the CGU ranging from 19% to 23%.

The growth rates and margins used to estimate future performance are based on past performance and our experience of growth rates and margins achievable in our key markets as a guide. We believe that the assumptions used in estimating the future performance of the savoury and dressings CGU are consistent with past performance

The projections covered a period of 10 years as we believe this to be a suitable timescale over which to review and consider annual performance before applying a fixed terminal value multiple to the final year cash flows of the detailed projection. Stopping the detailed projections after five years and applying a terminal value multiple thereafter would not result in a materially different estimate of the value in use.

The growth rates used to estimate future performance beyond the periods covered by our annual planning and strategic planning processes do not exceed the long-term average rates of growth for similar products.

We have performed sensitivity analysis around the base case assumptions and have concluded that no reasonable possible changes in key assumptions would cause the carrying amount of the savoury and dressings CGU to exceed its recoverable amount.

2.5   *IAS 23 Borrowing Costs* (revised December 2003 and March 2007)

The objective of IAS 23 is to prescribe the accounting treatment for borrowing costs. Originally it required immediate expensing but, under a revision in March 2007, capitalisation of borrowing costs that are directly attributable to the acquisition, construction or production of a qualifying asset must be undertaken. The standard should be applied in accounting for borrowing costs but it does not cover the actual or imputed costs of equity.

Definitions

Borrowing costs. Interest and other costs incurred by an enterprise in connection with borrowing of funds.

Qualifying asset. An asset which takes a substantial period of time to get ready for its intended use or sale.

Borrowing costs include interest on bank overdrafts, amortisation of discounts, amortisation of ancillary costs and finance lease charges.

Examples of qualifying assets include inventories requiring a substantial period of time to bring to a saleable condition, power generation facilities and investment properties. Assets that are ready for their intended use are not qualifying assets.

Borrowing costs – Required treatment

Recognition

Borrowing costs that are directly attributable to the acquisition, construction or production of a qualifying asset should be capitalised as part of the cost of that asset. That can occur when it is probable that they will result in future economic benefits to the enterprise and the costs can be measured reliably.

Borrowing costs eligible for capitalisation

Those borrowing costs that would have been avoided if the expenditure on the qualifying asset had not been made. When an enterprise borrows funds specifically to obtain a particular asset, the borrowing costs can be readily identified. It may be difficult to identify a direct relationship e.g. central co-ordination of finance, use of a range of debt instruments, loans in foreign currencies, operations in highly inflationary economies or from fluctuations in exchange rates. The exercise of judgement is required to determine the amount of borrowing costs to capitalise.

The IAS requires the use of actual borrowing costs less any temporary investment income where funds are borrowed specifically. To the extent that funds are borrowed generally then the amount capitalised should be determined by applying a weighted average capitalisation rate to the borrowings outstanding during the period. However, the amount of borrowing costs capitalised during a period should not exceed the amount of borrowing costs incurred during that period.

Example – Ballyclare Plc (Capitalisation of interest)

Ballyclare Plc, a retailing company with many high street shops, is considering a major expansion incorporating a major distinct initiative.

It is proposing to build a major new store which it will finance partly by bank borrowings and partly through existing cash resources. There will be substantial external and imputed interest costs both while the store is being built and on the inventories held once the store opens.

The Main arguments Advanced in Support of This Capitalisation

(1) Interest incurred as a consequence of a decision to acquire an asset is not intrinsically different from other costs that are commonly capitalised. If an asset requires a period of time to bring it to the condition and location necessary for its intended use, any interest incurred during that period as a result of expenditure on the asset is part of the cost of acquisition (IAS 23).

(2) A better matching of income and expenditure is achieved, in that interest incurred with a view to future benefits is carried forward to be expensed in the periods expected to benefit. A failure to capitalise would reduce current earnings artificially and not give a representative view of the benefits of the acquisition.

(3) It results in greater comparability between companies constructing assets and those buying similar completed assets. Any purchase price would normally include interest as the vendor would wish to recover all costs, including interest, on pricing the asset.

In Ballyclare's specific circumstances, examination of IAS 23 reveals a number of specific conditions which should be applied:

(1) Only those borrowing costs which are directly attributable to the construction of a property should be capitalised.

(2) The amount capitalised should not exceed the amount of borrowing costs incurred during the period.

(3) Capitalisation should commence only when:
  • borrowing costs are being incurred;
  • expenditure on the asset is being incurred; and
  • activity is in progress in getting the asset ready for use.

(4) Capitalisation should be suspended during extended periods in which activity is not taking place.

(5) Capitalisation should cease when all activities are complete. If the asset is built in parts, then capitalisation should cease on completion of each part.

(6) A weighted average of borrowing costs may be adopted, but no notional borrowing costs are to be included.

It is certainly fair to capitalise interest as the store is being built because this will bring the asset to its intended location and condition and thus ensure comparability between self-built and acquired stores. This was adopted in the past by most retail stores and hotel groups in the United Kingdom and Ireland, e.g. Marks and Spencer, Sainsbury, Jurys Hotel Group.

An additional problem is whether or not interest can be imputed to the balance sheet value for inventory as the cost of financing those inventories once the store opens. This policy is common for inventories which mature over a long period of time (e.g. whisky), or for long-term work in progress when financing costs are a material element of total cost. However, the costs must be concerned with improving the condition of that inventory. In Ballyclare's case, this seems unlikely as the stocks would not change in condition once they have arrived in the store, and stock turnover should be fast enough to make any interest cost immaterial.

Excess of the carrying amount of the qualifying asset over recoverable amount

When the carrying amount of the qualifying asset exceeds its recoverable amount or net realisable value, the carrying amount is written down. In certain circumstances the amount can be written back.

Commencement of capitalisation

Capitalisation should commence when:

(a)   expenditures for the asset are being incurred;
(b)   borrowing costs are being incurred; and
(c)   activities to prepare the asset for intended use are in progress

Only those expenditures that result in payments of cash, transfers of other assets or assumption of interest bearing liabilities may be capitalised. These are reduced by any progress payments and grants received. The average carrying amount of the asset during a period should normally be a reasonable approximation of the expenditure to which the capitalisation rate is applied in that period.

The activities necessary to prepare the asset encompass more than the physical construction of the asset. They include technical and administrative work prior to the commencement of physical construction. This excludes holding costs e.g. borrowing costs incurred while land acquired for building is held without any associated development activity.

Suspension of capitalisation

Capitalisation should be suspended during extended periods in which active development is interrupted. Capitalisation of borrowing costs is not normally suspended during a period when substantial, technical and administrative work is being carried out nor when a temporary delay is necessary to get an asset ready for intended use or sale e.g. high water levels delay construction of a bridge.

Cessation of capitalisation

Capitalisation should cease when substantially all the activities necessary to prepare the qualifying asset for its intended use or sale are complete. Normally, when physical construction is complete but if minor modifications are all that is outstanding would indicate that substantially all activities are complete.

When the construction of a qualifying asset is completed in parts and each part is capable of being used then capitalisation should cease when substantially all the activities necessary to prepare that part for use, are completed e.g. each building in a business park but not an industrial plant involving several processes carried out in sequence.

Disclosure

(a)   the accounting policy adopted for borrowing costs.
(b)   the amount of borrowing costs capitalised in the period.
(c)   the capitalisation rate used.

An example of a company complying with the revised IAS 23, is provided by a Cypriot company, Lanitis Development Public Limited.

Lanitis Development Year   Ended 31 December 2005 Public Limited

Extracts from the Notes to the Financial Statements

9. Finance Costs – Net

	2005 €£	2004 €£
Interest expense:		
Bank borrowings	1,657,685	1,301,780
Overdue taxation	9,179	75,802
Loan from parent company (Note 28 (e))	2,819	–
	1,669,683	1,377,582
Less interest capitalised for assets under construction	(440,675)	(1,267,643)
	1,229,008	109,939
Net foreign exchange transaction (gains/losses on financing activities	(169,265)	945
	1,059,743	110,884

3

Asset valuation:
Intangible assets

3.1   IAS 38 *Intangible Assets* (revised 2003)

The objective of IAS 38 is to prescribe the accounting treatment for intangible assets and how to recognise an intangible asset if, and only if, certain criteria are met. It also specifies how to measure the carrying amount of intangible assets and requires certain disclosures.

It should be applied to all intangible assets, except:

(a)   intangible assets covered by another standard, e.g. those for sale in ordinary course of business, deferred tax assets, leases under IAS 17, employee benefits under IAS 19, goodwill;
(b)   financial assets as defined per IAS 32 and IAS 39;
(c)   mineral rights and exploration for oil and gas expenditure; and
(d)   insurance contracts with policyholders (see IFRS 4).

Some intangibles may be contained in a physical asset, e.g. compact disc. Judgement is required to decide if IAS 16 or IAS 38 should be applied. Where software is not an integral part of related hardware, it is an intangible asset.

IAS 38 applies to advertising, training, start-up, and research and development. Licensing agreements, patents, copyrights, etc. are excluded from IAS 17 and fall within the scope of IAS 38.

Definitions

• *Intangible asset.* An intangible asset is an identifiable non-monetary asset without physical substance.

- *Research*. Original and planned investigation undertaken with the prospect of gaining new scientific or technical knowledge and understanding.
- *Development*. The application of research findings or other knowledge to a plan or design for the production of new or substantially improved materials, devices, products, processes, systems or services prior to the commencement of commercial production or use.
- *Intangible assets*. Examples include computer software, patents, copyrights, motion picture films, customer lists, mortgage servicing rights, fishing licences, import quotas, franchises, customer or supplier relationships, customer loyalty, market share and marketing rights.

To be capitalised they must meet the definition of an intangible asset, i.e. identifiability, control over a resource and the existence of future economic benefits. If it fails, then expenditure should be expensed unless part of a business combination when it should be treated as part of goodwill.

Identifiability

Goodwill, in a business combination, represents a payment in anticipation of future economic benefits from assets that are not capable of being individually identified and separately recognised.

An intangible asset meets the identifiability criterion in the definition of an intangible asset when it:

(a)   is separable, i.e. capable of being separated or divided from the entity and sold, transferred, licensed, rented or exchanged, either individually or together with a related contract, asset or liability or

(b)   arises from contractual or other legal rights, regardless of whether those rights are transferable or separable from the entity or from other rights and obligations.

Control

An entity controls an intangible asset if it has the power to obtain future economic benefits and restrict the access of others to those benefits. Capacity to control is usually via legal rights but that is not a necessary condition.

Market and technical knowledge may give rise to future economic benefits if it is protected by legal rights such as copyrights, a restraint of trade agreement or by a legal duty on employees to maintain confidentiality.

Skilled staff and specific management or technical talent are unlikely to meet the definition of an intangible asset unless it is protected by legal rights and also meets the other parts of the definition. An entity has no sufficient control over customer loyalty and customer relationships and thus is also unlikely to meet the definition, unless as part of a business combination.

Future economic benefits

This can include revenue from the sale of products or services, cost savings or other benefits resulting from the use of the asset, e.g. use of intellectual property may reduce future production costs rather than increase future revenues.

Recognition and initial measurement of an intangible asset

Recognition of an intangible asset requires an entity to demonstrate that the item meets the:

(a)   definition of an intangible asset; and
(b)   the recognition criteria set out in IAS 38.

An intangible asset shall be recognised if and only if:

(a)   it is probable that the future economic benefits attributable to the asset will flow to the entity; and
(b)   the cost of the asset can be measured reliably.

An entity shall assess the probability of future economic benefits using reasonable and supportable assumptions that represent management's best estimate of the set of economic conditions that will exist over the useful life of the asset. Greater emphasis will be given on external evidence when using judgement as to the degree of certainty attached to future cash flows.

An intangible asset shall be measured initially at cost.

Separate acquisition

The price an entity pays to acquire separately an intangible asset normally reflects expectations about the probability that the future economic benefits embodied in the asset will flow to the entity. Probability is already reflected in the cost of the acquired asset.

In addition, the cost of a separately acquired intangible asset can usually be measured reliably. That is specially the case if paid out in cash.

The cost of a separately acquired intangible asset comprises:

(a)   its purchase price, including import duties but after deducting trade discounts and rebates; and
(b)   any directly attributable expenditure on preparing the asset for its intended use, e.g. costs of employee benefits as per IAS 19, professional fees.

Costs incurred in using or redeploying intangible assets are excluded from the cost of those assets (e.g. costs incurred while the asset is capable of operating in the manner intended by management and initial operating losses).

Incidental operations are not necessary to bring an asset to its normal working condition, and thus they should be recognised immediately in the income statement and not included in the costs capitalised.

Acquisition as part of a business combination

Under IFRS 3 *Business Combinations*, the fair value of an intangible asset reflects market expectations about the probability that future economic benefits will flow to the entity. Probability is already reflected in the fair value measurement and thus the probability criterion is always satisfied for acquired intangible assets.

A non-monetary asset without physical substance must be identifiable to meet the definition of an intangible asset, i.e. when an asset is separable or arises from contractual or other legal rights. Sufficient evidence must exist to reliably measure a fair value that is separable from the entity.

It is unlikely that a workforce and its related intellectual capital would be measured with sufficient reliability to be separately recognised.

IAS 38 requires, at acquisition date, that an acquirer recognises all of the acquiree's intangible assets (excluding assembled workforces) separately from goodwill irrespective of whether those assets had been recognised in the acquiree's financial statements before the business combination. Research and development projects that meet the definition should be recognised separately.

Measuring the fair value of an intangible asset acquired in a business combination

Quoted market prices are the most reliable estimates of fair values of intangible assets. That is usually the current bid price or, if not available, the price of the most recent similar transaction provided no significant change in the economic circumstances occurred between the transaction date and the date of fair value.

If no active market exists, fair value is the amount that an entity would have paid for the asset, at acquisition date, in an arm's length transaction. Recent transactions should help in this situation.

Certain entities that are regularly involved in the purchase and sale of unique intangible assets have developed techniques for estimating their fair values indirectly. These techniques may be used to calculate the initial measurement of an intangible asset if their objective is to estimate fair value for that purpose.

Few examples of companies including new intangible assets on to the balance sheet on adoption of IAS 38 are provided below.

Brambles Industries Plc   Year Ended 31 December 2005

Until 2005, Brambles did not recognise any intangible assets other than good-will. This year, the company has restated business combinations after the date of transition and recognises $60 million of intangible assets, comprising principally acquired customer lists and agreements. In addition, the company recognised $14.7 million brands and software that it did not require on an acquisition in the year due to integration plans. It has wholly amortised these during the year, classifying the charge as accelerated amortisation. It explains that the brands and software were fair valued at the acquisition date without regard to its intentions for these assets.

IAS 38 *Intangible Assets* requires that software which is not an integral part of related hardware be treated as an intangible asset. Prior to 2005, Brambles accounted for software within tangible fixed assets. From 2005, the company follows IAS 38 and recognises $95.1 million software as an intangible asset.

Intangible assets

Intangible assets acquired are capitalised at cost, unless acquired as part of a business combination in which case they are capitalised at fair value as at the date of acquisition.

Following initial recognition, intangible assets are carried at cost less provisions for amortisation and impairment.

The costs of acquiring and developing computer software for internal use are capitalised as intangible non-current assets where it is used to support a significant business system and the expenditure leads to the creation of a durable asset.

Useful lives have been established for all non-goodwill intangible assets. Amortisation charges are expensed in the income statement on a straight-line basis over those useful lives. Estimated useful lives are reviewed annually.

The expected useful lives of intangible assets are generally:

*   customer lists and relationships   3–20 years;
*   computer software   3–7 years.

There are no non-goodwill intangible assets with indefinite lives.

Intangible assets are tested for impairment where an indicator of impairment exists, either individually or at the cash generating unit level.

Gains or losses arising from derecognition of an intangible asset are measured as the difference between the net disposal proceeds and the carrying amount of the asset and are recognised in the income statement when the asset is derecognised.

Fyffes Plc   Year Ended 31 December 2005

Intangible assets

Trademarks are carried at historic cost. The directors are of the opinion that the Fyffes trademark has an indefinite useful life and therefore it is not amortised, but subject to annual impairment testing. Other identifiable intangible assets, that are acquired by the Group, are stated at cost less accumulated amortisation and impairment losses, when separable or arising from contractual or other legal rights and reliably measurable.

Amortisation is expensed in the income statement on a straight-line basis over the estimated useful lives of intangible assets, unless such lives are indefinite from the date they are available for use. Intangible assets reflecting the value of customer relationships, which arise on acquisitions, are amortised over their useful lives ranging from one to ten years.

Under the terms of EU legislation, certain Group companies are granted rights to import bananas in the normal course of trading. In accordance with paragraph 23 of IAS 20 *Accounting for Government Grants and Disclosure of Government Assistance,* these rights have been accounted for as grants, at nominal value.

12. Goodwill and Intangible Assets

	Customer relationships (€'000)	Trademark (€'000)	Goodwill (€'000)	Total (€'000)
Cost				
Balance at 1 January 2004	–	2,319	21,261	23,580
Arising from business combinations	25,694	–	33,222	58,916
Foreign exchange movement	167	(6)	881	992
Balance at 31 December 2004	25,861	2,313	55,314	83,488
Arising from business combinations	722	–	14	786
Revisions to deferred consideration estimates	–	–	5,006	5,006
Reclassifications	115	–	(115)	–
Foreign exchange movement	(765)	41	(1,090)	(1,814)
Balance at 31 December 2005	25,933	2,354	59,129	87,416
Accumulated amortisation and impairment				
Balance at 1 January 2004	–	–	–	–
Amortisation for the year	1,718	–	–	1,713
Foreign exchange movement	–	–	–	–
Balance at 31 December 2004	1,718	–	–	1,713
Amortisation for the year	3,110	–	–	8,110
Foreign exchange movement	(1)	–	–	(1)
Balance at 31 December 2005	4,822	–	–	4,822
Carrying amount				
At 31 December 2004	24,148	2,313	55,314	81,775
At 31 December 2005	21,111	2,354	59,129	82,594

The carrying value of the trademark represents the cost of acquiring the worldwide rights to the Fyffes trademark. The trademark is tested for impairment at each balance sheet date. The Fyffes trademark is widely used in the business with ongoing success and therefore, in the opinion of the directors, does not have a finite useful life.

Customer relationships are amortised over their estimated useful lives, ranging from 1 to 10 years. Goodwill and intangible assets arise in connection with acquisitions, including revisions of estimates of deferred consideration payable in respect of acquisitions in previous years, as set out in Note 25.

Acquisition by way of a government grant

Some intangible assets could be acquired for free or for a nominal consideration, e.g. landing rights, import licences, licences to operate radio stations and so on. Under IAS 20, an entity may choose to recognise both the asset and the grant at fair value initially. If it chooses not to do that, the entity must recognise the asset initially at a nominal amount including any expenditure that is directly attributable to preparing the asset for its intended use.

Exchanges of assets

The cost of such an asset is measured at the fair value of the asset given up, adjusted by the amount of any cash or cash equivalents transferred. The fair value of the asset received is used to measure its cost if it is more clearly evident than the fair value of the asset given up.

The cost of an intangible asset acquired in exchange for a similar asset is measured at the carrying amount of the asset given up when the fair value of neither of the assets exchanged can be determined reliably.

Internally generated goodwill

Internally generated goodwill shall not be recognised as an asset. It is not an identifiable resource (i.e. it is not separable nor does it arise from contractual or other legal rights) controlled by the entity that can be measured reliably at cost.

Differences between the market value of an entity and the carrying amount of its identifiable net assets may capture a range of factors that affect the value of the entity. Such differences cannot be considered to represent the cost of intangible assets controlled by the entity.

Internally generated intangible assets

It is difficult to assess whether an identifiable internal intangible asset exists or not. Thus, in addition to ensuring that there are probable economic benefits flowing to the entity and measuring cost reliably, an entity must also classify the generation of the asset into its research and development phases. If it cannot separate between the two, it must be classified as research.

Research phase

No intangible asset can arise from the research phase and thus it must be written off as an expense. No demonstration of probable future economic benefits can exist. Examples include:

(a)   activities aimed at obtaining new knowledge;
(b)   the search for, evaluation and final selection of, applications of research findings;
(c)   the search for alternatives for materials, devices, products, processes, systems or services; and
(d)   the formulation, design, evaluation and final selection of possible alternatives for new or improved materials, products, devices, processes, systems or services.

Development phase

Should be recognised but if, and only if, an entity can demonstrate all of the following:

(a) The technical feasibility of completing the intangible asset so that it will be available for use or sale.
(b) Its intention to complete the intangible asset and use or sell it.
(c) Its ability to use or sell the intangible asset.
(d) How the intangible asset will generate probable future economic benefits. It shall demonstrate the existence of a market for the output of the intangible asset or, if used internally, its usefulness.
(e) The availability of adequate technical, financial and other resources to complete the development and to use or sell the intangible asset.
(f) Its ability to reliably measure the expenditure attributable to the intangible asset during its development phase.

These could be verified by an internal business plan or by lenders providing external finance for the project. Internal costing systems can often measure reliably the cost of generating an intangible asset internally such as salary and other expenditure in securing copyrights or licences or developing computer software.

Examples of development activities are:

(a) the design, construction and testing of pre-production or pre-use prototypes and models;
(b) the design of tools, jigs, moulds and dies involving new technology;
(c) the design, construction and operation of a pilot plant that is not of a scale economically feasible for commercial production; and
(d) the design, construction and testing of a chosen alternative for new or improved materials, devices, products, processes, systems or services.

Internally generated brands, mastheads, publishing titles, customer lists and items similar in substance shall not be recognised as intangible assets. They cannot be distinguished from the cost of developing the business as a whole.

Cost of an internally generated intangible asset

Reinstatement of expenditure recognised as an expense in previous years may not occur.

The cost of an internally generated intangible asset comprises all expenditure that can be directly attributable and is necessary to creating, producing and preparing the asset for it to be capable of operating in the manner intended by management. The cost includes, if applicable:

(a) expenditure on materials and services used or consumed in generating the intangible asset;
(b) the salaries, wages and other employment-related costs of personnel directly engaged in generating the asset; and

(c) any expenditure directly attributable to generating the asset, such as fees to register a legal right and the amortisation of patents and licences.

The following are not included:

(a) selling, administration and other general overheads unless directly attributable to the asset;
(b) clearly identified inefficiencies and initial operating losses;
(c) expenditure on training staff to operate the asset.

EXAMPLE

An entity is developing a new production process. During 20×5, expenditure incurred was 1,000, of which 900 was incurred before $1.12.20 \times 5$ and 100 was incurred in December. At $1.12.20 \times 5$ the production process met the criteria for recognition as an intangible asset.

At the end of 20×5 an intangible asset of 100 should be recorded with 900 being expensed (pre-criteria).

During 20×6 expenditure incurred is 2,000. At the end of 20×6 the recoverable amount of knowhow is estimated to be 1,900.

At the end of 20×6, the cost of the production process is 2,100 (100 + 2,000). An impairment loss of 200 needs to be recorded which may be reversed in a subsequent period if the requirements in IAS 36 are met.

Example – Cadogan Plc

Cadogan Plc has an extensive research facility involved in the research, development and promotion of various projects. Information regarding the research department's activities for the year ended 31 July 2007 is given below:

(1) £750,000 spent on a new gas ionising plant. Such plant is highly specialised and has minimal scrap value due to contamination. It has an expected life of 10 years and came into use from 1 July 2007.
(2) A contract was entered into with a cosmetics group on a cost plus 25 per cent basis to develop a kiss-proof lipstick. So far Cadogan Plc has incurred costs of £90,000 and has received £25,000 on account. Further costs of £35,000 to complete the contract are expected before 31 July 2008. The balance of the contract price is to be settled on completion.
(3) Dr Zod, a nuclear physicist, was employed at a cost of £25,000 to conduct investigations into subatomic wave motions. The work is vital to the future success of several current projects.
(4) £250,000 has been spent on the research and development of a new audio product. Forty per cent is attributable to development. The product will not be

marketable until 2009. Further total costs of some £400,000 are estimated, but financial backing is available from institutions and there are no doubts over the technical feasibility of the product. It is expected to have the same impact on home entertainment as television.

(5) Wallop, a new low-alcohol beverage, was launched on 1 February 2007 with an expected market life of four years. During the year £20,000 was spent on advertising. Development expenditure brought forward amounted to £300,000.

Suggested solution – Cadogan Plc

New gas ionising plant, £750,000

This is a fixed asset which should be capitalised and subsequently depreciated over its estimated useful life. However, if the asset is used specifically for development, then the depreciation charge may form part of overall development costs. No information is available concerning its use during 2007; thus it can be assumed that it is not used on qualifying development projects and depreciation should be written off to the income statement. With a life of 10 years and a charge for one month, depreciation should be £6,250 ($£750,000 \times 1/10 \times 1/12$) and the net book value is £743,750.

Development of kiss-proof lipstick

Although this is research expenditure, it is a contract with a third party to provide a service to that party, albeit on a contract exceeding one year. It thus falls under IAS 11's definition of a construction contract. As such it is not part of development expenditure under IAS 38. Turnover should be recorded on the basis of work carried out to date and cost of sales should be matched to the same period of time. As this is a straightforward cost plus 25% contract, then cost of sales would be fairly charged at £90,000 and turnover at $£90,000 \times 125\% = £112,500$. As payments on account amount to £25,000 to date, then receivables would be recorded at £87,500 ($£112,500 - £25,000$). No amount would be recorded as work in progress. However, if a more conservative view is taken of the profit to date, the turnover and related cost of sales can be reduced, thus creating a balance of costs not transferred to cost of sales, i.e. work in progress.

Employment of Dr Zod, £25,000

Dr Zod is a nuclear physicist and is probably an expert in the field of sub-atomic wave motions. However, the annual salary must be regarded as an expense unless it can be matched to a specific successful development project. If such a project cannot be identified then the cost of £25,000 should be written off straight to the income statement.

New audio product, £250,000

This product would appear to meet the five qualifying conditions to enable development expenditure to be capitalised under IAS 38. However, only 40% (£100,000) is in respect of development and £150,000 will need to be written off immediately to the income statement. The £100,000 may be carried forward in the balance sheet as an intangible asset, as well as the expected £400,000 when it is spent in future years. Assuming that £500,000 is eventually capitalised, this should be amortised to accounting periods on a systematic basis by reference to the periods over which it is expected that the new audio product will be sold. This could be on the basis of either time or units sold.

Wallop advertising (£20,000) and development costs (£300,000)

Development costs of £300,000 have already been capitalised in prior years. Amortisation should commence on 1 February 2007, the date of commencement of commercial production. With an expected market life of four years, annual amortisation will be £75,000 per annum assuming a straight-line allocation. For 2007, six months should be charged, i.e. £37,500. Development costs would be stated at £262,500 under intangible assets in the balance sheet. In addition, the movement for the year should be disclosed in the notes to the accounts. The advertising expenditure of £20,000 could be carried forward as an asset, provided that it meets the definition of an asset under the Framework, i.e. it is probable that future revenues will result from the expenditure and the asset has a cost or value which can be sufficiently reliably measured (general recognition tests). It would then be subsequently amortised to the income statement over the period from which future benefits will derive. However, prudence would probably dictate an immediate write-off. For Plcs and public interest bodies, this expenditure fits under the heading of *investment for the future* and should be disclosed in the *Operating and Financial Review.*

Recognition of an expense

Expenditure on an intangible item shall be expensed when incurred unless:

(a) it forms part of the cost of an intangible asset that meets the recognition criteria or

(b) the item is acquired in a business combination and cannot be recognised as an intangible asset. In this case it forms part of goodwill.

Research is always expensed when incurred. Other examples include costs of start-up activities unless included as a fixed asset under IAS 16, training expenditure, advertising, and relocation and reorganisation expenses.

Expenditure initially expensed in previous years may not be reinstated as part of an asset at a later date.

Subsequent expenditure

Subsequent expenditure shall be expensed when incurred unless:

(a) it is probable that the expenditure will increase future economic benefits beyond that originally assessed prior to the expenditure taking place and

(b) the expenditure can be attributed to the asset and can be reliably measured.

If both conditions are met any subsequent expenditure should be added to the cost of the intangible asset. Normally the nature of such assets is that it is not possible to determine whether or not the subsequent expenditure is likely to enhance or maintain future economic benefits. Only rarely they will pass (a) and (b) above.

Subsequent expenditure on brands, mastheads, customer lists, publishing titles should always be expensed to avoid the recognition of internally generated goodwill.

Research and development that:

(a) relates to an in-process research or development project acquired separately or in a business combination and recognised as an intangible asset and

(b) is incurred after the acquisition of that project

The research phase and development phase should be accounted for as above. Effectively that means that subsequent expenditure should be expensed if it is in the nature of research expenditure, expensed if development but fail to satisfy the criteria as an intangible asset and added to the asset if satisfies the recognition criteria.

An example of companies who have changed their accounting policy are French companies Compagnie de Richemont SA and Saint-Gobain who now capitalise development for the first time.

Compagnie de Richemont SA

In 2004, all research and development costs were expensed as incurred. From 2005, Richemont states that development costs relating to projects in the development phase meeting the criteria set by IAS 38 *Intangible Assets* are capitalised as intangible assets. Accordingly, it recognises €23 million of development costs within its €67 million intangible assets and adds that capitalised expenditure is amortised over its useful economic life, although no explicit period is disclosed.

(c) Research and development, patents and trademarks:

Research expenditures are recognised as an expense as incurred. Costs incurred on development projects are recognised as intangible assets when it is probable that the project will be a success, considering its commercial and technological feasibility, and costs can be measured reliably. Other development expenditures are recognised as an expense as incurred. Development costs previously recognised as an expense are not recognised as an asset in a subsequent period. Development costs that have a finite useful life and that have been capitalised are amortised from the commencement of commercial production of the product on the straight-line method over the period of its expected benefit.

Saint-Gobain   Year Ended 31 December 2005

Last year any research and development costs all were expensed as incurred. This year Saint-Gobain states that development costs relating to significant projects in the development, validation or manufacturing phase meeting the criteria set by IAS 38 *Intangible Assets* are capitalised as intangible assets. Accordingly, it recognises €29 million of development costs within its €2.3 billion intangible assets.

Other intangible assets

Other intangible assets primarily include patents, brands, software and development costs.

Acquired retail brands and certain manufacturing brands are treated as intangible assets with indefinite useful lives as they have a strong reputation on a national and/or international scale. These brands are not amortised but are tested for impairment on an annual basis. Other brands are amortised over their useful lives not to exceed 40 years. Patents and purchased software are amortised over their estimated useful lives. The applicable useful lives for patents do not exceed 20 years and those for purchased software range from three to five years.

Research costs are expensed as incurred. Development costs meeting the recognition criteria under IAS 38 are included in intangible assets.

The greenhouse gas emission allowances granted to the Group as at 31 December 2005 were not recognised in the consolidated accounts at that date, as IFRIC 3 – Emission Rights – has been withdrawn. A provision is recorded in the consolidated financial statements to cover any difference between the Group's emissions and the emission rights granted. Details relating to the measurement of emissions allowances available at the balance sheet date are provided in Note 4.

Measurement subsequent to initial recognition

Benchmark treatment

Shall be carried at cost less accumulated amortisation and impairment losses.

Allowed alternative treatment

Shall be carried at a revalued amount, being its fair value at the date of the revaluation less any subsequent accumulated amortisation and impairment losses. Fair value should refer to an active market. Revaluations should be carried out with sufficient regularity so that the carrying values are not materially different from the fair value at the balance sheet date.

It is uncommon to find an active market in intangible assets but they can occur, e.g. taxi licences, fishing licences, production quotas and so on. However, it cannot exist for brands, newspaper mastheads, music and film publishing rights, patents or trademarks because each asset is unique and transactions are infrequent.

The frequency of revaluations depends on the volatility of the fair values and, if they are significant, an annual valuation may be necessary.

If an intangible asset is revalued, any accumulated amortisation at the date of revaluation is either:

(a) restated proportionately with change in the gross carrying amount of the asset so that the carrying amount of the asset after revaluation equals its revalued amount or
(b) eliminated against the gross carrying amount of the asset and the net amount restated to the revalued amount of the asset.

If an intangible asset is revalued, all the other assets in that class shall also be revalued unless there is no active market for those assets. That is to prevent selective revaluation and reporting of a mixture of costs and values as at different dates.

If there is no active market then the class of asset must be carried at cost less accumulated amortisation and impairment losses. Also if the fair value can no longer be determined by reference to an active market, the carrying amount of the asset shall be its revalued amount at the date of the last revaluation less accumulated amortisation and impairment losses. The fact that there is no active market should also trigger off an impairment review.

Any increase on a revaluation should normally be credited directly to equity but to income to the extent it reverses a revaluation decrease of the same asset that has previously been recognised as an expense.

Any decrease on a revaluation should be expensed unless there is a previous revaluation surplus on the same asset in which case it should be used to reverse the surplus first. Any excess is then expensed.

The cumulative revaluation surplus included in equity may be transferred directly to retained earnings when the surplus is realised, i.e. on retirement or disposal of the asset.

Useful life

An entity shall assess whether the useful life of an intangible asset is infinite or finite. An indefinite life is one where there is no foreseeable limit to the period over which the asset is expected to generate net cash inflows for the entity.

An intangible asset with a finite life shall be amortised but not an intangible asset having an indefinite life.

Many factors must be considered in determining the useful life including:

(a) the expected usage of the asset and whether it can be managed efficiently;
(b) typical product life cycles;
(c) technical, technological, commercial or other types of obsolescence;
(d) the stability of the industry in which the asset operates and changes in market demand;
(e) expected actions by competitors;
(f) the level of maintenance expenditure required to obtain future benefits;
(g) the period of control over the asset; and
(h) whether the useful life is dependent on the useful life of other assets in the entity.

Examples illustrating the determination of useful life for different intangible assets and their subsequent accounting are provided by the standard and these are listed below:

Examples

An acquired customer list

A direct mail company acquires a customer list and expects to derive benefit for at least one year but not more than three years. The customer list would be amortised over best estimate of useful life, say 18 months. Even the intention to add customer names to the list must be ignored as the asset relates only to the list of customers that existed at the date it was acquired. It should also be reviewed for impairment under IAS 36.

An acquired patent that expires in 15 years

The patent is protected for 15 years. There is a commitment to sell the patent after five years to a third party for 60% of the fair value of the patent at the date it was acquired.

The patent should be amortised over five years with a residual value of 60% of the present value of the patent's fair value at the date it was acquired. It should also be reviewed for impairment under IAS 36.

An acquired copyright that has a remaining legal life of 50 years

Assume an analysis of consumer habits provides evidence that there are only 30 years left of future benefits. The asset must now be amortised over the new expected remaining estimated useful life of 30 years as well as reviewing the asset for impairment.

An acquired broadcast licence that expires in five years

The licence is renewable every 10 years but can be renewed indefinitely at little cost and the entity intends to renew the licence. The technology is not expected to be replaced in the foreseeable future.

The licence would be treated as having an indefinite useful life thus the licence would not be amortised until its useful life is determined to be finite. The licence would be tested for impairment at the end of each annual reporting period and whenever there is an indication of impairment.

The broadcast licence is revoked

Assume the licensing authority will no longer renew the licences but decide to auction them. There are three years before the licence expires. The useful life is no longer infinite and must be amortised over the remaining useful life of three years as well as being tested for impairment.

An acquired airline route authority between two major cities expires in three years

The route authority may be renewed every five years and these are routinely granted at minimal cost and historically have been renewed. The acquiring entity expects to service the route indefinitely and cash flow analysis supports that view. The intangible asset therefore has an indefinite life and should not be amortised until its useful life is determined to be finite. It must, however, be tested annually for impairment and whenever there is an indication of an impairment.

An acquired trademark used to identify and distinguish a leading consumer product that has been a market leader for the past eight years

A trademark has a legal life of 5 years but is renewable every 10 years at little cost and the entity intends to renew. This asset has an indefinite life and should not be amortised until useful life is determined to be definite. It should also be tested for impairment annually or when there is an indication of impairment.

A trademark acquired 10 years ago that distinguishes a leading consumer product

Unexpected competition has emerged which will reduce future sales by 20% but management expects that the 80% will continue indefinitely. An impairment must be recognised immediately to recoverable amount but would continue to be subject to annual impairment although not amortised.

A trademark for a line of products acquired several years ago in a business combination

This is a well established product, going for 35 years. There is an expectation that there was no limit to period of time it would contribute to cash flows thus it has not been amortised. Management has recently decided that the product line will be discontinued over next four years. It must now be tested for impairment and subsequently amortised over the next four years.

The term indefinite does not mean infinite. A conclusion that the useful life is indefinite should not depend on planned future expenditure in excess of that required to maintain the asset at that standard of performance.

Computer software is susceptible to changes in technology and should written off over a short useful life.

The useful life may be very long but uncertainty justifies estimating the useful life on a prudent basis but it does not justify an unrealistically short life.

The useful life of an intangible asset that arises from contractual or other legal rights should not exceed the period of the legal or contractual rights but may be shorter. The useful life may include a renewal period but only if there is evidence to support renewal by the entity without significant cost. If there are both legal and economic factors influencing the useful life of an intangible asset, then economic factors determine the period over which benefits will be received but legal factors may restrict the period over which the entity controls access to those benefits. The useful life is the shorter of the periods determined by these factors.

Intangible assets with finite useful lives

Amortisation period and amortisation method

The depreciable amount of an intangible asset should be allocated over its useful life. Amortisation should be allocated on a systematic basis over its useful life from the day it is available for use. It should reflect the pattern of economic benefits being consumed but straight line should be adopted if it cannot be determined reliably. The standard requires it to be expensed unless permitted by another standard to be capitalised, e.g. IAS 2 *Inventories.*

The method should be applied consistently but it would be rare for persuasive evidence to support a method which would result in lower amortisation than that achieved by straight line.

Residual value

It should be assumed to be zero unless:

(a)   there is a commitment by a third party to purchase the asset at the end of its useful life
or
(b)   there is an active market for the asset:
   • residual value can be determined by reference to the market and
   • it is probable that such a market will exist at the end of the asset's useful life.

The depreciable amount is determined after deducting residual value but the latter is based on prices prevailing at the date of the estimate and is reviewed at each balance sheet date. Any change in that value is treated as an adjustment to future amortisation.

Review of amortisation period and amortisation method

The amortisation period and method shall be reviewed at the end of each annual reporting period. If the expected useful life is different from previous estimates, the amortisation period shall be changed. If there is a change in the expected pattern of consumption of future benefits, the amortisation period shall be accounted for as a change in accounting estimates as per IAS 8, e.g. it may become apparent that the diminishing balance method is more appropriate than straight line.

Intangible assets with indefinite useful lives

An intangible asset with an indefinite useful life shall not be amortised. However, it is required to be tested annually for impairment and whenever there is an indication of an impairment.

Review of useful life assessment

Should be reviewed each period to determine whether events and circumstances support an indefinite useful life. If not, the change should be treated as a change in accounting estimate by amortising the asset over its remaining useful life.

A reassessment of useful life is a sign that the asset should be tested for impairment. Any excess of the carrying amount over the recoverable amount should be treated as an impairment loss.

Recoverability of the carrying amount – impairment losses

To determine whether an intangible asset is impaired, an entity applies IAS 36 which explains when and how an entity reviews the carrying amount of its assets, how it determines the recoverable amount of an asset and when it recognises or reverses an impairment loss.

Retirements and disposals

An intangible asset should be derecognised on disposal or when no future economic benefits are expected from its use or disposal.

Gains or losses should be calculated as the difference between the net disposal proceeds and the carrying amount of the asset, and shall be recognised as income/expenses in the period in which the retirement or disposal occurs. The date of disposal should be determined by applying IAS 18 and the consideration should be valued initially at fair value. If the latter is deferred then it should be recognised at the cash price equivalent. The difference between the nominal amount of the consideration and the cash price equivalent is recognised as interest revenue under IAS 18 according to the effective yield on the receivable.

Amortisation should not cease on temporary idleness unless already fully depreciated.

Disclosure

General

The following should be disclosed for each class of intangible assets – split between internally generated and other intangible assets:

(a) Whether the useful lives are indefinite or finite and, if the latter, their useful lives or amortisation rates used.
(b) The amortisation methods adopted.
(c) The gross carrying amount and accumulated amortisation at start and end of the period.
(d) The line item of the income statement in which the amortisation charge is included.
(e) A reconciliation of the carrying amount at start and end of the period showing.
  • additions, split between internal, acquired and via business combinations;
  • retirements and disposals;
  • revaluations;
  • impairment losses;
  • impairment losses reversed;
  • amortisation during the period;
  • net exchange differences; and
  • other changes in carrying amount.

A class of intangible assets may include:

(a) brand names;
(b) mastheads and publishing rights;
(c) computer software;
(d) licences and franchises;
(e) copyrights, patents and other industrial property rights;
(f) recipes, formulae, models, designs and prototypes; and
(g) intangible assets under development.

Further disaggregation may be required if it involves providing more relevant information. The financial statements shall also disclose:

(a) if an intangible asset has an indefinite useful life, the carrying amount and the reasons supporting the assessment of that life. The significant factors should be described;
(b) a description, the carrying amount and remaining amortisation period of any individual intangible asset that is material to the entity as a whole;
(c) for acquired intangibles via grant – the initial fair value, their carrying amount and whether carried under the benchmark or allowed alternative treatment for subsequent measurement;
(d) the existence and carrying amounts of intangibles whose title is restricted or pledged for security;
(e) the amount of contractual commitments for the acquisition of intangibles.

Intangible assets carried under the allowed alternative treatment

The following shall be disclosed:

(a) By class of intangible assets:
  • the effective date of the revaluation;
  • the carrying amount; and
  • the carrying amount had the benchmark treatment been adopted (historic cost)
(b) The amount of the revaluation surplus at start and end of period indicating any changes and any restrictions on distribution.
(c) The methods and significant assumptions applied in estimating the asset's fair values.

Research and development expenditure

The aggregate amount of research and development expenditure expensed during the period.

Other information

An entity is encouraged to disclose the following:

(a) A description of any fully amortised intangible asset that is still in use.
(b) A brief description of significant intangible assets controlled by the entity but not recognised as assets as they failed to meet the recognition criteria in IAS 38 or were generated prior to IAS 38 being made effective.

SIC Intangible assets – Website costs (January 2003)

Issue

A website arising from internal development should be recognised as an asset if, and only if, the general conditions for recognition of an internally generated intangible asset are satisfied. Costs incurred on a website developed solely or primarily for promoting and advertising the entity's products should be expensed as incurred, since the entity will be unable to demonstrate that such a website will generate probable future economic benefits.

3.2   IAS 17 *Leases* (December 2003)

The objective of IAS 17 is to prescribe, for lessees and lessors, the appropriate accounting policies and disclosures to apply to both operating and finance leases.

The standard should apply to all leases other than:

(a)   leases to explore for minerals, oil, natural gas, etc.
(b)   licensing agreements for motion pictures, videos, plays, manuscripts, patents and copyrights.

There is also an exemption to the measurement of investment properties held by lessees under finance leases and vice versa to investment properties let out as operating leases by lessors as well as those relating to biological assets governed by IAS 41.

Definitions

- *Lease.* An agreement whereby the lessor coveys to the lessee the right to use an asset in return for a payment or series of payments for an agreed period of time.
- *Finance lease.* A lease that transfers substantially all the risks and rewards attached to an asset to a lessee. Title may or may not eventually be transferred (incident to ownership).
- *Operating lease.* A lease other than a finance lease.
- *Net investment in the lease.* The gross investment in the lease less unearned finance income.
- *Interest rate implicit in the lease.* The discount rate that, at the inception of the lease, causes the present value of (a) the minimum lease payments (MLPs) and (b) the unguaranteed residual value to be equal to the sum of the fair value of the leased asset and any initial direct costs of the lessor.

Classification of leases

This is based on the extent to which risks and rewards incident to ownership lie with the lessee or lessor. Risks include idle capacity losses, obsolescence, variations in returns, etc., and rewards include expectation of future profits and appreciation in the value of the residual value.

A lease is classified as finance if it transfers substantially all the risks and rewards and an operating lease vice versa.

There should be consistent treatment between lessor and lessee but the application of common definitions could still result in the same lease being classified differently by both parties.

The decision as to whether or not there is a finance lease depends on the substance of the transaction rather than its legal form. Normally a finance lease results where:

(a) lease transfers ownership of the asset to the lessee at the end of the lease term;
(b) lessee has option to purchase the asset at a price sufficiently lower than the fair value at the date the option becomes exercisable such that, at the inception of the lease, it is reasonably certain that the option will be exercised;
(c) the lease term is for a major part of the asset's economic life;
(d) at the inception of the lease, the present value of the MLPs amounts to substantially all of the fair value of the leased asset;
(e) the leased assets are of a specialised nature such that only the lessee can use them without major modifications being made.

Indicators of situations that individually or in combination could also lead to a lease being classified as a finance lease are as follows:

(a) If the lessee can cancel the lease and the losses of cancellation are borne by the lessee.
(b) Gains/losses from fluctuations in fair values of the residual values fall to the lessee, e.g. rent rebate equal to most of the sale proceeds at the end of the lease.
(c) The lessee has the ability to continue the lease for a secondary period at a rent substantially lower than market rent.

The decision is made at the inception of the lease but if both parties substantially alter the terms of the lease in a manner that would have resulted in a different classification then the revised agreement should be treated as a new agreement.

Leases of land and buildings should be classified in the same way. However land has an indefinite life and if title does not change hands then the lessee does not have substantially all the risks and rewards incident to ownership. In that case a premium paid for such a leasehold represents pre-paid lease payments which are amortised over the lease term in accordance with the pattern of benefits provided.

Accounting for leases in the financial statements of lessees

Finance lease

Should be recognised as an asset and a liability in the balance sheet of a lessee at amounts equal, at the inception of the lease, to the fair value of the leased property, net of grants and any tax credits receivable by the lessor. However, if the present value of the MLPs is lower, that value should be adopted.

The discount rate adopted should be the implicit rate of return in the lease, if practicable, or if not, the lessee's incremental borrowing rate.

By capitalising finance leases the substance of the transaction is recognised and thus financial ratios such as gearing are not distorted. It is not appropriate to net off finance lease assets and liabilities.

Initial direct costs are included as part of the amount recognised as an asset under the lease.

Lease payments should be apportioned between the finance charge and the reduction of the outstanding liability. The finance charge should be allocated to periods during the lease term so as to produce a constant rate of interest on the remaining balance of the liability for each period. Some form of approximation, however, is acceptable, e.g. sum of the digits method.

A finance lease gives rise to a depreciation charge as well as a finance cost for each period. The depreciation policy should be consistent with purchased assets and as per IAS 16 and IAS 38. If there is no reasonable certainty that the lessee will obtain ownership by the end of the lease term, the asset should be fully depreciated over the shorter of the lease term or its useful life.

It would be rare for the sum of the depreciation charge and finance cost to be the same as the lease payments made, thus the asset and related liability are unlikely to be equal after the inception of the lease. If a leased asset appears to be impaired, IAS 36 should be applied.

Disclosures

The following disclosures must be made:

(a) For each class of asset, the net carrying amount at the balance sheet date:

Inbev Accounts   Year Ended 31 December 2005

Leased assets

The company leases land and buildings as well as equipment under a number of finance lease agreements. The carrying amount of leased land and buildings was 12m euro (2004; 12m euro) and leased plant and equipment was 7 m euro (2004; 7m euro).

A reconciliation between the total of minimum lease payments (MLPs) at the balance sheet date and their present value. In addition the total of MLPs at the balance sheet date and their present value for each of the following periods:

- not later than one year;
- later than one year but not later than five years; and
- later than five years;

(b) Contingent rents recognised in income for the period.

(c) The total of future minimum sublease payments expected to be received under non-cancellable subleases at the balance sheet date.

(d) A general description of the lessee's significant leasing arrangements including, but not limited to, the following:
- the basis on which contingent rent payments are determined;
- the existence and terms of renewal or purchase options and escalation clauses; and
- restrictions imposed by lease arrangements, such as those concerning dividends, additional debt and further leasing.

BAE Systems Plc provides a good example of the accounting policy for and disclosures required for finance leases.

BAE Systems Plc   Year Ended 31 December 2005

Leases

Assets obtained under finance leases are included in property, plant and equipment at cost and are depreciated over their useful lives, or the lease term, whichever is the shorter. Future instalments under such leases, net of financing costs, are included within loans. Rental payments are apportioned between the finance element, which is included in finance costs, and the capital element, which reduces the outstanding obligation for future instalments, so as to give a constant charge on the outstanding obligation.

Payments, including any incentives, made under operating leases are recognised in the income statement on a straight-line basis over the lease term.

Assets held for leasing out under operating leases are included in property, plant and equipment at cost less accumulated depreciation and accumulated impairment losses. Rental income is recognised in revenue on a straight-line basis.

Assets leased out under finance leases cease to be recognised in the balance sheet after the inception of the lease. Instead, a finance lease receivable, representing the discounted future lease payments to be received from the lessee plus any discounted unguaranteed residual value, is recorded as long-term financial assets. Interest income is recognised in the income statement as it accrues, taking into account the effective yield on the asset.

Finance lease obligations

The Group has a number of non-cancellable finance lease arrangements predominantly in respect of aircraft as part of the Commercial Aerospace business. The maturity of these lease liabilities from the balance sheet date is shown below:

	2005 (£m)	2004 (£m)
Finance lease liabilities – minimum lease payments due:		
Not later than one year	46	112
Later than one year and not later than five years	77	78
Later than five years	1	7
	124	197
Future finance charges on finance leases	(16)	(25)
Present value of finance lease liabilities	108	172
Present value of finance lease liabilities – payments due:		
Not later than one year	38	112
Later than one year and not later than five years	69	53
Later than five years	1	7
	108	172

Under the terms of the lease agreements, no contingent rents are payable.

The interest rate inherent in these finance leases is fixed at the contract date for all of the lease term. The average interest rate on finance lease payables at 31 December 2005 was 7% (2004: 7%).

Operating leases

Lease payments should be recognised as an expense in the income statement on a straight-line basis over the lease term unless another systematic basis is representative of the time pattern of the user's benefit.

Example – Hinch Ltd

Hinch Ltd manufactures 'Poteen' and to improve efficiency has scrapped all its existing plant and replaced it as follows:

(1)   On 1 December 2007 Hinch Ltd agreed to rent an 'Imperial Distiller' from Mick & Gerry at a cost of £1,500 per month payable in advance. The agreement is terminable at three months' notice by either party but is for five years.

(2)   On 1 June 2008 Hinch Ltd entered into an agreement with Saintfield for the lease of a 'Potillier.' terms included:
   (a)   neither party could cancel;
   (b)   Hinch Ltd is to have responsibility for maintenance;
   (c)   six instalments of £7,500 are payable half-yearly in advance.
      The cash price of a 'Potillier' on 1 June 2008 was £40,000 and the machine is considered to have a residual value of £5,000 at the end of a five-year life. The rate of interest implicit in the lease is 5.0% semi-annually.

(3)   A 'Finn McCool' was bought on 1 September 2008 from Causeway Ltd. The price of £120,000 is payable in 10 equal quarterly instalments starting 1 September 2008.

A 'Finn McCool' is expected to have negligible value at the end of its 12-year life.

   Other than the above items no amounts were unpaid at 30 November 2008. Hinch Ltd uses a straight-line basis for depreciation from the date of purchase.

Suggested solution – Hinch Ltd

Profit on ordinary activities before taxation
   Profit on ordinary activities before taxation is after changing the following:

	£
Depreciation (£4,000 + £2,500)	6,500
Hire of plant and machinery	18,000
Finance changes	1,625

Property, plant and equipment

	Plant and Machinery £
Cost	
Balance at 1.12.07	xxx
Additions	160,000
Disposals	(xxx)
Balance at 30.11.08	xxx

Accumulated depreciation

Balance at 1.12.07	xxx
Charge for the year	6,500
Disposals	(xxx)
Balance at 30.11.08	xxx

Net book value at 30.11.08   xxx

Included within plant and machinery are assets held under finance leases £36,000.

Current liabilities

	£
Obligations under finance lease	13,669
Other loans	48,000

Non-current liabilities

	£
Obligations under finance lease	20,456
Other loans	60,000

Obligations under finance leases

	£
Amounts falling due	
Within one year (2 × £7,500)	15,000
Between two and five year (3 × £7,500)	22,500
	37,500
Finance charges in suspense	
(5,000–1,625)	3,375
	34,125

Commitments under operating leases

Under one year	18,000
Between two and five years	72,000
	90,000

Imperial Distiller

The agreement is terminable at three months' notice by either party and would therefore probably constitute an operating lease since the risks and rewards of ownership still rest with the lessor. The payments during the year (12 × £1,500 = £18,000) should be written off through the income statement.

Potillier

This could constitute a finance lease as it would appear that the present value of the minimum lease payments of £45,000 would at least cover the fair value of the machine costing £40,000.

In addition the contract is non-cancellable and the lessee has responsibility for maintenance, indicating that the risks have passed to the lessee.

	£
Finance lease rentals 6 × £7500	45,000
Cash price 1.6.08	40,000
Finance charge	5,000

	Opening balance £	Paid £	Liability £	Finance charge (5%) £	Closing balance £
30.11.08	40,000	7,500	32,500	1,625	34,125
31.05.09	34,125	7,500	26,625	1,331	27,956
30.11.09	27,956	7,500	20,456	1,023	21,479
31.05.10	21,479	7,500	13,979	698	14,677
30.11.10	14,677	7,500	7,177	323	7,500
1.12.11	7,500	7,500			

At 30.11.08 the balance sheet liability will be:	£
Current: £7,500 × 2 = £15,000–£1,331=	13,669
Long-term: £7,500 × 3 = £22,500 − £2,044=	20,456

The income statement charges will be:

	£
Finance charge	1,625
Depreciation (£40,000 ÷ 5years × 1/2years)	4,000

Note: We must assume that the secondary period for the lease exceeds two years and therefore the useful life is less than the lease term for the Potillier. The residual value of £5,000 has been ignored in calculating the depreciation charge.

Finn McCool

This asset was purchased on 1 September 2008 and the quarterly instalments merely indicate a hire purchase agreement. The asset must be capitalised at £120,000 and the liability recorded at the same price, assuming that the loan is interest free.

The liability will be reduced by the instalments paid over the 10 quarters.

	£
Total payments due	120,000
Paid 1.9.08	12,000
Due at 30.11.08	108,000

Split between current liabilities (4 × £12,000 = £48,000) and long-term liabilities (£60,000). Depreciation £120,000 ÷ 12 years × 1/4 year = £2,500.

Disclosures

The following disclosures should be made:

(a)   The total of future MLPs under non-cancellable operating leases for each of the following periods:
   • not later than one year;
   • later than one year and not later than five years; and
   • later than five years;
(b)   The total of future minimum sublease payments expected to be received under non-cancellable subleases at the balance sheet date.
(c)   Lease and sublease recognised in income for the period, with separate amounts for MLPs, contingent rents and sublease payments.
(d)   A general description of the lessee's significant leasing arrangements including, but limited to, the following:

   • the basis on which contingent rent payments are determined;
   • the existence and terms of renewal or purchase options and escalation clauses; and
   • restrictions imposed by lease arrangements, such as those concerning dividends, additional debt and further leasing.

BAE also provide disclosures of their operating leases as follows:

BAE Systems Plc   Year Ended 31 December 2005

Notes to the Accounts (Extract)

Operating lease commitments – where the Group is the lessee

The Group leases various offices, factories, shipyards and aircraft under non-cancellable operating lease agreements. The leases have varying terms, escalation clauses and renewal rights.

The future aggregate minimum lease payments under non-cancellable operating leases and associated future minimum sublease income are as follows:

Payments due	2005 (£m)	2004 (£m)
Not later than one year	66	125
Later than one year and not later than five years	273	258
Later than five years	552	493
	891	876
Total of future minimum sublease income under non-cancellable subleases	118	133

Reckitt Benckiser also provide details of the amounts expected to be received under non-cancellable subleasing arrangements.

Reckitt Benckiser   Year Ended 31 December 2005

Notes to the Accounts (Extract)

24. Operating Lease Commitments

Group	2005		2004	
	Land and buildings £m	Plant and Equipment £m	Land and buildings £m	Plant and equipment £m
Total commitments under non-cancellable operating leases due				
Within one year	19	4	20	4
Later than one and less than five years	58	2	48	6
After five years	50	–	54	–
	127	6	122	10

Operating lease rentals charged to the income statement in 2005 were £21m (2004; £18m) in respect of land and buildings and £5m (2004; £7m) in respect of plant and equipment.

Accounting for leases in the financial statements of lessors

Finance leases

Lessor should recognise these as receivables in their balance sheet at amounts equal to the net investment in the lease.

The recognition of finance income should be based on a pattern reflecting a constant periodic rate of return on the lessor's net investment outstanding in respect of the finance lease.

Any lease payments should be applied against the gross investment in the lease to reduce both the principal and the unearned finance income. Estimated unguaranteed residual values are reviewed regularly and, if a reduction occurs, the income allocation over the lease term is revised and any reduction in respect of amounts already accrued is recognised immediately.

Initial direct costs such as commissions and legal fees can be either recognised immediately in income or allocated against income over the lease term.

Example – Lessor Plc

Lessor Plc leases plant (cost £50,000) to Lessee Ltd for four years from 1 January 2007 at a rental of £8,000 per half-year, payable in advance. Corporation tax is 35%, and capital allowances on the plant are 25% per annum, reducing balance basis. The rate of return (post-tax) on the lessor's net investment is 5.4% per half-year. The plant is assumed to have no residual value at the end of the lease term. Corporation tax is payable 12 months after the year end (31 December).

Suggested solution – Lessor Plc

Financial statements

Income Statement (extracts) for years ended 31 December

	2007 £	2008 £	2009 £
Rental income	16,000	16,000	16,000
Capital repaid (Bal. Fig.)	9,498	11,508	13,529
Profit before tax (W2)	6,502	4,492	2,471
Taxation (bal. figure)	2,276	1,572	865
Net profit (W1 & W2)	4,226	2,920	1,606

Balance Sheet (extracts) as at 31 December

Assets	2003 £	2004 £	2005 £
Net investment in finance lease	40,502	28,994	15,465
Deferred taxation (W3)	–	–	1,970

Note: £50,000 − £9,498 = £40,502 − £11,508 = £28,994, £28,994 − £13,529 = £15,465

Liabilities	2007 £	2008 £	2009 £
Current tax (W1)	1,225	2,319	3,139
Deferred tax (W3)	1,051	304	–

Periodic rate of return on average net investment

	2007 £	2008 £	2009 £
Profits before taxation	6,502	4,492	2,471
Average net cash investment			
2004 (42,000 + 36,268 ÷ 2)	39,134		
2005 (30,226 + 23,858 ÷ 2)		27,042	
2006 (18,371 + 11,363 ÷ 2)			14,867
Percentage return	16.6	16.6	16.6

Workings

(1) Calculation of rate of return

Period	Net investment £	Rental received £	Tax effect £	Average net investment £	Rate of Return (5.4%) £	Closing balance £
1	50,000	(8,000)		42,000	2,268	44,268
2	44,268	(8,000)		36,268	1,958	38,226

3	38,226	(8,000)		30,226	1,632	31,858
4	31,858	(8,000)		23,858	1,288	25,146
5	25,146	(8,000)	1,225	18,371	992	19,363
6	19,363	(8,000)		11,363	614	11,977
7	11,977	(8,000)	2,319	6,296	340	6,636
8	6,636	(8,000)				

Tax	Rentals	Capital allowances (25%)	Taxable profits	Corporation Tax (35%)
	£	£	£	£
2007	16,000	12,500	3,500	1,225
2008	16,000	9,375	6,625	2,319
2009	16,000	7,031	8,969	3,139
2010	16,000	5,273	10,727	3,754

(2) Calculation of annual profit

	Net	Gross
2007	£2,268 + £1,958 = £4,226 × 100/65 =	£6,502
2008	£1,632 + £1,288 = £2,920 × 100/65 =	£4,492
2009	£992 + £614 = £1,606 × 100/65 =	£2,471

(3) Calculation of deferred taxation

	2007 £	2008 £	2009 £
Tax charge per profit and loss	2,276	1,572	865
Corporation tax	1,225	2,319	3,139
Transfer to/(from) deferred tax	1,051	(747)	(2,274)

Example – Dungiven Clothes Plc

Dungiven Clothes Plc manufactures a machine that prints on sports shirts at a cost of £126,000. It either sells the machine for £160,748 cash or leases the machine on a three-year lease.

Lease with Limavady Shirts Plc

On 1 January 2008 Dungiven Clothes Plc entered into a three-year non-cancellable lease with Limavady Shirts Plc on the following terms:

(1) Lease rentals were £56,000 payable annually in advance.
(2) Initial direct costs of £8,400 incurred in commission and legal fees were borne by Dungiven Clothes Plc and charged to the income statement account on a systematic basis.

(3)   There was a guaranteed residual value of £28,000.
(4)   The interest rate implicit in the lease with Limavady Shirts Plc was 18%.

Transaction with Strabane Sales Ltd

On 1 January 2008 Dungiven Clothes Plc entered into an arrangement with Strabane Sales Ltd. Strabane Sales Ltd had purchased a machine from Dungiven Clothes Plc but, having run into cash flow problems, the company arranged a sale and lease-back of the machine to Dungiven Clothes Plc. The arrangement was that Strabane Sales Ltd sold the machine to Dungiven Clothes Plc for £124,575 and immediately leased it back for four years at a rental of £37,500 payable yearly in advance. At the time of the sale the book value of the machine was £75,000 which was arrived at after the provision of depreciation on the company's normal straight-line basis. It was agreed that the machine should revert to Dungiven Clothes Plc at the end of the four-year period when its scrap value was estimated to be nil. The lease is non-cancellable and Dungiven Clothes Plc is reasonably confident that the lease payments will be met. The interest rate implicit in the lease with Strabane Sales was 14%.

Suggested solution – Dungiven Clothes Plc

Limavady Shirts Plc

Entries in the income statement of Dungiven Clothes Plc

Profit and Loss account for the year ended 31 December 2008

	£
Sales	160,748
Less cost of sales	126,000
Gross profit	34,748
Interest receivable under finance lease	18,855
Lease expenses (1/3 × £8,400)	2,800

Entries in the balance sheet of Dungiven Clothes Plc

Balance Sheet as at 31 December

	2009 £	2008 £
Current assets		
Amount receivable under finance lease	51,772	43,831
Prepayments	2,800	5,600

Non-current assets
Amount receivable under finance lease   28,000   79,772
Workings   £   £

Gross investment in lease
  Rentals three years @ £56,000pa   168,000
  Guaranteed residual value   28,000
                                                          196,000

Net investment in lease
  Minimum lease payments (present value)
  £56,000 × (1.00 + 0.848 + 0.718)   143,696
  £28,000 × 0.609   17,052
                                                          160,748
Total finance income   35,252

Allocation of total finance income

Year	Opening net investment	Lease payments	Net investment outstanding	Interest income 18%	Reduction in net investment	Closing net investment
	£	£	£	£	£	£
2008	160,748	56,000	104,748	18,855	37,145	123,603
2009	123,603	56,000	67,603	12,169	43,831	79,772
2010	9,772	56,000	23,77 2	4,228	51,772	28,000

Strabane Sales Ltd

			£	£
(1)	Dr	Bank	124,575	
	Cr	Plant and machinery		75,000
		Deferred income		49,575

Being sale of machine back to leasing company at a price of £124,575

(2)	Dr	Paid under finance lease	124,575	
	Cr	Finance lease obligation		124,575

Being recording of loan received from the leasing company on leaseback of machine

(3)	Dr	Finance lease obligation	37,500	
	Cr	Bank		37,500

Being annual rental of £37,500 payable annually in advance

(4)	Dr	Finance lease interest	12,191	
	Cr	Finance lease obligation		12,191

Being the annual interest on the capital amount outstanding of (£124,575 – £37,500) × 14%

(5)	Dr	Depreciation – profit and loss	31,144	
	Cr	Accumulated depreciation		31,144

Being the annual depreciation charge £124,575÷4 years on a straight-line basis

(6)	Dr	Deferred income	12,394	
	Cr	Profit on sale and leaseback		12,394

Being overall profit on sale and leaseback of machine spread evenly over the leaseback period of four years. ˙

Workings

	£
Sales price to Strabane Sales Ltd	124,575
Net book value at date of sale	75,000
Capital gain	49,575

The lease entered into with Dungiven Clothes Plc is a finance lease. Therefore, in accordance with IAS 17, the profit on sale should be recorded and spread over the shorter of the life of the asset or the lease term, to provide an annual gain of £12,394. Depreciation is based on the same scenario and is also spread over four years in this case.

Manufacturer/lessors

Manufacturer or dealer lessors should recognise their selling profit/loss in income in accordance with normal sales. If artificially low rates of interest are quoted, selling profit should be restricted to that which would apply if a commercial rate were charged. Initial direct costs should be expensed in the income statement at the inception of the lease.

These contracts lead to the creation of two types of income:

(a) Profit/loss equivalent to outright sale.
(b) The finance income over the lease term.

The difference between the sales revenue (i.e. fair value of the asset) and the cost of sale (i.e. cost or carrying amount of the leased property less present value of the unguaranteed residual value) is selling profit which should be accounted as per the normal policy for sales.

Manufacturer or dealer lessors sometimes quote artificially low rates of interest in order to attract customers. The use of such a rate would result in an excessive portion of the total income from the transaction being recognised at time of sale. If artificially low rates of interest are quoted, selling profit would be restricted to that which would apply if a commercial rate were charged. Initial costs are immediately expensed as they relate mainly to earning the manufacturer's/dealers profit.

The following should be disclosed:

(a) A reconciliation between the total gross investment in the lease at the balance sheet date and the present value of MLPs at the balance sheet date. In addition, the total gross investment in the lease and the present value of MLPs receivable at the balance sheet date, for each of the following periods:
   • not later than one year;
   • later than one year and not later than five years;
   • later than five years;
(b) Unearned finance income.
(c) The unguaranteed residual values accruing to the benefit of the lessor.
(d) The accumulated residual values accruing to the benefit of the lessor.
(e) The accumulated allowance for uncollectible MLPs receivable.

(f)   Contingent rents recognised in income; and

(g)   A general description of the lessor's significant leasing arrangements.

South African company Dimension Data Holdings Plc provide relevant disclosure for their lessor operations.

Dimension Data Holdings Plc   Year Ended
30 September 2006

The Group as lessor

Amounts due from lessees under finance leases are recorded as receivables at the amount of the Group's net investment in the leases. Finance lease income is allocated to accounting periods so as to reflect a constant periodic rate of return on the Group's net investment outstanding in respect of the leases.

Rental income from operating leases is recognised on a straight-line basis over the term of the relevant lease. Initial direct costs incurred in negotiating and arranging an operating lease are added to the carrying amount of the leased asset and recognised on a straight-line basis over the lease term.

	2006 $'000	Restated 2005 $'000

31. Operating Lease Arrangements continued

The Group as Lessor

Property rental income earned during the year was $13.5 million (2005: $13.8m) which is included in other operating income.

At balance sheet date, the Group had contracted with tenants for the following MLPs:

	2006 $'000	Restated 2005 $'000
Within one year	6,246	7,816
In the second to fifth years inclusive	8,551	26,762
After five years	11,017	4,177
	25,814	38,755

Operating leases

Lessors should record assets in balance sheets according to their nature.

Lease income should be recognised on a straight-line basis unless a more systematic basis would be more representative of the time pattern in which the benefits deriving from the asset are diminished.

Initial direct costs are either deferred and allocated to income over the lease term in proportion to rent income or are recognised as expenses in the income statement in the period they are incurred.

Depreciation should be on a basis consistent with the lessor's normal depreciation policy for similar assets and calculated as per IAS 16. If the asset becomes impaired, IAS 36 must be applied.

No selling profit is recognised as the agreement is not the equivalent of a sale.
Lessors should disclose the following:

(a)   The future MLPs under non-cancellable operating leases, in aggregate, and for each of
the following periods:
   • not later than one year;
   • later than one year but not later than five years; and
   • later than five years;
(b)   Total contingent rents recognised in income.
(c)   A general description of the lessor's significant leasing arrangements.

Belgian brewer Inbev discloses operating lease information as follows:

Inbev   Year Ended 31 December 2005

Leases as lessor

The company leases out part of its property under operating leases. Non-cancellable
operating leases are receivable as follows:

Million euro	2005	2004
Less than one year	23	41
Between one and five years	159	167
More than five years	102	106
	284	314

In 2005, 102m euro (2004; 76m euro) was recognized as rental income in the
income statement.

Sale and leaseback transactions

The lease payment and the sale price are usually interdependent as they are negotiated as a
package. The accounting treatment depends on the type of lease involved.

Finance lease

Any excess of sales proceeds over carrying value should not be immediately expensed but,
instead, it should be deferred and amortised over the lease term. Effectively, the lessor provides finance to the lessee, with the asset as security, thus it is not appropriate to regard an
excess of sales proceeds over the carrying amount as income. Such excess is deferred and
amortised over the lease term.

Operating lease

Any profit/loss should be recognised immediately. If the sale price is below fair value,
any profit/loss should be recognised immediately except that if the loss is compensated
by future lease payments at below market price; it should be deferred and amortised in

proportion to the lease payments over the period for which the asset is expected to be used. If the sale price is above fair value, the excess over fair value should be deferred and amortised over the period for which the asset is expected to be used. It is effectively a normal sale transaction and any profit/loss is recognised immediately.

If the fair value at the time of sale and leaseback is less than the carrying amount of the asset, a loss equal to the amount of the difference between the carrying amount and fair value should be recognised immediately.

Disclosures for lessees/lessors should be the same as for other lease disclosures for lessees and lessors.

In 2005, BT did not address sale and leaseback transactions in its accounting policies note. In 2006, where a sale and leaseback transaction results in a finance lease, it states that it follows IAS 17 and any excess of the sale proceeds over the carrying amount is deferred in the income statement over the lease term. This amounts to £42 million at 31 March 2005. Where a sale and leaseback transaction results in an operating lease, any profit or loss is recognised in the income statement immediately. This too follows IAS 17 for sale and leaseback transactions where the sale is at fair value.

BT Plc   Year Ended 31 March 2006

(iv) Leases

Leases of property, plant and equipment where the group holds substantially all the risks and rewards of ownership are classified as finance leases.

Finance lease assets are capitalised at the commencement of the lease at the lower of the present value of the minimum lease payments or the fair value of the leased asset. The obligations relating to finance leases, net of finance charges in respect of future periods, are recognised as liabilities. Leases are subsequently measured at amortised cost using the effective interest method. If a sale and leaseback transaction results in a finance lease, any excess of sale proceeds over the carrying amount is deferred and recognised in the income statement over the lease term.

Leases where a significant portion of the risks and rewards are held by the lessor are classified as operating leases. Rentals are charged to the income statement on a straight-line basis over the period of the lease. If a sale and leaseback transaction results in an operating lease, any profit or loss is recognised in the income statement immediately.

(i) Differences between IFRS and United States generally accepted accounting principles (US GAAP)

The following are the main differences between IFRS and US GAAP which are relevant to the group's consolidated financial statements.

(a) Sale and leaseback of properties

Under IFRS, the sale of BT's property portfolio is treated as a disposal and the vast majority of the subsequent leaseback is an operating lease. Under US GAAP as BT has a continuing interest in the properties, these properties are recorded on the balance sheet at their net book value, a leasing obligation is recognised and the gain on disposal is deferred until the properties are sold and vacated by BT and the corresponding lease obligation is terminated. Rental payments made by BT are reversed and replaced by a finance lease interest charge and a depreciation charge.

Example – Farset Ltd

Farset Ltd prepares financial statements to 31 March each year. On 1 April 2006, Farset Ltd sold a freehold property to another company, Lagan Plc. Farset Ltd had purchased the property for £500,000 on 1 April 1998 and had charged total depreciation of £60,000 on the property for the period 1 April 1998 to 31 March 2008. Lagan Plc paid £850,000 for the property on 1 April 2008, at which date its true market value was £550,000.

From 1 April 2008 the property was leased back by Farset Ltd on a 10-year operating lease for annual rentals (payable in arrears) of £100,000. A normal annual rental for such a property would have been £50,000.

Lagan Plc is a financial institution which, on 1 April 2006, charged interest of 10.56% per annum on 10-year fixed-rate loans.

Suggested solution – Farset Ltd

Journal entries to record the sale of property to Lagan Plc and the payment of the first rental

Date				£	£
1 April 2008	Dr		Bank account	850,000	
		Cr	Loan account		300,000
			Disposal of property account		550,000
being the sale of property at market value					
	Dr		Disposal of property account	500,000	
		Cr	Property		500,000
being the cost of property sold transferred to disposal of property account					
	Dr		Accumulated depreciation – property	60,000	
		Cr	Disposal of property account		60,000
being accumulated depreciation on property sold					

	Dr	Disposal of property account	110,000	
	Cr	Income statement		110,000

being profit on disposal of property

These journal entries record the sale and disposal of property to/from Lagan Plc in accordance with the substance of the transaction. The profit on sale is the difference between the fair value of the property and its carrying value at the date of sale.

			£	£
31 March 2009	Dr	Income statement (leasing charges)	50,000	
		(interest 10.56% × £300,000)	31,680	
		Loan account		
		(capital repaid £50,000 – £31,680)	18,320	
	Cr	Bank account		100,000

Being the first rental payment to Lagan Plc, which is a combination of an operating lease and a repayment of interest and capital on the loan

The rental repayment reveals the recording of the substance of the sale and lease-back transaction undertaken by Lagan Plc, which is a combination of an operating lease rental (for the continued use of the property) and the repayment of interest and capital on the loan.

SIC 15 Operating leases – Incentives (July 1999)

Issue

In negotiating a new or renewed operating lease, the lessor may provide incentives for the lessee to enter into the agreement. Examples include up front cash to the lessee or the reimbursement or assumption by the lessor of costs to the lessee, e.g. relocation costs, lease-hold improvements and so on. Alternatively initial periods of the lease term may be agreed to be rent free or at a reduced rent.

The issue is how incentives in an operating lease should be recognised in the financial statements of both lessor and lessee.

Consensus

All incentives for the agreement of a new or renewed operating lease should be recognised as an integral part of the net consideration agreed for the use of the leased asset, irrespective of the incentive's nature or form or timing of payments.

The lessor should recognise the aggregate cost of incentives as a reduction of rental income over the lease term, on a straight-line basis unless another systematic basis is representative of the time pattern over which the benefit of the leased asset is diminished.

The lessee should recognise the aggregate benefit of incentives as a reduction in rental expense over the lease term, on a straight-line basis unless another systematic basis is representative of the time pattern of the lessee's benefit from the use of the leased asset.

Costs incurred by the lessee, including costs in connection with a pre-existing lease, should be accounted for by the lessee in accordance with IASs applicable to those costs, including costs which are effectively reimbursed through an incentive arrangement.

J.D. Wetherspoon Plc   Year Ended 30 July 2006

Under SIC 15 "Operating leases – incentives," the lessee recognises the leasing incentives as a reduction of rental expense over the lease term. Previously, Wetherspoon disclosed that where, on acquisition of a property, a reverse premium or capital contribution is granted by the lessor, it is released to profit from the date on which the pub opened through the date of the first rent review to market value, usually on the fifth anniversary of the lease. In 2005, following adoption of IFRS, the company accounts for lease incentives as a reduction of rental expense over the lease term and, for 2005, it reverses £221,000 in the income statement and recognises £5.1 million deferred income within non-current liabilities. In 2006, within provisions and other liabilities, but with no quantification, the company includes incentives on leases and adds that the weighted average period to maturity of the liabilities is 17.9 years.

Lease premiums

Payments made on entering into or acquiring leaseholds which are accounted for as operating leases represent prepaid lease payments. These are amortised on a straight-line basis over the lease term.

27. Transition to IFRS continued

2. Leases

Under UK GAAP lease incentives on leases where the lessor retains substantially all of the risks and benefits of ownership of the asset are recognised as a reduction in rent paid over the period up to the first rent review. Under IFRS, lease incentives on leases where the lessor retains substantially all of the risks and benefits of ownership of the asset are recognised as a reduction in rent paid over the lease term.

SIC 27 Evaluating the substance of transactions in the legal form of a lease

This SIC outlines the approach that must be taken when assessing an arrangement involving the legal form of a lease that should be undertaken to determine whether, in substance, the arrangement results in a lease under IAS 17. Where the arrangement does not meet the definition of a lease, IAS 17 is not applicable and the principles of the Framework for the

Preparation and Presentation of Financial Statements, and other relevant standards, should be used to determine the appropriate accounting for this arrangement.

Deutsche Post AG   Year Ended 31st December 2002

A note discloses that Deutsche Post leases to companies electronic sorting systems although it remains the beneficial and legal owner of all the assets which remain available without material restrictions to Deutsche Post for its operating activities. The note refers to SIC 27 and discloses that the net present value benefit from the transactions has been recognised immediately which results in income of €136 million and expenses of €40 million being recognised. In addition to a description of the arrangement, SIC 27 requires disclosure of its life and other significant terms although Deutsche Post is silent on this.

Note to the accounts

Note 8 special factors
Under the terms of certain leasing transactions (qualified technical equipment – QTE leases), Deutsche Post AG leased the electronic sorting systems at mail and freight centres to various US companies. They are accounted for in accordance with SIC 27. Deutsche Post AG remains the beneficial owner of all the assets included in the transactions when the contracts are entered into, and they remain available to the Company for its operating activities without any material restrictions.

Because the criteria set out in SIC 27.8 are met, the net present value benefit from the transactions was recognised immediately. This produced income of €136 million (previous year: €29m), which was recognised in income in the MAIL and EXPRESS segments. This income is partially offset by expenses amounting to €40 million (previous year: €6m).

Asset valuation: Inventories and construction contracts

4.1 IAS 2 *Inventories* (December 2003)

The objective of IAS 2 is to prescribe the accounting treatment for inventories and to determine the cost to be recognised as an asset, which will be subsequently expended. It also provides guidance on cost formulas to adopt and when to write-down inventories to net realisable value (NRV).

The standard applies only to inventories. It does not apply to:

(a) work in progress arising in construction and service contracts (see IAS 11);
(b) financial instruments (see IAS 39);
(c) biological assets related to agricultural activity (see IAS 41);
(d) inventories of agricultural and forest products and mineral ores to the extent that they can be measured at NRV, i.e. crops harvested (see IAS 41); and
(e) commodity broker traders who measure inventories at NRV, e.g. active market, sale assumed under forward contracts.

Definitions

- *Inventories* are assets:

(a) held for sale in the ordinary course of business;
(b) in the process of production; or
(c) in the form of materials, supplies to be consumed in production or rendering of services.

- *Net realisable value*. The estimated selling price in the ordinary course of business less estimated costs of completion and estimated selling costs.

   Examples of inventories include retail merchandise, land held for resale and finished goods.

Measurement of inventories

Inventories should be measured at the lower of cost and NRV.

(1) *Cost of inventories*
All costs of purchase, costs of conversion and other costs in bringing the inventories to their present location and condition.

(2) *Costs of purchase*
These comprise the purchase price, import duties, transport and handling costs. However, trade discounts and rebates must be deducted.

(3) *Costs of conversion*
These include direct labour and a systematic allocation of overheads, both fixed and variable, incurred in converting materials into finished goods.

Fixed overheads (maintenance, depreciation, factory management costs) should be allocated on the basis of normal capacity, i.e. which could be achieved on average over a number of periods or seasons. The actual may be adopted if it approximates normal activity. Unallocated overheads are expended.

In abnormally high production periods the allocation should be decreased so that inventories are not measured above cost.

Variable production overheads are allocated on the basis of the actual use of the production facilities.

Where joint products are being produced a suitable allocation method should be adopted, e.g. relative sales value. By-products should be measured at NRV and deducted from the cost of the main product.

(4) *Other costs*
Only permitted if they bring inventories to their present location and condition, e.g. cost of specific designing of products for customers.

Examples of specific exclusions:

    (a)   abnormal costs, e.g. wasted materials, labour
    (b)   storage costs
    (c)   administration overheads
    (d)   selling costs.

However, borrowing costs are included provided they meet the criteria in IAS 23.

(5) *Costs of a service provider*
Should primarily be labour and personnel costs plus attributable overheads. Selling and administrative costs are not included. No profit margins may be included either. Costs of agricultural produce harvested from biological assets – as per IAS 41 value at fair value less costs of sale at harvest.

(6) *Cost of agricultural produce harvested from biological assets*
These are measured initially at their fair value less estimated point of sale costs at the point of harvest.

(7) *Techniques for the measurement of cost*
Standard cost and the retail gross margin method may be adopted if their results approximate cost. They must, however, be regularly reviewed and revised, if necessary. The retail method must be careful to deduct gross margins but care is particularly

required in cases of marked down inventories not to reduce stocks below cost, where they are clearly worth more.

Cost formulas

Costs should be specifically identified to specific projects, where possible. That, however, is not appropriate where there are large numbers of items of inventories that are ordinarily interchangeable. In those cases the method selected should be first-in, first-out (FIFO) basis or weighted average.

The same formula should be adopted for all inventories having a similar nature and use to the entity. However, a difference in geographical location, by itself, would not be sufficient to justify the use of different cost formulas.

FIFO results in inventory valuations being up to date. Last-in, first-out (LIFO) method would not be an acceptable method as inventories tend to be valued at out-of-date prices.

Net realisable value

Where the cost of inventories may not be recoverable, e.g. damaged, obsolete, selling prices declined, etc. then inventories should not be carried in excess of the amounts expected to be realised from their sale or use.

Inventories are usually written down to NRV on an item-by-item basis. It is not appropriate to write-down inventories based on a general classification, e.g. finished goods, or all inventories in a particular industry.

Estimates of NRV are based on the most reliable evidence of amounts expected to realise and should take into account price fluctuations of post balance sheet data to the extent that they can confirm conditions at that data.

If inventories are for a specific contract, reference should be made only to the contract price of that specific contract but if they are for sale generally, then reference should be made to general selling prices.

Materials are not written down below cost, provided that the finished products in which they will be incorporated are expected to be sold at or above cost. However, if a decline in material prices indicates that the cost of finished goods exceeds NRV then the materials should be written down to NRV, using replacement cost as the best available measure.

NRV should be reviewed in every subsequent period and if circumstances reveal that the write-down is no longer appropriate, it should be reversed.

Example – Derg Ltd

The following information relates to Derg Ltd for its first year of trading to 31 December 2007:

COSTS	£'000	£'000
Wages and salaries		
Factory	90	
Administration	48	
Selling	28	
		166

Overheads		
Rent and rates	10	
Heat and power	6	
Depreciation		
Factory buildings and machinery	6	
Salesmen's motor vehicles	2	
Office building and furniture	2	
Sundry overheads		
Factory	12	
Administration	4	
Selling	6	
		48
Direct material cost of goods sold (80,000 kg)		160
Closing inventories at cost – material value		
Raw materials (20,000 kg)		40
Work in progress (8,000 kg, half completed)		16
Finished goods (16,000 kg)		32

The factory occupies 75% of the total area. Working a 40-hour week it was operational for 48 weeks of the year with a four-week allowance for holidays. This will be the operating level. The turnover for the period was £331,000.

Suggested solution – Derg Ltd

Inventory valuations

Raw materials inventories

20,000 kg at £2 per kg   £40,000

Assume that this is lower than NRV. Even if NRV is lower, as long as the raw material can be incorporated into a finished product which will recover the £2 per kg, the cost is the correct value.

Work in progress inventories

	£
Material 8,000 kg × £2 per kg	16,000
Conversion costs 8,000 kg × 1/2	
= 4,000 kg × £1.21 per kg (W2)	4,840
	20,840

Assume that cost is lower than NRV.

Finished goods inventories

Total cost of production (W2)	£3.21 per kg
NRV (W3)	£3.69 per kg

This stock must be valued at the lower of cost and NRV, i.e. 16,000 kg × £3.21 per kg = £51,360.

Notes to the balance sheet

Accounting policies (extract)

Inventories

Inventories have been valued in accordance with standard accounting practice at the lower of cost and NRV. Costs include all those factories and other overheads required to bring the inventories to their present condition and location.

Inventories

Inventories comprise the following

	£'000
Raw materials and consumables	40
Work in progress	21
Finished goods	51
	112

Income Statement for the Year Ended 31 December 2007

	£'000	£'000	£'000
Sales			331
Cost of sales			
Material		160	
Labour (90 × 80%)		72	
Factory overhead (7.5 + 5.4 + 6+12) × 80%		24.7	
			256.7
Gross profit			74.3
Administration expenses			
Wages and salaries	48		
Rent and rates	2.5		
Heat and power	0.6		
Depreciation – office building and furniture	2		
Sundry overheads	4		
		57.1	

Selling and distribution costs

Wages and salaries	28	
Depreciation – salesmen's motor vehicles	2	
Sundry overheads	6	
		36
		93.1

Net loss for the year (18.8)

Workings

(1) Production

	kg
Sales	80,000
Closing inventories – finished goods	16,000
Closing inventories – work in progress	4,000
	100,000

(2) Factory cost of production

	£'000	£ per kg
Direct materials (£160,000 ÷ 80,000)		2.0
Wages and salaries – factory	90	
Rent and rates (75%)	7.5	
Heat and power (say 90%)	5.4	
Depreciation – factory	6	
Sundry overheads – factory	12	
	120.9	1.21
		3.21

(3) Determination of NRV

	£'000	£ per kg
Sales (80,000 kg)	331	4.14
Less selling expenses (80,000 kg)		
Wages and salaries	28	(0.35)
Depreciation – salesmen's motor vehicles	2	(0.03)
Sundry overheads	6	(0.07)
	36	(0.45)
	295	3.69

The NRV of £3.69 per kg is greater than the cost of £3.21 per kg; therefore, inventories of finished goods should be valued at the lower cost figure.

Example – Donard Ltd

Donard Ltd is a chemical manufacturing company. The following items, in relation to the company's manufacturing processes, have been included in stocks and work in progress as on 31 July 2007:

(1) Inventories of Banoline have been valued at £426,000 based on the following amounts:

	£
Raw materials – cost	200,000
Other direct costs	144,000
Proportion of factory overheads	38,000
Proportion of selling office expenses	44,000
	426,000

Banoline is a steady selling product which shows reasonable profit margins.

(2) Laboratory costs to 31 July 2007 of £348,000 on research into a new tranquilliser called Calmdown. The research is being sponsored by a government agency on a one-year programme. The agency has agreed to reimburse the company on a cost plus 6% basis at the end of the programme, up to a maximum contribution of £500,000.

(3) Inventories of 1,300 kg, held in bulk, of a chemical substance known as Apentone, and valued as follows:

	£
Raw materials – cost	340,000
Other direct costs	260,000
Proportion of factory overheads	47,000
Proportion of selling office expenses	59,000
	706,000

A competitor of Donard Ltd has recently introduced to the market a similar substance, which it is selling in handy 100 g packs at £35 each. To meet the competition, Donard Ltd will also have to pack in 100 g containers. The cost of packing the inventory held will be £20,000, and additional advertising costs to clear the inventory are estimated at £30,000.

(4) Laboratory costs to 31 July 2007 of £365,000 on research into a new chemical substitute for Supositone, of which demand exceeds the world supply. These costs include £100,000 for special items of plant required for the research programme.

Suggested solution – Donard Ltd

(1) Banoline inventories

In accordance with the definition of cost described in IAS 2, it would appear that the value of these inventories is overstated. It is incorrect to include a proportion of selling expenses as these have not been incurred in bringing the unsold inventory to its present condition or location.

The inclusion of a proportion of factory overheads seems appropriate and therefore inventories would be valued fairly at £382,000.

Consideration of NRV is unlikely to change this value, as the product is selling steadily and showing good profit margins.

The valuation of Banoline should be disclosed in the balance sheet under the heading of current assets. The accounting policy concerning the valuation of inventories should be included as part of the company's accounting policy section of the financial statements.

(2) Research costs – Calmdown

Although £348,000 has been spent on research into a new tranquilliser, it is to be reimbursed by a government agency. Therefore it should be accounted for as work in progress and not as research and development expenditure.

As the work is performed over the course of the contract, then a proportion could be recorded as turnover representing cost plus 6%, and the cost up to that stage could be written off to cost of sales.

However, if any of the debt is likely to become irrecoverable then provision should be made for the probable loss in accordance with IAS 11's concept of expected losses.

(3) Apentone inventories

As with the Banoline inventories, selling expenses should be excluded and thus the cost value of the stock is £706,000 – £59,000 = £647,000.

Under IAS 2 it is a requirement to ensure that the NRV is not lower than cost. In the case of Apentone, the NRV would be calculated as follows:

	£	£
Estimated sale proceeds		
(13,000 × 100 g packs at £35 each)		455,000
Less further packing costs	20,000	
Additional advertising costs	30,000	
Proportion of selling office expenses	59,000	
		109,000
NRV		346,000

As the NRV of £346,000 is lower than the cost of £647,000, inventories should be valued at that reduced amount. The inventories should be recorded under current assets in the balance sheet and the accounting policy must be disclosed in the financial statements.

(4) Laboratory costs

These are research costs, which relate to the company's own products. As such they are not the subject matter of IAS 2. This expenditure is governed by IAS 38, and if the project is only in the embryo stages with no likelihood of future revenue then £265,000 should be written off immediately as an expense.

In addition, any capital expenditure, albeit capitalised, should be depreciated and written off directly to the income statement.

Under IAS 38, research expenditure should be disclosed in the notes to the accounts. The net book value of the property, plant and equipment should be included in the balance sheet under property, plant and equipment. The accounting policies for research expenditure should also be disclosed.

Example – PAR

A newly established electronics company, manufacturing components for a wide range of customers, has budgets for the first year indicating that approximately 60% of turnover would be represented by one special component marketed under the name 'PAR'. The remainder would be represented by products manufactured specifically to customer specifications and design ('special orders').

Development expenditure relating to the 'PAR' product is £396,000. This amount is being amortised over five years on the straight-line basis. Technological changes now indicate that the product may be replaced in three years. The following information has been obtained about the company's first three months in business:

	£'000
(1) Production costs	
Purchases of raw materials	
Wiring	92
Others	348
Production labour costs	348
Fixed production overheads	128
Depreciation of equipment and factory buildings	102
(2) Sales analysis	
'PAR' brand sales	641
'Special order' sales	109

(3) Raw materials (other than wiring) purchased specifically for the 'special orders' amounted to £97,000. In addition, wiring material with an estimated cost of £10,000 was also used on these orders.

(4) 14,000 units of 'PAR' were manufactured in the three-month period. The company expects to manufacture 100,000 units per annum, representing 70% of full capacity.

(5) 50% of the labour and overhead costs are estimated to be attributable to the 'PAR' product, and 50% to the 'special orders'.

(6) At 31 March 2004, the following details of inventories were available:

Finished product – 'PAR'	3,000 units
Work in progress	Nil
Raw materials – wiring (at cost)	£7,000
Raw materials – other (at cost)	
'PAR'	£42,000
'Special orders'	£5,000

(7) The managing director is concerned about the profitability of the first three-months' trading and about the way in which closing inventories will be valued in preparing the financial statements for the three-month period.

Possible solution – PAR

The effect on reported profits of the valuation of inventories

	PAR		Others		Total	
	£'000	£'000	£'000	£'000	£'000	£'000
						750
Sales (Note 2)		641		109		
Opening inventories:						
Raw materials	Nil		Nil		Nil	
Purchases	333		107		440	
	333		107		440	
Less closing inventories:						
Raw material (Note 6)	49		5		54	
Cost of raw material						
Consumed	284		102		386	
Direct labour costs	174		174		348	
Production overheads:						
Fixed	64		64		128	
Depreciation	51		51		102	
Amortisation of development	33		–		33	
Cost of manufacture	606		391		997	
Closing inventories:						
Finished goods	(116)		–		(116)	
Cost of sales		490		391		881
Net Profit/(Loss)		151		(282)		131

Value of finished goods inventory
At cost
3,000 units × £38.634 (working) = £115,902 (say £116,000)

Net realisable value
Average selling price of PAR = £641,000 ÷ 11,000 units sold = £58.27

Assuming that selling and distribution costs do not exceed £58.27–£38.634 then production cost is lower than NRV.

Workings

Production costs relating to 14,000 units of PAR – 3 months ended 31 March 2008

	£'000	£'000	£'000
Wiring (purchases) (Note 1)		92	
Less: Special order transfer (Note 3)	10		
closing inventory (Note 6)	7		
		17	
Cost of wiring consumed			75
Other raw material purchases (Note 1)		348	
Less: Special order transfer (Note 3)	97		
closing inventory (Note 6)	42		
		139	
			209
Total raw materials consumed			284
Direct labour costs (£348,000 × 50%) (Note 5)			174
			458

Production cost per unit of output £458,000 ÷ 14,000 = £32.714 per unit

Production overheads	£'000
Fixed production overheads £128,000 × 50% (Note 5)	64
Depreciation of equipment and factory buildings £102,000 × 50% (Note 5)	51
Amortisation of development expenditure £396,000 ÷ 3 years × 1/4 year	33
	148

Overhead recovery rate £148,000 ÷ 25,000 units (normal capacity 100,000 units per annum – Note 4) =	£5.92 per unit
Total cost of production for inventory valuation £32.714 + £5.92 per unit=	£38.634 per unit

Recognition as an expense

When inventories are sold, they should be expended in the period when the revenue is recognised. Any write-downs or reversals should be recorded in the period they occur.

If some inventories are used in the construction of property, plant, etc. they should be capitalised and expended over the useful life of the fixed assets created.

Disclosure

The financial statements should disclose the following:

(a)   The accounting policies adopting in measuring inventories, including cost formulas.
(b)   The total carrying amount of inventories broken into appropriate classifications.
(c)   The carrying amount at fair value less costs to date.
(d)   The amount expended in the period.
(e)   The amount of any write-downs of inventories.
(f)   The amount of any reversal of any write-downs.
(g)   The circumstances or events that led to the write-down(s).
(h)   The carrying amount of inventories pledged as security for liabilities.

Common classifications include retail merchandise, production supplies, materials, work in progress and finished goods.

A typical example of both accounting policy and note disclosure is that of George Wimpey Plc:

George Wimpey Plc   Year Ended 31 December 2005

Inventories

Inventories are stated at the lower of cost and NRV. Cost comprises direct materials, direct labour costs and those overheads, which have been incurred in bringing the inventories to their present location and condition. Cost in certain circumstances also includes notional interest as explained in the accounting policy for finance income and costs. NRV represents the estimated selling price less all estimated costs of completion and costs to be incurred in marketing and selling.

Land inventory is recognised at the time a liability is recognised – generally after exchange of unconditional contracts.

13. Inventories

	Group	
	2005 (£m)	2004 (£m)
		Restated
Land held for development	2,153.4	1,932.3
Construction work in progress	735.3	651.4
Part exchange properties	1.5	25.6
Other inventories	42.0	34.9
	2,932.2	2,647.2

The Directors consider all inventories to be current in nature. The operational cycle is such that the majority of inventories will not be realised within 12 months. It is not possible to determine with accuracy when specific inventory will be realised, as this will be subject to a number of issues such as consumer demand and planning permission delays. The value of land expensed in 2005 was £737.4 million. At this level of activity and ignoring the effect of other factors such as inflation and exchange rate volatility, approximately 66% of inventory is estimated to be realised in excess of 12 months.

In accordance with the accounting policies on finance income and costs as set out on page 47 the Group adds to the cost of inventory certain notional interest; representing the unwinding discount on long-term creditors for land to which the Group has neither title nor access. Interest included within land held for development has moved as follows:

	Group	
	2005 (£m)	2004 (£m)
In land inventory at 1 January	4.2	2.8
Added to land inventory (Note 3)	3.4	1.4
In land inventory at 31 December	7.6	4.2

Another good example with slightly more normal inventories is that provided by Rio Tinto Plc:

Rio Tinto Plc   Year Ended 31 December 2005

I. Inventories

Inventories are valued at the lower of cost and NRV on a 'FIFO' basis. Cost for raw materials and stores is the purchase price and for partly processed and saleable products, the cost is generally the cost of production. For this purpose, the costs of production include:

- labour costs, materials and contractor expenses which are directly attributable to the extraction and processing of ore;
- the depreciation of mining properties and leases and of property, plant and equipment used in the extraction and processing of ore; and
- production overheads.

Stockpiles represent ore that has been extracted and is available for further processing. If there is significant uncertainty as to when the stockpiled ore will be processed it is expensed as incurred. Where the future processing of this ore can be predicted with confidence, e.g. because it exceeds the mine's cut off grade, it is valued at the lower of cost and NRV. If the ore will not be processed within 12 months after the balance sheet date it is included within non-current assets. Work in progress inventory includes ore stockpiles and other partly processed materials. Quantities are assessed primarily through surveys and assays.

17. Inventories

	2005 (US$m)	2004 (US$m)
Raw materials and purchased components	277	302
Consumable stores	428	344
Work in progress	553	498
Finished goods and goods for resale	931	876
	2,189	2,020
Comprising:		
Expected to be used within one year	2,048	1,952
Expected to be used after more than one year	141	68
	2,189	2,020

(a) No inventories were pledged as security for liabilities at 31 December 2005 (2004: $nil).

(b) The increase in inventories during 2005 reported in the cash flow statement, was US$249 million (2004: US$217m), which excludes the effects of subsidiaries sold and changes in exchange rates on translation into US dollars.

Readymix Plc provide a note, which incorporates details of write-downs to NRV as required by the standard:

Readymix Plc   Year Ended 31 December 2005

17. Inventories

	2005 (€m)	2004 (€m)
Raw materials	408.2	320.1
Work in progress	112.6	80.9
Finished goods	1,201.8	907.9
Total inventories at the lower of cost and NRV	1,722.6	1,308.9

Write-downs of inventories recognised as an expense within cost of sales amounted to €16.5 million (2004: £6.2m).

The aggregate amount of costs incurred and recognised profits (less recognised losses) for all contracts in progress at the balance sheet date was €418.1 million (2004: €293.4m).

None of the above carrying amounts has been pledged as security for liabilities entered into by the Group.

4.2   IAS 11 *Construction Contracts* (1978, revised 1993)

The basic principle of IAS 11 is that when the outcome of a construction contract can be estimated reliably, contract revenue and associated costs with the construction contract should be recognised as revenue and expenses respectively by reference to the stage of completion of the contract activity at the balance sheet date. An expected loss on the construction contract should be recognised as an expense immediately.

The objective of IAS 11 is to prescribe the accounting treatment of revenue and costs associated with construction contracts.

Definitions

*   *Construction contracts.* A construction contract is a contract specifically negotiated for the construction of an asset or group of inter-related assets. Construction contracts include contracts for architectural, engineering, demolition and other services related to the construction of an asset.

Under IAS 11, if a contract covers two or more assets, the construction of each asset should be accounted for separately if:

(a)   Separate proposals were submitted for each asset.
(b)   The portions of the contract relating to each contract were negotiated separately.
(c)   The costs and revenues of each asset can be measured.

Otherwise, the contract should be accounted for in its entirety. Two or more contracts should be accounted for as a single contract if they were negotiated together and the work is inter-related.

If a contract gives the customer an option to order one or more additional assets, the construction of each additional asset should be accounted for as a separate contract if either (a) the additional asset differs significantly from the original asset(s), or (b) the price of the additional asset is separately negotiated.

Contract revenue and costs

Contract revenue

Contract revenue should comprise:

(a)   the initial amount of revenue agreed in the contract; and
(b)   variations in contract work, claims and incentive payments:
  (i)   to the extent that it is probable that they will result in revenue; and
  (ii)   they are capable of being reliably measured.

Contract costs

Contract costs should comprise:

(a)   costs that relate directly to the specific contract;
(b)   costs that are attributable to contract activity in general and can be allocated to the contract; and

(c) such other costs as are specifically chargeable to the customer under the terms of the contract.

Costs that relate directly to a specific contract include:

(a) site labour costs, including supervision;
(b) costs of materials used in construction;
(c) depreciation of plant used on the contract;
(d) costs of moving plant and materials to and from the contract;
(e) costs of hiring plant;
(f) costs of design and technical assistance directly attributable to the contract;
(g) the estimated costs of rectification and guarantee work including expected warranty costs; and
(h) claims from third parties.

Borrowing costs may be capitalised under IAS 23.

Determining when contract revenue and expenses may be recognised

Fixed price contracts

In the case of a fixed price contract, the outcome of a construction contract can be estimated reliably when all the following conditions are satisfied:

(a) The total contract revenue can be measured reliably.
(b) It is probable that the economic benefits associated with the contract will flow to the enterprise.
(c) Both the contract costs to complete and the stage of completion at the balance sheet date can be measured reliably.
(d) The contract costs attributable to the contract can be clearly identified and measured reliably so that actual contract costs incurred can be compared with prior estimates.

Cost plus contracts

In the case of a cost plus contract, the outcome of a construction contract can be estimated reliably when all the following conditions are satisfied:

(a) It is probable that the economic benefits associated with the contract will flow to the enterprise.
(b) The contract costs attributable to the contract, whether or not specifically reimbursable, can be clearly identified and measured reliably.

The stage of completion of a contract may be determined in a variety of ways. The enterprise uses the method that measures reliably the work performed. Depending on the nature of the contract, the methods may include:

(a) the proportion that contract costs incurred for work performed to date bear to the estimated total contract costs;
(b) surveys of work performed; and
(c) completion of a physical proportion of the contract work.

Progress payments and advances from customers often do not reflect the work performed.

When the stage of completion is determined by reference to the contract costs incurred to date; only those contract costs that reflect work performed are included in costs incurred to date. Examples of contract costs which are excluded are:

(a)   contract costs that relate to future activity on the contract such as costs of materials that have been delivered to a contract site or set aside for use in a contract but not yet installed, used or applied during contract performance, unless the materials have been made specifically for the contract; and

(b)   payments made to sub-contractors in advance of work performed under the sub-contract.

When the outcome of a construction contract cannot be estimated reliably:

(a)   Revenue should be recognised only to the extent of contract costs incurred that it is probable will be recoverable.

(b)   Contract costs should be recognised as an expense in the period in which they are incurred.

An expected loss on the construction contract should be recognised as an expense immediately.

Expected losses on contract

When it is probable that total contract costs will exceed total contract revenue, the expected loss should be recognised as an expense immediately.

Example – Hilltown Ltd

Hilltown Ltd designs and builds luxury yachts to order. The company prepares its financial statements to 31 December each year and at 31 December 2007 had three contracts still to be completed. The following information is available:

| | Contracts | | |
	1	2	3
Start date	1 January 2007	1 November 2007	1 January 2007
Completion date	31 August 2008	31 December 2008	31 December 2008
	£'000	£'000	£'000
Contract price	10,800	8,400	18,200
Invoiced to date:			
Received	5,830	850	8,000
Outstanding	20	–	–
Costs incurred to date	5,350	980	8,960
Costs certified to date	5,290	800	7,750
Costs to complete	3,250	5,900	10,200

Additional information

(1) Under the terms of each of the contracts, Hilltown Ltd is responsible for certain post-completion rectification work. This cost is not included in the 'costs to complete' shown above, and is estimated by management at 2% of the contract price.

(2) It is the company's policy to adjust cost of sales (which includes foreseeable losses, where appropriate) by the amount of attributable profit/loss to be recognised in the period (if appropriate) in order to arrive at turnover. This is done on a contract-by-contract basis.

Suggested solution – Hilltown Ltd

Income Statement for the Year Ended 31 December 2007 (Extract)

	£'000
Turnover (£6,480 + £800 + £7,750)	15,030
Cost of sales (£5,290 + £800 + £7,750)	(13,840)
Provision for foreseeable loss	(1,324)
Gross loss	(134)

Balance Sheet as at 31 December 2007

	£'000
Work in progress (£60 + £180 − £1,210)	1,450
Trade receivables	350
Provisions for foreseeable losses	(1,324)
Trade payables (50 + 250)	(300)

Workings

Estimate of total profit/(loss) on contracts

	Contract 1	Contract 2	Contract 3
	£'000	£'000	£'000
Contract price	10,800	8,400	18,200
Costs to date	5,350	980	8,960
Estimated costs to complete contract	3,250	5,900	10,200
Rectification work to complete (2% price)	216	168	364
Estimated total contract costs	8,816	7,048	19,524
Estimated total contract profit/(loss)	1,984	1,352	(1,324)
Stage of completion	12/20 months = 60%		2/14 months = 14%
Costs certified/estimated total costs	£5,290/8,816 = 60%		£800/7,048 = 11%
Attributable profit/(loss)	1,190	149	(1,324)

Turnover

	£'000	£'000	£'000	£'000
Costs certified to date	5,290	800	7,750	13,840
Attributable profit	1,190	–		
	6,480	800	7,750	15,030

Work in progress

	£'000	£'000	£'000	£'000
Costs incurred to date	5,350	980	8,960	15,290
Cost of sales (certified to date)	5,290	800	7,750	13,840
	60	180	1,210	1,450

Receivables – amounts recoverable on contract

	£'000	£'000	£'000	£'000
Turnover	6,480	800	7,750	15,030
Payments on account	5,830	850	8,000	14,680
	650	(50)	(250)	350

Example – Eagle Rock Ltd

Eagle Rock Ltd is a civil engineering company which at 31 July 2007 had three construction contracts in progress, information about which is as follows:

		Contract	
	A	B	C
Costs to date	£910,000	£1,500,000	£222,000
Future costs to complete	£545,000	£495,000	£666,000
Project started	1 February 2006	1 December 2005	1 October 2006
Likely completion	31 January 2008	15 April 2008	30 November 2007
Progress payments received	£757,000	£1,600,000	£200,000
Progress payments due but unpaid	–	£50,000	–
Tender value	£1,700,000	£2,100,000	£875,000

Income statement

	£'000
Turnover (1,063 + 1,579 + 219)	2,861
Cost of sales (910 + 1,500 + 222)	2,632

Expenses

Provision for expected losses on contract	10

Workings

Revised income statement/balance sheet

(1) Calculation of overall profit/(loss)

	A	B	C
	£'000	£'000	£'000
Tender price	1,700	2,100	875
Cost to date	(62.5%) 910	(75%) 1,500	(25%) 222
Future costs to complete	(37.5%) 545	(25%) 495	(75%) 666
	1,455	1,995	888
Profit/(Loss) on contract	245	105	(13)

Suggested solution – Eagle Rock

IAS 11

Balance sheet

	£'000
Work in progress at cost	Nil
Trade receivables (306 + 19)	325
Payables (included in current liabilities)	21
Provision for expected losses on construction contracts (included in non-current liabilities)	10

Note:

Costs to date as a proportion of estimated total costs are charged to income and turnover is matched by crediting the same proportion of total turnover.

Disclosure requirements

An enterprise should disclose:

(a) the amount of contract revenue recognised as revenue in the period;
(b) the methods used to determine the contract revenue recognised in the period; and
(c) the methods used to determine the stage of completion of contracts in progress.

An enterprise should disclose each of the following for contracts in progress at the balance sheet date:

(a) The aggregate amount of costs incurred and recognised profits less recognised losses to date.

(b)   The amount of advances received.

(c)   The amount of retentions.

Retentions are amounts of progress billings which are not paid until the satisfaction of conditions specified in the contract for the payment of such amounts or until defects have been rectified. Progress billings are amounts billed for work performed on a contract whether or not they have been paid by the customer. Advances are amounts received by the contractor before the related work is performed.

An enterprise should present:

(a)   The gross amount due from customers for contract work as an asset.

(b)   The gross amount due to customers for contract work as a liability.

CRH Plc provide a joint policy note encompassing both their policy on inventories and also on construction contracts and in the notes the amount due from customers is clearly seen within trade receivables.

CRH Plc   Year Ended 31 December 2005

Inventories and construction contracts

Inventories are stated at the lower of cost and NRV. Cost is based on the FIFO principle (and weighted average, where appropriate) and includes all expenditure incurred in acquiring the inventories and bringing them to their present location and condition. Raw materials are valued on the basis of purchase cost on a FIFO basis. In the case of finished goods and work in progress, cost includes direct materials, direct labour and attributable overheads based on normal operating capacity and excludes borrowing costs. NRV is the estimated proceeds of sale less all further costs to completion, and less all costs to be incurred in marketing, selling and distribution.

Contract costs are recognised as incurred. When the outcome of a construction contract cannot be estimated reliably, contract revenue is recognised only to the extent of contract costs incurred that are likely to be recoverable. When the outcome of a construction contract can be estimated reliably and it is probable that the contract will be profitable, contract revenue is recognised over the period of the contract. When it is probable that total contract costs will exceed total contract revenue, the expected loss is immediately recognised as an expense. The percentage-of-completion method is used to determine the appropriate amount to recognise in a particular reporting period with the stage of completion assessed by reference to the proportion that contract costs incurred at the balance sheet date bear to the total estimated cost of the contract.

Amounts recoverable on construction contracts, which are included in debtors, are stated at the net sales value of the work done less amounts received as progress payments on account. Cumulative costs incurred, net of amounts transferred to cost of sales, after deducting foreseeable losses, provision for contingencies and payments on account not matched with turnover, are included as construction contract balances in inventories. Cost includes all the expenditure related directly to specific projects and an allocation of fixed and variable overheads incurred in the Group's contract activities based on normal operating capacity.

18. Trade and Other Receivables

	2005 (€m)	2004 (€m)
All current		
Trade receivables	1,924.8	1,560.7
Amounts receivable in respect of construction contracts	170.7	110.8
Other receivables	226.4	186.2
Amounts receivable from associates	4.3	1.7
Prepayments and accrued income	150.2	113.7
Total	2,476.4	1,973.1

Retentions held by customers included in other receivables at the balance sheet date amounted to €10.3 million (2004: €7.7m).

Spanish company, Grupo Ferrovial SA go in to some detail on their revenue earning policy on construction contracts:

Grupo Ferrovial SA   Year Ended 31 December 2005

2.4.22.1 Construction business

When recognising the results obtained from the construction business, the Company follows the criteria established by IAS 11.

In accordance with IAS 11, paragraph 22 when the results from a construction contract may be reliably estimated, ordinary income and associated costs from the contract concerned must be recorded in the income statement as such, making reference to the percentage of completion.

Of the methods established by IAS 11, paragraph 30 to determine the percentage of completion of a contract, the Company normally follows the policy of examining the completed work (paragraph 30b).

This method may be used since all contracts generally include:

- a definition of each project unit that must be executed to complete the whole project;
- measurement of each of these project units; and
- the price at which each unit is certified.

In order to put this method into practice at the end of each month, a measurement of completed units is measured for each project. The resulting total is the amount of the construction work performed at the contractual price that should be recognised as project revenue from the inception. The difference with respect to the corresponding figure a month earlier gives the production for the month, which is the figure that is recorded as income.

Construction work costs are recognised for accounting purposes on an accruals basis, and the expenses actually incurred in the execution of the project units completed and those that, although they may be incurred in the future, have to be allocated to the project units now completed, are recognised as expense.

As is indicated in IAS 11, paragraph 29, the application of this income recognition method is combined with the preparation of a budget made for each construction work contract by the project unit. This budget is used as a key management tool in order to maintain detailed monitoring, project unit by project unit, of fluctuations between actual and budgeted figures.

In those exceptional cases in which it is not possible to estimate the margin for the entire contract, the total costs incurred are recognised and the income is deemed to be sales that are reasonably ensured with respect to the completed work (IAS 11, p. 32).

Recognition of changes to the main contract

During performance of construction work unforeseen events not envisaged in the primary contract may occur that increase the volume of work to be performed.

These changes to the contract initially entered into require the customer's technical approval and subsequent financial approval. This approval permits, from that moment, the issuance of certificates for and collection on this additional work.

The policy followed by Ferrovial Group in this respect is in line with the matters indicated in IAS 11, paragraph 14, and the income for this additional work is not recognised until approval is reasonably ensured by the customer (paragraph 13(a) and the amount that is likely to be accepted by the customer may be measured with sufficient reliability (paragraph 13(b)).

However, the costs associated with these project units are recognised when they arise regardless of the degree of customer approval of the work.

5

Balance sheet: Liabilities

5.1 IAS 37 *Provisions, Contingent Liabilities and Contingent Assets* (May 1975, revised September 1988)

IAS 37 prescribes the accounting and disclosure for all provisions, contingent liabilities and contingent assets, except for:

(a) financial instruments carried at fair value (see IAS 39);
(b) executory contracts (neither party performed nor both partially performed), except where onerous;
(c) insurance enterprises from contracts with policyholders (see IFRS 4);
(d) those covered by another IAS, e.g. IAS 11, 12, 17, 19 or any revenue covered by IAS 18; and
(e) reduction in asset values, e.g. depreciation and doubtful debts.

The objective of IAS 37 is to ensure that appropriate recognition criteria and measurement bases are applied to provisions, contingent liabilities and contingent assets and that sufficient information is disclosed in the notes to enable users to understand their nature, timing and amount.

Restructuring provisions are included in IAS 37 but additional disclosures may be required by IFRS 5 on Discontinued Operations.

Definitions

- *Provision*. A liability of uncertain timing or amount.
- *Legal obligation*. An obligation that derives from a contract, legislation or other operation of law.

- *Constructive obligation.* An obligation that derives from an enterprise's actions where:
  - (a) by an established pattern of past practice, published policies or a sufficiently specific current statement, the enterprise has indicated to other parties that it will accept certain responsibilities; and
  - (b) as a result, the enterprise has created a valid expectation on the part of those parties that it will discharge those responsibilities.
- *Contingent liability*
  - (a) A possible obligation that arises from past events and whose existence will be confirmed only by the occurrence or non-occurrence of one or more uncertain future events not wholly within the control of the enterprise; or
  - (b) A present obligation that arises from past events but is not recognised because:
    - (i) it is not probable that an outflow of resources embodying economic benefits will be required to settle the obligation; or
    - (ii) the amount of the obligation cannot be measured with sufficient reliability.
- *Contingent asset.* A possible asset that arises from past events and whose existence will be confirmed only by the occurrence or non-occurrence of one or more uncertain future events not wholly within the control of the enterprise.

Provisions and other liabilities

What distinguishes provisions from other liabilities is uncertainty about the timing or amount of future expenditure. Trade payables are certain liabilities to pay for goods or services received and accruals are certain liabilities for goods or services received not invoiced or formerly agreed as due to employees/suppliers.

Provisions, due to their uncertain nature, are reported separately whereas accruals are reported as part of trade and other payables.

Relationship between provisions and contingent liabilities

The key difference between provisions and contingencies is that the latter are not recognised because their existence will be confirmed only by the occurrence or non-occurrence of one or more uncertain future events not wholly within the entity's control or else they fail to meet the recognition criteria for liabilities.

- *Provisions.* Liabilities – present obligation – probable outflow of resources required to settle.
- *Contingent liabilities.* Possible obligations or fail to pass recognition criteria, i.e. not probable or no reliable estimate of the amount of the obligation.

Recognition

Provisions

A provision should be recognised when:

- (a) an enterprise has a legal or constructive obligation;
- (b) it is probable that an outflow of resources will be required to settle the obligation; and
- (c) a reliable estimate can be made of the obligation.

In rare cases where it is not clear whether or not there is an obligation, a past event is deemed to give rise to a present obligation if it is more likely than not that a present obligation exists at the balance sheet date. All available evidence should be considered including the opinion of experts.

The financial statements deal with the financial position at the period end, not with the future. No provision can be recognised for costs that need to be incurred in the future. It must only be those that existed at the balance sheet date.

However, provisions are required for penalties, clean-up costs and decommissioning costs as these are legal obligations. In contrast, expenditure to operate in a future way by fitting smoke filters would not be permitted as it could change its method of operation to avoid the liability.

For a liability to be created it is not necessary to know the identity of the party to whom the liability is owed – it may be to the public at large. A Board decision, by itself, does not result in a constructive obligation unless that decision has been communicated before the balance sheet date to those affected by it.

An event may not immediately give rise to an obligation but may do so in the future because of a change in law or statement to make the obligation constructive. If a new law is yet to be finalised, then an obligation only arises when the legislation is virtually certain to be enacted.

An entity should be able to determine a range of possible outcomes and therefore make an estimate of the obligation that is sufficiently reliable to use when recognising a provision. In extremely rare cases where no reliable estimate can be made, a liability exists that cannot be recognised. Instead it should be disclosed as a contingent liability.

Contingent liabilities

An enterprise should not recognise a contingent liability. Instead it should be disclosed unless the possibility of an outflow of resources is remote.

Where an entity is jointly and severally liable for an obligation, the part that is expected to be met by other parties is treated as a contingent liability. They must be assessed continually to determine whether an outflow has become probable. If that is the case, it will become a provision in the year in which the change in probability occurs.

Contingent assets

An entity should not recognise a contingent asset as this may result in the recognition of income that may never be realised. However, when realisation is virtually certain, then the related asset should be recognised.

A contingent asset should be disclosed where an inflow of benefits is probable.

Contingent assets are not recognised as this may result in recognition of income that may never be realised. However, when realisation is virtually certain then the related asset is not a contingent asset and should be recognised. Contingent assets should be continually assessed to ensure that they are appropriately accounted for.

Measurement

Best estimate

The amount recognised as a provision should be a best estimate of the expenditure required to settle the present obligation at the balance sheet date.

It is the amount an entity would rationally pay to settle at the balance sheet date or to transfer it to a third party. Often that amount would be prohibitive to settle. However, the estimate that would rationally be paid would be the best estimate of expenditure required to settle.

The estimates of outcomes and financial effect should be determined by the judgement of management supplemented by experience of similar transactions and independent experts. That should include any additional evidence discovered in the post balance sheet period.

Where a large population is involved, the obligation should be estimated by weighing up all possible outcomes by their associated probabilities, i.e. expected value. Where there is a continuous range of possible outcomes and each point in that range is as likely as any other, the midpoint of the range is used.

EXAMPLE

An entity sells goods with a warranty that covers defects within first six months after purchase. If minor defects were detected repair costs of £1 million would be incurred and, if major, £4 million. Past experience and future expectations indicate that 75% of goods sold will have no defects, 20% minor and 5% major.

Expected value of cost of repairs is 75% × Nil + 20% × £1m + 5% × £4m = £400,000

Where a single obligation is being measured the most likely outcome should be chosen. However, an entity must consider other outcomes, e.g. if it must rectify a serious fault and assumes that the most likely outcome to be £1,000 a provision for a larger amount is made if there is a significant chance that the further attempts to rectify the fault will be necessary.

The provision should be measured before tax. Any tax consequences are dealt with in IAS 12.

Risks and uncertainties

The risks and uncertainties surrounding events should be considered in reaching the best estimate of a provision. Risk describes the variability of outcomes. A risk adjustment may require an increase in a liability. However, the existence of uncertainty does not justify the creation of excessive provisions.

Disclosure of the uncertainties surrounding the amount of the expenditure is required.

Present value

Where the time value of money is material, the amount of a provision should be its present value. The discount rate should be a pre-tax rate that reflects the risks for which future cash flows estimates have been adjusted.

Future events that may affect the amount required to settle an obligation should be reflected in the amount of a provision where there is sufficient evidence that they will occur.

It is appropriate to include expected cost reductions associated with past experience in applying existing technology but it cannot anticipate the development of new technology unless that is supported by objective evidence.

The effect of possible new legislation is considered when measuring an existing obligation, if the legislation is virtually certain to be enacted. Evidence is required for both what the legislation will demand and whether or not it is virtually certain to be enacted and implemented. In many cases sufficient objective evidence will not exist until the new legislation is actually enacted.

Gains from the expected disposal of assets should not be taken into account in measuring a provision. Instead an entity recognises gains on disposal at the time specified in more specific IASs, when dealing with the assets concerned.

Reimbursements

Where some of the expenditure is expected to be reimbursed by another party, the reimbursement should be recognised when and, only when, it is virtually certain that reimbursement will be received if the entity settles the obligation. It should be treated as a separate asset. The reimbursement should not exceed the provision.

In the income statement, the expense relating a provision may be presented net of the amount recognised for a reimbursement.

Changes in provisions

Provisions should be reviewed at each balance sheet date and adjusted to reflect the current best estimate. If it is no longer probable that an outflow of resources embodying economic benefits will be required to settle, the provision should be reversed.

Where discounting is used, the carrying amount of the provision increases each period to reflect the passage of time and the increase is recognised as a borrowing cost.

Use of provisions

A provision should be used only for expenditures for which the provision was originally recognised. There should be no virement across provisions.

Application of the recognition and measurement rules

Provisions should not be recognised for future operating losses. They neither meet the definition of a liability nor the general recognition criteria. However, it may indicate impairment testing under IAS 36.

Onerous contracts

A provision should be made for any contract which is onerous. Where certain rights and obligations make a contract onerous a liability should be recognised. Executory contracts fall outside the scope of the standard.

It is onerous when, in a contract, any unavoidable costs of meeting the obligations under the contract exceed any economic benefits. The former represent the least net cost of exiting from the contract, i.e. lower of fulfilling it or penalties from failure to fulfil.

Any impairment losses must be recognised first, however, under IAS 36.

Restructuring

The following are examples of events that may fall under the definition of restructuring:

(a)   Sale or termination of a line of business.
(b)   The closure or relocation of business activities.
(c)   Changes in management structure.
(d)   Fundamental reorganisations having a material effect on the nature and focus of an entity's operations.

A constructive obligation arises only when an entity has the following:

(a)   A detailed formal plan for restructuring by identifying at least; the part of business concerned; the principal locations affected; the location, function and number of employees being terminated; and the expenditures to be undertaken and when the plan will be implemented.
(b)   Raised a valid expectation in those affected that it will carry out the restructuring by starting to implement the plan or announcing its main features to those affected by it.

Commencement could be evidenced by selling off assets, dismantling plant or the public announcement of its main features. For a constructive obligation the implementation should take place as soon as possible and be completed in a timeframe that makes significant changes to the plan unlikely. Long delays are unlikely to achieve that objective.

A board decision to restructure, before the balance sheet date, does not give rise to a constructive obligation unless the entity has:

(a)   started to implement the restructuring plan or
(b)   announced its main features sufficiently well to those affected that it will clearly result in a valid expectation that the entity will carry out the restructuring.

Any post balance sheet disclosure may be disclosed under IAS 10 *Events after the Balance Sheet Date* as a non-adjusting event.

In some countries which have a two-tiered board system with employees on the secondary board – if they are informed then a constructive obligation could exist.

No obligation arises for the sale of an operation until the entity is committed to the sale, i.e. there is a binding sale agreement.

A restructuring provision should only include the direct expenditures arising from the restructuring which are those that are both:

(a)   necessarily entailed by the restructuring and
(b)   not associated with the ongoing activities of the enterprise.

It does not include retraining costs, marketing or investment in new systems. These relate to the future. Future operating losses are also excluded unless they are related to an onerous contract.

Two examples are provided showing how IAS 37 should be applied:

Example – Killyleagh Plc

Killyleagh Plc, a company which prepares its accounts to 31 December each year, has two independent income streams: the power generation and the recycling and disposal of nuclear waste.

The company has no subsidiary or associate undertakings and no goodwill is carried on the company's balance sheet. All property, plant and equipment are stated at depreciated historical cost. The net assets directly involved in the power generation and nuclear waste income streams are being carried at £160 million and £180 million, respectively, at 31 December 2008. In addition, there are head office net assets with a carrying value of £15 million at the same date. Head office resources are used by the power generation and nuclear waste income streams in the proportion 40:60.

Before the financial statements for the year ended 31 December 2008 can be finalised, a number of issues need to be resolved. These are set out below.

Outstanding issues

(1) During 2008, there was a significant adverse change in the power generation regulatory environment, suggesting that the net assets of this income stream might not be fully recoverable. The company's power generation licensing agreement expires on 31 December 2018, and management estimate that the useful life of the existing assets is approximately 10 years. Company-approved budgets for the power generation income stream indicate that future net cash inflows for the next 10 years are estimated at £20 million per annum, before taking account of cash outflows of £4 million per annum relating to tax and financing costs. The net realisable value of the power generation net assets at 31 December 2008 is estimated at £100 million, after selling costs of £10 million. The current weighted average cost of capital of a listed company, whose cash flows have similar risk profiles to those of the power generation income generating unit, is 7%. This weighted average cost of capital has been calculated on a pre-tax basis.

(2) Increased competition and stricter safety regulations have put pressure on profit margins with respect to the recycling and disposal of nuclear waste. Accordingly, management has prepared a formal plan to reorganise this part of the company's business and they wish to include a provision of £15 million in the financial statements for the year ended 31 December 2008 to cover redundancies and relocation costs associated with the proposed reorganisation. Management has decided that, given the competitive nature of the business, a public announcement regarding the reorganisation would not be appropriate at this time.

(3)   On 1 January 2008, legislation dealing with emission levels came into effect. As a result, Killyleagh was required to fit special filters by 30 June 2008. Due to management changes and cash flow problems, the company was unable to install the new filters during 2008. The company hopes to start and complete this work during the first half of 2009, at an estimated cost of £5 million. No provision has yet been made in the 2008 financial statements for this, nor for the fines of £1 million payable at 31 December 2008 under the legislation. It is estimated that additional fines of £750,000 will become payable before the filters are fitted and operational.

(4)   On 1 January 2008, Killyleagh entered into a five-year contract with the government to dispose of nuclear waste in the North Sea. Under the terms of the contract, Killyleagh is responsible for restoring the sea bed at the end of the contract. It is estimated that this will cost £6 million. No provision has been made in the 2008 financial statements for this future expenditure, but the management intends to disclose in the notes to the financial statements their obligation to restore the sea bed. The current weighted average cost of capital of a listed company, whose cash flows have similar risk profiles to those of the recycling and disposal of nuclear waste cash generating unit, is 7%. The risk-free rate is 4%.

Suggested solution – Killyleagh Plc

Issue 1 Impairment of power generation cash generating stream – IAS 36

	Power generation unit (£m)	
Direct net assets attributable to power generation	160	
Share of head office net assets (£15m × 40% given)	6	
NBV	166	
Recoverable amount is the higher of NRV and NPV		
NRV (£110m − £10 selling costs)	100	
NPV		Higher figure is £140.468m
£20m per annum × 10 years × 7% WACC £20m × 7.0234	140.468	
(Cash flows relating to tax and financing should not be considered)		

Under IAS 36 *Impairment of Assets*, property, plant, etc. should not be carried at more than their recoverable amount, which is the higher of NRV and net present value (NPV). The impairment at 31 December 2008 is £166m − £140.468 = £25.532m.

This write-down should be reflected within operating costs, and if material, it should be recorded as an exceptional item in the notes to the financial statements. The impairment should be recorded within cumulative depreciation as the property, plant and equipment have been carried on an historic cost basis.

Impairment losses recognised when IAS 36 was first implemented should be recorded as changes in accounting estimate and should not be treated as changes in accounting policy. The IASB believes that the IAS is simply codifying existing practice and thus any adjustments should be treated as adjustments to current estimated lives and therefore treated as additional depreciation.

Issue 2 Provision for reorganisation of nuclear waste plant – IAS 37

IAS 37 *Provisions, Contingent Liabilities and Contingent Assets* states that a provision should only be created when an entity has a present obligation (i.e. either legal or constructive) as a result of a past transaction or event. It should also be probable (i.e. more than 50% chance of occurring) and be capable of being reliably measured.

In the case of a reorganisation, a provision should only be created if a constructive obligation exists. This is deemed to have arisen when an entity not only has a detailed formal plan but also has actually started to implement the plan or at least has announced the main features of the plan to those people affected by the decision. It must raise a valid expectation in those affected that it will carry out the restructuring.

IAS 37 notes that, by actually starting to implement the plan, it makes those people affected realise that the plan will be carried out. Examples of such events that trigger constructive obligations include the decommissioning of plant, the selling off of assets or the making of a public announcement. The announcement, however, must be outlined in sufficient detail, setting out main features of the plan so that it gives rise to a valid expectation in other parties, e.g. customers, suppliers, employees, trade unions, etc., that the entity will actually carry out the restructuring.

It is not acceptable, post-implementation of IAS 37, simply to include the £15 million provision because, at the year end, Killyleagh Plc has not started to implement the plan or announced its main features to those affected by it. The company, therefore, does not have a constructive obligation.

IAS 37 does not permit the inclusion of certain costs in restructuring provisions. These include retraining or relocation costs. These relate to the future operation of the business.

The standard expects that there will not be a long delay between creating the provision and commencing the reorganisation. If there were a significant delay, it is unlikely that the plan would raise an expectation on the part of others that the entity was committed to the restructuring. Under the disclosure requirements of IAS 37, reporting entities must now disclose when the provision is likely to crystallise.

Issue 3 Fitting of special filters – IAS 37

At 31 December 2008, there is no obligation for the costs of fitting the filters because no obligating event has occurred (i.e. the fitting of filters). However, the appendix to IAS 37 suggests that an obligation to pay fines does exist due to non-compliance with the regulations. The company should therefore provide for £1 million in fines but should not provide for the additional £750,000 as there is not a present obligation at the balance sheet date.

However, an opposing opinion would suggest that the entity must ultimately comply with the new legislation and therefore £5 million should be provided at once. This may be discounted to its present value if it is unlikely to be paid in the near future.

The disclosures required under IAS 37 include a brief description of the obligation, the expected timing of any resulting transfer of economic benefits and an indication of the uncertainties about the amount or timing of those transfers.

Details are also required of the carrying amount at the start and end of the accounting period, any additional provisions created or reversed in the period and the discount rate applied.

Issue 4 Provision for decommissioning costs – IAS 37

Under IAS 37, Killyleagh Plc has a legal obligation to restore the seabed at the end of the contract. This should be provided at once. However, it may be discounted to its present value. It could be argued that the correct double entry would be to create property, plant and equipment which is then depreciated over the period of the contract. It is regarded as a 'negative' residual value because when the entity enters the contract it has to put the seabed back to its original state and it is therefore part of the cost of purchasing the contract in the first place.

The measurement of the liability at present value means that interest has to be accounted for to unwind the discount. The finance cost is purely notional as no interest is paid. However, it must be regarded as part of interest payable and it should not be treated as an operating expense.

The details of the costs to be charged to income and the balance sheet assets and liabilities are computed as follows:

Year	Operating costs (£)	Finance costs (£)	Property, etc. (NBV) (£)	Property, etc. (provision) (£)
31.12.2008	986,280	197,256	3,945,120	5,128,656
31.12.2009	986,280	205,146	2,958,840	5,333,802
31.12.2010	986,280	213,352	1,972,560	5,547,154
31.12.2011	986,280	221,886	986,280	5,579,040
31.12.2012	986,280	230,960	Nil	6,000,000
	4,931,400	1,068,600		

Depreciation	£6m × 0.8219 (annuity for 4 years at 4% risk-free rate) = £4,931,400/ 5 years = £986,280

Finance costs	£4,931,400 × 4% = £197,256	2008
	£5,128,656 × 4% = £205,146	2009
	£5,333,802 × 4% = £213,352	2010
	£5,547,154 × 4% = £221,886	2011
	£5,579,040 × 4% = £230,960	2012 (Bal. fig.)

Example – Beragh Plc

Assume the following provisions have been accounted for by Beragh Plc. Are they acceptable under IAS 37 *Provisions, Contingent Liabilities and Contingent Assets*:

Provisions and long-term commitments

(i) Provision for decommissioning the group's radioactive facilities is made over their useful life and covers complete demolition of the facility within 50 years of it being taken out of service together with any associated waste disposal. The provision is based on future prices and is discounted using a current market rate of interest.

	£m
Provision for decommissioning costs	
Balance at 1.12.07	675
Adjustment arising from change in price levels charged to reserves	33
Charged in the year to income	125
Adjustment due to change in knowledge (charged to reserves)	27
Balance at 30.11.08	860

There are still decommissioning costs of £1,231 million (undiscounted) to be provided for in respect of the group's radioactive facilities as the company's policy is to build up the required provision over the life of the facility.

Assume that adjustments to the provision due to change in knowledge about the accuracy of the provision do not give rise to future economic benefits.

(ii) The company purchased an oil company during the year. As part of the sale agreement, oil has to be supplied for a five-year period to the company's former holding company at an uneconomic rate. As a result, a provision for future operating losses has been set up of £135 million, which relates solely to the uneconomic supply of oil. Additionally, the oil company is exposed to environmental liabilities arising out of its past obligations, principally in respect of remedial work to soil and ground water systems, although currently there is no legal obligation to carry out the work. Liabilities for environmental costs are provided for when the group determines a formal plan of action on the closure of an inactive site and when expenditure on remedial work is probable and the cost can be measured with reasonable certainty. However, in this case, it has been decided to provide for £120 million in respect of the environmental liability on the acquisition of the oil company. Beragh has a reputation of ensuring that the environment is preserved and protected from the effects of its business activities.

Suggested solution – Beragh Plc

(i)   Provision for decommissioning costs

IAS 37 *Provisions, Contingent Liabilities and Contingent Assets* has had a major impact on accounting for decommissioning costs. In the past, most extractive/oil companies gradually built up a provision over the life of the associated mine/oilfield. The provision was often created on a unit of production basis so as to match the cost of decommissioning with the associated revenue being created from the sale of associated oil, etc. This was a profit and loss or accruals-based approach. This is the accounting treatment adopted by Beragh Plc.

Since the publication of IAS 37 these provisions must now comply with the balance sheet approach and it is argued that a nuclear energy company has an immediate obligation on the day that the damage occurs, i.e. on the opening up of the radioactive facilities, etc. A provision must be created in full immediately and, if not payable for several years, then it should be discounted to its present value. In the case of the group, the discount rate adopted is market rate. Under IAS 37 companies should adopt a real interest rate or future prices discounted by a nominal rate. A risk-free rate should be adopted where a prudent estimate of future cash flows already reflects risk (e.g. government bond rate).

The unwinding of the discount should be charged to income, not as part of decommissioning costs, but as part of finance costs.

(ii)   Provision for future operating losses

Under IAS 37 no provision for future operating losses may be created. However, if the company has entered into an onerous contract then a provision should be created. An onerous contract is one in which the entity cannot avoid the excess costs over revenues of fulfilling a contract. Clearly the company has entered such a contract and the provision of £135 million should be set up for the uneconomic supply of oil.

IAS 37 does not spell out specifically any rules on environment liabilities. However, in the appendix, it is recommended that where legislation has been broken or if the entity has a dark green policy then provisions should be made for such costs on the grounds that they are clearly legal or constructive obligations. If the company has created a valid expectation that the environmental liabilities will be paid out then a provision should be set up. It will depend on the subjective judgement of both auditor and preparer.

The company only sets up a provision when a formal plan of action on the closure of an inactive site has been set up and when the expenditure on remedial work is probable and the cost can be measured with reasonable certainty. This would appear to be a satisfactory basis on which to set up a provision. The provision of £120 million should therefore be permitted.

Zenitel, a Belgian voice and data provision company, discloses that restructuring provisions comprise employee termination payments and are recognised in the period in which it becomes legally or constructively committed to the obligation. During the year, the company recognised a provision for restructuring of €4.9 million and a note disclosed that of this, €1.8 million related to restructuring programmes in The Netherlands, France and Caribbean that have been announced after the year end. However, Zenitel has failed to follow IAS 37 by recognising a provision before announcing the restructuring plans.

Disclosure

For each class of provision:

(a)   the net book value (NBV) at start and end of the period;
(b)   additional provisions made in the period, including increases to existing provisions;
(c)   amounts used in the period;
(d)   unused amounts reversed during the period; and
(e)   the increase during the period in the discounted amount arising from the passage of time and any change in the discount rate.

Comparatives are not required.
In addition an entity should disclose the following:

(a)   A brief description of the nature of the obligation and expected timing of any result-ing outflows of economic benefits.
(b)   An indication of the uncertainties about the timing or amount of any outflows including the major assumptions adopted.
(c)   The amount of any expected reimbursement, stating the amount of any asset recog-nised for that expected reimbursement.

Two good examples of provision disclosure are provided by Unilever Plc and BP Plc, the latter providing details of the unwinding of their long-term decommissioning provisions. Both also provide full movements in their material provisions and a short description of what the provisions are for and their likely timing.

Unilever Plc   Year Ended 31 December 2005

27. Provisions

	Restructuring (Note 1)	Profit sharing and bonuses (Note 2)	Environmental compliance (Note 3)	Other (Note 4)	Total
	(£m)	(£m)	(£m)	(£m)	(£m)
At 1 January 2005	(11)	(7)	(25)	(4)	(47)
Exchange differences	–	–	(2)	–	(2)
Charge for the year	–	(3)	(9)	(1)	(13)
Utilised	8	2	2	–	12
Transfers	–	–	(2)	–	(2)
At 31 December 2005	(3)	(8)	(36)	(5)	(52)
At 31 December 2005					
Current liabilities	(2)	(2)	(12)	(2)	(18)
Non-current liabilities	(1)	(6)	(24)	(3)	(34)
	(3)	(8)	(36)	(5)	(52)
At 31 December 2004					
Current liabilities	(7)	(2)	–	–	(9)
Non-current liabilities	(4)	(5)	(25)	(4)	(38)
	(11)	(7)	(25)	(4)	(47)

Notes:

(i)   Restructuring

The provision relates primarily to amounts set aside for various reorganisations within the Group, principally continental European operations. Most of the utilisation of these provisions is likely to take place within the next year.

(ii)   Profit sharing and bonuses

The Group operates various profit sharing and bonus schemes, including the cash settled phantom share option scheme. These provisions are long term, with the timing of their utilisation being dependent on various performance criteria being met.

(iii)   Environmental compliance

Environmental compliance includes £9 million (2004: £nil) of omission rights in the Glass businesses, the utilisation of which is likely within the next year. The balance mainly relates to the United States and is long term in nature with the timing of utilisation unknown.

(iv)   Others

Other provisions include £4 million (2004: £2m) relating to onerous property contracts in the United Kingdom, the timing of the utilisation of which is in accordance with those contracts and £1 million (2004: £1m) relating to business disposals, the amount of the final liability and timing of payment, if any, being dependent upon the outcome of ongoing negotiations.

BP Plc   Year Ended 31 December 2005

41. Provisions

	Decommissioning	Environmental	Litigation and others	Total ($m)
At 1 January 2005	5,572	2,457	1,570	9,599
Exchange adjustments	(38)	(32)	(35)	(105)
New provisions	1,023	565	1,464	3,052
Write-back of unused provisions	–	(335)	(86)	(421)
Unwinding of discount	122	47	32	201
Utilisation	(128)	(366)	(650)	(1,144)
Deletions	(101)	(25)	–	(126)
At 31 December 2005	6,450	2,311	2,295	11,056
Of which				
– expected to be incurred within one year	162	489	451	1,102
– expected to be incurred in more than one year	6,288	1,822	1,844	9,954

	Decommissioning	Environmental	Litigation and others	Total ($m)
At 1 January 2004	4,720	2,298	1,581	8,599
Exchange adjustments	213	21	25	259
New provisions	286	587	298	1,171
Write-back of unused provisions	–	(151)	(64)	(215)
Unwinding of discount	118	55	23	196
Change in discount rate	434	40	1	475
Utilisation	(87)	(393)	(294)	(774)
Deletions	(112)	–	–	(112)
At 31 December 2004	5,572	2,457	1,570	9,599
Of which				
– expected to be incurred within one year	124	513	78	715
– expected to be incurred in more than one year	5,448	1,944	1,492	8,884

	Decommissioning	Environmental	Litigation and others	Total ($m)
At 1 January 2003	4,168	2,122	1,546	7,836
Exchange adjustments	257	28	28	313
New provisions	1,159	599	331	2,089
Write-back of unused provisions	–	(84)	(64)	(148)
Unwinding of discount	107	46	20	173
Utilisation	(121)	(337)	(273)	(731)
Deletions	(850)	(76)	(7)	(933)
At 31 December 2003	4,720	2,298	1,581	8,599
Of which				
– expected to be incurred within one year	99	272	364	735
– expected to be incurred in more than one year	4,621	2,026	1,217	7,864

The group makes full provision for the future cost of decommissioning oil and natural gas production facilities and related pipelines on a discounted basis on the installation of those facilities. At 31 December 2005, the provision for the costs of decommissioning these production facilities and pipelines at the end of their economic lives was $6,450 million (2003: $4,720m). The provision has been estimated using existing technology, at current prices and discounted using a real discount rate of 2.0% (2004: 2.0% and 2003: 2.5%). These costs are expected to be incurred over the next 30 years. While the provision is based on the best estimate of future costs and the economic lives of the facilities and pipelines, there is uncertainty regarding both the amount and the timing of incurring these costs.

Provisions for environmental remediation are made when a clean-up is probable and the amount reasonably determinable. Generally, this coincides with commitments to a formal plan of action or, if earlier, on divestment or closure of inactive sites. The provision for environmental liabilities at 31 December 2005 was $2,311 million (2004: $2,457m and 2003: $2,298m). The provision has been estimated using existing technology, at current prices and discounted using a real discount rate of 2.0 % (2004: 2.0% and 2003: 2.5%). The majority of these costs are expected to be incurred over the next 10 years. The extent and cost of future remediation programmes are inherently difficult to estimate. They depend on the scale of any possible contamination, the timing and extent of corrective actions, and also the group's share of liability.

The group also holds provisions for litigation, expected rental shortfalls on surplus properties, and sundry other liabilities, included within the new provisions made for 2005 is an amount of $700 million in respect of the Taxes City incident of which $492 million has been disbursed to claimants. To the extent that these liabilities are not expected to be settled within the next three years, the provisions are discounted using either a nominal discount rate of 4.5% (2004: 4.5% and 2003: 4.5%) or a real discount rate of 2.0% (2004: 2.0% and 2003: 2.5%) as appropriate.

For all possible contingent liabilities the following should be disclosed together with a brief description of the nature of the contingent liability:

(a)   An estimate of its financial effect.
(b)   An indication of the uncertainties relating to the amount or timing of any outflow.
(c)   The possibility of any reimbursement.

Disclosures may be aggregated provided their nature is sufficiently similar for a single statement to fulfil the above requirements.

Where an inflow of economic benefits is probable an entity should disclose a brief description of the nature of the contingent asset at the balance sheet date and, if practicable, an estimate of their financial effect.

Where any of the above disclosure is not practicable, the fact should be disclosed. In extremely rare cases disclosure may seriously prejudice the entity in a dispute with other parties. In that case an entity need not disclose the information but should, instead, disclose the general nature of the dispute together with the fact that, and the reason why, the information has not been disclosed.

An example of this is provided by Innogenetics SA, a Belgium company in the biopharmaceutical industry. A note continues to disclose the details of claims against Innogenetics in respect of alleged patent infringements and breach of a distribution agreement. Following along the lines of IAS 37, the company invokes the prejudicial override on the grounds that disclosure of additional information can be expected to prejudice the outcome of the litigation seriously.

Innogenetics SA   Year Ended 30 December 2005

Note 18 – Contingencies

In November 1998, a claim was filed against Innogenetics alleging patent infringement relating to HIV-2, following earlier descriptive seizure proceedings. The claim seeks damages based on sales of particular types of products. The plaintiff's claim for damages amounts to €6.2 million, subject to further increases in the course of the proceedings. The case is pending before the Antwerp Court of First Instance. On 23 September 2005, the Court issued an interlocutory decision whereby it appointed an expert to render an opinion to the Court as to (i) whether or not the invoked patent complies with the requirements of novelty, inventive step, sufficient disclosure, and correspondence between the granted patent and the patent application and (ii) whether or not Innogenetics' activities infringe the plaintiff's patent. The mission of the expert is ongoing. Management strongly disputes this claim and believes that it lacks a proper basis in fact and law.

On 3 November 2005, a second descriptive seizure was performed at the Innogenetics premises by an expert appointed by the court at the request of the same plaintiffs. The aim of the descriptive seizure was to obtain all manufacturing, marketing and sales information relating to HIV immunoassays manufactured by Innogenetics in view of a second patent owned by the plaintiffs in the field of HIV-2, distinct from the patent asserted against Innogenetics in the above-mentioned court case. So far, no claim as to the merits has been received in connection with this second descriptive seizure. Management continues to believe that damages relating to this matter, if any, will not have a material impact on the Company's financial position, results, operations or cash flow in future years.

At the end of 1998, Innogenetics was subject to descriptive and seizure proceedings based on the allegation that the Company would be infringing two European patents relating to hepatitis C virus (HCV). In the subsequent proceedings with regard to the merits filed before the Gent Court of First Instance, the plaintiff originally claimed a provisional amount of €744,000, adaptable in the course of the proceedings. In the plaintiff's briefs of argument filed in February 2001, this amount was increased to €25 million if the Company were to be found to have infringed the plaintiff's patents in bad faith, or €12.5 million if the Company were to be found to have infringed the plaintiff's patents in good faith. On 6 February 2002, the Court issued an interlocutory order, appointing a court expert with the following mission: (i) to provide an opinion on whether the plaintiff's two patents are valid, more specifically taking into account the invalidation arguments developed by the Company; (ii) to provide an opinion on whether certain HCV related products of the Company contain all essential characteristics of plaintiffs two patents; and (iii) to give an opinion on what extent and in what sense polynucleotides, primers, probes, assays, etc. are essential characteristics of the two patents. The mission of the expert is ongoing. Similar proceedings with regard to the merits have been filed by the same plaintiff in France based on the allegation that the Company would be infringing one (of the previously indicated two) European patents relating to HCV. Management strongly disputes this claim and believes that it lacks a proper basis in fact and law. The position of the Company was strengthened by a European Patent Office decision rendered in 2000, which greatly reduced the scope of one of the plaintiff's patents that formed part of the basis of their claim in Belgium, as well as court and/or patent office decisions between the plaintiff and third parties in other jurisdictions. Furthermore, Management believes the amount of the claim is strongly exaggerated.

Innogenetics is also subject to certain other legal proceedings and claims that have arisen in the ordinary course of its business and to a court action with its former Italian distributor claiming compensation in the framework of the alleged breach and the termination of its distribution agreement. In the latter proceedings initiated before the Cent Commercial Court, the plaintiff's claims were entirely dismissed in First Instance in June 2002 and by the Gent Court of Appeal in February 2005. A Supreme Court Appeal ('Hof van Cassatie') lodged by the plaintiff is pending.

On 29 September 2005, Innogenetics filed complaints against two US-based companies in the United States District Court for the Western District of Wisconsin, for patent infringement of one of its HCV genotyping patents. One complaint was filed against Abbott Laboratories (Chicago, IL) and the other against Third Wave Technologies Inc (TWT) (Madison, Wl). In the complaints, Innogenetics claims that both Abbott Laboratories and TWT have been infringing Innogenetics' US Patent No. 5 846 704, for a process for typing of HCV isolates. Both TWT and Abbott filed counterclaims, alleging that (i) the invoked patent is invalid and/or unenforceable and (ii) their respective activities are not infringing. Innogenetics strongly disputes these counterclaims. Innogenetics expects that the trial court will issue a ruling (in first instance) within a period of no more than 12 months that could have a material impact on the Company's financial position (see Note 20).

In the opinion of the Management, resolution of the matters described above is not expected to have a materially adverse effect on the consolidated financial position of Innogenetics. However, depending on the amount and timing of such resolution, an unfavourable resolution of some or all of these matters could materially affect the Company's future results of operations or cash flows in a particular quarter. The Company believes it has adequately accrued for these matters until 31 December 2005, and continues to periodically review the accrual. Legal fees related to such matters are expensed as incurred. The information usually required by IAS 37 is not disclosed on the grounds that it can be expected to prejudice the outcome of the litigation seriously.

Delta Plc provides an outstanding legal case as a classic example of a contingent liability note:

Delta Plc   Year Ended 31 December 2005

37. Contingent Liabilities

£m	At 31 December 2005	At 1 January 2005
Financial guarantees	5.3	2.7

It is not expected that any loss will arise in respect of these financial guarantees all of which were undertaken in the ordinary course of business.

European Commission investigation

During January 2001, the European Commission's competition directorate-general commenced an investigation into allegations of anti-competitive behaviour among certain manufacturers of copper plumbing fittings, including the Group's former plumbing fittings business. Notwithstanding the Group's subsequent disposal of that business, the Group retains some responsibility in relation to the outcome of the Commission's investigation. On 10 March 2004, the Group submitted a leniency application and has co-operated fully with the Commission. The Commission issued a statement of objections on 22 September 2005, and the Group provided a written response to such statement on 5 December 2005. Representatives of the Group and legal counsel, together with other parties subject to this investigation, attended a hearing convened by the European Commission in Brussels on 26–27 January 2006. The Group expects a decision by the Commission later in 2006. The investigation is expected to result in a fine. Legal counsel has advised that applicable regulations limit the maximum level of fines that could be imposed at 10% of the Group's total turnover in the business year preceding the imposition of the fine. The Commission is afforded considerable discretion in the determination of such fines, as well as in the reduction of fines imposed on parties, such as the Group, which seek leniency and co-operate with the Commission At this stage in the investigation, and given the Commission's considerable discretion in determining the level of any fines, it is not possible to estimate reliably the level of fine that might be imposed upon the Group. Any decision by the Commission could be appealed to the European Courts, although an appeal would not automatically suspend payment of any fine. Consequently no provision has been raised in respect of this matter except for legal expenses expected to be incurred in connection with the investigation.

Another short example of contingent liabilities which includes a possible infringement of EC legislation has been provided by Fyffes Plc:

Fyffes Plc   Year Ended 31 December 2005

(d)   Contingencies

(i)   From time to time, the Group is involved in other claims and legal actions, which arise in the normal course of business. Based on information currently available to the company, and legal advice, the directors believe such litigation will not, individually or in aggregate, have a material adverse effect on the financial statements and that the Group is adequately positioned to deal with the outcome of any such litigation.

(ii)   The European Commission is currently undertaking an investigation into whether there have been infringements of Article 81 of the Treaty of Rome and Article 53 of the European Economic Area (EEA) agreement by businesses involved in the supply of bananas and pineapples within the EEA. In June 2005, the Commission carried out inspections of a number of companies operating in these markets, including Fyffes. At this time, it is not possible for the Group to determine the final outcome of these investigations including whether the European Commission may seek to impose any fines and, if so, the level of any such fines. Fyffes has recently received a request for information from the Commission and intends to continue to co-operate with it in relation to this matter.

A similar example is provided by British Airways Plc (BA). In 2005, BA stated that it was under investigation by several regulatory authorities in respect of alleged anti-competitive activity related to its air cargo business and was a defendant in several lawsuits in connection with the allegations. It follows along the lines of IAS 37 and states that it is not possible to predict whether these actions will have an adverse effect on its financial position or on results of operations.

British Airways Plc   Year Ended 31 March 2006

32. Contingent Liabilities

There were contingent liabilities at 31 March 2006 in respect of guarantees and indemnities entered into as part of, and claims arising from, the ordinary course of business, upon which no material losses are likely to arise. The Company is under investigation by the European Commission, the US Department of Justice, the Competition Commission in Canada and the New Zealand Commerce Commission in connection with alleged anti-competitive activity related to its cargo business. The Company is named as a defendant in a number of lawsuits that have been filed in various parts of the United States and Canada in connection with these allegations. It is not possible to predict whether these actions will have an adverse effect on the Group's financial position or on results of operations. A number of other lawsuits and regulatory proceedings are pending the outcome of which in the aggregate is not expected to have a material effect on the Group's financial position or on results of operations.

The Group and the Company have guaranteed certain borrowings, liabilities and commitments which at 31 March 2006 amounted to £204 million (2005: £259m) and £410 million (2005: £577m) respectively. For the Company these included guarantees given in respect of the fixed perpetual preferred securities issued by subsidiary companies and, for the year ended 31 March 2005, the Convertible Capital Bonds.

IAS 37 provides a number of illustrative examples to demonstrate how to apply the standard. These are provided below:

Example 1 – Warranties

A manufacturer gives warranties to its customers. Under the terms of the contract it promises to remedy any defects that become apparent within three years from the date of sale. On past experience, it is probable that there will be some claims under the warranties.

Present obligation as a result of a past obligating event
The sale of the product – gives rise to legal obligation.

Outflow of resources
Probable for warranties as a whole.

Conclusion
A provision is recognised for the best estimate of costs of making goods under warranty products sold before the balance sheet date.

Example 2A – Contaminated land – Legislation virtually certain to be enacted

An oil company causes contamination. In one country there is no legislation requiring cleaning up but contamination has occurred for several years. At 31 December 2008, it is virtually certain that a draft law will be enacted shortly after the year end.

Present obligation as a result of a past obligating event
The obligating event is the contamination of the land because of virtual certainty of clean-up.

Outflow of resources
Probable

Conclusion
A provision is recognised for the best estimate of the costs of clean-up.

Example 2B – Contaminated land and constructive obligation

An oil company causes environmental damage in a country with no legislation to clean-up but the entity has a widely published environmental policy in which it undertakes to clean-up all contamination that it causes. It normally honours that pledge.

Present obligation as a result of a past obligating event
The obligating event is the contamination of the land giving rise to a constructive obligation to clean-up.

Outflow of resources
Probable

Conclusion
A provision for the best estimate of the costs of clean-up.

Example 3 – Offshore oilfield

An agreement requires the removal of an oil rig and the restoration of the seabed. Ninety per cent of costs relate to removal of rig and restoration of damage and 10% to extraction of oil. At year end the rig was constructed but no oil extracted.

Present obligation as a result of a past obligating event
Construction of oil rig creates a legal obligation. At the balance sheet date, however, there is no obligation to rectify the damage caused by the extraction of oil.

Outflow of resources
Probable

Conclusion
A provision is recognised for the best estimate of 90% of the eventual costs that relate to the removal of the oil rig. These costs are included as part of the cost of the oil rig. The 10% are recognised as a liability as the oil is extracted.

Example 4 – Refunds policy

A retail store has a policy of refunding purchases by dissatisfied customers and this is generally known.

Present obligation as a result of a past obligating event
The obligating event is the sale of the product – constructive obligation – valid expectation by customers that the store will refund purchases.

Outflow of resources
Probable, a proportion of goods are returned for refund.

Conclusion
A provision is recognised for the best estimate of the costs of the refunds.

Example 5A – Closure of a division – No implementation before balance sheet date

Assume in December 2008 the board of an entity decides to close down a division. Before the year end (31.12.08) the decision was not communicated to any of those affected.

Present obligation as a result of a past obligating event
There has been no obligating event and so no obligation.

Conclusion
No provision is recognised.

Example 5B – Closure of a division – Communication/implementation before balance sheet date

Assume in December 2008 the board of an entity decides to close down a division. Before the year end (31.12.08) a detailed plan for closing down the division was agreed by the board and letters sent to customers warning them to seek an alternative source of supply. Redundancy notices were also sent to employees.

Present obligation as a result of a past obligating event
The obligating event is the communication of the decision to customers and staff – constructive contract.

Outflow of resources
Probable

Conclusion
A provision should be recognised for the best estimate of the costs of closing the division.

Example 6 – Legal requirements to fit smoke filters

Under new legislation an entity is required to fit smoke filters by 30 June 2008. It has not fitted these.

(a)   At 31.12.2007
No obligation as no obligating event either for costs of fitting the filters or for fines. No provision is recognised.
(b)   At 31.12.2008
Still no obligation for fitting the filters but could be for fines.
Need to assess the probability of incurring fines and penalties by non-compliance thus a provision is recognised for the best estimate of any fines and penalties that are more likely than not to be imposed.

Example 7 – Staff retraining as a result of changes in the income tax system

A number of changes to the tax systems have resulted in a need to retrain a large proportion of its administrative and sales workforce to ensure compliance with financial services regulations. No retraining had taken place by the year end.

Present obligation as a result of a past obligating event
No obligation because no obligating event (retraining) has taken place.

Conclusion
No provision is recognised.

Example 8 – An onerous contract

During December, 2008 the entity relocates to a new factory. The lease on the old factory continues for the next four years, cannot be cancelled or relet.

Present obligation as a result of a past obligating event
The obligating event is the signing of the lease contract – legal obligation.

Outflow of resources
When the lease becomes onerous, an outflow is probable.

Conclusion
A provision is recognised for the best estimate of the unavoidable lease payments.

Example 9 – A single guarantee

During 2007, A guarantees certain borrowings of B. During 2008, B's financial condition deteriorates and in June 2008, files for protection from creditors.

(a) At 31 December 2007
The obligating event is the giving of the guarantee – legal obligation.
No outflow of benefits is probable.
No provision is recognised. The guarantee is a contingent liability unless probability of outflow is remote.
(b) At 31 December 2008
The obligating event is the giving of the guarantee – legal obligation.
Probable an outflow of resources will occur
Provision is recognised for the best estimate of the obligation.

Example 10 – A court case

Ten people died after a wedding, of food poisoning, possibly from goods sold by the company. Legal proceedings have started but they are being disputed by the company. In 2007, the legal advisors felt that the loss was not probable but during 2008 they have changed their mind.

(a) At 31 December 2007
No obligation exists and thus no provision should be created. It is disclosed as a contingent liability, unless liability is remote.
(b) At 31 December 2008
There is a present obligation. It is probable and a provision should be made for the best estimate of the amount to settle the obligation.

Example 11 – Repairs and maintenance

Where a major overhaul is required, IAS 16 permits component accounting.

Example 11A   No legislative requirement
No obligation exists even if, e.g. a furnace needs to be relined every five years. No provision is permitted as this is still only an intention. Instead the relining costs should be capitalised when incurred and depreciated over the subsequent five years.

Example 11B   Legislative requirement

An airline is required by law to overhaul its aircraft every three years. No obligation and no provision as it is still only an intention. The company can avoid the expenditure by selling the aircraft. Once again depreciation should be accelerated via component accounting and subsequent overhaul costs capitalised.

A number of examples of disclosure are also provided by IAS 37 as follows:

Example 1 – Warranties

A manufacturer gives warranties at the time of sale to purchasers of its three product lines. Under the terms of the warranty, the manufacturer undertakes to repair or replace items that fail to perform satisfactorily for two years from the date of sale. At the balance sheet date, a provision of 60,000 has been recognised. The provision has not been discounted as the effect of discounting is not material. The following information is disclosed:

A provision of 60,000 has been recognised for expected warranty claims on products sold during the last three financial years. It is expected that the majority of this expenditure will be incurred in the next financial year, and all will be incurred within two years of the balance sheet date

Example 2 – Decommissioning costs

In 2007, an entity involved in nuclear activities recognises a provision for decommissioning costs of £300 million. The provision is estimated using the assumption that decommissioning will take place in 60–70 years time. However, there is a possibility that it will not take place until 100–110 years time, in which case the present value of the costs will be significantly reduced. The following information is disclosed:

'A provision of £300 million has been recognised for decommissioning costs. These costs are expected to be incurred between 2060 and 2070; however, there is a possibility that decommissioning will not take place until 2100–2110. If the costs were measured based upon the expectation that they would not be incurred until 2100–2110 the provision would be reduced to 136 million. The provision has been estimated using existing technology, at current prices, and discounted using a real discount rate of 2%'.

Example 3 – Disclosure exemption

An entity is involved in a dispute with a competitor, who is alleging that the entity has infringed patents and is seeking damages of £100 million. The entity recognises a provision for its best estimate of the obligation, but discloses none of the information due to its seriously prejudicial outcome. The following information is disclosed:

> 'Litigation is in process against the company relating to a dispute with a competitor who alleges that the company has infringed patents and is seeking damages of £100 million. The information usually required by IAS 37, Provisions, Contingent Liabilities and Contingent Assets, is not disclosed on the grounds that it can be expected to prejudice seriously the outcome of the litigation. The directors are of the opinion that the claim can be successfully resisted by the company'.

6

Performance measurement

6.1 IAS 18 *Revenue Recognition* (November 1984)

IAS 18 deals with the bases for recognition of revenue in the income statements of enterprises, particularly from the following:

- the sale of goods;
- the rendering of services; and
- the use of resources yielding interest, royalties and dividends.

The following specialised aspects are excluded:

(a) Dividends received under the equity method (see IAS 28)
(b) Revenue arising from construction contracts (see IAS 11)
(c) Revenue arising from lease agreements (see IAS 17)
(d) Revenue arising from government grants (see IAS 20)
(e) Revenue of insurance companies (see IFRS 4).

Revenue also does not include realised and unrealised gains from selling/holding non-current assets, unrealised holding gains due to changes in the value of current assets, natural increases in agricultural and forest products, changes in foreign exchange rates, discharges of obligations at less than their carrying amount and unrealised gains from restating the carrying amount of obligations.

Definitions

- *Revenue.* Gross inflow of cash, receivables or other consideration arising in the course of the ordinary activities of an enterprise from the sale of goods, from the rendering of services and from the use by others of enterprise resources yielding interest, royalties and dividends. It excludes third-party collections such as VAT (value added tax). In an agency relationship revenue is the amount of the commission.

- *Completed contract method.* Recognises revenue only when the sale of goods or the rendering of services is complete or substantially completed.
- *Percentage of completion method.* Recognises revenue proportionately with the degree of completion of goods and services.

Revenue recognition

Revenue from sales or service transactions should be recognised when performance is satisfied. However, if it is unreasonable to expect ultimate collection then it should be postponed.

Sale of goods

Performance will be achieved if the following conditions are satisfied:

(a) The seller has transferred the significant risks and rewards of ownership to the buyer.
(b) No significant uncertainty exists regarding:
- the consideration to be derived from the sale of goods;
- the associated costs incurred in producing/purchasing the goods;
- the extent to which the goods may be returned.

If a seller retains significant risks, it is not appropriate to recognise a sale. However, if a non-significant risk is retained by a seller this will not normally preclude the recognition of revenue e.g. collectability of the debt.

In most cases, the transfer of legal title coincides with the transfer of risks but in other cases, they may occur at different times. Each transaction must be examined separately.

In certain specific industries e.g. harvesting of crops, extraction of mineral ores, performance may be substantially complete prior to the execution of the transaction generating revenue.

Rendering of services

In rendering services, performance should be measured either under the completed contract method or the percentage of completion method. Performance is achieved if no significant uncertainty exists regarding:

(a) the consideration that will be derived from rendering the service and
(b) the associated costs.

Use by others of enterprise resources yielding interest, royalties and dividends

Revenues yielding interest, royalties and dividends should only be recognised when no significant uncertainty exists as to their measurability or collectability. They are recognised as follows:

- Interest – on a time proportion basis.
- Royalties – on an accruals basis in accordance with the terms of the agreement.
- Dividends – when a right to receive payment is established.

In foreign countries revenue recognition may need to be postponed if exchange permission is required and a delay in remittance is expected.

Effect of uncertainties on revenue recognition

Recognition of revenue requires that revenue is measurable. Where the ability to assess the ultimate collection with reasonable certainty is lacking, revenue recognition is postponed. In such cases, it may be appropriate to recognise revenue only when cash is collected.

If the uncertainty relates to collectability, a more appropriate approach would be to make a separate provision for bad debts.

Uncertainties may involve doubt over the collectability of the consideration, costs or returns and, in all cases, revenue recognition should be postponed if they cannot be adequately measured.

Non-monetary consideration

The fair value of assets/services is normally used to determine the amount of revenue involved.

Disclosure

In addition to normal accounting policy notes, an enterprise should also disclose the circumstances in which revenue recognition has been postponed pending the resolution of significant uncertainties.

Reed Elsevier provides a clear description of their revenue recognition policy covering normal sales, subscriptions and splitting of revenue between independent components.

Reed Elsevier Plc

Revenue

Revenue represents the invoiced value of sales less anticipated returns on transactions completed by performance, excluding customer sales taxes and sales between the combined businesses.

Revenues are recognised for the various categories of turnover as follows: subscriptions – on periodic despatch of subscribed product or ratably over the period of the subscription where performance is not measurable by despatch; circulation – on despatch; advertising – on publication or over the period of online display; exhibitions – on occurrence of the exhibition; educational testing contracts – over the term of the contract on percentage completed against contract milestones.

Where sales consist of two or more independent components, revenue is recognised on each component, as it is completed by performance, based on attribution of relative value.

Below are two further examples of accounting policies. BAT Industries Plc note the exclusion of excise duties from their revenue and concentrate on the transfer of significant risks and rewards to a third party. A slightly more detailed accounting policy note covers construction contracts as well as the elimination of inter-company sales and discounts (Hanson Plc):

BAT Industries Plc

Revenue

Revenue comprises sales of cigarettes, cigars, leaf and other tobacco products to external customers. Revenue excludes duty, excise and other taxes and is after deducting rebates, returns and other similar discounts. Revenue is recognised when the significant risks and rewards of ownership are transferred to a third party.

Hanson Plc

Turnover

Turnover is recognised by the group when the risks and rewards associated with the transaction have been transferred to the purchaser which is demonstrated when all the following conditions are most evident of a binding arrangement existence (generally, purchase orders): products have been delivered, services have been rendered, there is no future performance required and amounts are collectable under normal payment terms. Turnover represents the net amounts charged or chargeable in respect of services rendered and goods supplied, excluding inter-company sales, VAT and other sales taxes. Turnover is recognised net of any discounts given to the customer. Turnover on long-term construction contracts is recognised as the value of measured works, claims and variations on contracts in the year, based on the stage of completion. Claims and variations are only recognised where they have been agreed with the customer. Where it is foreseen that a loss will arise to the group on a long-term contract, full provision is made for that loss during the year.

6.2   IAS 8 *Accounting Policies Changes in Accounting Estimates and Errors* (December 2003)

The objective of IAS 8 is to prescribe the criteria for selecting and changing accounting policies together with the disclosure and accounting treatment of changes in accounting policies, accounting estimates and corrections of errors. It is also to enhance the relevance and reliability of financial statements and their comparability. It should be applied in selecting and applying accounting policies, and accounting for changes in accounting policies, changes in accounting estimates and corrections of prior period errors.

Definitions

- *Accounting policies.* The specific principles, bases, conventions, rules and practices applied by an entity in preparing and presenting its financial statements.
- *Change in accounting estimate.* An adjustment to the carrying amount of an asset/liability or the amount of the periodic consumption of an asset that results from the assessment of the present status of, and expected future benefits and obligations associated with, assets and liabilities. They are not errors caused by new information or developments.
- *Prior period errors.* Omissions or misstatements for one or more prior periods due to a failure to use or a misuse of reliable information that:
  - (a) was available when financial statements for those periods were authorised and
  - (b) could have reasonably be obtained and taken into account while preparing and presenting those financial statements.

Includes mathematical mistakes, mistakes in applying policies, oversights and fraud.

Accounting policies

Selection and application of accounting policies

Should apply the appropriate standard if it applies specifically to a transaction. In the absence of an IFRS/IAS/SIC, management must use their judgement in developing and applying an accounting policy that results in information that is:

- (a) relevant to the economic decision-making needs of users and
- (b) reliable as it purports faithfully the financial statements, reflects their substance, is neutral, prudent and complete in all material respects.

Management must consider the IFRSs, etc. first and then the framework in deciding the most appropriate policies. They are also encouraged to look to other standard setters having the same framework, accounting literature and accepted industry practice in making their choice.

Consistency of accounting policies

Must adopt consistent accounting policies for similar transactions unless an IFRS/IAS requires a more specific policy to be adopted.

Changes in accounting policies

Can only change an accounting policy if:

- (a) required by an IFRS or IAS or
- (b) it results in financial statements providing more reliable and relevant information about the effects of transactions on the entity's financial position, performance or cash flows.

The following are not changes in accounting policies:

(a) the application of accounting policies for transactions that differ in substance from those previously undertaken and
(b) the application of a new policy that did not occur previously or was immaterial.

Applying changes in accounting policy

On first application of a standard, the change must be applied retrospectively unless specific transitional arrangements in the IFRS/IAS apply.

Opening reserves should be adjusted for the earliest prior period presented as if the new policy had always applied (retrospective application).

If it is impracticable to apply retrospective application to prior periods then the entity should apply the new policy to the carrying amounts of assets and liabilities as at the start of the earliest period for which retrospective application is practicable. That may be the current period.

Disclosure

An entity should disclose the following (unless it is impracticable to determine the amount of the adjustment) on a change of accounting policy:

(a) the title of the standard or SIC/IFRIC;
(b) that the change in policy is made in accordance with any transitional provisions (if applicable);
(c) the nature of the change in accounting policy;
(d) a description of the transitional provisions, if applicable;
(e) the transitional provisions if they have an effect on future periods, if applicable;
(f) for current and prior periods, the amount of the adjustment for each item effected as well as its impact on EPS;
(g) for periods prior to those presented, the impact, if practicable;
(h) if retrospective application is impracticable, the circumstances causing that condition and how the change in policy has been applied.

When a voluntary change in policy affects the current or any prior period but it is impracticable to determine its amount an entity should disclose:

(a) the nature of the change in accounting policy;
(b) the reasons why applying the new policy provides more reliable and relevant information;
(c) for the current and each prior period, to the extent practicable, the amount of the adjustment for each line item effected as well as its impact on EPS;
(d) for periods prior to those presented, the impact, if practicable;
(e) if retrospective application is impracticable, the circumstances causing that condition and how change in policy has been applied.

When an entity has not applied a new IFRS or SIC/IFRIC that is published but not effective, the entity should disclose that fact and estimate the possible impact that its application will have on its financial statements.

Changes in accounting estimates

Many items in financial statements cannot be measured with precision but must be estimated. These involve judgements based on the latest available information. Examples where this would be applied include bad debts, inventory obsolescence, useful lives, warranty obligations and so on.

Estimates need to be revised if circumstances change as a result of new information or experience. A change in measurement base is, however, a change in policy. If it is difficult to distinguish between a policy and an estimate change, then the change should be treated as a change in estimate.

A change in estimate is charged prospectively in the income statement in the current and future years. Any related asset/liability should equally be adjusted in the period of change.

Disclosure

The nature and amount of a change in accounting estimate and its effect on both current and future periods should be disclosed unless the amount is impracticable to estimate. If the amount of the effect on future years is not disclosed, due to impracticality, that fact must be disclosed. Disclosure of future standards to be applied should be provided. The Yell Group provides evidence of this. Yell adopted IFRS for its financial statements from 1 April 2005 and following IFRS 1 *First-time adoption of International Financial Reporting Standards* disclosed information explaining how the transition affected its reported financial position together with reconciliation statements for the year 2005. Profit before tax increased by £80 million caused mainly by elimination of goodwill amortisation and net assets increased from £884 million to £925 million as a result of an increase in goodwill and a derecognition of dividends, offset by recognition of pension deficit.

Following the disclosure requirements of IAS 8 'Accounting policies, changes in accounting estimates and errors', Yell provided information in relation to Standards which had been issued but were not yet effective and stated that no material impact was expected following their future adoption (see below). Additionally, Yell disclosed that it had adopted early the amendment to IAS 19 'Employee benefits' in relation to full recognition of all actuarial gains and losses.

Standards, interpretations and amendments to published standards that are not yet effective

Certain new standards, amendments and interpretations to existing standards have been published that are mandatory for accounting periods beginning on or after 1 April 2006 or later periods but which the Group has chosen not to early adopt. The new standards that could be relevant to the Group's operations are as follows:

IAS 39 (Amendment) Cash Flow Hedge Accounting of Forecast Intragroup Transactions (effective from 1 April 2006)

The amendment allows the foreign currency risk of a highly probable forecast intragroup transaction to qualify as a hedged item in the consolidated financial statements, provided that (a) the transaction is denominated in a currency other than the functional currency of the entity entering into that transaction and (b) the foreign currency risk will affect consolidated income. We do not believe this amendment will have a significant effect on our report of operations.

IAS 39 (Amendment) The Fair Value Option (effective from 1 April 2006)

This amendment changes the definition of financial instruments classified at fair value through income and restricts the ability to designate financial instruments as part of this category. We believe that this amendment should not have a significant impact on the classification of financial instruments, as we should be able to comply with the amended criteria for the designation of financial instruments at fair value through income. We will apply this amendment from annual periods beginning 1 April 2006.

Errors

Material prior period errors should be corrected retrospectively as soon as discovered by:

(a)   restating the comparatives for the prior periods presented or
(b)   if the error occurred before the earliest period presented, by adjusting the opening balances of assets, liabilities and equity for the earliest period presented.

An example of an error and its consequential prior period adjustment is provided by AGI Therapeutics Plc:

AGI Therapeutics Plc

Income statement	Notes	2005 (€)	2004 (as restated) (€)
For the year ended 31 December 2005			
Revenue		–	–
Cost of sales		–	–
Gross profit		–	–
Research and development costs		(4,369,045)	(2,341,497)
Administration expenses		(230,583)	(361,867)
Operating loss from continuing operations		(4,599,628)	(2,703,364)
Finance revenue	3	104,723	140,000
Finance costs	4	(705,322)	(558,069)

		2005	2004
Loss from continuing operations Before taxation	5	(5,200,227)	(3,121,433)
Tax expense	6	–	–
Loss for the year from continuing operations		(5,200,227)	(3,121,433)
Retained loss brought forward As previously stated Prior year adjustments	7	(3,439,032) 317,599	– –
Restated loss brought forward		(3,121,433)	–
Retained loss carried forward		(8,321,660)	(3,121,433)

7.   Prior Year Adjustment

	2005 (€)	2004 (€)
Reversal of transaction costs	238,000	–
Reversal of amortisation of intangible assets	79,599	–
	317,599	–

7.1   The financial statements have been adjusted to reflect the correction of error made in the financial statements for the year ended 31 December 2004, which has led to the restatements of the 2004 results. This arose due to amount of €238,000 being charged to the income statement rather than the reduction of the share premium arising on issue of ordinary preference shares.

7.2   The financial statements have been restated to reverse amounts amortised in-process research and development, which were incorrectly amortised in the prior year. This results in a reversal of €79,599 against administration expenses in the income statement.

Limitations on retrospective restatement

An error should be corrected retrospectively unless impracticable. If that is the case, the entity must restate the opening balances of assets, liabilities and equity for the earliest period for which retrospective restatement is practicable.

If impracticable to determine the cumulative impact for all prior periods, the entity shall restate the comparative information to correct the error prospectively from the earliest date practicable.

The correction of prior period errors are not included in arriving at the profit or loss for the year.

Disclosure of prior period errors

The following should be disclosed:

(a) the nature of the prior period error;
(b) for each prior period presented, to the extent practicable, the amount of the correction for each line item affected and for EPS;
(c) the amount of the correction at the start of the earliest period presented;
(d) if retrospective application is impracticable, the circumstances that led to the existence of that condition and a description of how and from when the error has been corrected.

This is only required in the year of discovery. It is not required in future years.

6.3   IAS 33 *Earnings Per Share* (October 1998)

Background

One of the key financial ratios adopted by financial analysts has been the price/earnings ratio (P/E ratio). It is a widely used performance indicator and is published in the *Financial Times* on a daily basis. If the P/E ratio starts to veer away from the 'norm' for the industrial sector concerned, analysts may well advise their fund managers to sell shares in the company, resulting in a fall in the share price of that company and its overall value to shareholders.

The P/E ratio is defined as:

$$\frac{\text{Current market share price}}{\text{Earnings per share}} \quad \text{e.g.} \quad \frac{580\text{p}}{72.5\text{p}} = 8$$

In the example above it would take an investor eight years of current earnings of 72.5p to recover the initial investment of 580p.

IAS 33 was published to clarify and standardise the calculation of the bottom line of that ratio, earnings per share (EPS), which is published at the foot of the income statement for every listed company in their annual report. This should serve to enhance comparability across listed companies. It only applies to listed companies, although if published by unlisted companies, the calculations must be the same.

Definition

Basic earnings per share should be calculated by dividing the net profit or loss for the period attributable to ordinary shareholders by the weighted average number of ordinary shares outstanding during the period.

IAS 33 also permits the adoption of alternative EPS figures based on other versions of profits. If adopted, a listed company must reconcile the alternative EPS back to the official EPS by itemising and quantifying the adjustments. The additional version must not be disclosed on the face of the income statement.

A further alternative EPS may be calculated based on the first *Statement of Investment Practice* published by the Institute of Investment Management and Research (IIMR), which excludes non-trading items, such as the profits/losses on termination of a discontinued operation, profits/losses on the sale of fixed assets and any permanent diminutions in the value of fixed assets from the calculation of earnings. It is, therefore, now possible to calculate three different basic versions of EPS – the official, alternative and IIMR.

Basic earnings per share – Problems

Preference dividends unpaid

Deduct if cumulative or if participating (fixed proportion).

The discount/premium on any increasing rate preference shares should be included as part of the finance cost for non-equity shares.

Example – Increasing rate preference dividends

An entity issued non-convertible, non-redeemable class A cumulative preference shares of 100 par value on 1 January 2001. They are entitled to a 7% annual dividend, starting in 2004.

The market rate dividend yield, in 2001, was 7%. To compensate for no dividend for three years the shares are issued at 81.63 (a discount of 18.37 – present value of 100 discounted at 7% over three years).

The discount is amortised to income and treated as a preference dividend. The following imputed dividend is deducted:

	Carrying value 1 January 2001	Imputed dividend	Carrying value 31 December	Dividend paid
2001	81.63	5.71	87.34	
2002	87.34	6.12	93.46	
2003	93.46	6.54	100.00	
Thereafter	100.00	7.00	107.00	(7.00)

Losses

Should still calculate losses per share in the same manner as earnings.

Changes in share capital

(i)   Issue at full market price.
(ii) Capitalisation or bonus issue.
(iii) Share-for-share exchange.
(iv) Rights issue at less than market price.

(i)   *Issue at full market price*

Where new equity shares are issued for cash at full market price, the new shares should be included on a weighted average time basis on the grounds that the cash received will generate earnings only for the period after the cash is received.

EXAMPLE

	Normal	
Earnings year 2	£10m	Assume 1:5 full market price issue at £2/share on 30.6.08
Number of shares prior to issue	5m	
Earnings per share	£2	
Weighted average shares	1m × 1/2 year = 0.5m + 5m = 5.5m	

Assume earnings of £10m incorporate additional earnings boosted by the cash received for the second half of the year.

Earnings £10m ÷ 5.5m = £1.81 per share

(ii) *Capitalisation or bonus issue*

Where new equity shares are issued by way of conversion of reserves into equity capital, no increase in earnings has occurred but the bottom line has increased. To ensure comparability with prior years both the current and prior year are boosted *in full* by the issue of shares regardless of the date of issue.

EXAMPLE

	Normal	
Earnings year 2	£10m	Assume 1:5 bonus issue on 30.6.08
Number of shares prior to issue	5m	
Earnings per share	£2	
Shares	1m × full year = 1m + 5m = 6m	

Assume earnings of £10m are unaffected by the issue of shares as no cash has been received.

Earnings £10m ÷ 6m = £1.67 per share

Assume prior year EPS was £1.8, then prior year EPS is restated to £1.8 × 5/6 = £1.5.

(iii) *Share-for-share exchange*

Where shares are exchanged in an acquisition for shares in the acquiree the shares are assumed to be included on a weighted average basis from the period from which the profits of the acquiree are included in the consolidated accounts.

EXAMPLE

Earnings year 2	£10m	Original shares	5m
Earnings of acquiree		Shares in exchange	
(1.4–31.12 only)	£4m	(4m × 3/4)	3m
	£14m	8m	

Earnings per share £14m÷8m shares = £1.75 per share

(iv) *Rights issue*

Where shares are issued at a discount from their normal market price, the issue of shares is really a mixture of a full market price issue and a free bonus issue, i.e. a mixture of (i) and (ii) above.

EXAMPLE

	Normal	
Earnings year 2	£10m	Assume 1:5 rights issue on 31.03.04 @ £4 per share
Number of shares pre-rights issue	5m	(i.e. discount of 20% from market price of £5 per share)
Earnings per share	£2	

Number of shares pre-rights	5m @	£5 cum	£25m
Rights issue (1:5)	1m @	£4	£4m
Total shares	6m	£4.83	£29m

Adjustment factor £5/£4.83 = 1.035

Pre-rights	5m × 1.035 × 1/4 year = 1.294m
Post-rights	6m × 3/4 year = 4.500m
	5.794m

Earnings per share £10m ÷ 5.794m = £1.73 per share

Prior year (say £9m ÷ 5m) adjusted £9m ÷ (5m × 1.035) = £1.74 per share

Diluted earnings per share – Problems

If a company has issued a separate class of equity shares which do not rank immediately for dividends in the current period (but will do so in the future), or if it has certain types of convertible loans or warrants which have the right to convert into ordinary shares at some future date, then these may well dilute earnings per share in the future. Users of financial statements should therefore be made aware of their likely impact.

As a result, a second version of EPS is required to be disclosed on the face of the income statement, if the diluted EPS is either equal to or below the basic EPS. It is not disclosed above basic EPS as it is argued that it will not happen because it would not be in the interests of the holders of those securities to exercise their rights.

There are three main types of diluting instrument:

(i)   Convertible preference shares.
(ii)   Convertible loan stock.
(iii) Share options or warrants.

(i)   *Convertible preference shares*
       There will be a saving in preference dividends and holders are assumed to transfer at the best conversion rate.

EXAMPLE

Basic earnings per share (assume)	£1.50	10% convertible preference shares	1m
Basic share structure (assume)	2m	(convertible 0.5 ordinary for every £1	
Basic earnings	£3m	ordinary)	

Diluted earnings per share £3m + £0.1m = £3.1m ÷ (2m + 0.5m) = £1.24 per share, which is dilutive and therefore must be disclosed.

(ii) *Convertible loan stock*

There will be a saving in interest payments but because these are tax allowable the company will also lose the tax relief that it is currently saving. The net interest to be saved is therefore added back to basic earnings.

The bottom line will be increased by the maximum shares, which the loan holders can earn if they convert into equity.

EXAMPLE

Basic earnings (as above)	£3.00m	£4m 8% convertible loan stocks convertible as follows (assume tax at 30%):
Add net interest saved	£2.24m	
	£5.24m	1.0m year 5
		1.2m year 6
		1.5m year 7
		2.0m year 8
Basic shares (assume)	2m	
Add convertible loans	2m	
(£4m × year 8 = 2m)	4m	
Basic earnings per share	£3m ÷ 2m = £1.50 per share	
Diluted earnings per share	£5.24m ÷ 4m = £1.31 per share, a dilution and therefore disclosable	

(iii) *Share options*

The company is assumed to have to pay out shares to their employees/directors at an exercise price which is lower than current market, thus resulting in a dilution in earnings for existing shareholders. No dividends or interest are currently being paid to option holders, so no adjustment is made to the top line of the ratio.

The bottom line is assumed to be increased by the discounted element of the number of shares to be issued.

EXAMPLE

Assume that there are 5m of share options. Option holders can exercise their rights at a price of £2 per share. Currently the shares have a market value of £3 each.

Basic and adjusted earnings		£3m
Basic shares (assume)	2m	
Share options 5m×1/3rd	1.67m	
Total shares		3.67m
Basic earnings per share	£3m ÷ 2m = £1.50 per share	
Diluted earnings per share	£3m ÷ 3.67m = £0.82 per share, a dilution and therefore disclosable	

IAS 33 also provides guidance on the order in which to include dilutive securities in the calculation of the weighted average number of shares.

Example – Determining the order in which to include dilutive securities in the calculation of weighted average number of shares

Earnings	£
Net profit attributable to continuing operations	16,400,000
Less preference dividends	(6,400,000)
Profit from continuing operations attributable	
To ordinary shareholders	10,000,000
Loss from discontinued operations	(4,000,000)
Net profit attributable to ordinary shareholders	6,000,000
Ordinary shares outstanding	2 m
Average market price of one ordinary share during year	£75

Potential ordinary shares	
Options	100,000 with exercise price of £60
Convertible preference shares	800,000 convertible 2:1
	£8 per share cumulative dividend
5% Convertible bond	100 m each 1,000 convertible into 20 ordinary shares
Tax rate	40%

Increase in earnings attributable to ordinary shareholders on conversion of potential ordinary shares

	Increase in earnings (£)	Increase in number of ordinary shares	Earnings per incremental share (£)
Options			
Increase in earnings	Nil		
Incremental shares			
100,000 × (75 − 60)/75		20,000	Nil
Convertible preference shares			
Increase in earnings			
8 × 800,000	6,400,000		
Incremental shares			
2 × 800,000		1,600,000	4
5% Convertible bonds			
Increase in earnings			
100m × 5% × 0.6	3,000,000		
Incremental shares		2,000,000	1.50

Ranking – (1) options, (2) convertible loans, (3) convertible preference shares

Computation of diluted earnings per share

	Net profit attributable (£)	Ordinary shares	Per share (£)
As reported	10,000,000	2,000,000	5.00
Options		20,000	
	10,000,000	2,020,000	4.95 dilutive
5% Convertible bonds	3,000,000	2,000,000	
	13,000,000	4,020,000	3.23 dilutive
Convertible preference shares	6,400,000	1,600,000	
	19,400,000	5,620,000	3.45 antidilutive

The convertible preference shares are ignored in calculating the dilutive earnings per share as they are antidilutive.

Computation of basic and diluted earnings per share

	Basic	Diluted
Profit from continuing operations	£5.00	£3.23
Loss from discontinued operations	*(2.00)	*(0.99)
Net profit	£3.00	£2.24

*(£4,000,000 ÷ 2m) = (£2.00)
 (£4,000,000 ÷ 4.02m) = (£0.99)

Example – Dundrum Plc

The directors of Dundrum plc have supplied you with summarised income statement information for the years ended 30 September 2007 and 2008 as follows:

	30 September 2008 (£'000)	30 September 2007 (£'000)
Profit before tax	1,747	1,492
Taxation	(523)	(395)
Profit after tax	1,224	1,097
Minority interests	(87)	(57)
Dividends – ordinary	(100)	(100)
preference	(35)	–
	1,002	940

The figure of profit after taxation for the year ended 30 September 2008 supplied to you is after charging exceptional items of £279,000 net of taxation.

The earnings per share for the year ended 30 September 2007 was disclosed as 10.40p, there having been no changes in the number of shares in issue during that year.

On 1 January 2008, the company had a one-for-four rights issue at 60p per share which was fully subscribed. The price at the close of trading on 31 December 2007 was 84p and 10,000,000 50p ordinary shares were in issue at that date.

On 1 July 2008, to raise funds for additional working capital, the company issued a package of units each comprising one £1.7% convertible preference share plus one warrant for one ordinary share. The issue realised a total of £2.4 million with the preference shares being issued at a premium of 20p. The conversion terms were as follows:

£100 nominal preference shares in June 2018	110 ordinary 50p shares
or in June 2019	120 ordinary 50p shares
or in June 2020	130 ordinary 50p shares

and one warrant for one ordinary share with the consideration being 60p at the date on which the holder exercises his conversion rights.

The dividend on the preference shares is declared annually on 30 June. The price of 2.5% consolidated stock at 30 June 2008 was 27 × d.

Assume a corporation tax rate of 35%.

Suggested solution – Dundrum Plc

Calculation of basic earnings per share

2008	£'000	£'000
Earnings		
Profits after taxation		1,224
Less minority interests	87	
Preference dividends	35	
		122
		1,102

IAS 33: computation of adjustment factor

$$\frac{(10\text{m} \times 84\text{p}) + (2.5\text{m} \times 60\text{p})}{10\text{m} + 2.5\text{m}} = 79.2\text{p}$$

$$\frac{\text{Cum } 84.0\text{p}}{\text{Ex } 79.2\text{p}} = 1.06$$

$$\begin{aligned}4 \times 84\text{p} &= 3.36 \\ 1 \times 60\text{p} &= 0.60 \\ \overline{5} \times 79.2\text{p} &\ \overline{3.96}\end{aligned}$$

$$\frac{£1,102,000}{(10\text{m} \times 1.06 \times 3/12) + (12.5\text{m} \times 9/12)} = 9.2\text{p} \quad \text{or} \quad \frac{£1,102,000}{12,027,000}$$

Calculation of diluted earnings per share   IAS 33

2008	£'000
Earnings	
Basic earnings (as above)	1,102
Add saving on preference dividend	35
	1,137

Number of shares	
Basic number of shares	12,027
Add preference shares 1.7.07	
£2.4m ÷ £1.20 = 2,000,000 × 1.3 (highest conversion)	
= 2,600,000 × 1/4 year issue	650
Warrants 2,000,000 (as above) × 1/4 year × $\frac{24p}{84p}$ discount	
	142,847
	12,819.847

Note also the need, under IAS 33, to disclose both basic and diluted earnings per share on an inclusive and exclusive basis of discontinued operations.

IAS 33: Calculation of Diluted Earnings Per Share

Increase in earnings attributable to ordinary shareholders on conversion of potential ordinary shares

	Increase in earnings £'000	Increase in number of ordinary shares £'000	Earnings per incremental share £'000
Warrants			
Increase in earnings	Nil		
Incremental shares issued for no consideration			
2,000,000 × ((84p − 60p) ÷ 84p) × 1/4		142.847	Nil[1]
Preferences shares			
Increase in net profit	35		
Incremental shares		650 (1/4 × 2,600)	5.38[2]

Computation of diluted earnings per share

	Net profit attributable £	Ordinary shares £	Earnings per incremental share £
As reported	1,102,000	12,027,000	9.2p
Warrants	–	142,857	
	1,102,000	12,169,857	9.06p
Convertible preference shares	35,000	650,000	
	1,137,000	12,819,857	8.87p

The diluted earnings per share is 8.87p and *must* be disclosed under IAS 33.

The second example is more complicated as it includes the issue of both bonus and full market issues of ordinary shares during the year as well as the requirement to use the ranking process in determining the order in which dilutable securities should be brought into the calculation of diluted earnings per share. The example includes both profits from continuing and from discontinued operations, the latter of which must initially be excluded in the calculation of diluted earnings per share. Under the revised IAS 33 *Earnings Per Share*, the diluted earnings per share will have to be calculated twice, one inclusive and one exclusive of discontinued operations. The example, therefore, covers most of the situations likely to be encountered in practice.

Example – Mourne Plc

The following financial statement extracts for the year ended 31 May 2007 relate to Mourne, a public limited company.

	£'000	£'000
Operating profit		
Continuing operations	26,700	
Discontinued operations	(1,120)	25,580
Continuing operations		
Profit on disposal of property, plant and equipment		2,500
Discontinued operations		
(Loss) on sale of operations		(5,080)
		23,000
Interest payable		(2,100)
Profit on ordinary activities before taxation		20,900
Tax on ordinary activities		(7,500)
Profit on ordinary activities after tax		13,400
Minority interests – equity		(540)
Profit attributable to members of parent company		12,860
Dividends:		
Preference dividend on non-equity shares	290	
Ordinary dividend on equity shares	300	
		(590)
Retained profit for year		12,270

Capital as at 31 May 2007	£'000
Allotted, called-up and fully paid ordinary shares of £1 each	12,500
7% convertible redeemable preference shares of £1	3,000
	15,500

Additional information

(1) On 1 January 2007, 3.6 million ordinary shares were issued at £2.50 in consideration of the acquisition of June Ltd for £9 million. These shares do not rank for dividend in the current period. Additionally, the company purchased and cancelled £2.4 million of its own £1 ordinary shares on 1 April 2007. On 1 July 2007, the company made a bonus issue of one for five ordinary shares before the financial statements were issued for the year ended 31 May 2007.

(2) The company has a share option scheme under which certain directors can subscribe for the company's shares. The following details relate to the scheme: Options outstanding 31 May 2006:
   (i)   1.2 million ordinary shares at £2 each;
   (ii) 2 million ordinary shares at £3 each, both sets of options are exercisable before 31 May 2008.

   Options granted during the year 31 May 2007:
   One million ordinary shares at £4 each exercisable before 31 May 2010, granted 1 June 2006.
   During the year to 31 May 2007, the options relating to the 1.2 million ordinary shares (at a price of £2) were exercised on 1 March 2007.
   The average fair value of one ordinary share during the year was £5.

(3) The convertible cumulative redeemable preference shares are convertible at the option of the shareholder or the company on 1 July 2008, 2009, 2010 on the basis of two ordinary shares for every three preference shares. The preference share dividends are not in arrears. The shares are redeemable at the option of the shareholder on 1 July 2008, 2009, 2010 at £1.50 per share. The 'other appropriations – non-equity shares' item charged against the profits relates to the amortisation of the redemption premium and issue costs on the preference shares.

(4) Mourne issued £6 million of 6% convertible bonds on 1 June 2006 to finance the acquisition of Saintfield Ltd. Each bond is convertible into two ordinary shares of £1. Assume a corporation tax rate of 35%.

(5) The interest payable relates entirely to continuing operations and the taxation charge relating to discontinued operations is assessed at £100,000 despite the accounting losses. The loss on discontinued operations relating to the minority interest is £600,000.

Suggested solution – Mourne Plc

Earnings per share – basic

		£'000
Profit attributable to members of parent company		12,860
Less: Preference dividend	(290)	
		(290)
Basic earnings		12,570
Weighted average number of shares ('000)		

	Shares	Weight	No.
1 June 2006	10,100	1.0	10,100
1 January 2007	3,600	5/12	1,500
(Note 1 – non-ranking)			
1 March 2007	1,200	3/12	300
1 April 2007	(2,400)	2/12	(400)
	12,500		11,500
Bonus issue (post-year/end but prior to issue) (1:5)			2,300
			13,800

Basic earnings $\dfrac{12.570}{13.800} \times 100 = 91.08\,\text{p}$

Weighted average shares

Diluted earnings per share

	£'000
Basic earnings	12,570
Add: Interest saved on 6% convertible bonds	234
Preference dividends	290
	13,094
Number of shares	29,340

Diluted earnings per share $\dfrac{13,094}{29,340} \times 100$ 44.6p

Ranking of dilutive securities

	Increase in earnings (£'000)	Increase in shares (£'000)	Increase in earnings/share (£'000)
Options	Nil	$1,000 \times \dfrac{5-4}{5} = 200$	Nil
		$2,000 \times \dfrac{5-3}{5} = 800\checkmark$	
		$1,200 \times \dfrac{9}{12} \times \dfrac{5-2}{5} = 540$	Nil
Convertible preference shares	290	$3,000 \times 2/3 = 2,000$	£0.145
Convertible bonds (6% × 6,000 × 65%)	234	$6,000 \times 2 = 12,000$	£0.0112
Basic shares		15,540	
		13,800	
		29,340	

Ranking – 1 options, 2 convertible bonds and 3 convertible preference shares

Computation of dilutive/antidilutive EPS

	£'000	Ordinary shares	Per share
Net profit from continuing operations	18,270	13,800	132p
Options	Nil	1,540	
	18,270	15,340	119p dilutive
6% bonds	234	12,000	
	18,504	27,340	67.7p dilutive
Convertible preference shares	290	2,000	
	18,794	29,340	64.1 dilutive

		£'000
Net profit from continuing operations		
Profit as per basic		12,860
Add discontinued loss (1,120 + 100)		1,220
Loss on sale of operations (5,080 − 600)		4,480
Non-equity shares appropriations		(290)
Net profit from continuing operations		18,270

Presentation

Basic and diluted EPS should be presented on the face of the income statement with equal prominence given to both ratios. If diluted EPS is necessary, then it must be provided for all periods presented.

The basic and diluted EPS for a discontinued operation, for both basic and diluted, should be disclosed either on the face of the income statement or in the notes.

The standard requires an entity to present basic and diluted EPS, even if the amounts are negative (i.e. loss per share).

Disclosure

An entity shall disclose the following:

(a) Amounts used in the numerators and a reconciliation to net profit/loss.
(b) The weighted average number of ordinary shares used as the denominator in calculating basic and diluted EPS and a reconciliation to each other.
(c) Instruments that could potentially dilute basic EPS but were not included in the diluted EPS as antidilutive at present.
(d) a description of ordinary share transactions that occur after the balance sheet date but before the issue of the financial statements that would significantly change the number of ordinary shares outstanding at the end of the period had they occurred before the end of the reporting period.

Examples included in (d) would include:

- the issue of shares for cash;
- the issue of shares as part of a repayment of debt or preference shares;

- the redemption of ordinary shares outstanding;
- the conversion or exercise of potential ordinary shares into ordinary;
- the issue of warrants, options or convertible securities;
- the achievement of conditions that would result in the issue of contingently issuable shares.

The disclosure of terms and conditions should be encouraged as they may determine whether any potential ordinary shares are dilutive.

If an entity discloses amounts per share in addition to basic and dilutive EPS required by IAS 33, they should be calculated using the weighted average number of ordinary shares. Equal prominence should be presented for basic and diluted amounts per share and presented in the notes. An entity should indicate the basis on which the numerator is determined and if a component is used that is not reported as a line item, a reconciliation should be provided between the component and the line item in the income statement. A good example of an accounting policy and detailed disclosure of calculation required by IAS 33 is provided by UTV Plc:

UTV Plc   Year Ended 31 December 2005

11. Earnings Per Share

Basic earnings per share is calculated based on the profit for the financial year attributable to equity holders of the parent and on the weighted average number of shares in issue during the period.

Adjusted earnings per share is calculated based on the profit for the financial year attributable to equity holders of the parent adjusted for the exceptional items and foreign exchange recorded in the year. This calculation uses the weighted average number of shares in issue during the period.

Diluted earnings per share is calculated based on profit for the financial year attributable to equity holders of the parent after adjusting for the net interest payable on the Convertible Loan Notes. The weighted average number of shares is adjusted to reflect the dilutive potential of the Convertible Loan Notes and the Share Option Schemes.

Diluted adjusted earnings per share is calculated based on profit for the financial year attributable to equity holders of the parent before exceptional items and foreign exchange, and after adjusting for the net interest payable on the Convertible Loan Notes. The weighted average number of shares is adjusted to reflect the dilutive potential of the Convertible Loan Notes and the Share Option Schemes.

The following reflects the income and share data used in the basic, adjusted, diluted and diluted adjusted earnings per share calculations:

Net profit	2005 (£'000)	2004 (£'000)
Net profit attributable to equity holders	14,356	12,590
Net interest on convertible loan notes	–	24
Net profit attributable to ordinary shareholders for diluted earnings per share	14,356	12,614
Exceptional costs	1,235	–
Foreign exchange gains	(413)	–
Taxation relating to above items	(247)	–
Net profit attributable to ordinary shareholders for adjusted diluted earnings per share	14,931	12,614
Net interest on convertible loan notes	–	(24)
Net profit attributable to ordinary shareholders for adjusted earnings per share	14,931	12,590

Weighted average number of shares	2005 Thousands	2004 Thousands
Weighted average number of shares for basic and adjusted earnings per share	54,423	53,904
Effect of dilution:		
• Share options		
• Convertible Loan Notes	597	609
	–	314
Adjusted weighted average number of ordinary shares for diluted earnings per share	55,020	54,827

Earnings per share	2005	2004
Diluted	26.09p	23.01p
Basic	26.38p	23.36p
Adjusted	27.43p	23.36p
Diluted adjusted	27.14p	23.01p

Note the use of an adjusted EPS beyond that required by the standard.

The second example, from Glanbia Plc provides a more detailed explanation of how both basic and diluted EPS were calculated.

Glanbia Plc   Year Ended 31 December 2005

14. Earnings Per Share

Basic

Basic earnings per share is calculated by dividing the net profit attributable to equity holders of the Company by the weighted average number of ordinary shares in issue during the year excluding ordinary shares purchased by the Group and held as treasury shares (Note 28):

	2005 (€'000)	2004 (€'000)
Profit attributable to equity holders of the Company	61.327	61,119
Weighted average number of ordinary shares in issue	291,469,902	290,617,359
Basic earnings per share (cent per share)	21.04	21.03

The basic earnings per share, excluding the result of discontinued operations, for the year 2004 is 21.58 cent per share.

Diluted

Diluted earnings per share is calculated by adjusting the weighted average number of ordinary shares outstanding to assume conversion of all dilutive potential ordinary shares. Share options are dilutive potential ordinary shares. In respect of share options, a calculation is done to determine the number of shares that could have been acquired at fair value (determined as the average annual market share price of the Company's shares) based on the monetary value of the subscription rights attached to outstanding share options. The number of shares calculated is compared with the number of shares that would have been issued assuming the exercise of the share options.

	2005	2004
Weighted average number of ordinary shares in issue	291,469,902	290,617,359
Adjustments for share options	1,134,139	1,532,995
Adjusted weighted average number of ordinary shares	292,604,041	292,150,354
Diluted earnings per share (cent per share)	20.96	20.92

The diluted earnings per share, excluding the result of discontinued operations, for the year 2004 is 21.47 cent per share.

At year end options, over 1,505,000 ordinary shares could potentially dilute basic earnings per share in the future but are antidilutive during the year ended 31 December 2005.

Adjusted	2005 (€'000)	2004 (€'000)
Profit attributable to equity holders of the Company	61,327	61,119
Exceptional items	(521)	(1,294)
	60,806	59,825
Adjusted earnings per share (cent per share)	20.86	20.59
Diluted adjusted earnings per share (cent per share)	20.78	20.48

6.4   IFRS 5 *Non-current Assets Held for Sale and Presentation of Discontinued Operations* (March 2004)

The objective of this IFRS is to improve the information about assets and disposal groups that are about to be disposed of and discontinued operations. It does this by specifying:

- the measurement, presentation and disclosure of non-current assets and disposal groups and
- the presentation and disclosure of discontinued operations.

The IFRS applies to all recognised non-current assets except:

(a) deferred tax assets (see IAS 12);
(b) contractual rights under IFRS 4;
(c) assets arising from employee benefits (see IAS 19);
(d) financial assets included within the scope of IAS 39; and
(e) non-current assets under the fair value model in IAS 40.

A disposal group could be a group of cash generating units (CGUs) or part of a CGU. It is really the disposal of a group of assets and liabilities as part of a single transaction.

Classification of non-current assets as held for sale

Classified as such if the asset will be recovered principally through a sale rather than through continuing use. Such a classification is only required when certain criteria are met:

(a) management are committed and have the authority to approve the action to sell;
(b) the asset or disposal groups are available for immediate sale in their present condition subject to the usual terms:

Example

An entity is committed to a plan to sell its headquarters (HQ) and has initiated action to find a buyer.

(a)   The entity intends to transfer the building to a buyer after it vacates the building. The time to vacate is normal. The criterion is met at the plan commitment date.

(b)   The entity will continue to use the building until a new HQ is built. The building will not be transferred until construction is completed. The delay demonstrates that the building is not available for immediate sale and thus the criterion is not met even if a firm purchase commitment is obtained earlier.

Example

An entity is committed to a plan to sell a manufacturing facility and has initiated action to locate a buyer but there is a backlog of customer orders.

(a)   The entity intends to sell the manufacturing facility with its operations. Any uncompleted orders will transfer to the buyer. The criterion will be met at plan commitment date.

(b)   The entity intends to sell the manufacturing facility but without its operations. It does not intend to transfer until it eliminates the backlog of orders. The delay means that the facility is not available for immediate sale and thus the criterion is not met until the operations cease even if a firm purchase commitment was obtained earlier.

Example

An entity acquires a property via foreclosure comprising land and buildings that it intends to sell.

(a)   The entity does not intend to sell until it completes renovations. The delay means the property is not available for immediate sale until the renovations are completed.

(b)   After renovations are completed and the property classified as held for sale, the entity is aware of environmental damage. The property cannot be sold until remediation takes place. The property is thus not available for immediate sale and the criterion would not be met. It would have to be reclassified.

(c)   an active programme to locate a buyer is initiated;

(d)   the sale is highly probable and is expected to qualify for recognition as a completed sale within one year from the date of classification as 'held for sale';

Example

An entity in the power generation industry is committed to plan to sell a disposal group that represents a significant portion of its regulated operations. The sale requires regulatory approval which could extend beyond one year. Actions to obtain approval cannot be initiated until a buyer is located and a firm purchase commitment is obtained. However, the commitment is highly probable and thus it may be classified as 'held for sale' even though it extends beyond one year.

Example

An entity is committed to sell a manufacturing facility but after a firm purchase commitment is obtained, the buyer's inspection identifies environmental damage which must be made good and this will extend beyond one year. However, the entity has initiated remediation and rectification is highly probable hence it can still be classified as 'held for resale'.

Example

An entity is committed to sell a non-current asset and classifies the asset as held for sale at that date:

(a) During the initial one year period, market conditions deteriorate and the asset is not sold within one year and no reasonable offers received. The asset continues to be actively marketed. At the end of the first year the asset would continue to be classified as 'held for sale'.

(b) During the following year, market conditions deteriorate further and the asset is not sold. The sale price has not been reduced and thus, in the absence of a price reduction, the asset is not available for immediate sale and the criterion is therefore not met and the asset will need to be reclassified.

(e) the asset or disposal group is being actively marketed for sale at a reasonable price in relation to its fair value; and

(f) actions required to complete the plan indicate that it is unlikely that significant changes to the plan will be made or the plan will be withdrawn.

As can be seen from some of the examples above, events may extend the period to complete the sale beyond one year. An extension does not preclude an asset or disposal group from being classified as held for sale if the delay is caused by events beyond the entity's control and there is sufficient evidence that the entity remains committed to its plan to sell the asset. As a result, an exception to the one year requirement shall therefore apply in the following situations:

(a)   at the date, an entity commits itself to a plan to sell it reasonably expects that others will impose conditions on the transfer of the asset that will extend the period beyond one year, and:
- actions cannot be initiated until after a firm purchase commitment is obtained and
- a firm purchase commitment is highly probable within one year;

(b)   an entity obtains a firm purchase commitment and a buyer unexpectedly imposes conditions to extend the period beyond one year, and:
- timely actions necessary to respond have been taken and
- a favourable resolution of the delaying factors is expected;

(c)   during the initial one year period, circumstances arise which were previously considered unlikely:
- during the initial one year the entity took action to respond to change in circumstances and
- the non-current asset is being actively marketed given change in circumstances; and
- the criteria in (a) to (f) above are met.

When an entity acquires a non-current asset exclusively with a view to subsequent disposal, it shall classify the non-current asset as held for sale at the acquisition date only if the one year is met and it is highly probable that any other criteria that are not met will be met within a short period following the acquisition.

If the criteria are met after the balance sheet date, but before they are authorised, an entity shall not classify a non-current asset as held for sale. However, the entity should disclose the information in the notes.

Impairment losses and subsequent increases in fair values less costs to sell off assets that were previously revalued

Any asset carried at a revalued amount under another IFRS shall be revalued under that IFRS immediately before it is classified as held for sale under this IFRS. Any impairment loss that arises on reclassification of the asset shall be recognised in the income statement.

Subsequent impairment losses

Any subsequent increases in costs to sell should be recorded in income. Any decreases in fair value should be treated as revaluation decreases in accordance with the IFRS under which the assets were revalued before their classification as held for sale.

Subsequent gains

Any subsequent decreases in costs to sell should be recognised in income. For individual assets that were revalued prior to classification were revalued under another IFRS, any subsequent increase should be treated as a revaluation increase. For disposal groups, any subsequent increases in fair value should be recognised to the extent that the carrying value of the non-current assets in the group after the increase has been allocated does not exceed their fair value less costs to sell. The increase should be treated as a revaluation increase in accordance with the IFRS under which the assets were revalued.

Non-current assets to be abandoned

These are not included as 'held for sale' as it will be recovered through use. However, if the disposal group to be abandoned is a component of an entity than the entity shall present the results and cash flows of the disposal group as discontinued on the date it ceases to be used.

A non-current asset that has been temporarily taken out of use as if abandoned should not be accounted for.

Example

An entity ceases to use a manufacturing plant because demand has declined. However, the plant is maintained in workable condition and it is expected to be brought back into use if demand picks up. It is not therefore abandoned.

Example

In October 2007, an entity decides to abandon all of its cotton mills (major line of business). All work stops during 2008. For 2007, the results and cash flows should be treated as continuing operations but in 2008, the entity discloses the information for discontinued operations including a restatement of any comparative figures.

Measurement of a Non-current asset (or disposal group) classified as held for sale

An entity should measure a non-current asset (or disposal group) classified as 'held for sale' at the lower of its carrying amount and fair value less costs to sell.

If a newly acquired asset meets the criteria as 'held for sale', it should be measured initially at fair value less costs to sell.

Where, rarely, the sale takes more than one year to complete, it should be measured at present value.

The carrying amounts of any assets not covered by the IFRS but included in a disposal group should be measured in accordance with other IFRSs before the fair value less costs to sell is measured.

For assets that have not been revalued an entity should recognise:

(a)   an impairment loss for any initial write-down to fair value less costs to sell and
(b)   a gain for any subsequent increase in fair value less costs to sell but not in excess of the cumulative impairment loss recognised under this IFRS.

Changes to a plan of sale

If previously classified as 'held for sale' but now the criteria are no longer met, then the entity should cease to classify the asset or group as 'held for sale'.

On cessation as 'held for sale' a non-current asset should be valued at the lower of its:

1. carrying amount before the asset or group was classified, as adjusted for depreciation that would have been recognised had the asset not been classified and
2. its recoverable amount at the date of the subsequent decision not to sell.

The entity should include, in income from continuing operations, any required adjustments to the carrying value of a non-current asset that ceases to be classified as held for sale.

Presentation and disclosure

Information should be presented to enable users to evaluate the financial effects of discontinued operations and disposals of non-current assets.

Presenting discontinuing operations

A component of an entity comprises operations and cash flows that can clearly be distinguished from the rest of the entity. It may be a CGU or any group of CGUs.

A discontinued operation is a component of an entity that has either been disposed of or is classified as 'held for sale' and:

(a) represents a separate major line of business or geographical area of operations;
(b) is part of a single coordinated plan to dispose of a separate major line of business or geographical area of operations or
(c) is a subsidiary acquired exclusively with a view to resale.

An entity shall disclose for all periods presented:

(a) Single amount on the face of the income statement comprising:
 • Post-tax profit/loss of discontinued operations;
 • Post-tax gains/losses on measurement to fair value or on disposal of discontinued operations;
(b) Analysis of (a) into:
 • revenue, expenses and pre-tax profits/losses of discontinued operations;
 • related tax expense;
 • gains/losses on measurement to fair value or on disposal of discontinued operations; and
 • related tax expense;
(c) The net cash flows attributable to the operating, investing and financing activities of discontinued operations.

The disclosures required by (a) must be on the face of the income statement but the others may be presented in the notes or on the face of the income statement.

Prior periods for disclosures (a) to (c) are also required.

Adjustment to previous discontinued operations of prior periods should be classified separately e.g. resolution of uncertainties.

Example – XYZ Group – Income Statement for the year ended 31 December 20 × 2 (by function)

Continuing operations	20 X 2	20 X 1
Revenue	X	X
Cost of sales	(X)	(X)
Gross profit	X	X
Other income	X	X
Distribution costs	(X)	(X)
Administrative expenses	(X)	(X)
Other expenses	(X)	(X)
Finance costs	(X)	(X)
Share of profit of associates	X	X
Profit before tax	X	X
Income tax expense	(X)	(X)
Profit for the period from continuing operations	X	X
Discontinued operations		
Profit for the period from discontinued operations*	X	X
Profit for the period	X	X
Attributable to:		
Equity holders of the parent	X	X
Minority interest	X	X
	X	X

*The required analysis would be given in the notes.

Gains or losses relating to continuing operations

Any gain/loss on remeasurement of a non-current asset that does not meet the definition of a component shall be included in the profit/loss from continuing operations.

Presentation of a non-current asset or disposal group classified as held for sale

These should be separately disclosed from other assets. The liabilities of a disposal group classified as 'held for sale' shall be presented separately from other liabilities. These assets and liabilities must all not be offset but separately disclosed on the face of the balance sheet.

A good example of disclosure and presentation of IFRS 5 has been provided by Cadbury Schweppes Plc:

Cadbury Schweppes Plc   Period for the 52 Weeks Ended 1 January 2006

Consolidated Income Statement for the 52 weeks ended 1 January 2006 (Note 1)

Notes		2005 (£m)	2004 (£m)
	Continuing operations		
2	Revenue	6,508	6,085
3	Trading coils	(5,452)	(5,131)
4	Restructuring costs	(72)	(140)
15	Amortisation and impairment of intangibles	(6)	(7)
5	Non-trading items	25	18
	Profit from operations	**1,003**	**825**
17	Share of result in associates	28	22
	Profit before financing and taxation	**1,031**	**847**
9	Investment revenue	42	48
10	Finance costs	(230)	(253)
	Profit before taxation	**843**	**642**
11	Taxation	(140)	145
	Profit for the period from continuing operations	**703**	**497**
32	Discontinued operations		
	Profit for the period from discontinued operations	73	50
	Profit for the period	**776**	**547**
	Attributable to:		
	Equity holders of the parent	765	525
	Minority interests	11	22
		776	547
	Earnings per share		
	From continuing and discontinued operations		
13	Basic	37.3p	25.9p
13	Diluted	36.9p	25.7p
	From continuing operations		
13	Basic	33.8p	23.4p
13	Diluted	33.4p	23.3p

Consolidated Balance Sheet at 1 January 2006 (Note 1)

Notes		2005 (£m)	2004 (£m)
	Assets		
	Non-current assets		

14	Goodwill	2,299	2,352
15	Brand intangibles	3,200	3,261
15	Software intangibles	149	144
16	Property, plant and equipment	1,446	1,464
17	Investment in associates	372	324
24	Deferred tax assets	123	17
20	Trade and other receivables	70	67
18	Other investments	2	11
		7,661	**7,640**
	Current assets		
19	Inventories	713	709
	Short-term investments	47	21
20	Trade and other receivables	1,180	1,150
	Tax recoverable	47	30
	Cash and cash equivalents	332	325
28	Derivative financial instruments	67	–
		2,386	**2,235**
21	Assets held for sale	945	5
	Total assets	**10,992**	**9,880**
	Liabilities		
	Current liabilities		
22	Trade and other payables	(1,543)	(1,546)
	Tax payable	(237)	(150)
27	Short-term borrowings and overdrafts	(1,194)	(610)
23	Short-term provisions	(42)	(67)
27	Obligations under finance leases	(20)	(20)
28	Derivative financial instruments	(61)	–
		(3,097)	**(2,393)**
	Non-current liabilities		
22	Trade and other payables	(32)	(27)
27	Borrowings	(3,022)	(3,520)
25	Retirement benefit obligation	(369)	(485)
	Tax payable	(138)	(184)
24	Deferred tax liabilities	(954)	(895)
23	Long-term provisions	(11)	(10)
27	Obligations under finance leases	(43)	(66)
		(4,569)	**(5,187)**
	Liabilities directly associated with assets classified as held for sale	(291)	–
	Total liabilities	**(7,957)**	**(7,580)**
	Net assets	**3,035**	**2,300**
	Equity		
29	Share capital	260	259
29	Share premium account	1,135	1,098
29	Other reserves	223	(32)
29	Retained earnings	1,390	746
29	Equity attributable to equity holders of the parent	3,008	2,071

30	Minority interest	27	229
	Total equity	3,035	2,300

On behalf of the Board and

Directors: Todd Stitzer
               Ken Hanna

13 March 2006

21. Assets held for sale

	2005 (£m)	2004 (£m)
At 2 January 2005	5	9
Exchange rate adjustments	–	–
Additions	3	–
Transfer of discontinued operations	941	–
Disposals	(4)	(4)
At 1 January 2006	**945**	**5**

As discussed in Note 32, the Group announced the disposal of its Europe Beverages business in 2005.

32. Discontinued operations

On 1 September 2005, the Group announced its intention to sell its Europe Beverages business. From this date the segment has been classified as a discontinued operation. On 21 November 2005, the Group received a binding offer to buy its Europe Beverages business conditional upon receiving European Union regulatory approval. The disposal was effected in order to allow the Group to focus on its faster growing confectionery and other beverage businesses. The disposal completed on 2 February 2006.

(a)   **The results of the discontinued operations which have been included in the consolidated income statement are as follows:**

	2005 (£m)	2004 (£m)
Revenue	649	653
Trading costs	(537)	(537)
Restructuring costs	(14)	(26)
Amortisation/impairment of intangibles	–	–

Non-trading items	–	1
Profit from operations	98	91
Share of result in associates	=	(1)
Profit before financing and taxation	98	90
Investment income	–	–
Finance costs	(1)	–
Profit before taxation	97	90
Taxation	(15)	(40)
Disposal costs	(9)	–
Attributable tax expense	–	–
Net profit attributable to discontinued operations	73	50

The disposal costs relate to transaction costs incurred before the year end.

(e) The major classes of assets and liabilities comprising the operations classified as held for sale are as follows:

Assets	2005 (£m)
Non-current assets	
Goodwill	230
Brand intangibles	370
Software intangibles	2
Property, plant and equipment	153
Investment in associates	30
Deferred tax assets	1
Trade and other receivables	1
	787
Current assets	
Inventories	20
Short-term investments	3
Trade and other receivables	116
Tax recoverable	3
Cash and cash equivalents	11
Derivative financial instruments	–
	153
Non-current assets held for sale	1
Total assets	941
Liabilities	
Current liabilities	
Trade and other payables	(160)
Tax payable	(3)
Short-term borrowings and overdrafts	(8)
Short-term provisions	(4)
Current instalments of finance leases	(2)
Derivative financial instruments	–

	(177)
Non-current liabilities	
Trade and other payables	(1)
Borrowings	–
Retirement benefit obligation	(12)
Tax payable	–
Deferred tax liabilities	(94)
Long-term provisions	(3)
Obligations under finance leases	(4)
	(114)
Total liabilities	(291)
Net assets	650

IFRS 5 requires that the total assets and total liabilities of discontinued operations are each shown separately and excluded from the individual line items of the Balance Sheet. However no representation of the prior period is required and the assets and liabilities are included in the individual line items. Hence only amounts in respect of 2005 are shown above.

Example – Presenting discontinued operations

At the end of 20 × 5 an entity decides to dispose of part of its assets and directly associated liabilities. This disposal which meets the criteria as held for sale takes the form of two disposal groups as follows:

	NBV after classification as held for sale	
	Disposal group 1	Disposal group 2
Property, plant and equipment	4,900	1,700
Asset for sale financial asset	1,400*	–
Liabilities	(2,400)	(900)
NBV of disposal group	3,900	800

*An amount of 400 relating to these assets has been recognised directly in equity.

The presentation in the entity's balance sheet of the disposal groups classified as held for sale can be shown as follows:

	20 X 5	20 X 4
Assets		
Non-current assets		
AAA	X	X
BBB	X	X
CCC	X	X

	X	X
Current assets		
DDD	X	X
EEE	X	X
	X	X
Non-current assets classified as held for sale	8,000	–
	X	X
Total assets	X	X
	20 × 5	20 × 4
Equity and liabilities		
Equity attributable to equity holders of the parent		
FFF	X	X
GGG	X	X
Amounts recognised directly in equity relating to non-current		
Assets held for sale	400	X
	X	X
Minority interest	X	X
Total equity	X	X
Non-current liabilities		
HHH	X	X
III	X	X
JJJ	X	X
	X	X
Current liabilities		
KKK	X	X
LLL	X	X
MMM	X	X
Liabilities directly associated with non-current assets		
Classified as held for sale	3,300	–
	X	X
Total liabilities	X	X
Total equity and liabilities	X	X

7

Employee costs

7.1 IAS 19 *Employee Benefits* (December 1998, amended 2000)

Introduction

There are five categories of employee benefits:

(1) Short-term – wages, salaries, paid leave, profit sharing, bonuses and non-monetary benefits such as medical care, housing, cars or subsidised goods.
(2) Post-employment benefits, e.g. pensions, medical care, life insurance.
(3) Other long-term employee benefits, e.g. long-service leave, sabbaticals, long-term disability payments.
(4) Termination benefits, e.g. early retirement, redundancy payments.
(5) Equity compensation benefits.

Short-term employee benefits should be recognised when the employee has rendered service in exchange for the benefits.

Post-employment benefit plans are classified as defined contribution (DC) or defined benefit (DB). IAS 19 also covers multi-employer plans, state plans and plans with insured benefits.

Under defined contribution, fixed contributions are paid into a fund – the employer has not further legal or constructive obligation to pay more into the fund if there are not sufficient assets to pay employee benefits. IAS 19 requires immediate expense of defined contributions when employees have rendered service in exchange for those contributions.

All other post-employment benefit plans are defined benefit plans. These may be unfunded or wholly or partly funded. IAS 19 requires an enterprise to:

(a) account for all legal and constructive obligations;
(b) determine the present value of defined benefit obligations and the fair value of any plan assets with sufficient regularity that the amounts recognised in the financial statements

do not materially differ from the amounts that would be determined at the balance sheet date;

(c)   use the projected unit credit method;

(d)   accrue benefit to periods of service under the plan's benefit formula unless an employee's service in later years will lead to a higher level of benefits than in earlier years;

(e)   use unbiased and mutually compatible actuarial assumptions re demographic and financial variables. Financial assumptions should be based on market expectations at the balance sheet date; and

(f)   discount rate should be based on high quality corporate bonds of a currency and term consistent with the currency and term of the post-employment benefit obligations.

Objective

The objective of IAS 19 is to prescribe the accounting treatment and disclosure for employee benefits (i.e. all forms of consideration given by an entity in exchange for services rendered by employees). The principle underlying all of the detailed requirements of the standard is that the cost of providing employee benefits should be recognised in the period in which the benefit is earned by the employee rather than when it is paid or payable.

Scope

IAS 19 applies to wages and salaries, paid vacation and sick leave, profit sharing plans, medical and life assurance benefits during employment, housing benefits, free or subsidised goods or services given to employees, pension benefits, post-retirement medical and life insurance benefits, long-service or sabbatical leave, deferred compensation programmes, termination benefits and equity compensation benefits.

Definitions

*   *Employee benefits*. All forms of consideration given by an enterprise in exchange for services rendered by employees.
*   *Short-term employee benefits*. Employee benefits (bar termination and equity compensation benefits) which fall wholly within 12 months after the end of the period in which the employees render the related service.
*   *Post-employment benefits*. Employee benefits (bar termination and equity compensation benefits) which are payable after the completion of employment.
*   *Defined contribution plans*. Post-employment benefit plans in which an enterprise pays fixed contributions into a separate entity fund. There are no legal or constructive obligations to pay further contributions if the fund is insufficient to pay all employee benefits.
*   *Defined benefit plans*. Post-employment benefit plans other than defined contribution plans.
*   *Multi-employer plans*. Defined contribution or defined benefit plans (other than state plans) that:
    (a)   pool the assets contributed by various enterprises not under common control and
    (b)   use those assets to provide benefits to employees of more than one enterprise, on the basis that contribution and benefit levels are determined without regard to the identity of the enterprise that employs the employees concerned.

- *Other long-term employee benefits.* Employee benefits (other than post-employment benefits, termination and equity compensation benefits) which do not fall due within 12 months after the end of the period in which employees render the related service.
- *Termination benefits.* Employee benefits payable as a result of either:
  - (a)   an enterprise's decision to terminate an employee's employment before normal retirement date or
  - (b)   an employee's decision to accept voluntary redundancy in exchange for those benefits.
- *Equity compensation benefits.* Employee benefits under which either:
  - (a)   employees are entitled to receive equity financial instruments issued by the enterprise or
  - (b)   the amount of the enterprise's obligation to employees depends on the future price of equity financial instruments issued by the enterprise.
- *Current service costs.* The increase in the present value of the defined benefit obligation resulting from employee service in the current period.
- *Interest cost.* The increase during a period in the present value of a defined benefit obligation which arises because the benefits are one period closer to settlement.
- *Return on plan assets.* Interest, dividends and other revenue derived from the plan assets together with realised and unrealised gains or losses on the plan assets, less any cost of administering the plan and less any tax payable by the plan itself.
- *Past-service cost.* The increase in the present value of the defined benefit obligation for employee service in prior periods, resulting from the introduction of, or changes to, post-employment benefits or other long-term employee benefits. Can be positive or negative (i.e. benefits are improved or reduced).
- *Actuarial gains and losses*
  - (a)   experience adjustments (i.e. differences between previous actuarial assumptions and what occurred) and
  - (b)   the effects of changes in actuarial assumptions.

Short-term employee benefits

Accounting for short-term benefits is fairly simple as there are no actuarial assumptions to make and there is no requirement to discount future benefits.

Recognition and measurement

All short-term employee benefits

When an employee has rendered service the enterprise should recognise the undiscounted amount of short-term benefits expected to be paid in exchange for that service:

(a)   As a liability (accrual) after deduction of amounts paid. If payments exceeds the benefits, then the excess should be treated as an asset (prepayment) to the extent that it will lead to a reduction in future payments or a cash refund.

(b)   As an expense unless another IAS permits or requires the inclusion of employment costs as part of the cost of an asset, e.g. IAS 2 and 16.

Short-term absences

An enterprise should recognise the expected cost of short-term employee benefits when:

(a)   the employees render service that increases their entitlement to future compensated absences and

(b)   when the absences occur.

Examples include unused holiday leave which is expensed when employees render services, i.e. an accumulating entitlement.

EXAMPLE

An enterprise has 100 employees, who are each entitled to five working days of paid sick leave each year. Unused sick leave may be carried forward for one year. Sick leave is taken first out of the current years entitlement and then out of any balance brought forward from the previous year (i.e. LIFO basis). At 31.12.20 × 1, the average unused entitlement is two days per employee. Based on past experience, 92 employees will take no more than five days of paid sick leave in 20 × 2 and that the remaining eight employees will take an average of 6.5 days each.

The enterprise expects to pay an additional 12 days of sick pay (8 employees × 1.5 days) thus a liability equal to 12 days sick pay should be accrued.

Other non-accumulating absences, e.g. sick leave are only paid when they occur but there is no accumulated entitlement. No liability or expense occurs until the time of the absence.

Profit sharing and bonus plan

An enterprise should recognise the expected cost of profit sharing and bonus payments only when both:

(a)   the enterprise has a legal or constructive obligation to make such payments and

(b)   a reliable estimate of the obligation can be made.

EXAMPLE

A profit sharing plan requires an enterprise to pay a specified proportion of its net profit for the year to employees who serve throughout the year. If none leave, the total payments will be 3% of net profit. The enterprise estimates that staff turnover will reduce this to 2.5% of net profit.

The enterprise should recognise a liability and an expense of 2.5% of net profit.

A constructive obligation can only exist if:

(a)   the formal terms of the bonus plan contain a formula for determining the size of the benefit;

(b)   the enterprise determines the amounts to be paid before the financial statements are authorised for issue; and

(c)   past practice gives clear evidence of the amount of the obligation.

Disclosure

No specific disclosures are required re short-term employee benefits but other IASs may require disclosures, e.g. IAS 24 re employee benefits for key management personnel and IAS 1 re staff costs.

Post-employment benefits

Most employers provide post-employment benefits for their employees after they have retired. These benefits not only include pension schemes but also post-employment death benefits, medical care. These benefit schemes are often referred to as 'plans'.

The plans receive regular contributions from employers (and sometimes employees) and the monies are invested in assets such as stocks and shares, bonds and property. The benefits are paid out of the income derived from the plan assets or the sale of some plan assets.

There are two types or categories of plans:

(1)   *Defined contribution*
       The contributions paid in are defined and the size of the benefit will depend on the performance of the plan assets, i.e. the risk is with the employee.
(2)   *Defined benefit*
       The size of the benefits are determined in advance. The employer must contribute to meet those benefits and if the assets are insufficient then any deficit must be made good by the employer by making additional contributions. If, however, there is a surplus then an employer may take a contribution holiday or even obtain a refund from the fund. The risk, however, is clearly borne by the employer.

A clear distinction must be made between the funding of a pension scheme (i.e. actual cash contributions into the scheme) and its accounting treatment (i.e. cost to be charged to the income and other performance statements).

Multi-employer plans

IAS 19 requires all multi-employer schemes to be classified as either defined benefit or defined contribution. If it is defined benefit, the entity should account for its proportionate share of the defined benefit obligation, plan assets and costs in the same way as for other defined benefit schemes and provide full disclosure.

However, where there is insufficient information (e.g. cannot get access to share of plan assets/liabilities), it should be accounted for as a defined contribution scheme and provide additional disclosures that it is a defined benefit scheme and the reasons why the information is not available.

In addition, to the extent that a surplus/deficit may affect the amount of future contributions, the following should be disclosed:

(i)   any available information about the surplus/deficit;
(ii) the basis used in determining the surplus/deficit; and
(iii) the implications, if any, for the enterprise.

Multi-employer plans must be distinguished from group administration plans. The latter is an aggregation of single employer plans combined to allow participating employers to pool their assets for investment purposes and reduce administration costs but the claims of different employers are segregated. These, therefore, should be treated in the normal way for defined benefit purposes.

State plans

These are established by legislation and operated by government. They cannot be controlled or influenced by the enterprise. They should, therefore, be treated in the same way as multi-employer schemes. In most state plans, the enterprise has no legal or constructive obligation to pay future benefits; thus, its only obligation is to pay the contributions as they fall due and if the enterprise ceases to employ the members of the state plan, there is no further obligation. They are usually, therefore, classified as defined contribution schemes but in rare cases they could be defined benefit and the enterprise must follow the disclosure as per multi-employer schemes.

Insurance benefits

Insurance premiums should be treated as defined contributions to the plan unless the employer has a legal or constructive obligation to pay the benefits directly to the employees, or to make further payments in the event that the insurance company does not pay all the post-employment benefits for which the·insurance has been paid.

Defined contribution schemes

These schemes are relatively straightforward as:

(a) The obligation is determined by the amount paid into the plan each period.
(b) There are no actuarial assumptions.
(c) There is no discounting involved, if the obligation is settled in the current period.

IAS 19 requires the following:

(a) Contributions should be recognised as an expense in the period payable.
(b) Any liability for unpaid contributions should be accrued as a liability.
(c) Any excess contributions, should be treated as prepayments but only to the extent that they will lead to a refund or reduction in future payments.
(d) If the contributions do not fall within 12 months, they should be discounted.

An enterprise must disclose a description of the plan as well as the amount recognised as an expense in the period.

Defined benefit plans

This is much more complex than defined contribution schemes for the following reasons:

(a)   The future benefits cannot be estimated exactly – need actuarial assumptions.
(b)   The obligations are payable in future years and therefore there is a need for these to be discounted to present value.
(c)   If the actuarial assumptions change or experience differs from those assumptions, then actuarial gains and losses will arise.

These factors mean that the actual contributions paid into the fund in a particular period is not a fair charge for that period. Defined benefit plans may be funded or unfunded and, if funded, contributions are paid into a fund that is legally separate from the reporting enterprise.

Recognition and measurement

The following are the steps required in order for an employer to account for the expense and liability of a defined benefit plan:

(1)   Actuarial assumptions must be used to make a reliable estimate of the amount of future benefits that employees have earned from service in relation to the current and prior years. These include life expectancy, inflation, labour turnover, salary increases, etc.
(2)   The future benefits should be discounted using the projected unit credit method in order to provide a total present value of future benefit obligations arising from past and current periods of service.
(3)   The fair value of the plan assets should be established.
(4)   The total actuarial gain/loss should be determined and the amount that should be recognised.
(5)   Where a plan has been improved, the additional cost arising from past service should be determined.
(6)   Where a plan has been curtailed or cancelled, the resulting gain or loss.

These procedures must be followed individually for each defined benefit scheme the enterprise has. IAS 19 makes it very clear that an entity must account for all constructive obligations. Thus it may have an informal practice, whereby the entity has no realistic alternative but to pay employee benefits, thus it should provide for those obligations, e.g. where a change in the enterprise's formal practices would cause unacceptable damage to its relationship with employees.

Projected unit credit method

Under this actuarial method, it is assumed that each period of service by an employee gives rise to an additional unit of future benefits. The present value of that unit can be calculated and attributed to the period in which the service is given. The units, each measured separately, add up to the total overall obligation. The accumulated present value of discounted future benefits will incur interest over time and thus an interest expense should be recognised.

Example – Projected unit credit method

Assume an employer pays a lump sum to employees when they retire. The lump sum is equal to 1% of their salary in the final year of service, for every year of service given.

(a) An employee is expected to work for five years (actuarial assumption).
(b) His/her salary is expected to rise by 8% per annum (actuarial assumption).
(c) His/her salary in 20×1 is £10,000.
(d) The discount rate is 10% per annum.

Based on a current salary of £10,000 and an annual rise of 8% the salary in 20×5 should be £13,605. His/her lump sum entitlement is therefore expected to be £136 for each year's service, i.e. £680 in total.

Assuming no change in the actuarial assumptions and that no employees leave, the calculations are as follows:

Future benefit attributable to:	20×1 (£)	20×2 (£)	20×3 (£)	20×4 (£)	20×5 (£)
Prior years	0	136	272	408	544
Current year (1% of final salary)	136	136	136	136	136
Prior and current years total	136	272	408	544	680

The future benefit builds up to €680 over the five years, at the end of which the employee is expected to retire and the benefit is payable.

These figures, however, need to be discounted:

	20×1 (£)	20×2 (£)	20×3 (£)	20×4 (£)	20×5 (£)
Opening obligation	–	93	204	336	494
Interest at 10%	–	9	20	34	50
Current service cost	93	102	112	124	136
Closing obligation	93	204	336	494	680

Note that interest is the opening obligation multiplied by the discount rate.

Balance Sheet

Under IAS 19, the following net total should be recognised as a defined benefit liability on the balance sheet:

(a) the present value of the defined benefit obligation at the balance sheet date;
(b) plus – any actuarial gains or minus – any actuarial losses not yet recognised;
(c) minus – any past service costs not yet recognised; and
(d) minus – the fair value of the assets in the plan out of which future obligations to current and past employees will be directly settled.

The present value of defined benefit obligations and plan assets should be determined with sufficient regularity that the amounts recognised in the financial statements do not differ materially from the amounts that would be determined at the balance sheet date. IAS 19 does not require but does encourage the use of a qualified actuary in the measurement process.

If the total is negative, i.e. an asset, then it should be disclosed in the balance sheet as the lower of (a) and (b) below:

(a)   the figure as calculated above;
(b)   the total of the present values of:
    (i)   any unrecognised actuarial losses and past service costs;
    (ii)   any refunds expected from the plan; and
    (iii) any reductions in future contributions, due to the surplus.

EXAMPLE

A DB plan has the following characteristics:

Present value of the obligation	1,100
Fair value of plan assets	(1,190)
	(90)
Unrecognised actuarial losses	(110)
Unrecognised past service cost	(70)
Unrecognised increase in the liability on initial adoption of IAS 19	(50)
	(320)
Present value of available future refunds and reductions in future contributions	100

The limit is computed as follows:

Unrecognised actuarial losses	(110)
Unrecognised past service costs	(70)
Present value of available future refunds and reductions in future contributions	(100)
Limit	(280)

280 is less than 320. Therefore, the enterprise recognises an asset of 280 and discloses that the limit reduced the carrying amount of the asset by 40.

Income statement

The expense to be recognised in the income statement is the net total of the following:

(a)   the current service cost;
(b)   interest;
(c)   expected return on plan assets and reimbursement rights;
(d)   actuarial gains and losses to the extent recognised;
(e)   past service costs to the extent recognised; and
(f)   the effect of any curtailments or settlements.

Recognition and measurement: Present value of defined benefit obligations and current service cost

There are many variables affecting the ultimate cost of a defined benefit scheme, e.g. final salaries, labour turnover, mortality, medical cost trends, etc. In order to measure the present value of the post-employment benefit obligations and related current service cost it is necessary to:

(a) apply an actuarial valuation method, i.e. the projected unit credit method (see example earlier);
(b) attribute benefit to periods of service; and
(c) make actuarial assumptions.

Attribute benefits to periods of service

These should be attributed under the plan's benefit formula. However, if an employee's service in later years leads to a materially higher level of benefit than in earlier years, an enterprise should attribute benefit on a straight-line basis from:

(a) the date when service by the employee first leads to benefits under the plan; until
(b) the date when further service by the employee will lead to no material amount of further benefits under the plan, other than from further salary increases.

EXAMPLE

Assume a defined benefit plan provides for an annual pension for former employees on retirement. The size of the pension is 2.5% of the employee's final salary, for each year of service. The pension is payable from the age of 65.

The annual payment obligation of 2.5% should first be converted to a present value lump sum as at the date of retirement, using actuarial assumptions. The current service cost is the present value of that obligation, i.e. the present value of monthly pension payments of 2.5% of final salary, multiplied by the number of years of service to date. For example, if an employee is expected to earn £10,000 in his/her final year and live for 15 years after retirement, the benefit payable for each year of employment would be the discounted value, as at retirement date, of £250 per annum for 15 years. This should then be converted to a present value to determine the current service cost for the year for that employee.

Probabilities should be taken into consideration. Assume a benefit of £1,000 for every year of service is payable to employees when they retire at 60, provided they remain with the employer until that time. Also assume an employee joins the company at the age of 40, with 20 years still to work.

The benefit attributable to each year of service is £1,000 × probability that the employee will remain with the employer until he/she is 60. Since the benefit is payable at retirement as a lump sum it should be discounted, i.e. the present value of £40,000 (40 years × £1,000) multiplied by the same probability.

No added obligations arise after all significant post-employment benefits have vested. Suppose employees have an entitlement to a lump sum on retirement of £2,000 for every year they have worked, up to a maximum of 10 years, i.e. maximum of £20,000 and this vests after 10 years. A benefit of £2,000 should be attributed to each of the first 10 years of an employee's service. The current service cost in each of the 10 years should be the present value of £2,000. If an employee has 25 years to go before retirement, there should be a service cost in each of the first 10 years and none in the last 15 thereafter.

The following is a further example of how the rules should be applied:

EXAMPLE
Inter Plc's defined benefit plan provides all employees with a paid lump sum retirement benefit of £100,000. They must be still employed aged 55 after 20 years of service, or still employed at the age of 65, no matter what their length of service.

(i) For employees joining before age 35, service first leads to benefits at age 35 because he/she could leave at 30 and return at 33 with no effect on the amount/timing of benefits. Also beyond age 55 no further benefits will arise. Inter Plc should allocate £100,000 ÷ 20 = £5,000 to each year between the ages of 35 and 55.

(ii) For employees joining between the ages of 35 and 45, service beyond 20 years will lead to no further benefit. Inter Plc should, therefore, allocate £100,000 ÷ 20 = £5,000 to each of the first 20 years.

(iii) Employees joining at 55 exactly will receive no further benefit past 65; so, Inter Plc should allocate £100,000 ÷ 10 years = £10,000 to each of the first 10 years.

Actuarial assumptions

These should be unbiased and mutually compatible. They are the enterprise's best estimate of the variables that will determine the ultimate cost of providing post-retirement benefits. They comprise:

(a) *Demographic assumptions* – mortality rates, employee turnover, disability and early retirement, proportion of members eligible for benefits and medical claim rates.

(b) *Financial assumptions* – discount rate, future salary and benefit levels, future increase in medical costs, expected return on assets, etc. These should be based on market expectations, at the balance sheet date, for the period over which the obligations are to be settled.

The discount rate adopted should be determined by reference to market yields on high quality fixed rate corporate bonds but, in their absence, yields on comparable government bonds should be used.

Actuarial gains and losses

These arise because of the following:
• Actual events differ from the actuarial assumptions.
• Actuarial assumptions are revised.
• Actual returns on plan assets differ from expected returns.

These are inevitable and thus IAS 19 takes the view that they should not be recognised until they become significant. They are not recognised, however, if they fall within a tolerable range or 'corridor'.

IAS 19 requires the following:

(a) As a general rule, actuarial gains and losses should be recorded in the income statement as an expense/income and as part of the defined benefit liability/asset on the balance sheet.

(b) However, only a portion should be recognised if the net cumulative actuarial gains/losses exceed the greater of:

    (i)   10% of the present value of the defined benefit obligation (i.e. before deducting plan assets) and

    (ii) 10% of the fair value of the plan assets.

This must be carried out separately for each plan. The excess calculated as above should then be divided by the expected average remaining working lives of participating employees to arrive at the charge to go through the income statement.

IAS 19 does permit, however, any systematic method to be adopted if it results in faster recognition of actuarial gains and losses. The same basis must be applied to both gains and losses and applied consistently from period to period. An immediate write-off to reserves and the SORIE is permitted and is consistent with the approach adopted in the United Kingdom in FRS 17 *Retirement Benefits*.

Past service cost

These should be expensed on a straight-line basis over the average period until the benefits become vested. To the extent that the benefits are already vested immediately following the introduction of, or changes to, a defined benefit plan, an enterprise should recognise past service costs immediately.

EXAMPLE

An enterprise operates a pension plan that provides for a pension of 2% of final salary for each year of service. On 1 January 20 × 5, the enterprise improves the pension to 2.5% of final salary for each year of service starting from 1 January 20 × 1. At the date of the improvement, the present value of the additional benefits for service from 1 January 20 × 1 to 1 January 20 × 5 is as follows:

Employees with more than 5 years service at 1.1.20 × 5	150
Employees with less than 5 years service at 1.1.20 × 5 (average vesting period: 3 years)	120
	270

The enterprise should recognise 150 immediately because those benefits are already vested. The enterprise should recognise 120 on a straight-line basis over three years from 1 January 20 × 5.

Past service costs exclude:

(a)   the effect of differences between actual and previously assumed salary increases;
(b)   under/over estimates of discretionary pension increases where a constructive obliga-
      tion exists;
(c)   estimates of benefit improvements resulting from actuarial gains already recognised in
      the financial statements if the enterprise is obliged to use a surplus for the benefit of
      participants even if no award is formally made;
(d)   the increase in vested benefits when employees complete vesting requirements; and
(e)   the effect of plan amendments that reduce benefits for future service (curtailments).

Recognition and measurement: Plan assets

The contributions into a plan by the employer (and sometimes also employees) are invested
in assets such as stocks and shares, property, bonds, etc. The fair value of these plan assets
are deducted from the defined benefits obligation in calculating the balance sheet liability.

Where no market price is available, the fair value is estimated by discounting future cash
flows using a discount rate that reflects both the risk and maturity of those assets. They
exclude any unpaid contributions. Where plan assets include qualifying insurance policies
that exactly match the amount and timing of some or all of the benefits payable under
the plan, the fair value of those insurance policies is deemed to be the present value of the
related obligations.

When it is virtually certain that another party will reimburse some or all of the expenditure required to settle a defined benefit obligation, an enterprise should recognise its right
to reimbursement as a separate asset. This should be measured at fair value. In all other
respects, an enterprise should treat that asset in the same way as plan assets, the expense
should be presented net of any reimbursement.

EXAMPLE

Present value of obligation	1,241
Unrecognised actuarial gains	17
Liability recognised on balance sheet	1,258
Rights under insurance policies that exactly match the amount and timing of some of the benefits payable under the plan. Those benefits have a present value of 1,092	1,092

The unrecognised actuarial gains of 17 are the net cumulative actuarial gains on the obligation and on the reimbursement rights.

Return on plan assets

The expected return on plan assets is one component of the expense recognised in the
income statement. The difference between the expected return on plan assets and the actual

return is an actuarial gain or loss. It is included with the actuarial gains/losses in determining the net amount that is compared with the limits of the 10% corridor.

The expected return is based on market expectations at the start of the period. Administration expenses are deducted in determining the expected and actual return on plan assets.

EXAMPLE

At 1.1.20 × 1, the fair value of plan assets was 10,000 and net cumulative unrecognised actuarial gains were 760. On 30.6.20 × 1, the plan paid benefits of 1,900 and received contributions of 4,900. At 31.12.20 × 1, the fair value of plan assets was 15,000 and the present value of the defined benefit obligation was 14,792. Actuarial losses for 20 × 1 on the obligation were 60.

At 1.1.20 × 1 the entity made the following estimates, based on market prices at that date:

	%
Interest and dividend income after tax	9.25
Realised and unrealised gains on plan assets after tax	2.00
Administration costs	(1.00)
Expected rate of return	10.25

For 20 × 1 the expected and actual return on plan assets are as follows:

Return on 10,000 held for 12 months at 10.25%	1,025
Return on 3,000 held for 6 months at 5% (equivalent to 10.25% annually compounded every 6 months)	150
Expected return on plan assets for 20 × 1	1,175
Fair value of plan assets at 31.12.20 × 1	15,000
Less fair value of plan assets at 1.1.20 × 1	(10,000)
Less contributions received	(4,900)
Add benefits paid	1,900
Actual return on plan assets	2,000

The difference between the expected return on plan assets (1,175) and the actual return on plan assets (2,000) is an actuarial gain of 825. Therefore, the cumulative net unrecognised gains are 1,525 (760 + 825 – 60). The limits of the corridor are set at 1,500 (greater of 10% × 15,000 and 10% of 14,792). In the following year (20 × 2) the entity recognises in income an actuarial gain of 25 (1,525 – 1,500) divided by the expected average remaining life of the employees concerned.

Business combinations

For acquisitions, an entity should recognise the present value of the obligations less the present value of any plan assets arising from post-employment benefits. The present value includes the following even if the acquiree has not recognised them at the date of acquisition:

(a)   actuarial gains and losses that arose before the date of the acquisition;
(b)   past service cost that arose from benefit changes before the date of acquisition; and
(c)   amounts, under transitional arrangements, that the acquiree had not recognised.

Curtailments and settlements

Should recognise gains/losses when the curtailment or settlement occurs and a gain/loss should comprise:

(a)   any resulting change in the present value of the plan liabilities;
(b)   any resulting change in the fair value of plan assets; and
(c)   any related actuarial gains/losses and past service cost not previously recognised.

However, an entity should first determine the effect of a curtailment/settlement by remeasuring the obligation using current actuarial assumptions.

A curtailment occurs when there is a material reduction in the number of employees in the plan or when a plan is materially changed so that current employees no longer qualify for benefits or for reduced benefits. They are often linked to restructuring.

A settlement occurs when an entity eliminates all further legal or constructive obligations under a defined benefit plan.

When a curtailment relates to only some of the employees, the gain/loss includes a proportionate share of the previously unrecognised past service cost and actuarial gains/losses. That is determined on the basis of the present value of obligations before and after curtailment or settlement unless another more rational basis is appropriate.

EXAMPLE
A business segment is discontinued and employees will earn no further benefits. Using actuarial assumptions immediately prior to the curtailment, the net present value of the obligation is 1,000. Plan assets have a fair value of 820 and net cumulative unrecognised actuarial gains are 50. IAS 19 was adopted one year earlier and the net liability has risen by 100 (recognised over five years).

The effect of the curtailment is as follows:

	Before curtailment	Curtailment gain	After curtailment
Net present value of obligation	1,000	(100)	900
Fair value of plan assets	(820)	–	(820)
	180	(100)	80
Unrecognised actuarial gains	50	(5)	45
Unrecognised transitional amount (100 × 4/5)	(80)	8	(72)
Net liability recognised in balance sheet	150	(97)	53

Offset

Only offset an asset on one plan against a liability on another plan if there is a legally enforceable right to use a surplus in one plan against a deficit on another and the entity intends to settle its obligations on a net basis or to realise the surplus and settle its obligation simultaneously.

Current/non-current distinction

IAS 19 does not distinguish between current and non-current portions of assets and liabilities under post-employment benefit plans.

Financial components of post-employment benefit costs

IAS 19 does not specify whether an entity should present current service cost, interest cost and the expected return on plan assets as components of a single item of income/expense on the face of the income statement.

The following should be disclosed about defined benefit plans:

(a)   Accounting policy for recognising actuarial gains/losses.
(b)   General description of the type of plan.
(c)   Reconciliation of assets and liabilities recognised on balance sheet showing, at least:
    (i)   present value of defined benefit obligations wholly unfunded;
    (ii)   present value of defined benefit obligations wholly or partly funded;
    (iii) fair value of any plan assets at the balance sheet date;
    (iv)   the net actuarial gains/losses not recognised in the balance sheet;
    (v)   the past service cost not yet recognised on the balance sheet;
    (vi)   any amount not recognised as an asset;
    (vii) the fair value of any reimbursement right recognised as an asset; and
    (viii) the other amounts recognised in the balance sheet.
(d)   The amounts included in the fair value of plan assets for:
    (i)   each category of an entity's own financial instruments and
    (ii)   any property occupied by, or other assets used by, the reporting entity.
(e)   A reconciliation showing movements during the period in the net liability recognised.
(f)   The total expense in income for:
    (i)   current service cost;
    (ii)   interest cost;
    (iii) expected return on plan assets;
    (iv)   expected return on any reimbursement right recognised as an asset;
    (v)   actuarial gains and losses;
    (vi)   past service costs; and
    (vii) the effect of any curtailment or settlement.
(g)   The actual return on plan assets and on any reimbursement right.
(h)   The principal actuarial assumptions including:
    (i)   the discount rates;
    (ii)   the expected rates of return on plan assets;

(iii)   the expected rates of return for periods presented on any reimbursement right;
(iv)   the expected rates of salary increase;
 (v)   medical cost trend rates; and
(vi)   any other material actuarial assumptions used.

Actuarial assumptions must be disclosed in absolute terms not relative.

Other long-term employee benefits

These include:

(a)   long-term compensated absences, e.g. sabbatical leave;
(b)   jubilee or long-term benefits;
(c)   long-term disability benefits;
(d)   profit sharing and bonuses payable; and
(e)   deferred compensation paid after more than 12 months.

These are not as complicated as post-employment benefits – they need a simple model as their measurement is not usually subject to the same degree of uncertainty. The method differs from post-employment benefits as follows:

(a)   actuarial gains and losses are recognised immediately – no 'corridor' is applied and
(b)   all past service costs are recognised immediately.

Recognition and measurement

The liability should be the net total of the following:

(a)   the present value of defined benefit obligations at the balance sheet date and
(b)   minus the fair value at the balance sheet date of plan assets used to settle the obligations.

The liability should be measured as per defined benefit schemes.

The net total should be expensed except to the extent that another IAS requires or permits their inclusion in the cost of an asset:

(a)   current service cost;
(b)   interest cost;
(c)   expected return on plan assets and on any reimbursement right recognised as an asset;
(d)   actuarial gains and losses which should be recognised immediately;
(e)   past service cost recognised immediately; and
(f)   the effect of any curtailments or settlements.

If there is a long-term disability benefit, the obligation arises when the service is rendered and the measurement of that obligation reflects the probability that payment will be required and the length of time when it will be paid.

Disclosure

No specific disclosures are required but under IAS 24 an entity should disclose information about other long-term employee benefits for key management personnel.

Termination benefits

An entity should recognise termination benefits as a liability and an expense when, and only when, the entity is demonstrably committed to either:

(a)   terminate the employment of an employee/s before the normal retirement date or
(b)   provide termination benefits as a result of an offer made to encourage voluntary redundancy.

An entity is demonstrably committed to a termination date when the entity has a detailed formal plan for the termination. The plan should include, as a minimum:

(a)   the location, function and approximate number of employees of termination;
(b)   the termination benefits for each job; and
(c)   the time at which the plan will be implemented.

Termination benefits are usually lump sum payments but also include:

(a)   enhancement of retirement benefits and
(b)   salary until the end of a specified notice period if the employee does not render further service.

As these benefits do not provide an entity with future economic benefits they are, therefore, expensed immediately.

If the benefits fall due after more than 12 months they should be discounted. The measurement of a voluntary redundancy programme should be based on the expected number of employees expected to accept the offer.

Disclosure

Where uncertainty exists, a contingent liability should be disclosed under IAS 37. Under IAS 8 the nature and amount of an expense, if exceptional, should be disclosed as well as termination benefits for key management personnel, under IAS 24.

Equity compensation benefits

These include such benefits as:

(a)   shares, share options and other equity issued to employees at less than fair value and
(b)   cash payments whose amount depends on the future market price of the shares.

There are no specific recognition and measurement requirements in the standard on equity compensation payments.

Equity compensation benefits may affect:

(a)   an entity's financial position by having to issue equity and
(b)   an entity's performance and cash flows by reducing cash or increasing expenses.

An entity should disclose:

(a)   the nature and terms of equity compensation plans;
(b)   the accounting policy for equity compensation plans;

(c)   the amounts recognised for equity compensation plans;
(d)   the number and terms of equity instruments that are held by equity compensation plans at the start and end of the period. The extent to which the employees' entitlements to those instruments are vested at the start and end of the year should be specified;
(e)   the number and terms of equity instruments issued by the entity to equity compensation plans or to employees during the period and the fair value of any consideration received from the equity compensation plans or the employees;
(f)   the number, exercise dates and exercise prices of share options exercised under equity compensation plans during the period;
(g)   the number of share options held by equity compensation plans or held by employees under the plans that lapsed during the period; and
(h)   the amount, and principal terms of any loans or guarantees granted by the entity to or on behalf of equity compensation plans.

In addition the entity should also disclose:

(a)   the fair value at start and end of the period of the entity's own equity instruments held by equity compensation plans and
(b)   the fair value, at date of issue, of the entity's own equity instruments issued by the entity to equity compensation plans or to employees or by equity compensation plans to employees during the period.

If it is not practicable to determine the fair value of equity instruments, that fact should be disclosed.

If there is more than one equity instrument, the disclosures can be carried out individually or in suitable groupings. If the latter, disclosures should be provided in the form of weighted averages or in the form of relatively narrow ranges. It might be useful to distinguish 'out of the money' options separately.

Additional disclosures may be required under IAS 24 if an entity:

(a)   provides equity compensation benefits to key management personnel;
(b)   provides equity compensation benefits via instruments issued by the entity's parent; or
(c)   enters into related party transactions with equity compensation plans.

IFRS 2 *Share-Based Payment* now requires both extensive disclosure and a fair charge to be expensed for these benefits (see Section 7.3).

Transitional provisions

On first adoption of IAS 19, the transitional liability for defined benefit schemes is determined as:

(a)   the present value of the obligation at date of adoption;
(b)   minus the fair value, at date of adoption, of plan assets out of which obligations will be settled; and
(c)   minus any past service cost that should be recognised in later periods.

If the liability is larger than the previous accounting policy the entity should recognise irrevocably the increase as:

(a)   immediate as per IAS 8 or
(b)   as an expense on a straight-line basis up to five years from the date of adoption but the entity must apply the 10% limit in measuring the asset, disclose the amount still unrecognised and the amount recognised in the period, limit the actuarial gain only to the extent that net cumulative unrecognised actuarial gains exceed the unrecognised part of the transitional liability. Also it must include the related part of the unrecognised transitional liability in determining any subsequent gain or loss on settlement or curtailment.

Any decreases should be recognised immediately under IAS 8.

EXAMPLE
At 31.12.2008 a pension liability of 100 exists on the balance sheet. IAS 19 is adopted from 1.1.2009 when the present value of the obligation is 1,300 and the fair value of plan assets is 1,000. On 1.1.2003 the entity improved pensions (cost for non-vested benefits 160 – average remaining period 10 years).
    Transitional effect is as follows:

Present value of the obligation	1,300
Fair value of plan assets	(1,000)
Less past service cost to be recognised in later periods (160 × 4/10)	(64)
Transitional liability	236
Liability already recognised	100
Increase in liability	136

The entity may choose to recognise the increase of 136 immediately or over up to five years but the choice is irrevocable.

At 31.12.2009 the present value of the obligation is 1,400 and the fair value of plan assets is 1,050. Net cumulative unrecognised actuarial gains since adopting the standard is 120. The expected average working life of employees in the plan was eight years. The policy is to recognise all actuarial gains and losses immediately.
    The effect of the limit is as follows:

Net cumulative unrecognised actuarial gains		120
Unrecognised part of the transitional liability	(136 × 4/5)	(109)
Maximum gain to be recognised		11

Illustrative example

The following information is provided about a defined benefit plan. To keep the example simple, all transactions are assumed to occur at the year end. The present value of the obligation and the fair value of the plan assets were both 1,000 at 1.1.20 × 1. Net cumulative unrecognised actuarial gains at that date were 140.

	20 × 1	20 × 2	20 × 3
Discount at start of the year (%)	10.0	9.0	8.0
Expected rate of return on plan assets at start of year (%)	12.0	11.1	10.3
Current service cost	130	140	150
Benefits paid	150	180	190
Contributions paid	90	100	110
Present value of obligation, 31 December	1,141	1,197	1,295
Fair value of plan assets, 31 December	1,092	1,109	1,093
Expected average remaining working lives of employees (years)	10	10	10

In 20 × 2 the plan was amended to provide additional benefits with effect from 1.1.20 × 2. The present value as at 1.1.20 × 2 of additional benefits for employee service before 1.1.20 × 2 was 50 for vested benefits and 30 for non-vested benefits. As at 1 January 20 × 2, the enterprise estimated that the average period until the non-vested benefits would become vested was three years; the past service cost arising from additional non-vested benefits is therefore recognised on a straight-line basis over three years. The past service cost arising from additional vested benefits is recognised immediately. The enterprise has adopted a policy of recognising actuarial gains and losses under the minimum requirements of IAS 19.

Changes in the present value of the obligation and in the fair value of the plan assets

The first step is to summarise the changes in fair value of the obligation and in the fair value of the plan assets and use this to determine the amount of the actuarial gains or losses for the period. These are as follows:

	20 × 1	20 × 2	20 × 3
Present value of obligation, 1 January	1,000	1,141	1,197
Interest cost	100	103	96
Current service cost	130	140	150
Past service cost – non-vested benefits	–	30	–
Past service cost – vested benefits	–	50	–
Benefits paid	(150)	(180)	(190)
Actuarial (gain)/loss on obligation (Bal. fig.)	61	(87)	42
Present value of obligation, 31 December	1,141	1,197	1,295
Fair value of plan assets, 1 January	1,000	1,092	1,109
Expected return on plan assets	120	121	114
Contributions	90	100	110
Benefits paid	(150)	(180)	(190)
Actuarial gain/(loss) on plan assets (Bal. fig.)	32	(24)	(50)
Fair value of plan assets, 31 December	1,092	1,109	1,093

Limits of the corridor

The next step is to determine the limits of the corridor and then compare these with the cumulative unrecognised actuarial gains and losses in order to determine the net actuarial gain or loss to be recognised in the following period. The limits are set at the greater of:

(a) 10% of the present value of the obligation before deducting plan asset and
(b) 10% of the fair value of any plan assets.

These limits and the recognised and unrecognised actuarial gains and losses, are as follows:

	20 × 1	20 × 2	20 × 3
Net cumulative unrecognised actuarial gains/(losses), 1 January	140	107	170
Limits of corridor, 1 January	100	114	120
Excess (a)	40	–	50
Average expected remaining working lives (years) (b)	10	10	10
Actuarial gain/(loss) to be recognised (a/b)	4	–	5
Unrecognised actuarial gains/(losses), 1 January	140	107	170
Actuarial gain/(loss) for year – obligation	(61)	87	(42)
Actuarial gain/(loss) for year – plan assets	32	(24)	(50)
Subtotal	111	170	78
Actuarial gain/(loss) recognised	(4)	–	(5)
Unrecognised actuarial gains/(losses), 31 December	107	170	73

Amounts recognised in the balance sheet and income statement, and related analyses

The final step is to determine the amounts to be recognised in the balance sheet and income statement, and the related analyses to be disclosed under paragraphs 120 (c), (e), (f) and (g) of the Standard. These are as follows:

	20 × 1	20 × 2	20 × 3
Present value of the obligation	1,141	1,197	1,295
Fair value of plan assets	(1,092)	(1,109)	(1,093)
	49	88	202
Unrecognised actuarial gains/(losses)	107	170	73
Unrecognised past service cost – non-vested benefits	–	(20)	(10)
Liability recognised in Balance Sheet	**156**	**238**	**265**
Current service cost	130	140	150
Interest cost	100	103	96
Expected return on assets	(120)	(121)	(114)
Net actuarial (gain)/loss recognised in year	(4)	–	(5)
Past service cost – non-vested benefits	–	10	10
Past service cost – vested benefits	–	50	–
Expense recognised in Income Statement	**106**	**182**	**137**

Movements in the net liability recognised in the balance sheet, to be disclosed under paragraph 120 (e):

Opening net liability	140	156	238
Expense as above	106	182	137
Contributions paid	(90)	(100)	(110)
Closing net liability	156	238	265

Actual return on plan assets, to be disclosed under paragraph 120 (g):

Expected return on assets	120	121	114
Actuarial gain/(loss) on plan assets	32	(24)	(50)
Actuarial return on plan assets	152	97	64

Illustrative disclosures

Employee benefit obligations

The amounts recognised in the balance sheet are as follows:

	Defined benefit pension plans		Post-employment medical benefits	
	20 × 2	20 × 1	20 × 2	20 × 1
Present value of funded obligations	12,310	11,772	2,819	2,721
Fair value of plan assets	(11,982)	(11,188)	(2,480)	(2,415)
	328	584	339	306
Present value of unfunded obligations	6,459	6,123	5,160	5,094
Unrecognised actuarial gains/(losses)	(97)	(17)	31	72
Unrecognised past service cost	(450)	(650)	–	–
Net liability in balance sheet	6,240	6,040	5,530	5,472
Amounts in the Balance Sheet:				
Liabilities	6,451	6,278	5,530	5,472
Assets	(211)	(238)	–	–
Net liability in balance sheet	6,240	6,040	5,530	5,472

The pension plan assets include ordinary shares issued by the enterprise with a fair value of 317 (20 × 1: 281). Plan assets also include property occupied by the enterprise with a fair value of 200 (20 × 1: 185)

The amounts recognised in the income statement are as follows:

	Defined benefit pension plans		Post-employment medical benefits	
	20 × 2	20 × 1	20 × 2	20 × 1
Current service cost	1,679	1,554	471	411
Interest on obligation	1,890	1,650	819	705
Expected return on plan assets	(1,392)	(1,188)	(291)	(266)
Net actuarial losses (gains) recognised in year	90	(187)	–	
Past service cost	200	200	–	
Losses (gains) on curtailments and settlements	221	(47)	–	–
Total, included in 'staff costs'	2,688	1,982	999	850
Actual return on plan assets	1,232	1,205	275	254

Movements in the net liability recognised in the balance sheet are as follows:

	Defined benefit pension plans		Post-employment medical benefits	
	20 × 2	20 × 1	20 × 2	20 × 1
Net liability at start of year	6,040	5,505	5,472	5,439
Net expense recognised in the income statement	2,688	1,982	999	5,439
Contributions	(2,261)	(1,988)	(941)	(817)
Exchange differences on foreign plan	(227)	221	–	–
Liabilities acquired in business combinations	–	320	–	–
Net liability at end of year	6,240	6,040	5,530	5,472

Principal actuarial assumptions at the balance sheet date (expressed as weighted averages):

	20 × 2 (%)	20 × 1 (%)
Discount rate at 31 December	10.0	9.1
Expected return on plan assets at 31 December	12.0	10.9
Future salary increases	5.0	4.0
Future pension increases	3.0	2.0
Proportion of employees opting for early retirement	30.0	30.0
Annual increase in health care costs	8.0	8.0
Future changes in maximum state health care benefits	3.0	2.0

The group also participates in an industry wide defined benefit plan which provides pension benefits linked to final salaries and is funded on a pay-as-you-go basis. It is not practicable to determine the present value of the group's obligation or the related current service cost as the plan computes its obligations on a basis that differs materially from the basis used in the enterprise's financial statements. On that basis, the plan's financial statements to 30 June 20 × 0 show an unfunded liability of 27,525. The unfunded liability will result in future payments by participating employers. The plan will result in future payments by participating employers. The plan has approximately 75,000 members, of whom approximately 5,000 are current or former employees of the enterprise or their dependants. The expense recognised in the income statement, which is equal to contributions due for the year, and is not included in the above amounts, was 230 (20 × 1: 215). The group's future contributions may be increased substantially if other enterprises withdraw from the plan.

An excellent example of a practical application of the disclosure required by the standard has been provided by Reckitt Benckiser.

Reckitt Benckiser   Year Ended 31 December 2005

(d) Pension and other Post-Retirement Commitments

The Group operates a number of defined benefit and defined contribution pension schemes around the world covering many of its employees, which are principally of the funded type. The Group's two most significant defined benefit pension schemes (UK and US) are both funded by the payment of contributions to separately administered trust funds.

The Group also operates a number of other post-retirement schemes in certain countries. The major scheme is in the US (US retiree health care scheme), where salaried participants become eligible for retiree health care benefits after they reach a combined 'age and years of service rendered' figure of 70, although the age must be a minimum of 55. As at 31 December 2005 there were 2,816 (2004: 2,765) eligible retirees and 1,470 (2004: 1,517) current employees potentially eligible. This scheme is unfunded.

Pension costs for the year are as follows:

	2005 (£m)	2001 (£m)
Defined contribution schemes	11	11
Defined benefit schemes (net charge)	14	11
Total pension costs recognised in the income statement (Note 2)	25	22

For the UK scheme, a full independent actuarial valuation was carried out at 5 April 2004 and updated at 31 December 2005. For the US scheme, a full independent actuarial valuation was carried out at 1 January 2005 and updated at 31 December 2005. The projected unit valuation method was used for the UK and US scheme valuations. The major assumptions used by the actuaries for the three major schemes as at 31 December 2005 were:

	2005				2004	
	UK	US (pension)	US (medical)	UK	US (pension)	US (pension)
	%	%	%	%	%	%
Rate of increase in pensionable salaries	4.8	5.0	–	4.8	5.0	–
Rate of increase in pension payments and deferred pensions	2.8	–	–	2.8	–	–
Discount rate	4.8	5.5	5.5	5.3	5.8	5.8
Inflation assumption	2.8	4.0	–	2.8	4.0	–
Annual medical cost inflation	–	–	10.5–4.5	–	–	10.5–4.5
Long-term expected rate of return on:						
Equities	7.4	10.8	–	7.8	10.0	–
Bonds	4.3	5.0	–	4.3	7.0	–
Others	5.9	–	–	6.1	–	–

The expected rate of return on plan assets is based on market expectation at the beginning of the period for returns over the entire life of the benefit obligation. For the UK scheme the mortality assumptions were based on PMA92 and PFA92 tables, with allowance for projected improvements in mortality rates in 2004. In addition, the net discount rate has been reduced by 0.25% to allow for further improvements in mortality.

4 Employees (continued)

The movements in the amounts recognised in the balance sheet are as follows:

| Movement in net liability assets during the year | 2005 | | | | | 2004 | | | | |
	UK £m	US (pension) £m	US (medical) £m	Others £m	Total £m	UK £m	US (pension) £m	US (medical) £m	Others £m	Total £m
Surplus/(deficit) at 1 January	(59)	2	(92)	(100)	(249)	11	(11)	(94)	(95)	(189)
Current service cost	(8)	(3)	(1)	(5)	(17)	(7)	(3)	(1)	(4)	(15)
Contributions	5	–	8	6	19	–	14	6	2	22
Past service cost	–	–	–	1	1	–	–	–	–	–
Other finance income	4	4	(5)	(1)	2	6	2	(5)	1	4
Actuarial gain/(loss)	8	(13)	(10)	1	(14)	(69)	(1)	–	(6)	(76)
Exchange adjustments	–	–	(7)	(11)	4	–	1	2	2	5
(Deficit)/surplus at 31 December	(50)	(10)	(107)	(87)	(254)	(59)	(2)	(92)	(100)	(249)

The actual return of plan assets was £103 million (2004: £50m) for the UK scheme and £10 million (2004: £11m) for the US scheme.

Changes in the present value of scheme liabilities are as follows:

| | 2005 | | | | | 2004 | | | | |
	UK £m	US (pension) £m	US (medical) £m	Others £m	Total £m	UK £m	US (pension) £m	US (medical) £m	Others £m	Total £m
Present value of liabilities at 1 January	625	113	92	153	983	529	121	94	146	890
Service cost	8	3	1	4	16	7	3	1	4	15
Interest cost	88	7	5	5	50	30	7	5	2	44
Benefits paid	(24)	(17)	(8)	(11)	(60)	(24)	(17)	(6)	(7)	(54)
Actuarial losses/(gains)	58	13	10	4	85	83	1	–	11	95
Exchange adjustments	–	17	7	(26)	(2)	–	(2)	(2)	(3)	(7)
Present value of liabilities at 31 December	700	136	107	129	1,072	625	113	92	153	983

Changes in the fair value of plan assets are as follows:

| | 2005 | | | | 2004 | | | |
	UK £m	US (pension) £m	Others £m	Total £m	UK £m	US (pension) £m	Others £m	Total £m
Fair value of plan assets at 1 January	566	115	53	734	540	110	51	701
Expected rate of return	37	11	4	52	36	9	3	48
Contributions	5	–	6	11	–	14	2	16
Benefits paid	(24)	(17)	(11)	(52)	(24)	(17)	(7)	(48)
Actuarial gains/flosses)	66	–	5	71	14	–	5	19
Exchange adjustments	–	17	(15)	2	–	(1)	(1)	(2)
Fair value of plan assets at 31 December	650	126	42	818	566	115	53	734

Cumulative actuarial gains and losses recognised in equity:

	2005 (£m)	2004 (£m)
At 1 January	(76)	–
Net actuarial less recognised in the year	(14)	(76)
At 31 December	(90)	(76)

History of experience gains and losses:

	2005 (£m)	2004 (£m)
Experience adjustments arising on scheme assets:		
Amount (£m)	71	19
Percentage of scheme assets (%)	8.7	2.6
Experience adjustments arising on scheme liabilities:		
Amount (£m)	(85)	(95)
Percentage of scheme liabilities (%)	7.9	9.7
Present value of scheme abilities	(1,072)	(983)
Fair value of scheme assets	818	734
Net pension liability	(254)	(249)

Expected employer contributions to be paid to funded defined benefit schemes in 2006 are £7 million (UK: £5m, other schemes: £2m).

4 Employees (continued)

Impact of medical cost trends rates

A one percentage point change in the assumed health care cost trend rates would have the following effects:

	+1% (£m)	−1% (£m)
Effect on service cost and interest cost	1	(1)
Effect on post-retirement benefit obligation	14	(11)

(d) Pension and other post-retirement commitments (continued)

The amounts recognised in the balance sheet are determined as follows:

	2005					2004				
	UK	US (pension)	US (medical)	Other	Total	UK	US (pension)	US (medical)	Other	Total
	£m	£m	£m	£m	£m	£m	£m	£m	£m	£m
Total equities	354	83	–	23	460	326	75	–	26	427
Total bonds	217	43	–	14	274	172	40	–	14	226
Total other assets	79	–	–	5	84	68	–	–	13	81

Fair value of plan assets	650	126	–	42	818	566	115	–	53	734
Present value of scheme liabilities	(700)	(136)	(107)	(129)	(1,072)	(625)	(113)	(92)	(153)	(983)
Net (liability) asset recognised in the Balance Sheet	(50)	(10)	(107)	(87)	(254)	(59)	(2)	(92)	(100)	(249)

Other represents the total of post-retirement benefits and Group defined benefit scheme not material for individual disclosure. The net pension liability is recognised in the balance sheet as follows:

	2005 (£m)	2004 (£m)
Non-current asset:		
Funded scheme surplus	7	4
Non-current liability:		
Funded scheme deficit	(73)	(82)
Unfunded scheme liability	(188)	(171)
Retirement benefit obligation	(261)	(253)
Net pension liability	(254)	(249)

None of the pension schemes assets include an investment in shares of the Company.
The amounts recognised in the income statement are as follows:

	2005					2004				
	UK	US (pension)	US (medical)	Other	Total	UK	US (pension)	US (medical)	Other	Total
	£m	£m	£m	£m	£m	£m	£m	£m	£m	£m
Current service cost	(8)	(3)	(1)	(5)	(17)	(7)	(3)	(1)	(4)	(15)
Past service cost	–	–	–	1	1	–	–	–	–	–
Expected return on pension scheme assets	37	11	–	4	52	36	9	–	3	48
Interest on pension scheme liabilities	(33)	(7)	(5)	(5)	(50)	(30)	(7)	(5)	(2)	(44)
Total charge to the income statement	(4)	1	(6)	(5)	(14)	(1)	(1)	(6)	(3)	(11)

The amounts recognised in shareholders' equity for the Group are as follows:

	2005 (£m)	2004 (£m)
Actual return less expected return on pension scheme assets	71	19
Experience gains and losses on scheme liabilities	(19)	(5)
Changes in assumptions underlying present value of scheme liabilities	(66)	(90)
Actuarial (loss)/gain recognised	(14)	(76)

Another excellent example of the accounting policy note for pensions is BAE Systems Plc which also incorporate the accounting treatment required under IFRS 2 *Share-Based Payment* (see Section 7.3).

BAE Systems Plc

Employee benefits:

Retirement benefit plans

Obligations for contributions to defined contribution pension plans are recognised as an expense in the income statement as incurred.

For defined benefit retirement plans, the cost of providing benefits is determined periodically by independent actuaries and charged to the income statement in the period in which those benefits are earned by the employees. Actuarial gains and losses are recognised in full in the period in which they occur, and are recognised in the statement of recognised income and expense. Past service cost is recognised immediately to the extent the benefits are already vested, or otherwise is amortised on a straight-line basis over the average period until the benefits become vested.

The retirement benefit obligations recognised in the balance sheet represents the present value of the defined benefit obligations as adjusted for unrecognised past service cost and as reduced by the fair value of scheme assets.

Long-term service benefits:

Equity and equity-related compensation benefits

The Group issues equity-settled and cash-settled share options to employees. In accordance with the requirements of IFRS 2 *Share-Based Payments* (IFRS 2), the Group has applied IFRS 2 to all equity-settled share options granted after 7 November 2002 that were unvested as of 1 January 2005 and all cash-settled options outstanding at the balance sheet date.

As explained in Note 26, equity-settled share options are measured at fair value at the date of grant using an option pricing model. The fair value is expensed on a straight-line basis over the vesting period, based on the Group's estimate of the number of shares that will actually vest.

Cash-settled share options are measured at fair value at the balance sheet date using an option pricing model. The Group recognises a liability at the balance sheet date based on these fair values, and taking into account the estimated number of the options that will actually vest and the relative completion of the vesting period. Changes in the value of this liability are recognised in the income statement for the year.

22. Retirement benefit obligations

Pension plans

BAE Systems Plc operates pension plans for the Group's qualifying employees in the UK, US and other countries. The principal plans in the UK and US are funded defined benefit plans and the assets are held in separate trustee administered funds. The plans in other countries are unfunded. Pension plan valuations are regularly carried out by independent actuaries to determine pension costs for pension funding and to calculate the IAS 19 deficit.

The disclosures below relate to post-retirement benefit plans in the UK, US and other countries which are accounted for as defined benefit plans in accordance with IAS 19. The valuations used for the IAS 19 disclosures are based on the most recent actuarial valuation undertaken by independent qualified actuaries and updated to take account of the requirements of IAS 19 in order to assess the deficit of the plans at 31 December each year. Plan assets are shown at the bid value at 31 December each year.

The plan in Germany relates to the arrangements for Atlas Elektronik GmbH. The obligations for these arrangements have been presented as liabilities directly associated with non-current assets and disposal groups held for sale following the classification of Atlas Elektronik as a disposal group (Note 19).

Post-retirement benefits other than pensions

The Group also operates a number of non-pension post-retirement benefit plans, under which certain employees are eligible to receive benefits after retirement, the majority of which relate to the provision of medical benefits to retired employees of the Group's subsidiaries in the US. These plans are generally unfunded. The latest valuations of the principal plans, covering retiree medical and life insurance plans in certain US subsidiaries, were performed by independent actuaries as at 1 January 2005. The method of accounting for these is similar to that used for defined benefit pension plans.

A relatively simple example of how to calculate the accounting entries for the income statement and balance sheet is provided below:

Example – Klondike

Klondike operates a defined benefit post-retirement plan for its employees. The plan is reviewed annually. Klondike's actuaries have provided the following information:

	At 31 March 2007 £'000	At 31 March 2008 £'000
Present value obligation	1,500	1,750
Fair value of plan assets	1,500	1,650
Current service cost – year to 31 March 2007		160
Contributions paid – year to 31 March 2007		85
Benefits paid to employees – year to 31 March 2007		125
Net cumulative unrecognised gains at 1 April 20027	200	
Expected return on plan assets at 1 April 2006 is	12%	
Discount rate for plan liabilities al 1 April 2006	10%	

The average remaining working lives of Klondike's employees at 31 March 2006 is 10 years.

Prepare extracts of Klondike's financial statements for the year to 31 March 2008 in compliance with IAS 19 *Employee Benefits* in so far as the information permits.

Solution – Klondike

Income Statement (Extracts)

	£'000
Current service costs	160
Interest cost (10% × 1,500)	150
Expected return on assets (12% × 1,500)	(180)
Recognised actuarial gain (W3)	(5)
Post-retirement cost	125

Balance Sheet (Extracts)

	£'000
Present value of obligations	1,750
Fair value of plan's assets	(1,650)
	100
Unrecognised actuarial gains (W1)	140
Liability recognised in balance sheet	240

Workings

W1 Unrecognised actuarial gains

Unrecognised actuarial gain at 1st April 2007	200
Actuarial gain on plan assets (W2)	10
Actuarial loss on plan liability (W2)	(65)
Gain recognised (W3)	(5)
	140

W2 Movement in plan assets and plan liabilities

	Plan assets £'000	Plan liabilities £'000
Balance at 1st April 2001	1,500	1,500
Current service costs		160
Interest (1,500 × 10%)		150
Expected return (1,500 × 12%)	180	
Contributions paid	85	
Benefits paid to employees	(125)	(125)
Actuarial gain (Bal. fig.)	10	
Actuarial loss (Bal. fig.)		65
	1,650	1,750

> **W3 Calculation of excess surplus on defined benefit scheme**
>
> | | |
> |---|---:|
> | Net cumulative unrecognised actuarial gains at 1st April 2007 | 200 |
> | 10% corridor (1,500 × 10%) | 150 |
> | Excess | 50 |
>
> £50,000/10 years = £5,000 actuarial gain to be recognised.

7.2   IAS 26 *Accounting and Reporting by Retirement Plans* (1994)

Objective

The objective of IAS 26 is to specify measurement and disclosure principles for the reports of retirement benefit plans. All plans should include in their reports a statement of changes in net assets available for benefits, a summary of significant accounting policies and a description of the plan and the effect of any changes in the plan during the period.

Scope

This standard should be applied in the reports of retirement benefit plans where such reports are prepared.

The plan should be separate from the employers. It covers reporting by the plan to all participants, not to individuals. It complements IAS 19 which applies to the cost of retirement plans in an employer's own financial statements.

The plans may be defined contribution or defined benefit. They may require the creation of separate funds to which contributions are made and from which retirement benefits are paid. IAS 26 applies regardless of whether or not a fund is created. Similarly funds invested through insurance companies are also covered.

It does not cover employment termination indemnities, long-service leave benefits, special early retirement or redundancy plans, health and welfare plans, etc.

Definitions

- *Retirement benefit plans.* Arrangements whereby an entity provides benefits for its employees on or after termination of service when such benefits can be determined or estimated in advance of retirement from the provisions of a document or from the entity's practices.
- *Defined contribution plans.* Retirement benefit plans under which retirement benefits are determined by contributions to a fund together with investment earnings thereon.
- *Defined benefit plans.* Retirement benefit plans under which retirement benefits are determined by reference to a formula usually based on employees' earnings and years of service.
- *Funding.* The transfer of assets to a fund separate from the employer's entity to meet future obligations for the payment of retirement benefits.

Most plans are based on formal agreements but some plans permit employers to limit their obligations under the plans but it is usually difficult to cancel a plan if the employees are to be retained. The same accounting treatment should apply to both formal and informal plans.

Any hybrid plans should be considered to be defined contribution for the purposes of IAS 26.

Defined contribution plans

The report of a defined contribution plan should contain a statement of net assets available for benefits and a description of the funding policy.

Future benefits are determined by the contributions paid by the employer and investment earnings thereon. There is no need for actuarial advice and the employer's obligation is a closed end liability.

However, an employer is interested in the efficient and fair operation of the plan and participants are concerned about proper control being exercised to protect their rights.

The objective of reporting by a defined contribution plan is to periodically provide information about the plan and the performance of its investments. That is achieved by providing a report including the following:

(a)   A description of significant activities for the period and the effect of any changes relating to the plan, its membership and terms and conditions.
(b)   Statements reporting on the transactions and investment performance for the period and the financial position of the plan at the end of the period.
(c)   A description of the investment policies.

Defined benefit plans

The report of a defined benefit plan should contain either:

(a)   a statement that shows:
    (i)   the net assets available for benefits;
    (ii)   the actuarial present value of promised retirement benefits, distinguishing between vested benefits and non-vested benefits; and
    (iii) the resulting excess or deficit; or
(b)   a statement of net assets available for benefits including either:
    (i)   a note disclosing the actuarial present value of promised retirement benefits, distinguishing between vested benefits and non-vested benefits or
    (ii)   a reference to this information in an accompanying actuarial report.

If an actuarial valuation has not been prepared at the date of the report, the most recent valuation should be used as a base and the date of the valuation disclosed.

The actuarial present value should be based on the benefits promised under the terms of the plan based on service to date using either current or projected salary levels, with disclosure of the basis. The effect of any changes in actuarial assumptions having a significant effect on the actuarial present value of promised benefits should also be disclosed.

The report should explain the relationship between the actuarial present value of promised actuarial benefits and net assets available, and the policy for funding.

The payment of promised benefits depends on the financial position of the plan and the ability to make future contributions as well as investment performance and operating efficiency. It requires actuarial advice to assess the financial position, review the assumptions and recommend future contribution levels.

The objective of reporting by a defined benefit plan is to periodically provide information about the financial resources and activities of the plan that is useful in assessing the relationships between the accumulation of resources and plan benefits over time. The objective is usually achieved by providing a report including the following:

(a) a description of significant activities for the period and the effect of any changes relating to the plan, its membership and terms and conditions;

(b) statements reporting on the transactions and investment performance for the period and the financial position of the plan at the end of the period;

(c) actuarial information either as part of the statements or by way of a separate report; and

(d) a description of the investment policies.

Actuarial present value of promised retirement benefits

The present value of future expected payments may be calculated using either current or expected salary levels.

The reasons for adopting a current salary approach include:

(a) the actuarial present value can be calculated more objectively than with projected salary levels as it involves fewer assumptions;

(b) increases in benefits due to salary increases become an obligation of the plan at the time of the salary increase; and

(c) the amount of the actuarial present value is more closely related to the amount payable in the event of a termination or discontinuance of the plan.

The reasons for adopting a projected salary approach include:

(a) financial information should be prepared on a going concern basis, irrespective of the assumptions and estimates made;

(b) under final pay schemes, benefits are determined by reference to salaries at or near retirement date – salaries, contribution levels and rates of return must be projected; and

(c) failure to incorporate salary projections may result in an apparent overfunding.

The actuarial value of benefits based on current salaries is disclosed in the report of a plan to indicate the obligation for benefits earned to the date of the report. The actuarial value of benefits based on projected salaries is disclosed to indicate the magnitude of the potential obligation on a going concern basis.

In addition, sufficient explanation might be needed to indicate clearly the context in which the actuarial valuation should be read. It may give the form of providing information on the adequacy of future funding and of the funding policy based on salary projections. This can be provided in the financial information or in the actuary's report.

Frequency of actuarial valuations

In many countries actuarial valuations are obtained every three years. If not prepared at the date of the report, the most recent valuation should be used as the base and the date of valuation disclosed.

Report content

For defined benefit plans the information should be provided in one of the following formats:

(a) a statement in the report showing the net assets, the actuarial present value of benefits and the excess/deficit. The report should also contain statements of changes in net assets and in the actuarial present value of benefits. It may include a separate actuary's report supporting the actuarial present value of promised retirement benefits;

(b) a report that includes a statement of net assets and a statement of changes in those benefits. The actuarial present value of benefits is disclosed in the notes. The report may also include a report from an actuary supporting the actuarial present value of promised benefits;

(c) a report that includes a statement of net assets and a statement of changes in net assets with the actuarial value of promised retirement benefits contained in a separate actuarial report.

In each format a trustee's report and an investment report may accompany the statements.

All plans

Valuation of plan assets

Investments should be valued at fair value – for marketable securities, i.e. market value. If the fair value is not possible, disclosure should be made of the reason why it is not adopted.

Disclosure

The following information should also be provided:

(a) a statement of changes in net assets available for benefits;
(b) a summary of significant accounting policies; and
(c) a description of the plan and the effect of any changes in the plan during the period.

Net assets

Statement of net assets available for benefits disclosing:

(i)   assets at the end of the period suitably classified;
(ii)   the basis of valuation of assets;
(iii) details of any single investment exceeding 5% of the net assets available for benefits;
(iv)   details of any investment in the employer; and
(v)   liabilities other than the actuarial present value of promised retirement benefits.

Statement of changes in net assets available for benefits disclosing:

(i)   employer contributions;
(ii)   employee contributions;
(iii)   investment income – interest and dividends;
(iv)   other income;
(v)   benefits paid or payable;
(vi)   administration expenses;
(vii)   other expenses;
(viii) taxes on income;

(ix) profits and losses on disposal of investments and changes in their value; and

(x) transfers to and from other plans.

A description of the funding policy

For defined benefit plans, the actuarial present value of promised retirement benefits based on benefits promised, service rendered to date and using either current salary levels or projected salary levels.

For defined benefit plans, a description of the significant actuarial assumptions made and the method used to calculate the actuarial present value of promised retirement benefits.

A description of the plan, either as part of the financial information or in a separate report

(a) the names of the employers and groups concerned;

(b) the number of participants receiving benefits and the number of other participants, classified as appropriate;

(c) the type of plan – defined contribution or defined benefit;

(d) a note as to whether participants contribute to the plan;

(e) a description of the retirement benefits promised;

(f) a description of any plan termination terms; and

(g) changes in items (a) to (f) during the period covered by the report.

7.3   IFRS 2 *Share-Based Payment* (April 2004)

Introduction

Share options are a common feature of employee remuneration. In addition, some entities issue share options to suppliers. However, until this IFRS was issued, there was no IFRS on the subject.

Objective

The objective of this IFRS is to specify the financial reporting by an entity when it undertakes a *share-based payment transaction,* particularly its impact on profit or loss and financial position.

Scope

An entity shall apply this IFRS for all share-based payment transactions including:

(a) equity-settled share-based payment transactions;

(b) cash-settled share-based payment transactions; and

(c) transactions in which the entity receives or acquires goods or services and the terms provide a choice of settling in cash or by issuing equity.

Transfers of an entity's equity instruments by its shareholders to suppliers are share-based payment transactions.

A transaction with an employee in his/her capacity as a holder of equity of the entity is not a share-based payment transaction.

Goods include inventories, consumables, property, plant and equipment, intangible assets and other non-financial assets. However, IFRS 2 does not apply to a business combination (see IFRS 3 *Business Combinations*). Hence, equity issued in a business combination in exchange for control of the acquiree is not within the scope of this IFRS. However, equity granted in capacity as employees (e.g. in return for continued service) is within the scope of this IFRS.

This IFRS does not apply to a contract within the scope of paragraphs 8–10 of IAS 32 *Financial Instruments: Disclosure and Presentation* or paragraphs 5–7 of IAS 39 *Financial Instruments: Recognition and Measurement*.

Definitions

- *Cash-settled share-based payment transaction.* A share-based payment transaction in which the entity acquires goods or services by incurring a liability to transfer cash or other assets to the supplier of those goods or services for amounts that are based on the price (or value) of the entity's shares or other equity instruments of the entity.
- *Equity instrument.* A contract that evidences a residual interest in the assets of an entity after deducting all of its liabilities.
- *Equity-settled share-based payment transaction.* A share-based payment transaction in which the entity receives goods or services as consideration for equity instruments of the entity (including shares or share options).
- *Grant date.* The date at which the entity and another party (including an employee) agree to a share-based payment arrangement, being when the entity and the counterparty have a shared understanding of the terms and conditions of the arrangement. At grant date the entity confers on the counterparty the right to cash, other assets, or equity instruments of the entity, provided the specified vesting conditions, if any, are met. If that agreement is subject to an approval process (e.g. by shareholders), grant date is the date when that approval is obtained.
- *Intrinsic value.* The difference between the fair value of the shares to which the counterparty has the (conditional or unconditional) right to subscribe or which it has the right to receive, and the price (if any) the counterparty is (or will be) required to pay for those shares. For example, a share option with an exercise price of £15, on a share with a fair value of £20, has an intrinsic value of £5.
- *Market condition.* A condition upon which the exercise price, vesting or exercisability of an equity instrument depends is related to the market price of the entity's equity instruments, such as attaining a specified share price or a specified amount of intrinsic value of a share option, or achieving a specified target that is based on the market price of the entity's equity instruments relative to an index of market prices of equity instruments of other entities.
- *Measurement date.* The date at which the fair value of the equity instruments granted is measured for the purposes of this IFRS. For transactions with employees and others providing similar services, the measurement date is grant date. For transactions with parties other than employees (and those providing similar services), the measurement date is the date the entity obtains the goods or the counterparty renders service.
- *Reload feature.* A feature that provides for an automatic grant of additional share options whenever the option holder exercises previously granted options using the entity's shares, rather than cash, to satisfy the exercise price.

- *Reload option.* A new share option granted when a share is used to satisfy the exercise price of a previous share option.
- *Share-based payment transaction.* A transaction in which the entity receives goods or services as consideration for equity instruments of the entity (including shares or share options), or acquires goods or services by incurring liabilities to the supplier of those goods or services for amounts that are based on the price of the entity's shares or other equity instruments of the entity.
- *Share option.* A contract that gives the holder the right, but not the obligation, to subscribe to the entity's shares at a fixed or determinable price for a specified period of time.
- *Vest.* To become an entitlement. Under a share-based payment arrangement, a counterparty's right to receive cash, other assets, or equity instruments of the entity vests upon satisfaction of any specified vesting conditions.
- *Vesting conditions.* The conditions that must be satisfied for the counterparty to become entitled to receive cash, other assets or equity instruments of the entity, under a share-based payment arrangement. Vesting conditions include service conditions, which require the other party to complete a specified period of service, and performance conditions, which require specified performance targets to be met (such as a specified increase in the entity's profit over a specified period of time).
- *Vesting period.* The period during which all the specified vesting conditions of a share-based payment arrangement are to be satisfied.

Recognition

An entity must recognise the goods or services received or acquired in a share-based payment transaction when it obtains the goods or as the services are received. The entity must recognise a corresponding increase in equity if the goods or services were received in an equity-settled share-based payment transaction, or a liability if the goods or services were acquired in a cash-settled share-based payment transaction.

When the goods or services received do not qualify as assets, they must be expensed.

Typically, an expense arises from the consumption of goods or services. Services are typically consumed immediately, in which case an expense is recognised as counterparty renders service. Goods might be consumed over a period of time, in which case an expense is recognised when the goods are consumed or sold. However, sometimes it is necessary to recognise an expense before the goods or services are consumed or sold, because they do not qualify for recognition as assets. For example, an entity might acquire goods as part of the research phase of a project. Although those goods have not been consumed, they might not qualify for recognition as assets under the applicable IFRS.

Equity-settled share-based payment transactions

Overview

For equity-settled share-based payment transactions, the entity must measure the goods or services received, and the corresponding increase in equity, directly, at the fair value of the goods or services received, unless that fair value cannot be estimated reliably. If the entity cannot estimate reliably the fair value of the goods or services received, the entity must measure their value, and the corresponding increase in equity, indirectly, by reference to the fair value of the equity instruments granted.

For transactions with *employees and others providing similar services*, fair value of the services received are referred to the fair value of the equity granted, as it is not possible to estimate reliably the fair value of the services received. The fair value of equity should be measured at *grant date*.

Typically share options are granted to employees as part of their remuneration package. Usually, it is not possible to measure directly the services received for particular components of the employee's remuneration package. It might also not be possible to measure the fair value of the total remuneration package independently, without measuring directly the fair value of equity instruments granted as share options are sometimes granted as part of a bonus arrangement (e.g. as an incentive to the employees to remain in the entity's employ or to reward them for their efforts in improving the entity's performance). By granting shares or share options, the entity is paying additional remuneration to obtain additional benefits. Estimating the fair value of those additional benefits is likely to be difficult. Because of the difficulty of measuring directly the fair value of the services received, the entity must measure the fair value of the employee services received by reference to the fair value of the equity instruments granted.

For parties other than employees, there is a rebuttable presumption that the fair value of the goods or services received can be estimated reliably. It is measured at the date the entity obtains the goods or the counterparty renders service. In rare cases, if the entity rebuts this presumption because it cannot estimate reliably the fair value of the goods or services received, the entity must measure the goods or services received, and the corresponding increase in equity, indirectly, by reference to the fair value of the equity instruments granted. These should be measured at the date the entity obtains the goods or the counterparty renders service.

Transactions in which services are received

If the equity *vests* immediately, the services rendered are assumed to have been received. In this case, on grant date, the entity must recognise the services received in full, with a corresponding increase in equity.

If the equity does not vest until the counterparty completes a specified period of service, the services will be received in the future, during the *vesting period*. The entity must account for those services as they are rendered by the counterparty during the vesting period, with a corresponding increase in equity. For example:

(a) If an employee is granted share options conditional upon completing three years service, over that three-year vesting period.

(b) If an employee is granted share options conditional upon, say, a condition being satisfied, and the length of the vesting period varies, the entity must presume that the services rendered by the employee as consideration will be received in the future, over the expected vesting period. The entity must estimate the length of the expected vesting period at grant date, based on the most likely outcome of the performance condition. If the performance condition is a *market condition*, the estimate of the length of the expected vesting period shall be consistent with the assumptions used in estimating the fair value of the options granted, and shall not be subsequently revised. If the performance condition is not a market condition, the entity must revise its estimate of the length of the vesting period, if necessary, if subsequent information indicates that the length of the vesting period differs from previous estimates.

Example 1 – Equity-settled share-based payment transactions

Background

An entity grants 100 options to each of its 500 employees. Each is conditional on the employee working for the entity over the next three years. Assume the fair value is £15. Based on weighted average probability, 20% of employees will leave during the three-year period and thus forfeit their rights. The total fair value of options granted = 500 × 100 options × £15 × 80% = £600,000.

The entity also estimates that the departures will occur evenly over three years.

Application

Scenario 1

If everything turns out as expected		Cumulative	Expense
Year 1	50,000 options × 80% × £15 × 1/3 years	200,000	200,000
Year 2	50,000 options ×·80% × £15 × 2/3 years	400,000	200,000
Year 3	50,000 options × 80% × £15 × 3/3 years	600,000	200,000
Total over 3 years			600,000

Scenario 2

During year 1 – 20 employees leave then the entity revises its estimate of total departures from 20% to 15%.
During year 2 – 22 employees leave then the entity revises its estimate of total departures from 15% to 12%
During year 3 – 15 employees leave thus 57 in total forfeited their rights leaving 443 × 100 options vested.

	Cumulative	Expense
Year 1 50,000 options × 85% × £15 × 1/3 years	212,500	212,500
Year 2 50,000 options × 88% × £15 × 2/3 years	440,000	227,500
Year 3 44,300 options × £15 × 3/3 years	664,500	224,500
Total over 3 years		664,500

Transactions measured by reference to the fair value of the equity instruments granted

Determining the fair value of equity instruments granted

The fair value of equity instruments granted at the *measurement date* is based on market prices if available, taking into account the terms and conditions upon which those equity instruments were granted.

If market prices are not available, the entity shall estimate the fair value of the equity using a valuation technique to estimate what the price of those equity instruments would have been on the measurement date in an arm's length transaction between knowledgeable, willing parties. The valuation technique shall be consistent with generally accepted valuation methodologies for pricing financial instruments, incorporating all factors and assumptions that knowledgeable, willing market participants would consider in setting the price.

Treatment of vesting conditions

A grant of equity instruments might be conditional upon satisfying specified *vesting conditions*, e.g. the employee remaining in the entity's employ for a specified period of time. There might be performance conditions that must be satisfied, e.g. achieving a specified growth in profit or specified increase in the entity's share price. Vesting conditions should not be taken into account when estimating the fair value at the measurement date. Instead, vesting conditions are used to adjust the number of equity instruments included in the measurement of the transaction amount so that, ultimately, the amount recognised for goods or services received as consideration for the equity instruments granted shall be based on the number of equity instruments that eventually vest. Hence, on a cumulative basis, no amount is recognised for goods or services received if the equity instruments granted do not vest because of failure to satisfy a vesting condition, e.g. the counterparty fails to complete a specified service period, or a performance condition is not satisfied.

The entity should recognise an amount for the goods/services received during the vesting period based on the best available estimate of the number of equity instruments expected to vest and it must revise that estimate if subsequent information indicates that the number of equity instruments expected to vest differs from previous estimates. On vesting date, the entity must revise the estimate to equal the number of equity instruments that ultimately vested.

Market conditions, such as a target share price must be taken into account when estimating the fair value of the equity instruments granted.

Treatment of a reload feature

A *reload option* should be accounted for as a new option grant when a reload option is subsequently granted.

After vesting date

No subsequent adjustment must be made to total equity after vesting date. No reversal occurs if the vested equity instruments are later forfeited or not exercised. However, the entity may transfer within equity, i.e. a transfer from one component of equity to another.

If the fair value of the equity instruments cannot be estimated reliably

In rare cases, the entity may be unable to estimate reliably the fair value of the equity instruments granted at the measurement date. In these cases, the entity shall instead:

(a) Measure the equity instruments at their *intrinsic value*, initially at the date the entity obtains the goods or the counterparty renders service and subsequently at each reporting date and at the date of final settlement, with any change in intrinsic value recognised in profit or loss. For a grant of share options, the share-based payment arrangement is finally settled when the options are exercised, are forfeited (e.g. upon cessation of employment) or lapse (e.g. at the end of the option's life).

(b) Recognise the goods or services received based on the number of equity instruments that ultimately vest or (where applicable) are ultimately exercised. The amount recognised for goods or services received during the vesting period shall be based on the number of share options expected to vest. The entity shall revise that estimate, if necessary, if subsequent information indicates that the number of share options expected to vest differs from previous estimates. On vesting date, the entity shall revise the estimate to equal the number of equity instruments that ultimately vested. After vesting date, the entity shall reverse the amount recognised for goods or services received if the share options are later forfeited, or lapse at the end of the share option's life.

Modifications to the terms and conditions on which equity instruments were granted, including cancellations and settlements

If an entity reduces the exercise price of options granted to employees (i.e. reprice the options), it increases the fair value of those options. IFRS 2 must also be applied equally to share-based payment transactions with parties other than employees that are measured by reference to the fair value of the equity instruments granted.

As a minimum, the services received should be measured at the grant date fair value of the equity instruments granted, unless those equity instruments do not vest because of failure to satisfy a vesting condition (other than a market condition) that was specified at grant date. This applies irrespective of any modifications or a cancellation or settlement of that grant of equity instruments. In addition, the entity shall recognise the effects of modifications that increase the total fair value of the share-based payment arrangement or are otherwise beneficial to the employee.

If the entity cancels or settles a grant of equity during the vesting period (other than forfeiture):

(a) The entity shall account for the cancellation/settlement as an acceleration of vesting, and therefore recognise immediately the amount that otherwise would have been recognised for services received over the remainder of the vesting period.

(b) Any payment made to the employee on the cancellation or settlement of the grant must be accounted for as a repurchase of an equity interest, i.e. as a deduction from equity, except to the extent that the payment exceeds the fair value of the equity instruments granted, measured at the repurchase date. Any such excess is recognised as an expense.

(c) If new equity is granted to the employee and, on grant date, the entity identifies the new equity as replacement equity for the cancelled equity, the entity must account for replacement equity in the same way as a modification of the original grant. The incremental fair value granted is the difference between the fair value of the replacement equity instruments and the net fair value of the cancelled equity instruments, at the date replacement equity instruments are granted. The net fair value of the cancelled equity instruments is their fair value, immediately before the cancellation, less the amount of any payment made to the employee on cancellation of the equity that is accounted for as a deduction from equity in accordance with (b) above. If the entity does not identify new equity granted as replacement equity for the cancelled equity instruments, the entity must account for the new equity as a new grant of equity instruments.

If an entity repurchases vested equity, the payment made to the employee must be accounted for as a deduction from equity, except to the extent that the payment exceeds the fair value of the equity repurchased, measured at the repurchase date. Any excess should be expensed.

Example 2 – Equity-settled share-based payment transactions (performance condition – Vesting period varies)

Background

At start of year 1 an entity grants 100 shares to 500 employees conditional on staying for vesting period.

Shares vest at end of year 1 if earnings increase by more than 18%.
Shares vest at end of year 2 if earnings increase by more than an average of 13% per annum over two-year period.
Shares vest at end of year 3 if earnings increase by more than an average of 10% per annum over three-year period.
Fair value at start of year 1 is £30 per share and no dividends are expected over the three years.

End of year 1 – earnings increased by 14% and 30 employees left – expect earnings to increase similarly in year 2 and thus vest at end of year 2. However, a further 30 employees are expected to leave.

End of year 2 – earnings increased by only 10%. 28 employees left during the year and expect a further 25 to leave during year 3. Earnings are expected to rise by a further 6% and thus achieve an average of 10% per annum.

End of year 3 – 23 employees left and earnings rose by 8% – an average of 10.67% over three years 419 employees received 100 shares at the end of year 3.

Application

		Cumulative	Expense
Year 1	440 employees × 100 shares × £30 × 1/3 years	440,000	440,000
Year 2	417 employees × 100 shares × £30 × 2/3 years	834,000	394,000
Year 3	419 employees × 100 shares × £30 × 3/3 years	1,257,000	423,000
Total charged during the 3-year period			1,257,000

Example 3 – Equity-settled share-based payment transactions (performance condition – Number of equity instruments varies)

Background

At start of year 1 – A grants options to 100 employees to vest after three years provided employees stay for period and sales volumes increase by 5% per annum.

If sales volumes are between 5% and 10% employees receive 100 options.
If sales volumes are between 10% and 15% employees receive 200 options.
If sales volumes exceed 15% employees receive 300 options.

The fair value at date of grant is £20 per option.
Grant date-assume growth between 10–15% and 20% of employees will leave.
End of year 1 – 7 employees left but still expects 20 in total to leave by end of year 3. Sales increase by 12% and expect this to continue.
End of year 2 – 5 employees left but only expects three more to leave. Sales increased by 18% – average 15% for two years but expect sales to achieve a 15% plus growth over a three-year period.
End of year 3 – 2 employees left. Sales growth was 16% over three-year period.

Application

	Cumulative	Expense
Year 1 80 employees × 200 options × £20 × 1/3 years	106,667	106,667
Year 2 85 employees × 300 options × £20 × 2/3 years	340,000	233,333
Year 3 86 employees × 300 options × £20 × 3/3 years	516,000	176,000
Total expense over 3 years		516,000

Cash-settled share-based payment transactions

Goods or services acquired and the liability incurred should be measured at the fair value of the liability. Until the liability is settled, it should be remeasured at each reporting date and at the date of settlement, with any changes in fair value being recognised in profit or loss.

Share appreciation rights to employees as part of their remuneration package is popular, whereby the employees will become entitled to a future cash payment based on the increase in the entity's share price from a specified level over a specified period of time or an entity might grant its employees a right to receive a future cash payment by granting them a right to shares (including shares to be issued upon the exercise of share options) that are redeemable, either mandatorily (e.g. upon cessation of employment) or at the employee's option.

An entity should recognise services received and a liability, as the employees render service. Some share appreciation rights (SARs) vest immediately, and the employees are therefore not required to complete a specified period of service to become entitled to the cash payment. In the absence of evidence to the contrary, the entity should presume that the services rendered by the employees in exchange for the SARs have been received. Thus, the entity shall recognise immediately the services received and a liability to pay for them. If the SARs do not vest until the employees have completed a specified period of service, the entity shall recognise the services received, and a liability to pay for them, as the employees render service during that period.

The liability should be measured, initially and each reporting date until settled, at the fair value of the SARs, by applying an option pricing model, taking into account the terms and conditions on which the SARs were granted, and the extent to which the employees have rendered service to date.

Example 4 – Cash-settled share-based payment transactions

Background

An entity grants 100 cash share appreciation rights (SARs) as long as an employee stays three years.

During year 1 – 35 employees leave. The entity estimates that a further 60 will leave during years 2 and 3.

During year 2 – 40 employees leave and the entity estimates a further 25 will leave during year 3.

During year 3 – 22 employees leave and at the end of year 3, 150 employees exercise their SARs, another 140 exercise at the end of year 4 and the remaining 113 at the end of year 5.

	Fair value (£)	Intrinsic value (£)
Year 1	14.40	
2	15.50	
3	18.20	15.00
4	21.40	20.00
5		25.00

Application

		Cumulative	Expense
Year 1 Expense for services received and consumed, and the year end liability (500–95 employees × 100 SARs × £14.40 × 1/3		194,400	194,400
Year 2 (500–100 employees × 100 SARs × £15.50 × 2/3		413,333	218,933
Year 3 (500–97 left–150 exercised × 100 SARs × £18.20 × 3/3	460,460		
150 exercised × 100 exercised × £15	225,000	685,460	272,127
Year 4 150 exercised × 100 SARs × £15	225,000		
140 exercised × 100 SARS × £20	280,000		
(500–97 left–290 exercised × 100 SARs × £21.40	241,820	746,820	61,360
Year 5 150 exercised × 100 SARs × £15	225,000		
140 exercised × 100 SARs × £20	280,000		
113 exercised × 100 SARs × £25	282,500	787,500	40,680
Total charged over the 5 years			787,500

Share-based payment transactions with choice of settlement

For transactions which provide either the entity or the counterparty with the choice of whether the entity settles in cash or by issuing equity, the entity should account for that transaction as a cash-settled share-based payment transaction if it has incurred a liability to settle in cash or as an equity-settled transaction if no such liability has been incurred.

This covers the situation where the entity has granted a compound financial instrument, which includes a debt and an equity component. For transactions with parties other than employees the entity should measure the equity component of the compound as the difference between the fair value of the goods or services received and the fair value of the debt component, at the date when the goods or services are received.

For other transactions, including those with employees, the entity should measure the fair value of the compound instrument at the measurement date, taking into account the terms and conditions on which the rights to cash or equity instruments were granted.

The entity must first measure the fair value of the debt component, and then the fair value of the equity component. The fair value of the compound financial instrument is the sum of the fair values of the two components. However, share-based payment transactions in which the counterparty has the choice of settlement are often structured so that the fair value of one settlement alternative is the same as the other, e.g. the counterparty might have the choice of receiving share options or cash-settled SARs. In such cases, the fair value of the equity component is zero, and thus the fair value of the compound instrument is the same as the fair value of the debt component. Conversely, if the fair values of the settlement alternatives differ, the fair value of the equity component usually will be greater than zero, in which case the fair value of the compound instrument will be greater than the fair value of the debt component.

Any goods/services received or acquired in respect of each component of the compound instrument should be accounted for separately. For the debt component, the goods/services acquired and liability to pay for those goods/services should be reported as the counterparty supplies goods or renders service, in accordance with cash-settled transactions. For the equity component (if any), the entity should recognise the goods/services received, and an increase in equity, as the counterparty supplies goods or renders service, in accordance with the requirements applying to equity-settled transactions.

At the date of settlement, the liability should be remeasured to fair value. If the entity issues equity on settlement rather than paying cash, the liability should be transferred direct to equity, as the consideration for the equity instruments issued.

If the entity pays in cash on settlement rather than issuing equity, that payment should be applied to settle the liability in full. Any equity component previously recognised shall remain within equity. By electing to receive cash, the counterparty forfeited the right to receive equity. However, this does not preclude the entity from recognising a transfer within equity, i.e. a transfer from one component of equity to another.

Share-based payment transactions in which the terms of the arrangement provide the entity with a choice of settlement

Where the terms provide an entity with the choice of whether to settle in cash or by issuing equity, the entity must determine whether it has a present obligation to settle in cash and account for it accordingly. The entity has a present obligation to settle in cash if the choice of settlement in equity has no commercial substance or the entity has a past practice or a stated policy of settling in cash, or generally settles in cash whenever the counterparty asks for cash settlement.

If the entity has a present obligation to settle in cash, it must account for the transaction in accordance with cash-settled transactions but if no such obligation exists it should be accounted for as an equity-settled share-based payment transactions. Upon settlement:

(a)   if entity elects to settle in cash, the cash payment shall be accounted for as a repurchase of an equity interest, i.e. as a deduction from equity, except as noted in (c) below;

(b)   if the entity elects to settle by issuing equity, no further accounting is required (other than a cross equity transfer), except as noted in (c) below; and

(c)   if the entity elects the settlement alternative with the higher fair value, as at the date of settlement, the entity shall recognise an additional expense for the excess value given, i.e. the difference between the cash paid and the fair value of the equity that would otherwise have been issued, or the difference between the fair value of the equity issued and the amount of cash that otherwise would have been paid, whichever is applicable.

Example 5 – Share-based payment arrangements with cash alternatives

Background

An entity grants employees a choice – 1,000 phantom shares (cash) or 1,200 shares conditional on three-years service. If choose latter must hold shares for a further three years after vesting date.

Grant date – share price £50 and at end of years 1, 2 and 3 – £52, £55 and £60 respectively.

No dividends are expected to be paid out during the three years.

After taking into account effects of post-vesting transfer restrictions the entity estimates that the grant date fair value of the share alternative is £48 per share.

End of year 3 – employee chooses (1) cash or (2) equity.

Application

Fair value of equity is £57,600 (1,200 shares × £48)
Fair value of cash is £50,000 (1,000 phantom shares × £50)
Fair value of equity component of compound is £7,600

			Cumulative liability	Cumulative equity	Expense
Year 1	Liability	(1,000 × £52 × 1/3 years)	17,333		17,333
	Equity	(£7,600 × 1/3 years)		2,533	2,533
Year 2	Liability	(1,000 × £55 × 2/3 years)	36,666		19,333
	Equity	£7,600 × 2/3 years)		5,066	2,533
Year 3	Liability	(1,000 × £60 × 3/3 years)	60,000		23,334
	Equity	(£7,600 × 3/3 years)		7,600	2,534
Total expense under both scenarios					67,600
Scenario (1)					
End year 3		Paid	(60,000)		
			Nil		
Scenario (2)					
End year 3			(60,000)	60,000	
			Nil	67,600	

Disclosures

Information must be provided to enable users to understand the nature and extent of share-based payment arrangements.

At least the following should be disclosed:

(a)   A description of each type of share-based payment, including general terms and conditions.
(b)   The number and weighted average exercise prices of share options for each of the following groups of options:
   (i)   outstanding at the beginning of the period;
   (ii)   granted during the period;
   (iii) forfeited during the period;
   (iv)   exercised during the period;
   (v)   expired during the period;
   (vi)   outstanding at the end of the period; and
   (vii) exercisable at the end of the period.
(c)   For share options exercised, the weighted average share price at the date of exercise.
(d)   For share options outstanding at the end of the period, the range of exercise prices and weighted average remaining contractual life. If the range is wide, the options should be divided into meaningful ranges for assessing the number and timing of additional shares that may be issued or cash that may be received on exercise.

Further information that enables users to understand how the fair value of the goods or services received, or the fair value of equity granted was determined should be provided including the option pricing model adopted, the expected volatility and how other features of option grants were incorporated into fair value. Details of any modifications and the overall expense must also be provided.

Two examples are provided below of companies disclosing the information under IFRS 2 but adopting different valuation techniques – BAE Systems adopting three different methods – Monte Carlo, Binomial and Dividend Valuation Model:

BAE Systems Plc   Year Ended 31 December 2005

26. Share-based payments

Details of the terms and conditions of each share option scheme are given in the Remuneration Report on pages 62 to 63.

Executive Share Option Scheme (ExSOS)

Equity-settled options

	2005		2004	
	Number of shares	Weighted average exercise price	Number of shares	Weighted average exercise price
	000	£	000	£
Outstanding at the beginning of the year	63,475	2.76	53,627	2.97
Granted during the year	10,569	2.89	13,060	2.09

Exercised during the year	(992)	1.65	(165)	1.70
Expired during the year	(1,653)	3.35	(3,047)	3.65
Outstanding at the end of the year	71,399	2.78	63,475	2.76
Exercisable at the end of the year	2,850	3.18	3,346	2.73

Cash-settled options

	2005		2004	
	Number of shares	Weighted average exercise price	Number of shares	Weighted average exercise price
	000	£	000	£
Outstanding at the beginning of the year	61,957	2.90	50,204	3.11
Granted during the year	8,946	2.71	11,753	2.02
Exercised during the year	(6)	2.40	–	–
Expired during the year	(1,769)	2.68	–	–
Outstanding at the end of the year	69,129	2.88	61,957	2.90
Exercisable at the end of the year	–	–	–	–

	2005		2004	
	Equity-settled	Cash-settled	Equity-settled	Case-settled
Range of exercise price of outstanding options (£)	1.72–4.87	1.72–4.21	1.72–2.41	1.72–4.21
Weighted average remaining contracted life (years)	7	7	7	7
Weighted average fair value of options granted (£)	1.00	1.62	0.67	0.83
Expense recognised for the year (£m)	8	27	4	8

Performance Share Plan (PSP)

Equity-settled options

	2005 Number of shares 000	2004 Number of shares 000
Outstanding at the beginning of the year	14,462	7,570
Granted during the year	5,261	6,915
Expired during the year	(806)	(23)
Outstanding at the end of the year	18,917	14,462
Exercisable at the end of the year	–	–

Cash-settled options

	2005		2004	
	Number of shares	Weighted average exercise price	Number of shares	Weighted average exercise price
	000	£	000	£
Outstanding at the beginning of the year	16,924	2.46	12,094	2.48
Granted during the year	4,424	3.56	4,830	2.40
Exercised during the year	(557)	2.56	–	–
Expired during the year	(6,403)	2.66	–	–
Outstanding at the end of the year	14,388	2.70	16,924	2.46
Exercisable at the end of the year	3,093	2.71	5,553	2.72

	2005		2004	
	Equity-settled	Cash-settled	Equity-settled	Case-settled
Range of exercise price of outstanding options (£)	0.93–3.21	1.72–3.56	0.93–3.21	1.72–2.72
Weighted average remaining contracted life (years)	2	2	3	2
Weighted average fair value of options granted (£)	–	1.15	0.65	0.58
Expense recognised for the year (£m)	3	9	2	1

Share Investment Plan

At 31 December 2005 there were no options outstanding under this plan (2004: £nil).

Details of options granted in period

The fair value of both equity-settled and cash-settled options granted in the period have been measured using the weighted average inputs below and the following valuation models:

PSP – Monte Carlo
RSP – Dividend valuation model
ExSOS and SAYE – Binomial model

	2005	2004
Range of share price at date of grant (£)	2.62–3.86	2.01–2.40
Exercise price (£)	0–3.56	0–2.40
Expected option life (years)	3–5	3–5
Volatility (%)	27–42	39–45
Spot dividend yield (%)	2.6	3.4
Risk-free interest rate (%)	4.1–4.2	4.3–4.5

Volatility was calculated with reference to the Group's weekly share price volatility, after allowing for dividends and stock splits, for the greater of 30 weeks or for the period until vest date.

The average share price in the year was £2.94 (2004: £2.10).

The liability in respect of the cash-settled elements of the schemes shown above and reported within provisions at 31 December 2005 is £80 million (2004: £19m).

The intrinsic value of cash-settled options that have vested at 31 December 2005 is £3 million (2004: £nil).

British American Tobacco (BAT) Industries Plc provide an excellent accounting policy on share options as well as a detailed disclosure note in accordance with IFRS 2.

BAT Industries Plc　Year Ended 31 December 2005

Share-based payments

The Group has equity-settled and cash-settled share-based compensation plans. IFRS2 has been applied to all equity-settled grants that were unvested as at 1 January 2004. IFRS2 has also been applied to all cash-settled grants not settled as at 1 January 2004. The comparative figures for 2004 have been adjusted accordingly in respect of both types of grant.

Equity-settled share-based payments are measured at fair value at the date of grant. The fair value determined at the grant date of the equity-settled share-based payments is expensed over the vesting period, based on the Group's estimate of awards that will eventually vest. For plans where vesting conditions are based on total shareholder returns, the fair value at date of grant reflects these conditions, whereas earnings per share vesting conditions are reflected in the calculation of awards that will eventually vest over the vesting period. For cash-settled share-based payments, a liability equal to the portion of the services received is recognised at its current fair value determined at each balance sheet date.

Fair value is measured by the use of Black-Scholes and Monte-Carlo option pricing models. The expected life used in the models has been adjusted, based on management's best estimate, for the effects of non-transferability, exercise restrictions and behavioural considerations.

27. Share-Based Payments

During the period ended 31 December 2005, the following material share-based payment arrangements existed, which are described below:

Type of arrangement	Long-Term Incentive Plan	Deferred Share Bonus Scheme	Sharesave Scheme	Share Option Scheme	Share Reward Scheme	Share Participation Scheme
Timing of grant	Annually in March (2005 – May)	Annually in March	Annually in November	See note (a)	Annually in April	Last grant made in April 2002
Number of options/shares granted in 2005	3,472,111	2,275,558	3 year – 224,885 5 year – 190,160	n/a	305,888	n/a
Number of options/shares granted in 2004	3,208,521	2,266,749	3 year – 305,110 5 year – 409,513	3,735,654	582,482	n/a
Fair value per share for 2005 grant	£7.29	£8.12	3 year – £3.12 5 year – £3.33	n/a	£9.31	n/a
Fair value per share for 2004 grant	£5.67	£7.02	3 year – £2.44 5 year – £2.61	£1.97	£8.17	n/a
Method of settlement	Both equity and cash-settled grants	Both equity and cash-settled grants	Equity	Both equity and cash-settled grants	Equity	Equity
Contractual life	10 years	3 years	3.5 or 5.5 years	10 years	3 years	n/a
Vesting conditions	See note (b)	See note (c)	See note (d)	See note (e)	See note (f)	See note (g)

Notes:

(a) The granting of options under this scheme ceased with the last grant made in March 2004.

(b) NI-cost options exercisable three years from date of grant, with payout subject to performance conditions based on earnings per share relative to Inflation (50 per cent of grant) and total shareholder return, combining the share price and dividend performance of the Company by reference to two comparator groups (50 percent grant). Participants are not entitled to dividends prior to the exercise of the options. For grants made in 2005 and thereafter, a cash equivalent dividend will accrue through the vesting period and will be paid on vesting.

(c) Free shares released three years from date or grant and may be subject to forfeit if participant leaves employment before the end of the three year holding period. Participants receive a separate payment equivalent to a proportion or dividend during the holding period.

(d) Options granted by invitation at a 20 per cent discount to the market price. Options are exercisable at the end of a three year or five year savings contract. Participants are not entitled receive dividends prior to the exercise of the options.

(e) Options exercisable three years from date of grant and subject to earnings per share performance condition relative to inflation. Participants are not entitled to receive dividends in the period prior to the exercise of the options.

(f) Free shares granted (maximum £3,000 in any year) subject to a three year holding period and may be subject to forfeit if the employee leaves within this period. Participants are entitled to receive dividends during the holding period which are reinvested to buy further shares.

(g) Free shares issued subject to a two year holding period and no forfeiture conditions. Participants are entitled to receive dividends during the holding period. The final appropriation of shares made in April 2002 was released in April 2005.

During the period, the Company operated a Partnership Share Scheme, which was open to all eligible employees, where employees can allocate part of their pre-tax salary to purchase shares in British American Tobacco. The maximum amount that can be allocated in this way to any individual is £1,500 in any tax year. The shares purchased are held in a UK-based trust and are normally capable of transfer to participants tax free after a five-year holding period.

During 2005, the last of the former BAT Industries Employee Share 'E' Option Scheme options were exercised prior to the outstanding options expiry date of 30 June 2005.

During 2004, the last of the former BAT Industries Employee Share 'D' Option Scheme options were exercised prior to the outstanding options expiry date of 31 May 2004.

Further details on the operation of share-based payment arrangements can be found in the Remuneration Report.

Share Option Schemes

Details of the movements for equity-settled share option schemes during the year ended 31 December 2005 covering the Share Option, Sharesave and BAT Industries Employee Share 'E' Option Schemes were as follows:

	2005		2004	
	Number of options	Weighted average exercise price per share (£)	Number of options	Weighted averages exercise price per share (£)
Outstanding at start of year	17,352,182	5.97	19,219,742	5.11
Granted during the period	415,045	9.77	4,295,259	7.84
Exercised during the period	(4,864,295)	5.20	(5,664,819)	4.5
Forfeited during the period	(254,237)	5.89	(498,000)	5.75
Outstanding at end of year	12,648,695	6.39	17,352,182	5.97
Exercisable at end of year	3,267,697	5.19	3,637,252	4.16

In addition to the above options, the movement in nil-cost equity-settled options from the Long-Term Incentive Plan are as follows:

	2005 Number of options	2004 Number of options
Outstanding at start of year	9,851,735	12,165,089
Granted during the period	3,099,082	2,983,377
Exercised during the period	(2,078,722)	(3,577,038)
Forfeited during the period	(1,468,843)	(1,719,693)
Outstanding at end of year	9,403,252	9,851,735
Exercisable at end of year	744,082	763,514

The weighted average British American Tobacco p.l.c. share price at the date of exercise for share options exercised during the period was £10.05 (2004: £8.23). A detailed breakdown of the range of exercise prices for options outstanding at 31 December 2005 is shown in the table below:

Range of exercise prices	2005			2004		
	Number outstanding attend of year	Weighted average remaining contractual life in years	Weighted average exercise price per share (£)	Number outstanding at end of year	Weighted average remaining contractual life in years	Weighted average exercise price per share (£)
Nil-cost	9,403,252	8.0	n/a	9,851,735	8	n/a
£2.53 to £4.99	966,689	1.8	3.46	2,533,298	2.4	3.35
£5.00 to £6.99	7,330,469	5.5	5.81	10,598,085	6.4	5.85
£7.00 to £8.99	3,936,492	7.4	7.83	4,220,799	8.4	7.84
£9.00 to £12.50	415,045	4.4	9.77			
Total	22,051,947	6.7	3.66	27,203,917	6.9	3.81

The weighted average fair value of equity-settled share option schemes' shares granted during 2005 was £6.81 (2004: £3.54).

Assumptions used in the Black-Scholes models to determine the fair value of share options at grant date were as follows:

| | 2005 | | | 2004 | |
	Long-Term Incentive Plan	Sharesave Scheme*	Share Option Scheme	Long-Term Incentive Plan	Sharesave Scheme*
Share price at date of grant (£)	10.37	12.21	8.09	8.09	8.29
Exercise price (£)	nil-cost	9.77	8.09	nil-cost	6.63
Volatility (%)	27	24	38	38	36
Average expected term to exercise (years)	3.5	3.2/5.2	4.0	3.5	3.2/5.2
Risk-free rate (%)	4.3	4.2/4.2	4.5	4.5	4.4/4.5
Expected dividend yield (%)	4.0	3.5	4.7	4.7	4.5

*Where two figures have been quoted for the Sharesave schemes, the first number represents the assumptions for the three year savings contract and the second number for the five years savings contract'.

The last grant under the Share Option Scheme was made in March 2004. Eligible individuals are now entitled to participate in the Long-Term Incentive Plan and/or Deferred Share Bonus Scheme.

Market condition features were incorporated into the Monte-Carlo models for the total shareholder return elements of the Long-Term Incentive Plan, in determining fair value at grant date. Assumptions used in these models were as follows:

	2005 (%)	2004 (%)
Average share price volatility FTSE 100 comparator group	34	38
Average share price volatility FMCG comparator group	26	32
Average correlation FTSE 100 comparator group	24	23
Average correlation FMCG comparator group	16	15

The expected British American Tobacco p.l.c. share price volatility was determined taking account of the daily share price movements over a five year period. The respective FMCG and FTSE 100 share price volatility and correlations were also determined over the same periods. The average expected term to exercise used in the models has been adjusted, based on management's best estimate, for the effects of non-transferability, exercise restrictions and behavioural conditions, forfeiture and historical experience.

The risk free rate has been determined from market yield curves for government gilts with outstanding terms equal to the average expected term to exercise for each relevant grant The expected dividend yield was determined by calculating the yield from the last two declared dividends divided by the grant share price.

For grants containing earnings per share performance conditions, the payout calculation is based on the average of expectations published in analysts' forecasts.

Other equity share-based payment arrangements (other than share options)

Details of the movements of other equity share-based payment arrangements during the year ended 31 December 2005, covering the Deferred Share Bonus, Share Reward and Share Participation Schemes, were as follows:

	2005 **Number of shares**	2004 Number of shares
Outstanding at start of year	7,284,592	7,615,935
Granted during the period	2,310,273	2,726,346
Exercised during the period	(2,461,386)	(2,979,889)
Forfeited during the period	(132,208)	(77,800)
Outstanding at end of year	7,001,271	7,284,592
Exercisable at end of year	643,825	633,797

The shares outstanding for the year ended 31 December 2005 had a weighted average contractual life of 6.1 years (2004: 6.0 years).

8

Foreign trading

8.1 IAS 21 *The Effects of Changes in Foreign Exchange Rates* (revised December 2003)

Objective

An entity may carry on foreign activities in two ways – transactions and translation. In addition it may present its financial statements in a foreign currency. IAS 21 prescribes how transactions and foreign operations should be accounted and how to translate financial statements into a presentation currency.

The principal issues are which exchange rates to use and how to report the effects of those changes in exchange rates.

Scope

The standard should be applied to:

(a) accounting for transactions and balances in foreign currencies;
(b) translating foreign operations in preparation for consolidation; and
(c) translating an entity's results into a different presentation currency.

The standard does not deal with hedge accounting (see IAS 39).

It does not cover cash flows arising from transactions in a foreign currency nor with the translation of cash flows of a foreign operation (see IAS 7).

Definitions

• *Functional currency*. Currency of the primary economic environment in which the entity operates.

The following factors should be considered: the currency in which sales prices are denominated and settled; the country whose competitive forces and regulations mainly determine the sales prices of its goods/services; the currency in which labour and other costs are denominated and settled; the currency in which funds from financing activities are generated and the currency in which receipts from operating activities are usually retained.

When the entity is a foreign operation the following additional factors are considered:

(a) Whether the activities of the foreign operation represent an extension of the reporting entity.
(b) Whether transactions with the foreign entity are a high or a low proportion of the foreign operation's activities.
(c) Whether the cash flows of the foreign operation directly affect the cash flows of the reporting entity.
(d) Whether the cash flows of the foreign operation are sufficient to service existing and expected debt obligations.

Where the indicators are mixed, management must exercise its judgement as to the functional currency which it needs to adopt so that it best reflects the underlying transactions.

- *Foreign currency.* A currency other than the functional currency of the entity.
- *Presentation currency.* The currency in which the financial statements are presented.
- *Exchange rate.* The ratio of exchange for two currencies.
- *Spot exchange rate.* The exchange rate for immediate delivery.
- *Closing rate.* The spot exchange rate at the balance sheet date.
- *Exchange difference.* Difference resulting from translating one currency into another currency at different exchange rates.
- *Foreign operation.* A subsidiary, associate, joint venture or branch whose activities are based in a country or currency other than those of the reporting entity.
- *Net investment in a foreign operation.* The amount of the interest in the net assets of that operation. They include long-term receivables or loans but do not include trade receivables or trade payables.
- *Monetary items.* Money and assets/liabilities held to be received/paid in fixed or determinable amounts. Examples include deferred tax, pensions and provisions. The feature of a non-monetary item is the absence of a right to receive a fixed or determinable amount of money (includes prepayments, goodwill, intangible assets, inventories, property, and so on.)
- *Fair value.* The amount for which an asset could be exchanged by willing parties in an arm's length transaction.

Summary of the approach required by this standard

Each entity must determine its functional currency as per the definition above. Many reporting entities are groups, and each individual entity should be translated into the currency in which the group statements are to be presented. The standard permits the presentation currency to be any currency. If the functional currency differs from the presentational currency, then the results and position should be translated in accordance with paras 20–37 and 49 of the standard (use of a presentation currency other than the functional currency).

The standard also permits a standalone entity to adopt a different presentation currency. The rules are in accordance with paras 38–49 (use of a presentation currency other than the functional currency).

Reporting foreign currency transactions in the functional currency

Initial recognition

A foreign-currency transaction is a transaction denominated or requires settlement in a foreign currency including:

(a)   buying or selling of goods or services whose price is denominated in a foreign currency;
(b)   borrowing or lending of funds in a foreign currency; or
(c)   otherwise acquires or disposes of assets denominated in a foreign currency.

A foreign currency transaction shall be recorded initially by applying the spot rate at the date of the transaction. For practical reasons, an average rate for a period may be adopted unless the rate fluctuates significantly.

Reporting at subsequent balance sheet dates

At each balance sheet date:

(a)   monetary items should be translated at closing rate;
(b)   non-monetary items measured at historic cost are translated at the exchange rate at the date of the transaction; and
(c)   non-monetary items are measured at the fair value using the exchange rate when the value was determined.

The carrying amount is determined in accordance with other accounting standards e.g. IAS 16, IAS 2 and, if an impairment, IAS 36. When the asset is non-monetary the carrying amount is determined by comparing the cost or carrying value and the NRV. The effect could be a write-down or vice versa.

When several exchange rates are available, the rate to be used should be that at which future cash flows could be settled. If exchangeability is temporarily lacking, the first subsequent rate at which exchanges could be made is used.

Recognition of exchange differences

IAS 39 deals with hedge accounting, e.g. exchange differences that qualify as a hedging instrument are recognised in equity to the extent that the hedge is effective.

Exchange differences on the settlement of monetary items should be expended in the period they arise with the exception of para 32 differences (see below).

Where a gain/loss on a non-monetary item is recognised directly in equity any exchange component of that gain/loss shall also be recognised directly in equity. Conversely when a gain/loss on a non-monetary item is recognised in profit or loss, any exchange component of that gain/loss shall be recognised in profit or loss.

Para 32 insists that exchange differences on a monetary item that forms part of an entity's net investment in a foreign operation be recognised as income/expense in the separate financial statements of the reporting entity or foreign operation as appropriate. They should be recorded initially in a separate component of equity and then subsequently recognised in profit/loss on disposal of the net investment (i.e. they are recycled).

When a monetary item that forms part of an entity's net investment in a foreign operation is denominated in the functional currency of the reporting entity, an exchange difference should be recorded in equity. In addition, a monetary item that forms part of the net investment in a foreign operation may be denominated in a currency other than the functional currency. Exchange differences should be recognised in equity.

When an entity keeps its books in a currency other than its functional currency, all amounts are remeasured in the functional currency, i.e. monetary items at closing rate and non-monetary at date of transaction.

Change in functional currency

When there is a change in functional currency, the translation procedures applicable to the new functional currency shall be applied from the date of the change. A change should only be made, however, if there is a change to those underlying transactions.

The effect is accounted for prospectively. All items are translated using the new functional exchange rate at the date of the change. These are then treated as their historical cost. Exchange differences previously recognised in equity are not recognised as income or expenses until the disposal of the operation and are then recycled through profits.

Example – Neagh Plc

Neagh Plc, whose registered office is in London, conducts operations and transactions both in the United Kingdom and overseas. During the year ended 31 December 2007 the company was involved in various transactions in foreign currencies. Relevant exchange rates, except where given separately in the individual circumstances, were as scheduled below:

At	Rolads (R) R = £1	Nidars (N) N = £1	Krams (K) K = £1	Sarils (S) S = £1
31 December 2006	1.6	0.52	6.9	2,210.0
27 February 2007			7.0	
4 March 2007		0.65		
25 May 2007	1.5		6.7	
25 August 2007		0.50		
2 September 2007				2,224.0
11 November 2007	1.8			
31 December 2007	2.0	0.54	7.5	2,250.0
Average for 2007	1.7			

The transactions concerned are identified by the letters (a) to (f) and are detailed thus:

(a) Neagh Plc bought equipment (as a fixed asset) for 130,000 nidars on 4 March 2007 and paid for it on 25 August 2007 in sterling.

(b) On 27 February 2007 Neagh Plc sold goods which had cost £46,000 for £68,000 to a company whose currency was krams. The proceeds were received in krams on 25 May 2007.

(c) On 2 September 2007 Neagh Plc sold goods which had cost £17,000 for £24,000 to a company whose currency was sarils. The amount was outstanding at 31 December 2007 but the proceeds were received in sarils on 7 February 2008 when the exchange rate was S2,306.0 = £1. The directors of Neagh Plc approved the final accounts on 28 March 2008.

(d) Neagh Plc borrowed 426,000 rolads on 25 May 2007 and repaid it in sterling on 11 November 2007.

(e) On 9 November 2006 Neagh Plc had acquired an equity investment at a cost of 196,000 krams when the rate of exchange was K7.3 = £1. This investment was hedged by a loan of 15,000 nidars, at an exchange rate of N0.56 = £1, obtained on the same day.

(f) Neagh Plc has an overseas wholesale warehouse which is financed locally in rolads and is treated as an independent branch for accounting purposes. The net investment in the branch was R638,600 on 1 January 2007 and R854,700 on 31 December 2007. During the year 2007 the branch had made a net profit of R423,400, of which R207,300 had been remitted to the UK parent company; these had realised £116,727.

In accounting for the branch, Neagh Plc uses the average annual rate in translating income statement items.

Suggested solution – Neagh Plc

Transaction A

		£	£
4.3.07	Dr Property, plant, etc. (130,000 nidars ÷ 0.65)	200,000	
	Cr Payables		200,000
25.8.07	Dr Payables	200,000	
	Exchange loss – income statement	60,000	
	Cr Bank (130,000 nidars ÷ 0.50)		260,000

This is a normal trading transaction and should be written off as 'other operating expenses' in the income statement.

Transaction B

		£	£
27.2.07	Dr Receivables (476,000 krams ÷ 7/£1)	68,000	
	Cr Sales		68,000
27.2.07	Dr Cost of sales	46,000	
	Cr Inventories		46,000
25.5.07	Dr Bank (476,000 krams ÷ 6.7/£1)	71,045	
	Cr Receivables		68,000
	Exchange gain – income statement		3,045

This is a normal trading transaction and should be disclosed under the appropriate headings of sales, cost of sales and gross profit. The exchange gain should be included under the heading 'other operating income' in the income statement.

Transaction C

		£	£
2.9.07	Dr Receivables (53.376m sarils ÷ 2,224/£1)	24,000	
	Cr Sales		24,000
2.9.07	Dr Cost of sales	17,000	
	Cr Inventories		17,000
31.12.07	Dr Exchange loss – income statement	277	
	Cr Receivables (53.376 m ÷		277
	2,250/£1 = 23,723–24,000 = 277 loss)		
7.2.08	Dr Bank (53.376 m ÷ 2,306/£)	23,147	
	Cr Receivables		23,147
7.2.08	Dr Exchange loss – income statement	576	
	Cr Receivables (23,147 –23,723)		576

This is a normal trading transaction and should be disclosed under the appropriate headings of sales, cost of sales and gross profit. The receivables must be restated at the exchange rate at the year end as it is monetary in nature and the loss of £277 must be written off to the income statement in 2007. The subsequent loss of £576 is caused by an event which occurred after the year end and is thus non-adjusting. It would only be disclosed in the notes if it is regarded to be material and necessary to give the user a proper understanding of the financial statements.

Transaction D

		£	£
25.5.07	Dr Bank (426,000 rolads ÷ 1.5/£1)	284,000	
	Cr Loan		284,000
11.11.07	Dr Loan	284,000	
	Cr Bank (426,000 rolads ÷ 1.8/£1)		236,667
	Exchange gain		47,333

Although this is not a trading profit it should be written off in the income statement under the heading 'finance costs'.

Transaction E

		£	£
9.11.06	Dr Investment (196,000 krams ÷ 7.3/£1)	26,849	
	Cr Loan (15,000 nidars ÷ 0.56/£1)		26,786
	Bank		63
31.12.06	Dr Investment (196,000 krams ÷	1,557	
	6.9/£1 = 28,406 − 26,849 = 1,557)		
	C Exchange gain		1,557
	Dr Exchange loss	2,060	
	Cr Loan (15,000 nidars ÷ 0.52/£1 =		2,060
	28,846 − 26,786 = 2,060)		

The exchange loss of £2,060 can be offset against the exchange gain of £1,557. The excess loss of £503 must be charged to income statement under 'finance costs'. The offset of £1,557 is carried out within the reserves provided strict hedging criteria are met and the hedge is effective.

		£	£
31.12.07	Dr Exchange loss	2,273	
	Cr Investment (196,000 krams ÷ 7.5 =		2,273
	26,133 − 28,406)		
	Dr Loan (15,000 nidars ÷ 0.54 = 27,778 28,846)	1,068	
	Cr Exchange gain		1,068

The exchange loss of £2,273 on the loan is offset against the exchange gain in the reserves, but only to the extent of £1,068. The excess loss of £1,205 would be charged to the income statement as in 2006, but only if hedging is effective.

Transaction F

Branch current account (head office)

		Rolads	R/£1	£		Rolads	R/£1	£
1.1.07	Balance b/d	638,600	1.6	399,125	2007 Bank Exchange loss	207,300	1.7	121,941
2007	Net profit	423,400	1.7	249,059				98,893
					Dec. Bal. c/d	854,700	2.0	427,350
		1,062,000		648,184		1,062,000		648,184

Composition of exchange losses
Exchange loss on remittance

		£	£
207,300 ÷ 1.7/£1 average			121,941
207,300	actual		116,727
			5,214

Retranslation loss		£
Opening balance	638,600 Rs ÷ 1.6/£1	399,125
	638,600 Rs ÷ 2/£1	319,300
		79,825

Net profit restated		
(423,400–207,300) 1.7/£1	127,118	
(423,400–207,300) 2/£1	108,050	
		19,068
		98,893

The exchange loss of £5,214 is really a trading item and should be written off as an 'other operating expense'. The retranslation loss is unrealised and has no impact at present on cash flow. This loss should therefore be taken direct to reserves.

Use of a presentation currency other than the functional currency (Paras 38–49)

Translation to the presentation currency

The financial statements may be presented in any currency. If the presentation currency differs from the functional, its results and financial position need to be translated into the presentation currency. The group, in particular, needs a common currency.

The results and position of an entity whose functional currency is not the currency of a hyperinflationary economy shall be translated into a different presentation currency as follows:

(a)   Assets and liabilities at closing rate.
(b)   Income and expenses at the exchange rates at the dates of the transactions.
(c)   All exchange differences in equity, as a separate component.

For practical reasons an average rate may be adopted unless exchange rates were to fluctuate significantly.

The exchange differences arise from:

(a)   translating income and expenses at transaction rate and assets/liabilities at closing rate and
(b)   translating opening net assets at an exchange rate different from that previously reported.

These exchange differences are not recognised as income or expenses as they have little or no direct effect on present and future cash flows from operations. If a foreign operation is not 100% owned, exchange differences should be attributable to minority interests.

The results and position of an entity whose functional currency is the currency of a hyperinflationary economy shall be translated as follows:

(a)   All amounts at closing rate except when amounts are being translated into the currency of a non-hyperinflationary economy.

(b)   Comparative amounts should be those that were presented as current year amounts in the relevant year (i.e. not adjusted for either subsequent changes in prices or exchange rates).

When the functional currency is that of a hyperinflationary economy then its financial statements shall be restated under IAS 29 *Financial Reporting in Hyperinflationary Economies*. The accounts must be restated before the translation method is applied. Once it ceases to be hyperinflationary, it shall use the amounts restated to the price level at the date it ceases, as the historical costs for translation into the presentation currency.

Translation of a foreign operation

The incorporation of a foreign operation should follow normal consolidation procedures e.g. elimination of inter company balances (see IAS 27.).

However, an intragroup monetary asset/liability cannot be eliminated against a corresponding intragroup asset/liability without showing the results of currency fluctuations in the consolidated accounts. Such exchange differences should continue to be recognised as income/expenses or in equity as appropriate.

IAS 27 permits the use of different reporting dates as long as these are no greater than three months and adjustments are then made for the effects of any significant transactions between those dates. In such cases, the exchange rate to adopt is that at the balance sheet date of the foreign operation. The same approach should be applied to the equity method for associates and joint ventures.

Any goodwill and fair-value adjustments should be treated as assets and liabilities of the foreign operation. They therefore must be expressed in the functional currency of the foreign operation and translated at the closing rate.

Disposal of a foreign operation

Any cumulative exchange differences in equity shall be recognised as income or expenses when the gain or loss on disposal is recognised (i.e. they are all recycled through profits).

Tax effects of all exchange differences

Gains and losses on foreign currency transactions may have associated tax effects and these should be accounted for under IAS 12.

Disclosure

All references are to the functional currency of the parent if referring to a group.
    An entity should disclose:

(a)   the amount of exchange differences included in profit or loss except those arising from IAS 39;
(b)   net exchange differences classified as a component of equity and a reconciliation at start and end of the year;
(c)   when the presentation currency is different from the functional currency, that fact shall be disclosed as well disclosure of the functional currency and the reason for using a different presentation currency;

(d)   when there is a change in the functional currency of either the reporting entity or a significant foreign operation, that fact and reason for the change should be disclosed; and

(e)   when an entity presents its financial statements in a currency different from its functional, it should describe the statements as complying with IFRSs only if they comply with all of the requirements of each applicable standard and SIC/IFRIC including the translation method.

Where the requirements listed in (e) are not met, an entity should:

(a)   clearly identify the information as supplementary;
(b)   disclose the currency in which the supplementary information is displayed; and
(c)   disclose the entity's functional currency and method of translation used to determine the supplementary information.

Amvescap plc covers the disclosure of a change in presentation currency in their accounting policies note as well as the normal accounting treatment for foreign-currency translation.

Amvescap Plc   Year Ended 31 December 2005

Basis of accounting and consolidation

The company has changed its presentation currency from sterling to US dollars with effect from December 31, 2005. The comparative figures have been presented in US dollars applying the exchange rates outlined in Note 29. On December 8, 2006, the Parent rede-nominated its share capital from sterling to U.S. dollars and changed its functional currency from sterling to U.S. dollars. The U.S. dollar more accurately reflects the currency of the underlying operations and financing of the Parent. See Note C to the Parent financial statements for additional information.

Foreign currencies

Transactions in foreign currencies (currencies other than the functional currencies of the operation) are recorded at the rates of exchange prevailing on the dates of the transactions. At each balance sheet date, monetary assets and liabilities that are denominated in foreign currencies are retranslated at the rates prevailing at the balance sheet date. Gains and losses arising on retranslation are included in the income statement, with the exception of differences on foreign currency borrowings that provide an effective designated hedge against a net investment in a foreign entity. These differences are taken directly to equity until the disposal of the net investment, at which time they are recognized in the income statement. In the Parent's financial statements, a fair value hedge is utilized to revalue certain foreign currency investments in subsidiaries, allowing the revaluation of these assets to offset the revaluation of external foreign currency debt in the Parents income statement.

> The company's presentation currency and the functional currency of the Parent is US dollars. On consolidation, the assets and liabilities of company subsidiary operations whose functional currencies are currencies other than the US dollar ('foreign operations') are translated at the rates of exchange ruling at the balance sheet date.

Another good example of an accounting policy disclosure note including the functional currencies is Reed Elsevier Plc. Note the recycling of translation differences on disposal of operations and the need to record translation differences in a separate reserve awaiting transfer to income on disposal (Note 30):

Reed Elsevier Plc   Year Ended 31 December 2005

Foreign exchange translation

The combined financial statements are presented in both pounds sterling and euros, being the respective functional currencies of the two parent companies, Reed Elsevier PLC and Reed Elsevier NV.

Transactions in foreign currencies are recorded at the rate of exchange prevailing on the date of the transaction. At each balance sheet date, monetary assets and liabilities that are denominated in foreign currencies are retranslated at the rate prevailing on the balance sheet date. Exchange differences arising are recorded in the income statement other than where hedge accounting applied [see Financial Instruments].

Assets and liabilities of foreign operations are translated at exchange rates prevailing on the balance sheet date. Income and expense items of foreign operations are translated at the average exchange rate for the period. Exchange differences arising are classified as equity and transferred to the translation reserve. When operations are disposed of, the related cumulative translation differences are recognised within the income statement in the period.

As permitted under the transition rules of IFRS1 – First Time Adoption of International Financial Reporting Standards, cumulative translation differences in respect of foreign operations have been deemed to be nil at the date of transition to IFRS.

Reed Elsevier uses derivative financial instruments, primarily forward contracts, to hedge its exposure to certain foreign exchange risks. Details of Reed Elsevier's accounting policies in respect of derivative financial instruments are set out below.

30. Translation Reserve

	2005 (£m)	2004 (£m)	2005 (€m)	2004 (€m)
At start of year	(122)	–	(175)	–
Exchange differences on translation of foreign operations	180	(121)	346	(196)
Other exchange translation differences	31	(1)	(41)	21
At end of year	89	(122)	130	(175)

8.2   IAS 29 *Financial Reporting in Hyperinflationary Economies* (December 2003)

Objective

The objective of IAS 29 is to establish specific standards for entities reporting in the currency of a hyperinflationary economy, so that the financial information provided is meaningful.

Scope

The standard should apply to the primary financial statements, including consolidated financial statements, of any entity whose functional currency is the currency of a hyperinflationary economy.

In a hyperinflationary economy, reporting in local currency is not useful as money loses purchasing power and therefore the accounts become misleading.

The standard does not establish an absolute rate. It is a matter of judgement when the standard becomes necessary but the following characteristics should be reviewed:

(a)   The general population prefers to invest in non-monetary assets or in a relatively stable currency.
(b)   The general population regards monetary amounts, not in terms of local currency, but in terms of a relatively stable currency.
(c)   Credit sales and purchases take place at prices adjusted for the expected loss in purchasing power, even if the credit period is short.
(d)   Interest rates, wages and prices are linked to a price index.
(e)   The cumulative inflation rate over three years is approaching or exceeds 100%.

It is preferable that all enterprises in the same hyperinflationary economy apply the standard from the same date. It applies to the start of the reporting period in which hyperinflation is identified.

The restatement of financial statements

Prices change over time due to supply and demand as well as general forces pushing up the general level of prices. In most countries, the primary statements are prepared on a historical cost basis except for the revaluation of property, etc. Some enterprises, however, adopt a current cost approach using specific price increases.

In a hyperinflationary economy, financial statements must be expressed in terms of an up-to-date measuring unit if they are to be useful.

The financial statements of an entity whose functional currency is that of a hyperinflationary economy, whether historic or current cost, must be restated in current measuring unit terms as well as corresponding figures for the previous period. The gain/loss on the net monetary position should be included within income and separately disclosed.

This approach must be consistently applied from period to period. That is more important than precise accuracy.

Historical cost financial statements

Balance sheet

Balance sheet amounts should be restated by applying a general price index. However, monetary items are not restated as they are already recorded in current monetary terms.

Index linked bonds and loans are adjusted in accordance with the agreement. All other non-monetary assets must be restated unless they are already carried at NRV or market value.

Most non-monetary assets require the application of a general price index to their historic costs and accumulated depreciation from the date of acquisition to the balance sheet date. Inventory work in progress should be restated from the dates on which the costs of purchase and of conversion were incurred.

If detailed records of acquisition dates are not available or capable of estimation, then in rare circumstances, an independent professional assessment may form the basis for their restatement.

If a general price index is not available then an estimate should be based on movements in the exchange rate between the functional and a relatively stable foreign currency.

Some non-monetary assets are revalued. These need to be restated from the date of revaluation. Where fixed assets are impaired they must be reduced to their recoverable amount and inventories to NRV.

An investee that is accounted for under the equity method may report in the currency of a hyperinflationary economy. The balance sheet and income statement are restated in accordance with this standard in order to calculate the investor's share of its net assets and results. If expressed in a foreign currency they are translated at closing rates.

It is not appropriate both to restate the capital expenditure financed by borrowing and to capitalise that part of the borrowing costs that compensates for inflation during the same period.

It should be expensed. Also if undue effort or cost is needed to impute interest, such assets are restated from the payment date, not the date of purchase.

On first application of the standard, owners' equity must be restated by applying a general price index from the dates that different components of equity arose. Any revaluation surplus is eliminated.

At the end of the first period, and subsequently, all components of owners' equity are restated by applying a general price index from the start of the period to date of contribution and any movements disclosed as per IAS 1.

Income statement

All items must be expressed in terms of current measuring units at the balance sheet date, i.e. by being restated from the dates when initially recorded by the general price index.

Gain or loss on net-monetary position

Any excess of monetary assets loses purchasing power and vice versa. The gain/loss is the difference resulting from the restatement of non-monetary assets, owners' equity and income statement items and the adjustment of index-linked assets and liabilities. The gain/loss may be estimated by applying the change in a general price index to the weighted average for the period of the difference between monetary assets and monetary liabilities.

The gain or loss is included in net income. Other income statement items, e.g. interest, foreign exchange differences are also associated with the monetary position. They should be presented together with the gain or loss on the net monetary position in the income statement.

Current cost financial statements

Balance sheet. Items stated at current cost are not restated, already in current measurement units.

Income statement. All amounts need to be restated from their current cost at date of transactions to the balance sheet date by applying a general price index.

Gain or loss on net monetary position. This is accounted for in accordance with the historic cost approach.

Taxes. Restatement may give rise to deferred tax consequences – see IAS 12.

Cash flow statement

All items in the cash flow statement are expressed in current measuring units at the balance sheet date.

Corresponding figures

These are restated by applying a general price index so that comparative financial statements are presented in terms of current measuring units at the end of the reporting period.

Consolidated financial statements

Subsidiaries reporting in the hyperinflationary economy must be restated by applying a general price index and if that is a foreign subsidiary then its restated financial statements should be translated at closing rates. If not in hyperinflationary economies, then they should report in accordance with the IAS 21 *The Effects of Changes in Foreign Exchange Rates*.

If one adopts different reporting dates these need to be restated into current measuring units at the date of the consolidated financial statements.

Selection and use of the general price index

All enterprises that report in the currency of the same economy should use the same index.

Economies ceasing to be hyperinflationary

When an economy ceases to be hyperinflationary and an entity discontinues using this standard, it should treat the amounts expressed at the end of the previous period as the basis for its subsequent financial statements.

Disclosures

(a) The fact that the financial statements and the corresponding periods have been restated for changes in general purchasing power and are restated in terms of current measurement units at the balance sheet date.

(b) Whether the financial statements are based on historic cost or current cost.

(c) The identity and level of the price index at the balance sheet date and the movement in the index during the current and previous reporting period.

9

Cash flow statements

9.1 IAS 7 *Cash Flow Statements* (revised 1992)

The income statement and the balance sheet of an enterprise show important aspects of its performance and position. However, users of financial statements are also interested in how the enterprise generates and uses its cash resources. In particular, users are concerned about the overall solvency and liquidity of the enterprise.

IAS 7 is designed to aid users in that regard and requires a cash flow statement to be drawn up summarising the cash flows during a period classified into three separate sections:

(a) Operating activities
(b) Investing
(c) Financing

Operating activities

Although an enterprise may have generated a profit during the year and increased its assets, it is recognised that it might not necessarily create readily accessible cash as the money could be tied up in inventories, receivables, etc. Also, in arriving at a profit, a number of non-cash deductions and additions could have been included, e.g. depreciation. These need to be taken into account when calculating the actual cash generated.

IAS 7 permits two methods of calculating operating cash flows – the direct and the indirect methods. The indirect method requires the profit to be reconciled to the cash flow being generated by operations. This is carried out as in the previous paragraph. The direct method, in contrast, identifies the actual cash receipts from customers and the actual cash payments to suppliers and employees. Both methods lead to the same figure. The direct method is illustrated below and the indirect method is illustrated as part of an overall specimen format:

Direct method

As an alternative, the net cash flow from operating activities of 1,560 may be arrived at by adopting the direct method as shown below:

Cash flows from operating activities

Cash receipts from customers	30,150
Cash paid to suppliers and employees	(27,600)
Cash generated from operations	2,550
Interest paid	(270)
Income taxes paid	(900)
Cash flow before extraordinary item	1,380
Proceeds from earthquake disaster settlement	180
Net cash from operating activities	1,560

Investing activities

Under this heading are included purchases and sales of long-term assets and the purchase and sales of investments not qualifying as cash equivalents.

Interest and dividends received may be classified under this heading but they may also be included under operating activities or financing. The specimen provided in the IAS includes them as investing.

Only one figure for cash should be provided for subsidiaries acquired or disposed, with disclosure by note of the assets and liabilities acquired/disposed.

Investing and financing transactions that do not require the use of cash or cash equivalents should be excluded from a cash flow statement. They should be disclosed elsewhere in the financial statements and should not form part of the cash flow statement itself; however, users should have all the relevant information.

The following should be disclosed, in aggregate, for all acquisitions and separately for all disposals:

(a) The total purchase/disposal consideration.
(b) The portion of the consideration discharged via cash or cash equivalents.
(c) The amount of cash and cash equivalents in the acquisition/disposal.
(d) The amount of assets and liabilities other than cash or cash equivalents in the subsidiary acquired/disposed, summarised by each major category.

Financing activities

This should represent claims on future cash flows or sources of future cash flows and they would include:

(a) cash proceeds from the issue of shares;
(b) cash payments to redeem/acquire the enterprise's shares;

(c)   cash proceeds from the issue of debentures, loans, etc.;
(d)   cash repayments of loans, etc.; and
(e)   cash payments by a lessee to repay principal of finance lease liabilities.

Cash and cash equivalents

The end product of the cash flow statement or balancing figure will be the increase or decrease in cash and cash equivalents. Cash equivalents are defined in IAS 7 as 'short-term, highly liquid investments that are readily convertible to known amounts of cash and which are subject to an insignificant risk of changes in value'.

An unusual feature, which is required by IAS 7, is the need to provide a separate note to the financial statements detailing out the individual components of cash and cash equivalents and requiring a reconciliation to the amounts reported in the balance sheet. If there are any cash or cash equivalent balances held by the enterprise, but are not available for use by the group then these should be disclosed, together with a commentary by the management.

Other issues

Foreign currency cash flows

Cash flows arising from transactions in a foreign currency should be recorded in an enterprise's reporting currency by applying to the foreign currency amount the exchange rate between the reporting currency and the foreign currency at the date of the cash flow.

On translation, the cash flows should be translated at the exchange rates between the reporting currency and the foreign currency at the dates of the cash flows.

Equity accounted investments

For associates, the only cash to be recorded is the actual dividends received and NOT the share of profit included in the income statement.

Proportionate consolidation

Joint ventures, reporting under IAS 31 *Financial Reporting of Interests in Joint Ventures* and that have adopted the policy of proportionate consolidation, should include their proportionate share of the jointly controlled entity's cash flows. An enterprise, however, adopting the equity method, should include the cash flows in respect of its investments in the jointly controlled entity only.

Reporting cash flows on a net basis

Cash flows arising from the following operating, investing or financing activities may be reported on a net basis:

(a)   cash receipts and payments on behalf of customers when the cash flows reflect the activities of the customer rather than those of the enterprise and
(b)   cash receipts and payments for items in which the turnover is quick, the amounts are large, and the maturities are short.

Examples of cash receipts and payments referred to in (a) include:

(a)   the acceptance and repayment of demand deposits of a bank;
(b)   funds held for customers by an investment enterprise; and
(c)   rents collected on behalf of, and paid over to, the owners of properties.

Examples of cash receipts and payments referred to in (b) are advances made for, and the repayment of:

(a)   principal amounts relating to credit card customers;
(b)   the purchase and sale of investments; and
(c)   other short-term borrowings, e.g. those that have a maturity period of three months or less.

Segment information

The disclosure of segmental cash flows enables users to obtain a better understanding of the relationship between the cash flows of the business as a whole and those of its component parts and the availability and variability of segmental cash flows. An example of disclosure is provided in Note D of the specimen format.

Specimen format

Indirect method

Cash flows from operating activities

Net profit before taxation, and extraordinary item	3,350	
Adjustments for:		
Depreciation	450	
Foreign exchange loss	40	
Investment income	(500)	
Interest expense	400	
Operating profit before working capital changes	3,740	
Increase in trade and other receivables	(500)	
Decrease in inventories	1,050	
Decrease in trade payables	(1,740)	
Cash generated from operations	2,550	
Interest paid	(270)	
Income taxes paid	(900)	
Cash flows before extraordinary item	1,380	
Proceeds from earthquake disaster settlement	180	
Net cash from operating activities		1,560

Cash flows from investing activities

Acquisition of subsidiary X net of cash acquired (Note A)	(550)	
Purchase of property, plant and equipment (Note B)	(350)	
Proceeds from sale of equipment	20	
Interest received	200	
Dividends received	200	
Net cash used in investing activities		(480)

Cash flows from financing activities

Proceeds from issuance of share capital	250
Proceeds from long-term borrowings	250
Payment of finance lease liabilities	(90)
Dividends paid*	(1,200)
Net cash used in financing activities	(790)
Net increase in cash and cash equivalents	290
Cash and cash equivalents at beginning of period (Note C)	120
Cash and cash equivalents at end of period (Note C)	410

*This could also be shown as an operating cash flow.

Note:

One major criticism of the specimen format is the inclusion of non-cash movements such as depreciation on the face of the statement. Many companies have decided to move the 'reconciliation of net profit before taxation to cash generated from operations' to the notes and therefore commence the statement with 'cash generated from operations 2,550'.

Notes to the Cash Flow Statement (direct and indirect method)

A   Acquisition of subsidiary

During the period the group acquired subsidiary X. The fair value of assets acquired and liabilities assumed were as follows:

Cash	40
Inventories	100
Accounts receivable	100
Property, plant and equipment	650
Trade payables	(100)
Long-term debts	(200)
Total purchase price	590
Less: Cash of X	(40)
Cash flow on acquisition net of cash acquired	550

B   Property, plant and equipment

During the period, the group acquired property, plant and equipment with an aggregate cost of 1,250 of which 900 was acquired by means of finance leases. Cash payments of 350 were made to purchase property, plant and equipment.

C   Cash and cash equivalents

Cash and cash equivalents consist of cash on hand and balances with banks and investments in money market instruments. Cash and cash equivalents included in the cash flow statement comprise the following balance sheet amounts:

Cash on hand and balances with banks	40	25
Short-term investments	370	135
Cash and cash equivalents as previously reported	410	160
Effect of exchange rate changes	–	(40)
Cash and cash equivalents as restated	410	120

Cash and cash equivalents at the end of the period include deposits with banks of 100 held by a subsidiary which are not freely remittable to the holding company because of currency exchange restrictions.

The group has undrawn borrowing facilities of 2,000 of which only 700 may be used for future expansion.

D   Segment information

	Segment A	Segment B	Total
Cash flows from:			
Operating activities	1,700	(140)	1,560
Investing activities	(640)	160	(480)
Financing activities	(570)	(220)	(790)
	490	(200)	290

Example – Squire

The following draft financial statements relate to Squire, a public limited company:

Draft Group Balance Sheet at 31 May 2008

	2008 (£m)	2007 (£m)
Non-current assets		
Intangible assets	80	65
Tangible non-current assets	2,630	2,010
Investment in associate	535	550
	3,245	2,625
Retirement benefit asset	22	16
Current assets		
Inventories	1,300	1,160
Trade receivables	1,220	1,060
Cash at bank and in hand	90	280
	2,610	2,500
Total assets	5,877	5,141
Capital and reserves		
Called up share capital	200	170
Share premium account	60	30
Revaluation reserve	92	286
Accumulated profits	508	505
	806	991
Minority interest	522	345
Non-current liabilities	1,675	1,320
Provisions for deferred tax	200	175
Current liabilities	2,620	2,310
Total equity and liabilities	5,877	5,141

Draft Group Income Statement for the Year Ended 31 May 2008

	£m
Revenue	8,774
Cost of sales	(7,310)
	1,464
Distribution and administrative expenses	(1,030)
Share of operating profit in associate	65
Profit from operations	499
Exchange difference on purchase of non-current assets	(9)
Finance costs	(75)
Profit before tax	415
Income tax expense (including tax on income from associate £20 million)	(225)
Profit after tax	190
Minority interests	(92)
Profit for period	98

Draft Group Statement of Recognised Gains and Losses for the Year Ended 31 May 2008

	£m
Profit for period	98
Foreign exchange difference of associate	(10)
Impairment losses on non-current assets offset against revaluation surplus	(194)
Total recognised gains and losses	(106)

Draft Statement of Changes in Equity for the Year Ended 31 May 2008

	£m
Total recognised gains and losses	(106)
Dividends paid	(85)
New shares issued	60
Total movements during the year	(131)
Shareholders' funds at 1 June 2007	991
Shareholders' funds at 31 May 2008	860

The following information relates to Squire:

(i) Squire acquired a 70% holding in Hunsten Holdings, a public limited company, on 1 June 2007. The fair values of the net assets acquired were as follows:

	£m
Tangible non-current assets	150
Inventories and work in progress	180
Provisions for onerous contracts	(30)
	300

The purchase consideration was £200 million in cash and £50 million (discounted value) deferred consideration which is payable on 1 June 2009. The provision for the onerous contracts was no longer required at 31 May 2008 as Squire had paid compensation of £30 million in order to terminate the contract on 1 December 2007. The group amortises goodwill over five years. The intangible asset in the group balance sheet comprises goodwill only. The difference between the discounted value of the deferred consideration (£50m) and the amount payable (£54m) is included in 'interest payable'.

(ii)   There had been no disposals of tangible non-current assets during the year. Depreciation for the period charged in cost of sales was £129 million.

(iii)   Current liabilities comprised the following items:

	2008 (£m)	2007 (£m)
Trade payables	2,355	2,105
Interest payable	65	45
Taxation	200	160
	2,620	2,310

(iv)   Non-current liabilities comprised the following items:

	2008 (£m)	2007 (£m)
Deferred consideration – purchase of Hunsten	54	–
Liability for the purchase of non-current assets	351	–
Loans repayable	1,270	1,320
	1,675	1,320

(v)   The retirement benefit asset comprised the following:

Movement in year:	£m
Surplus at 1 June 2007	16
Current and past service costs charged to income statement	(20)
Contributions paid to retirement benefit scheme	26
Surplus at 31 May 2008	22

Required:

Prepare a group cash flow statement using the indirect method for Squire group for the year ended 31 May 2008 in accordance with IAS 7 *Cash Flow Statements*.

Solution – Squire

Cash Flow Statement for the Year Ended 31 May 2008

Net cash inflow from operating activities

	£m	£m
Cash flows from investing activities		521
Purchase of property, plant and equipment (W1)	(451)	
Acquisition of subsidiary (200 + 30 onerous)	(230)	
Dividends from associates (W3)	50	(631)
Cash flows from financing activities		
Issue of ordinary shares (30 + 30)	60	
Repayment of long-term borrowings (1,320 − 1,270)	(50)	
Dividends paid	(85)	
Dividends paid to minority interests (W2)	(5)	(80)
Net decrease in cash and cash equivalents (280 − 90)		(190)

Reconciliation of operating profit to net cash inflow from operating activities

	£m	£m
Net profit before taxation		415
Adjustments		
Depreciation on property, plant and equipment	129	
Amortisation of goodwill (W2)	25	
Exchange difference on non current assets	9	
Retirement benefit expense	20	
Share of operating profit in associate	(65)	
Interest payable	75	
Decrease in inventories (1,300 − (1,160 + 180 acq.)	40	
Increase in trade receivables (1,220 − 1,060)	(160)	
Increase in trade payables (2,355 − 2,105)	250	323
		738
Interest paid (W5)	(51)	
Income tax paid (W4)	(140)	
Retirement benefits paid	(26)	
		(217)
		521

Workings

W1   Property, plant and equipment

	£'000		£'000
Opening balance	2,010	Impairment losses	194
Acquisition – Hunsten	150	Depreciation	129
Purchases (Bal. fig.)	793	Closing balance	2,630
	2,953		2,953

Cash paid is purchases of £793 million plus exchange difference of £9 million less £351 still owed equals £451 million.

W2   Acquisition of Hunsten

	£'000		£'000
Purchase consideration		Share of net assets acquired	
(200 + 50)	250	(300 × 70%)	210
		Goodwill	40
	250		250

	Goodwill		
	£'000		£'000
Opening balance	65	Amortisation (Bal. fig)	25
Acquisition of Hunsten	40	Closing balance	80
	105		105

Note: Amortisation of goodwill is no longer permitted under IFRS 3 but used in this example to illustrate a non-monetary movement.

	Minority interest		
	$'000		$'000
Dividend paid (Bal. fig.)	5	Opening balance	345
Closing balance	522	Acq. of Hunsten (30% ×	
		300)	90
		Profit for year	92
	527		527

W3   Associates

	Investment in associate		
	£'000		£'000
Opening balance	550	Foreign exchange loss	10
Profit for the year (65 − 20 tax)	45	Dividends received	
		(Bal. fig.)	50
		Closing balance	535
	595		595

W4   Income taxes

	Income taxes		
	£'000		£'000
Tax paid (Bal. fig)	140	Opening balance	
		(160+ 175)	335
Closing balance (200 + 200)	400	Income for year (225 − 20)	205
	540		540

W5   Interest paid

	Interest payable (£'000)		(£'000)
Unwinding of discount	4	Opening balance	45
Cash paid (Bal. fig.)	51	Income statement	75
Closing balance	65		
	120		120

Included below are two examples of companies presenting their cash flow statements in different ways. The first, Vislink Plc, prepares its cash flow statement in line with the traditional approach of moving the reconciliation of operating profit to cash flow from operating activities to the notes to the accounts which ensures that only real cash in and out are included in the cash flow statement. The second example is taken from the Grafton Group Plc. It follows the illustrative example in IAS 7 and includes the indirect method as part of the cash flow statement. However, strangely, it does deliberately exclude the movement in working capital from inclusion in the cash flow statement and this is included in the notes to the accounts. However, the group does provide excellent extensive disclosures of its acquisitions effect on cash flow:

Vislink Plc

Consolidated Group Cash Flow Statement for the Year Ended 31 December 2005

	Notes	2005 (£'000)	2004 (£'000)
Cash flow from operating activities			
Cash generated from/absorbed by) operations	31	9,602	(2,613)
Interest received		96	93
Interest paid		(567)	(590)
Taxation paid		(2,670)	(737)
Net cash generated from/(absorbed by) operating activities		6,461	(3,847)
Cash flows from investing activities			
Acquisition of subsidiary (net of cash acquired)	32	(2,445)	–
Proceeds from sale of property, plant and equipment		130	2
Purchase of property plant and equipment		(1,014)	(749)
Expenditure on capitalised development costs		(1,054)	(1,012)
Acquisition of investments		(43)	–
Net cash (absorbed by) investing activities		(4,426)	(1,759)
Cash flows from investing activities			
Net proceeds from issue of ordinary share capital		4,687	–
Net proceeds from sale of own shares		51	–

Repayment of borrowings	(3,138)	(275)
Dividend paid to shareholders	(246)	(202)
Net cash generated from/(absorbed by) financing activities	1,354	(477)
Effect of foreign exchange rate changes	514	(238)
Net increase/(decrease) in cash and cash equivalents	3,903	(6,321)
Cash and cash equivalents at 1 January	3,219	9,540
Cash and cash equivalents at 31 December	17	7,122	3,219

The Grafton Group Plc

Group Cash Flow Statement for the Year Ended 31 December 2005

	Note	2005 (a'000)	2004 (€'000)
Profit before taxation		**192,181**	145,826
Interest income		**(17,574)**	(10,559)
Interest expense		**48,803**	33,339
Income from financial assets		**–**	(1,541)
Property profit		**(9,640)**	(7,521)
Operating profit		**213,770**	159,544
Property development profit		**–**	6,729
Depreciation		**48,248**	34,626
Intangible amortisation		**2,176**	–
Share based payments change		**2,220**	892
Net profit on sale of plant and equipment		**(2,564)**	(2,179)
Contributions to pension schemes in excess of IAS 19 charge		**(10,888)**	(1,791)
Increase in working capital	32	**(28,485)**	(19,641)
Cash generated from operations		**224,477**	178,180
Interest paid		**(39,233)**	(27,111)
Income taxes paid		**(15,226)**	(7,301)
Cash flows from operating activities		**170,018**	143,768
Investing activities			
Inflows			
Proceeds from sale of property, plant and equipment		**32,793**	25,437
Interest received		**7,738**	4,849
Dividends received		**–**	2,364
		40,531	32,650
Outflows			
Acquisition of subsidiary undertakings and businesses	33	**(395,451)**	(61,805)
Net cash/(debt) acquired with subsidiary undertakings	33	**22,097**	718
Deferred acquisition consideration		**(6,844)**	(3,750)
Purchase of property, plant and equipment		**(100,559)**	(88,917)
Purchase of financial assets		**–**	(13,351)
		(479,957)	(167,105)
Cash flows from investing activities		**(439,426)**	(134,455)

Financing activities
Inflows

Proceeds from the issue of share capital		**178,658**	1,288
Proceeds from long-term borrowings		**373,078**	69,843
		551,736	71,131

Outflows

Repayments of long-term borrowings	9	**(35,673)**	(5,673)
Redemption of redeemable shares	9	**–**	(23,392)
Purchase of A ordinary shares		**(33,751)**	(2,131)
Payment of finance lease liabilities		**(2,061)**	(23,834)
Redemption of loan notes payable		**(25,237)**	(24,758)
Dividend paid	9	**–**	(53)
		(96,722)	(79,841)
Cash flows from financing activities		**455,014**	(8,71)
Net increase in cash and cash equivalents		**185,606**	603
Cash and cash equivalents at 1 January		**105,822**	106,557
Effect of exchange rate fluctuations on cash held		**416**	(1,338)
Cash and cash equivalents at 31 December		**291,844**	105,822

Cash and cash equivalents are broken down as follows:

Cash at bank and short-term deposits		**334,023**	135,868
Overdrafts		**(42,179)**	(30,046)
		291,844	105,822

32. Movement in Working Capital

Group	Inventory	Trade and other receivables	Trade and other payables	Total
	(€'000)	(€'000)	(€'000)	(€'000)
At 1 January 2005	237,680	318,165	(310,706)	245,059
Translation adjustment	5,140	9,509	(8,425)	6,304
Interest accruals and other movements	(21)	1,257	(10,419)	(9,183)
Acquisitions	90,011	152,542	(155,980)	86,573
Movement in 2005	23,837	17,755	(13,107)	28,485
At 31 December 2005	356,647	499,308	(498,717)	357,238
Movement in 2004	34,414	29,312	(44,085)	19,641

Company	Trade and other receivables	Trade and other payables	Total
	(€'000)	(€'000)	(€'000)
At 1 January 2005	292,264	(91,959)	200,305
Translation adjustment	9,251	(8,792)	459
Interest accrual and other movements	8	56	64
Movement in 2005	205,037	(342,219)	(137,182)
At 31 December 2005	506,560	(442,914)	63,646
Movement in 2004	19,560	(4,703)	14,857

33. Acquisition of Subsidiary Undertakings and Businesses

During the year the Group made three Irish and fourteen UK acquisitions at a total cost of €471 million including net debt acquired. In Ireland the Group acquired Heiton Group Plc on 7 January 2005, Garveys, a single branch builders merchant based in Roscommon, and Davies, a specialist merchant trading from two branches in the greater Dublin area were acquired on 1 December 2006.

The UK acquisitions added seven builders and twelve plumbers merchanting branches. These included seven single branch builders merchanting businesses located at Bolton, Lancashire; Sudbury, Suffolk; Hadleigh, Suffolk; Douglas, Isle of Man; Longridge, Lancashire; Sandy, Bedfoidshine and Belfast, of Northern Ireland.

The seven plumbers merchanting businesses acquired added twelve branches. The Five single branch businesses trade from the following locations; Fort William, Invernesshire; Barnhall, Cheshire; Darwen, Lancashire; Heathfield, East Sussex and Kirkintillock in Scotland. The two multi branch plumbers merchanting businesses acquired were: Camberley Plumbing and Heating trading from four branches in Camberley and Woking, Surrey; Liphook, Hampshire and from Reading in Berkshire, and Domestic Plumbing and Heating Supplies, a three branch business located in Preston and Morecambe, Lancashire and Kendal in Cumbria.

In the year ended 31 December 2004, the Group made seventeen UK acquisitions at a total cost of €85 million which comprised twenty builders and two plumbers merchanting branches. These included Five two branch builders merchants as follows: Thompson Builders Merchants based in Preston, Lancashire; Hall & Rogers located in central Manchester and Everton, Liverpool; Keelsupply which trades from Newton-le-Willows, St Helens and from Leyland, Lancashire; Slocombe & Butcher based in Weston-Super-Mare, North Somerset and Wellington, Somerset and Castle Builders Merchants based in Little lever, Bolton and Crewe in Cheshire.

The Group also acquired ten single branch builders merchanting businesses located at Coleraine and Bangor, Northern Ireland: Horncastle, Lincolnshire; Rushden, Northamptonshire; Ashton in Makerfield, St Helens; Airdrie, Scotland; Shrewsbury, Shropshire; Warrington and Stockport; Harrogate, North Yorkshire and two plumbers merchanting businesses located at Ely, Cambridge shire and Blandfort Forum in Dorset.

Acquisitions would have contributed €57.8 million and €6.8 million to operating profit in the year ended 31 December 2005 and 2004, respectively, assuming that had been acquired on 1 January of both years.

In 2005, Heitons contributed revenue of €607.7 million and operating profit of €48.8 million in the period since acquisition (7 January 2005).

	2005 (€'000)	2004 (€'000)
The fair values of assets and liabilities acquired are set out below:		
Intangible assets	17,695	–
Property, plant and equipment	176,711	17,761
Financial assets	39	17
Inventories	90,011	9,290
Trade and other receivables	152,542	23,424
Trade and other payables	(155,980)	(14,986)
Deferred consideration	(4,141)	–
Employee benefits	(25,014)	–
Corporation tax	(6,198)	(1,503)
Deferred tax liability	(12,762)	(842)
Deferred tax asset	20,381	1,808
Finance leases acquired	(7,934)	(1,388)
Bank debt acquired	(76,864)	–
Loan notes acquired	(12,655)	–
Net assets, acquired excluding cash and overdrafts	155,831	33,581
Goodwill	278,892	38,071
Consideration	434,723	71,652
Satisfied by:		
Cash paid	221,828	61,805
Cash acquired	(26,468)	(4,221)
Bank overdrafts assumed on acquisition	3,571	3,503
Net cash outflow	198,931	61,087
Shares issued*	173,623	–
Further payments accrued	10,055	–
Deferred acquisition consideration	–	1,480
Loan notes issued to vendors of businesses acquired	867	9,085
Investment held in business acquired at start of year	46,808	–
Fair value adjustment at 1 January 2006	53,974	–
Fair value eliminated on consolidation of Heitons	(49,535)	–
	434,723	71,652

21.4 million Grafton Units were issued at a share price of €8.12 (share price on 6 January 2005).

Other acquisitions

- Fixed assets have been fair valued to market value at date of acquisition.
- Under IFRS 3 stocks have been valued at selling price adjusted for costs of disposal and a reasonable profit allowance for selling effort.
- Deferred tax has been provided on the above adjustments under IAS 12 *Income Taxes*.

Goodwill has arisen on the above transactions due to synergies between the acquired entities and the Group.

The fair value of net assets acquired of €155,831,000 includes the Heiton Group Plc acquisition which constituted a material acquisition for the Group.

	Fair value (€'000)	Consideration (€'000)	Goodwill (€'000)
Heiton Group Plc	107,498	320,768	213,270
Other acquisitions	48,333	113,955	65,622
	155,831	434,723	278,892

The fair values were calculated as follows:

	Book value (€'000)	Fair value adjustment (€'000)	Fair value (€'000)
Heiton Group Plc			
Intangible assets	–	17,695	17,695
Financial assets	2,832	(2,832)	–
Property, plant and equipment	147,481	–	147,481
Working capital	79,412	(5,438)	73,974
Deferred consideration	(4,141)	–	4,141
Employee benefits	(24,249)	–	24,249
Corporation tax	(4,724)	(500)	5,224
Deferred tax liability	(9,255)	(2,307)	11,562
Deferred tax asset	3,031	–	3,031
Finance leases	(7,646)	–	7,646
Bank debt	(69,206)	–	69,206
Loan notes	(12,655)	–	12,655
	100,880	6,618	107,498
Other acquisitions			
Financial assets	39	–	39
Property, plant and equipment	27,980	1,250	29,230
Working capital	12,479	120	12,599
Employee benefits	(765)	–	(765)
Corporation tax	(974)	–	(974)
Deferred tax liability	(925)	(275)	(1,200)
Deferred tax asset	17,350	–	17,350
Finance leases	(288)	–	(288)
Bank debt	(7,658)	–	(7,658)
	47,288	1095	48,333

The fair values adjustments noted above have arisen as follows:

Heiton Group Plc

- Recognition of intangible assets for brands and customer relationships under IFRS 3 *Business Combinations* and IAS 38 *Intangible Assets*.
- Financial assets were reduced for impairment as required by IAS 36 *Impairment of Assets*.
- The assets and liabilities have been fair valued at the date of acquisition.
- Under IFRS 3 stocks have been valued at selling price adjusted for costs of disposal and a reasonable profit allowance for selling effort.
- Under IAS 12 *Income Taxes* corporation and deferred tax has been provided on the above adjustments.

Disclosure standards

10.1 IAS 10 *Events After the Balance Sheet Date* (December 2003)

Introduction

The main impact of IAS 10 *Events After the Balance Sheet Date* (revised 1999) is the removal of dividends declared after the balance sheet date, as adjusting events. Instead they should be disclosed in the notes. They do not meet the definition of a liability under IAS 37 *Provisions, Contingent Liabilities and Contingent Assets*.

Similarly dividends receivable from associates/subsidiaries, relating to a period prior to the balance sheet date, are now classified as non-adjusting.

There is also no exceptional provision in IAS 10 to use prudence to reclassify a non-adjusting event as adjusting.

Objective

(a) To prescribe when an entity should adjust its financial statements for events after the balance sheet date (i.e. adjusting events).

(b) To prescribe the disclosures about the date of authorisation of the financial statements, for both adjusting and non-adjusting events, and also the disclosure of non-adjusting events themselves.

IAS 10 also includes a requirement that an entity should not prepare its financial statements on a going concern basis if events after the balance sheet date indicate that it is no longer appropriate.

Scope

The standard should apply in accounting for and disclosure of events after the balance sheet date.

Definitions

Events after the balance sheet date

These occur between the balance sheet date and the date the financial statements are authorised for issue. These are of two types:

(1)   those providing evidence of conditions existing at the balance sheet date (adjusting) and
(2)   those that are indicative of conditions arising after the balance sheet date (non-adjusting).

If an entity submits its accounts to shareholders for approval AFTER the financial statements are issued, then the authorisation date is the date of original issuance and not the date of approval of the financial statements by the shareholders.

EXAMPLE 1

Completion of draft financial statements	28 February 20 × 2
Board reviews and authorises for issue	*18 March 20 × 2
Profit announcement	19 March 20 × 2
Available to shareholders	1 April 20 × 2
AGM	15 May 20 × 2
Filed with regulatory body	17 May 20 × 2

*Correct date of authorisation for issue

EXAMPLE 2

Management reviews and authorises for issue	*18 March 20 × 2
Supervisory Board approves	26 March 20 × 2
Available to shareholders	1 April 20 × 2
AGM	15 May 20 × 2
Filed with regulatory body	17 May 20 × 2

*Correct date of authorisation for issue

Events after the balance sheet date include all events up to the date when the financial statements are authorised for issue.

Recognition and measurement

(1) Adjusting events after the balance sheet date

An entity should adjust the amounts recognised in its financial statements to reflect adjusting events after the balance sheet date.
Examples include:

(a)   settlement after the balance sheet date of a court case confirming a liability;
(b)   receipt of information after the balance sheet or date indicating that an asset was impaired at the balance sheet date, e.g., bankruptcy of customer or sale of inventories lower than their cost;
(c)   the determination, after the balance sheet date, of the cost of assets purchased or proceeds sold before the balance sheet date;
(d)   the determination after the balance sheet date of the amount of profit/bonus payments provided there was a legal or constructive obligation at the balance sheet date; and
(e)   the discovery of fraud or error.

(2)   Non-adjusting events after the balance sheet date

An entity should not adjust the amounts recognised in the financial statements to reflect non-adjusting events after the balance sheet date.

An example would be a decline in the market value of investments. It reflects circumstances arising in the following period.

(3)   Dividends

If dividends are declared after the balance sheet date, no liability should be recognised at that date. Instead they should be disclosed in the notes as a contingent liability. They do not meet the definition of a liability under IAS 37.

Paddy Power Plc has prepared an excellent note to meet this requirement:

> ## Paddy Power Plc   Year Ended 31 December 2005
>
> ### Notes to the Accounts
>
> #### 24. Events after the Balance Sheet Date
>
> In respect of the current year, the directors proposed that a final dividend of 12.84c per share (2004: 12.52c per share) would be paid to shareholders on 19 May 2006. This dividend is subject to approval by shareholders at the Annual General Meeting and has not been included as a liability in these financial statements. The proposed dividend is payable to all shareholders on the Register of Members on 10 March 2006. The total estimated dividend to be paid amounts to €6,416,000 (2004: €6,234,000).

(4)   Going concern

An entity cannot prepare its financial statements under the going concern basis if management intends to liquidate the business after the balance sheet date or ceases trading or has no realistic alternative to do so. IAS 1 outlines the required disclosure in such cases.

Disclosure

(1)   Date of authorisation of issue

The date and who gave the authorisation should be disclosed. Also if the owners or others have powers to amend the financial statements after that date, that fact should be disclosed as well.

(2)   Updating disclosure about conditions at the balance sheet date

If an entity receives information after the balance sheet date about conditions at the balance sheet date, the entity should update disclosures that relate to these conditions in the light of any new information.

An example would be a contingent liability becoming a provision, then the disclosures relating to these contingent liabilities need to be updated (as per IAS 37).

(3)   Non-adjusting events after the balance sheet date

If material, these could influence user decisions. Thus the following should be disclosed:

(a)   the nature of the event and
(b)   an estimate of its financial effect or a statement that such an estimate cannot be made.

Examples include:

(a)   A major business combination/disposal after the balance sheet date.
(b)   An announcement of a plan to discontinue an operation or entering into binding agreements to sell.
(c)   Major purchases/disposals of assets or expropriations of major assets by government.
(d)   The destruction of a major production plant by fire.
(e)   The announcement or commencing of a major restructuring.
(f)   Major ordinary share and potential share transactions.
(g)   Abnormal large changes in prices or foreign exchange rates.
(h)   Changes in tax rates/laws enacted or announced after the balance sheet date.
(i)   Entering into significant commitments, e.g. guarantees.
(j)   Commencement of major litigation arising solely out of events that have occurred after the balance sheet date.

Some unusual examples are provided below, some of which relate prior to the advent of IAS 10 but are still relevant today:

Friends Provident   Year Ended 31 December 2005

Notes to the Accounts

47. Post Balance Sheet Event

On 10 March 2006, an announcement was made by one of F&C's investment trust clients, F&C Latin American Trust PLC, that it has decided to appoint a new manager. Whilst the exact timing on the termination of the management contract is uncertain, it is expected to be imminent. Annualised revenues from this trust are approximately £3m.

The expected loss of this business constitutes an indicator of potential impairment in the related intangible which was recognised as part of the F&C acquisition, and as such, an impairment review of the investment trust management contracts will be undertaken in 2006. This review will reassess the carrying value of the relevant assets, including their estimated remaining economic life, and determine whether any further impairment will arise.

Corus Group Plc   Year Ended 31 December 2002

Notes to the Accounts (Extract)

36. Post Balance Sheet Events

(i) As discussed in Note 20, on 30 Dec 2002 the Company reduced its main available bank facility by voluntary cancellation of €460m, of which €260 m would have matured in Jan 2003 and €100 million in Mar 2003. The facility now stands at €1,400m of which €455m was utilised as at 31 Dec 2002.

(ii) On 23 Oct 2002, Corus announced that it had agreed in principle to the sale of its Aluminium Rolled Products and Extrusions businesses to Pechiney SA for €861m (approximately £543m). It was intended that a definitive sale and purchase agreement would be entered into following completion of internal consultation, advice and approval processes. However, the Supervisory Board of Corus Nederland BV decided on 10 Mar 2003 to reject the recommendation to proceed with the sale. On 11 Mar 2003 Corus Group Plc announced that it would commence proceedings before the Enterprise Chamber of the Amsterdam Court of Appeal to seek redress in respect of this decision. However, this request was unsuccesfull and, since no appeal procedure was available to resolve the issue in time for the sale to proceed, Corus accepted the Court's decision as final. Pechiney has been informed that Corus will not proceed with the sale now and as a result, a break fee of €20m is payable to Pechiney.

(iii) In the light of the Company's performance, the Board including Mr Tony Pedder, Chief Executive, concluded that a change of leadership was required. Mr Pedder tendered his resignation on 13 Mar 2003 and this was accepted with immediate effect. The procedure for the recruitment of a new Chief Executive is underway. Mr Stuart Pettifor, a main Board Executive Director, was appointed Chief Operating Officer, taking responsibility for all operational matters. Sir Brian Moffat agreed to defer his planned retirement to become full-time Chairman until his successor is appointed.

Granada Plc   Year Ended 30 September 2002

Notes to the Accounts (Extract)

36. Post Balance Sheet Events

On 16 October 2002 Carlton and Granada Plc announced agreed terms for a proposed merger to pave the way for a fully consolidated ITV. The merger is conditional on regulatory clearances, including those from the competition authorities. A joint submission by Carlton and Granada was filed with the Office of Fair Trading on 25 November 2002.

One of the most obvious of non-adjusting events was the effects of the aftermath of the 9/11 tragedy in New York and WH Smith Plc have provided an example of that for their accounts to 31 August 2001, and in particular, on the effects on their US retail business. It was based on the United Kingdom standard, SSAP 17 *Accounting for Post Balance Sheet Events* but the concepts are the same as IAS 10:

WH Smith Plc   12 Months Ended 31 August 2001

Notes to the Accounts (Extract)

The tragic events in the United States on 11 September 2001 and their aftermath had an material adverse effect on the trading of WH Smith USA Travel Retail. The majority of WH Smith USA Travel Retail's stores are based in airports and city centre hotels. Like-for-like sales in WH Smith USA Travel Retail have fallen 24 per cent in the six weeks to 13 October 2001.

The Group has initiated a restructuring of the WH Smith USA Travel Retail operations to align the business with the current market conditions but it is too early to estimate the full continuing financial effect of 11 September 2001.

In accordance with SSAP 17 *Accounting for Post Balance Sheet Events*, the events of 11 September 2001 and their aftermath constitute a 'non-adjusting event', as they do not relate to conditions that existed at the balance sheet date. Accordingly, it is not appropriate to reflect any financial effect of these events in the balance sheet at 31 August 2001.

The costs of restructuring, together with any adjustments to asset carrying values and additional liabilities that may arise as a result of the events of 11 September 2001 and any subsequent developments, will therefore be included in the accounts for the year ending 31 August 2002.

Following is an example, which brings out the main points in the standard:

Example – Cashel Plc

You are the accountant of Cashel Plc, a small but diverse group. You are in the process of drafting the financial statements for the year to 30 June 2007, and the following issues have been referred to you for resolution or comment:

(1) Subsequent to 30 June 2007, a subsidiary, Caher Ltd, suffered a flood at a warehouse that destroyed inventory with a book value of £350,000. The insurance company has agreed a claim for £250,000 in respect of the inventory.

In addition, a major customer of Caher Ltd has just been placed in receivership. The amount owed to Caher Ltd at 30 June 2007 was £34,000 but a further delivery at an invoiced value of £40,000 was made on 2 July 2007. Caher Ltd has no reservation of title clauses in its trading terms and no provision has so far been made in respect of these balances, which remain outstanding.

The draft accounts of Caher Ltd for the year disclose a profit before tax of £180,000 and net assets of £1,260,000.

(2) The group acquired the freehold interest in a listed building for £850,000 during the year through a wholly owned subsidiary, Bandon Ltd, which was incorporated specifically for that purpose. Bandon Ltd currently leases the property to a third party at arm's length but your managing director is considering moving the group head office personnel into this building when the lease expires. The building is recorded in the books at cost, but has been valued at £1 million.

(3) On 1 August 2007, a major design fault was found in a new product and it was withdrawn from the market. Inventories of the product have been returned to Cashel Plc's supplier for a full refund. The company had committed itself to an advertising schedule for this new product involving total expenditure of £300,000, to be written off evenly over three years. £150,000 had been spent in the first year to 31 June 2007.

(4) On 15 September 2007 torrential rain caused flooding at the company's riverside warehouse, resulting in an uninsured inventory loss totalling £200,000.

(5) Bills receivable of £120,000 had been discounted at the bank on 15 June 2007. The bills were dishonoured on presentation at the maturity date on 16 September 2007.

Suggested solution – Cashel Plc

(1)   Inventory destroyed

The event (i.e. the flood) occurred after the year end and is therefore non-adjusting. The net loss after insurance is expected to be £100,000. This should be disclosed if its non-disclosure would affect the user's ability to reach a proper understanding of the financial statements. As this represents over 55% of the profits before tax, it is certainly material and should be disclosed. In next year's accounts it should be written off as an exceptional item within the figure for profit before tax.

Receivable in receivership

The event (i.e. the receivable of £34,000) existed at the year end and the subsequent evidence indicates that the receivable may not be recovered due to the receivership of the company. The provision for bad debts should be based on the likely non-recovery at the time of the accounts being approved but prudence may dictate 100% provision if no evidence exists at that time.

The additional sale of £40,000 occurred after the year end and should be matched against a bad debt provision in the next year. No provision should be made at this stage as the event did not exist at the year end. However, this represents over 20% of profits and therefore could be considered to be sufficiently material to be disclosed as a non-adjusting event.

Note 19. Events after the balance sheet date

(1) Subsequent to the year end, a severe flood at the Company's warehouse in Romcard destroyed inventory to the value of £350,000. Insurance proceeds have recovered £250,000 of this loss but a net loss of £100,000 has been incurred.

(2) One of Caher's major customers, Brickbat Ltd, went into receivership after the year end. Full provision has been made in the accounts for amounts owing at the year end but £40,000 sales since then have not been provided as they relate to next year.

(2)   Listed building

Under IAS 40 *Investment Property*, if an asset is held by the group purely for investment potential with a rental income at arm's length, then it need not be depreciated. It should be recorded in the books at its open market value of £1 million. This is an uplift of £150,000 from its original cost, which must be credited to the income statement for the year. However, the asset may still be treated as a normal property and depreciated accordingly. The former option is the more popular since the uplift is recorded as a profit for the year.

Bandon Ltd was set up this year to acquire the listed building and it is 100% owned by the group. The company should be consolidated as it is no longer permissible, under the Companies Act 1989 and IAS 27 *Consolidated and Separate Financial Statements*, to argue that Bandon's activities are so dissimilar that consolidation would be misleading.

The proposal to move group head office would mean that the building no longer meets the criteria as an investment property because property let to another group company is specifically excluded. The building would then need to be depreciated unless maintenance expenditure renders the charge immaterial or residual values are considered to be as high as cost. The building needs no longer be revalued, but if it is, then the revaluation should follow the rules set out in IAS 16 and revaluation should take place on a regular basis to ensure that the values are kept up to date.

(3)   Withdrawal of faulty design products

The major design fault was discovered on 1 August 2007, one month after the year end. Therefore, although the event did not exist at (i.e. was not discovered before) the year end, it could be argued that the inventories did exist in a faulty state at that time. It would therefore be treated as an adjusting post balance sheet event under IAS 10.

The committed advertising expenditure of £300,000 should be written off and fully accrued by the year end as it is unlikely to be recovered. However, if the unspent £150,000 could be avoided or switched to other products then only the

£150,000 expenditure incurred to date would need to be expensed. The write-off may be so material that it is abnormal in relation to usual expenditure and it should therefore be disclosed as an exceptional item in the annual accounts. However, under IAS 37 the committed but unspent expenditure of £150,000 would be treated as a mere intention and not an obligation. Therefore it may not be provided as a liability in 2007.

The inventories returned will be refunded in full to the customer but hopefully this will be countered by a refund to Brickbat Ltd from its own suppliers. This is a counterclaim contingency. If it is probable that a refund will be received and thus no loss crystallises, then the financial statements should record the liability and separately a probable asset. If, however, it is only possible that a refund will be received, then the liability should be accrued and any possible gain ignored, following the prudence concept. These recommendations are in accordance with IAS 37 *Provisions, Contingent Liabilities and Contingent Assets*. Under IAS 37 a counterclaim should be treated completely separately from the accounting treatment for the claim, as it is argued to be illegally offsetting an asset against a liability.

It is important to understand that the likelihood of success and the probable amounts of the claim/counterclaim must be separately assessed and disclosed, if appropriate. Only if the possibility of the loss is remote should no disclosure be made. If a possible material contingency is disclosed, the following are required:

(a) The nature of the contingency.
(b) Any uncertainties expected to affect its ultimate outcome.
(c) A prudent estimate of its financial effect or a statement to the effect that it is not practicable to make such an estimate.

In addition, under the *Framework*, it is unlikely that the advertising expenditure would result in future economic benefits. Therefore it must not be capitalised and should be written off to the income statement.

(4)   Flood at warehouse destroying stock

The uninsured inventory loss of £200,000 was caused by a torrential downpour of rain resulting in a flood at the company's new riverside warehouse. This event occurred after the year end, therefore the condition did not exist at the year end. The loss would be considered as non-adjusting under IAS 10 unless it could affect the going concern of the business. If the latter were the case then the accounts would need to be prepared on a break-up basis.

However, assuming that the company is a going concern, the non-adjusting event would require the following disclosures if non-disclosure would affect the user's ability to reach a proper understanding of the financial statements:

(a) The nature of the event.
(b) An estimate of the financial effect before accounting for taxation, and any tax implications, to effect a proper understanding of the financial position.

(5)   Bills dishonoured

The bills were discounted by the bank two weeks before the year end. They subsequently became dishonoured on maturity after the year end. This is a post balance sheet event and gives additional evidence of a condition existing at the year end. It should be treated as an adjusting event under IAS 10 and the loss of £120,000 should be accrued in the financial statements.

The company would obviously take action to make a counterclaim. If success is probable then, under IAS 37, the probable gain would have been offset against the liability to the bank. However, if success is no more than possible then, under the prudence concept, no disclosure can be made. IAS 37, however, has effectively banned the offsetting procedure and the claim liability must be kept separate from the probable counterclaim asset.

10.2   IAS 14 *Segment Reporting* (1997)

Objective

To establish principles for reporting segment information, both products, services, etc. and geographical. This is to help users:

(a)   better understand past performance;
(b)   better assess the entity's risks and returns; and
(c)   make more informed judgements about the entity as a whole.

Consolidated data by itself does not provide that information and needs to be disaggregated to achieve the objectives above.

Scope

IAS 14 should apply to the full financial statements that comply with IASs and be applied by entities whose equity or debt is publically traded or are in the process of issuing those instruments in the public securities markets. Further voluntary disclosure, however, for other entities is encouraged but they must comply in full with IAS 14.

Normally it is required only for consolidated accounts but if a subsidiary is itself publically traded then it must also be presented in its own separate financial report. Similar requirements also exist for associates or joint ventures.

Definitions

* *Business segment.* A distinguishable component of an entity that is engaged in providing an individual product or service or a group of related products/services and that is subject to risks and returns that are different from those of other business segments. Factors to consider include:
  (a)   the nature of the products/services;
  (b)   the nature of the production processes;

(c)   the type or class of customer for the products or services;

(d)   the methods used to distribute the products or provide the services; and

(e)   if applicable, the nature of the regulatory environment e.g. banking, insurance, etc.

• *Geographical segment.* A distinguishable component of an entity that is engaged in providing products or services within a particular economic environment and is subject to risks and returns that are different from those of components operating in other economic environments. Factors to consider include:

(a)   similarity of economic and political conditions;

(b)   relationships between operations in different geographical areas;

(c)   proximity of operations;

(d)   special risks associated with a particular area;

(e)   exchange control regulations; and

(f)   the underlying currency risks.

It can be a single country, group of two or more countries or even a region within a country.

Most organisations are organised and managed on the basis of predominant risks thus an entity's organisational structure and internal financial reporting systems would be relevant in deciding the basis for identifying its segments.

Geographical segments may be based on either the location of its operations (origin) or the location of its markets and customers (destination). The organisational structure should normally help to determine which is the more important of the two.

The determination of segments is judgmental and must involve a consideration of the qualitative characteristics of relevance, reliability and comparability over time as well as its usefulness in assessing the risks and returns of the entity as a whole.

• *Segment revenue.* This represents revenue that is directly attributable to a segment and the relevant portion of enterprise revenue that can be allocated on a reasonable basis to a segment. That can arise from external sales or from internal segments of the same entity. It does not include extraordinary items, interest or dividend income unless it is a financial segment, nor should it include gains on the sale of investments or extinguishment of debt unless it is a financial segment.

It does include, however, an entity's share of profits/losses of associates and joint ventures accounted for under the equity method as well as a joint venturer's share of the revenue of a jointly controlled entity that is accounted for by proportionate consolidation in accordance with IAS 31 *Financial Reporting of Interests in Joint Ventures.*

• *Segment expense.* These represent expenses that are directly attributable to a segment and the relevant portion of an expense that can be allocated on a reasonable basis to the segment, including those relating to both external customers and internal segments. It does not include extraordinary items; interest unless a financial segment; losses on sale of investments unless a financial segment; losses on sale of investments; share of associates/joint venture losses nor income tax or general administration expenses that relate to the business as a whole.

It does, however, include a joint venturer's share of expenses that are proportionately consolidated in accordance with IAS 31.

For a financial segment interest income and expenses should be reported as a single net amount only if they are reported as such in the consolidated financial statements.

- *Segment result.* Segment revenue less segment expense before any adjustments for minority interests.
- *Segment assets.* Operating assets employed by the segment for operating activities and are either directly attributable to the segment or can be allocated on a reasonable basis. If the segment result includes interest income then segment assets should include the related income producing assets.
- Income tax assets are not included and equity accounted investments only if the profit/loss from such investments is included within segment revenue. However, proportionately consolidated joint venture operating assets should be included.

EXAMPLES

> Current assets used in operating activities of the segment
> Property, plant and equipment
> Finance leases
> Intangible assets
> Share of operating assets used by two or more segments, provided a reasonable
>   allocation can be made.
> Goodwill directly attributable to a segment or allocated on a reasonable basis.

Revaluations and prior period adjustments to business combination segment assets must be reflected in segment disclosure.

- *Segment liabilities.* Operating liabilities resulting from the operating activities of a segment and are either directly attributable to a segment or can be allocated to the segment on a reasonable basis. If the segment result includes interest expense segment liabilities should include related interest bearing liabilities. However, it should include a joint venturer's share of the liabilities of a jointly controlled entity that is accounted for by proportionate consolidation under IAS 31. Income tax liabilities are excluded.

EXAMPLES

> Trade and other payables
> Accrued liabilities
> Customer advances
> Product warranty provisions.

It is expected that the internal reporting system should enable reporting entities to identify attributable revenues, expenses, assets and liabilities to reporting segments. However, in some cases, these could be argued to be arbitrary or difficult to understand by external users. Such an allocation would not be on a reasonable basis. Conversely some items may not have been allocated internally but a reasonable basis for doing so exists, in which case they should be allocated.

Identifying reportable segments

Primary and secondary segment reporting formats

The dominant source and nature of an entity's risks and returns should govern whether its primary reporting format should be business or geographical segments. If they are affected predominantly by differences in the products/services it produces then its primary format should be business segments with secondary information being reported geographically and vice versa.

An entity's internal organisational and management structure and its system of internal financial reporting should normally be the basis for identifying the predominant source and nature of risks and differing rates of return and thus which reporting format is primary, except in rare cases where:

(a)   if it is affected both by differences in products/services and geographically as evidenced by a 'matrix approach' to managing the company and reporting internally, then business segments should be primary and geographical secondary and

(b)   if internal reporting is not based on either approach, the directors should determine which is the more appropriate basis to adopt as the primary format.

IAS 14 does not require but it does not prohibit the adoption of a matrix presentation (i.e. both treated as primary) if it is felt appropriate. In the case of (b) above the objective is to achieve a reasonable degree of comparability with other entities, enhance comparability and meet the expressed needs of investors, creditors and others for information about product/service related and geographically related risks and returns.

Business and geographical segments

The business and geographical segments for external reporting should be in line with internal reporting units that are used by the CEO and Directors to evaluate past performance and make decisions about future allocations of resources within the entity.

If the internal reporting systems are based neither on products/services, etc., nor on geography the directors should choose either business segments or geographical segments as the entity's primary segment reporting format based on their assessment of which format best reflects the primary source of the enterprise's risks and returns. The decision should be based on the factors in the definitions of both consistent with the following:

(a)   if one or more segments are based on the definition but others are not, (b) below should apply to those not covered by the definitions;

(b)   management should look to the next lower level of internal segmentation that reports on product/geographical lines and if such a level meets the definition of a segment then it should be treated as an identifiable reportable segment itself.

This approach of looking to an enterprise's organisational and management structure and its internal reporting system to identify the entity's business and geographical segments for external reporting purposes is sometimes called the 'management approach'.

Reportable segments

Two or more internally reported business segments or geographical segments that are substantially similar may be combined as a single business or geographical segment. That is only if:

(a)   they exhibit similar long-term financial performance;

(b)   they are similar in all of the factors in the appropriate definition of either a business or geographical segment.

A reportable segment should be identified if a majority of its revenue is earned from sales to external customers and:

(a)   its revenue from sales to external customers and from other segments amounts to 10% or more of total revenue (internal and external);
(b)   its segment result is 10% or more of the combined result of all segments in profit or in loss whichever is greater; or
(c)   its assets are 10% or more of total assets of all segments.

However, if an internally reported segment fails all of the above thresholds:

(a)   it may be designated as a reportable segment despite its size;
(b)   it may be combined into a separately reportable segment with one or more other similar segments that are also below the thresholds; and
(c)   if not treated as (a) or (b) it should be included as an unallocated reconciling item.

If total external revenue attributable to reportable segments is less than 75% of the total consolidated revenue, additional segments should be identified as reportable segments even if they fail the 10% thresholds until the 75% revenue threshold is met.

IAS 14 does not limit reporting segments to those that earn a majority of their revenue externally. For example, an oil company could report upstream activities (exploration and development) as a separate segment from downstream (refining and marketing) despite the fact that most of the upstream product is transferred internally. IAS 14 encourages voluntary disclosure along these lines with appropriate disclosure of the basis of pricing inter-segment transfers.

If an entity reports vertically integrated activities as separate segments and the entity does not choose to report them externally as business segments, the selling segment should be combined into the buying segment in identifying externally reportable business segments unless there is no reasonable basis for doing so, in which case the selling segment should be included as an unallocated reconciling item.

If a segment meets the threshold in a preceding period but not the current then it should continue to be reported as a separate segment, unless impracticable to do so.

Segment accounting policies

Segment information should be prepared in conformity with the accounting policies adopted for preparing and presenting the financial statements of the consolidated group.

IAS 14 does not prevent the disclosure of additional segment information prepared on a basis other than the accounting policies adopted for consolidated statements provided that (a) the information is reported internally to the board for making decisions on allocating resources and (b) the basis of measurement is clearly described.

Assets that are jointly used by two or more segments should be allocated only if their related revenues and expenses are also allocated to those segments. For example, an asset is included in segment assets only if the related depreciation or amortisation is deducted in measuring segment result.

Disclosure

Primary reporting format

The disclosure requirements below should be applied to each reportable segment based on an entity's primary reporting format:

1. Segment revenue with separate disclosure of external and internal.
2. Segment result with clear description if adopt accounting policies other than those for the consolidated financial statements. Should normally be net profit/loss. If cannot allocate expenses, except arbitrarily, then could use gross margin on sales.
3. The total carrying amount of segment assets.
4. Segment liabilities.
5. Capital expenditure incurred on an accruals basis.
6. Total depreciation and amortisation included in the segment result for the period.
7. Encouraged but not required to disclose the nature and amount of any items of segment revenue and expense that are of such size, nature or incidence that their disclosure is relevant to explain performance for the period, i.e. exceptional items. The decision regarding materiality should, however, be based on segments not on the entity as a whole.
8. Significant non-cash expenses other than depreciation and amortisation.
9. Entities providing the voluntary segment disclosure under IAS 7 *Cash Flow Statements* need not disclose depreciation, amortisation or non-cash expenses.
10. Share of net profit/loss of associates, joint ventures, etc. adopting the equity method if substantially all operations are within that single segment. If disclosed then the aggregate investments in those associates/joint ventures should also be disclosed by reportable segment.
11. A reconciliation between the segmental information and the consolidated accounts is required – segment revenue to total, segment result to entity operating profit/loss as well as to net profit/loss and segment assets and liabilities to entity total assets and liabilities.

Secondary segment information

If an entity's primary format for reporting segment information is business segments, it should also report the following information:

(a) segment revenue from external customers by geographical area based on the geographical location of its customers for each segment which exceeds 10% or more of total external sales;
(b) the total carrying amount of segment assets, for each geographical segment whose assets are 10% or more of total assets; and
(c) the total cost incurred during the period to acquire segment fixed assets for each geographical segment that exceeds 10% or more of all geographical segments.

If an entity's primary format for reporting segment information is geographical segments (location of assets or of customers) must also report the following secondary information.

For each business segment which exceeds 10% or more of total revenue or total assets:

(a) segment revenue from external customers;
(b) the total carrying amount of segment assets;
(c) the total cost incurred during the period to acquire segment fixed assets.

If an entity's primary format for reporting segment information is geographical segments (location of assets) and if location of its customers is different from the location of its assets, then the entity should also report revenue from sales to external customers for each customer-based geographical segment whose revenue from sales to external customers is 10% or more of total entity revenue to external customers.

If an entity's primary format for reporting segment information is geographical segments (location of customers) and if location of its assets is different from the location of its customers then the following should be reported for each asset-based geographical segment whose revenue from external sales or segment assets is 10% or more of group amounts:

(a) the total carrying amount of segment assets by geographical location and
(b) the total cost incurred in the period to acquire segment fixed assets, by location of assets.

Other disclosure matters

If a business segment for which information is reported to the CEO or Board is not a reportable segment because it earns a majority of its income from internal sales but still sells 10% or more of total entity revenue, the entity should disclose that fact and the amounts of revenue from (a) sales to external customers and (b) internal sales.

The basis of transfer pricing should be disclosed.

Changes in accounting policies adopted for segment reporting that has a material effect on segment information presented for comparative information should be restated unless it is impracticable to do so. Such disclosure should include a description of the nature of the change, the reasons for the change, the fact that comparative information has been restated or that it is impracticable to do so and the financial effect of the change, if reasonably determinable. If an entity changes the identification of its segments and it does restate prior periods then the entity should report segment data for both the old and the new bases of segmentation in the year in which it changes the identification of its segments.

An enterprise should disclose the types of products/services included in each segment and indicate the composition of each reported geographical segment, *both primary and secondary, if not otherwise disclosed in the financial report.*

The latter should help users assess the impact of changes in demand, changes in price of inputs, development of alternative products, the impact of changes in the economic and geographical environment, etc.

Summary of required primary disclosures

Primary format – business	Primary format – geographic location of assets	Primary format – geographic location of customers
Required primary disclosures		
Revenue from external customers by business segment	Revenue from external customers by location of assets	Revenue from external customers by location of customers
Revenue from transactions with other segments by business segment	Revenue from transactions with other segments by location of assets	Revenue from transactions with other segments by location of customers
Segment result by business segment	Segment result by location of assets	Segment result by location of customers
Carrying amount of segment assets by business segment	Carrying amount of segment assets by location of assets	Carrying amount of segment assets by location of customers
Segment liabilities by business segment	Segment liabilities by location of assets	Segment liabilities by location of customers
Cost to acquire property, plant, equipment and intangibles by business segment	Cost to acquire property, plant, equipment and intangibles by location of assets	Cost to acquire property, plant, equipment and intangibles by location of customers
Depreciation and amortisation by business segment	Depreciation and amortisation by location of assets	Depreciation and amortisation by location of customers
Non-cash expenses by business segment	Non-cash expenses by location of assets	Non-cash expenses by location of customers
Share of net profit/loss and investment in equity method associates or joint ventures by business segment (if substantially all within one segment)	Share of net profit/loss and investment in equity method associates or joint ventures by location of assets (if substantially all within one segment)	Share of net profit/loss and investment in equity method associates or joint ventures by location of customers (if substantially all within one segment)
Reconciliation of revenue, result, assets and liabilities by business segment	Reconciliation of revenue, result, assets and liabilities	Reconciliation of revenue, result, assets and liabilities

Summary of required secondary disclosures

Primary format – business	Primary format – geographic location of assets	Primary format – geographic location of customers
Required secondary disclosures		
Revenue from external customers by location of customers	Revenue from external customers by business segment	Revenue from external customers by business segment
Carrying amount of segment assets by location of assets	Carrying amount of segment assets by business segment	Carrying amount of segment assets by business segment
Cost to acquire property, plant, equipment and intangibles by location of assets	Cost to acquire property, plant, equipment and intangibles by business segment	Cost to acquire property, plant, equipment and intangibles by business segment
	Revenue from external customers by geographical customers if different from location of assets	
		Carrying amount of segment assets by location of assets if different from location of customers
		Cost to acquire property, plant, equipment and intangibles by location of assets if different from location of customers
Revenue for any business or geographical segment whose external revenue is more than 10% of entity revenue but that is not a reportable segment because a majority of its revenue is from internal transfers	Revenue for any business or geographical segment whose external revenue is more than 10% of entity revenue but that is not a reportable segment because a majority of its revenue is from internal transfers	Revenue for any business or geographical segment whose external revenue is more than 10% of entity revenue but that is not a reportable segment because a majority of its revenue is from internal transfers
Basis of pricing inter-segment transfers and any changes therein	Basis of pricing inter-segment transfers and any changes therein	Basis of pricing inter-segment transfers and any changes therein
Changes in segment accounting policies	Changes in segment accounting policies	Changes in segment accounting policies
Types of products and services in each business segment	Types of products and services in each business segment	Types of products and services in each business segment
Composition of each geographical segment	Composition of each geographical segment	Composition of each geographical segment

Illustrative layout – information about business segments (£m)

	Paper Products 2002	Paper Products 2001	Office Products 2002	Office Products 2001	Publishing 2002	Publishing 2001	Other Operations 2002	Other Operations 2001	Eliminations 2002	Eliminations 2001	Consolidated 2002	Consolidated 2001
Revenue												
External sales	55	50	20	17	19	16	7	7				
Inter-segment sales	15	10	10	14	2	4	2	2	(29)	(30)		
Total revenue	70	60	30	31	21	20	9	9	(29)	(30)	101	90
Result												
Segment result	20	17	9	7	2	1	0	0	(1)	(1)	30	24
Unallocated corporate expenses											(7)	(9)
Operating profit											23	15
Interest expense											(4)	(4)
Interest income											2	3
Share of net profits of associates	6	5					2	2			8	7
Income taxes											(7)	(4)
Profit from ordinary activities											22	17
Extraordinary loss: uninsured earthquake damage to property		(3)										(3)
Net profit											22	14
Other information												
Segment assets	54	50	34	30	10	10	10	9			108	99
Investment in equity accounted associates	20	16					12	10			32	26
Unallocated corporate assets											35	30
Consolidated total assets											175	155
Segment liabilities	25	15	8	11	8	8	1	1			42	35
Unallocated corporate liabilities											40	55
Consolidated total liabilities											82	90
Capital expenditure	12	10	3	5	5	5	4	3				
Depreciation	9	7	9	7	5	3	3	4				
Non-cash expenses other than depreciation	8	2	7	3	2	2	2	1				

Note business and geographical segments

Business segments: For management purposes, the Company is organised on a world-wide basis into three major operating divisions – paper products, office products and publishing – each headed by a senior vice president. The divisions are the basis on which the Company reports its primary segment information. The paper products segment produces a broad range of writing and publishing papers and newsprint. The office products segment manufactures labels, binders, pens and markers and also distributes office products made by others. The publishing segment develops and sells loose-leaf services, bound volumes and CD-ROM products in the fields of taxation, law and accounting. Other operations include development of computer software for specialised business applications for unaffiliated customers and development of certain former productive timberlands into vacation sites. Financial information about business segments is presented in Schedule A.

Geographical segments: Although the Company's three divisions are managed on a world-wide basis, they operate in four principal geographical areas of the world. In the United Kingdom, its home country, the Company produces and sells a broad range of papers and office products. Additionally, all of the Company's publishing and computer software development operations are conducted in the United Kingdom, though the published loose-leaf and bound volumes and CD-ROM products are sold throughout the United Kingdom and Western Europe. In the European Union, the Company operates paper and office products manufacturing facilities and sales offices in the following countries: France, Belgium, Germany and the Netherlands. Operations in Canada and the United States are essentially similar and consist of manufacturing papers and newsprint that are sold entirely within those two countries. Most of the paper pulp comes from company owned timberlands in the two countries.

Operations in Indonesia include the production of paper pulp and the manufacture of writing and publishing papers and office products, almost all of which is sold outside Indonesia, both to other segments of the company and to external customers.

Sales by market: The following table shows the distribution of the company's consolidated sales by geographical market, regardless of where the goods were produced:

| | Sales revenue by Geographical market | |
	20 × 2	20 × 1
United Kingdom	19	22
Other European Union countries	30	31
Canada and the United States	28	21
Mexico and South America	6	2
Southeast Asia (principally Japan and Taiwan)	18	14
	101	90

Assets and additions to property, plant, equipment and intangible assets by geographical area: The following tables show the carrying amount of segment assets and additions to property, plant, equipment and intangible assets by geographical area in which the assets are located:

	Carrying amount of segment assets		Additions to property, plant, equipment and intangible assets	
	20 × 2	20 × 1	20 × 1	20 × 1
United Kingdom	72	78	8	5
Other European Union countries	47	37	5	4
Canada and the United States	34	20	4	3
Indonesia	22	20	7	6
	175	155	24	18

Segment revenue and expense: In Belgium, paper and office products are manufactured in combined facilities and are sold by a combined sales force. Joint revenues and expenses are allocated to the two business segments. All other segment revenues and expenses are directly attributable to the segments.

Segment assets and liabilities: Segment assets include all operating assets used by a segment and consist principally of operating cash, receivables, inventories and property, plant and equipment, net of allowances and provisions. While most such assets can be directly attributed to individual segments, the carrying amount of certain assets used jointly by two or more segments is allocated to the segments on a reasonable basis. Segment liabilities include all operating liabilities and consist principally of accounts, wages and taxes currently payable and accrued liabilities. Segment assets and liabilities do not include deferred income taxes.

Inter-segment transfers: Segment revenue, segment expenses and segment result include transfers between business segments and between geographical segments. Such transfers are accounted for at competitive market prices charged to unaffiliated customers for similar goods. Those transfers are eliminated in consolidation.

Unusual item: Sales of office products to external customers in 20 × 2 were adversely affected by a lengthy strike of transportation workers in the United Kingdom, which interrupted product shipments for approximately four months. The company estimates that sales of office products were approximately half of what they would have been during the four-month period.

Investment in equity method associates: The company owns 40% of the capital stock of Europaper Ltd, a specialist paper manufacturer with operations principally in Spain and the United Kingdom. The investment is accounted for by the equity method. Although the investment and the company's share of Europaper's net profit are excluded from segment assets and segment revenue, they are shown separately in conjunction with data for the paper products segment. The company also owns several small equity method investments in Canada and the United States whose operations are dissimilar to any of the three business segments.

Extraordinary loss: As more fully discussed in Note 6, the company incurred an uninsured loss of £3 million caused by earthquake damage to a paper mill in Belgium in November 20 × 1.

Unilever provide an excellent example of the disclosure requirements of IAS 14 using geographic regions as the primary segmentation:

Unilever Plc   Year Ended 31 December 2005

Notes to the Accounts (Extract)

3. Segment information

Our primary reporting segments are geographic, comprising our three operating regions of Europe. The Americas and Asia Africa. The home countries of the Unilever Group are the Netherlands and the United Kingdom. The United States is the only country for which third party turnover is required to be separately reported, on the basis that it exceeds 10% of the Group total.

The analysis of turnover by geographical area is stated on the basis of origin. Turnover on a destination basis would not be materially different. Inter-segment sales between geographical areas and between product areas as are not material. Total assets and capital expenditure are based on the location of the assets. Segment results are presented on the basis of operating profit. Segment assets consist primarily of property, plant and equipment, goodwill and other intangible assets, inventories and receivables. Corporate assets consist of financial assets, cash and cash equivalents, other non-current investments and pension and deferred tax assets. Segment liabilities consist primarily of trade payables and other liabilities. Corporate liabilities include borrowings, tax balances payable, restructuring and other provisions and pension and deferred tax liabilities. Capital expenditure comprises additions to property, plant and equipment and other intangible assets, including additions resulting from acquisitions. Other non-cash charges include charges to the income statement during the year in respect of share-based compensation, restructuring and other provisions.

Analysis by geographical segment	Europe	The Americas	Asia Africa	Total
	€m	€m	€m	€m
2005				
Turnover	16,211	13,179	10,282	39,672
Operating profit	2,304	1,719	1,291	5,314
Net finance costs				(618)
Share of net profit/(loss) of joint ventures	11	36	–	47
Share of net profit/(loss) of associates	(25)	1	(1)	(25)
Other income from non-current investments				33
Profit before taxation				4,751
Taxation				(1,249)
Net profit from continuing operations				3,502
Net profit from discontinued operations				473
Net profit				3,975

2004

Turnover	16, 650	12,296	9,620	38,566
Operating profit	2,303	896	1,040	4,239
Net finance costs				(630)
Share of net profit/(loss) of joint ventures	6	31	2	39
Share of net profit/(loss) of associates	(2)	3	1	2
Other income from non-current investments				54
Profit before taxation				3,704
Taxation				(810)
Net profit from continuing operations				2,894
Net profit from discontinued operations				47
Net profit				2,941

Assets

2005

Segment assets	15,237	13,626	5,106	33,969
Joint ventures/associates	26	37	21	84
Total assets by geographical segment	15,263	13,663	5,127	34,053
Corporate assets				5,323
Total assets				39,376

2004

Segment assets	15,569	11,465	4,353	31,387
Joint ventures/associates	17	21	16	54
Total assets by geographical segment	15,586	11,486	4,369	31,441
Corporate assets				5,417
Total assets				36,858

Liabilities

2005

Segment liabilities	4,485	1,914	2,244	8,643
Joint ventures/associates	20	11	6	37
Total liabilities by geographical segment	4,505	1,925	2,250	8,680
Corporate liabilities				21,931
Total liabilities				30,611

2004

Segment liabilities	4,370	1,748	1,835	7,953
Joint ventures/associates	9	5	2	16
Total liabilities by geographical segment	4,379	1,753	1,837	7,969
Corporate liabilities				21,260
Total liabilities				29,229

Capital expenditure

2005	447	305	298	1,050
2004	497	297	305	1,099

Depreciation of property, plant and equipment

2005	379	205	157	741
2004	383	212	155	750

Amortisation of finite-lived intangible assets and software

2005	52	38	9	99
2004	37	24	3	64

Impairment charges

2005				
Property, plant and equipment	46	51	21	118
Goodwill	–	129	2	131
Intangible assets	–	241	10	251
Total impairment charge	46	421	33	500

2004				
Property, plant and equipment	95	104	73	272
Goodwill	147	793	63	1,003
Total impairment charge	242	897	136	1,275

Reversal of impairment charges

2005				
Property, plant and equipment	15	26	28	69

2004				
Property, plant and equipment	9	13	11	33

Other non-cash charges				
2005	228	311	53	592
2004	446	472	194	1,112

Although the Group's operations are managed on a geographical basis, the two Foods and Home and Personal Care categories manage brands which we group into six main product areas; these are our secondary reporting segments and are:

- Savoury and dressings – including sales of soups, bouillons, sauces, snacks, mayonnaise, salad dressings and olive oil.
- Spreads and cooking products – including sales of margarines and spreads and cooking products such as liquid margarines.
- Beverages – including sales of tea, weight management products, and nutritionally enhanced staples sold in developing markets.
- Ice cream and frozen foods – including sales of ice cream and frozen food.
- Personal care – including sales of skin care and hair care products, deodorants and anti-perspirants and oral care products.
- Home care and other operations – including sales of home care products, such as laundry powders and liquids, and a wide range of cleaning products. To support our consumer brands, we own tea plantations and palm oil plantations, the results of which are reported within this segment.

Analysis by product area	Savoury and dressings	Spreads and cooking products	Beverages	Ice cream and frozen foods	Foods	Personal Care	Home care and other	Home and personal care	Total
	€m	€m	€m	€m	€m	€m	€m	€m	€m
2005									
Turnover	8,369	4,364	3,054	6,373	22,160	10,485	7,027	17,512	39,672
Operating profit	1,286	756	48	767	2,857	1,801	656	2,457	5,314
Net finance costs									(618)
Share of net profit/(loss) of joint ventures	4	6	38	(2)	46	1	–	1	47
Share of net profit/(loss) of associates	–	–	–	–	–	–	(25)	(25)	(25)
Other income from non-current investments									33
Profit before taxation									4,751
Taxation									(1,249)
Net profit from continuing operations									3,502
Net profit from discontinued operations									473
Net profit									3,975
2004									
Turnover	8,172	4,494	3,012	6,286	21,964	9,780	6,822	16,602	38,566
Operating profit	1,226	681	(508)	709	2,108	1,508	623	2,131	4,239
Net finance costs									(630)
Share of net profit/(loss) of joint ventures	1	4	31	–	36	1	2	3	39
Share of net profit/(loss) of associates	–	–	–	–	–	–	2	2	2
Other income from non-current investments									54
Profit before taxation									3,704
Taxation									(810)
Net profit from continuing operations									2,894
Net profit from discontinued operations									47
Net profit									2,941

Assets

2005

Segment assets	18,788	2,501	2,098	3,357	26,744	3,622	3,603	7,225	33,969
Joint ventures/associates	9	14	33	(2)	54	9	21	30	84
Total assets by product area	18,797	2,515	2,131	3,355	26,798	3,631	3,624	7,255	34,053
Corporate assets									5,323
Total assets									39,376

2004

Segment assets	17,384	2,508	2,258	3,206	25,356	3,393	2,638	6,031	31,387
Joint ventures/associates	8	–	18	–	26	5	23	28	54
Total assets by product area	17,392	2,508	2,276	3,206	25,382	3,398	2,661	6,059	31,441
Corporate assets									5,417
Total assets									36,858

Capital expenditure

2005	235	98	62	209	604	260	186	446	1,050
2004	234	87	61	206	588	321	190	511	1,099

10.3   IFRS 8 *Operating Segments* (November 2006)

Introduction

IFRS 8 should be applied for periods beginning on or after 1 January 2009 but earlier application is encouraged. Comparatives should be restated for prior year unless the cost is excessive. IFRS 8 supersedes IAS 14.

Scope

IFRS 8 should be applied by all entities that have traded in a public market or are in the process of filing with a securities commission but if an entity voluntarily chooses to disclose segment information it must not describe the information as segment information.

Operating segments

An operating segment is a component of an entity:

(a)   that engages in business activities from it may earn revenue and incur expenses;
(b)   whose operating results are regularly reviewed by the entity's chief operating decision maker (CODM) to make decisions about resource allocation and assessment of performance; and
(c)   for which discrete financial information is available.

Not every part of an entity is an operating segment, e.g. a corporate HQ is incidental to operations. Retirement benefit plans are similarly not regarded as operating.

The chief operating officer identifies a function not an individual – it could be a group of executive directors.

Generally an operating segment has a segment manager (again a function) who is directly accountable to and maintains regular contact with its chief operating decision maker. There may be more than one operating segment for a single manager.

Sometimes managers are responsible for overlapping sets of components and may adopt a matrix form of organisation with different geographical and product/services. In that case products/services would constitute the operating segments.

Reportable segments

An entity should separately report information about each operating segment that:

(a)   has been identified in accordance with the above definition and
(b)   exceeds the quantitative thresholds listed below.

Aggregation criteria

Operating segments often exhibit similar long-term financial performance if they have similar economic characteristics e.g. have similar long-term average gross margins.

Two or more operating segments may be aggregated into a single segment if consistent with core principle of the standard. The segments must be similar in each of following respects:

(a)   the nature of products and services;
(b)   the nature of the production processes;
(c)   the type or class of customer for products and services;
(d)   the methods used to distribute the products and services; and
(e)   the nature of the regulatory environment, if applicable.

Quantitative thresholds

Operating segments should be separately disclosed that meets any of the following quantitative thresholds:

(a)   Its reported revenue including sales to external customers is 10% or more of combined revenue of all operating segments, both internal and external;
(b)   The absolute amount of its reported profit/loss is 10% or more of:
   (i)   combined profit of all operating segments in profit and
   (ii) combined loss of all operating segments in loss.
(c)   Its assets are 10% or more of combined assets of all operating segments.

Additional operating segments not meeting any of the above may still be reported separately, if useful to users.

Operating segments below the thresholds may be aggregated only if share a majority of the aggregation criteria listed above.

If the total external revenue reported by operating segments is less than 75% of the entity's revenue need to identify additional operating segments until at least 75% of revenue is included in reportable segments.

Information about other business activities not reportable should be combined and disclosed in 'other segments' category separately from other reconciling items.

If a segment was identified in the previous period as separable that segment should continue to be reported separately in the current period.

Prior periods should be restated to reflect newly reported segments even if they did not satisfy the requirements in a prior period.

There is no practical limit to number of segments but if exceeds 10 the entity should consider whether a practical limit has been reached.

Disclosure

Information should be disclosed to enable users to evaluate the nature and financial effects of the types of business activities in which it engages and the economic environments in which it operates.

The following should be disclosed:

(a)   general information;
(b)   information about reported segment profit or loss and basis of measurement; and
(c)   reconciliations of totals of segment revenues, segment profit or loss, segment assets and other material segment items to corresponding amounts in previous period.

Reconciliations are required at each balance sheet date for balance sheet items and prior periods should be restated:

(a) General information (see example 1)

The following should be disclosed:

(i)   factors used in identifying operating segments – products/services, geographical areas, regulatory environments (see example 3); and
(ii) types of products/services from which each reportable segment derives its revenues.

(b) Information about profit or loss and assets (see example 4)

Should be reported separately for each segment. The following should also be provided if regarded as being regularly provided to the CODM:

(a)   revenues from external customers;
(b)   revenues with other operating segments;
(c)   interest revenue;
(d)   interest expense;
(e)   depreciation and amortisation;
(f)   material items of income and expense;
(g)   the entity's interest in associates and joint ventures profit/loss – per equity method;
(h)   income tax expense or income; and
(i)   material non-cash items other than depreciation and amortisation.

Interest revenue should be reported separately from interest expense for each operating segment unless a majority of a segment's revenues are from interest and the CODM relies primarily on net interest revenue to assess performance.

The following should be disclosed about each reportable segment even if not included in determining segment assets:

(a)   amount of investment in associates and joint ventures accounted for under equity method, and
(b)   total expenditures for additions to non-current assets other than deferred tax assets, retirement benefits, financial instruments and insurance contracts.

Measurement

The amount of each segment item reported shall be the measure reported to the CODM for making resource allocation decisions. Adjustments to the financial statements are only included if included by CODM for measuring a segment's profit or loss. Similarly, only assets used by CODM shall be reported for that segment.

If the CODM uses only one measure to allocate resources and assess performance segments should be reported only using that measure. If adopt more than one measure the reported measures should be those that management believes are determined in accordance with the measurement principles most consistent with those used in measuring the corresponding amounts in the entity's financial statements.

An entity should provide an explanation of the measurements of segment profit or loss and segment assets for each reportable segment. The following should be disclosed as a minimum (see example 2):

(a) basis of accounting for any transactions between reportable segments;
(b) the nature of differences between reportable segment profits/losses and entity's profit or loss; could include accounting policies and policies for allocating jointly used assets;
(c) the nature of any differences between the measurements of reportable segments' assets and entity's assets; could include accounting policies and policies for allocating jointly used assets;
(d) the nature of any differences between the measurements of reportable segments' liabilities and entity's liabilities – could include accounting policy and jointly utilised liabilities;
(e) the nature of any changes from prior periods;
(f) the nature and effect of any asymmetrical allocations to reportable segments e.g. an entity might allocate depreciation to a segment without allocating related depreciation.

Reconciliations (see example 5)

A reconciliation must be provided of all the following:

(a) total of reportable segments revenues to entity's revenue;
(b) total of reportable segments' measure of profit or loss to entity's profit before tax and discontinued operations;
(c) total of reportable segments assets to entity's assets;
(d) total of reportable segments amounts for every other material item of information.

All material reconciling items should be separately identified e.g. different accounting policies should be separately identified.

Restatement of previously reported information

If an entity changes its internal structure that causes the composition of its reportable segments to change the corresponding information for earlier periods should be restated unless the information is not available and the cost to develop would be excessive. An entity shall disclose whether it has restated or not.

If an entity changes its internal structure that causes the composition of its reportable segments to change and if segment information is not restated for earlier periods the entity should disclose in the year in which the change occurs segment information for the current year on both the old and new basis unless the necessary information is not available and the cost is excessive.

Information about geographical areas (see example 6)

The following should be disclosed unless its cost is excessive:

(a) Revenues from external revenues (i) attributed to country of domicile and (ii) attributed to all foreign countries in total. If an individual country is material it should be separately disclosed. The basis for attributing revenues from external customers to individual countries should also be disclosed.

(b)   Non-current assets, deferred tax assets, retirement benefit assets and insurance contract assets (i) located in country of domicile and (ii) located in all foreign countries in total. If an individual country is material it should be disclosed separately.

The amounts reported should be based on the financial information used to produce the statutory accounts. If the information is not available and cost excessive, that fact must be disclosed.

Information about major customers (see example 7)

Information on extent of reliance on major customers should be disclosed. If revenues with a single customer amount to 10% or more of an entity's revenues that fact should be disclosed. The identity of a major customer need not be disclosed nor amount of revenues from that customer. A group of entities under common control shall be considered a single customer.

Implementation guidance

Examples are provided below to illustrate the disclosures required by the standard.

Descriptive information about an entity's reportable segments

The following is an illustration of the disclosure of descriptive information about an entity's reportable segments.

EXAMPLE 1

Description of types of products and services from which each reportable segment derives its segments

Diversified Company has five reportable segments: car parts, motor vessels, software, electronics and finance. The car parts segment produces replacement parts for sale to car parts retailers. The motor vessels segment produces small motor vessels to serve the offshore oil industry and similar businesses. The software segment produces application software for sale to computer manufacturers and retailers. The electronics segment produces integrated circuits and related products for sale to computer manufacturers. The finance segment is responsible for portions of the company's financial operations including financing customer purchases of products from other segments and property lending operations.

EXAMPLE 2

Measurement of operating segment profit or loss and assets

The accounting policies of the operating segments are the same as those described in the summary of significant accounting policies except that pension expense for each operating segment is recognised and measured on the basis of cash payments to the pension plan. Diversified Company evaluates performance on the basis of profit or loss from operations before income tax expense not including non-recurring gains and losses and foreign exchange gains and losses.

Diversified Company accounts for inter-segment sales and transfers as if the sales or transfers were to third parties, i.e. at current market sales.

EXAMPLE 3

Factors management used to identify the entity's reportable segments

Diversified Company's reportable segments are strategic business units that offer different products and services. They are managed separately because each business requires different technology and marketing strategies. Most of the businesses were acquired as a unit, and the management at the time of the acquisition was retained.

Information about reportable segment profit or loss and assets

The following table illustrates a suggested format for disclosing information about reportable segment profit or loss and assets. Diversified Company does not allocate tax or non-recurring gains and losses to reportable segments. In addition, not all reportable segments have material non-cash segments other than depreciation and amortisation in profit or loss.

EXAMPLE 4

	Car parts	Motor vessels	Software	Electronics	Finance	All others	Totals
	CU	CU	CU	CU	CU	CU	CU
Revenues from external customers	3,000	5,000	9,500	12,000	5,000	1,000 (a)	35,500
Inter-segment revenues	–	–	3,000	1,500	–	–	4,500
Interest revenue	450	800	1,000	1,500	–	–	3,750
Interest expense	350	600	700	1,100	–	–	2,750
Net interest revenue (b)	–	–	–	–	1,000	–	1,000
Depreciation and amortisation	200	100	50	1,500	1,100	–	2,950
Reportable segment profit	200	70	900	2,300	500	100	4,070
Other material non-cash items: Impairment of assets	–	200	–	–	–	–	200
Reportable segment assets	2,000	5,000	3,000	12,000	57,000	2,000	81,000
Expenditures for reportable segment non-current assets	300	700	500	800	600	–	2,900

(a)   Revenues from segments below the quantitative thresholds are attributable to four operating segments of Diversified Company. Those segments include a small property business, an electronics equipment rental business, a software consulting practice and a warehouse leasing operation. None of those segments has ever met any of the quantitative thresholds for determining reportable segments.

(b)   The finance segment derives a majority of its revenue from interest. In addition, management primarily relies on net interest revenue, not the gross revenue and expense amounts, in managing that segment. Therefore, as permitted by paragraph 22, only the net amount is disclosed.

Reconciliations of reportable segment revenues, profit or loss and assets

EXAMPLE 5

Revenues

	CU
Total revenues for reportable segments	39,000
Other revenues	1,000
Elimination of inter-segment revenues	(4,500)
Entity's revenues	35,500

Profit or loss

	CU
Total profit or loss for reportable segments	3,970
Other profit or loss	100
Elimination of inter-segment profits	(500)
Unallocated amounts:	
Litigation settlement received	500
Other corporate expenses	(750)
Adjustment to pension expense in consolidation	(250)
Income before income tax expense	3,070

Assets

	CU
Total assets for reportable segments	79,000
Other assets	2,000
Elimination of receivable from corporate headquarters	(1,000)
Goodwill not allocated to reportable segments	4,000
Other unallocated amounts	1,000
Entity's assets	85,000

Other material items

	Reportable segment totals CU	Adjustments CU	Entity totals CU
Interest revenue	3,750	75	3,825
Interest expense	2,750	(50)	2,700
Net interest revenue (finance segment only)	1,000	–	1,000
Expenditures for assets	2,900	1,000	3,900
Depreciation and amortisation	2,950	–	2,950
Impairment of assets	200	–	200

Geographical information

EXAMPLE 6

Geographical information	Revenues (a) CU	Non-current assets CU
United States	19,000	11,000
Canada	4,200	–
China	3,400	6,500
Japan	2,900	3,500
Other countries	6,000	3,000
Total	35,500	24,000

(a)   Revenues are attributed to countries on the basis of the customer's location.

Information about major customers

EXAMPLE 7

Revenues from one customer of Diversified Company's software and electronics segments represent approximately CU 5,000 of the Company's total revenues.

10.4   IAS 24 *Related Party Disclosures* (December 2003)

Objective

To ensure that the disclosure of information about related party relationships draws attention to the possibility that the entity's financial position and performance may have been effected by the existence of related parties and by transactions and outstanding balances between an entity and its related parties.

Scope

The standard should apply in:

(a)   identifying related party relationships, transactions and outstanding balances;
(b)   identifying the circumstances in which disclosure is required in the financial statements;
(c)   determining the disclosures to be made.

Disclosure is also required of related party transactions and balances in the separate financial statements of a parent, venturer or investor as per IAS 27.

Purpose of related party disclosures

Related party relationships are a normal feature of commerce but they could have an effect on profit/loss, financial position and cash flows. Related parties may enter contracts that unrelated parties may not, e.g. transfer of goods to a parent at cost.

The mere existence of a related party relationship may be sufficient to affect the transactions with other parties. One party may refrain from acting because of the significant influence of another, e.g. a subsidiary may be instructed by a parent not to engage in research and development.

Thus knowledge of related party transactions, balances and relationships may affect assessments of an entity's operations, risks, etc. and should be disclosed.

Definitions

Related party

A party is related to an entity if:

(a)   Directly, or indirectly through one or more intermediaries, it:
    (i)   controls, or is controlled by, or is under common control with the entity;
    (ii)   has an interest in the entity that gives it significant influence over that entity;
    (iii)   has joint control over the entity;
(b)   It is an associate as defined in IAS 28.
(c)   It is a joint venture as defined in IAS 31.
(d)   It is a member of the key management personnel of the entity or its parent.
(e)   It is a close member of the family of any individual referred to above.
(f)   It is an entity in which a controlling or jointly controlling interest over voting power is owned.
(g)   It is a post-employment benefit plan.

Related party transaction

A transfer of resources, services or obligations between related parties, regardless of whether or not a price is charged.

Control

The power to govern the financial and operating policies of an entity to obtain benefits from its activities.

Joint control

Contractually agreed sharing of control over an economic activity.

Significant influence

The power to participate in the financial and operating policy decisions but not control. This can be achieved by share ownership, statute or agreement.

Close members

Family members expected to influence or be actually influenced by an individual in their dealings with the entity. This includes:

(a)   the individual's domestic partner and children;
(b)   children of the individual's domestic partner; and
(c)   dependants of the individual or individual's domestic partner.

In all cases attention is given to the substance of the relationship, not merely the legal form. The following are specifically mentioned as NOT being related parties:

(a)   two entities simply because they have common directors;
(b)   two venturers simply because they share joint control over a joint venture;
(c)   providers of finance, trade unions, public utilities and government departments;
(d)   economic dependent entities e.g. major customers, suppliers, distributors, franchisors, etc.

Disclosure

Disclosure of control

Relationships between parents and subsidiaries should be disclosed irrespective of whether or not there have been transactions between those parties.

Where an entity is controlled by another party, the name of that party and, if different, the ultimate controlling party should be disclosed. If the ultimate party is not known, that fact should be disclosed. If neither the entity's parent nor ultimate controlling party publishes financial statements for public use then it needs next most senior parent to be disclosed.

Disclosure of key management personnel compensation

Must be disclosed in total and for the each of the following:

(a)   short-term employee benefits;
(b)   post-employment benefits;
(c)   other long-term benefits;
(d)   termination benefits;
(e)   equity compensation benefits.

Disclosure of transactions

The nature of the relationship between the parties should be disclosed as well as the following MINIMUM information:

(a)   The amount of the transactions.
(b)   The amount of outstanding balances.
   (i)   their terms and conditions including details of security and nature of consideration and
   (ii)   details of any guarantees provided or received.
(c)   provisions for doubtful debts.
(d)   bad debts written off.

The above must be disclosed separately for each of the following categories – the parent, entities with joint control, subsidiaries, associates, joint ventures, key management and other related parties.

The following are examples of transactions that should be disclosed with a related party:
• Purchases and sale of goods
• Purchases and sales of property and other assets
• Rendering of services

- Leases
- Transfer of research and development
- Transfer under licence arrangements
- Transfers under finance arrangements
- Provision of guarantees or collateral
- Settlement of liabilities on behalf of the entity or by the entity on behalf of another party.

Disclosure that terms were on an arms length basis should only be provided if the disclosures could be substantiated.

Similar items can be aggregated except if separate disclosure is necessary for an understanding of the effects of related party transactions on the financial statements.

A good example of a number of related parties and their required disclosures including key management, joint ventures and associates as well as the chairman of the group is provided by Unilever Plc:

Unilever Plc   Year Ended 31 December 2005

Accounting policies and notes to the accounts (Extracts)

32. Related party transitions

The following related party balances existed with associate or joint venture businesses at 31 December:

Related party balances	€m 2005	€m 2004
Trading and other balances due to/from Joint ventures	85	87
Trading balances due to/from associates	(8)	29

Joint ventures

As discussed in Note 28 on p. XXX. Unilever completed the restructuring of its Portuguese foods business during the year. Balances owed by FIMA at 31 December 2005 were €85 million (2004: €87m).

In July 2004 in the United Kingdom, Unilever formed a joint venture with Arlington Science Park Ltd. and sold its property at the Colworth site for a total consideration of €46 million.

Associates

After the sale of Diversey Lever, our Institutional and Industrial cleaning business, to Johnson Professional Holdings Inc. in 2002, Unilever has a one-third equity stake in the combined Johnson Diversey business, with an option to exit the business from 2007. At 31 December 2005 the outstanding balance payable to Johnson Diversey Holdings Inc. was €8 million (2004:€29m receivable). Sales agency fees to Johnson Diversey were incurred of approximately €76 million in 2005 (2004: €68m).

Langholm Capital Partners invests in private European companies with above average longer term growth prospects. It has invested in Physcience, a French natural food supplements business, and Nolro, the leading company in the mass prestige personal care market in Finland. To build business opportunities that fit our core business interests in foods and home and personal care, we have committed €97 million to Langholm Capital Partners on a total of €242 million raised funds. At 31 December 2005 the outstanding balance with Langholm Capital Partners was immaterial.

Other related parties

In 2004 Patrick Cescau, the then Chairman of Unilever PLC, and his wife purchased a house from immobilla Transholrne B.V., a group company ultimate owned by NV. for €3,348,000 (£2,270,000). The full Boards, acting on the recommendation of the remuneration committee and without the participation of Mr Cescau, gave their prior approvals to the purchase, which was made at full market value based on two independent valuations of the property.

33. Key management personnel

For 2004 key management personnel included the Executive Directors, Non-Executive Directors and Business Presidents described on pp. XXX and XXX of the 2004 Report and Accounts. Following a change in the management structure which took place in 2005 key management for 2005 for reporting purposes became the members of the UEX together with the Non-Executive Directors described on p. XXX.

Key management compensation	2005 €m	2004 €m
Salaries and short-term employee benefits	13	21
Non-Executive Director's fee	1	1
Post-employment benefits	4	5
Other long-term benefit (all share-based)	1	13
Termination payments	1	2
	20	42
Of which		
Executive Directors	16	24
Non-Executive Directors	1	1
Other	3	17
	20	42

Details of the remuneration of Directors are given in the auditable part of the report of the Remuneration committee as defined on p. XXX see also Note 32 above for information on related party transactions.

11

Group reporting

11.1 IAS 27 *Consolidated and Separate Financial Statements* (December 2003)

Scope

This standard should be applied in the preparation and presentation of consolidated financial statements for a group of enterprises under the control of a parent.

IAS 27 should also be applied to accounting for investments in subsidiaries in a parent's separate financial statements.

The standard does not deal with:

(a) methods of business combinations (see IFRS 3);
(b) accounting for investments in associates (see IAS 28); and
(c) accounting for investments in joint ventures (see IAS 31).

Definitions

* *Control.* Power to govern the accounting and financial policies of another entity so as to obtain benefits from its activities.
* *Subsidiary.* An entity that is controlled by another (the parent).
* *Parent.* An entity that has one or more subsidiaries.
* *Consolidated financial statements.* Financial statements of a group presented as those of a single economic entity.
* *Minority interest.* Portion of the net results and net assets of a subsidiary attributable to interests not owned directly or indirectly by the parent.

Presentation of consolidated financial statements

A parent should present consolidated financial statements in which it consolidates its investments in subsidiaries in accordance with IAS 27.

However, a parent need not present consolidated financial statements if and only if:

(a) the parent itself is a 100% owned subsidiary or is partially owned by another entity whose owners have been informed and do not object to the parent not preparing consolidated accounts;
(b) the parent's debt or equity instruments are not traded publicly;
(c) the parent did not file nor is it in the process of filing its financial statements with a securities commission for the purpose of going on the public market; and
(d) the ultimate or any intermediate parent of the parent publishes consolidated financial statements available for public use that comply with IFRSs.

Scope of consolidated financial statements

A parent should consolidate all subsidiaries, foreign and domestic, other than those referred to below.

Control is presumed to exist when the parent owns over 50% of the voting power of an enterprise unless, in exceptional circumstances, it can be clearly demonstrated that such ownership does not constitute control. Cyprus Airways provide a good example where substance over legal form ensures that a 100% legal owned entity is not recorded as a subsidiary but as an associate due to the appointment of the Board of Directors by the Minister of Finance. Details of the basis of consolidation and the elimination of intercompany balances are also provided:

Cyprus Airways   Year Ended 31 December 2005

Accounting Policies (Extracts)

Basis at consolidation

The Group financial statements consolidate the financial statements of the Company, its wholly owned subsidiaries: Eurocypria Airlines Limited, Cyprair Tours Limited, Zenon NDC Limited and Hellas Jet S.A, made up to 31 December 2005 and are expressed in Cyprus Pounds.

The subsidiary companies are consolidated from the date on which control is transferred to the Group and cease to be consolidated when control is transferred outside the Group. Control is affected when the parent company controls directly or indirectly more than 50% of the share capital of the company with voting rights or is in a position to affect its financial and operational decisions or when it controls the appointment or the resignation of the majority of the members of the Board of Directors.

Associated company

The investment in the associated company is accounted for using the equity method.

Although Cyprus Airways (Duty-Free Shops) Limited is wholly owned by Cyprus Airways Public Limited, the former is treated in accordance with International Accounting Standard No.28 'Investments in Associates' as an associate, because the Board of Directors of the company is appointed by the Minister of Finance, Extracts from the financial statements of Cyprus Airways (Duty-Free Shops) Limited are disclosed in Note 43 of these financial statements.

Transactions eliminated on consolidation

Intragroup balances and any unrealised gains and losses or income and expenses arising from intragroup transactions are eliminated in preparing the consolidated financial statements. Unrealised gains arising from transactions with associates are eliminated to the extent of the Group's interest in the entity. Unrealised losses are eliminated in the same way as unrealised gains, but only to the extent that there is no evidence of impairment.

Control also exists where there is:

(a)   power over more than 50% of voting rights through an agreement with other investors;
(b)   power to govern the financial and operating policies under statute or agreement;
(c)   power to appoint or remove the majority of members of the board; and
(d)   power to cast the majority of votes at meetings of the board of directors.

In making this judgement consideration should also be given to the existence and effect of potential voting rights held by another entity, e.g. share warrants, call options, convertible shares/debt, etc.

An example of the inclusion of special purpose entities (SPEs) is provided by BAE Systems Plc:

BAE Systems Plc   Year Ended 31 December 2005

Accounting Policies (Extract)

Basis of consolidation

The financial statements of the Group consolidate the results of the Company and its subsidiary entities, and include its share of its joint ventures' and associates' results accounted for under the equity method, all of which are prepared to 31 December.

A subsidiary is an entity controlled by the Group. Control is the power to govern the financial and operating policies of the entity so as to obtain benefits from its activities. Subsidiaries include the SPEs that the Group transacted through for the provision of guarantees in respect of residual values and head lease and finance payments on certain regional aircraft sold.

A subsidiary should be excluded from consolidation when:

(a) control is only temporary as it is expected to be disposed in the near future (12 months) and
(b) management is actively seeking a buyer.

Bayerische Hypo-Und Vereinsbank AG   Year Ended 31 March 2003

In their notes to the accounts HVB has increased to 61.7% its holding in a company. It adds that 28.1% of the interest has been acquired with the intention of reselling and thus it is not consolidated. The holding was sold in early 2004.

Such subsidiaries should be accounted for in accordance with IAS 39.

A subsidiary is not excluded just because its activities are dissimilar from those of the group nor if there are severe restrictions that impair its ability to transfer funds to the parent. Control must be lost for exclusion to occur. Better information is provided by full consolidation backed up by segment reporting, under IAS 14.

Example – Aughnacloy Plc

The directors of Aughnacloy Plc are proposing to set up a new company, Bearnagh Plc, to which it would transfer patent rights that had been developed by Aughnacloy Group companies with a view to Bearnagh Plc entering into licensing agreements which would provide a long-term source of finance for the group.

Bearnagh Plc was to be formed with a share capital that would comprise 1,000,000 ordinary shares of 25p each to be held by Aughnacloy Plc and 1,000,000 ten per cent voting convertible preference shares of 25p each to be held by a third party that was friendly to Aughnacloy Plc.

The preference shares would be convertible in 15 years and Aughnacloy Plc would have a call option to acquire the shares after 10 years and the holders of the shares would have a put option to sell the shares to Aughnacloy Plc after 12 years.

Should Bearnagh Plc fall to be treated as a subsidiary under the provisions of IAS 27 in any consolidated accounts that Aughnacloy Group prepares? What additional information in this regard would be required to be able to provide proper guidance?

If it were the case that the directors of Aughnacloy Plc have been successful in establishing a structure which ensures that the legal effect is that Bearnagh Plc is a controlled non-subsidiary whereas the commercial effect is that it is a subsidiary undertaking, then explain the measures being taken by the accounting profession, such as the proposals in SIC 12 to ensure that consolidated accounts provide the holding company shareholders with information, i.e. relevant, understandable, reliable and comparable.

Suggested solution – Aughnacloy Plc

Is Bearnagh Plc to be treated as a subsidiary under IAS 27?

The definition of a subsidiary has been changed with the implementation of IAS 27. Underlying the philosophy behind the standard is the concept of reflecting economic substance/control within group accounting. The revised definition is more widely drawn to try and 'bring back into the net' certain 'subsidiaries' which previously were not legally defined as subsidiaries but which were very largely dependent upon a 'parent undertaking'.

The new definition states that an undertaking is a parent of another if any of the following statements apply:

(1) It holds a majority of the voting rights in that undertaking. Aughnacloy owns 50% but not a majority.
(2) It is a member of the other undertaking and can appoint or remove a majority of its board of directors. No information is provided for Aughnacloy.
(3) It has a right to exercise a dominant influence over the other undertaking either through provisions in the entity's articles/memorandum or through a control contract. No information is provided for Aughnacloy.
(4) It is a member and controls, in agreement with others, a majority of the voting rights in the other undertaking. No information is provided for Aughnacloy.

On balance, the information appears to indicate that a subsidiary undertaking has been created, but confirmation would be required to ensure that the parent has in fact dominant influence over Bearnagh Plc.

*The effect of SIC12 **Consolidation – Special Purpose Entities***

SIC 12 requires companies to include all SPEs which currently fail the IAS 27 definition. This is achieved by requiring a company to record transactions so that their commercial effect is fairly reflected.

In terms of quasi-subsidiaries, control is defined as control through the medium of another enterprise, whereby effective control exists over and risks arise from the assets of another enterprise as if it were a subsidiary.

Quasi-subsidiaries (SPEs) should also be consolidated in the group accounts. Under IAS 27, they fail to meet the statutory definition of a subsidiary.

Consolidation procedures

The parent and its subsidiaries are combined on a line-by-line basis by adding together items such as assets, liabilities, equity, income and expenses. The following steps are then taken:

(a) The parent's investment in each subsidiary and the parent's portion of equity of each subsidiary are eliminated.
(b) Minority interests in the net income of subsidiaries are identified and adjusted against group income to arrive at the net income attributable to the parent.

(c) Minority interests in the net assets are identified and presented separately from liabilities. Minority interests in net assets consist of:
   (i)   the amount at the date of the original combination as per IFRS 3 and
   (ii) the minority's share of movements in equity since combination.

Where there are potential voting rights in existence, the proportions of profit or loss and changes in equity allocated to the parent and minority interests are determined on the basis of present ownership interests and they should not reflect the possible exercise or conversion of those potential voting rights.

Taxes should be computed in accordance with IAS 12.

Intragroup balances and transactions should be eliminated in full. Unrealised losses should also be eliminated unless their cost cannot be recovered. Unrealised profits on inventory and fixed assets should be eliminated in full and any timing differences dealt with in accordance with IAS 12.

The financial statements should be drawn up to the same reporting date for all entities in the group. However, if the financial statements are drawn up to different dates, adjustments should be made for the effects of significant transactions that occur between those dates. In any case, the difference between reporting dates should be no longer than three months.

Consistency dictates that the length of the reporting periods should be the same from period to period.

Agrana Beteiligungs AG   Year Ended 28 February 2004

Accounting Policies (Extract)

The subsidiaries prior to 2004 were consolidated with financial statements drawn up to different accounting dates that fell within a three-month window. From 2003 on the balance sheet dates of all subsidiaries have been harmonised to the end of February. It resulted in an increase of €40m in revenue and €2m in profit after tax.

Uniform accounting policies must be adopted for similar transactions and appropriate adjustments must be made in preparing the consolidated financial statements.

The subsidiary should be included in the consolidated accounts from the date of acquisition, i.e. the date on which control is effectively transferred to the buyer, in accordance with IFRS 3. The results of subsidiaries disposed are included in the consolidated income statement until the date of disposal, i.e. the date on which control ceases. The difference between the proceeds from disposal and the carrying amount should be included in the income statement at the date of disposal. This includes the cumulative amount of any exchange differences that relate to the subsidiary recognised in equity in accordance with IAS 21 (i.e. recycling is compulsory).

An investment should be accounted for in accordance with IAS 39, from the date it ceases to fall within the definition of a subsidiary and does not become an associate under IAS 28. The carrying amount is regarded as its cost thereafter.

Minority interest must be presented within equity but separate from the parent shareholders' equity. Minority interests in the income statement should also be separately presented.

The losses recorded may exceed the minority interest in the equity and this excess must be charged to the majority except to the extent that the minority has a binding obligation and is able to make good those losses. If the subsidiary subsequently reports profits, the majority interest is allocated all such profits until the minority's share of losses has been recovered.

If the subsidiary has cumulative preference shares held by a minority, and classified as equity, the parent should compute its share of profits or losses after adjusting for the dividends on such shares, whether or not these dividends have been declared.

Accounting for investments in subsidiaries, jointly controlled entities and associates in separate financial statements

Where separate financial statements are prepared, investments in subsidiaries should be either:

(a) carried at cost or
(b) accounted for as available for sale financial assets as per IAS 39.

The same accounting treatment should be applied for each category of investments.

Investments in subsidiaries, jointly controlled entities (JCEs) and associates that are accounted for in accordance with IAS 39 in the consolidated accounts should be accounted for in the same way as in the investor's separate financial statements.

Disclosure

The following disclosures should be made:

(a) The fact that a subsidiary is not consolidated.
(b) Summarised financial information of subsidiaries, either individually or in groups, that are not consolidated, including the amounts of total assets, liabilities, revenues and profits or losses.
(c) The nature of the relationship between the parent and a subsidiary when the parent does not own, directly or indirectly through subsidiaries, more than 50% of the voting power.
(d) The reasons why ownership, directly or indirectly, of more than 50% of the voting power does not give control.
(e) The reporting date of a subsidiary, if different from the parent, and the reason for using it.
(f) The nature and extent of any significant restrictions on the ability of subsidiaries to transfer funds to the parent through cash dividends or to repay loans or advances.

When separate financial statements are prepared for a parent that elects not to prepare consolidated financial statements, those separate financial statements should disclose the following:

(a) The fact that the financial statements are separate; that the exemption from consolidation has been used; the name and country of incorporation or residence of the entity publishing consolidated accounts in accordance with IFRSs; the address where consolidated accounts are available.
(b) A list of significant investments in subsidiaries, JCEs and associates, including the name, country of incorporation or residence, proportion of ownership interest and, if different, proportion of voting power held.

(c) A description of the method used to account for the investments listed in (a).

When a parent, venturer or investor in an associate prepares separate financial statements, those statements must disclose the following:

(a) The fact that the statements are separate and the reasons why prepared, if not by law.
(b) A list of significant investments in subsidiaries, JCEs and associates, including the name, country of incorporation or residence, proportion of ownership interest and, if different, proportion of voting power held.
(c) A description of the method used to account for the investments listed under (b).

SIC 12 *Consolidation – Special Purpose Entities* *(November 1998)*

Issue

An entity may be created to accomplish a narrow and well-defined objective, e.g. to effect a lease, research and development activities or a securitisation. Such an SPE may take the form of a corporation, trust, partnership or unincorporated entity. SPEs often include strict limits on their decision-making powers.

The sponsor frequently transfers assets to the SPE, obtains the right to use assets held by the SPE or performs services for the SPE whereas other parties (capital providers) may provide the funding to the SPE. An entity that engages in transactions with an SPE may in substance control the SPE.

A beneficial interest in an SPE may take the form of a debt instrument, an equity instrument, a participation right, a residual interest or a lease. In most cases the sponsor retains a significant beneficial interest in the SPE's activities, even though it may own little or none of the SPE's equity.

IAS 27 does not provide explicit guidance on the consolidation of SPEs.

The issue is under what circumstances an entity should consolidate an SPE. It does not apply to post-employment benefit plans or equity compensation plans.

Consensus

An SPE should be consolidated when the substance of the relationship between an entity and an SPE indicates that the SPE is controlled by that entity.

In the context of an SPE, control may arise through the predetermination of the activities of the SPE (autopilot) or otherwise. Control may exist when less than 50% of the voting power rests with the reporting entity. Judgement is required to decide whether or not control exists in the context of all relevant factors.

In addition to IAS 27, the following circumstances may indicate a relationship in which an entity controls an SPE and consequently should consolidate the SPE:

(a) in substance, the activities of the SPE are being conducted on behalf of the entity according to its specific business needs so that the entity obtains benefits from the SPE's operation;

(b) in substance, the entity has the decision-making powers to obtain the majority of the benefits of the activities of the SPE or, by setting up an 'autopilot' mechanism, the entity has delegated these decision-making powers;

(c) in substance, the entity has rights to obtain the majority of the benefits of the SPE and therefore may be exposed to risks incident to the activities of the SPE; or

(d) in substance, the entity retains the majority of the residual or ownership risks related to the SPE or its assets in order to obtain benefits from its activities.

Predetermination of the ongoing activities of an SPE by an entity would not represent the type of restrictions referred to in IAS 27.

Some Indicators of Control over an SPE are provided in an appendix. These include the following:

(a) Activities. The activities are, in substance, being conducted on behalf of the reporting entity and include situations where the SPE is principally engaged in providing a source of long-term capital to the entity or it provides a supply of goods and services consistent with the entity's major operations. Economic dependence of an entity on the reporting enterprise does not, by itself, lead to control.

(b) Decision-making. The reporting entity, in substance, has the decision-making powers to control or obtain control of the SPE or its assets, including certain decision-making powers coming into existence after the formation of the SPE. Such decision-making powers may have been delegated by establishing an 'autopilot' mechanism. Examples include the power to unilaterally dissolve an SPE, the power of change to the SPE's charter or the power to veto the proposed changes of the SPE's charter.

(c) Benefits. The reporting entity, in substance, has rights to obtain a majority of the benefits of the SPE's activities through a statute, contract, agreement, etc. Such rights may be indicators of control when they are specified in favour of an entity that is engaged in transactions with an SPE and that enterprise stands to gain those benefits from the financial performance of the SPE. Examples are rights to a majority of any economic benefits or rights to majority residual interests such as a liquidation.

(d) Risks. An indication of control may be obtained by evaluating the risks of each party engaging in transactions with an SPE. This could be a guarantee to outside investors providing most of the capital to the SPE. Examples are the capital providers who do not have a significant interest in the underlying net assets of the SPE, and they also do not have rights to future economic benefits of the SPE. The capital providers are not substantively exposed to the inherent risks of the underlying net assets or operations of the SPE or in substance, they receive mainly consideration equivalent to a lender's return through a debt or equity interest.

IAS 27 *Consolidated and Separate Financial Statements* (revised January 2008)

When IAS 27 was last revised in 2003, no consideration was given to the fundamental approach undertaken by the standard. In January 2008, IAS 27 was amended as part of the second phase of the IASB's business combinations project. This was a joint project with FASB. The amendments are related primarily to:

(i)   non-controlling interests and
(ii) loss of control of a subsidiary.

These must be applied for annual periods beginning on or after 1 July 2009.

Main features of the revised standard

To enhance the relevance, reliability and comparability of information that a parent provides in its separate financial statements and its consolidated accounts IAS 27 (revised) specifies:

(a) the circumstances when an entity must consolidate;
(b) how to account for changes in the level of ownership interest of a subsidiary;
(c) how to account for the loss of control of a subsidiary; and
(d) what information needs to be disclosed.

Presentation of consolidated financial statements. A parent must consolidate all its subsidiaries but there is a limited exception for some non-public entities.

Consolidation procedures. The group must adopt uniform accounting policies and eliminate inter-group transactions and balances.

Non-controlling interests (formerly minority interests). These must now be presented within equity, separately from the owners of the parent. Total comprehensive income must also be attributed to the owners of the parent and to the non-controlling interests even if in deficit.

Changes in the ownership interests. Any changes in a parent's interest in a subsidiary that does not result in a loss of control must be accounted for within equity and when a parent loses control of a subsidiary it should derecognise the assets, liabilities and related equity components of the subsidiary. Any resulting gain or loss must be included in profit/(loss). Any investment still retained in the subsidiary should be measured at fair value at the date control is lost.

Separate financial statements. When a reporting entity elects or is required to present separate financial statements, investments in subsidiaries, JCEs and associates must be accounted for at cost or in accordance with IAS 39.

Disclosure. Information regarding the nature of the relationship between a parent and its subsidiaries must be provided.

11.2   IFRS 3 *Business Combinations*

IAS 22 *Business Combinations* permitted two methods of accounting – the pooling of interests and the purchase method. Although IAS 22 restricted the use of pooling, analysts indicated that two methods impaired comparability and created incentives for structuring those transactions to achieve a particular accounting result.

This, combined with the prohibition of pooling by United States, Canada and Australia prompted the IASB to seek harmonisation.

In addition, various jurisdictions dealt differently with goodwill and IAS 22 permitted two methods of applying the purchase method – benchmark (combination of fair value of acquirer's ownership interest and pre-acquisition carrying amounts for minority interests) or allowed alternative to measure all assets at fair value.

The IASB seeks to ensure that similar transactions are not accounted for in dissimilar ways as this impairs their usefulness.

The IFRS was an attempt to improve the quality of accounting and seek international convergence on accounting for business combinations, including:

(a) the method of accounting for business combinations;
(b) the initial measurement of identifiable net assets acquired;
(c) the recognition of liabilities for terminating the activities of an acquiree;
(d) the treatment of any excess of an acquirer's interest in fair values of identifiable net assets acquired; and
(e) the accounting treatment for goodwill and intangible assets.

Objective

To specify the financial reporting by an entity when it combines with one or more entities

Scope

IFRS 3 should apply to all business combinations except for:

(a) joint ventures;
(b) business combinations under common control;
(c) business combinations involving two or more mutual entities; and
(d) business combination entities brought together by contract alone to form a reporting entity.

Identifying a business combination

It is a bringing together of separate entities into one single reporting entity. It may be structured in a number of ways for legal, taxation or other reasons.

It may result in the creation of a parent–subsidiary relationship in which the acquirer is the parent and the acquiree the subsidiary. The acquirer should apply the IFRS to its consolidated statements. In its own accounts it records the investment under IAS 27 *Consolidated and Separate Financial Statements* as an investment in a subsidiary.

It may result in the purchase of net assets, including goodwill but not the purchase of the entity itself. This does not result in a parent–subsidiary relationship.

Included within the IFRS are business combinations where one entity obtains control of another entity but the acquisition date does not coincide with the date of acquiring an ownership interest, e.g. share buyback arrangements. It does not apply to joint ventures (see IAS 31 *Financial Reporting of Interests in Joint Ventures*).

Business combinations involving entities under common control

These occur where all of the combining entities are ultimately controlled by the same party both before and after the date of business combination. A group of individuals are regarded as controlling an entity if, as a result of contractual arrangements, they collectively have the power to govern its financial and operating policies. These are outside the scope of the IFRS. The extent of minority interests is not relevant to determining whether or not the entity is under common control. They will be dealt with in a subsequent standard.

Method of accounting

All business combinations should be accounted for under the purchase method. This method recognises that the net assets are acquired by the acquirer and that the measurement of the acquirer's own net assets are not affected by the transaction.

Application of the purchase method

The following steps should be undertaken in the purchase method:

(a) identification of an acquirer;
(b) measuring the cost of a business combination; and
(c) allocating at the acquisition date, the cost to net assets acquired.

Identification of an acquirer

An acquirer should be identified for all business combinations. The acquirer is the entity that obtains control of the other combining entity. The purchase method always assumes an acquirer. Control is the power to govern the financial and operating policies of an entity to obtain benefits. Normally this requires more than 50% of an entity's voting rights. Even if this is not the case the following could result in an acquirer:

(a) Power over more than 50% of voting rights through an agreement with other investors.
(b) Power to govern the financial and operating policies of the other entity under statute or an agreement.
(c) Power to appoint or remove a majority of the board of directors.
(d) Power to cast a majority of votes at meetings of the board of directors.

Although it may be difficult to identify an acquirer, there are usually indications that one exists. For example:

(a) if the fair value of one of the combining entities is significantly greater than the other;
(b) if there is an exchange of voting ordinary shares for cash; and
(c) if the management of one dominates the selection of the management team of the combined entity.

In a business combination through an exchange of equity, the entity that issues the equity shares is usually the acquirer. However, all pertinent facts must be considered in determining which of the combining entities has the power to govern the operating and financial policies of the other entity. In some business combinations, e.g. reverse acquisitions, the acquirer is the entity whose equity interests itself have been acquired. That occurs when a private operating entity arranges to have itself acquired by a non-operating or dormant public entity as a means of obtaining a stock exchange listing. Although legally the public entity is the parent, the circumstances could indicate that the smaller entity has acquired a larger entity.

When a new entity is formed, one of the combining entities must be adjudged to be the acquirer on the evidence available.

Measuring the costs of a business combination

The acquirer shall measure the cost of a business combination as the aggregate of:

(a) the fair values of assets given (usually cash), liabilities incurred (e.g. loans) and equity issued by the acquirer in exchange for control of the acquiree; plus
(b) any costs directly attributable to business combination.

The acquisition date is the date when the acquirer effectively obtains control of the acquiree. When achieved through a single transaction the date of exchange coincides with the acquisition date. However, if the entity is acquired in stages:

(a) the cost is the aggregate of individual transactions and
(b) the date of exchange is the date of each exchange transaction whereas the acquisition date is the date on which an acquirer obtains control.

When settlement of any part of the cost is deferred, the fair value is determined by discounting the amounts payable to their present value at the date of exchange.

The published price at the date of exchange of a quoted equity provides the best evidence of the instrument's fair value. Other evidence should only be used in rare circumstances when the published price is unreliable and where that other evidence is a more reliable measure, e.g. thinness of the market. One example would be to use an estimate of their proportional interest in the fair value of the acquirer or by reference to their proportionate interest in the fair value of the acquiree obtained, whichever is more clearly evident. In any event, all aspects of the combination should be considered.

The cost of a combination includes liabilities incurred by the acquirer in exchange for control of the acquiree. However, future losses shall not be included as part of that cost. Costs should include professional fees incurred but not general administration expenses. The costs of arranging and issuing financial liabilities, however, are part of the cost of issuing the financial instrument and are not part of the costs of the business combination. Similarly the costs of issuing equity instruments are an integral part of the equity issue but they should not be included in the costs of a business combination.

Adjustments to the cost of a business combination contingent on future events (earn out clauses). In these situations, the acquirer should include an amount of the adjustment in the cost of combination if the contingency is probable and can be measured reliably. It could be paid after a specified level of income has been achieved in the future or on the market price being maintained. If the future events do not occur then the cost can be adjusted accordingly. It should not be included if it is not probable or cannot be measured reliably but if future events make it probable then it can be adjusted to the entity's cost of acquisition.

In some circumstances, the acquirer may be required to make a subsequent payment to the seller as compensation for a reduction in the value of assets given. This occurs if the acquirer has guaranteed the market price of equity or debt instruments issued. In such cases, no increase in the cost of the business combination is recognised. In the case of debt instruments, the additional payment is regarded as a reduction in the premium or an increase in the discount on the initial issue.

Allocating the cost of a business combination to the assets acquired and liabilities and contingent liabilities assumed

The acquirer, at acquisition date, should allocate the cost of a business combination by recognising the acquiree's identifiable net assets at fair value. Any difference between the cost of the combination and the acquirer's interest in the net fair value of identifiable assets should be accounted for as goodwill. However, non-current assets held for sale and discontinued operations are valued at fair value less costs to sell (as per IFRS 5).

The acquirer should recognise separately the acquiree's identifiable net assets at acquisition date only if they satisfy the following criteria:

(a) For an asset other than an intangible asset, it is probable that any associated future economic benefits will flow to the acquirer and it can be measured reliably.
(b) For a liability other than contingencies, it is probable that an outflow of economic benefits will occur and its fair value can be reliably measured.
(c) For intangible assets, their fair value can be measured reliably.
(d) For contingent liabilities, its fair value can be reliably measured.

The acquirer's income statement shall incorporate the acquiree's post-acquisition profits and losses in the income statement. Expenses should be based on the cost of the business combination, e.g. depreciation should be based on the fair values of those depreciable assets at the acquisition date, i.e. based on their cost to the acquirer.

It is not necessary for a transaction to be closed or finalised at law before the acquirer effectively obtains control. All pertinent facts should be considered in assessing when the acquirer has effectively obtained control.

Any minority interest in the acquiree should be stated at the minority's proportion of the net fair values of those items.

Acquiree's identifiable assets and liabilities. Only those identifiable net assets that existed at the acquisition date and satisfy the recognition criteria in (a) to (d) above may be recognised separately by the acquirer. Thus:

(a) the acquirer should recognise liabilities for terminating an acquiree only when the acquiree has an existing liability for restructuring, recognised through IAS 37 *Provisions, Contingent Liabilities and Contingent Assets* and
(b) the acquirer may not recognise liabilities for future losses.

A payment contractually agreed to make to employees or suppliers, in the event it is acquired, is an obligation but it is contingent until it becomes probable that a business combination will occur. The identifiable net assets might include some previously never recognised assets, e.g. tax benefit due to acquiree's tax losses when acquirer has adequate future taxable profits against which the losses can be offset.

Acquiree's intangible assets. An intangible asset of the acquiree may only be recognised if it meets the definition of an intangible asset under IAS 38 and its fair value can be reliably measured. A non-monetary asset must be identifiable and be separate from goodwill. Thus this can only happen if it:

(a) is separable, i.e. it is capable of being separated and sold, transferred, licensed, rented or exchanged or
(b) arises from contractual or other legal rights.

Some examples are provided in the appendix to the standard but these are not intended to be exhaustive.

Examples of intangible assets – Separate from goodwill

It must be a non-monetary asset without physical substance and be separate from goodwill, i.e. it must arise from contractual or other legal rights.

(A) Marketing related intangible assets
(1) Trademarks, trade names, service marks, collective marks and certification marks
(2) Internet domain names
(3) Trade dress (unique colour, share or package design)
(4) Newspaper mastheads
(5) Non-competition agreements.

(B) Customer related intangible assets
(1) Customer lists
(2) Order or production backlogs
(3) Customer contracts and the related customer relationships
(4) Non-contractual customer relationships.

(C) Artistic related intangible assets
Normally arise from contractual or legal rights such as copyrights. These include:

(1) Plays, operas and ballets
(2) Books, magazines, newspapers and other literary works
(3) Musical works
(4) Pictures and photographs
(5) Video material including films, music videos, television programmes.

(D) Contract based intangible assets
(1) Licensing, royalty agreements
(2) Advertising contracts
(3) Lease agreements
(4) Construction permits
(5) Franchise agreements
(6) Operating and broadcasting rights
(7) Drilling rights for water, air and minerals
(8) Servicing and mortgage service contracts
(9) Employment contracts.

E. Technology based intangible assets

(1) Patented technology
(2) Computer software and mask works
(3) Unpatented technology

(4) Databases
(5) Trade secrets, e.g. recipes.

Acquiree's contingent liabilities. These may only be recognised if their fair values can be measured reliably. If not, they should be disclosed in accordance with IAS 37.

After initial recognition, the acquirer should measure recognised contingent liabilities at the higher of:

(a) the amount that would be recognised per FAS 37 and
(b) the initial amount less cumulative amortisation per IAS 18.

The above points do not apply to contracts under IAS 39. However, loan commitments excluded from IAS 39 are accounted for as contingent liabilities if it is not probable that an outflow will be required to settle the obligation or it cannot be reliably measured.

Example – Rostrevor Plc

You are the group accountant at Rostrevor Plc and need to make adjustments to the draft accounts for the year ended 30 June 2007 to reflect the acquisition of a subsidiary, and to calculate the earnings per share.

Information in respect of the new subsidiary is as follows:

(1) On 1 October 2006, Rostrevor Plc acquired a 90% interest in Warrenpoint Inc, US corporation. The consideration of £2,450,000 comprised £1,500,000, satisfied by the issue of 5,000,000, 25p ordinary shares in Rostrevor Plc to the vendors and £950,000 cash payable as to £750,000 at completion and £200,000 on 1 October 2007.

(2) The financial statements of Warrenpoint Inc at 30 September 2006 showed net assets of $4,370,000, before deducting costs totalling $380,000 in respect of redundancies which were identified at acquisition and subsequently paid.

(3) At a board meeting to approve the acquisition, the directors of Rostrevor Plc were informed that an investment in plant and machinery would be required in Warrenpoint Inc. of $300,000 in the period to 30 June 2007.

(4) Professional fees for advice in respect of the acquisition amounted to £30,000 and your finance director has estimated that the time and expenses incurred by the directors of Rostrevor Plc in negotiating and completing the deal amounted to £20,000.

(5) Warrenpoint Inc. valued inventories on the LIFO (last in first out) method in its financial statements. On 30 September 2006, the value of inventories held by Warrenpoint Inc. would have been $150,000 greater if valued on the FIFO method consistent with that used by Rostrevor Plc.

(6) The share capital of Rostrevor Plc at 1 July 2006 comprised 47,500,000 ordinary shares of 25 pence each. Except for the transaction described above, there were no other movements in share capital during the ensuing year.

(7) The exchange rate at 1 October 2006 was £1 = $1.8.

(8) Rostrevor Plc amortise goodwill arising on consolidation over a three-year period.

Suggested solution – Rostrevor Plc

Calculation of fair value of Warrenpoint Inc as at 1 October 2006

	$'000		£'000
Net assets per Warrenpoint Inc 30.9.06 (Note 2)	4,370		
Adjustments to reflect fair value			
Redundancy costs (Note 2)	–		
Uniformity of accounting policies (Note 5)	150		
Fair value of Warrenpoint Inc	4,520	$1.8/£1	2,511

Redundancy costs (Note 2)

The costs are clearly defined and identified at acquisition and are confirmed by subsequent payments. Undoubtedly these would have been considered by Rostrevor Plc in calculating the purchase price for Warrenpoint Inc. However, IFRS 3 would appear to preclude such a provision as it represents the acquirer's future intentions in controlling the new subsidiary. Therefore, it should be recorded as a post-acquisition expense.

Investment in plant and machinery (Note 3)

These are prospective acquisitions. If Warrenpoint Inc. had invested in plant prior to the takeover, either cash/bank or creditors would also have been affected, thereby leaving net assets unaffected. It is merely a switch within the individual components of the same total net assets. No adjustment is therefore needed to fair value as at 1 October 2006.

Professional fees and directors' time and expenses (Note 4)

These are costs incurred by Rostrevor Plc to help the directors to decide whether or not to purchase Warrenpoint Inc. As such they relate to the cost of the investment and not to the fair value of the net assets of Warrenpoint Inc.

Only the professional fees have been included in the fair value of consideration as the directors' time and expenses are not evidenced by a market transaction and should be disregarded.

Inventories (Note 5)

Part of the fair value exercise should be to ensure uniformity of accounting policies, and under IAS 2 the LIFO method for inventory valuation is not permitted.

An adjustment has therefore been made to increase the net assets of Warrenpoint Inc. at acquisition by $150,000.

Calculation of goodwill in the consolidated Balance Sheet at 30 June 2007

	£'000	£'000
Fair value of consideration 1.10.06		
Ordinary shares (5m × 25p) at 30p market value		1,500
Cash – paid	750	
– deferred	200	
		950
		2,450
Acquisition costs: Professional fees		30
Fair value of consideration		2,480
Fair value of net assets acquired 1.10.06		
£2,511,000 (from a) × 90% interest		2,260
Goodwill arising on consolidation 1.10.06		220

If amortisation were permitted the charges and net book values would have been as follows:

	£'000
Amortisation to 30.6.07 9/12 × 1/3 × 220=	55
Net book value 30.6.07 (220–55)=	165

However, under IFRS 3, no amortisation is permitted but instead an annual impairment review must take place under IAS 36 *Impairment of Assets*.

Goodwill

The acquirer should:

(a) recognise goodwill as an asset and
(b) initially measure it at cost being the excess of cost over an acquirer's interest in the fair value of identifiable net assets.

Goodwill represents future economic benefits that are not capable of being individually identified and separately recognised. Goodwill is essentially the residual cost after allocating fair values to identifiable net assets taken over.

After initial recognition, the acquirer should measure goodwill at cost less accumulated impairment losses. It should not be amortised but instead tested annually for impairment, or more frequently, if events indicate that it might be impaired, in accordance with IAS 36.

Negative goodwill

If the fair value of net assets acquired exceeds the cost then the acquirer must:

(a) reassess the identification and measurement of the net assets acquired and
(b) recognise immediately in profit or loss any excess remaining after that reassessment.

A gain in that situation could arise from the following:

(a) Errors in measuring the fair value of the cost of the combination and the fact that future costs are not reflected correctly in the fair value of the acquiree's identifiable net assets.
(b) A requirement in an accounting standard to measure identifiable net assets at an amount that is not fair value but treated for this purpose as its fair value.
(c) A bargain purchase.

Business combination achieved in stages

Each exchange transaction should be treated separately by the acquirer to determine goodwill. This results in a step-by-step comparison of the cost of the individual investments with the acquirer's percentage interest in the fair values of the acquiree's identifiable net assets.

In that situation the fair values may be different at the date of each exchange transaction because:

(a) the acquiree's net assets are notionally restated to fair value at each exchange transaction and
(b) the acquiree's identifiable assets must be valued at their fair values at acquisition date.

Any adjustment to those fair values relating to previously held interests of the acquirer is a revaluation but it does not signify that the acquirer has elected to apply a general policy of revaluation under IAS 16 *Property, plant and equipment.*

Initial accounting determined provisionally

Initially, fair values need to be assigned to the acquiree's identifiable net assets. If these can only be determined provisionally at the end of the first reporting period then these values may be adopted. However, the acquirer should recognise any adjustments, after finalising the initial accounting, to those provisional values within 12 months of the acquisition date.

Also any adjustments should be recognised from the acquisition date. Thus:

(i) the book value of adjusted net assets should be adjusted to fair value at that date;
(ii) goodwill should be adjusted; and
(iii) comparatives should be adjusted, e.g. additional depreciation.

Adjustments after the initial accounting is complete

Except for contingent consideration or finalisation of any deferred tax assets, adjustments are made to the initial accounting after an initial accounting is complete and can only be recognised to correct an error in accordance with IAS 8 *Accounting policies, changes in accounting estimates and errors.* In that case, a prior period adjustment should be recorded.

Recognition of deferred tax assets after the initial
accounting is complete

If the potential benefit of the acquiree's income tax loss carry forwards did not satisfy the criteria for separate recognition, on initial accounting, but is subsequently realised then, in addition, the acquirer should:

(a) reduce goodwill to an amount that would have been recognised if the deferred tax asset had been recognised as an identifiable asset from acquisition date and
(b) recognise the reduction in the carrying amount of goodwill as an expense.

However, this procedure should not result in the creation of negative goodwill.

Disclosure

An acquirer should disclose sufficient information that enables users to evaluate the nature and financial effect of business combinations that were affected:

(a) during the reporting period and
(b) after the balance sheet date but before the financial statements are authorised.

To achieve this, the following information should be provided for each business combination affected during the reporting period:

(a) The names and descriptions of the combining entities.
(b) The date of acquisition.
(c) The percentage of voting equity instruments acquired.
(d) The cost of the combination and a description of the components of that cost. When equity instruments are issued the following should also be disclosed:
  (i) the number of equity instruments issued and
  (ii) the fair value of those instruments and the basis for determining that fair value. If no published price exists or that price has not been used as a reliable indicator, then that fact must be disclosed together with the reasons and the method and assumptions actually adopted as well as disclosing the aggregate amount of the difference between the value attributed to and the published price of equity instruments.
(e) Details of operations that the entity has decided to dispose.
(f) The amounts recognised for each class of the acquiree's net assets at acquisition date together with their carrying amounts immediately prior to the combination.
(g) The amount of any excess recognised in profit or loss on the creation of negative goodwill.
(h) A description of the factors contributing to the recognition of goodwill.
(i) The amount of the acquiree's profit or loss since the acquisition date included in the acquirer's profit or loss for the period, unless impracticable. If impracticable, that fact must be disclosed.

The information above may be disclosed in aggregate for business combinations that are individually immaterial. If the initial accounting was only provisionally determined then that fact should also be disclosed together with an explanation of why this is the case.

The following should also be provided unless it would be impracticable:

(a) The revenue of the combined entity for the period as though the acquisition date was at the start of the reporting period.

(b) The profit or loss of the combined entity for the period as though the acquisition date was at the start of the reporting period.

If it would be impracticable then that fact must be disclosed.

An acquirer should disclose information that enables users to evaluate the financial effects of gains, losses, error corrections and other adjustments recognised in the current period that relate to business combinations that were effected in the current or in previous periods. In that regard the following should be disclosed:

(a) The amount and explanation for any gain/loss recognised in the current reporting period that:

(i) relates to the identifiable assets acquired or liabilities assumed in a business combination effected in a previous reporting period and

(ii) is of such size, nature or incidence that disclosure is relevant to an understanding of the combined entity's financial performance.

(b) If the initial accounting is provisional, the amounts and explanations of adjustments made to provisional values during the reporting period.

(c) Information about error corrections required to be disclosed under IAS 8.

An entity should disclose an intangible fixed asset schedule for goodwill, which requires a reconciliation of goodwill between the start and end of the reporting period showing separately:

(a) The gross amount and accumulated impairment losses at the start of the period.

(b) Additional goodwill recognised in the period.

(c) Adjustments resulting in the subsequent recognition of deferred tax assets.

(d) Goodwill included in a disposal group (per IFRS 5) and derecognised in the period if not included in a disposal group.

(e) Impairment losses recognised in accordance with IAS 36.

(f) Net exchange differences arising during the period (per IAS 21).

(g) Any other changes in the carrying amount during the period.

(h) The gross amount and accumulated impairment losses at the end of the period.

Entities should also disclose any additional information as is necessary to meet the objectives of enabling users to properly evaluate the nature and financial effect of business combinations.

A good practical illustration of a business combination and its required disclosure is provided by Hanson Plc:

Hanson Plc   Year Ended 31 December 2005

Accounting Policy (Extract)

Business combinations

The results of companies and businesses acquired are dealt with in the consolidated accounts from the date of acquisition. Upon the acquisition of a business, the fair values that reflect their condition at the date of acquisition are attributed to the identifiable assets (including separately identifiable intangible assets) acquired and liabilities and contingent liabilities assumed. Adjustments are also made to bring the accounting policies of businesses acquired into alignment with those of the group. Where the consideration paid for a business exceeds the fair value of net assets acquired and liabilities and contingent liabilities assumed, the difference is treated as goodwill.

The detail in the notes is provided below. Note the inclusion of intangible assets as part of the business combination but no details are provided of their content:

25. Business Combinations

Total cash acquisitions spend for 2005 was £342.9m (£88.4m). On January 4, 2005, Hanson Building Products, UK, acquired the assets of UK brick manufacturer Marshalls Clay Products for £64.7m and Thermalite, a market leader in air-crete blocks, on March 7 for £124.2m. On June 17, Hanson Aggregates, North America, acquired the assets of Mission Valley Rock, Berkeley Ready Mix and Berkeley Asphalt, and Hanson Building Products, North America, acquired the assets of Sherman Pipe, a concrete pipe and precast concrete products business for a total of £108.0m. Other acquisitions made in the year consisted of three quarries in Southern Indiana by Hanson Aggregates, North America, in December, and a further six acquisitions totalling £46.0m.

During 2004, Hanson Building Products, North America, acquired the assets of US brick manufacturer Athens Brick for £22.0m on February 19. The assets of concrete pipe manufacturers Waco Precast and WPC Florida, the assets of a roof tile manufacturer in Fort Myers and an aggregates quarry in Sylvania were also acquired by Hanson Aggregates, North America, on May 14, July 16, June 25 and November 12 respectively for a total of £22.2m. Hanson Aggregates, UK, acquired contractor Cumbrian Industrials Ltd on September 15 and Hanson Building Products, UK, acquired brick manufacturer Wilnecole on November 12 for a total of £41.6m. Within Hanson Australia and Asia Pacific two further bolt-on acquisitions totalling £2.6m were made.

| | 2006 | 2005 | | 2004 | | |
	Total carrying value (£m)	Fair value adjustments (£m)	Total fair value (£m)	Total carrying value (£m)	Fair value adjustments (£m)	Total fair value (£m)
Intangible assets (other than goodwill)	–	25.6	25.6	–	4.4	4.4
Property, plant and equipment	107.6	26.2	133.8	29.6	9.8	39.4

Inventories	22.8	(0.4)	22.4	7.6	(0.3)	7.3
Receivables	20.8	6.2	27.0	11.3	(0.4)	10.9
Cash and cash equivalents	0.1	–	0.1	4.1	–	4.1
Payables	(20.5)	(9.2)	(29.7)	(11.0)	(0.5)	(11.5)
Borrowings	(1.9)	–	(1.9)	(1.9)	–	(1.9)
Provisions	(1.6)	(0.8)	(2.4)	(0.1)	(0.2)	(0.3)
Deferred tax (liabilities)/assets	(6.9)	(13.9)	(20.8)	0.9	–	0.9
	120.4	33.7	154.1	40.5	12.8	53.3
Goodwill on acquisition			190.1			35.1
			344.2			88.4
Consideration: Cash paid			340.5			87.7
Other consideration			1.3			–
Acquisition costs (primarily legal and accounting fees)			2.4			0.7
Total consideration			344.2			88.4

Included in the goodwill recognised above are items that cannot be individually separated and reliably measured due to their nature. These include new customers and synergy benefits.

For the period since acquisition turnover of £143.8 million and operating profit of £17.1 million in respect of the current year acquisitions is included within the income statement as continuing operations. If the acquisitions had taken place at the beginning of the financial year, the continuing operating profit of the group would have been £491.4 million (£417.0m) and turnover from continuing operations would have been £3,777.9 million (£3.581.5m).

The preliminary allocation of the purchase consideration to net assets and liabilities will be reviewed based on additional information up to 31 December 2006. The Directors do not anticipate that any net adjustments resulting from such reviews will have a material effect on the financial position or results of Hanson's operations. In respect of acquisitions in 2004, there were no material subsequent amendments to the preliminary allocations made.

Goodwill of £36.9 million arising on current year acquisitions is deductible for tax purposes.

Transitional provisions and effective date

The IFRS applies to business combinations for which the agreement date is set on or after 31 March 2004. It should apply to:

(a) goodwill arising from a business combination for which the agreement date is on or after 31 March 2004 or

(b) any negative goodwill for an agreement date on or after 31 March 2004.

Previously recognised goodwill

The IFRS should apply on a prospective basis. Thus an entity must:

(a) from the start of the first annual reporting period beginning on or after 31 March 2004, discontinue amortising goodwill for 'old' business combinations;
(b) from the start of the first annual reporting period on or after 31 March 2004, eliminate the carrying amount of accumulated amortisation with a corresponding reduction in goodwill; and
(c) from the start of the first annual reporting period beginning on or after 31 March 2004, test goodwill for impairment in accordance with IAS 36 *Impairment of Assets.*

If goodwill was previously written off against annually (per SSAP 22), an entity should not recognise that goodwill in the income statement when it disposes all or part of the business to which it relates or when a CGU is impaired.

Previously recognised negative goodwill

Should be derecognised starting on or after 31 March 2004 with a corresponding adjustment to opening retained earnings.

Previously recognised intangible assets

These should be reclassified as goodwill if that intangible asset does not, at the 31 March 2004, meet the identifiability criterion in IAS 38.

Equity accounted investments

For equity accounted investments the IFRS should apply in accounting for:

(a) any goodwill included in the carrying amount of the investment and
(b) any negative goodwill, that should be treated as an income.

For investments accounted for by applying the equity method and acquired before the IFRS was issued:

(a) should be applied on a prospective basis and therefore should discontinue amortisation of goodwill.
(b) should derecognise any negative goodwill with a corresponding adjustment to retained earnings.

IFRS 3 *Business Combinations* (revised January 2008)

The revised FRS is a joint effort between FASB in the United States and the IASB as part of the international convergence process. This is the result of the second phase of the project.

The primary conclusion in Phase 1 was that acquisition accounting was the only acceptable method of accounting for business combinations. Phase 2 addresses how acquisition accounting should be applied in practice.

The revised standard comes into effect for periods commencing on or after 1 July 2009.

Main features of the revised IFRS

The objective of the revised IFRS is to enhance the relevance, reliability and comparability of accounting information provided in a business combination. It achieves this by establishing principles and requirements for how an acquirer:

(a) recognises and measures identifiable assets acquired, liabilities assumed and any non-controlling interest in the acquiree;
(b) recognises and measures goodwill; and
(c) determines what information should be disclosed to evaluate the nature and financial effects of the combination.

The Core Principle of the standard is to ensure that an acquirer recognises assets acquired and liabilities assumed at acquisition date and discloses sufficient information so that users can evaluate the nature and financial effects of an acquisition.

Applying the acquisition method

(1)   Must apply the acquisition method unless it is a combination under common control.
(2)   One party must be identified as the acquirer.
(3)   Must recognise net assets assumed and any non-controlling interests in the acquiree.
(4)   Each identifiable asset/liability is measured at acquisition date at fair value.
(5)   Non-controlling interests are measured at fair value or as the non-controlling interest's proportionate share of the acquiree's net identifiable assets.

The difference between the consideration paid (measured at fair value) and the net identifiable assets acquired should be recorded as goodwill or as a gain from a bargain purchase.

There are special rules on reacquired rights, contingent liabilities, contingent consideration and indemnification assets.

Disclosures. An entity must disclose sufficient information to evaluate the nature and financial effect of business combinations that occur during an accounting period or for combinations that arise before the accounts are finalised.

11.3   IAS 28 *Accounting for Investments in Associates* (December 2003)

Scope

Should be applied by an investor in accounting for investments in associates.

Definitions

*   *Associate.* An entity in which the investor has significant influence and which is neither a subsidiary nor a joint venture of the investor.
*   *Significant influence.* The power to participate in the financial and operating policy decisions of the investee but has not got control over those policies.

- *The equity method.* A method of accounting whereby the investment is initially recorded at cost and adjusted thereafter for the post-acquisition change in the investor's share of net assets of the investee. The income statement reflects the investor's share of the results of operations of the investee.
- *The cost method.* The investment is recorded at cost. The income statement reflects income only to the extent that the investor receives dividends from the investee subsequent to the date of acquisition.

Significant influence

If an investor holds, directly or indirectly, 20% or more of the voting power of the investee, it is presumed that it has significant influence, unless it can be clearly demonstrated that this is not the case. Conversely, if it holds less than 20%, the presumption is that the investor does not have significant influence. A majority shareholder by another investor does not preclude an investor having significant influence.

Its existence is usually evidenced in one or more of the following ways:

(a) representation on the board of directors;
(b) participation in the policy making processes;
(c) material transactions between the investor and the investee;
(d) interchange of managerial personnel; or
(e) the provision of essential technical information.

Equity method

The investment is initially recorded at cost and its carrying amount is increased/decreased to recognise the investor's share of profits/losses of the investee after the date of acquisition. Dividends received from the investee reduce the carrying amount of the investment.

Cost method

The investment should be recorded at cost. Income should only be included to the extent that it receives dividends from post-acquisition profits. Dividends received in excess of such profits should be recorded as a reduction of the cost of the investment.

Consolidated financial statements

An investment in an associate should be accounted for in the consolidated accounts under the equity method except when:

(a) the investment is acquired and held exclusively with a view to its subsequent disposal in the near future or
(b) it operates under severe long-term restrictions.

In these latter cases, the investments should be accounted for in accordance with IAS 39.

Dividends received may bear little relationship to the performance of the associate. As the investor has significant influence over the associate, the investor has a measure of responsibility for the associate's performance and it should account for this stewardship by extending the scope of consolidation to include the investor's share of results of such an associate. As a result, the application of the equity method provides more informative reporting of both net assets and net income of the investor.

An investor should discontinue the use of the equity method from the date that:

(a) it ceases to have significant influence but retains either in part or in whole its investment or
(b) the use of the equity method is no longer appropriate as the associate operates under severe long-term restrictions.

The carrying value should be regarded as cost thereafter.

Separate financial statements of the investor

An investment in an associate, for an entity publishing consolidated accounts, should be:

(a) carried at cost;
(b) accounted for using the equity method as per IAS 28; or
(c) accounted for as an 'available for sale financial asset' as per IAS 39.

An investment in an associate, for an entity not publishing consolidated accounts, should be:

(a) carried at cost;
(b) accounted for using the equity method if the equity method would be appropriate for the associate if the investor had issued consolidated accounts; or
(c) accounted for under IAS 39 as an 'available for sale financial asset'.

Basically, an investor should provide the same information about its investments in associates as those entities that issue consolidated accounts.

Application of the equity method

Many of the procedures appropriate for applying equity accounting are similar to consolidation under IAS 27.

On acquisition any difference between the cost of acquisition and the investor's share of the fair values of the net identifiable assets is accounted for under IFRS 3. Appropriate adjustments to post-acquisition share of profits are made to account for depreciation based on fair values.

The most recent available financial statements of the associate are used by the investor in applying the equity method and they are usually drawn up to the same date as the investor. When the dates differ, the associate often prepares statements specifically for the investor to the same date but if this is impracticable then a different date may be used. However, the length of the reporting periods should be consistent from period to period.

When different dates have to be adopted, any adjustments for significant events occurring between the date of the associate's statements and the date of the investor's financial statements must be made.

Uniform accounting policies should be adopted and appropriate adjustments are made to the associate's statements but if this is not practicable, that fact must be disclosed.

If an associate has outstanding cumulative preferred shares held by outsiders, the investor must compute its share of profits/losses after adjusting for preferred dividends, whether these are declared or not.

If an investor's share of losses exceeds the carrying amount of the investment, the investor should stop including its share of losses and instead report the investment at £nil.

Additional losses are only provided to the extent that the investor has incurred obligations, which it has guaranteed to the investee. If subsequently the associate does report profits, the investor can only resume inclusion of its share of the investee profits once its share of profits equals the share of losses not recognised.

Impairment losses

If there is an indication of impairment losses in an associate, an entity should apply IAS 36. In determining value in use, an entity estimates:

(a) its share of the present value of estimated future cash flows expected to be generated by the investee as a whole, including the proceeds on ultimate disposal or
(b) the present value of estimated future cash flows expected to arise from dividends and ultimate disposal.

Both methods give the same result, under appropriate assumptions. Any impairment loss is then allocated as per IAS 36. It must, therefore, be allocated first to goodwill.

The recoverable amount of an investment is assessed for each individual associate unless that associate does not generate independent cash flows.

The example below shows how to integrate the results of an associated undertaking into the consolidated financial statements of a group using equity accounting. It also examines situations where a decision must be made as to whether a reporting entity is an associate or not in cases of complicated shareholdings:

Example – Cushendall Plc

Cushendall Plc has acquired interests in subsidiary and associated companies as follows:

Glendun Ltd	80% holding
Glenwhirry Ltd	70% holding
Glenshesk Ltd	25% holding (associated company).

Glenshesk Ltd is a holding company with a 90% holding in Glencorp Ltd.

Cushendall Plc, Glendun Ltd and Glenshesk Ltd have each acquired holdings in Glentaisie Ltd as follows:

Cushendall Plc – 12%   Glendun Ltd – 5%   Glenshesk Ltd – 24%

Fifty-five per cent of the shares in Glentaisie Ltd are held by a major shareholder.

The directors of Cushendall Plc are of the opinion that the results of Glenshesk Ltd are not material but those of Glentaisie Ltd are material, within the context of the financial statements of Cushendall Plc. Cushendall Plc prepared a draft on group financial statements for the year ended 31 May 2007. The following notes were appended there to.

Notes to the Income Statement

(1) Analysis of turnover

	£
Cushendall Plc	500,000
Glendun Ltd	100,000
Glenwhirry Ltd	80,000
Glenshesk Ltd	40,000
Glentaisie Ltd	300,000
As per income statement	1,020,000

(2) This note gave an analysis, similar to note (1), of depreciation; total as per the income statement – £56,000.

(3)

	Profit before tax (£)	Tax (£)	Profit after tax (£)
Cushendall Plc (actual for year)	126,000	31,000	95,000
Glendun Ltd (actual for year)	24,000	10,000	14,000
Glenwhirry Ltd (actual for year)	(14,000)	–	(14,000)
Glenshesk Ltd (25% of actual for year)	3,000	1,000	2,000
Glentaisie Ltd (22% of actual for year)	22,000	5,000	17,000
As per income statement	161,000	47,000	114,000

(4) Minority interests in current year's profits:

	£
Glendun Ltd 20% £14,000	2,800
Glenwhirry Ltd 30% (£14,000)	(4,200)
As per income statement	(1,400)

(5) Retained current year profits were £112,600 (i.e. £114,000–£1,400).

(6) This note gave detailed information as to how the profit brought forward was apportioned between pre-acquisition profits, minority interests and the group's share of post-acquisition profits.

(7) This showed the figure for retained profits carried forward.

(8) Shares in associated companies are stated in the balance sheet at £120,000. This total is made up as follows:

	£	£
25% net assets (excluding goodwill) – Glenshesk Ltd		20,000
22% net assets (excluding goodwill) – Glentaisie Ltd		60,000
		80,000
25% goodwill – Glenshesk Ltd		30,000
Premium on purchase – Glenshesk Ltd	15,000	
Discount on purchase – Glentaisie Ltd	(5,000)	
		10,000
		120,000

(9) Loans amounted to £150,000. They comprised the following:

	£
Loan from Laharna Ltd	120,000
Loan from Glenshesk Ltd	60,000
Loan to Glentaisie Ltd	(30,000)
	150,000

Suggested solution – Cushendall Ltd

(1) *Turnover*. Both subsidiaries and the holding company should be included (Glendun, Glenwhirry and Cushendall – see Appendix) but neither Glenshesk nor Glentaisie should have been in the turnover.

Glentaisie is not an associated undertaking as control of 17% would be below the normal 20% presumption in IAS 28 for significant influence. There could be evidence to rebut this but a major shareholder controls 55% of the company, so it would seem unlikely that the company could exercise sufficient influence. Turnover from Glentaisie should, therefore, be excluded.

(2) *Depreciation*. For the same reasons as (1) above, the depreciation of both Glenshesk Ltd and Glentaisie Ltd should be excluded.

(3) *Profit before tax/tax*. Once again Glentaisie Ltd should be excluded because it is not an associated undertaking. However, 25% of Glenshesk's profit before tax and tax charges should be included. The information for the associates should be disclosed separately from the group companies.

(4) *Minority interests*. The calculations are correct. If a minority holds shares in an associate then that share should be reflected in the minority interest account.

(5) to (7) *Retained profits*. The retained profits for the year should be analysed between holding company, subsidiaries and associated undertaking (i.e. Cushendall £95,000, subsidiaries (£1,400) (2,800 – 4,200) and associated undertakings £2,000).

If Glentaisie is not considered to be an associate, the dividend received/receivable should be included.

(8) *Balance sheet – associated undertakings*

The only associated undertaking is Glenshesk Ltd, which should be valued as follows:

	£	
Share of net tangible assets	20,000	
Share of goodwill	30,000	can be
Goodwill on acquisition	15,000	combined
	65,000	

Glentaisie Ltd should be included as an investment at cost.

(9) *Loans*. The loan from Glenshesk Ltd (associate) should be separately disclosed. That to Glentaisie Ltd should be included with other loans to companies outside the group.

Appendix

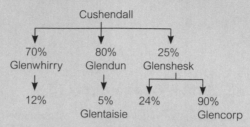

Group structure of Cushendall Ltd

Cushendall

70% Glenwhirry   80% Glendun   25% Glenshesk

12%   5% Glentaisie   24%   90% Glencorp

55% Major shareholders

Glenwhirry Ltd. Clearly a subsidiary requires full consolidation.

Glendun Ltd. Clearly a subsidiary requires full consolidation.

Glenshesk Ltd. Presumed to be an 'associated undertaking' because more than 20% of the shares are controlled. Evidence is required of significant influence by way of, perhaps, board representation and active involvement in strategic decision-making in the company.

It could be a subsidiary if there is evidence of 'dominant influence' by Cushendall Ltd, i.e. control over the operating and financial policies of Glenshesk Ltd.

Glencorp Ltd. This is a subsidiary of Glenshesk Ltd and therefore should be included with the group accounts of Glenshesk Ltd. Twenty-five per cent of that combined result will be included as an 'associated undertaking' of Cushendall Ltd.

Glentaisie Ltd. For an associated company status it is permissible to add the 12% directly held by Cushendall plus 5% through its subsidiary Glendun. The 24% held by an associate must be excluded; 17% would not be classified as an associated undertaking under normal circumstances. Again, this can be rebutted if Cushendall is able to exercise significant influence over the affairs of Glentaisie Ltd.

Income taxes

These should be accounted for in accordance with IAS 12.

Contingencies

In accordance with IAS 37 an investor discloses:

(a) its share of contingent liabilities and capital commitments of an associate and

(b) those contingent liabilities arising because the investor is severally liable for ALL the liabilities of the associate.

Disclosure

The following disclosures should be made:

(a) An appropriate listing and description of significant associates, including the proportion of ownership interest and, if different, the proportion of voting power held.
(b) The methods used to account for such investments.

Investments in associates should be classified as long-term assets and disclosed separately in the balance sheet. The investor's share of profits/losses should be disclosed separately in the income statement. A good example of the disclosure required by IAS 28 is provided by Party Gaming Plc:

Party Gaming Plc   Year Ended 31 December 2005

Accounting Policies and Notes (Extract)

Associates

Where the Group has the power to exercise significant influence over (but not control) the financial and operating policy decisions of another entity, it is classified as an associate. Associates are initially recognised in the consolidated balance sheet at cost. The Group's share of post-acquisition profits and losses is recognised in the consolidated income statement, except that losses in excess of the Group's investment in the associate are not recognised unless there is an obligation to make good those losses.

Profits and losses arising on transactions between the Group and its associates are recognised only to the extent of unrelated investors' interests in the associate. The investor's share in the associate's profits and losses resulting from these transactions is eliminated against the carrying value of the associate.

Any premium paid for an associate above the fair value of the Group's share of the identifiable assets, liabilities and contingent liabilities acquired is capitalised and included in the carrying amount of the associate and subject to impairment in the same way as goodwill arising on a business combination described below.

Investments in associates held by the Company are carried at cost less any impairment in value.

11. Investments

Group

The Group acquired a 35% interest in the ordinary share capital of a company incorporated in England and Wales, in the period ended 31 December 2005, for a cash consideration of $1.8 million (this represents 35% of the voting rights). This is accounted for under the equity method. The Group's share of losses for the period ended 31 December 2005 was $0.8 million, resulting in a carrying value of $1.0 million.

Group

	$m
As at 1 January and 31 December 2004	–
Additions	1.8
Share of loss of associate	(0.8)
As at 31 December 2005	1.0

Another excellent example of the required disclosure is provided by UTV Plc including details of the summarised financial information of its associates' accounts:

UTV Year Ended 31 December 2005

Accounting Policies and Notes (Extracts)

Investment in associate

The Group's investment in its associate is accounted for under the equity method of accounting. This is an entity in which the Group has significant influence and which is neither a subsidiary nor a joint venture. The financial statements of the associate are used by the Group to apply the equity method. The reporting dates of the associate and the Group are identical and both use consistent accounting policies.

The investment in associate is carried in the balance sheet at cost plus post-acquisition changes in the Group's share of net assets of the associate, less any impairment in value. The income statement reflects the share of the results of operations of the associate. Where there has been a change recognised directly in the associates' equity, the Group recognises its share of any changes and discloses this, when applicable in the statement of changes in equity.

16. Investments

(a) Group

	Investment in associates £'000	Other investments £'000	Total £'000
Cost and net book value			
At 1 January 2005	–	–	–
Acquired through the acquisition of subsidiary undertakings	194	32	226
Group share of retained earnings of associate	109	–	109
Dividend received from associate	(35)	–	(35)
At 31 December 2005	268	32	300

The investment in the Group accounts comprise of:

	Country of incorporation	Percentage of Share held of (%)	Nature business
Associate, undertakings			
Digital Radio Group (London) Ltd	England	*30.2	Commercial radio
Dec 106.3	England	*21.7	Commercial radio
Other investments			
Somthin' Else Productions Ltd	England	*8.0	Radio and TV production

*Held by a subsidiary undertaking

The following illustrates the summarised financial information of the Group's associate undertaking:

	2005 (£000)	2004 (£000)
Share of associates balance sheet		
Non-current assets	67	–
Current assets	340	–
Share of gross assets	407	–
Current liabilities	154	
Non-current liabilities	–	–
Share of gross liabilities	154	–
Share of net assets	253	–

	2005 (£000)	2004 (£000)
Revenue	388	–
Net profit	109	–

11.4 IAS 31 *Interests in Joint Ventures* (December 2003)

Scope

This standard should be applied in accounting for interests in joint ventures and the reporting of joint venture assets, liabilities, income and expenses in the financial statements of venturers and investors, regardless of the structures under which the activities take place.

It does not apply, however, to interests held by venture capitalists or mutual funds/unit trusts classified as held for trading under IAS 39.

A venturer with an interest in a jointly controlled entity is exempted from proportional consolidation and equity accounting when it meets the following conditions:

(a) there is evidence that the interest is acquired and held exclusively with a view to disposal within 12 months from acquisition and management is actively seeking a buyer;
(b) the exception in IAS 27 permitting a parent not to prepare consolidated accounts applies; or
(c) all of the following apply:
  (i) the venturer is 100% owned or the minority are aware and have given permission not to apply proportionate consolidation or the equity method;
  (ii) the venturer's debt or equity are not traded in a public market;
  (iii) the venturer did not file nor is in the process of filing its statements publically; and
  (iv) the ultimate or intermediate parent publishes consolidated accounts.

Definitions

(a) *Joint venture.* A contractual agreement whereby two or more parties undertake an economic activity which is subject to joint control.
(b) *Joint control.* The contractually agreed sharing of control over an economic activity.
(c) *Venturer.* A party to a joint venture and having joint control over that joint venture.
(d) *Proportionate consolidation.* A method of accounting and reporting whereby a venturer's share of each of the assets, liabilities, income and expenses of a jointly controlled entity is combined on a line-by-line basis with similar items in the venturer's financial statements or reported as separate line items.
(e) *Equity method.* Initially the investment is carried at cost and adjusted thereafter for the post-acquisition change in the venturer's share of net assets of the jointly controlled entity. The income statement reflects the venturer's share of results of operations of the jointly controlled entity.

Forms of joint venture

IAS 31 identifies three broad types of joint venture activity:

(1) jointly controlled operations;
(2) jointly controlled assets; and
(3) jointly controlled entities.

They all have the common characteristics of having two or more joint venturers bound under contract and establishing joint control.

Joint control. May be precluded when an investee is in legal reorganisation or in bankruptcy or operates under severe long-term restrictions on its ability to transfer funds to the venturer.

Contractual arrangement. The existence of a contract distinguishes interests involving joint control from investments in associates in which an investor has significant influence.

The contract may be evidenced by way of formal contract or minutes of discussions between the venturers. In some cases, it may be incorporated in the articles of the joint venture. It is usually in writing and deals with such matters as:

(a) the activity, duration and reporting obligations of the joint venture;
(b) the appointment of the board of directors of the joint venture and voting rights of venturers;
(c) capital contributions by the venturers; and
(d) the sharing by the venturers of the output, income, expenses or results of the joint venture.

No single venturer is in a position to control activity unilaterally but instead requires the consent of all the venturers to undertake essential decisions.

Jointly controlled operations

Some joint ventures involve the use of assets and other resources rather than the establishment of a corporation, partnership or other entity. Each venturer uses its own assets and incurs its own expenses and raises its own finance.

The joint venture agreement usually provides a means by which revenue from the sale of the joint product and any expenses are shared among the venturers. An example might be a joint venture to manufacture, market and distribute jointly a particular product such as an aircraft. Different parts of the manufacturing process are carried out by each of the venturers and each venturer takes a share of the revenue from the sale of the aircraft but bears its own costs.

A venturer should recognise in its financial statements the following:

(a) the assets it controls and the liabilities it incurs and
(b) the expenses it incurs and its share of the income it earns from the sale of goods or services by the joint venture.

No adjustments or other consolidated procedures are required as the elements are already included in the separate statements of the investor.

Separate accounting records may not be required for the joint venture but the venturers may prepare management accounts to assess the performance of the joint venture.

Jointly controlled assets

Some joint ventures involve joint control by the venturers over one or more assets which are dedicated for the purposes of the joint venture. Each venturer may take a share of the output and bear an agreed share of the expenses incurred.

No corporation, however, is established. Many activities in oil and gas and mineral extraction involve jointly controlled assets, e.g. an oil pipeline. Another example is the joint control of property, each taking a share of the rents received and bearing a share of the expenses.

A venturer should recognise in its financial statements:

(a) its share of jointly controlled assets, classified according to their nature;
(b) any liabilities it has incurred;

(c) its share of any liabilities jointly incurred with other venturers;

(d) any income from the sale or use of the share of the output of the joint venture together with its share of any expenses incurred; and

(e) any expenses incurred regarding its interest in the joint venture.

No adjustments or other consolidation adjustments are required as the assets, liabilities, income and expenses are already recognised in the separate financial statements of the venturer.

The treatment of jointly controlled assets reflects the substance and economic reality and usually the legal form of the joint venture. Separate accounting records for the joint venture may be limited to those expenses incurred in common. Financial statements may not be prepared for the joint venture but management accounts may be needed to assess performance.

Jointly controlled entities

In this case, a corporation is established and operates as per other legal entities except that there is a contractual arrangement between the venturers that establishes joint control over the economic activity of the entity.

A jointly controlled entity controls the assets of the joint venture, incurs liabilities and expenses and earns income. It may enter contracts in its own name and raise finance for itself and each venturer is entitled to a share of the results of the jointly controlled entity.

An example is when two entities combine their activities in a particular line of business by transferring relevant assets and liabilities into a jointly controlled entity or it could be a joint venture by establishing a joint entity with a foreign government.

In substance, they are often similar to jointly controlled operations or jointly controlled assets. However, it does maintain its own accounting records and prepares its financial statements in the same way as other normal entities in conformity with appropriate national regulations.

Each venturer usually contributes cash or other resources to the jointly controlled entity. These contributions are included in the accounting records of the venturer and recognised in its financial statements as an investment in the jointly controlled entity.

Financial statements of a venturer

Proportionate consolidation

A venturer should report its interest in a jointly controlled entity using one of two reporting formats for proportionate consolidation or using the equity method.

It is essential that a venturer reflects the substance and economic reality of the arrangement. The application of proportionate consolidation means that the consolidated balance sheet of the venturer includes its share of the assets it controls jointly and its share of the liabilities for which it is jointly responsible. The consolidated income statement includes the venturer's share of the income and expenses of the jointly controlled entity. Many of the procedures are similar to consolidation procedures set out in IAS 27.

There are different reporting formats to give effect to proportionate consolidation:

(i)   Combine share of each of the assets, liabilities, income and expenses of the jointly controlled entity with similar items in the consolidated statements on a line-by-line basis, e.g. its share of inventory with inventory of the consolidated group.

(ii) May include separate line items for its share of the jointly controlled entity's assets, etc., e.g. may show its share of a current asset of the jointly controlled entity separately as part of its current assets; it may show its share of the property, etc., of the jointly controlled entity separately as part of property, etc.

Both methods are acceptable under the standard and both result in identical profits being recorded and of each major classification of assets. However, regardless of format, it is inappropriate to offset any assets or liabilities unless a legal right of set off exists and the offsetting represents the expectation as to the realisation of the asset or settlement of the liability. Proportionate consolidation should be discontinued from the date on which it ceases to have joint control over a jointly controlled entity. This could happen when the venturer disposes of its interest or when external restrictions mean that it can no longer achieve its goals.

Equity method

As an alternative, a venturer should report its interest in a jointly controlled entity using the equity method as per IAS 28. The equity method is supported by those who argue that it is inappropriate to combine controlled items with jointly controlled items. The standard does not recommend the use of the equity method because proportional consolidation better reflects the substance and economic reality of a venturer's interest in a jointly controlled entity. However, the standard does permit its adoption as an alternative treatment.

A venturer should discontinue the use of the equity method from the date it ceases to have joint control over or have significant influence in a jointly controlled entity.

Exceptions to proportional consolidation and equity method

A venturer should account for the following interests in accordance with IAS 39:

(a) An interest held exclusively with a view to its subsequent disposal in the near future.

(b) From the date on which a jointly controlled entity becomes a subsidiary of a venturer, the venturer accounts for its interest in accordance with IAS 27.

(c) From the date on which a jointly controlled entity becomes an associate of a venturer, the venturer should account for its interest in accordance with IAS 28.

Example – Castlerock Plc

The following financial statements relate to Castlerock, a public limited company.

Income Statement for Year Ended 31 December 2007

	£m	£m
Turnover		212
Cost of sales		(170)
Gross profit		42
Distribution costs	17	
Administration expenses	8	(25)
		17
Other operating income		12
		29
Exceptional item		(10)
Finance costs		(4)
Profit on ordinary activities before tax		15
Income tax		(3)
		12

Balance Sheet at 31 December 2007

	£m	£m
Non-current assets		
Property, plant and equipment	30	
Goodwill	7	
		37
Current assets	31	
Current liabilities	(12)	
Net current assets		19
Total assets less current liabilities		56
Non-current liabilities		(10)
		46
Equity and reserves		
Called up share capital		
Ordinary share capital		10
Share premium account		4
Retained profits (36–4 dividend paid)		32
		46

(i) Castlederg, a public limited company, acquired 30% of the ordinary share capital of Castlerock Plc at a cost of £14 million on 1 January 2006. The share capital of Castlerock has not changed since acquisition when the retained profits of Castlerock was £9 million.

(ii) At 1 January 2006 the following fair values were attributed to the net assets of Castlerock Plc but not incorporated in its accounting records.

	£m
Property, plant and equipment	30 (carrying value £20m)
Goodwill (estimate)	10
Current assets	31
Current liabilities	20
Non-current liabilities	8

(iii) Aghadowey, an associated company of Castlederg, also holds a 25% interest in the ordinary share capital of Castlerock. This was acquired on 1 January 2007.

(iv) During the year to 31 December 2007, Castlerock sold goods to Castlederg to the value of £35 million. The inventory of Castlederg Plc at 31 December 2007 included goods purchased from Castlerock Plc on which the company made a profit of £10 million.

(v) The policy of all companies in the Castlederg group is to depreciate tangible fixed assets at 20% per annum on the straight-line basis.

(vi) Castlerock does not represent a material part of the group.

Suggested solution – Castlerock Plc

Distinguish between trade investment and associate. The main difference between an associate and an ordinary trade investment is that, in the latter case, the investor takes a passive role in the running of the business but in the former the shareholders exercise considerable influence over the operating and financial policies of the investee. The associate normally implements accounting policies that are consistent with those of the investor. Under IAS 28 *Accounting for Associates*, the investor must actually exercise a significant influence so as to ensure that the investor secures a contribution to its activities by the exercise of control or influence.

IAS 28 states that a holding of 20% or more of the voting rights suggests, but does not ensure, that the investor exercises significant influence. There is a presumption that the investor is involved in the strategic decisions made by the company. The IAS also suggests that the attitude towards the investee's dividend policy may indicate the status of the investment. To have associate status it would appear that the investor should have board representation in order for it to be able to participate in the decision-making process. The investor must be able not only to exercise influence but it should also be able to exercise it actively.

Distinguish between a jointly controlled operation/asset and a jointly controlled entity. A joint venture may be both a legal and a joint arrangement. A jointly controlled entity is normally a limited company, partnership or incorporation association which has been set up to carry on a business or trade of its own. One example of a jointly controlled operation or asset would be a number of oil companies that would be setting up a pipeline in the Alaskan tundra as a joint arrangement. This would be set up as it is too expensive and also environmentally unfriendly for a number of pipelines to be set up separately by each of the companies. All significant decisions are taken by all the participants.

However, a jointly controlled entity is where a separate entity has been set up and all parties require the consent of each other for any decision to be taken. Joint ventures are set up, however, for the purpose of making profits.

The accounting treatment of a joint arrangement is that the investor should record its own share of its joint venture's assets and liabilities and its incomes/expenses. However, in joint ventures, they can opt for proportionate consolidation as per jointly controlled operations or can adopt equity accounting, the same as associates.

How should the investment in Castlerock Plc be treated in the consolidated balance sheet and income statement?
The investment should be disclosed as a single line under IAS 28 as follows:

Calculation of goodwill

	At 1 January 2007 – Fair value of assets (£m)
Property, plant and equipment	30
Current assets	31
Current liabilities	(20)
Non-current liabilities	(8)
	33
Shareholding 30% × £33m	9.9
Fair value of investment (Note i)	14
Goodwill (Bal. fig.)	4.1

	£m
Disclosure in Balance Sheet	
Cost of investment	14
Post-acquisition profits 30% × (32–10 share capital plus 9 retained reserves)	3.9
Additional depreciation charge (2 years × 20% × (30 fair value – 20 cost) × 30%	(1.2)
Investment in associate	16.7
Alternative disclosure	
Share of net assets (46 – share of inventory profits 10)	36
Revaluation of property, plant and equipment	10
Additional depreciation (£10m × 20% = £2m × 2 years)	(4)
	42
Shareholding 30% × £42m	12.6
Share of goodwill	4.1
Investment in associate	16.7

The alternative disclosure is more correct since it does not disclose any element of profit as part of the investment.

Disclosure in the income statement

	£m
Share of operating profit in associate (30% × £29m = £8.7m – inter-co. profit 3 – depreciation 0.6.m)	5.1
Exceptional item – associate (30% × £10m)	(3.0)
Finance costs – associate (30% × £4m)	(1.2)
Tax on profit on ordinary activities Associate (30% × £3m)	(0.9)

The treatment of Castlerock Plc could change if Castlerock were classified as an investment in joint venture And the company adopted proportionate consolidation

Joint venture – proportionate consolidation

	Consolidated income statement (£m)
Consolidated income statement	
Turnover: Group and share of joint ventures	X + 53.1
(£212m gross less inter-company turnover £35m × 30%)	
Consolidated balance sheet	
Share of gross assets	*23.3
Share of gross liabilities (30% × 12 + 10)	(6.6)
	16.7

*Computation of share of gross assets.

Property, etc.	£37m + £10m revaluation – 4 additional depreciation	= 43 × 30% =	12.9
Inventories	£31m – 10 inter-company profit on stocks	= 21 × 30% =	6.3
			19.2m
Goodwill			4.1m
			23.3m

Separate financial statements of a venturer

In many countries separate financial statements are presented by a venturer to meet legal or other requirements. These are provided for a variety of needs but the standard does not indicate a preference for any particular treatment.

Transactions between a venturer and a joint venture

When a venturer contributes or sells assets to a joint venture, recognition of any portion of a gain or loss should reflect the substance of the transaction. While the assets are retained by the joint venture and provided the venturer has transferred the significant risks and rewards of ownership, the venturer should recognise only that portion of the gain or loss, which is attributable to the interests of the other venturers. The venturer should recognise the full amount of any loss when the sale provides evidence of a reduction in the NRV of current assets or an impairment loss.

When a venturer purchases assets from a joint venture, the venturer should not recognise its share of the profits of the joint venture until it resells the assets to an independent party. A venturer should recognise its share of the losses in the same way as profits except the losses should be recognised immediately when they represent a reduction in the NRV of current assets or an impairment loss under IAS 36.

Reporting interests in joint ventures in the financial statements of an investor

An investor in a joint venture which does not have joint control, should report its interest in a joint venture in its consolidated accounts, under IAS 39 or, if significant influence, under IAS 28.

Operators of joint ventures

Operators or managers of a joint venture should account for any fees in accordance with IAS 18. The fees are accounted for by the joint venture as an expense.

Disclosure

A venturer should disclose the aggregate amount of the following contingent liabilities, unless the probability of loss is remote, each separately:

(a) any contingent liabilities incurred in relation to its interest in joint ventures and its share in each contingent liability incurred jointly with other venturers;
(b) its share of contingent liabilities of the joint ventures for which it is contingently liable; and
(c) those contingent liabilities that arise because the venturer is contingently liable for the liabilities of the other venturers of a joint venture.

A venturer should disclose the aggregate amount of the following commitments regarding interests in joint ventures separately from other commitments:

(a) any capital commitments regarding joint ventures and its share in capital commitments incurred jointly with other venturers and
(b) its share of capital commitments of the joint ventures themselves.

A venturer should disclose a listing and description of interests in significant joint ventures and the proportion of ownership interest held in JCEs. An entity that adopts line-by-line reporting for proportionate consolidation or the equity method should disclose the aggregate amounts of each of its current assets, long-term assets, current liabilities, long-term liabilities, income and expenses related to interests in joint ventures.

A venturer that does not publish consolidated accounts, because it has no subsidiaries, should disclose the above information as well.

SIC 13 *Jointly Controlled Entities – Non-Monetary Contributions by Venturers* (November 1998)

Issue

There is no explicit guidance in IAS 31 on the recognition of gains and losses resulting from contributions of non-monetary assets to JCEs.

Contributions to a JCE are transfers of assets by venturers in exchange for an equity interest in the JCE. Such contributions may take various forms and can be made simultaneously by the venturers either upon setting up the JCE or subsequently. The consideration received by the venturer in exchange for assets contributed to the JCE may also include cash or other consideration that does not depend on future cash flows of the JCE.

The issues are:

(a) when the appropriate portion of gains or losses resulting from the contribution of a non-monetary asset to a JCE in exchange for an equity interest in the JCE should be recognised by the venturer in the income statement;

(b) how additional consideration should be accounted for by the venturer; and

(c) how any unrealised gain or loss should be presented in the consolidated statements of the venturer.

The SIC deals with the venturer's accounting for non-monetary contributions to a JCE in exchange for an equity interest in the JCE that is accounted for using the equity method or proportionate consolidation.

Consensus

In applying IAS 31 to non-monetary contributions to a JCE in exchange for an equity interest in the JCE, a venturer should recognise in the income statement the portion of the gain or loss attributable to the equity interests of the other venturers except when:

(a) the significant risks and rewards of ownership of the contributed non-monetary assets have not been transferred to the JCE;

(b) the gain or loss on the non-monetary contribution cannot be reliably measured;

(c) the non-monetary assets contributed are similar to those contributed by the other venturers. Non-monetary assets are similar to those contributed by other venturers when they have a similar nature, a similar use in the same line of business and a similar fair value. A contribution meets the similarity test only if all of the significant component assets thereof are similar to those contributed by the other venturers.

Where any of (a) to (c) applies, the gain/loss would be considered unrealised and therefore not recognised in income.

If, in addition to receiving an equity interest in the JCE, a venturer receives monetary or non-monetary assets dissimilar to those it contributed, an appropriate portion of gain/loss on the transaction should be recognised by the venturer in income.

Unrealised gains/losses on non-monetary assets contributed to JCEs should be eliminated against the underlying assets under the proportionate consolidation method or equity method. Such unrealised gains/losses should not be presented as deferred gains or losses in the venturer's consolidated balance sheet.

Two of the best overall disclosures for joint ventures are provided by BAE Systems Plc and Anglo American Plc, the former revealing the extent of its involvement in Airbus SAS. BAE Systems Plc adopts equity accounting and Anglo American Plc adopt proportionate consolidation.

BAE Systems Plc   Year Ended 31 December 2005

Notes to the Accounts (Extract)
14. Equity accounted investments

The following represent the Group's share of the assets, liabilities and results of equity accounted investments:

	2005 (£m)	2004 (£m)
Assets		
Non-current assets	3,453	3,725
Current assets	5,764	4,256
	9,217	7,981
Liabilities		
Non-current liabilities	(3,550)	(2,989)
Current liabilities	(3,946)	(3,523)
	(7,496)	(6,512)
Carrying value	1,721	1,469

Share of results of equity accounted investments by business group

	2005 (£m)	2004 (£m)
Share of results excluding finance costs and taxation expense:		
Electronics, Intelligence & Support	5	(1)
Land & Armaments	(1)	(2)
Programmes	1	–
Customer Solutions & Support	18	16
Integrated Systems & Partnerships	68	115
Commercial Aerospace	274	216
HQ and other businesses	8	4
	373	348
Finance costs	(11)	(27)
Taxation expense	(149)	(105)
	213	216

Carrying value of equity accounted investments

	Share of net assets (£m)	Purchased goodwill (£m)	Carrying value (£m)
At 1 January 2004	(169)	1,626	1,457
Share of results after tax	216	–	216
Reclassification	35	–	35
Transfer to subsidiary company	(5)	–	(5)
Reduction in shareholding	2	–	2
Dividends receivable	(66)	–	(66)
Actuarial losses on defined benefit pension schemes, net of tax	(111)	–	(111)
Foreign exchange adjustment	(56)	(3)	(59)
At 31 December 2004	(154)	1,623	1,469
Adoption of IAS 39	770	–	770
At 1 January 2005	616	1,623	2,239
Share of results after tax	213	–	213
Acquired through acquisition	23	–	23
Disposal	140	(136)	4
Reduction in shareholding	(62)	(68)	(130)
Dividends receivable	(88)	–	(88)
Market value adjustments in respect of derivative financial instruments, net of tax	(470)	–	(470)
Actuarial losses on defined benefit pension schemes, net of tax	(47)	–	(47)
Foreign exchange adjustment	(8)	(15)	(23)
At 31 December 2095	317	1,404	1,721

As stated in Note 1, the Group has adopted IAS 39 from 1 January 2005. As a result, the Group is required to recognise its share of the market value of the equity accounted investments' derivative contracts as at 1 January 2005.

On 25 February 2005, the Group announced the sale of 13.2 million B series shares in the capital of Saab AB for a net consideration of £125 million. Following the sale and subsequent conversion of 1.2 million A series shares to B series shares and the exercise of the over allotment option of a further 1.8 million B series shares. BAE Systems owns 20.5% of Saab AB.

The market value of the Group's shareholding in Saab AB at 31 December 2005 was £278 million (2004: £336m).

Additional disclosures in respect of the Group's share of Airbus SAS

	2005 (£m)	2004 (£m)
Sales	3,002	2,666
Profit before taxation	254	235
Taxation	(115)	(54)
Profit after taxation	139	181

Assets (excluding goodwill)		
Non-current assets (including aircraft let under operating leases)	1,701	1,685
Current assets	3,083	974
	4,784	2,659
Liabilities		
Non-current liabilities	(2,951)	(2,028)
Current liabilities	(1,723)	(855)
	(4,674)	(2,883)
Share of net assets/(liabilities)	110	(224)
Goodwill at 31 December	1,063	1,063
Carrying value	1,173	839

Anglo American Plc   Year Ended 31 December 2005

Accounting Policies and Notes to the Accounts (Extract)

Joint venture entitles

A Joint venture entry is an entity in which the Group holds a long-term interest and shares joint control over the strategic, financial and operating decisions with one or more other venturers under a contractual arrangement.

The Group's share of the assets, liabilities, income, expenditure and cash flows of JCEs are accounted for using proportionate consolidation.

Proportionate consolidation combines the Group's share of the results of the joint venture entity on a line-by-line basis with similar items in the Group's financial statements.

Joint venture operations

The Group has contractual arrangements with other participants to engage in joint activities other than through a separate entity. The Group includes its assets, liabilities, expenditure and its share of revenue in such joint venture operations with similar items in the Group's financial statements.

17. Joint ventures

The Group's share of the summarised financial information of joint venture entities that is proportionately consolidated in the Group financial statements, is as follows:

US$m	2005	2004
Total non-current assets	1,468	1,531
Total current assets	832	653
Total current liabilities	(132)	(194)
Total non-current liabilities	(359)	(512)
Share of joint venture entities' net assets, proportionately consolidated	1,809	1,478

Revenue	1,331	1,195
Total operating costs	(797)	(749)
Net finance costs	(28)	(26)
Income tax expense	(85)	(73)
Share of joint venture entities results	421	347

The Group's share of joint venture entities' contingent liabilities incurred jointly with other ventures is nil (2004: $3m) and its share of capital commitments is $8 million (2004: $3m).

Details of principal joint ventures are set out in Note 42.

	Country of incorporation	Business	Percentage of equity owned®	
			2005 (%)	2004 (%)
Joint ventures				
Aylesford Newsprint Holdings Limited	United Kingdom	Newspirit	50	50
Comparia Minera Donalnes de Collahuasi SGM	Chile	Copper	44	44
Mondi Shanduka Newsprint (Pty) Ltd	South Africa	Newsprint	54	54
United Marine Holdings Ltd	United Kingdom	Construction materials	50	50

	Location	Business	Percentage owned	
			2005 (%)	2004 (%)
Proportionately consolidated jointly controlled operations*				
Drayton	Australia	Coal	88	88
Moranbah North	Australia	Coal	88	88
Dartbrook	Australia	Coal	78	78
German Creek	Australia	Coal	70	70
Dawson	Australia	Coal	51	51

*The wholly owned subsidiary Anglo Coal Holdings Australia Limited holds the proportionately consolidated jointly controlled operations.

ED 9 *Joint Arrangements* (September 2007)

ED 9 sets out requirements for the recognition and disclosure of interests in joint arrangements. Its objective is to enhance the faithful representation of joint arrangements and it achieves this by requiring an entity:

(a) to recognise its contractual rights and obligations arising from its joint arrangements. The legal form of the arrangement is no longer the most significant factor in determining the right accounting treatment and

(b) to provide enhanced disclosures about its interest in joint arrangements.

This is part of the short-term convergence project undertaken by the IASB and FASB in the United States. It will, if implemented, supersede IAS 31 and SIC 13.

Core principle

The parties to a joint arrangement recognise their contractual rights and obligations arising from the arrangement.

General requirements

ED 9 applies to interests in joint arrangements except for those held by venture capital organisations, mutual funds, unit trusts, etc., if these are measured at fair value and changes recognised within profit.

A joint arrangement is a contractual arrangement whereby two or more parties undertake an economic activity together and share decision-making relating to the activity. There are three types – joint operations, joint assets and joint ventures.

ED 9 requires a party to recognise its contractual rights and obligations as assets and liabilities. Contractual rights to individual assets and contractual obligations for expenses represent interests in joint operations or joint assets.

An interest in a joint venture must use the equity method. Proportionate consolidation will no longer be acceptable.

ED 9 also requires disclosure of a description of the nature of operations an entity conducts through joint arrangements as well as a description of and summarised financial information relating to its interests in joint ventures.

12 Financial instruments

12.1 IAS 32 *Financial Instruments: Disclosure and Presentation* (revised 2003)

Objective

The dynamic nature of international financial markets has led to a widespread use of a variety of financial instruments ranging from primary to various forms of derivatives. The objective of IAS 32 is to enhance users' understanding of the significance of financial instruments to an entity's position, performance and cash flows.

IAS 32 prescribes requirements for presentation and the information that must be disclosed. It classifies instruments between equity and liabilities as well as details how to present and disclose related interest, dividends, losses and gains. The disclosure includes factors that affect the amount, timing and certainty of an entity's future cash flows relating to financial instruments. It also covers information about the nature and extent of an entity's use of financial instruments, their associated risks and management's policies for controlling those risks. For accounting periods beginning on or after 1 January 2007, however, the disclosure requirements are dropped and most of these have been transferred to a separate IFRS 7 *Financial Instruments: Disclosure*.

Scope

IAS 32 applies to all financial statements giving a true and fair view except that paras 42–95 on disclosure should only apply to banks and Plcs having capital instruments listed.

IAS 32 should be applied to all types of financial instruments except:

(a) those interests in subsidiary, quasi-subsidiary and associated undertakings, partnerships and joint ventures accounted for under IAS 27 and IAS 28. It should be applied to subsidiaries held exclusively for resale;

(b)   employers rights and obligations under IAS 19 and IAS 26;

(c)   rights and obligations under insurance contracts (see IFRS 4);

(d)   contracts for contingent consideration in a business combination (i.e. earn-outs);

(e)   contracts requiring a payment based on climatic, geological or other physical variables.

It applies to both recognised and unrecognised financial instruments.

Other standards specific to particular types of financial instruments contain additional presentation and disclosure requirements e.g. IAS 17 *Leases*, IAS 19 *Employee benefits*.

IAS 32 should be applied to those contracts to buy or sell a non-financial item that can be settled net in cash or by some other financial instrument as if they were financial instruments. Examples include contracts to buy or sell commodities at a fixed price at a future date.

Definitions

- *Financial instrument.* Any contract giving rise to both a financial asset of one entity and a financial liability or equity instrument of another entity.
- *Financial asset.* Any asset that is:
    (a)   cash;
    (b)   a contractual right to receive cash or another financial asset from another entity (i.e. trade receivables);
    (c)   a contractual right to exchange financial instruments with another entity under conditions that are potentially favourable; or
    (d)   an equity instrument of another entity.
- *Financial liability.* A contractual obligation:
    (a)   to deliver cash to another entity (e.g. trade payables) and
    (b)   to exchange financial instruments with another entity under conditions that are potentially unfavourable.
- *Equity instrument.* Any contract evidencing a residual interest in the assets of an entity after deducting all of its liabilities.
- *Fair value.* The amount for which an asset could be exchanged in an arm's length transaction.
- *Market value.* The amount obtainable from the sale or payable of a financial instrument in an active market.

Financial instruments include both primary and derivative instruments. Derivatives create rights and obligations that transfer one or more of the financial risks inherent in an underlying primary financial instrument between the parties to the instrument. They do not result in a transfer of the underlying primary instrument and a transfer does not necessarily occur on maturity of the contract.

Physical and intangible assets (patents/trademarks) are not financial assets nor are prepayments or deferred revenue, as the latter are associated with the delivery of goods and services. Income taxes are not financial liabilities. They are created as a result of statutory requirements.

Commitments to buy or sell non-financial items do not meet the definition of a financial instrument, nor do operating leases for the use of a physical asset that can be settled only by the receipt or delivery of non-financial assets.

Minority interest is not a financial liability nor an equity instrument of the parent.

Presentation

Liabilities and equity

An issuer must classify a financial instrument, on initial recognition, as a liability or as equity in accordance with the substance of the contract and the definitions of a financial liability and an equity instrument.

Some financial instruments take the legal form of equity but are liabilities in substance and others combine features of both. Their classification should be based on substance and that classification continues at each reporting date until the instrument is derecognised.

The critical feature in differentiating a financial liability from equity is the existence of a contractual obligation of one party to a financial instrument either to deliver cash to the other party or to exchange another financial instrument under conditions that are potentially unfavourable to the issuer.

When a financial instrument does not give rise to a contractual obligation it should be classified as equity. When a preferred share provides for mandatory redemption by the issuer for a fixed or determinable amount at a fixed or determinable future date (or gives the holder the right to require the issuer to redeem the share at a particular date or amount) then the instrument meets the definition of a financial liability and is classified as such.

Where an entity issues a financial instrument to be settled by cash or other financial assets depending on the occurrence/non-occurrence of certain uncertain future events, e.g. consumer price index, it should be classified as a financial liability. The issuer does not have an unconditional right to avoid settlement.

If an entity issues a 'puttable instrument' (i.e. it gives the holder the right to put the instrument back to the issuer for cash based on an index) even if its legal form gives the holder the right to the residual interest, the inclusion of the option meets the definition of a financial liability.

An entity may have a contract of a fixed amount or a variable amount that fluctuates in response to an external variable. If the entity can settle by delivery of its own equity instruments it is still a financial liability of the entity.

If the number of an entity's own shares required to settle an obligation varies with changes in their fair value it is still a financial liability.

Classification of compound instruments by the issuer

An issuer of a financial instrument containing both a liability and an equity element must classify the component parts separately.

It is a matter of form, not substance, that a single instrument can represent both equity and debt features. An issuer recognises separately the component parts of a financial instrument (e.g. convertible loan) that:

(a)   creates a financial liability of the issuer (to deliver cash) and
(b)   grants an option to convert it into equity (a call option to convert into shares).

The economic effect is the same as issuing simultaneously a debt instrument with an early settlement provision and warrants to purchase common shares.

Classification is not revised as a result of a change in the likelihood that a conversion option will be exercised. The issuer's obligation remains outstanding until extinguished through conversion, maturity or other transaction.

The following example shows how the compound should be split for a convertible debenture:

Facts

An entity issues 2,000 convertible loans at par with a three-year life with a face value of £1,000 per bond. Total proceeds are £2 million. Interest is payable at 6% in arrears. The loans can be convertible into 250 ordinary shares at any time. Assume a normal loan without any convertibility would cost 9%.

Solution

	£
Present value of principal £2m discounted at 9% and payable in three years	1,544,367
Present value of interest £120,000 payable annually for three years	303,755
Total liability	1,848,122
Equity component (bal. fig.)	151,878
	2,000,000

A financial instrument may contain components that are neither financial liabilities nor equity, e.g. the right to receive in settlement a non-financial asset, commodity and an option to exchange that right for a fixed number of shares of the issuer. The equity instrument should be disclosed separately from the liability element whether the liabilities are financial or non-financial.

Equity instruments represent a residual interest and should be assigned the residual amount after deducting from the total, the amount separately determined for the liability. The sum assigned to the liability and equity components on initial recognition is always equal to the carrying amount ascribed to the instrument as a whole. No gain or loss arises on initial recognition.

The issuer of a convertible bond, therefore, must first determine the carrying amount of the liability. The carrying amount of the equity instrument, represented by the option to convert the instrument into shares, is calculated by deducting the carrying amount of the financial liability from the amount of the compound instrument as a whole (see above).

BAE Systems Plc provides an example of how to apply the compound instrument rules:

BAE Systems Plc   Year Ended 31 December 2005

Notes to the Accounts (Extract)

Preference shares

The 7.75p (net) cumulative redeemable preference shares of 25p each are convertible into ordinary shares of 2.5p each at the option of the holder on 31 May in any of the years up to 2007, on the basis of 0.47904 ordinary shares for every preference share. During the year 187,489 shares were converted for 89,814 ordinary shares. The Group may redeem all of the remaining preference shares at any time after 1 July 2007 and, in any case, will redeem any remaining shares on 1 January 2010, in each case at 100p per share together with any arrears and accruals of dividend. The maximum redemption value of the preference shares, ignoring any arrears or accruals of dividend, is therefore £266 m.

As stated in Note 1, the Group has adopted IAS 39 from 1 January 2005. In accordance with IAS 32 the convertible preference shares are considered to be a compound financial instrument consisting of both a debt element and an equity component which require separate accounting treatment. Under IAS 32, the equity option element of preference shares of £78 m is included as a separate component of equity. The debt component is recognised within loans and overdrafts (Note 20).

Transactions in an entity's own equity instruments

Treasury shares

If an entity reacquires its own equity, those 'treasury shares' should be deducted from equity. No gain or loss is recognised and any consideration paid or received is recognised directly in equity. The amount of treasury shares should be disclosed separately in the notes or on the balance sheet itself.

Derivatives based on an entity's own equity instruments

A derivative should be classified as equity if it is settled by the exchange of a fixed number of an entity's own equity instruments for a fixed amount of cash. Any consideration received is added directly to equity. Any consideration paid is deducted directly from equity. Changes in the fair value of a derivative in that case are not recognised.

A derivative is not classified as equity solely because it may result in the receipt or delivery of an entity's own equity instruments. A derivative that requires to be settled on a net basis in cash is a derivative asset/liability. Similarly a derivative that requires settlement on a net basis in an entity's own equity instruments is a derivative asset/liability.

If a derivative has more than one settlement alternative (e.g. cash, equity or exchange of equity for cash) the contract is a derivative asset/liability unless the entity:

(a) has an unconditional right and ability to settle by exchanging a fixed number of its own equity for a fixed amount of cash;

(b) has an established practice of settling such contracts by exchanging a fixed number of its own equity for a fixed amount of cash; and

(c) intends to settle the contract by exchanging a fixed number of its own equity for a fixed amount of cash.

In these situations, the contract should be classified as equity.

Where an entity enters into a derivative contract (e.g. a forward contract that requires settlement by cash), that instrument ceases to meet the definition of equity and is therefore a financial liability. Its cost (the present value of the redemption amount) is reclassified from equity to debt. If the contract expires without delivery of cash it is then reclassified to equity.

A derivative whose fair value fluctuates in response to changes in external variables is clearly not equity and must be classified as a derivative asset/liability.

Interest, dividends, losses and gains

All of the above relating to financial liabilities should be recognised in the income statement as expenses/incomes. However, dividends paid to equity holders must be charged directly to equity and any transaction costs deducted from equity net of any tax benefit. The latter must, however, be incremental external costs directly attributable to the equity transaction.

Transaction costs for hybrids must be allocated to the components in proportion to the allocation of proceeds and, if related to more than one transaction, they must be allocated on a rational and consistent basis. Those costs deducted from equity must be disclosed separately.

Dividends can be disclosed separately or with interest but if there are significant tax differences between the two, then separate disclosure is desirable.

It is the classification of instruments between equity/liabilities that determines where related interest/expenses are charged.

Offsetting of a financial asset and a financial liability

A financial asset and a financial liability should be offset and the net amount reported in the balance sheet when, and only when, an entity:

(a)   has a legally enforceable right of set off and
(b)   intends to settle on a net basis or to realise the asset and settle the liability simultaneously.

Offsetting differs from ceasing to recognise a financial asset or liability. The latter not only does remove items from the balance sheet, but it may also result in the recognition of a gain or loss.

The existence of a legal right of setoff affects the rights and obligations associated with a financial asset and a financial liability and may significantly affect an entity's exposure to credit and liquidity risk. The existence of the right itself, however, is not a sufficient basis for offsetting. In the absence of an intention to exercise the right to settle means that the amount of the entity's future cash flows are not affected. Where the intention is to exercise, the presentation on a net basis reflects more appropriately the amounts and timing of the expected future cash flows, as well as the risks to which the cash flows are exposed. An intention to settle net without a legal right to do so is not sufficient to justify offsetting because the rights and obligations remain unaltered.

Intentions may reflect normal business practice, the needs of the financial markets and any other circumstances that could limit the ability to settle net or simultaneously (i.e. at the same moment).

Offsetting is usually inappropriate when:

(a) several different financial instruments are used to emulate the features of a single financial instrument (a 'synthetic instrument');
(b) financial assets and liabilities arise from instruments having the same primary risk exposure (e.g. portfolio of forward contracts) but involving different counterparties;
(c) financial or other assets pledged as collateral for non-recourse financial liabilities;
(d) financial assets set aside in trust by a debtor to discharge an obligation without those assets having been accepted by the creditor in settlement; or
(e) obligations incurred by events giving rise to losses expected to be recovered from a third party via an insurance policy claim.

A 'master netting arrangement', providing for a single net settlement of all financial instruments covered by the agreement in the event of a default, commonly creates a right of setoff that becomes enforceable only following a specified event of default or other circumstances not normally expected in the normal course of business.

Normally a master netting arrangement does not provide a basis for offsetting unless both the criteria (a) and (b) at the start of this section are satisfied. If not offset then details of credit-risk exposure must be provided.

Disclosure (now transferred to IFRS 7)

The purpose of the disclosures in IAS 32 is to provide information to enhance an understanding of the significance of financial instruments to an entity's financial position, performance and cash flows that will assist in assessing the amounts, timing and certainty of future cash flows associated with those instruments.

In particular, the required disclosure is to help assess the following risks related to financial instruments:

(1) *Market risk*
  • Currency risk – value fluctuates due to changes in foreign exchange rates.
  • Fair value interest risk – value fluctuates due to changes in interest rates.
  • Price risk – value fluctuates due to changes in market prices whether specific or affecting all securities traded in the market.
(2) *Credit risk.* The risk that one party will fail to discharge an obligation and cause the other party to incur a financial loss.
(3) *Liquidity risk.* The risk encountered in raising funds to meet commitments.
(4) *Cash flow interest rate risk.* The risk that future cash flows will fluctuate due to changes in interest rates.

Format and location

IAS 32 does not prescribe the location nor the format of the information required under the standard. If it is disclosed on the face of the financial statements, it does need to be repeated in the notes. The format may contain both a quantitative and a narrative element, as appropriate.

The extent of detail of disclosure requires judgment and an ability to strike a balance between providing excessive detail and obscuring significant information by too much aggregation. Details of individual instruments may be important if they represent a significant component of an entity's capital structure but similar instruments may well be combined.

Classification distinguishing between cost and fair-value items would seem preferable.

Risk management policies and hedging activities

An entity should describe its financial risk management objectives and policies, including its policy for hedging each major type of forecast transaction for which hedge accounting is used.

These will include policies on matters such as hedging of risk exposures, avoidance of undue concentration of risk and requirements for collateral to mitigate credit risk. This is a valuable independent perspective that is gathered from the specific instruments held.

The following should be disclosed separately for designated fair value hedges, cash flow hedges and hedges of a net investment in a foreign operation as per IAS 39:

(i)   a description of the hedge;
(ii) a description of the financial instruments designated as hedging instruments and their fair values at the balance sheet date;
(iii) the nature of the risks being hedged;
(iv) for hedges of forecast transactions, the periods in which the forecast transactions are expected to occur, when they are expected to enter into the determination of profit or loss, and a description of any forecast transaction for which hedge accounting had previously been used but which is no longer expected to occur.

If gains/losses on derivative and non-derivative financial assets and liabilities designated as hedging instruments in cash flow hedges have been recognised, by remeasuring the hedging instrument, an entity must disclose the amount so recognised during the period and provide an explanation of how the gains/losses have been dealt with in the financial statements.

Terms, conditions, and accounting policies

For each class of financial asset, financial liability and equity instrument, an entity should disclose:

(a)   information about the extent and nature of the financial instruments, including significant terms and conditions that might affect the amount, timing and certainty of future cash flows and
(b)   the accounting policies and methods adopted, including the criteria for recognition and the basis of measurement applied.

Terms and conditions of contracts are very important in assessing future cash flows. These should be disclosed for individual contracts, if significant, but the information may be presented by reference to appropriate groupings of like instruments.

If financial instruments create a potentially significant exposure to risks then the terms and conditions that should be disclosed include:

(a)   the principal on which future payments are based;
(b)   the date of maturity, expiry or execution;

(c) early settlement options including the period when they can be exercised prices;

(d) options held to convert instruments into others including the period of exercise and the exchange ratio;

(e) the amount and timing of scheduled cash flows of the principal amount;

(f) stated rate of interest, dividend or other return on principal;

(g) collateral held or pledged;

(h) for instruments denominated in a foreign currency other than presentation, that currency;

(i) for exchanges items (a) to (h);

(j) any condition which would significantly alter the other terms of the contract.

Where the presentation differs from the legal form, the entity should explain in the notes, the nature of the instrument.

Any relationship between individual instruments that can affect the amount, timing or certainty of future cash flows would be useful, e.g. hedging relationships.

All significant accounting policies should be disclosed including the general principles adopted in applying the principles to significant transactions. Disclosures include:

(a) the criteria applied in determining when to recognise a financial asset or liability and when to derecognise it;

(b) the basis of measurement applied to financial assets and liabilities initially and subsequently; and

(c) the basis on which income and expenses arising from financial assets and liabilities are recognised and measured.

If IAS 39 is not being applied it would be particularly important to provide adequate information for users to disclose for cost-based instruments:

(a) costs of acquisition;

(b) premiums/discounts on monetary financial assets and liabilities;

(c) changes in the estimated determinable future cash flows associated with a monetary instrument such as an indexed linked bond;

(d) changes in circumstances resulting in significant uncertainty about the timely collection of amounts due from monetary assets;

(e) declines in the fair value of financial assets below their carrying amount; and

(f) restructured financial liabilities.

For fair-value instruments an entity should disclose whether they are determined from quoted market prices, independent appraisals, discounted cash flow analysis or other appropriate method as well as disclosing any significant assumptions.

The basis of reporting unrealised gains, losses and interest should be provided and this includes information about the basis on which income and expenses arising from financial instruments, held for hedging, are recognised. If income and expenses are presented net, even though corresponding assets and liabilities have not been offset, the reason for that presentation should be disclosed, if significant.

Interest rate risk

For each class of financial assets and liabilities, an entity must disclose information about its exposure to interest rate risk, including:

(a)   contractual repricing or maturity dates, whichever are earlier;
(b)   effective interest rates, when applicable.

It is important that exposure to the effects of future changes in the prevailing level of interest rates and how changes in market rates affect cash flows be provided.

Information regarding maturity dates provides useful information as to the length of time that rates are fixed and the levels at which they are fixed. Disclosure provides users with a basis for evaluating the fair value interest rate risk to which an entity is exposed and thus the potential for gain or loss.

To supplement the above, an entity may elect to disclose information about repricing or maturity dates if those dates differ significantly from the contractual dates. Such information is particularly relevant when predicting the amount of fixed-rate mortgage loans that will be repaid prior to maturity and it uses the information as the basis for managing its interest rate risk exposure.

An entity indicates which of its financial assets/liabilities are:

(a)   exposed to fair value interest rate risk;
(b)   exposed to cash flow interest rate risk, e.g. floating rates; and
(c)   not directly exposed to interest rate risk, e.g. investments in equity securities.

An entity may become exposed to interest rate risk, e.g. commitment to lend funds at a fixed rate. The entity should disclose information that permits users to understand the nature and extent of its exposure. That normally includes the stated principal, interest rate and term to maturity of the amount to be lent as well as the significant terms of the transaction giving rise to the exposure to risk.

Exposure to interest rate risk can be presented in tables, in narrative form or as a combination of the two. If the entity has a significant number of instruments exposed to fair value or cash flow interest rate risk, it may adopt one or more of the following approaches while presenting information:

(1)   The carrying amounts exposed to interest rate risk may be presented in tabular form, grouped by those contracted to mature or be repriced in the following periods after the balance sheet date:
  • not later than one year;
  • later than one year and not later than two years;
  • later than two years and not later than three years;
  • later than three years and not later than four years;
  • later than four years but not later than five years; and
  • later than five years.

(2)   Where performance is significantly affected by exposure to interest rate risk more details are required. A bank, for example, may disclose separate groupings of instruments to mature or be repriced:
  • within one month of the balance sheet date;
  • more than one month and less than three months from the balance sheet date; and
  • more than three months and less than twelve months from the balance sheet date.

(3) Similar cash flow interest rate risk exposure may be provided indicating groups of floating rate financial assets/liabilities maturing within various future time periods.

(4) Interest rate information may be disclosed for individual instruments or weighted average rates or a range of rates may be presented for each class of instrument.

In some cases, the effects of hypothetical changes in market interest rates on fair values and future earnings/cash flows would be useful. Such interest rate sensitivity, when disclosed, should indicate the basis on which it has prepared the information, including any significant assumptions.

Credit risk

For each class of financial assets and other credit exposures, an entity should disclose information about its exposure to credit risk, including:

(a) the amount that best represents its maximum credit risk exposure at the balance sheet date, without taking account of the fair value of any collateral, in the event of other parties failing to perform their obligations under financial instruments; and

(b) significant concentrations of credit risk.

The first requirement of ignoring collateral is to provide users with a consistent measure of the amount exposed to risk and to take into account the possibility that the maximum exposure to loss may differ from the carrying value of the financial assets.

Where an entity has entered one or more master netting arrangements that serve to mitigate its exposure to credit loss and this significantly reduces the credit risk associated, an entity must provide additional information indicating that:

(a) the credit risk is eliminated only to the extent that financial liabilities due to the same counterparty will be settled after the assets are realised and

(b) the extent to which an entity's overall exposure to credit risk is reduced through a master netting arrangement. The disclosure of terms may also be useful.

Concentrations of credit risk should be disclosed if they are not apparent from other disclosures about the nature of the business and financial position of the entity and result in a significant exposure to loss in the event of default by other parties. Identification of significant concentrations requires judgement by management taking into account the circumstances of the entity and its debtors. IAS 14 may provide guidance in this regard.

Characteristics giving rise to significant concentrations of credit risk include the nature of the activities undertaken by debtors such as the industry in which it operates, the geographical area in which activities take place and the level of creditworthiness of groups of borrowers, e.g. bank lending to less developed nations.

Disclosure of credit risk includes a description of the shared characteristic that identifies each concentration and the amount of the maximum credit-risk exposure associated with all financial assets sharing that characteristic.

Fair value

For each class of financial assets and liabilities, an entity should disclose the fair value of that class of assets and liabilities in such a way that it permits it to be compared with the corresponding amount in the balance sheet. IAS 39 provides guidance on how the fair value should be determined.

If IAS 39 is being applied and unquoted investments are valued at cost (no reliable fair value) that fact should be disclosed together with a description of the instruments, their carrying amount, an explanation of why fair value cannot be measured reliably and, if possible, the range of estimates within which fair value is highly likely to lie. If these financial assets are then sold that fact, their carrying value at date of sale and the amount of gain/loss should be disclosed.

An entity should disclose:

(a)   the methods and significant assumptions applied in determining fair values of financial assets and liabilities, separately for significant classes;

(b)   the extent to which fair values are determined directly through market prices or are estimated using a valuation technique;

(c)   the extent to which fair values are determined in full or in part using a valuation technique based on assumptions that are not supported by observable market prices;

(d)   if a fair value estimated using a valuation technique is sensitive to valuation assumptions that are not supported by observable market prices, a statement of this fact and the effect on the fair value of using a range of reasonably possible alternative assumptions; and

(e)   the total amount of the change in fair value estimated using a valuation technique that was recognised in profit or loss during the period.

Fair values are widely used in business and they provide relevant information to users as well as permitting comparisons of financial instruments having the same economic characteristics, regardless of their purpose and when or by whom they are issued. If fair values are not included within the balance sheet they should be disclosed as supplementary disclosure.

Disclosure of fair value information includes disclosure of the method used to determine fair value and any significant assumptions made, e.g. prepayment rates, discount rates and rates of estimated credit losses.

For financial instruments such as short-term trade receivables and payables, no disclosure of fair value is required when their carrying value approximates fair value.

Fair values should be grouped only into classes and offset to the extent that their related carrying amounts are offset in the balance sheet.

Other disclosures

The following should also be disclosed for financial instruments:

(1)   Significant incomes, expenses, gains and losses resulting from financial assets and liabilities whether included in the performance statements or on the balance sheet. In particular, the following should be disclosed:

- total interest income and interest expense for financial assets and liabilities not designated as held for trading (historic cost basis);
- for financial assets that are available for sale, the amount of any gain or loss recognised directly in the performance statement during the period; and
- the amount of any interest income accrued on impaired loans.

(2) If the entity has sold or transferred a financial asset, but it does not qualify for derecognition in full or in part:
- the nature of the assets transferred;
- the nature of the continuing involvement in the assets transferred;
- the extent of such transfers; and
- information about the risks retained in any portion of a transferred asset that the transferor continues to recognise.

(3) If the entity has entered into a securitisation agreement and has a continuing involvement in all or a portion of the securitised financial assets at the balance sheet date, for each major asset type:
- the nature of the assets transferred;
- the extent of such transactions, including quantitative information about the key assumptions used in calculating fair values; and
- the total principal amount outstanding, any portion derecognised and the portion that continues to be recognised;

(4) If IAS 39 forces the entity to reclassify a financial asset at cost rather than at fair value, the reason for that reclassification.

(5) The nature and amount of any impairment loss recognised for a financial asset, separately for each significant class.

(6) The carrying amount of financial assets pledged as collateral for liabilities, the carrying amount of financial assets pledged as collateral for contingent liabilities, and any significant terms and conditions relating to pledged assets.

(7) When an entity has accepted collateral:
- the fair value of collateral that it is permitted to sell or repledge in the absence of default;
- the fair value of collateral that it has sold and has an obligation to return; and
- any significant terms and conditions associated with its use of collateral.

(8) If the entity has designated non-derivative financial liabilities as held for trading, the difference between their carrying amount and the amount the entity would be contractually required to pay to the holders of the obligations at maturity.

(9) If the entity has issued an instrument containing both a liability and an equity amount and the instrument has multiple embedded derivative features whose values are interdependent, the existence of these features and the effective yield on the liability element.

(10) With respect to defaults of principal, interest, sinking fund, or redemption provisions during the period on loans payable recognised at the balance sheet date, and any other breaches during the period of loan agreements when those breaches can permit the lender to demand repayment:
- details of those breaches;
- the amount recognised at the balance sheet date in respect of loans payable on which the breaches occurred; and
- with respect to amounts disclosed above, whether the default has been remedied or the terms of the loans payable renegotiated before the date the financial statements were authorised for issue.

An excellent example of the required disclosure required by IAS 32 is provided by Rexam Plc. Particularly note the narrative disclosure required on the overall risks and strategies devised by the company to meet those risks:

Rexam Plc   Year Ended 31 December 2005

Notes to the Accounts (Extract)

16. Available for Sale Financial Assets

	2005 (£m)	2004 (£m)
At 1 January	–	–
Adaption of IAS 32 and IAS 39	28	–
Exchange differences	3	–
Income for the year	1	–
Transfers	(2)	–
At 31 December	30	–
Non-current assets	26	–
Current assets	4	–
	30	–

Available for sale financial assets at 31 December 2005 include £25 million of investments used to satisfy certain pension obligations, of which £21 million comprises listed investments, the fair value of which are determined directly by reference to published price quotations in an active market, and £4 million comprises cash and cash equivalents. Also included in available for sale financial assets at 31 December 2005 are life insurance policies of £3 million and unlisted investments of £2 million.

23. Derivative Financial Instruments

	2005 (£m)	2004 (£m)
Non-current assets	92	90
Current assets	43	11
	135	101
Current liabilities	(20)	(2)
Total derivative financial instruments	115	99

See Notes 24 and 25 for further details of derivative financial instruments.

24. Financial Instruments – 2005

(i)   Financial risk management

Rexam's financial risk management is based upon sound economic objectives and good corporate practice. Derivative financial instruments are used to manage trading exposures, liabilities and assets under parameters laid down by the Board of Directors and are monitored by its Finance Committee. Derivatives financial instruments are used as economic hedges to manage interest rate, foreign exchange and commodity risks. Rexam has not used derivatives for purposes other than for hedging. Hedge accounting treatment has not been applied, following the adoption of IFRS, to all hedging activities due in part to the onerous level of compliance required under IAS 39. All derivative financial instruments are measured at fair value at each balance sheet date.

The Group's major operational hedging activities, mainly associated with the European beverage can operation, comply with IFRS hedge accounting requirements. For the smaller trading exposures in its other businesses, Rexam has derivative hedges which are effective from an economic standpoint, but where hedge accounting has not been applied. Fair value gains and losses on these hedges are recognised in the consolidated income statement at each reporting date. The income statement volatility resulting from these exposures is not significant.

Rexam has entered into interest rate swap transactions to fix its US dollar interest payments. These US dollar interest rate swaps hedge floating interest payable on sterling to US dollar cross currency swap associated with Rexam's issue of £250 million sterling medium-term notes in 2002. These medium-term notes were subsequently swapped into US dollars as a cost efficient way of raising US dollar bond debt at the time of issue. The interest rate swaps fail to get hedge accounting treatment under IAS 39 as they are hedging other derivatives. Fair value gains and losses on these interest rate swaps have to be taken to the consolidated income statement at each reporting date. The amount taken to the consolidated income statement each year will be determined by movements in US dollar interest rates on bonds and swaps with equivalent maturities, which can neither be predicted nor, under current IFRS rules, managed. The swaps continue to fulfil their original objective of fixing part of the Group's US dollar interest cash payments, even though the IFRS accounting treatment means that there is associated volatility in the consolidated income statement.

When the fixed euro medium-term notes were issued in 2002, they were immediately swapped to floating rates, so as to maintain the balance between fixed and floating rates. Rexam then entered into interest rate swap transactions to fix a part of its euro interest payments. Under IFRS, these two sets of interest rate swaps, entered into at different times and at different rates, are now effectively offsetting the volatility each would otherwise generate, whilst the fixed rate notes provide the fixed rate level of funding sought.

In 2005 there was a net gain of £9 million on financing derivatives recorded within interest in the consolidated income statement. This comprised a £5 million gain on the US dollar interest rate swaps, a £6 million gain on the offsetting euro interest rate swaps and a £2 million loss on other cross currency swaps.

Interest rate risk

The objective of interest rate risk management is to reduce the Group's exposure to the effects of rising short-term interest rates. Its effect is to fix the interest cash flows, using interest rate swaps, for a significant part of the Group's borrowings. The interest rate risk profile of the Group is set out in [iv] below.

The issue of longer-term borrowings through the MTN programme is a key element of the Group's debt and financial risk management process. Fixed rate MTNs, in sterling (£250m) and euros (euros 550m) were issued in 2002 to meet strong investor demand for public issuance in those currencies, which helped the pricing of the notes issued. However, the Group's fixed to floating rate debt proportions were relatively high at that time and its own funding needs were for floating rate euros and US dollars. To satisfy both investor demand and meet its own funding needs, the Group entered into a series of swap transactions simultaneously with the pricing of the notes. A further MTN issue of £ 120 million was made in February 2003 and, again simultaneous to issue, it was swapped into floating rate US dollar interest rates to its maturity. Additional smaller private issues of MTNs have been made in response to investor enquiries Most of these notes have been issued at floating rates to fit more readily into the Group's funding profile. This has enabled the Group to continue to manage the fixed to floating rate proportion of its borrowings and the duration of the fixed rate borrowings independently of the sourcing of the funding.

Interest rate swaps have been used to fix a proportion of the US dollar interest paid by the Group. These interest rate swaps cannot be treated as hedges under IFRS rules, so fair value gains and losses are recognised in the consolidated income statement.

Refinancing risk

It is the Group's policy to maintain a range of maturity dates for its borrowings, and to refinance them at the appropriate time so as to reduce refinancing risk. The Group also has a committed syndicated bank facility of £775 million, reduced from £875 million at 31 December 2004, due in 2010.

Foreign exchange translation risk

With substantially all of the Group's businesses located outside the United Kingdom, and therefore with net assets denominated in foreign currencies, hedging the consolidated balance sheet position is very important. The translation of foreign currency net assets does not affect their underlying local currency value but does affect their sterling value for reporting in the consolidated financial statements. The Group has its borrowings largely denominated in foreign currencies, which, with the use of forward foreign exchange (FX) contracts and cross currency swaps, provide hedges for its foreign currency net assets. These amounts are included in the consolidated financial statements by translation into sterling at the reporting date and, where hedge accounted, offset in equity against the translation movements in net assets.

Interest expenses, which mirrors the currency denomination of borrowings, is also largely in foreign currencies and acts as a partial hedge on the income earned by overseas businesses. In addition, income of overseas businesses is translated in the consolidated financial statements at the average FX rates, for the year, and provides some protection against volatility.

As well as hedging net assets this strategy helps protect gearing and borrowing covenant ratios against adverse currency movements.

Foreign exchange transaction risk

A number of the Group's businesses are involved in cross border trade transactions which inevitably introduce currency risks related to FX movements. Where appropriate, hedging strategies using forward FX contracts and other derivatives are put in place for managing these exposures. The Group usually hedges a higher proportion of the nearer term currency exposures than the expected, but not contractually committed, sales or purchases to be made further into the future. This active management of risk means that more cover is taken out when exchange rates are judged to be favourable or to protect against increased risk.

Longer-term FX contracts have been entered into to hedge future sales and purchasing contracts of the European beverage can operation. As a result, a proportion of FX hedges extend beyond the end of 2006 into 2007 and 2008.

None of the FX derivative financial instruments at 31 December 2005 related to derivative trading activity, although some fair value gains and losses were taken to the consolidated income statement because IFRS hedge accounting was not applied. FX derivative contracts are used for hedging general business exposures in foreign currencies such as the purchase and sale of goods, capital expenditure and dividend flows. Where IFRS hedge accounting treatment is obtained, gains or losses on the derivative hedges are held in equity and only recognised in the consolidated income statement when the losses or gains on the hedged transactions are recognised in the consolidated income statement.

Commodity risk

The objective of commodity risk management is to identify those businesses that have exposures to commodities traded on commodity markets and to then determine which, if any, commodity market instruments are appropriate for hedging those exposures. To manage such exposures, the Group uses mainly over the counter instruments transacted with banks, which are themselves priced through a recognised commodity exchange such as the London Metal Exchange. In addition, the Group makes use of physical supply contracts which effectively pass commodity risks through to customers.

Rexam manages the purchase of certain raw materials, including aluminium and energy costs through physical supply contracts which, in the main, relate directly to commodity price indices. The supply contracts can be hedged with appropriate derivative contracts to fix and manage costs. The derivative hedge contracts may extend over several years. Usually a higher proportion of short-term exposures are hedged than those further forward. The extent of the forward cover taken is judged according to market conditions and prices of futures prevailing at the time. At 31 December 2005, hedges were in place with maturities in 2006, with lesser amounts hedged into 2007 and 2008.

None of the commodity derivative financial instruments at 31 December 2005 was related to derivative trading activity, although some fair value gains and losses were taken to the consolidated income statements because IFRS hedge accounting was not applied. The commodity hedges relate to contracted and expected future purchases of aluminium and energy. Where IFRS hedge accounting treatment is obtained, gains or losses on the derivative hedges are held in equity and recognised in the consolidated income statement when the losses or gains on the hedged transactions are recognised in the consolidated income statement.

Embedded derivatives

As part of the implementation of IFRS, contracts were reviewed to identify any embedded derivatives which are required to be separately accounted for. Certain supply contracts entered into by Group companies include embedded derivatives, used as part of the pricing mechanisms agreed with customers or suppliers. These embedded derivatives cannot be reported as being part of a hedging relationship, so fair value gains and losses are taken to the consolidated income statement. The effect of fair valuing these embedded derivatives is generally to recognise at the reporting date the impact, at current prices, of the pricing mechanism's embedded derivatives on the expected future supplies to be made under the contracts, even where a contract is in profit or would not otherwise require its future financial effects to be recognised.

(ii) Carrying amount and fair value of financial assets and liabilities at 31 December 2005:

	Carrying amount (£m)	Fair value (£m)
Financial assets		
Cash and cash equivalents	87	87
Available for sale financial assets	30	30
Derivative financial instruments	135	135
Financial liabilities		
Borrowings:		
Bank overdrafts	(91)	(91)
Bank loans	(369)	(369)
Medium-term notes	(815)	(845)
Finance leases	(36)	(38)
Convertible preference shares	(70)	(76)
Derivatives financial instruments	(20)	(20)

Market values have been used to determine the fair values of cash and cash equivalents, available for sale financial assets, cross currency swaps and bank borrowings.

The fair value of the medium-term notes has been determined by references to their quoted market prices at the close of businesses on 31 December 2005. The fair value of the convertible preference shares has been determined using a market rate for an equivalent non-convertible bond. The fair values of interest rate swaps, fixed rate loans and finance leases have been determined by discounting their cash flows at prevailing interest rates. The fair value of forward foreign exchange contracts has been determined by marking those contracts to market against prevailing forward foreign exchange rates. The fair value of forward aluminium commodity contracts has been determined by marking those contracts to market at prevailing forward aluminium prices. The fair value of embedded derivatives was calculated using valuation models incorporating market commodity prices and foreign exchange rates.

(iii)   Hedging activities

The net fair values of the Group's derivative financial instruments at 31 December 2005 designated, as hedging instruments are set out below.

	Non-hedge accounted	Fair value hedges	Cash flow hedges	Net investment hedges	Total
	£m	£m	£m	£m	£m
Derivative financial instruments					
Interest rate swaps	(8)	8	–	–	–
Cross currency swaps	4	64	–	6	74
Forward foreign exchange contracts	1	–	4	–	5
Forward aluminium commodity contracts	1	–	41	–	42
Embedded derivatives	(6)	–	–	–	(6)
	(8)	72	45	6	115

The fair values of the Group's non-derivative financial instruments at 31 December 2005 designated as hedging instruments are set out below.

	Net investment hedges (£m)
Bank loans	(106)
Medium-term notes	(410)
	(516)

Derivative financial instruments not hedge accounted

At 31 December 2005, the Group had interest rate swaps with principal amounts of euro 510 million and $356 million, whereby interest is payable at fixed interest rates varying from 3.8% to 4.7%, and interest rate swaps with principal amounts of euro 510 million and Czech Krone 150 million, whereby interest is receivable at fixed interest rates varying from 2.7% to 4.3%. These interest rate swaps all settle against the appropriate prevailing LIBOR rate, in some cases adjusted by a margin. The interest rate swaps mature between 2007 and 2009. At 31 December 2005, the Group had cross currency swaps of sterling for US dollars with principal amounts of £95 million and $159 million, whereby interest is payable and receivable at floating rates adjusted by a margin. The cross currency swaps mature between 2006 and 2009. At 31 December 2005, the Group had forward foreign exchange contracts with principal amounts equivalent to £198 million that mature between 2006 and 2007. At 31 December 2005, the Group had forward aluminium commodity contracts with principal amounts of $34 million that mature between 2006 and 2007. At 31 December 2005, the Group had embedded derivatives with principal amounts equivalent to £45 million representing metal price and foreign exchange derivatives within customer and supplier contracts that are due to expire over the next three years.

Fair value hedges

At 31 December 2005, the Group had an interest rate swap contract with a principal amount of £120 million, whereby interest is receivable at a fixed rate of 7.1% and payable at a floating rate plus a margin. At 31 December 2005, the Group had cross currency swaps which are separated for accounting purposes into interest rate swaps and cross currency swaps. The interest rate swaps element has a principal amount of £250 million, whereby interest is receivable at a fixed rate of 7.1% and payable at floating sterling UBCR plus a margin. The cross currency swaps element has principal amounts of $356 million and £250 million, whereby interest is payable and receivable at floating rates plus a margin. The £120 million interest rate swaps and £250 million interest rate swaps element referred to above both hedge the exposure to changes in the fair value of £370 million of medium-term notes and mature in 2009. The cross currency swaps element referred to above hedge changes in the fair value of US dollar intercompany loans and mature in 2009.

Cash flow hedges

At 31 December 2005, the Group had forward foreign exchange contracts and forward aluminium commodity contracts with principal amounts equivalent to £135 million and $282 million, respectively. The forward foreign exchange contracts and forward aluminium commodity contracts hedge the foreign currency and commodity price risks, respectively, of anticipated future purchases of aluminium. The associated fair value gains and losses will be transferred to inventory when the purchases occur over the next three years. During the year, certain forecast purchases of aluminium were no longer expected to occur and cash flow hedge accounting discontinued, resulting in recognition of a gain of £1 million in the consolidated income statement.

Net investment hedges

At 31 December 2005, the Group has borrowed amounts denominated in euros and US dollars of, euro 703 million and $121 million, which it has designated as hedges of net investments in its subsidiaries in the Eurozone and the United States. The amounts borrowed under the cross currency swaps mature in 2009.

(iv) Interest rate risk

The following tables set out the carrying amount, by maturity, of the Group's non-derivative financial instruments that are exposed to interest rate risk at 31 December 2005.

	Effective interest rate (%)	Within 1 year £m	1 to 2years £m	2 to 3 years £m	3 to 4 years £m	4 to 5 years £m	More than 5 years £m	Total carrying amount £m
Fixed rate								
Bank loans	4.6	(3)	(1)	(1)	–	–	–	(5)
Medium-term notes	6.9	(40)	(388)	–	(370)	–	–	(798)
Finance leases	7.5	(16)	(7)	(3)	(1)	(1)	(1)	(29)
Convertible preference shares	8.0	–	–	–	–	–	(70)	(70)
		(59)	(396)	(4)	(371)	(1)	(71)	(902)
Fixed rate								
Cash and cash equivalents		87	–	–	–	–	–	87
Bank overdrafts		(91)	–	–	–	–	–	(91)
Bank loans		(4)	(3)	(3)	(3)	(339)	(12)	(364)
Medium-term notes		(10)	–	(7)	–	–	–	(17)
Finance leases		–	–	(7)	–	–	–	(7)
		(18)	(3)	(17)	(3)	(339)	(12)	(392)

Cash at bank earns interest at floating rates based on daily bank deposit rates in the relevant currency. Short-term deposits are made for varying periods of between one day and three months depending on the immediate cash requirements of the Group and they earn interest at the respective short-term deposit rates. Other floating rate financial instruments above are at the appropriate UBOR interest rates as adjusted by variable margins. Interest on floating rate financial instruments is re-priced at intervals of less than one year. Interest on fixed rate financial instruments is fixed until maturity of the instrument.

The effect of interest rate swaps and cross currency swaps, including principal amounts only, is to modify the amounts and interest rates of medium-term notes as set out below.

	Effective interest rate (%)	Within 1 year £m	1 to 2 years £m	2 to 3 years £m	3 to 4 years £m	4 to 5 years £m	More than 5 years £m	Total carrying amount £m
Fixed rate	7.2	(40)	(384)	–	(205)	–	–	(629)
Floating rate		(10)	(4)	(7)	(111)	–	–	(132)
Medium-term notes after effects of hedging		(50)	(388)	(7)	(316)	–	–	(761)
Principal amounts of cross currency swaps		–	–	–	(54)	–	–	(54)
Medium-term notes before effects of hedging		(50)	(388)	(7)	(370)	–	–	(815)

(v)   Currency risk

Non-derivative financial instruments that create potentially significant currency exposures, since they are denominated in currencies other than the functional currency of the entities which hold them, are set out below.

	£m
Borrowings denominated in Brazilian reais by entities in Brazil with a US dollar functional currency	(25)
Borrowings denominated in US dollars by an entity in Sweden	(13)
Borrowings denominated in sterling by an entity in the United Kingdom with a euro functional currency	(5)
Cash denominated in local currencies held by entities in South America with a US dollar functional currency	13
Intercompany deposit denominated in US dollars by an entity in the United Kingdom with a euro functional currency	34

In addition, there are minor balances in currency bank accounts held by various entities for operational reasons as well as instruments in local currency hedged back to the entity's functional currency and currency borrowings used to fund loans to overseas subsidiaries in their functional currency or to provide net investment hedges. These financial instruments do not generate significant currency exposures.

(vi)   Credit risk

The maximum credit risk exposure of the Group's financial assets at 31 December 2005 is represented by the amounts reported under the corresponding balance sheet headings. There is no significant concentration of credit risk associated with financial instruments of the Group.

(vii)   Collateral

Included within borrowings are secured loans of £1 million the security for which is principally property.

12.2   IAS 39 *Financial Instruments: Recognition and Measurement* (revised 2003)

Objective

To establish principles for recognising and measuring financial assets and liabilities.

Scope

IAS 39 applies to all financial instruments giving a true and fair view and prepared under fair value accounting.

It applies to all types of financial instruments except:

(a)   Interest in subsidiaries, quasi-subsidiaries and associated undertakings. Those investments, however, held exclusively with a view to subsequent disposal are included;
(b)   Leases under IAS 17.
(c)   Employers rights and obligations under IAS 19.
(d)   Insurance contracts but is to derivatives embedded in insurance contracts.
(e)   Equity instruments issued by the entity including options and warrants.
(f)   Financial guarantee contracts including letters of credit made to reimburse the holder for a loss it incurs because a specified debtor fails to pay.
(g)   Contracts for contingent consideration in a business combination.
(h)   Contracts that require a payment based on climatic, geological or other physical variables as the payout is unrelated to the amount of an insured entity's loss.
(i)   Loan commitments that cannot be settled net in cash.

Sometimes a 'strategic investment' is made and, if under IAS 28/31, the equity method is not applied then the entity must apply IAS 39. It must also be applied to contracts to buy or sell a non-financial item that can be settled net in cash. An exception is that contracts entered into for the purpose of receipt or delivery of a non-financial item in accordance with the entity's expected purchase, sale or usage requirements.

Definitions

Most of the key definitions are covered in IAS 32. However a number of other definitions are also provided.

- *Derivative*. A financial instrument with all three of the following characteristics:
  (1)   Its value changes in response to the change in an underlying specified interest rate, security price, commodity price and foreign exchange rate;
  (2)   It requires no initial net investment or an initial net investment that is smaller than would be expected to changes in market factors;
  (3)   It is settled at a future date.

Financial instruments

Financial asset or liability at fair value through profit or loss (held for trading)

A financial instrument is classified as at fair value through profit or loss:

(a)   is acquired or incurred principally for the purpose of selling or repurchasing it in the near future;
(b)   is part of a portfolio of identified financial instruments that are managed together and for which there is evidence of a recent actual pattern of short-term profit-taking; or
(c)   is a derivative, except if used as a hedging instrument.

Held to maturity investments

Financial assets with fixed or determinable payments and fixed maturity that an entity has positive intent and ability to hold to maturity other than those the entity elects to designate as held for trading or meets the definition of loans and receivables.

Loans and receivables originated by the entity

Financial assets created by the entity to provide money, goods or services directly to a debtor other than:

(i)   those originated with the intent of sale immediately or in the short term and

(ii) designated as held for trading.

Available for sale financial assets

Financial assets that are not classified as:

(a)   loans and receivables originated by the entity;

(b)   held to maturity investments; or

(c)   held for trading.

Some examples of these instruments and their measurement rules are provided in the financial statements of Gallaher Plc as follows:

Gallaher Group Plc   Year Ended 31 December 2005

Accounting Policies (Extract)

Financial instruments are reported and measured in accordance with IAS 32 and IAS 39, respectively. Financial instruments comprise: non-derivative financial assets and liabilities, including cash, deposits and borrowings; and financial derivatives, whose value changes in line with movements in market rates. The Group uses derivative financial instruments to hedge exposure to interest rate and foreign exchange risks arising from operational, financing and investment activities. In accordance with its treasury policy, the Group does not hold or issue derivative financial instruments for trading purposes.

Non-derivative financial assets are classified as either loans and receivables, cash and cash equivalents or financial assets held at fair value through profit and loss.

Financial assets held at fair value through profit and loss are stated at their market value and changes in this value are taken to the income statement. Financial assets held at fair value principally comprise listed securities held as collateral for pension and excise duty obligations. All other financial assets are stated at the lower of their initial cost (including any transaction costs and accrued interest receivable) and their estimated recoverable amount. Cash and cash equivalents include cash in hand; deposits held on call with banks, other short-term highly liquid investments and accrued interest income thereon. Bank overdrafts are included within borrowings in current liabilities on the balance sheet.

Non-derivative financial liabilities include borrowings and finance leases. They are stated at their redeemable value, including accrued interest payable, less transaction costs that have not yet been recognised in the income statement.

Where the change in value of a financial liability or financial asset, due to the movement in market interest rates, has been hedged with financial derivatives, its value is adjusted for the change in market value due to the financial risk being hedged. Where such fair value hedging relationships exist, the changed value of the liability or asset being hedged should broadly offset the change in market value of the hedging instrument and any difference is recognised immediately in the income statement.

Derivative financial instruments are stated at their market value in the balance sheet and are classified as current assets or liabilities, unless they form part of a hedging relationship, where their classification follows the classification of the hedged financial asset or liability. Changes in the market value of derivative financial instruments are recognised immediately in the income statements, unless the derivative is designated as a hedge of a net investment in a foreign operation and comprises the cost of the investment, long-term intra-Group in value are taken direct to equity. A net investment in a foreign operation comprises the cost of the investment. Long-term intro-group receivables and payables that are not intended to be settled,are post-acquisition reserves. Where non-derivatives such as foreign currency borrowings are designated as net investment hedges, the relevant exchange differences are similarly taken to equity. Where gains and losses have been taken direct to equity, the accumulated gain or loss is subsequently transferred to the income statement in the same period in which the foreign operation is sold or otherwise disposed of.

Definitions relating to measurement

- *Amortised cost of a financial asset or liability.* The initial recognition minus principal repayments, plus or minus the cumulative amortisation using the effective interest method and minus any write-down for impairment.
- *Effective interest method.* A method of calculating amortised cost using the effective interest rate of a financial asset or liability. It is the rate that exactly discounts future cash payments or receipts through maturity or the next market-based repricing date to the net carrying amount of the financial asset or liability. The computation includes all fees and the rate is based on the estimated stream of cash receipts. The effective rate is sometimes termed the level yield to maturity or next repricing.
- *Transaction costs.* Incremental external costs directly attributable to the acquisition or disposal of a financial asset or liability.
- *Firm commitment.* A binding agreement for the exchange of a specified quantity of resources at a specified price on a specified future date or dates.

Definitions relating to hedge accounting

- *Hedged item.* An asset, liability or commitment that exposes the entity to risk of changes in fair value or future cash flows and is designated as being hedged.
- *Hedging instrument.* A designated derivative whose fair value or cash flows are expected to offset changes in the fair value of a hedged item.
- *Hedging effectiveness.* The degree to which offsetting changes in fair value or cash flows attributable to a hedged risk are achieved by the hedging instrument.

Elaboration on the definitions

Derivatives

Typical examples are futures and forward, swap and option contracts. It usually has a notional amount but the holder is not required to invest or receive the notional amount at the inception of the contract. Alternatively a derivative could require a fixed payment as a result of some future event unrelated to a notional amount, e.g. a fixed payment of 1,000 if six-month LIBOR increases by 100 basis points.

It includes contracts that are settled gross by delivery of the underlying item. It may have a contract to buy or sell non-financial items that can be settled net in cash.

One of the defining characteristics of a derivative is that it has an initial net investment that is smaller than would be required for other types of contracts. An option qualifies as the premium is less than the investment that would be required to obtain the underlying financial instrument to which the option is linked. A currency swap also qualifies as it has a zero initial net investment. Forward contracts also meet the definition.

Transaction costs

Fees and commissions paid to agents; levies by regulatory authorities and transfer taxes and duties. However they do not include debt premiums or discounts and any financing or internal administration expenses.

Financial assets and financial liabilities at fair value through profit or loss (held for trading)

These are used with the objective of generating a profit from short-term price fluctuations. However, designated trading items are not precluded simply because the entity does not intend to sell or repurchase in the near future. Under IAS 39 any financial instrument may be designated initially as 'Financial assets and financial liabilities at fair value through profit or loss (held for trading)'.

Financial liabilities held for trading include:

(a)   derivative liabilities not accounted for as hedging instruments;
(b)   obligations to deliver securities borrowed by a short seller;
(c)   financial liabilities incurred with an intention to repurchase them in the near future;
(d)   financial liabilities that are part of a portfolio managed together and for which there is evidence of a recent actual pattern of short-term profit trading; and
(e)   other financial liabilities designated as held for trading.

If an entity elects to designate as 'held for trading' instruments that are not for short-term profit then it should present them as 'available for sale' rather than as 'held for trading'.

Loans and receivables originated by the entity

An acquisition of an interest in a pool of loans/receivables, e.g. securitisation, is a purchase not an origination as the entity did not provide money, goods or services directly to the underlying debtors. In addition, a transaction that is, in substance, a purchase of a loan that was previously originated is not a loan originated by the entity. A loan acquired by an entity in a business combination is regarded as originated provided it was similarly classified by the acquired entity.

Any financial asset with fixed or determinable payments could potentially meet the definition. However financial assets quoted in an active market do not qualify. In addition, financial assets that are purchased by an entity after origination are not classified as loans or receivables originated by the entity. If they do not meet the definition they may be classified as 'held to maturity investments' if they meet the conditions for that classification.

Embedded derivatives

These are components of hybrid instruments that also include non-derivative host contracts. A derivative that is attached to a financial instrument but is contractually transferable independently is not an embedded derivative, but a separate financial instrument. IAS 39 does not address whether an embedded derivative shall be presented separately on the face of the financial statements.

An embedded derivative shall be separated from the host contract and accounted for as a derivative under IAS 39 if, and only if, all of the following conditions are met:

(a) The economic characteristics and risks of the embedded derivative are not closely related to those of the host contract.
(b) A separate instrument with the same terms as the embedded derivative would meet the definition of a derivative.
(c) The hybrid is not measured at fair value with changes in fair value reported in profit or loss.

If an embedded derivative is separated, the host contract should be accounted for under IAS 39 if it is a financial instrument.

If an entity is required to separate an embedded derivative from its host contract but is unable to measure the embedded derivative then it shall treat the entire combined contract as a financial instrument held for trading.

Measurement

Initial measurement of financial assets and financial liabilities

When a financial asset/liability is recognised initially an entity should measure it at cost which is the fair value of consideration given or received. Transaction costs that are directly attributable are included in the initial measurement.

Fair value should be referenced to the transaction price or other market prices. If these are not available then fair value should be the sum of all future cash payments/receipts discounted using prevailing market rates for similar instruments.

Subsequent measurement of financial assets

After initial recognition, an entity should measure financial assets at fair value without deduction for transaction costs, except for:

(a) loans and receivables originated by the entity must be measured at amortised cost using the effective interest method;

(b)   held to maturity investments must be measured at amortised cost using the effective interest method;

(c)   investments in equity instruments that do not have a quoted market price in an active market and whose fair value cannot be reliably measured, and derivatives linked to and settled by delivery of such unquoted equity instruments, must be measured at cost.

Financial assets designated as hedged items are subject to hedge accounting and all financial assets, other than those fair valued, are subject to impairment review.

If a financial asset is measured at fair value and its fair value is below zero then it should be accounted for as a financial liability.

EXAMPLE

Assume an asset is acquired for 100 + commissions of 2. Initially the asset should be recognised at 102. Next year the market price is 100 but a commission of 3 would be paid, thus the asset is measured at 100 and a loss of 2 reported in profit and loss.

Loans and receivables originated by an entity are measured at amortised cost without any regard to the entity's intention to hold them until maturity.

For floating rate financial assets, periodic re-estimation of cash flows to reflect movements in market rates should take place with any changes therein being recognised over the remaining term of the asset or the period to the next repricing date.

Held to maturity investments

An entity does not have a positive intention to hold to maturity a financial asset if ANY one of the following conditions is met:

(a)   the entity intends to hold the asset for an undefined period;

(b)   the entity stands ready to sell the asset in response to interest rate changes, liquidity needs, changes in yield on alternative investments or changes in foreign exchange risk; or

(c)   the issuer has a right to settle at an amount significantly below its amortised cost.

Most equity securities cannot be said as being 'held to maturity', either due to their indefinite life or because the amount a holder may receive can vary. Similarly if the terms of a perpetual debt instrument provide for interest for an indefinite period then that instrument cannot be classified as 'held to maturity' as there is no maturity date.

A financial asset that is puttable cannot be classified as 'held to maturity' as this is inconsistent with an intention to hold until maturity.

Any financial assets, which an entity has sold or reclassified more than an insignificant amount of, held to maturity investments during the year or previous two years may not be classified as held for maturity. However, a number of exceptions exist:

(a)   sales/reclassifications so close to maturity that changes in market rates would not significantly affect the asset's fair value;

(b)   sales/reclassifications occurring after the entity has already collected substantially all of the asset's original principal (e.g. 90%); or

(c)   sales/reclassifications due to an isolated event beyond the entity's control, is nonrecurring and could not have reasonably anticipated by the entity.

Fair value is more appropriate than amortised cost for most financial assets. However 'held to maturity' is an exception but only if the entity has a positive intention to hold the investment to maturity.

A 'disaster scenario', e.g. run on a bank, is not an event that should be considered in deciding whether or not there is a positive intention to hold to maturity.

Sales before maturity do not raise a question about 'intention to hold' if they are due to:

(a)   a significant deterioration in the issuer's credit worthiness, e.g. sale following a downgrade in credit rating;

(b)   a change in tax law eliminating or significantly reducing the tax exempt status of interest;

(c)   a major business combination necessitating the sale or transfer of held to maturity investments to maintain the entity's existing interest rate risk position or credit risk policy;

(d)   a change in statutory requirements causing an entity to dispose of a held to maturity investment;

(e)   a significant increase in capital needs causing the entity to downsize by selling 'held to maturity' investments; or

(f)   a significant increase in the risk weights of 'held to maturity' investments used for regulatory risk based capital purposes.

An entity does not have an ability to 'hold to maturity' a financial asset if either of the following conditions is met:

(a)   it does not have the financial resources to continue to finance until maturity or

(b)   it is subject to existing legal constraints that could frustrate its intention to hold the asset to maturity.

There could be other circumstances that do not have a positive intention to hold to maturity and an entity needs to assess its intention, not only when initially recognised but also at each subsequent balance sheet date.

Subsequent measurement of financial liabilities

After initial recognition, an entity should measure all financial liabilities other than those held for trading and derivatives, at amortised cost using the effective interest rate method. Financial liabilities held for trading and fair value derivatives, except for a derivative liability linked to and settled by delivery of an unquoted equity instrument whose fair value cannot be reliably measured, should be kept at cost. Financial liabilities designated as hedged items are subject to separate hedge accounting rules.

Reclassifications

Because the designation of a financial asset/liability held for trading is made on initial recognition, an entity shall not reclassify a financial instrument into or out of trading while it is held.

If it is no longer appropriate to carry a 'held to maturity' investment at amortised cost, it should be reclassified into the 'available for sale' category and remeasured at fair value, with any difference between carrying amount and fair value accounted for in accordance with fair value measurement considerations.

Similarly, if a reliable measure becomes available for a financial asset/liability for which there was no previously available fair value then it should be remeasured at fair value and the difference accounted for in accordance with fair value measurement considerations.

If, due to a change in intention, a reliable measure is no longer available or two preceding years have passed, it is appropriate to carry a financial asset at cost or amortised cost rather than at fair value with the fair value on that date becoming its new cost. If a previous gain or loss has gone directly to the equity statement, no adjustment should be made on the reclassification of the financial asset.

Fair value measurement considerations

In determining the fair value, an entity should presume that it is a going concern and is not to be valued as a forced transaction.

Active market: Quoted price

The existence of published price quotations in an active market is the best evidence of fair value and this is usually the current bid price. When current bid prices are unavailable, the price of the most recent transaction is sufficient evidence provided that there has not been a significant change in economic circumstances between the transaction date and the reporting date. If a published price quotation in an active market does not exist in its entirety, but active markets exist for its component parts, fair value is determined on the basis of relevant market prices for its component parts.

No active market: Unquoted price

If the market is not active, the best evidence of fair value is recent market transactions between willing parties in an arm's length transaction.

No active market: Valuation technique

If an entity has to use a valuation technique to assess fair value. This must:

(a)   incorporate all factors to be considered in setting a price and
(b)   be consistent with accepted economic theory for pricing.

Valuation techniques that are well established include reference to the current market value of another instrument that is substantially the same, discounted cash flow analysis and option pricing models.

If a measure is used commonly to price instruments then that measure should be adopted.

In applying discounted cash flow analysis, the discount rate should be equal to the prevailing rate of return for instruments having substantially the same terms and characteristics, including the creditworthiness of the debtor, the remaining term and the currency in which payments are made. When the terms extend beyond the period for which market prices are available, the valuation technique uses current market prices and extrapolates those prices for later periods.

The initial acquisition or origination of a financial asset or incurrence of a financial liability is a market transaction that provides a foundation for estimating fair value. A debt instrument can be valued by referring to the market conditions that existed at its acquisition or origination date and current market conditions or interest rates.

Alternatively, provided there is no change in credit risk, an estimate of the current market interest rate may be derived by using a benchmark interest rate reflecting a better credit quality than the underlying debt instrument and adjusting for the change in the benchmark interest rate from the origination date.

No active market: Equity instruments

For equity instruments, with no quoted market prices and which must be settled by delivery of an unquoted equity instrument, a reliable measure can be found if:

(a) the variability in the range of reasonable fair value estimates is not significant or
(b) the probabilities can be reasonably assessed.

Gains and losses

A recognised gain or loss arising from a change in fair value of a financial asset/liability that is not part of a hedging relationship should be recognised as follows:

(a) A gain or loss on a financial asset/liability held for trading should be recognised in profit or loss for the period in which it arises.
(b) A gain or loss on an available for sale financial asset should be recognised in the change in equity statement. However the amortisation charge, using the effective interest method, of any difference between the amount initially recognised and the maturity amount represents interest and is recognised in profit or loss.

For financial assets and liabilities carried at amortised cost, a gain or loss is recognised in profit or loss when the financial asset/liability is derecognised or impaired, as well as through the amortisation process.

An entity should apply IAS 21 *The Effect of Changes in Foreign Exchange Rates* to monetary items denominated in a foreign currency. An exception is a derivative designated as a hedging instrument.

Where financial assets are not classified as monetary items, any changes in fair value are accounted for as per the fair value approach. If hedging exists between a non-derivative monetary asset and a non-derivative monetary liability, changes in the foreign currency component should be recognised in profit or loss.

Impairment and uncollectability of financial assets

An entity should assess, at every balance sheet date, whether there is any objective evidence that a financial asset or group of assets is impaired. If so, the entity must apply 'amortised cost' or treat them as 'available for sale financial assets'.

Objective evidence exists if:

(a)   there is significant financial difficulty for the issuer;
(b)   there is a breach of contract, e.g. default in interest or principal;
(c)   the granting by the lender to the borrower of a concession that the lender would not otherwise consider;
(d)   there is a high probability of bankruptcy of the issuer;
(e)   there is recognition of an impairment loss on that asset in a prior period;
(f)   there is the disappearance of an active market for the financial asset due to financial difficulties;
(g)   there is an historical pattern of collections of groups of financial assets indicating that the entity will not be able to collect all amounts due (principal and interest).

The disappearance of an active market is not evidence of impairment nor is a downgrade of credit rating nor a decline in the fair value of a financial asset below cost. An adverse change in the technological, market, economic or legal environment may indicate that the asset may not be recovered. A significant and prolonged decline in fair value of an equity investment below cost is also objective evidence of impairment.

Financial assets carried at amortised cost

If there is objective evidence of impairment and it is probable that an entity will not be able to collect all amounts due (principal and interest), an impairment has occurred. The loss is the difference between the asset's carrying amount and the present value of expected future cash flows discounted at the original effective interest rate. The carrying amount of the asset shall be reduced to its estimated recoverable amount either directly or through use of an allowance account. The loss should go through profit and loss.

An entity first assesses whether or not there is objective evidence of impairment, either individually or collectively. If there is no objective evidence of individual impairment the asset must be included in a group of financial assets with similar credit risk characteristics that can be collectively assessed. Assets assessed individually for impairment are not included in the collective assessment for impairment.

Impairment of a financial asset carried at amortised cost should be measured at the instrument's original effective interest rate as discounting at current market rates would impose fair value measurement. If a loan has a variable interest rate, the discount rate should be the current effective interest rate determined under the contract. As a practical expedient, a creditor may measure impairment using an observable market price.

For collective evaluation of impairment, financial assets are grouped on the basis of similar credit risk characteristics.

Impairment losses recognised on a group basis represent an interim step pending the identification of impairment losses on individual assets. As soon as information is available to identify losses individually the assets must be removed from the group.

Expected cash flows for a group should be based on the contractual cash flows of the assets in the group and historical loss experience for assets with similar risk characteristics to the group. If there is insufficient experience, entities should use peer group experiences for comparable groups. Historical loss experience is adjusted to reflect current conditions. Estimates of changes in expected cash flows reflect changes in related observable data from period to period (e.g. unemployment rates, property prices, etc). The methodology and assumptions must be reviewed regularly.

In discounting groups of financial assets, an entity uses a weighted average of the original effective interest rates of the group assets. For example, if the original contractual rate is 12% and past experience is 10%, then the original effective rate should be the expected rate of 10%.

If subsequently the impairment decreases and this can be related objectively to an event occurring after the write-down, the write-down shall be reversed either directly or by adjusting an allowance account. The reversal must not result in a carrying amount of the financial asset exceeding what the amortised cost would have been had the impairment not been recognised.

Interest income after impairment recognition

Once impaired, interest income is thereafter based on the rate of interest used to discount the future cash flows for the purpose of measuring the recoverable amount. Additionally the entity reviews the asset for further impairment.

Financial assets carried at cost

If there is objective evidence of impairment of an unquoted equity instrument that is not carried at fair value because its fair value cannot be objectively determined, the loss is the difference between the carrying amount of the asset and the present value of expected future cash flows discounted at the current market rate of interest for similar assets. Such losses shall not be reversed.

Available for sale financial assets

A decline in the fair value of an available for sale financial asset that has been recognised in the change in equity statement should not subsequently be recognised in profit and loss if and when objective evidence of impairment is discovered.

Impairment losses recognised in profit or loss should not be reversed as long as the instrument is recognised.

Hedging

Hedging instruments

Qualifying instruments

IAS 39 does not restrict the circumstances in which a derivative may be designated as a hedging instrument provided the conditions listed in (a) to (e) later are met. However, a non-derivative financial asset may be designated as a hedging instrument only for a hedge of a foreign currency risk.

The potential loss on an option could be significantly greater than the potential gain in value of a related hedged item, i.e. a written option is not effective in reducing exposure and thus does not qualify unless designated as an offset to a purchased option. In contrast, a purchased option has potential gains equal to or greater than losses and thus it has the potential to reduce profit or loss exposure from changes in fair values or cash flows. It can thus qualify.

Held to maturity investments carried at amortised cost may be effective hedging instruments with respect to risks from changes in foreign currency exchange rates.

An investment in an unquoted equity instrument that is not carried at fair value, as that value cannot be reliably measured, cannot be designated as a hedging instrument.

An entity's own equity securities cannot be designated as hedging instruments.

For hedge accounting, only derivatives involving a party external to the entity can be designated as hedging instruments. Although individual entities within a group may enter hedging transactions with other entities in the group, any gains or losses are eliminated on consolidation. Therefore intercompany hedging transactions do not qualify for hedge accounting on consolidation.

Designation of hedging instruments

Normally there is a single fair value measure for a hedging instrument in its entirety. The only exceptions permitted are:

(a)   separating the intrinsic value and the time value of an option and designating only the change in the intrinsic value of an option as the hedging instrument and

(b)   separating the interest element and the spot price on a forward contract.

These are permitted only because the intrinsic value and the premium on the forward contract can be measured separately.

A proportion of the entire hedging instrument may be designated as the hedging instrument in a hedging relationship. However, a hedging relationship may not be designated for only a portion of the time period during which the time period remains outstanding.

A single hedging instrument may be designated as a hedge of more than one type of risk provided that:

(a)   the risks hedged can be identified clearly;

(b)   the effectiveness of the hedge can be demonstrated; and

(c)   it is possible to ensure that there is specific designation of the hedging instrument and different risk positions.

Two or more derivatives may be viewed in combination. However where a written option component is combined with a purchased option it does not qualify as a hedging instrument if it is, in effect, a net written option.

Hedged tems

Qualifying items

A hedged item can be a recognised asset or liability, an unrecognised firm commitment, an uncommitted but highly probable anticipated future transaction or a net investment in a foreign operation. The hedged item can be (a) a single asset, liability and commitment or (b) a group of assets, liabilities and commitments with similar characteristics.

A held to maturity investment cannot be a hedged item with respect to interest or prepayment risk because designation requires an intention to hold the investment until maturity without regard to changes in the fair value or cash flows. It can be a hedged item, however, with respect to foreign exchange and credit risks.

A firm commitment to acquire a business in a business combination cannot be a hedged item, except for foreign exchange risk because other risks being hedged cannot be specifically identified and measured.

An equity method investment cannot be a hedged item in a fair value hedge as it recognises in profit the investor's share of the associate's accrued profit or loss, rather than fair value changes. For similar reasons, an investment in a consolidated subsidiary cannot be a hedged item in a fair value hedge.

Designation of financial items as hedged items

If the hedged item is a financial asset/liability, it may be a hedged item with respect to the risks associated with only a portion of its cash flows provided that effectiveness can be measured, e.g. an identified and separately measurable portion of the interest rate exposure of an interest bearing asset may be designated as the hedged risk.

Designation of non-financial items as hedged items

If the hedged item is a non-financial liability, it shall be designated as a hedged item either (a) for foreign currency risks or (b) in its entirety for all risks, because of the difficulty of isolating and measuring the appropriate portion of the cash flows or fair value changes attributable to specific risks other than foreign currency risks.

If there is a difference between the terms of the hedging instrument and the hedged item, e.g. hedge of the forecast purchase of Brazilian coffee using a forward contract to purchase Colombian coffee, it may qualify provided the conditions are expected to be highly effective. However, the hedging relationship might result in ineffectiveness that would be recognised in profit or loss during the term of the hedging relationship.

Designation of groups of items as hedged items

If similar assets or liabilities are aggregated and hedged as a group, the change in fair value attributable to the hedged risk for each individual item in the group is expected to be approximately proportional to the overall change in fair value attributable to the hedged risk of the group.

For example, if a bank has 100 of assets and 90 of liabilities with risks and terms of a similar nature and hedges the net 10 exposure, it can designate 10 of those assets as the hedged item. This designation can be used if at fixed rates (fair value hedge) or at variable rates (cash flow hedge).

Similarly, if an entity has a firm commitment to purchase a foreign currency of 100 and a firm commitment to make a sale in a foreign currency of 90, it can hedge the net amount of 10 by acquiring a derivative and designating it as a hedging instrument associated with 10 of the firm purchase commitment of 100.

Hedge accounting

Hedge accounting recognises the offsetting effects on profit or loss of changes in the fair values of the hedging instrument and the hedged item.

Hedging relationships are of three types:

(1) *Fair value hedge.* A hedge of the exposure to changes in fair value of a recognised asset or liability or a previously unrecognised firm commitment to buy or sell an asset at a

fixed price, or an identified portion that is attributable to a particular risk and could affect reported profit or loss.

(2) *Cash flow hedge.* A hedge of the exposure to variability in cash flows that (i) is attributable to a particular risk or a forecast transaction and (ii) could affect profit or loss.

(3) *Hedge of a net investment in a foreign operation.* These are defined in IAS 21.

An example of a fair value hedge is a hedge of exposure to changes in the fair value of fixed rate debt as a result of changes in interest rates.

An example of a cash flow hedge is the use of a swap to change floating rate debt to fixed rate debt.

A hedge of a firm commitment e.g. a hedge by an airline to purchase an aircraft for a fixed amount of a foreign currency, or a hedge of a change in fuel price relating to an unrecognised contractual commitment by an electric utility to purchase fuel at a fixed price is a hedge of an exposure to a change in fair value – thus it is accounted for as a fair value hedge.

Under IAS 39 a hedging relationship qualifies for hedge accounting if, and only if, all of the following conditions are met:

(a) At the inception of the hedge there is formal documentation of the hedging relationship and the entity's risk management objective and strategy for undertaking the hedge. That includes identifying the hedging instrument, the related hedged item, the nature of the risk being hedged and how the entity will assess the hedging instruments' effectiveness.

(b) The hedge is expected to be highly effective in achieving offsetting changes in fair value or cash flows attributable to the hedged risk.

(c) For cash flow hedges, a forecast transaction must be highly probable and present an exposure to cash flow variations that could ultimately affect reported profit or loss.

(d) The effectiveness of the hedge can be reliably measured.

(e) The hedge is assessed on an ongoing basis and determined to have been highly effective throughout the financial reporting period.

Assessing hedge effectiveness

A hedge is normally highly effective if, at inception and throughout its life, the entity can expect changes in the fair value or cash flows of the hedged item to be almost fully offset by changes in the fair value or cash flows of the hedging instrument and if actual results are within a range of 80–125%.

EXAMPLE

If the loss on the hedging instrument is 120 and the gain on the cash instrument is 100, offset can be measured by 120/100 (120%) or by 100/120 (83%). It is therefore highly effective.

The method adopted for assessing hedge effectiveness depends on its risk management strategy and there could be different methods for different types of hedges. If the terms of the hedging instrument and hedged item are the same, the changes in fair values and cash flows may be likely to offset each other, e.g. an interest rate swap is likely to be effective if the notional and principal amounts, term, repricing dates, dates of interest and principal receipts/payments and basis for measuring interest rates are the same for both hedging instrument and hedged item.

Sometimes a hedge is only partially effective, e.g. in different currencies not moving in tandem.

To qualify for hedge accounting, the hedge must relate to a specific and designated risk, not merely to overall business risks, and must ultimately affect the entity's profit or loss. A hedge of the risk of obsolescence or expropriation of property by government would not be eligible for hedge accounting, as the risks are not reliably measured.

Hedge effectiveness may be assessed by preparing a maturity schedule for financial assets and liabilities showing the net interest rate exposure for each time period. There is no single method for assessing hedge effectiveness and so an entity must document its procedures. As a minimum, effectiveness should be computed at every interim and final year end. If the critical terms are the same for both hedged instrument and hedged item then an entity could conclude that changes in fair values/cash flows are expected to offset each other fully at inception and on an ongoing basis. A forecast purchase of a commodity with a forward contract will be highly effective and there will be no ineffectiveness to be recognised in profit or loss if:

(a) the forward contract is for the purchase of the same quantity of the same commodity at the same time and location as the hedged forecast purchase;
(b) the fair value of the forward contract at inception is zero;
(c) either the change in discount/premium on the forward contract is excluded from the assessment of effectiveness and included directly in profit or loss or the change in expected cash flows on the forecast transaction is based on the forward price for the commodity.

The time value of money should be considered. There is no need for perfect matching for either fixed or variable rates between the hedging instrument and hedged item.

Fair value hedges

If a fair value hedge meets the conditions of hedging it should be accounted for as follows:

(a) The gain or loss from remeasuring the hedging instrument at fair value (for a derivative) or the foreign currency component of its carrying amount (for a non-derivative) should be recognised immediately in profit or loss.
(b) The gain or loss on the hedged item attributable to the hedged risk shall adjust the carrying amount of the hedged item and be recognised immediately in profit or loss. This applies even if a hedged item is measured at fair value with changes in fair value recognised in the changes in equity statement. That also applies if the hedged item is measured at cost.

An entity shall discontinue prospectively the hedge accounting noted above if any one of the following occurs:

(a) the hedging instrument expires or is sold, terminated or exercised or
(b) the hedge no longer meets the criteria for hedge accounting.

An adjustment to the carrying amount of a hedged interest bearing financial instrument should be amortised to profit or loss. Amortisation may start as soon as an adjustment exists and no later than when the hedged item ceases to be adjusted for changes in its fair value attributable to the risk being hedged. The adjustment is based on a recalculated effective interest rate at the date when amortisation begins and should be amortised fully by maturity.

Cash flow hedges

If a cash flow hedge meets the conditions for hedging during the period, it should be accounted for as follows:

(a) the portion of the gain or loss on the hedging instrument that is determined to be an effective hedge should be reported on balance sheet and described as 'gains and losses arising on effective cash flow hedges not yet recognised in the profit and loss; and

(b) the ineffective portion of the gain or loss on the hedging instrument should be recognised immediately in profit or loss.

If a hedge of a forecast transaction subsequently results in the recognition of an asset or liability then the associated gains or losses that were reported on balance sheet shall be reclassified into profit or loss in the same period during which the asset acquired or liability incurred affects profit or loss. However, if an entity expects that all or a portion of a net loss reported amongst assets and liabilities will not be recovered it should recognise the amount not expected to be recovered, immediately into profit and loss.

For all cash flow hedges, other than those above, reported on balance sheet should be included in profit and loss in the same period during which the hedged forecast transaction affects profit or loss.

An entity should discontinue prospectively the hedge accounting specified above if any one of the following occurs:

(a) The hedging instrument expires, is sold, terminated or exercised. The cumulative gain or loss on the hedging instrument that was initially reported in the balance sheet when the hedge was effective should remain until the forecast transaction occurs. When the transaction occurs, the above accounting treatment will apply.

(b) The hedge no longer meets the criteria for hedge accounting. The cumulative gain or loss initially reported on balance sheet when the hedge was effective should remain until the forecast transaction occurs. When the transaction occurs, the above accounting treatment will apply.

(c) The forecast transaction is no longer expected to occur, in which case any related cumulative gain or loss that had been reported on balance sheet should be recognised in profit and loss for the period. A forecast that is no longer highly probable may still be expected to occur.

Hedges of a net investment

Hedges of a net investment in a foreign operation, including a hedge of a monetary item that is accounted for as part of the net investment should be accounted for as follows:

(a) the portion of the gain or loss on the hedging instrument that is determined to be an effective hedge should be recognised in the changes in equity statement.

(b) The ineffective portion should be recognised:
- immediately in profit or loss if the hedging instrument is a derivative; or in accordance with **Gains and Losses** section, in the limited circumstances in which the hedging instrument is not a derivative.

The amount of the gain or loss on the hedging instrument relating to the effective portion of the hedge that has been recognised in the changes in equity statement should not be reversed or adjusted at the disposal of the foreign operation.

Hedges that do not qualify for hedge accounting

If a hedge does not qualify for hedge accounting as it fails to meet the criteria, gains and losses arising from changes in the fair value of a hedged item that is measured at fair value after initial recognition are recognised in one of two ways (see **Gains and losses** section). Fair value adjustments of a hedging instrument that is a derivative would be recognised in profit or loss.

A good example of a detailed accounting policy for derivatives and hedging with a tabular back up note on derivative activity is provided by CRH Plc:

CRH Plc   Year Ended 31 December 2005

Accounting Policies and Notes to the Accounts (Extract)

Derivative financial instruments

The Group employs derivative financial instruments (principally interest rate and currency swaps and forward foreign exchange contracts) to manage interest rate risks and to realise the desired currency profile of borrowings. In accordance with its treasury policy, the Group does not trade in financial instruments nor does it enter into leveraged derivative transactions.

At the inception of a transaction entailing the usage of derivatives, the Group documents the relationship between the hedged item and the hedging instrument together with its risk management objective and the strategy underlying the proposed transaction. The Group also documents its assessment both at the inception of the hedging relationship and subsequently on an ongoing basis, of the effectiveness of the hedge in offsetting movements in the fair values or cash flows of the hedged items.

Derivative financial instruments are initially recognised at cost and are thereafter stated at fair value. Where derivatives do not fulfil the criteria for hedge accounting, they are classified as held-for-trading and changes in fair values are reported in the income statement The fair value of interest rate and currency swaps is the estimated amount the Group would pay or receive to terminate the swap at the balance sheet date taking into account current interest and currency rates and the creditworthiness of the swap counterparties. The fair value of forward exchange contracts is calculated by reference to current forward exchange rates for contracts with similar maturity profiles and equates to the quoted market price at the balance sheet date (being the present value of the quoted forward price).

Hedging

Fair value and cash flow hedges

The Group uses fair value hedges and cash flow hedges in its treasury activities. For the purposes of hedge accounting, hedges are classified either as fair value hedges (which entail hedging the exposure to movements in the fair value of a recognised asset or liability) or cash flow hedges (which hedge exposure to fluctuations in future cash flows derived from a particular risk associated with a recognised asset or liability, a firm commitment or a highly probable forecast transaction).

In the case of fair value hedges which satisfy the conditions for hedge accounting, any gain or loss stemming from the re-measurement of the hedging instrument to fair value is reported in the income statement. In addition, any gain or loss on the hedged item which is attributable to the hedged risk is adjusted against the carrying amount of the hedged item and reflected in the income statement. Where the adjustment is to the carrying amount of a hedged interest-hearing financial instrument, the adjustment is amortised to the Income Statement with the objective of achieving full amortisation by maturity.

Where a derivative financial instrument is designated as a hedge of the variability in cash flows of a recognised liability or a highly probable forecasted transaction, the effective part of any gain or loss on the derivative financial instrument is recognised as a separate component of equity with the ineffective portion being reported in the income statement. When a firm commitment or forecast transaction results in the recognition of an asset or a liability, the cumulative gain or loss is removed from equity and included in the initial measurement of the non-financial asset or liability. Otherwise, the associated gains or losses that had previously been recognised in equity transferred to the income statement contemporaneous with the materialisation of the hedged transaction. Any gain or loss arising in respect of changes in the time value of the derivative financial instrument is excluded from the measurement of hedge effectiveness and is recognised immediately in the Income Statement.

Hedge accounting is discontinued when the hedging instrument expires or is sold, terminated or exercised, or no longer qualifies for hedge accounting. At that point in time, any cumulative gain or loss on the hedging instrument recognised as a separate component of equity is kept in equity until the forecast transaction occurs. If a hedged transaction is no longer anticipated to occur, the net cumulative gain or loss recognised in equity is transferred to the Income Statement in the period.

Hedges of monetary assess and liabilities

Where a derivative financial instrument is used to economically hedge the foreign exchange exposure of a recognised monetary asset or liability, hedge accounting is not applied and any gain or loss accruing on the hedging instrument is recognised in the Income Statement.

Net investment hedges

Where foreign currency borrowings provide a hedge against a net investment in a foreign operation, foreign exchange differences are taken directly to a foreign currency translation reserve (being a separate component of equity). Cumulative gains and losses remain in equity until disposal of the net investment in the foreign operation at which point the related differences are transferred to the Income Statement as part of the overall gain or loss on sale.

Interest-bearing loans and borrowings

All loans and borrowings are initially recorded at cost being the fair value of the consideration received net of attributable transaction costs.

Subsequent to initial recognition, current and non-current interest-bearing loans and borrowings are measured at amortised cost employing the effective interest yield methodology. The computation of amortised cost includes any issue costs and any discount or premium materialising on settlement. Borrowings are classified as current liabilities unless the Group has an unconditional right to defer settlement of the liability for at least 12 months after the balance sheet date.

Gains and losses are recognised in the Income Statement through amortisation on the basis of the period of the loans and borrowings and/or on impairment and derecognition of the associated loans and borrowings.

23. Derivative Financial Instruments

Derivative financial instruments recognised as assets and liabilities in the Group Balance Sheet are analysed as follows:

	2005 (£m)	2004 (£m)
Non-current assets		
Fair value hedges	135.2	173.2
Net investment hedges	19.6	–
	154.8	173.2
Current assets		
Fair value hedges	4.8	0.7
Cash flow hedges	2.7	–
Net investment hedges	20.2	–
Not designated as hedges	3.0	0.4
	30.7	1.1
Total assets	185.5	174.3

Non-current liabilities		
Fair value hedges	(12.7)	(46.7)
Cash flow hedges	(0.3)	(0.1)
Net investment hedges	–	(4.2)
Not designated as hedges	(0.5)	(0.9)
	(13.5)	(51.9)
Current liabilities		
Fair value hedges	(1.3)	(15.7)
Cash flow hedges	(0.1)	(0.3)
Net investment hedges	(1.4)	(192.8)
Not designated as hedges	(1.8)	(1.6)
	(4.6)	(210.4)
Total liabilities	(18.1)	(262.3)
Net asset/liability) on derivative financial instruments	167.4	(88.0)

12.3   IFRS 7 *Financial Instruments: Presentation* (revised 2003)

Objective

The objective is to require entities to provide disclosures so that users can evaluate:

(a)   The significance of financial instruments regarding financial position and performance.

(b)   The nature and extent of risks arising from instruments that the entity is exposed to.

The standard will effectively replace the disclosure requirements of IAS 32 from 2007 onwards but still leave IAS 32 with the presentational aspects.

Scope

IFRS 7 applies to all financial instruments giving a true and fair view but the following are exempted:

(a)   subsidiary 90% or more voting rights controlled by group and

(b)   parent companies regarding single entity statements provided included in the consolidated accounts.

IFRS 7 applies to all types of financial instruments except:

(a)   subsidiaries, quasi-subsidiaries, associates, etc. – IAS 27, IAS 28. However, it must apply to derivatives of those entities.

(b)   employee benefit plans – IAS 19

(c)   contingent consideration – IFRS 3

(d)   insurance contracts – IFRS 6
(e)   share-based payment – IFRS 2.

IFRS 7 applies to both recognised and unrecognised financial instruments.

Classes of financial instruments and level of disclosure

Financial instruments are grouped into appropriate classes with similar characteristics. Sufficient information should be provided to permit reconciliation with the balance sheet.

Significance of financial instruments for financial position and performance

Disclosure should be sufficient to evaluate the significance of financial instruments to financial position and performance.

Balance sheet

Categories of financial assets and financial liabilities

The carrying amount of each of the following categories – balance sheet or notes

(a)   financial assets at fair value through profit or loss – separately initial and change of status;
(b)   held to maturity investments;
(c)   loans and receivables;
(d)   available for sale financial assets;
(e)   financial liabilities at fair value through profit or loss – separately initial and change of status;
(f)   financial liabilities at amortised cost.

Financial assets or financial liabilities at fair value through profit or loss

If financial liability shall disclose:

(a)   amount of change during period and cumulatively in the fair value of the liability attributable to changes in credit risk determined either:
  (i)   as the amount of change in fair value not attributable to changes in market conditions giving rise to market risk or
  (ii) using a alternative method which more faithfully represents changes in fair value.
  Changes in market conditions include changes in a benchmark interest rate, the price of another entity's financial instrument, a commodity price, foreign exchange rate or price index.
(b)   the difference between the carrying amount of liability and contractual repayment at maturity.

The entity shall disclose:

(a) the methods used to comply with the above;
(b) if disclosure does not provide faithful presentation in fair values, reasons should be provided.

Reclassification. If an entity reclassifies a financial asset:

(a) at cost or amortised cost rather than fair value or
(b) at fair value.

It must disclose the amount reclassified into and out of each category and reason for the reclassification.

Collateral. An entity should disclose:

(a) the carrying amount of financial assets pledged as collateral and
(b) the terms and conditions relating to the pledge.

When an entity holds collateral and is permitted to sell or pledge the collateral in absence of default, it should disclose:

(a) the fair value of collateral held;
(b) the fair value of collateral sold or repledged and whether obligation to return it; and
(c) the terms and conditions associated with the collateral.

Allowance account for credit losses. When financial assets are impaired by credit losses and these are recorded in a separate allowance account it should disclose a reconciliation of changes in that account during the period for each class of financial asset.

Compound financial instruments with multiple embedded derivatives. Where values are interdependent of multiple embedded derivatives, their existence should be disclosed.

Defaults and breaches. Loans payable – must disclose

(a) details of defaults of principal, interest, redemption, etc.
(b) carrying amount of loans payable in default; and
(c) whether default was remedied.

If there were breaches of loan agreement terms other than those above, an entity should disclose the same information if the breaches permitted the lender to demand accelerated repayment.

Income statement and equity

Items of income, expense, gains or losses

An entity should disclose the following on the face of the financial statements or in the notes:

(a) Net gains/losses on:
  (i) financial assets or liabilities at fair value through profit or loss;
  (ii) available for sale financial assets – separate equity, transferred from equity to profit and loss;
  (iii) held to maturity investments;

    (iv)   loans and receivables; and

    (v)   financial liabilities measured at amortised cost.

(b)   Total interest income and total interest expense for non-fair value assets/liabilities.

(c)   Fee income and expense arising from:

    (i)   financial assets/liabilities not at fair value and

    (ii)   trust and other fiduciary activities.

(d)   Interest income on impaired financial assets.

(e)   The amount of any impairment loss for each class of financial asset.

Other disclosures

Accounting policies

An entity must disclose material accounting policies.

If applying IFRS 7, without IAS 39, need adequate information for users to understand the basis on which financial assets and liabilities are measured. If measured at cost need information on:

(a)   costs of acquisition or issuance;

(b)   premiums and discounts;

(c)   changes in estimated amounts of determinable future cash flows;

(d)   changes in circumstances leading to considerable uncertainty re collection of all assets;

(e)   declines in fair value of financial assets below their carrying amount; and

(f)   restructured financial liabilities.

Fair values can be determined from quoted market prices, independent appraisals, discounted cash flows or another appropriate method. Disclosure of any significant assumptions should be provided.

An entity should disclose the basis of reporting in the income statement. When an entity presents income and expenditure on a net basis, the reason for that presentation and its effect, if significant.

Hedge accounting

An entity should disclose the following separately for each type of hedge:

(a)   a description of each type of hedge;

(b)   a description of instruments designated as hedging instruments and their fair values; and

(c)   the nature of risks being hedged.

For cash flow hedges an entity shall disclose:

(a)   the periods cash flows are expected to occur and when expected to affect profit;

(b)   a description of any forecast transaction for which hedge accounting previously used but is no longer expected to occur;

(c)   the amount recognised in equity in period;

(d)   the amount removed from equity and included in profit or loss;

(e)   the amount removed from equity and included in the initial cost or other carrying amount of a non-financial asset or liability.

An entity should disclose separately:

(a) In fair value hedges, gains or losses:
   (i)   on the hedging instrument and
   (ii) on the hedged item attributable to hedged risk.
(b) The ineffectiveness recognised in profit or loss arising from cash flow hedges.
(c) The ineffectiveness recognised in profit or loss arising from hedges of net investments in foreign operations.

Fair value

The fair value of each class of financial assets and liabilities should be disclosed so as to be comparable with their carrying amount.

Financial assets and liabilities should be grouped into classes but only be offset to extent carrying amounts are offset in the balance sheet.

An entity should disclose:

(a) Methods and assumptions applied in arriving at fair value.
(b) Whether fair values are determined in whole or in part to published prices or have used a valuation technique.
(c) Whether fair values are determined using a valuation technique not based on market prices – changes to assumptions should be disclosed if significant to change in fair value.
(d) The amount of change in fair value using a valuation technique that was recognised in profit or loss during the period.

If the market is not active a valuation technique may be used but the transaction price is the best evidence. Where fair value at initial recognition and the amount using a valuation technique is different the following should be disclosed, by class:

(a) Its accounting policy.
(b) The aggregate difference yet to be recognised in profit or loss, both at the start and end of the period.

Disclosures of fair value are not required:

(a) When the carrying amount is a reasonable approximate of fair value;
(b) For equity investments with no quoted price or fair value not determinable.
(c) For discretionary participation if the fair value cannot be measured reliably.

For (b) and (c) an entity should disclose information to help users make their own judgements including:

(a) Fact that fair value cannot be measured reliably.
(b) A description of the financial instruments, carrying amount and explanation why fair value cannot be measured reliably.
(c) Information regarding market for instruments.
(d) Information about whether or not intend to dispose of the instruments.
(e) If instruments are derecognised as no reliable measure, that fact, book value at derecognition and gain/loss recognised.

Nature and extent of risks arising from financial instruments

Disclosure should enable users to evaluate the nature and extent of risks arising from financial instruments to which the entity is exposed. Focus should be on credit risk, liquidity risk and market risk.

Qualitative disclosures

For each type of risk an entity should disclose:

(a) The exposures to risk and how they might arise.
(b) Its objectives, policies and processes for managing risk.
(c) Any changes from the previous year.

Quantitative disclosures

For each type of risk an entity should disclose:

(a) Summary quantitative data regarding exposure to that risk based on information internally provided to key management.
(b) The disclosures below to extent not covered in (a) unless the risk is not material.
(c) Concentrations of risk not apparent from (a) and (b).

If the quantitative data disclosed is unrepresentative of an entity's exposure to risk further information should be disclosed.

Credit risk. An entity should disclose, by class:

(a) Maximum exposure to credit risk without taking into account any collateral.
(b) A description of collateral held as security.
(c) Information re credit quality of financial assets not impaired.
(d) The carrying amount of financial assets that without negotiation would have been impaired.

Financial assets that are neither past due nor impaired. An entity should disclose, by class:

(a) An aged analysis of financial assets.
(b) An analysis of financial assets that are individually determined to be impaired.
(c) A description of collateral held by the entity as security.

Collateral and other credit enhancements obtained. An entity should disclose:

(a) The nature and carrying amount of assets obtained.
(b) When the assets are not readily convertible into cash, its policies for disposing such assets or using them in its operations.

Liquidity risk. An entity should disclose:

(a) a maturity analysis for financial liabilities and
(b) a description of how it manages the liquidity risk.

Market risk – Sensitivity analysis. An entity should disclose:

(a)   a sensitivity analysis for each type of market risk to which the entity is exposed;

(b)   the methods and assumptions used in preparing the sensitivity analysis; and

(c)   changes from the previous period in methods and assumptions used and reasons for changes.

If an entity prepares a sensitivity analysis that reflects interdependencies between risk variables, the entity should also disclose:

(a)   an explanation of the method used in preparing a sensitivity analysis and of the main parameters and assumptions underlying the data.

(b)   an explanation of the objective of the method used and of limitations.

Other market risk disclosures. If sensitivity analysis is unrepresentative of market risk, that fact should be disclosed and reason it believes it is unrepresentative.

Effective date and transition

Accounting periods starting on or after 1 January 2007 but earlier application is encouraged.

13

Sundry financial reporting standards

13.1 IAS 34 *Interim Reports* (1998)

Objective

The objective of IAS 34 is to prescribe the minimum content of an interim financial report and to prescribe the principles for recognition and measurement in interim reports.

Scope

The standard is not mandatory but instead strongly recommends to regulators that interim financial reporting should be a requirement for publicly traded securities. Specifically they are encouraged to:

(a) publish an interim report for at least the first six months of their financial year and
(b) it should be available no later than 60 days after the end of the interim period.

Definitions

- *Interim period.* A financial reporting period shorter than a full financial year.
- *Interim financial report.* A financial report containing either a complete set of financial statements or a set of condensed financial statements.

Content of an interim financial report

IAS 34 defines the minimum content of an interim report which should contain condensed financial statements together with selected explanatory notes but it should focus on new activities and events. Obviously, entities can disclose the following minimum content, if they wish:

(a) condensed balance sheet;
(b) condensed income statement;

(c)   condensed statement of all changes in equity or changes in equity other than those arising from capital transactions with owners and distributions to owners;

(d)   condensed cash flow statement; and

(e)   selected explanatory notes.

The condensed statements should include each of the headings and subtotals that were included in its most recent annual financial statements. Additional line items should be included if their omission would make the condensed interim statements misleading.

Basic and diluted EPS should be presented on the face of an income statement for an interim period.

Selected explanatory notes

IAS 34 is not concerned with relatively minor changes from its most recent annual financial statements. However, the notes to the interim report should include the following information (unless the information is contained elsewhere in the report):

(a)   A statement that the same accounting policies and methods of computation are followed in the interim statements as compared with the most recent annual statements or, if changed, a description of the nature and effect of the change.

(b)   Explanatory comments about the seasonality or cyclicality of interim operations.

(c)   The nature and amount of unusual items affecting assets, liabilities, incomes and expenses because of their nature, size or incidence.

(d)   The nature and amount of changes in estimates, if they have a material effect in the current interim period.

(e)   The issue or repurchase of equity or debt securities.

(f)   Dividends paid, separately for ordinary and other shares.

(g)   Segmental results for the primary basis of reporting i.e. either geographical or business.

(h)   Material events since the end of the interim period.

(i)   The effect of business combinations during the interim report.

(j)   Changes in contingent liabilities or contingent assets since the last annual balance sheet date.

Examples of the above include:
- write-downs of inventories to NRV and reversals;
- acquisitions, disposals, impairments of property, plant, etc., and reversals;
- litigation settlements;
- corrections of material errors;
- related party transactions.

Disclosure of compliance

If the interim report is in compliance with IAS 34, that fact should be disclosed.

Periods covered

- Balance sheet data at the end of the current interim period and comparative data at the end of the most recent financial year.

- Income statements for the current interim period and cumulative data for the current year to date together with comparative income statements for the comparable interim periods of the immediately preceding year.
- Cash flow statement cumulatively for the current financial year to date with a comparative statement for the comparable year to date period of the immediately preceding financial year.
- Changes in equity statement cumulatively for the current financial year to date with a comparative statement for the comparable year to date period of the immediately preceding financial year.

Materiality

Materiality should be assessed in relation to the interim period financial data. It should be recognised that interim measurements rely to a greater extent on estimates than on annual financial data.

Disclosure in annual financial statements

If an estimate of an amount reported in an interim report has changed significantly during the final interim report and a separate financial report has not been published for that period, then the nature and amount of that change in estimate should be disclosed in a note to the annual financial statements for that financial year.

Recognition and measurement

Same accounting policies as annual

The same accounting policies should be adopted in the interim report as are applied in the annual statements, except for accounting policy changes made after the date of the most recent annual financial statements that will be reflected in the next set of annual statements.

The guiding principle for recognition and measurement is that an enterprise should use the same recognition and measurement principles in its interim statements as it does in its annual financial statements, e.g. a cost would not be classified as an asset in the interim report if it would not be classified as such in the annual report.

Revenues received occasionally, seasonally or cyclically

Revenue which is received occasionally or seasonally should not be anticipated or deferred in interim reports. The principles of revenue recognition should be applied consistently to interim and annual reports.

Costs incurred unevenly during the financial year

These should only be anticipated or deferred if it would be appropriate to anticipate or defer the expense in the annual financial statements. It would be inappropriate, e.g., to anticipate part of the cost of a major advertising campaign later in the year for which no expenses have yet been incurred.

Appendix – Examples of application of recognition and measurement principles

Employer payroll taxes and insurance contributions

In some countries these are assessed on an annual basis but paid at an uneven rate during the year. It is therefore appropriate, in this situation, to adopt an estimated average annual tax rate for the year in an interim statement, not the actual tax paid. Taxes are an annual assessment but payment is uneven.

Cost of a planned major periodic overhaul

The cost of such an event must not be anticipated unless there is a legal or constructive obligation to carry out the work. A mere intention to carry out work later in the year is not sufficient justification to create a liability.

Year end bonus

This should not be provided in the interim report unless there is a constructive obligation to pay such a bonus and it can be reliably measured.

Intangible asset

IAS 34 must follow IAS 38 *Intangible Assets* and thus it would be inappropriate in an interim report to defer a cost in the expectation that it will eventually be part of a non-monetary intangible asset that has not yet been recognised.

Holiday pay

If holiday pay is an enforceable obligation on the employer, then any unpaid accumulated holiday pay may be accrued in the interim report.

Tax on income

An expense for tax should be included in the interim report and the tax rate should be the estimated average annual tax rate for the year.

EXAMPLE

Assume a quarterly reporting entity expects to earn 10,000 pre-tax each quarter and operates in a tax jurisdiction with a tax rate of 20% on the first 20,000 and 30% on all additional earnings. Actual earnings match expectations. The tax reported in each quarter is as follows:

| Tax expense | 2,500 | 2,500 | 2,500 | 2,500 | 10,000 |

Total estimate 40,000 (20,000 × 20% = 4,000 + 20,000 × 30% = 6,000, i.e. 10,000) 4 = 2,500.

Assume a quarterly reporting entity expects to earn 15,000 pre-tax in Q1 but losses of 5,000 in Q2–4. The tax rate is still 20%. The tax reported in each quarter is as follows:

Tax expense	3,000	(1,000)	(1,000)	(1,000)	Nil

Assume year end 30 June and taxable year end 31 December. Assume pre-tax earnings 10,000 each quarter and average tax rate 30% year 1 and 40% year 2.

Tax expense	3,000	3,000	4,000	4,000	14,000

Some countries give enterprises tax credits against the tax payable on the basis amounts of capital expenditure on research and development. These are usually awarded on an annual basis, thus it is appropriate to include anticipated tax credits within the estimated average tax rate for the year and apply it to calculate the tax on income for interim periods. However, if it relates to a one-off event it should be recognised in the interim period in which the event occurs.

Inventory valuations

Should be valued in the same way as for year end accounts but it will be necessary to rely more heavily on estimates for interim reports.

Depreciation

Depreciation should only be charged in the interim statement on assets that have been owned during the period but not on assets that will be acquired later in the financial year.

Foreign currency translation gains and losses

These should be calculated using the same principles as the year-end, in accordance with IAS 21.

Appendix – Use of estimates

Although accounting information must be reliable and free from material error, it may be necessary to sacrifice some accuracy and reliability for the sake of timeliness and costs/benefits. This is particularly the case in interim reporting where estimates must be used to a greater extent.

Some examples provided in the appendix are:

(a) Inventories – there is no need for a full inventory count but it is sufficient to estimate inventory values using sales margins.
(b) Provisions – it is inappropriate to bear the cost of experts to advise on the appropriate amount of a provision or an expert valuer to value fixed assets at the interim date.
(c) Income taxes – it is sufficient to apply an estimated weighted average tax rate to income earned in all jurisdictions. No need to calculate the tax rate in each country separately.

A full set of interim reports is provided by easyJet Plc and it incorporates an Operating and Financial Review as well as condensed primary statements. However, the company does clearly state it is not in accordance with IAS 34.

EasyJet Plc   Interim Report 2007

Operating and financial review

Half year 2007 compared with half year 2006

Key performance indicators

Return on equity

The Board has set return on equity as the key financial measure at easyJet, since it best represents the return attributable to the equity shareholders.

Return on equity for the half year ended 31 March 2007 was 1.3%, improved from 3.4% for the half year ended 31 March 2006. This was driven by a significant reduction in the loss for the period partially offset by an increase in other equity components, principally £15.8 million relating to the exercise of employee share options.

Return on equity for the year to 31 March 2007 was 11.9%, improved from 5.6% for the year to 31 March 2006.

Management is incentivised through the Long-Term Incentive Plan to deliver increases in return on equity to 15% by 2008.

Loss before tax per seat, revenue per seat and cost per seat

Loss before tax per seat is a measure used internally to allow all our people to understand and focus on the return on equity target, since the measures are closely related. It is the difference between revenue per seat and cost per seat, which are important measures that are used to monitor certain areas of the business. Loss before tax per seat improved in half year 2007 by 61.9% from £2.22 to £0.85 as a result of a-2.4% increase in revenue per seat from £34.67 to £35.51 (explained in more detail in 'Revenue' below) and a decrease in cost per seat of 1.4% from £36.89 to £36.36.

Cost per seat, excluding fuel

Even after the mitigation provided by easyJet's hedging activities, there is significant volatility in fuel costs which is largely dictated by external economic and political factors, we consider that the movement in cost per seat excluding fuel is the best indicator of management's performance in keeping unit costs low.

Cost per seat excluding fuel decreased by 2.1% from £27.75 in half year 2006 to £27.18 in half year 2007. This was mainly a result of direct management action to control overheads, in addition to the benefit from weaker US dollar and euro foreign exchange rates.

Seats flown

Seats flown is considered by the management to be the best measure of output units of production. The number of seats flown in half year 2006 increased by 11.5%

from 18.2 million in half year 2006 to 20.2 million in half year 2007, as a result of the introduction of new aircraft into the fleet.

Income statement

Revenue

easyJet's revenue increased 14.2% from £629.5 million to £719.0 million, from half year 2006 to half year 2007. Revenue per seat increased 2.4% from £34.67 to £35.51.

Passenger revenue, the largest component, comprises the price paid for the seat less government taxes, such as Air Passenger Duty and VAT. It increased by 12.4% from £571.0 million to £641.8 million, driven by a 10.7% growth in passenger numbers from £14.9 million to £16.4 million, and a 0.8% increase in passenger revenue per seat. This was despite the effect of the UK Government's decision to double Air Passenger Duty with effect from 1 February 2007, which resulted in additional taxes of £12.4 million. The number of passengers carried reflected a 14.3% increase in the size of the easyJet fleet in operation from an average of 100.8 aircraft to an average of 115.2 aircraft offset by a small decrease in the average load factor achieved from 81.8% to 81.2%.

Growth was particularly strong in continental Europe, with intra-European revenues growing by 47.7%.

Ancillary revenue includes fees and charges (including credit card fees, excess baggage charges, speedy boarding, sporting equipment fees, infant fees, change fees and rescue fees), profit share from in-flight sales (including food, beverages and boutique items) and commissions received from products and services sold (such as hotel bookings, car hire bookings and travel insurance), less chargebacks from credit cards. In half year 2007, £77.2 million was earned from ancillary revenues, up to 32.0% from half year 2006. This has been driven by the 10.7% growth in passengers carried, the positive effect of changes in arrangements for car hire, insurance and in-flight catering and increases in rates for change fees and credit card fees. It was also driven by the introduction of speedy boarding as a new product. Ancillary revenue per seat increased by 18.2% from £3.23 to £3.81.

Ground handling charges

easyJet's ground handling charges include the salaries of self-handling staff in Spain. These costs increased by 6.8% from £71.2 million to £76.1 million, from half year 2006 to half year 2007. The increase in ground handling charges reflects the 10.4% increase in the number of sectors flown, alongside mix costs as a result of network expansion decisions. Cost savings were achieved as a result of self-handling and renegotiated third-party handling in Spain. As a result, ground handling cost per seat decreased by 4.3% from £3.92 to £3.76.

Airport charges

easyJet's external airport charges increased by 13.6% from £115.7 million to £131.4 million from half year 2006 to half year 2007. This increase was attributable to the growth in passengers carried of 10.7% and inflationary cost increases at regulated airports. On a per-seat basis, costs increased by 1.8% from £6.37 to £6.49.

Fuel

easyJet's fuel costs increased by 12.1% from £165.9 million to £185.9 million from half year 2006 to half year 2007. A 2.7% decrease in easyJet's average US dollar fuel cost per tonne (excluding hedging) resulted in reduced costs to easyJet of £4.7 million. The strengthening of the value of sterling against the US dollar, the currency in which fuel prices are denominated, over the course of half year 2007 reduced costs by approximately £17.9 million. The impact of a significant increase in flying and our hedging activities amounted to £42.6 million additional fuel costs. On a per-seat basis, costs increased by 0.5% from £9.14 to £9.18.

Navigation charges

easyJet's navigation charges increased by 13.0% from £54.6 million to £61.7 million from half year 2006 to half year 2007. This increase was principally attributable to a 14.6% increase in the ASKs flown in half year 2007. Cost savings were derived from a weaker euro. On a per-seat basis, costs increased by 1.3% from £3.01 to £3.05.

Crew costs

easyJet's crew costs increased by 26.9% from £75.2 million to £95.5 million from half year 2006 to half year 2007. The increase in crew costs resulted from an increase in headcount during the half year 2007 to service the additional sectors and aircraft operated by easyJet during the half year the increase in salaries, following a new pay deal agreed with our flight crew and cabin crew employees, and the subsequent costs of recruitment and training. In addition, investments in crew have been made to ensure that the crew shortages experienced in summer 2006 are not repeated. Encouragingly, the business has experienced significantly less attrition compared to half year 2006. On a per-seat basis, costs increased by 13.8% from £4.14 to £4.71.

Maintenance

Maintenance expenses decreased by 8.8% from £51.4 million to £46.8 million from half year 2006 to half year 2007. easyJet's maintenance expenses consist primarily of the cost of routine maintenance and spare parts and provisions for the estimated future cost of heavy maintenance and engine overhauls on aircraft operated by easyJet pursuant to dry operating leases. The extent of the required annual maintenance reserve charges is determined by reference to the number of flight hours and cycles permitted between each engine shop visit and heavy maintenance overhaul on aircraft airframes. The decrease in maintenance costs was largely due to the exit of the Boeing 737-300 fleet and the benefits of new contractual arrangements being negotiated with lower prices, offset by the additional cost of a 10.4% increase in the number of sectors flown. On a per-seat basis, costs reduced by 18.3% from £2.83 to £2.31.

Advertising

easyJet continues to advertise to consolidate the awareness of the brand and its low fares philosophy. Advertising costs increased by 8.9% from £17.4 million to £18.9 million from half year 2006 to half year 2007. Advertising cost per seat decreased by 2.3% from £0.96 to £0.94.

Merchant fees and incentive pay

Merchant fees and incentive pay increased by 8.8% from £8.6 million to £9.4 million from half year 2006 to half year 2007. Merchant fees and incentive pay includes the costs of processing fees paid for all of easyJet's credit and debit card sales and the per-seat sold/transferred commission paid as incentive pay to easyJet's telesales staff. The increase is reflective of a larger volume of transactions but on a per-seat basis, costs have reduced marginally by 2.4% from £0.47 to £0.46.

Aircraft and passenger insurance

Aircraft and passenger insurance costs reduced by 18.4% from £8.2 million in half year 2006 to £6.7 million in half year 2007, despite a 10.7% increase in passenger numbers. This was as a result of lower rates being negotiated and the effect of the strengthening of sterling against the US dollar. On a per-seat basis, costs reduced by 26.8% from £0.45 to £0.33.

Other costs

Other costs increased by 38.5% from £34.0 million to £47.1 million from half year 2006 to half year 2007. Items in this cost category include administrative costs and operational costs not included elsewhere including some salary expenses. This cost category also includes compensation paid to passengers and other related disruption costs, the cost of share option schemes and management bonuses. On a per-seat basis, costs increased by 24.2% from £1.87 to £2.33.

Depreciation

Depreciation charges increased by 60.5% from £10.4 million to £16.7 million from half year 2006 to half year 2007. The depreciation charge reflects depreciation on owned and finance leased aircraft and capitalised aircraft maintenance charges, and also includes depreciation on computer hardware and other assets. easyJet has owned or leased under a finance lease an average of 47.2 Airbus A319 aircraft during the half year 2007 (half year 2006: 22.3 Airbus A319 aircraft). The increase in depreciation reflects the introduction of new owned Airbus aircraft. On a per-seat basis, depreciation increased by 44.6% from £0.57 to £0.82.

Aircraft dry lease costs

easyJet's aircraft dry lease costs comprise the lease payments paid by easyJet in respect of those aircraft in its fleet operated pursuant to dry operating leases and end of operating lease return costs. Aircraft dry lease costs decreased by 27.9% from £63.5 million to £45.9 million from half year 2006 to half year 2007. During the period 2 new Airbus A319 aircraft were added to the fleet on lease agreements, 2 Boeing 737-700s and 3 Boeing 737-300s were retired. The average number of leased aircraft in half year 2007 decreased by 15.1% to 74.9 by comparison with half year 2006. Half year over half year, easyJet has benefited from the strengthening of the value of sterling against the US dollar, the currency in which lease costs are denominated set off against rising dollar interest rates. There was also a reduction in the costs of lease returns. easyJet has seen its average leasing cost per aircraft decrease by around 15.0% half year on half year. On a per-seat basis aircraft dry lease costs decreased by 35.3% from £3.49 to £2.26.

Aircraft long-term wet lease costs

easyJet's aircraft wet lease costs comprise the lease payments paid by easyJet in respect of aircraft pursuant to wet leases (i.e. leases of aircraft plus crew, maintenance and insurance) of a duration of one month or more. The £1.0 million charge in 2007 relates to the costs incurred of leasing aircraft for the end of the summer 2006 season. Wet leased aircraft are not included in fleet numbers discussed elsewhere in the interim report.

Interest and other finance income

Interest and other finance income represent interest received or receivable by easyJet. Interest and other finance income increased by 52.9% from £15.6 million in half year 2006 to £23.9 million in half year 2007. This reflects an increase in the cash and restricted cash balances from £773.7 million at 31 March 2006 to £969.6 million at 31 March 2007.

Interest and other finance charges

Interest and other finance charges represent interest paid or payable by easyJet offset by the revaluation of financing assets and liabilities. Finance charges relate predominantly to easyJet's borrowings through either loans or sale and finance leasebacks. Interest and other finance charges increased by 84.4% from £9.0 million in half year 2006 to £16.6 million in half year 2007. This primarily reflects an increase in borrowings from £298.7 million at 31 March 2006 to £492.8 million at 31 March 2007 due to the financing of new Airbus aircraft. In addition there was an increase in US dollar and sterling interest rates. Foreign exchange revaluations on financing items produced net income of £1.0 million during half year 2007.

Share of profit after tax of The Big Orange Handling Company

The Big Orange Handling Company Limited is a company owned by Menzies Aviation Limited and easyJet. It was set up in January 2004 to provide ground handling services at London Luton airport. During the half year 2007, the share (26%) of the profit after tax attributable to easyJet was £0.1 million (2006: £0.1m).

Taxation

In half year 2007. easyJet recognised a tax credit of £4.4 million (half year 2006 – tax credit of £11.4m). The decrease in tax credit recognised is due to the decrease in pre-tax losses.

The net deferred tax liability decreased by £7.1 million from £31.7 million at 30 September 2006 to £24.6 million at 31 March 2007, primarily due to capital allowances taken being in excess of depreciation charges.

Loss after tax

For the reasons described above. easyJet's loss after tax decreased by 56.1% from £28.9 million in half year 2006 to £12.7 million in half year 2007.

Loss per share

The basic loss per share decreased by 57.4% from 7.17 pence in the half year 2006 to 3.06 pence in the half year 2007.

Balance sheet

Goodwill

Goodwill relates to the purchases of TEA Basel and Go Fly.

Property, plant and equipment

Property, plant and equipment comprises principally owned aircraft, spares and deposits paid to Airbus in respect of the delivery of future aircraft that are not to be financed according to sale and leaseback arrangements. The net book amount attributable to property, plant and equipment increased from £695.7 million at 30 September 2006 to £808.3 million at 31 March 2007. The increase is due to capital expenditure of £156.1 million, set out in more detail in 'capital expenditure' below, set off against disposals of £26.8 million and depreciation of £16.7 million.

Other non-current assets

Other non-current assets comprise principally capitalised software and software development costs, restricted cash, deposits paid in respect of Airbus aircraft to be financed by sale and leaseback which deliver in more than one year. The total of other non-current assets has increased from £31.1 million at 30 September 2006 to £36.6 million at 31 March 2007.

Cash and cash equivalents

Cash and cash equivalents, excluding restricted cash, have increased by 5.1% from £860.7 million to £904.5 million.

Other current assets

Other current assets comprise trade and other receivables, restricted cash and derivative financial instruments. Other current assets increased by 25.3% from £226.5 million at 30 September 2006 to £283.7 million at 31 March 2007.

Trade and other receivables comprise principally trade receivables, amounts due from credit card companies in respect of seat sales, supplier and lease deposits and prepayments. Trade and other receivables have increased by 13.4% from £213.3 million at 30 September 2006 to £241.8 million at 31 March 2007, principally due to the growth of the business.

Current liabilities

Current liabilities have increased by 35.9% from £509.0 million at 30 September 2006 to £691.7 million at 30 September 2007, principally due to growth and the cyclicality of the business, which means there are more sales in advance at 31 March compared with 30 September each year.

Non-current borrowings

Non-current borrowings all relate to debt related to owned aircraft and aircraft sold to lessors and leased back under finance leases. The amount increased by 2.2% from £446.9 million at 30 September 2006 to £456.9 million at 31 March 2007, due to the acquisition of more owned aircraft subject to debt finance arrangements, set off against the weakening of the US dollar compared with sterling.

Other non-current liabilities

Other non-current liabilities include provisions for maintenance liabilities, deferred surpluses on the sale and leaseback of aircraft, derivative financial instruments and deferred tax liabilities. The amount increased by 10.2% from £184.8 million at 30 September 2006 to £203.6 million at 31 March 2007. The deferred tax provision decreased by £6.7 million, the deferred surplus on sale and leaseback reduced due to the small number of aircraft taken under sale and leaseback during half year 2007, offset by increases in maintenance provisions and other maintenance liabilities.

Cash flow

Capital expenditure

Group capital expenditure on property, plant and equipment is summarised as follows:

	2007 (£m)	2006 (£m)
Aircraft	107.2	111.0
Prepayments on account – aircraft deposits	39.5	30.8
Leasehold improvements	4.8	0.8

Fixtures, fittings and equipment	3.3	0.7
Total cash capital expenditure	**154.8**	**143.3**
Aircraft spares received free of charge (non-cash capital expenditure)	1.3	1.9
Total capital expenditure	**156.1**	**145.2**

As a result of a purchase agreement approved by shareholders in March 2003 and the Class 1 circular approved by shareholders in December 2006, the Group is contractually committed to the acquisition of a further 95 new Airbus A319 aircraft with a list price of approximately US$4.2 billion, being approximately £2.1 billion (before escalations, discounts and deposits already paid). In respect of those aircraft deposit payments amounting to US$181.4 million or £97.3 million had been made as at 31 March 2007 (30 September 2006 US$164.3 million, £90.9 million) for commitments for acquisition of Airbus A319 aircraft. It is intended that these aircraft will be financed partly by cash holdings and internal cash flow and partly through external financing including committed facilities arranged prior to delivery. In addition certain of the aircraft will be sold and leased back under operating leases.

Working capital

At 31 March 2007, net current assets were £496.5 million, down £81.7 million from £578.2 million at 30 September 2006. This change principally reflects an increase in cash, an increase in debtors due to increased sales volumes offset by an increase in creditors. The increased sales volumes are due to the cyclicality of the business and growth.

Unearned revenue increased from £179.4 million to £356.0 million due to increased sales volumes.

Cash flow

Net cash inflow from operating activities totalled £161.8 million, an increase of £63.4 million from £98.4 million in half year 2006 primarily due to changes in working capital.

Financing arrangements

The following table sets out the movements in financing for the two half years ended 31 March 2007 and 31 March 2006:

	2007 (£m)	2006 (£m)
Balance at 1 October	479.7	217.3
New loans and finance leases raised	46.7	98.9
Capital repayments of loans and finance leases	(16.1)	(21.3)
Effect of exchange rates	(17.4)	3.8
Effect of deferred financing fees	(0.1)	–
Balance at 31 March	**492.8**	**298.7**

Of the 10 Airbus A319s that were delivered during the period, two were financed through US dollar or sterling mortgage loans, one was temporarily cash acquired with mortgage finance drawn after year-end, two were sold to lessors and leased back under operating leases, and five were cash acquired.

Share capital

The number of shares allotted, called up and fully paid on 31 March 2007 was 418.8 million (30 September 2006: −410.5m). During half year 2007, 8.3 million shares were issued on exercise of options under employee share option schemes (half year 2006: 6.5m).

Fleet

At the end of March 2007, the fleet comprised 30 Boeing 737s and 97 Airbus A319s, giving a total of 127 aircraft, up from the 35 Boeing 737s and 87 Airbus A319s at the start of the financial year. Details of the fleet at 31 March 2007 are as follows:

	Owned	Under operating lease	Under finance lease	Total	Changes in half year	Future deliveries (including exercised options)	Unexercised options (Note 1)
Airbus A319s	46	45	6	97	10	95	123
Boeing 737-700s	–	30	–	30	(2)	–	–
Boeing 737-300s	–	–	–	–	(3)	–	–
	46	75	6	127	5	95	123

Note 1:   Options may be taken as any Airbus A320 family aircraft and are valid until 2015.

A further 95 Airbus A319 aircraft are planned to be delivered through to December 2010. This will give us a modern fleet of aircraft that will underpin our high levels of asset utilisation and increase our operational efficiency. The average fleet age is currently 2.3 years (30 September 2006: 2.2 years).

EasyJet Plc   Interim Report 2007

Notes to the financial statements

For the six months ended 31 March 2007 (unaudited)

(1) Basis of preparation. The unaudited financial information included in this statement has been prepared in accordance with the FSA listing rules, accounting policies, methods of computation and presentation set out in the Annual Report and Accounts for the year ended 30 September 2006. These accounting policies are in accordance with International Financial Reporting Standards (IFRS).

As permitted under IFRS, easyJet has chosen not to adopt IAS 34 *Interim Financial Statements* in preparing its 2007 interim statement, and therefore this interim financial information is not in full compliance with the presentational and disclosure requirements of IFRS.

The financial information included in this statement does not constitute statutory accounts within the meaning of Section 240 of the Companies Act 1985. The financial information for the year ended 30 September 2006 included in this Interim Report is based upon easyJet's consolidated financial statements for that year. Those financial statements were reported on by easyJet's auditors and have been delivered to the Registrar of Companies. The report of the auditors was unqualified and does not contain a statement under Section 237 (2) or (3) of the Companies Act 1985.

The Drax Group, however, specifically state that the interim report has been prepared in accordance with IAS 34 and these have been reviewed by the auditors.

Drax Group Plc   Interim Report Ended
for Half Year   30 June 2006

Condensed consolidated Income Statements

	Notes	Six months ended 30 June		Year ended 31 December
		2006 (Unaudited) £'m	2005 £'m	2005 £'m
Continuing operations				
Revenue		650.0	403.6	928.6
Fuel costs		(329.9)	(264.0)	(539.5)
Other operating expenses excluding exceptional items		(99.0)	(85.7)	(180.9)
Other exceptional operating income	5	19.0	274.8	329.9
Other exceptional operating expenses	5	–	(11.3)	(66.6)
Total other operating (expenses)/income		(80.0)	177.8	82.4

Unrealised gains/(losses) on derivative contracts		89.1	(248.5)	(117.0)
Operating profit		**329.2**	**68.9**	**354.5**
Interest payable and similar charges		(18.2)	(58.9)	(114.4)
Interest receivable		5.7	2.7	23.5
Profit before tax		**316.7**	**12.7**	**263.6**
Tax (charge)/credit	6	(85.0)	77.1	18.8
Profit for the period attributable to equity share holders from continuing operations		**231.7**	**89.8**	**282.4**
Earnings per share from continuing operations expressed in pence per share				
Bask	7	56.9	31.8	98.0
Diluted		56.9	31.8	98.0

The results above relate to the continuing operations of the Group.

Condensed Consolidated Statement of Recognised Income and Expense

	Six months ended 30 June		Year ended 31 December
	2006 (Unaudited) £m	2005 £m	2005 £m
Profit for the period	231.7	89.8	282.4
Actuarial gains/(losses) on defined benefit pension schemes	9.8	(0.2)	(8.2)
Deferred tax in actuarial (gains)/losses on defined benefit pension schemes	(2.9)	0.1	2.5
Initial recognition of net mark-to-market liability on adoption of IAS 32 and IAS 39	–	(5.6)	(5.6)
Deferred tax recognised on adoption of IAS 32 and IAS 39	–	1.7	1.7
Fair value gains/(losses) on cash flow hedges	132.6	–	(109.7)
Deferred tax recognised on fair value (gains)/losses on cash flow hedges	(39.8)	–	32.9
Net gains/(losses) not recognised in income statement	**99.7**	**(4.0)**	**(86.4)**
Total recognised income for the period attributable to equity shareholders	**331.4**	**85.8**	**196.0**

Condensed Consolidated Balance Sheets

	Notes	As at 30 June		As at 31 December
		2006 (Unaudited) £m	2005 £m	2005 £m
Assets				
Non-current assets				
Property plant and equipment		1,044.5	1,051.3	1,050.5
Derivative financial instruments		19.5	–	0.3
		1,064.0	1,051.3	1,050.8
Current assets				
Inventories		75.6	56.8	67.8
Trade and other receivables		110.0	109.5	192.9
Derivative financial instruments		61.7	0.4	7.7
Cash at bank and in hand		298.2	109.7	99.1
		545.5	276.4	367.5
Liabilities				
Current liabilities				
Financial liabilities				
Borrowings	10	25.3	51.1	101.4
Derivative financial instruments		47.8	250.4	173.0
Trade and other payables		174.4	101.6	176.1
Current tax liabilities		32.1	0.9	5.2
		279.6	404.0	455.7
Net current assets/(liabilities)		265.9	(127.6)	(88.2)
Non-current liabilities				
Financial liabilities				
Borrowings	10	425.3	1,015.7	460.1
Derivative financial instruments		26.4	12.9	49.6
Deferred tax liabilities		287.2	167.8	185.3
Retirement benefit obligations		35.0	36.9	44.7
Other non-current liabilities		1.0	25.9	0.7
Provisions		2.1	1.5	2.0
		777.0	1,260.7	742.4
Net assets/(liabilities)		552.9	(337.0)	220.2
Shareholders' equity				
Issued equity	11	40.7	–	40.7
Share premium		420.7	0.5	420.7
Merger reserve		710.8	445.1	710.8
Capital reserve		–	293.5	–
Hedge reserve		16.0	–	(76.8)
Retained losses		(635.3)	(1,076.1)	(875.2)
Total shareholders' equity		552.9	(337.0)	220.2

Condensed Consolidated Statement of Changes in Equity

	Share capital £m	Share premium £m	Merger reserve £m	Capital reserve £m	Hedge reserve £m	Retained losses £m	Total £m
At 1 January 2005	–	0.5	445.1	293.5	–	(1,173.2)	(434.1)
Profit for the period	–	–	–	–	–	282.4	282.4
Actuarial losses on defined benefit pension schemes	–	–	–	–	–	(8.2)	(8.2)
Deferred tax on actuarial losses on defined benefit pension schemes	–	–	–	–	–	2.5	2.5
Initial recognition of net mark-to-market liability on adoption of IASs 32 and 39	–	–	–	–	–	(5.6)	(5.6)
Deferred tax recognised on adoption of IASs 32 and 39	–	–	–	–	–	1.7	1.7
Fair value losses on cash flew hedges	–	–	–	–	(109.7)	–	(109.7)
Deferred tax recognised on fair value losses on cash flow hedges	–	–	–	–	32.9	–	32.9
Share capital issued on refinancing and listing	40.7	–	–	–	–	–	40.7
Share premium arising on refinancing and listing	–	420.7	–	–	–	–	420.7
Reverse acquisition adjustments							
Share for share exchange	–	(0.5)	(27.8)	–	–	–	(28.3)
Transfer of capital reserve	–	–	293.5	(293.5)	–	–	–
LTIP – value of services provided	–	–	–	–	–	25.2	25.2
At 31 December 2005	40.7	420.7	710.8	–	(76.8)	(875.2)	220.2
At 1 January 2005	–	0.5	445.1	293.5	–	(1,173.2)	(434.1)
Profit for the period	–	–	–	–	–	89.8	89.8
Actuarial losses on defined benefit pension schemes	–	–	–	–	–	(0.2)	(0.2)
Deferred tax on actuarial losses on defined benefit pension schemes	–	–	–	–	–	0.1	0.1

Initial recognition of net mark-to-market liability on adoption of IAS 32 and IAS 39	–	–	–	–	–	(5.6)	(5.6)
Deferred tax recognised on adoption of IAS 32 and IAS 39	–	–	–	–	–	1.7	1.7
LTIP – value of services provided	–	–	–	–	–	11.3	11.3
At 30 June 2005	–	0.5	445.1	293.5	–	(1,076.1)	(337.0)
At 1 January 2006	40.7	420.7	710.8	–	(76.8)	(875.2)	220.2
Profit for the period	–	–	–	–	–	231.7	231.7
Actuarial gains on defined benefit pension schemes	–	–	–	–	–	9.8	9.8
Deferred tax on actuarial gains on defined benefit pension schemes	–	–	–	–	–	(2.9)	(2.9)
Fair value gains on cash flow hedges	–	–	–	–	132.6	–	132.6
Deferred tax recognised on fair value gains on cash flow hedges	–	–	–	–	(39.8)	–	(39.8)
Share-based payments – value of services provided	–	–	–	–	–	1.3	1.3
At 30 June 2006	40.7	420.7	710.8	–	16.0	(635.3)	552.9

Condensed Consolidated Cash Flow Statements

	Notes	Six months ended 30 June		Year ended 31 December
		2006 (Unaudited) £m	2005 £m	2005 £m
Cash generated from operations	12	338.3	320.2	462.3
Income taxes received/(paid)		1.1	(1.7)	(2.8)
Decrease in restricted cash		11.3	5.6	26.9
Interest paid on the refinancing and listing		–	–	(86.2)
Interest paid		(20.2)	(58.4)	(57.5)
Interest received		4.7	2.8	5.8
Net cash generated from operating activities		335.2	268.5	348.5
Cash flows from investing activities				
Purchase of property, plant and equipment		(12.2)	(12.4)	(25.0)

Net cash used in investing activities		(12.2)	(12.4)	(25.0)
Cash flows from financing activities				
Repayment of borrowings		(112.6)	–	–
Repayment of borrowings prior to the refinancing and listing		–	(216.5)	(267.6)
Repayment of borrowings on the refinancing and listing		–	–	(582.6)
Debt issued as a result of the refinancing and listing		–	–	577.0
Net cash used in financing activities		(112.6)	(216.5)	(273.2)
Net increase in cash and cash equivalents		210.4	39.6	50.3
Cash and cash equivalents at beginning of the period		87.8	37.5	37.5
Cash and cash equivalents at end of the period	12	298.2	77.1	87.8

Notes to the Condensed Consolidated Financial Statements

(1) General Information. Drax Group Plc (the 'Company') is a company incorporated in England and Wales under the Companies Act 1985. Drax Group Plc and its subsidiaries (together the 'Group') operate in the electricity generation industry within the United Kingdom. The address of Drax Group Plc's registered office and principal establishment is Drax Power Station, Selby, North Yorkshire, YO8 8PQ, United Kingdom.

(2) Basis of Preparation. The condensed consolidated financial statements have been prepared using accounting policies consistent with IFRS in accordance with IAS 34 *Interim Financial Reporting.*

The Refinancing and Listing of the Group, effective on 15 December 2005, resulted in the creation of a new holding company, Drax Group Plc. Under IFRS 3, the insertion of Drax Group Plc as the new holding company was accounted for as a reverse acquisition, whereby Drax Group Limited (being the previous Group holding company), the legal subsidiary, acquired Drax Group Plc, the legal parent company.

The information for the year ended 31 December 2005 does not constitute statutory accounts as defined in Section 240 of the Companies Act 1985. A copy of the statutory accounts for that year has been delivered to the Registrar of Companies. The auditors' report on those accounts was not qualified and did not contain statements under Section 237(2) or (3) of the Companies Act 1985.

The interim financial statements were approved by the Board of Directors on 11 September 2006.

(3) Significant Accounting Policies. The accounting policies adopted are consistent with those followed in the preparation of the Group's annual financial statements for the year ended 31 December 2005. The Group does not expect any significant changes in accounting policies in the remainder of 2006.

Independent Review Report to Drax Group Plc

Introduction

We have been instructed by the Company to review the financial information for the six months ended 30 June 2006 which comprises the condensed consolidated income statements, the condensed consolidated balance sheets, the condensed consolidated statement of total recognised income and expense, the condensed consolidated statement of changes in equity, the condensed consolidated cash flow statements and related Notes 1–12. We have read the other information contained in the interim report and considered whether it contains any apparent misstatements or material inconsistencies with the financial information.

This report is made solely to the Company in accordance with Bulletin 1999/4 issued by the Auditing Practices Board. Our work has been undertaken so that we might state to the Company those matters we are required to state to them in an independent review report and for no other purpose. To the fullest extent permitted by law, we do not accept or assume responsibility to anyone other than the Company, for our review work, for this report or for the conclusions we have formed.

Directors' responsibilities

The interim report, including the financial information contained therein, is the responsibility of, and has been approved by, the directors. The directors are responsible for preparing the interim report in accordance with the Listing Rules of the Financial Services Authority and the requirements of IAS 34 which require that the accounting policies and presentation applied to the interim figures are consistent with those applied in preparing the preceding annual accounts except where any changes, and the reasons for them, are disclosed.

Review work performed

We conducted our review in accordance with the guidance contained in Bulletin 1999/4 issued by the Auditing Practices Board for use in the United Kingdom. A review consists principally of making enquiries of Group management and applying analytical procedures to the financial information and underlying financial data and, based thereon, assessing whether the accounting policies and presentation have been consistently applied unless otherwise disclosed. A review excludes audit procedures such as tests of controls and verification of assets, liabilities and transactions. It is substantially less in scope than an audit performed in accordance with International Standards on Auditing (United Kingdom and Ireland) and therefore provides a lower level of assurance than an audit. Accordingly, we do not express an audit opinion on the financial information.

Review conclusion

On the basis of our review we are not aware of any material modifications that should be made to the financial information as presented for the six months ended 30 June 2006.

Deloitte & Touche LLP
Chartered Accountants
London
11 September 2006

13.2   IAS 41 *Agriculture* (February 2001)

Introduction

This specialised standard has been published because agriculture is very important in developing countries, as well as the developed world, in terms of GDP.

The main problem in developing such a standard is the great diversity in practice in accounting that exists in agriculture. It is also very difficult to apply traditional accounting methods to agricultural activities.

The main problems are:

(a)   When and how should entities account for critical events associated with biological transformation (growth, procreation, production and degeneration) which alter the substance of biological assets.
(b)   Balance sheet classification is made difficult by the variety and characteristics of the living assets of agriculture.
(c)   The nature of management of agricultural activities means that the unit of measurement is difficult to determine.

Definitions

*   *Agricultural activity.* The management by an enterprise of the biological transformation of biological assets for sale, into agricultural produce or into additional biological assets.
*   *Agricultural produce.* The harvested product of an enterprise's biological assets.
*   *Biological asset.* A living animal or plant.
*   *Biological transformation.* The processes of growth, degeneration, production and procreation that cause qualitative and quantitative changes in a biological asset.
*   *Group of biological assets.* An aggregation of similar living animals or plants.
*   *Harvest.* The detachment of produce from a biological asset or the cessation of a biological asset's life processes.

Scope

IAS 41 applies to the three elements that form part of, or result from, agricultural activity:

(1)   Biological assets
(2)   Agricultural produce at the point of harvest
(3)   Government grants

Biological assets	Agricultural produce	Products that are the result of processing after harvest
Sheep	Wool	Yarn, carpet
Trees in a plantation forest	Logs	Lumber
Plants	Cotton; Harvested cane	Thread, clothing; Sugar
Dairy cattle	Milk	Cheese
Pigs	Carcass	Sausages, cured hams
Bushes	Leaf	Tea, cured tobacco
Vines	Grapes	Wine
Fruit trees	Picked fruit	Processed fruit

The standard does not apply to agricultural land (see IASs 16 and 40) or intangible assets (see IAS 38). Also after harvest IAS 2 *Inventories* applies.

Biological assets

These are the core income producing assets of agricultural activity, held for their transformation abilities. Biological transformation leads to various different outcomes:

(a) Asset changes   – growth (increase in quantity and/or quality);
        – degeneration (decrease in quantity and/or quality).
(b) Creation of new assets – production (separable non-living products);
        – procreation (separable living animals).

Asset changes are critical to the flow of future economic benefits both in and beyond the current accounting period but their relative importance depends on the purpose of the agricultural activity.

The IAS distinguishes between two broad categories of agricultural production:

(a) consumable – animals/plants harvested;
(b) bearer – animals/plants that bear produce for harvest.

Biological assets are usually managed in groups of animal or plant classes with characteristics which permit sustainability in perpetuity and land often forms an integral part of the activity itself.

Recognition of biological assets

The recognition criteria are very similar to other assets as these may not be recognised unless the following conditions are met:

(a) The enterprise controls the asset as a result of past events.
(b) It is probable that the future economic benefits will flow to the enterprise.
(c) The fair value or cost can be measured reliably.

Measurement of biological assets

IAS 41 requires that, at each balance sheet date, all biological assets should be measured at fair value less estimated point of sale costs.

The IAS permits an alternative method of valuation if a fair value cannot be determined because market prices are not available. In that case it can be measured at cost less accumulated depreciation and impairment losses.

The alternative basis is only permitted on initial recognition. Fair value has greater relevance, reliability, comparability and understandability as a measure of future economic benefits.

Determining fair value

The primary indicator of fair value should be net market value as this provides the best evidence of fair value when an active market exists. Markets generally differentiate between differing qualities and quantities.

Recognition

The change in the carrying amount for a group of biological assets should be allocated between:

(a)   the change attributable to differences in fair value and
(b)   the physical change in biological assets held.

The total change in carrying value between the opening and closing periods thus consists of two components. IAS 41 insists that the separate disclosure of each is fundamental to appraising current period performance and future prospects. That is because they will not be reported in the same way in the financial statements.

The change in carrying amount attributable to the physical change must be recognised as income or expense and described as the change in biological assets. This should enable management performance to be evaluated and thus should be included in the 'operating' part of the change in carrying amount.

The change in carrying amount attributable to differences in fair value should be recognised in the statement of non-owner movements in equity and presented in equity under the heading of surplus/(deficit) on fair valuation of biological assets. This is the 'holding' part of the change in the carrying amount.

In the balance sheet the biological assets must be recorded at fair value after incorporating the consequences of all biological transformations. These assets, together with differing risk and return characteristics should be identified clearly.

The recommended method of separating the above components is to calculate the change attributable to the differences in fair value by restating biological assets on hand at the opening balance sheet using end of period fair values and comparing this with the closing carrying amount.

There are exceptions to this approach, e.g. where the production cycle is less than one year (broiler chickens, mushroom growing, cereal crops, etc.). In these cases the total change in carrying amount should be reported in the income statement as a single item of income or expense.

Any other events giving rise to a change in biological assets of such a size, nature or incidence that their disclosure is relevant to explain the entity's performance should be included in the change in biological assets recognised as an income or expense. They should be recorded as a separate item in the reconciliation required to determine the change attributable to biological transformation.

Presentation and disclosure

Balance sheet

Biological assets should be classified as a separate class of assets falling under neither current nor non-current classifications – unlimited life on a collective basis – it is the total exposure to the type of asset that is important.

Biological assets should also be sub-classified as follows:

(a)   class of animal or plant;
(b)   nature of activities (consumable or bearer); and
(c)   maturity or immaturity for intended purpose.

Where activities are consumable, the maturity criterion will be the attainment of harvestable specifications whereas in bearer activities it will be the attainment of sufficient maturity to sustain economic harvests.

In the income statement an analysis of income and expenses based on their nature should be presented rather than the cost of sales method.

IAS 41 also requires detailed disclosures to include the measurement base used for fair value, the details of the reconciliation of the change in carrying value for the year, etc.

Agricultural produce

This is recognised at the point of harvest, e.g. detachment from the biological asset. It is either incapable of biological process or such processes are dormant. Recognition ends once the produce enters trading activities or production processes within integrated agribusinesses.

Measurement and presentation

Should be measured at fair value at each balance sheet date. The change in the carrying amount of agriculture produce held at two balance sheet dates should be recognised as income or expenses in the income statement. This will be rare as such produce is usually sold or processed within a short time.

Agricultural produce that is harvested for trading or processing activities within integrated agricultural operations should be measured at fair value at the date of harvest and this amount is the deemed cost for application of IAS 2 to consequential inventories.

Presentation on the balance sheet

Agricultural produce should be classified as inventory in the balance sheet and disclosed separately either on the face of the balance sheet or in the notes.

Government grants

An unconditional government grant related to a biological asset measured at fair value less estimated point of sale costs should be recognised as income when, and only when, the grant becomes receivable.

If a grant requires an enterprise not to engage in agricultural activity an enterprise should only recognise the grant as income when the conditions are met.

IAS 20 normally does not apply to agricultural grants. However, if a biological asset is measured at cost less accumulated depreciation and impairment losses then IAS 20 does apply.

Overall disclosure

An enterprise should disclose the aggregate gain or loss arising during the current period on initial recognition of biological assets and agricultural produce and from the change in fair value less estimated point of sale costs of biological assets as well as a description of each group of biological assets.

If it is not disclosed elsewhere, the following should also be disclosed:

(a) The nature of its activities involving each group of biological assets.
(b) Non-financial measures or estimates of the physical quantities of:
    (i) each group of the enterprise's biological assets at the end of the period; and
    (ii) output of agricultural produce during the period.

The methods and significant assumptions applied in determining the fair value of each group of agricultural produce at the point of harvest and each group of biological assets should also be disclosed.

The fair value less estimated point of sale costs of agricultural produce harvested during the period, determined at the point of harvest, should be disclosed.

An enterprise should also disclose:

(a) the existence and carrying amounts of biological assets whose title is restricted, and the carrying amounts of biological assets pledged as security for liabilities;
(b) the amount of commitments for the development or acquisition of biological assets; and
(c) financial risk management strategies related to agricultural activity.

A reconciliation should be provided of changes in the carrying amount of biological assets between the start and the end of the current period and this should include:

(a) the gain or loss arising from changes in fair value less estimated point of sale costs;
(b) increases due to purchases;
(c) decreases due to sales;
(d) decreases due to harvest;
(e) increases resulting from business combinations;
(f) net exchange differences arising from the translation of financial statements of a foreign entity; and
(g) other changes.

Additional disclosures for biological assets where fair value cannot be reliably measured:

(a) a description of the biological assets;
(b) an explanation of why fair value cannot be reliably measured;
(c) if possible, the range of estimates within which fair value is highly likely to lie;
(d) the depreciation method used;
(e) the useful lives or the depreciation rates adopted;
(f) the gross carrying amount and the accumulated depreciation at the start and the end of the period.

If, during the current period, an enterprise measures biological assets at their cost less any accumulated depreciation and accumulated impairment losses, an enterprise should disclose any gain or loss recognised on disposal of such biological assets and the reconciliation required above should disclose amounts related to such biological assets separately. In addition, the reconciliation should include the following amounts included in the net profit or loss related to those biological assets:

(a) impairment losses;
(b) reversals of impairment losses; and
(c) depreciation.

If a previously measured biological asset at cost now becomes reliably measured at fair value the following should be disclosed for those assets:

(a) a description of the biological assets;
(b) an explanation of why fair value has become reliably measurable; and
(c) the effect of the change.

Government grants

The following should be disclosed:

(a) the nature and extent of government grants recognised in the financial statements;
(b) unfulfilled conditions and other contingencies attached to the grants; and
(c) significant decreases expected in the level of government grants.

Appendix A

Example 1 – XYZ Dairy Ltd

Balance Sheet

	Notes	31 December 20 × 1	31 December 20 × 0
Assets			
Non-current assets			
Dairy livestock – immature		52,060	47,730
Dairy livestock – mature		372,990	411,840
Biological assets	3	425,050	459,570
Property, plant and equipment		1,462,650	1,409,800
Total non-current assets		1,887,700	1,869,370
Current assets			
Inventories		82,950	70,650
Trade and other receivables		88,000	65,000
Cash		10,000	10,000

Total current assets	180,950	145,650
Total assets	2,068,650	2,015,020
Equity and liabilities		
Equity		
Issued capital	1,000,000	1,000,000
Accumulated profits	902,828	865,000
Total equity	1,902,828	1,865,000
Current liabilities		
Trade and other payables	165,822	150,020
Total current liabilities	165,822	150,020
Total equity and liabilities	2,068,650	2,015,020

Income Statement

Fair value of milk produced		518,240
Gains arising from changes in fair value less		
Estimated point of sale costs of dairy livestock	3	39,930
		558,170
Inventories used		(137,523)
Staff costs		(127,283)
Depreciation expense		(15,250)
Other operating expenses		(197,092)
		(477,148)
Profit from operations		81,022
Income tax expense		(43,194)
Net profit for the period		37,828

Statement of Changes in Equity

	Share capital	Accumulated profits	Year ended 31 December 20 × 1
Balance at 1 January 20 × 1	1,000,000	865,000	1,865,000
Net profit for the period		37,828	37,828
Balance at 31 December 20 × 1	1,000,000	902,828	1,902,828

Cash Flow Statement

	Notes	Year ended 31 December 20 × 1
Cash flows from operating activities		
Cash receipts from sales of milk		498,027
Cash receipts from sales of livestock		97,913
Cash paid for supplies and to employees		(460,831)
Cash paid for purchases of livestock		(23,815)
		111,294
Income taxes paid		(43,194)
Net cash flow from operating activities		68,100
Cash flows from investing activities		
Purchase of property, plant and equipment		(68,100)

Net cash used in investing activities	(68,100)
Net increase in cash	0
Cash at beginning of period	10,000
Cash at end of period	10,000

Notes to the financial statements

(1)   Operations and Principal Activities. XYZ Dairy Ltd ('the Company') is engaged in milk production for supply to various customers. At 31 December 20 × 1, the Company held 419 cows able to produce milk (mature assets) and 137 heifers being raised to produce milk in the future (immature assets). The Company produced 157,584 kg of milk with a fair value less estimated point-of-sale costs of 518,240 (that is determined at the time of milking) in the year ended 31 December 20 × 1.

(2)   Accounting Policies, Livestock and milk. Livestock are measured at their fair value less estimated point-of-sale costs. The fair value of livestock is determined based on market prices of livestock of similar age, breed and genetic merit. Milk is initially measured at its fair value less estimated point-of-sale costs at the time of milking. The fair value of milk is determined based on market prices in the local area.

(3)   Biological Assets

	20 × 1
Reconciliation of carrying amounts of dairy livestock	
Carrying amount at 1 January 20 × 1	459,570
Increases due to purchases	26,250
Gain arising from changes in fair value less estimated point-of-sale Costs attributable to physical changes	15,350
Gain arising from changes in fair value less estimated point-of-sale Costs attributable to price changes	24,580
Decreases due to sales	(100,700)
Carrying amount at 31 December 20 × 1	425,050

(4)   Financial Risk Management Strategies. The company is exposed to financial risks arising from changes in milk prices. The Company does not anticipate that milk prices will decline significantly in the foreseeable future and, therefore, has not entered into derivative or other contracts to manage the risk of a decline in milk prices. The Company reviews its outlook for milk prices regularly in considering the need for active risk management.

Example 2 – physical change and price change

The following example illustrates how to separate physical change and price change. Separating the change in fair value less estimated point-of-sale costs between the portion attributable to physical changes and the portion attributable to price changes is encouraged but not required by the standard.

A herd of 10.2-year-old animals was held at 1 January 20 × 1. One animal aged 2.5 years was purchased on 1 July 20 × 1 for 108, and one animal was born on 1 July 20 × 1. No animals were sold or disposed of during the period. Per unit fair values less estimated point-of-sale costs were as follows:

2-year-old animal at 1 January 20 × 1	100
Newborn animal at 1 July 20 × 1	70
2.5-year-old animal at 1 July 20 × 1	108
Newborn animal at 31 December 20 × 1	72
0.5-year-old animal at 31 December 20 × 1	80
2-year-old animal at 31 December 20 × 1	105
2.5-year-old animal at 31 December 20 × 1	111
3-year-old animal at 31 December 20 × 1	120

Fair value less estimated point-of-sale costs of herd at 1 January 20 × 1	(10 × 100)	1,000
Purchase on 1 July 20 × 1	(1 × 108)	108

Increase in fair value less estimated point-of-sale costs due to price change:

10 × (105 − 100)	50
1 × (111 − 108)	3
1 × (72 − 70)	2
	55

Increase in fair value less estimated point-of-sale costs due to physical change:

10 × (120 − 105)	150
1 × (120 − 111)	9
1 × (80 − 72)	8
1 × 70	70
	237

Fair value less estimated point-of-sale costs of herd at 31 December 20 × 1

11 × 120	1,320
1 × 80	80
	1,400

One group providing the required disclosure under IAS 41 is Diageo Plc:

Diageo Plc   Year Ended 30 June 2006

Accounting Policies (Extract)

Agriculture

Grape cultivation by the group's wine business is accounted for as an agricultural activity. Accordingly the group's biological assets (grape vines) are carried at fair value which is computed on the basis of a discounted cash flow computation. Agricultural produce (harvested grapes) is valued at market value on transfer into inventory.

13. Biological Assets

	Grape vine (£m)
Fair value	
At 1 July 2004	13
Harvested grapes transferred to inventories	(10)
Changes in fair value	11
At 30 June 2005	14
Exchange differences	(1)
Harvested grapes transferred to inventories	(19)
Changes, in fair value	19
At 30 June 2006	**13**

(a) Biological assets comprise grape vines and grapes on the vine. At 30 June 2006, grape vines comprise approximately 1,769 hectares (2005: 1,428ha) of vineyards, ranging from newly established vineyards to vineyards that are 87 years old.
(b) There are no outstanding commitments for the acquisition or development of vineyards.

Associated British Foods Plc discloses that it acquired during the year a sugar cane producer that has 60,000 hectares in various countries in Southern Africa. Unlike Diageo, which recognise biological assets as non-current, the company distinguishes its biological assets into current growing cane of £51 million and non-current cane roots of £46 million. In accordance with IAS 41, the company discloses within the accounting policies note that cane roots and growing cane are held at fair value. It explains the basis upon which they are measured with cane roots determined at escalated average cost, using inflation indices, for the remaining expected life with growing cane measured at the estimated sucrose price for the following season, less costs for harvesting and transport. Additionally, a table is published showing movements in the year.

Associated British Foods Plc   Year Ended
16 September 2006

Accounting Policies and Notes to the Accounts (Extract)

Biological assets

Cane roots and growing canes are valued at fair value determined on the following bases:

- Cane roots – the escalated average cost, using appropriate inflation related indices, of each year of planting adjusted for the remaining expected life.
- Growing cane – the estimated sucrose content valued at the estimated sucrose price for the following season, less the estimated costs for harvesting and transport.

11. Biological Assets

	Current growing cane £m	Non-current cane roots £m	Total £m
Carrying value			
At 17 September 2005	–	–	–
Acquired through business combination	51	47	98
Effect of movements in foreign exchange	–	(1)	(1)
At 16 September 2006	51	46	97

Cane roots	
Area under cane as at 16 September 2006	*Hectares*
South Africa	10,668
Malawi	18,381
Zambia	11,030
Swaziland	7,946
Tanzania	8,003
Mozambique	3,671
	59,699

Growing cane

The following assumptions have been used in the determination of the estimated sucrose tonnage at 16 September 2006:

	South Africa	Malawi	Zambia	Swaziland	Tanzania	Mozambique
Expected area to harvest (ha)	6,173	18,072	10,948	7,572	7,815	3,649
Estimated yield (tonnes cane/ha)	69.0	109.0	118.0	105.9	76.0	102.1
Average maturity of cane (%)	56.10	66.67	66.67	66.67	50.00	66.67

A final example of both the policy note and movement on balance sheet is provided by Finnish company UPM:

UPM   Year Ended 31 December 2006

Accounting Policies and Notes to the Accounts (Extract)

Biological Assets. Biological assets (i.e. living trees) are measured at their fair value less estimated point-of-sale costs. The fair value of biological assets other than young seedling stands is based on discounted cash flows from continuous operations. The fair value of young seedling stands is the actual reforestation cost of those stands. Continuous operations, the maintenance of currently existing seedling stands and the felling of forests during one rotation, are based on the Company's forest management guidelines. The calculation takes into account the growth potential and environmental restrictions and other reservations of the forests. Felling revenues and maintenance costs are calculated on the basis of actual costs and prices, taking into account the Company's projection of future price development.

Periodic changes resulting from growth, felling, prices, discount rate, costs and other premise changes are included in operating profit on the income statement.

8. Change in fair value of biological assets and wood harvested

	Year ended 31 December		
(€m)	2006	2005	2004
Biological assets harvested during the period	−107	−34	−42
Fair value change of biological assets	−19	68	57
Total	−126	34	15

20. Biological Assets

	As at 31 December	
(€m)	2006	2005
At 1 January	1,174	1,143
Purchases during the period	3	4
Sales during the period	−12	−7
Harvested during the period	−107	−34
Gains and losses arising from changes in fair values	−19	68
Translation differences	−2	−
At 31 December	1,037	1,174

The discount rate used in determining the fair value in 2006 was 7.50% (2005: 7.0%). A 1% decrease (increase) in discount rate would increase (decrease) the fair value of biological assets by approximately €120 million.

13.3   IFRS 4 *Insurance Contracts* (March 2004)

Background

IFRS 4 was introduced to prescribe the financial reporting required for insurance contracts by any entity issuing such contracts. It is applied to insurance contracts issued, reinsurance contracts held and financial instruments issued with a discretionary participation feature.

However, it does not apply to the following:

- Product warranties (covered by IASs 18 and 37).
- Employers' assets and liabilities under employee benefit plans (see IASs 19 and 26).
- Contractual rights that are contingent on the future use of or right to use a non-financial item and a lessee's residual value guarantees on finance leases (see IASs 17, 18 and 38).
- Financial guarantees entered into within the scope of IAS 39.
- Contingent consideration re business combination (see IFRS 3).
- Direct insurance contracts that an entity holds as a policy holder.

Key Points

IFRS 4 is only the first phase on the project on insurance contracts. The main points in the standard are as follows:

(1) It prohibits the recognition of a liability for provisions for future claims under insurance contracts that are not in existence at the reporting date, e.g. catastrophe and equalisation provisions.

(2) It requires an assessment to be made of the adequacy of recognised insurance liabilities and the recognition of any impairment of reinsurance assets.

(3) It requires an entity to keep insurance liabilities on the balance sheet until they are discharged or cancelled or expired and to ensure that insurance liabilities are presented without any offsetting against related reinsurance assets.

An entity is only permitted to change its accounting policies for insurance contracts if, as a result, its financial statements are more relevant or more reliable and no less relevant than previously. In particular, an entity must not introduce any of the following practices although, if currently adopted, it may continue to use them:

(1) measuring insurance liabilities on an undiscounted basis;

(2) measuring contractual rights to future investment management fees at an amount that exceeds their fair value as implied by a comparison with current fees charged by other market participants for similar services;

(3) using non-uniform accounting policies for the insurance contracts of subsidiaries;

(4) measuring insurance liabilities with excessive prudence.

There is a rebuttable presumption that an insurer's financial statements will become less relevant and reliable if it introduces an accounting policy that reflects future investment margins in measuring insurance contracts. When an insurer changes its accounting policies for insurance liabilities, it may reclassify some or all financial assets as 'at fair value through profit or loss'.

Sundry issues

IFRS 4 also specifies the following:

- An entity need not account for an embedded derivative separately at fair value if the embedded derivative meets the definition of an insurance contract.
- An entity is required to unbundle deposit components of some insurance contracts.
- An entity may apply 'shadow accounting' (i.e. account for both realised and unrealised gains or losses on assets in the same way relative to the measurement of insurance liabilities).
- Discretionary participation features contained in insurance contracts or financial instruments may be recognised separately from the guaranteed element and classified as a liability or as a separate component of equity.

Disclosures

IFRS 4 requires disclosure of the amounts in an entity's financial statements that arise from insurance contracts and the amount, timing and uncertainty of future cash flows from insurance contracts.

Legal and General Group Plc   Year Ended 31 December 2006

Accounting policies

Insurance contract liabilities. Under current IFRS requirements, insurance contract liabilities are measured using local generally accepted accounting principles (GAAP), as permitted by IFRS 4, 'Insurance Contracts'.

In the United Kingdom, insurance contract liabilities are determined following an annual investigation of the LTF in accordance with regulatory requirements. The liabilities are calculated on the basis of current information and using the gross premium valuation method. For participating contracts, the liabilities to policyholders are determined on a realistic basis in accordance with Financial Reporting Standard (FRS) 27, 'Life Assurance'. This includes an assessment of the cost of any future options and guarantees included in this business valued on a market consistent basis. The calculation also takes account of bonus decisions that are consistent with Legal & General Assurance Society's (Society's) Principles and Practices of Financial Management (PPFM). The shareholders' share of the future cost of bonuses is excluded from the assessment of the realistic liability. In determining the realistic value of liabilities for participating contracts, the value of non-participating business written in the with-profits part of the fund is accounted for as part of the calculation. The present value of future profits (VIF) on this business is separately determined and its value is deducted from the sum of the liabilities for participating contracts and the unallocated divisible surplus.

The long-term insurance contract liabilities for business transacted by overseas subsidiaries are determined on the basis of recognised actuarial methods which reflect local supervisory principles or, in the case of the USA, on the basis of US GAAP.

Long-term business liabilities can never be definitive as to their timing or the amount of claims and are therefore subject to subsequent reassessment on a regular basis.

Unallocated divisible surplus. The nature of benefits for participating contracts is such that the allocation of surpluses between ordinary equity holders and participating policyholders is uncertain. The amount of surplus which has not been allocated at the balance sheet date is classified within liabilities as the unallocated divisible surplus. Adjustments made to comply with FRS 27 are charged to the unallocated divisible surplus.

Notes to the financial statements

33. Insurance Contract Liabilities

(i) *Analysis of insurance contract liabilities*

	Gross 2006 £m	Reinsurance 2006 £m	Gross 2005 £m	Reinsurance 2005 £m
Life and pensions participating insurance contracts (iii)	12,660	(1)	13,180	(1)
Life and pensions non-participating insurance contracts (iv)	21,321	(1,237)	22,860	(2,649)
General insurance contracts (v)	281	(16)	292	(14)
Insurance contract liabilities	34,262	(1,254)	36,332	(2,664)

(ii) *Expected insurance contract net cash flows*

As at 31 December 2006	0–5 years £m	5–15 years £m	15–25 years £m	Over 25 years £m	Total £m	Carrying value £m
Life and pensions participating insurance contracts	7,124	7,086	1,403	470	16,083	12,659
Life and pensions non-participating insurance contracts	4,797	9,754	8,946	11,782	35,279	14,132
General insurance contracts	129	–	–	–	129	129
Insurance contract liabilities	12,050	16,840	10,349	12,252	51,491	26,920

	Date of cash flow					
As at 31 December 2005	0–5 years £m	5–15 years £m	15–25 years £m	Over 25 years £m	Total £m	Carrying value £m
Life and pensions participating insurance contracts	6,366	8,068	1,592	638	16,664	12,978
Life and pensions non-participating insurance contracts	4,378	8,774	8,422	11,165	32,739	14,598

| General insurance contracts | 278 | – | – | – | 278 | 278 |
| Insurance contract liabilities | 11,022 | 16,842 | 10,014 | 11,803 | 49,681 | 27,854 |

Insurance contract net cash flows are based on the expected date of settlement. Unit linked contracts have been excluded from the table due to the exact matching of cash flows to those of the linked backing assets.

(iii) *Movement in participating insurance contract liabilities*

	Gross 2006 £m	Reinsurance 2006 £m	Gross 2005 £m	Reinsurance 2005 £m
Balance at 1 January	13,180	(1)	12,388	(1)
New liabilities in the year	240	–	224	–
Liabilities discharged in the year	(1,671)	–	(1,142)	–
Unwinding of discount rates	432	–	402	–
Effect of change in non-economic assumptions	29	–	305	–
Effect of change in economic assumptions	487	–	1,148	–
Other	(37)	–	(145)	–
Balance at 31 December	12,660	(1)	13,180	(1)
Expected to be settled within 12 months (net of reinsurance)	1,431		1,153	
Expected to be settled after 12 months (net of reinsurance)	11,228		12,026	

In 2005, the largest impact of changes to non-economic assumptions was from the strengthening of the provision for claims on the endowment book (£240m). The assumption setting process is outlined in Note 37.

(iv) *Movement in non-participating insurance contract liabilities*

	Gross 2006 £m	Reinsurance 2006 £m	Gross 2005 £m	Reinsurance 2005 £m
Balance at 1 January	22,860	(2,649)	20,509	(2,887)
New liabilities in the year	1,995	(287)	2,370	(457)
Liabilities discharged in the year	(1,630)	75	(1,350)	215
Unwinding of discount rates	958	(134)	926	(225)
Effect of change in non-economic assumptions	90	(33)	(709)	706
Effect of change in economic assumptions	(417)	9	899	(1)
Foreign exchange adjustments	(176)	26	95	(19)
Other	(2,359)	1,756	120	19
Balance at 31 December	21,321	(1,237)	22,860	(2,649)

Expected to be settled within 12 months (net of reinsurance)	1,492		1,244
Expected to be settled after 12 months (net of reinsurance)	18,592		18,967

Included within effect of economic assumption changes is the impact of Society's review of its annuity investment policy as described in Note 2. In 2006, other includes £2,248 million gross (£1,756m reinsurance) relating to the impact of applying PS06/14. The implementation of PS06/14 is described in Note 2.

(v) *Analysis of General insurance contract liabilities*

	Gross 2006	Reinsurance 2006	Gross 2005	Reinsurance 2005
	£m	£m	£m	£m
Outstanding claims	101	(4)	97	(5)
Claims incurred but not reported	36	(1)	45	–
Unearned premiums	144	(11)	150	(9)
General insurance contract liabilities	281	(16)	292	(14)

(vi) *Movement in General insurance claim liabilities*

	Gross 2006	Reinsurance 2006	Gross 2005	Reinsurance 2005
	£m	£m	£m	£m
Balance at 1 January	142	(5)	180	(6)
Claims arising	247	(3)	272	(6)
Claims paid	(206)	2	(219)	6
Adjustments to prior year liabilities	(46)	1	(38)	1
	137	(5)	195	(5)
Disposal of Gresham	–	–	(53)	–
Balance at 31 December	137	(5)	142	(5)
Expected to be settled within 12 months (net of reinsurance)	85		91	
Expected to be settled after 12 months (net of reinsurance)	47		46	

(vii) *Unearned premiums*

	Gross 2006	Reinsurance 2006	Gross 2005	Reinsurance 2005
	£m	£m	£m	£m
Balance at 1 January	150	(9)	223	(16)
Earned in the period	(150)	(11)	(145)	(9)

Gross written premiums in respect of future periods	144	9	150	12
Disposal of Gresham		–	(78)	4
Balance at 31 December	144	(11)	150	(9)
Expected to be settled within 12 months (net of reinsurance)	131		138	
Expected to be settled after 12 months (net of reinsurance)	2		3	

(viii) *Claims development – General insurance*

Changes may occur in the amount of the Group's obligations at the end of a contract period. The top section of each table below illustrates how the estimate of total claims outstanding for each accident year developed over time. The bottom section of the table reconciles the cumulative claims to the amount appearing in the balance sheet. The claims development tables exclude amounts relating to Gresham which was disposed of in 2005.

Gross of reinsurance

Accident year	2002 (£m)	2003 (£m)	2004 (£m)	2005 (£m)	2006 (£m)	Total (£m)
Estimate of ultimate claims costs:						
At end of accident year	137	147	171	209	205	
One year later	133	145	166	195	–	
Two years later	133	141	160	–	–	
Three years later	132	142	–	–	–	
Four years later	133	–	–	–	–	
Estimate of cumulative claims	133	142	160	195	205	835
Cumulative payments	(131)	(135)	(151)	(172)	(121)	(710)
Outstanding claims provision	2	7	9	23	84	125
Prior period outstanding claims						9
Claims handling provision						3

Total claims liabilities recognised in the balance sheet						137

Net of reinsurance

Accident year	2002 (£m)	2003 (£m)	2004 (£m)	2005 (£m)	2006 (£m)	Total (£m)
Estimate of ultimate claims costs:						
At end of accident year	134	142	162	205	200	
One year later	130	140	161	193	–	
Two years later	130	137	157	–	–	
Three years later	129	139	–	–	–	
Four years later	129	–	–	–	–	
Estimate of cumulative claims	129	139	157	193	200	818
Cumulative payments	(127)	(132)	(149)	(171)	(119)	(698)
Outstanding claims provision	2	7	8	22	81	120
Prior period outstanding claims						9
Claims handling provision						3
Total claims liabilities recognised in the balance sheet						132

Old Mutual   Year Ended 31 December 2005

Insurance contracts

IFRS 4 *Insurance Contracts* requires or permits a company in some cases to unbundle its insurance contract and deposit components. Previously, contracts that did not include significant insurance risk were, nevertheless, classified by Old Mutual as insurance. Amounts received in respect of investment contracts were included within premium income whereas amounts paid out were classified as expenses. Following IFRS 4, the company unbundles those contracts and amounts received where there is no significant insurance risk classified as investment contract liabilities. Similarly, deferred acquisition costs have been disclosed previously without any further analysis but this year, the company disaggregates its £1 billion deferred acquisition costs: £936 million to insurance contracts including insurance contracts with discretionary policy features; £105 million to investment contracts and £32 million asset management costs.

Additionally, the company adopts shadow accounting which allows it to recognise unrealised gains or losses on insurer's assets and a gain of £117 million is recognised directly in equity. This follows IFRS 4 which permits the company to change its accounting policies and recognise the effects of unrealised gains or losses on insurer's assets directly in equity.

Last year, the company published voluntary supplementary disclosures in accordance with FRS 27 'Life assurance' although they were unaudited. This year, it continues to make voluntary disclosures under FRS 27 but states that it is not required to do so as it presents its financial statements under IFRS.

13.4   IFRS 6 *Exploration and Evaluation of Mineral Resources*

IFRS 6 applies to expenditures incurred by an entity in connection with the search for mineral resources. It applies to exploration and evaluation expenditures including minerals, oil and natural gas. This includes the determination of the technical feasibility and commercial viability. However, the following are excluded from its scope:

(a)   expenditures incurred before the entity has obtained legal rights to explore and
(b)   expenditures incurred after technical feasibility and commercial viability demonstrable.

Selection of accounting policies for exploration and evaluation assets

A wide variety is followed ranging from deferring on the balance sheet nearly all exploration and evaluation expenditures to recognising all in profit or loss. IFRS 6 does not require or prohibit any specific accounting policies but rather permits entities to continue to use existing policies provided they comply with IAS 8, i.e. result in information that is relevant and reliable.

Changes in accounting policies

Entities may change their accounting policies if more relevant or reliable using criteria in IAS 8 but a change must be justified as closer to meeting IAS 8 criteria.

Assets to be measured at cost at recognition

When first recognised on balance sheet exploration and evaluation assets must be measured at cost and costs therein should be applied consistently. IFRS 6 lists examples of costs that might be included such as acquisition of rights to explore; topographical, geological, geo-chemical and geophysical studies; exploratory drilling; trenching; sampling; and activities in relation to evaluating the technical feasibility and commercial viability of extracting a mineral resource.

When an entity incurs obligations for removal and restoration these must be recognised in accordance with IAS 37.

Subsequent measurement

After recognition, entities can apply either the cost model or the revaluation model to exploration and evaluation expenditure. Where revaluation model is selected should apply IAS 16 to tangible and IAS 38 to intangible assets.

Impairment

Because of difficulty of estimating future cash flows from exploration and evaluation assets, IFRS 6 modifies the rules of IAS 36. A detailed test is required in two circumstances:
- when technical feasibility and commercial viability become demonstrable – outside scope of IFRS 6 and is reclassified in the financial statements and
- when facts and circumstances suggest the asset's carrying amount may exceed its recoverable amount.

The following 'facts and circumstances' may indicate impairment testing is required:
- period of 'right to explore' has expired and not expected to be renewed;
- substantive expenditure on future exploration is neither budgeted nor planned;
- exploration for and evaluation has not led to discovery of commercially viable quantities of mineral resources and entity is discontinuing its activities in a specific area;
- although development likely to proceed, the carrying amount is unlikely to be recovered in full from successful development or by sale.

IFRS 6 permits greater flexibility as regards level at which the impairment assessment should be performed. CGUs should be determined by individual entities but should not be larger than a segment based on either the entity's primary or secondary reporting format under IAS 14.

Subject to the above, the measurement, recognition and disclosure of impairment should be in accordance with IAS 36.

Presentation

Must classify exploration and evaluation expenditure assets as tangible or intangible according to their nature. Examples of tangible assets include vehicles and drilling rigs and intangible assets include drilling rights.

Once technical feasibility and commercial viability become demonstrable any previously recognised exploration and evaluation assets fall outside the scope of IFRS 6 and is reclassified in accordance with other standards but they should be assessed for impairment first.

Disclosure

Entities are required to disclose information that identifies and explains the amounts recognised in the financial statements. The following should be disclosed:

- the accounting policies for exploration and evaluation expenditures and
- the amounts of assets, liabilities, income and expense and operating and investing cash flows arising from the exploration and evaluation of mineral resources.

These assets are treated as a separate class of assets.

Effective date

IFRS 6 is effective for annual periods beginning on or after 1 January 2006.

A good example of the disclosure required is provided by Vedanta Resources Plc:

Vedanta Resources Plc   Year Ended 31 December 2006

2a. Accounting policies continued

Property, plant and equipment, Mining properties and leases. Exploration and evaluation expenditure is written off in the year in which it is incurred.

The costs of mining properties and leases, which include the costs of acquiring and developing mining properties and mineral rights, are capitalised as property, plant and equipment under the heading 'Mining properties and leases' in the year in which they are incurred.

When a decision is taken that a mining property is viable for commercial production, all further pre-production primary development expenditure other than land, buildings, plant and equipment, etc., is capitalised as part of the cost of the mining property until the mining property is capable of commercial production. Capitalisation of pre-production expenditure ceases when the mining property is capable of commercial production. From that point, capitalised mining properties and lease costs are amortised on a unit-of-production basis over the total estimated remaining commercial reserves of each property or group of properties.

Stripping costs/secondary development expenditure incurred during the production stage of operations of an ore body are charged to the income statement immediately.

Exploration and evaluation assets acquired are recognised as assets at their cost of acquisition subject to meeting the commercial production criteria mentioned above and are subject to impairment review.

In circumstances where a property is abandoned, the cumulative capitalised costs relating to the property are written off in the period.

Commercial reserves are proved and probable reserves. Changes in the commercial reserves affecting unit of production calculations are dealt with prospectively over the revised remaining reserves.

Restoration, rehabilitation and environmental costs

An obligation to incur restoration, rehabilitation and environmental costs arises when environmental disturbance is caused by the development or ongoing production of a mine. Costs arising from the installation of plant and other site preparation work, discounted to net present value, are provided for and a corresponding amount is capitalised at the start of each project, as soon as the obligation to incur such costs arises. These costs are charged to the income statement over the life of the operation through the depreciation of the asset and the unwinding of the discount on the provision. The cost estimates are reviewed periodically and are adjusted to reflect known developments which may have an impact on the cost estimates or life of operations. The cost of the related asset is adjusted for changes in the provision due to factors such as updated cost estimates, changes to lives of operations, new disturbance and revisions to discount rates. The adjusted cost of the asset is depreciated prospectively over the life of the asset to which it relates. The unwinding of the discount is shown as a financing cost in the income statement.

Costs for restoration of subsequent site damage which is caused on an ongoing basis during production are provided for at their net present values and charged to the income statement as extraction progresses. Where the costs of site restoration are not anticipated to be material, they are expensed as incurred.

Another company providing detailed disclosures is Total SA:

Total SA Year   Ended 31 December 2006

H. Oil and gas exploration and producing properties

The Group applies IFRS 6 'Exploration for and Evaluation of Mineral Resources'. Oil and gas exploration and production properties and assets are accounted for in accordance with the successful efforts method.

(i) *Exploration costs.* Geological and geophysical costs, including seismic surveys for exploration purposes, are expensed as incurred.

Leasehold rights are capitalised as intangible assets when acquired. They are tested for impairment on a regular basis, property-by-property, based on the results of exploration activity and management's evaluation.

In the event of a discovery, the unproved leasehold rights are transferred to proved leasehold rights at their net book value as soon as proved reserves are booked.

Exploratory wells are tested for impairment on a well-by-well basis and accounted as follows:

(a) Costs of exploratory wells that have found proved reserves are capitalised. Capitalised successful exploration wells are then depreciated using the unit-of-production method based on proved developed reserves.

(b) Costs of dry exploratory wells and wells that have not found proved reserves are charged to expense.

(c) Costs of exploratory wells are temporarily capitalised until a determination is made as to whether the well has found proved reserves if both of the following conditions are met:

- the well has found a sufficient quantity of reserves to justify its completion as a producing well, if appropriate, assuming that the required capital expenditures are made;
- the Group is making sufficient progress assessing the reserves and the economic and operating viability of the project. This progress is evaluated on the basis of indicators such as whether additional exploratory works are under way or firmly planned (wells: seismic or significant studies), whether costs are being incurred for development studies and whether the Group is waiting for governmental or other third-party authorisation of a proposed project, or availability of capacity on an existing transport or processing facility.

Costs of exploratory wells not meeting these conditions are charged to expense.

(ii) *Oil and gas producing assets.* Development costs incurred for the drilling of development wells and in the construction of production facilities are capitalised, together with interest costs incurred during the period of construction and estimated discounted costs of asset retirement obligations. The depletion rate is equal to the ratio of oil and gas production for the period to proved developed reserves (unit-of-production method).

With respect to production sharing contracts, this computation is based on the portion of production and reserves assigned to the Group taking into account estimates based on the contractual clauses regarding the reimbursement of exploration and development costs (cost oil) as well as the sharing of hydrocarbon rights (profit oil).

Transportation assets are depreciated using the unit-of-production method based on throughput or by using the straight-line method whichever best reflects the economic life of the asset.

Proved leasehold rights are depreciated using the unit-of-production method based on proved reserves.

The final example, taken from Rio Tinto Plc, reveals compliance with IFRS 6 as well:

Rio Tinto Plc   Year Ended 31 December 2006

IFRS 6 permits a company to change its accounting policies for exploration and evaluation expenditure if the change makes the financial statements more relevant and no less reliable, or more reliable and no less relevant to the needs of users and requires the change to be justified.

In 2005, Rio Tinto adopted early IFRS 6 and continued its UK GAAP policy of commencing capitalisation of exploration expenditure on acquisition of a beneficial interest or option in mineral rights. Such expenditure was reviewed for impairment at the balance sheet date and a charge was made for full impairment, unless there was a high degree of confidence in a project's viability. If, as a result of subsequent developments, the expenditure was considered recoverable, such charges have been reversed.

In 2005, the company changed its accounting policy and now does not commence capitalisation until there is a high degree of confidence in a project's viability and it is considered probable that future economic benefits will flow to the company. Consequently, instead of disclosing separately movements in cost and in accumulated amortisation/impairment as previously, the company disclosed in a single table changes leading to the closing $196 million net book value, with $72 million capitalised expenditure disclosed in a single line. It added a table indicating that the income statement charge for the year was comprised of cash expenditure and changes in accruals, from which capitalised expenditure is deducted. Where successful development of an asset was not viable, irrecoverable costs were written off. Rio Tinto added that the consequent adjustments were not material to earnings or equity and that therefore prior periods were not restated.

(f) *Exploration and evaluation.* Exploration and evaluation expenditure comprises costs which are directly attributable to:

- researching and analysing existing exploration data;
- conducting geological studies, exploratory drilling and sampling;
- examining and testing extraction and treatment methods; and/or
- compiling pre-feasibility and feasibility studies.

Exploration and evaluation expenditure also includes costs incurred in acquiring mineral rights, the entry premiums paid to gain access to areas of interest and amounts payable to third parties to acquire interests in existing projects.

Capitalisation of exploration and evaluation expenditure commences when there is a high degree of confidence in the project's viability and hence it is probable that future economic benefits will flow to the Group.

Capitalised exploration and evaluation expenditure is reviewed for impairment at each balance sheet date. In the case of undeveloped properties, there may be only inferred resources to form a basis for the impairment review. The carrying values of these assets are reviewed twice per annum by management and the results of these reviews are reported to the *Audit committee.* The review is based on a status report regarding the Group's intentions for development of the undeveloped property. In some cases, the undeveloped properties are regarded as successors to ore bodies currently in production. It is intended that these will be developed and go into production when the current source of ore is exhausted.

Subsequent recovery of the resulting carrying value depends on successful development of the area of interest or sale of the project. If a project does not prove viable, all irrecoverable costs associated with the project and any related impairment provisions are written off.

(g) *Property, plant and equipment.* The cost of property, plant and equipment comprises its purchase price, any costs directly attributable to bringing the asset to the location and condition necessary for it to be capable of operating in the manner intended by management and the estimated close down and restoration costs associated with the asset. Once a mining project has been established as commercially viable, expenditure other than that on land, buildings, plant and equipment is capitalised under 'Mining properties and leases' together with any amount transferred from 'Exploration and evaluation'.

In open pit mining operations, it is necessary to remove overburden and other barren waste materials to access ore from which minerals can economically be extracted. The process of mining overburden and waste materials is referred to as stripping. During the development of a mine, before production commences, stripping costs are capitalised as part of the investment in construction of the mine.

Costs associated with commissioning new assets, in the period before they are capable of operating in the manner intended by management, are capitalised. Development costs incurred after the commencement of production are capitalised to the extent they are expected to give rise to a future economic benefit. Interest on borrowings related to construction or development projects is capitalised until the point when substantially all the activities that are necessary to make the asset ready for its intended use are complete.

(h) *Deferred stripping.* As noted above, stripping (i.e. overburden and other waste removal) costs incurred in the development of a mine before production commences are capitalised as part of the cost of constructing the mine and subsequently amortised over the life of the operation.

The Group defers stripping costs incurred subsequently, during the production stage of its operations, for those operations where this is the most appropriate basis for matching the costs against the related economic benefits and the effect is material. This is generally the case where there are fluctuations in stripping costs over the life of the mine, and the effect is material. The amount of stripping costs deferred is based on the ratio ('Ratio') obtained by dividing the tonnage of waste mined either by the quantity of ore mined or by the quantity of minerals contained in the ore. Stripping costs incurred in the period are deferred to the extent that the current period Ratio exceeds the life of mine Ratio. Such deferred costs are then charged against reported profits to the extent that, in subsequent periods, the current period Ratio falls short of the life of mine Ratio. The life of mine Ratio is based on proved and probable reserves of the operation.

The life of mine waste-to-ore ratio is a function of an individual mine's pit design and therefore changes to that design will generally result in changes to the Ratio. Changes in other technical or economic parameters that impact on reserves will also have an impact on the life of mine Ratio even if they do not affect the mine's pit design, changes to the life of mine Ratio are accounted for prospectively.

In the production stage of some operations, further development of the mine requires a phase of unusually high overburden removal activity that is similar in nature to preproduction mine development. The costs of such unusually high overburden removal activity are deferred and charged against reported profits in subsequent periods on a units of production basis. This accounting treatment is consistent with that for stripping costs incurred during the development phase of a mine, before production commences.

If the Group were to expense production stage stripping costs as incurred, there would be greater volatility in the year-to-year results from operations and excess stripping costs would be expensed at an earlier stage of a mine's operation.

Deferred stripping costs are included in 'Mining properties and leases', within property, plant and equipment or in investments in equity accounted units, as appropriate. These form part of the total investment in the relevant cash generating unit, which is reviewed for impairment if events or changes in circumstances indicate that the carrying value may not be recoverable. Amortisation of deferred stripping costs is included in operating costs or in the Group's share of the results of its equity accounted units, as appropriate.

12. Intangible Assets

Year ended 31 December 2006	Exploration and evaluation (a)	Other intangible assets (b)	Total (US$m)
Net book value			
At 1 January 2006	113	107	220
Adjustment on currency translation	5	10	15
Expenditure during year	72	118	190
Amortisation for the year	–	(27)	(27)
Disposals, transfers and other movements	6	(20)	(14)
At 31 December 2006	196	188	384
Cost	196	310	506
Accumulated amortisation	–	(122)	(122)

Year ended 31 December 2005	Exploration and evaluation	Other intangible assets	Total (US$m)
Net book value			
At 1 January 2005	91	98	189
Adjustment on currency translation	(5)	(4)	(9)
Expenditure during year	38	29	67
Amortisation for the year	–	(19)	(19)
Disposals, transfers and other movements	(11)	3	(8)
At 31 December 2005	113	107	220
Cost	113	327	440
Accumulated amortisation	–	(220)	(220)
At 1 January 2005			
cost	91	305	396
accumulated amortisation	–	(207)	(207)

(a) All of the net book value is related to intangible assets with finite lives. The following useful lives have been determined for the classes of intangible assets: Exploration and evaluation – useful life not determined until transferred to property, plant & equipment; other intangible assets: 2–20 years.
(b) There are no intangible assets either pledged as security or held under restriction of title.

Exploration and evaluation expenditure

The charge for the year and the net amount of intangible assets capitalised during the year are as follows:

	2006 (US$m)	2005 (US$m)
Cash expenditure in year (net of proceeds on disposal of undeveloped properties)	345	264
Changes in accruals (including non-cash proceeds on disposal of undeveloped properties)	(36)	24
Amount capitalised during year	(72)	(88)
Charge for year	237	250

IFRIC 13 Customer loyalty programmes

IFRIC 13 addresses accounting by entities that grant loyalty award credits (such as 'points' or travel miles) to customers who buy other goods or services. Specifically, it explains how such entities should account for their obligations to provide free or discounted goods or services ('awards') to customers who redeem award credits.

Key Provisions

- An entity that grants loyalty award credits must allocate some of the proceeds of the initial sale to the award credits as a liability (its obligation to provide the awards). In effect, the award is accounted for as a separate component of the sale transaction.
- The amount of proceeds allocated to the award credits is measured by reference to their fair value, i.e., the amount for which the award credits could have been sold separately.
- An entity must recognise the deferred portion of the proceeds as revenue only when it has fulfilled its obligations. It may fulfil its obligations either by supplying the awards itself or by engaging (and paying) a third party to do so.
- If at any time the expected costs of meeting the obligation exceed the consideration received, the entity has an onerous contract for which IAS 37 would require recognition of a liability.
- If IFRIC 13 causes an entity to change its accounting policy for customer loyalty awards, IAS 8 applies.

Effective date

IFRIC 13 is effective for annual periods beginning on or after 1 July 2008 but earlier application is permitted.

IFRIC 14 IAS 19 – The limit on a defined benefit asset, minimum funding requirements and their interaction

In many countries, laws or contractual terms require employers to make minimum funding payments for their pension or other employee benefit plans. This enhances the security of the retirement benefit promise made to members of an employee benefit plan.

Normally, such statutory or contractual funding requirements would not affect the measurement of the defined benefit asset or liability. This is because the contributions, once paid, become plan assets and the additional net liability would be nil. However, IAS 19 *Employee Benefits* limits the measurement of the defined benefit asset to the 'present value of economic benefits available in the form of refunds from the plan or reductions in future contributions to the plan'. IFRIC 14 addresses the interaction between a minimum funding requirement and the limit placed by IAS 19 on the measurement of the defined benefit asset or liability.

When determining the limit on a defined benefit asset in accordance with IAS 19, under IFRIC 14 entities are required to measure any economic benefits available to them in the form of refunds or reductions in future contributions at the maximum amount that is consistent with the terms and conditions of the plan and any statutory requirements in the jurisdiction of the plan. The entity's intentions on how to use a surplus (for instance, whether the entity intends to improve benefits rather than reduce contributions or get a refund) must be disregarded.

Such economic benefits are regarded as available to an entity if the entity has an unconditional right to realise them at some point during the life of the plan or when the plan is settled, even if they are not realisable immediately at the balance sheet date. Such an unconditional right would not exist when the availability of the refund or the reduction in future contribution would be contingent upon factors beyond the entity's control (e.g. approval by third parties such as plan trustees). To the extent the right is contingent, no asset would be recognised.

Economic benefits available as a refund

If an entity has an unconditional right to a refund:

(a)   during the life of the plan, without assuming that the plan liabilities must be settled in order to obtain the refund;

(b)   assuming the gradual settlement of the plan liabilities over time until all members have left the plan; or

(c)   assuming the full settlement of the plan liabilities in a single event (i.e. as a plan wind-up), it shall recognise an asset measured as the amount of the surplus at the balance sheet date that it has a right to receive as a refund. This is the fair value of the plan assets less the present value of the defined benefit obligation, less any associated costs, such as taxes.

If the refund is determined as the full amount or a proportion of the surplus, rather than a fixed amount, the amount must be calculated without further adjustment for the time value of money, even if the refund is realisable only at a future date, as both the defined benefit obligation and the fair value of plan assets are already measured on a present value basis.

Economic benefits available as a reduction in contributions

In the absence of a minimum funding requirement, IFRIC 14 requires entities to determine economic benefits available as a reduction in future contributions as:

(a) The present value of the future service cost to the entity (excluding costs borne by employees) over:
  •   the shorter of the expected life of the plan and
  •   the expected life of the entity;
(b) Determined using assumptions consistent with those used to determine the defined benefit obligation (including the discount rate).
(c) Based on conditions that exist at the balance sheet date.

  This means, an entity must assume:

•   no change to the benefits provided by a plan in the future until the plan is amended and
•   a stable workforce unless it is demonstrably committed at the balance sheet date to make a reduction in the number of employees covered by the plan.

  IFRIC 14 contains illustrative examples that outline the accounting treatments under a number of different scenarios.

  IFRIC 14 is effective for annual periods beginning on or after 1 January 2008 but earlier application is permitted. The interpretation is to be applied from the beginning of the first period presented in the financial statements for annual periods beginning on or after the effective date. The IFRIC had initially proposed full retrospective application, but decided to amend the transitional provisions reflecting concerns from constituents.

14

The International financial reporting interpretations committee

14.1   Introduction

The IASB's interpretative body, the former IASC's Standing Interpretations Committee (SIC), was reconstituted in December 2001 as the **International Financial Reporting Interpretations Committee (IFRIC)**. The IFRIC reviews, on a timely basis within the context of current International Financial Reporting Standards (IFRSs) and the IASB Framework, accounting issues that are likely to receive divergent or unacceptable treatment in the absence of authoritative guidance, with a view to reaching consensus on the appropriate accounting treatment. In developing interpretations, the IFRIC works closely with similar national committees.

The IFRIC meets about every six weeks. All technical decisions are taken at sessions that are open to public observation.

The IFRIC addresses issues of reasonably widespread importance, not issues that are of concern to only a small minority of entities. The interpretations cover both:

- newly identified financial reporting issues not specifically dealt with in IFRSs and
- issues where unsatisfactory or conflicting interpretations have developed, or seem likely to develop in the absence of authoritative guidance, with a view to reaching a consensus on the appropriate treatment.

Most of the SICs/IFRICs will only be adopted temporarily until a more permanent solution is found on the revision of the IASs/IFRSs. However, if extant, they must be complied with in order to provide a fair presentation of the financial statements. Currently the following are still applicable:

14.2   *Standing Interpretations*

SIC 7 *Introduction of the Euro*

SIC 7 requires IAS 21 to be strictly applied when a country joins the EU's Economic and Monetary Union. Thus:

- Foreign currency monetary assets and liabilities continue to be translated into the functional currency at closing rate.
- Resulting exchange gains/losses are recognised as incomes or expenses immediately except for hedging where it applies its existing policy.
- Cumulative exchange differences on translation continue to be classified in equity and are only recognised in income on disposal of the net investment in the foreign operation.
- Exchange differences resulting from translating liabilities denominated in participating countries are not included in the carrying amount of related assets.

SIC 10 *Government Assistance – No Specific Relation to Operating Activities*

Government assistance which is aimed at encouragement or long-term support of business activities either in certain regions or industry sectors. They may not be specifically related to the operating activities of the enterprise. These meet the definition of government grants under IAS 20 and such grants, therefore, should not be credited directly to shareholders interests.

SIC 12 *Consolidation – Special Purpose Entities*

This addresses when an SPE should be consolidated under IAS 27. Under SIC 12, an entity must consolidate an SPE when, in substance, the entity controls the SPE. Control may be indicated if:

- The SPE conducts its activities to meet the entity's specific needs.
- The entity has decision-making powers to obtain the majority of benefits of the SPE's activities.
- The entity is able to obtain the majority of the benefits through an 'auto pilot' mechanism.
- By having a right to majority of SPE's benefits, it is exposed to the SPE's business risks.
- The entity has the majority of residual interest in the SPE.

Examples would include entities set up to effect a lease, a securitisation of financial assets or R&D activities. Two examples are provided on next page.

Anglo American Plc   Year Ended 31 December 2006

SIC 12 '*Consolidation – Special Purpose Entities*' requires that a special purpose entity be consolidated, when the substance of the relationship indicates that it is controlled by a company. Anglo American discloses that it consolidates two charitable trusts in accordance with SIC 12. The trusts hold Anglo American shares. Whilst Anglo American has no voting rights and cannot appoint trustees, it has entered into agreements that give it a beneficial interest in the trusts' assets.

1. Accounting Policies (continued)

For some South African operations, annual contributions are made to dedicated environmental rehabilitation trusts to fund the estimated cost of rehabilitation during and at the end of the life of the relevant mine. The Group exercises full control of these trusts and therefore the trusts are consolidated. The trusts' assets are recognised separately on the balance sheet as non-current assets at fair value. Interest earned on funds invested in the environmental rehabilitation trusts are accrued on a time proportion basis and recognised as interest income.

SIC 13 *Jointly Controlled Entities – Non-monetary Contributions by Venturers*

SIC 13 clarifies the circumstances in which the appropriate portion of gains and losses resulting from a contribution of a non-monetary asset or jointly controlled entity (JCE) in exchange for an equity interest in the JCE should be recognised by the venturer in the income statement.

Marston Plc   Year Ended 31 December 2006

Accounting Policies (Extract)

The consolidated financial statements also incorporate the results of W&DB Issuer PLC, a company set up with the sole purpose of issuing debt secured on assets owned by the Group. The Directors consider this company meets the definition of a special purpose entity under SIC 12 '*Consolidation – Special Purpose Entities*' and hence for the purpose of the consolidated financial statements, it has been equity accounted for. Details of this company are provided in Note 35.

SIC interprets IAS 31 that recognition of gains or losses is appropriate unless:

(a)   significant risks and rewards related to non-monetary asset are not transferred to the jointly controlled entity;

(b)   the gain or loss cannot be measured reliably; or

(c)   similar assets are contributed by the other venturers.

SIC 15 *Operating Leases – Incentives*

SIC 15 indicates that lease incentives, e.g. rent-free periods or contributions to relocate lessee, should be considered an integral part of the consideration for the use of the leased asset. IAS 27 requires an enterprise to treat such incentives as a reduction of lease income or as a lease expense. As they are an integral part of the net consideration agreed for the use of the leased asset, incentives should be recognised by both lessor and lessee over the lease term with each party using a single amortisation method applied to the net consideration.

JC Sainsburys Plc   Year Ended 26 March 2006

Accounting Policies (Extract)

Leases

Sainsbury adopts IAS 17 '*Leases*' and capitalises as finance leases some leases previously considered operating leases, resulting in an increase of £37 million in fixed assets and £11 million reduction in net equity at the date of transition.

Previously, Sainsbury made no disclosure in its annual report about leases with incentives or predetermined fixed rental increases. Under SIC 15 the company now accounts for lease incentives on a straight line basis over the lease term, resulting in an increase of £21 million to deferred income gross of deferred tax at 26 March 2005.

In addition, the company discloses that it has leases with predetermined rental increases and has previously accounted for the increases in the year in which they arose. Following IAS 17, however, these are now amortised over the period of the lease so as to produce a constant periodic rate of interest, resulting in an increase in deferred income of £6 million gross of deferred tax at 26 March 2005.

SIC 21 *Income Taxes – Recovery of Revalued Non-Depreciable Assets*

Where a non-depreciable asset has been revalued (e.g. freehold land), the deferred tax liability or asset arising from the revaluation must be measured based on the tax consequences that would follow from the sale of the asset rather than through use. This could lead to a capital gains tax rate being applied rather than the rate applicable to corporate earnings.

Marston Plc   Year Ended 31 December 2006

SIC 21 requires that the deferred tax liability on revalued property be calculated on the basis of the tax consequences of recovery of the carrying amount through sale. Marston Plc applies SIC 21 to non-depreciable assets, but uses a 'mixed use' basis agreed, with its auditors, for depreciated property, under which a continuing use basis is applied to the depreciable amount and a sale basis is used for residual values and rolled over gains.

SIC 25 *Income Taxes – Changes in the Tax Status of an Enterprise or its Shareholders*

A change in tax status of an enterprise or its shareholders does not give rise to changes in the pre-tax amounts recognised directly in equity. SIC 25, therefore, concludes that the current and deferred tax consequences of the change in tax status should be included in net profit or loss for the period. However, where a transaction or event does result in a direct credit or charge to equity, e.g. revaluation of property under IAS 16, the related tax consequences would still be recognised directly in equity.

SIC 27 *Evaluating the Substance of Transactions in the Legal Form of a Lease*

Accounting for arrangements between an enterprise and an investor should reflect the substance of the arrangement. All aspects should be considered but SIC 27 lists a number of indicators that individually demonstrate that the arrangement may not be a lease.

If it is not a lease, then SIC 27 addresses whether a separate investment account and obligation that might exist represent assets and liabilities of the enterprise, how they should be accounted and how it should account for a fee it might receive from an investor.

Deutsche Post AG   Year Ended 31 December 2006

A note discloses that Deutsche Post leases to companies' electronic sorting systems, although it remains the beneficial and legal owner of all the assets which remain available without material restrictions to Deutsche Post for its operating activities. The note refers to SIC 27 and discloses that the net present value benefit from the transactions has been recognised immediately which results in income of €136 million and expenses of €40 million being recognised. In addition to a description of the arrangement, SIC 27 requires disclosure of its life and other significant terms although Deutsche Post is silent on this.

SIC 29 *Disclosure – Service Concession Arrangements*

SIC 29 prescribes the information that should be disclosed in the notes of a concession operator and provider when the two parties are joined by a service concession arrangement. This exists when an enterprise (the operator) agrees with another enterprise (the provider) to provide services that give the public access to major economic and social facilities.

Examples include water treatment, motorways, car parks, tunnels, bridges, airports, schools, hospitals, etc. Under SIC 29, the following should be disclosed:

- A description of the arrangement.
- Significant terms that may affect the amount, timing and certainty of future cash flows.
- The nature and extent of:
  - (i)   rights to use specified assets;
  - (ii) obligations to provide or rights to expect provision of services;

(iii)   obligations to acquire or build property, and so on;

(iv)   obligations to deliver or rights to receive specified assets at the end of concession period;

(v)   renewal and termination contracts;

(vi)   other rights and obligations, e.g. major overhauls; and

(vii)   changes in the arrangement occurring during the period.

SIC 31 *Revenue – Barter Transactions Involving Advertising Services*

Under IAS 18, revenue cannot be recognised unless it cannot be reliably measured. SIC 31 covers circumstances in which a seller can reliably measure revenue at the fair value of advertising services received or provided in a barter transaction. Under SIC 31 revenue from barter transactions cannot be measured reliably from services received but a seller can for the services it provides but only by reference to non-barter transactions that:

*   involve advertising similar to advertising in a barter;
*   occur frequently;
*   represent a predominant number of transactions and amount when compared to all transactions to provide advertising that is similar to the advertising in the barter transaction;
*   involve cash or other consideration that has a reliable measure; and
*   do not involve the same counterparty as in the barter transaction.

SIC 32 *Intangible Assets – Website Costs*

Identifies the following four stages of website development and the appropriate accounting treatment for each stage:

(a)   Website should be an intangible asset if, in addition to complying with IAS 38, it can demonstrate how the website will generate probable future economic benefits.

(b)   Planning stage – similar to research under IAS 38 and therefore expensed immediately.

(c)   Application and Infrastructure development – To the extent other than advertising, it is similar to development and should be capitalised if expenditure can be directly attributable to preparing the website for its intended use. However, expenditure initially expensed in previous periods cannot be capitalised at a later date.
*   Content development – should be expensed.
*   Operating – once website is complete, operating stage commences. Should be expensed when incurred.

(d)   A website recognised under SIC 32 should be measured subsequently by applying the requirements of IAS 38 and the best estimate of a useful life should be short.

14.3   *International Financial Reporting Interpretations Committee Statements*

IFRIC 1 *Changes in Existing Decommissioning, Restoration and Similar Liabilities*

Provides guidance on how changes in these provisions and in associated assets should be accounted for under both IAS 16 and 37. Changes may result from either (a) a revision in timing or amount of estimated decommissioning or restoration costs or from (b) a change in discount rate.

IAS 37 requires the amount recognised as a provision to be the best estimate to settle at the balance sheet date. This is measured at present value. IFRIC 1 covers three kinds of changes to an existing liability:

(a)   revision of estimated outflows;
(b)   revision of current market-based discount rate; and
(c)   unwinding of discount.

(a) and (b) If adopt cost model, then these changes are capitalised and depreciated prospectively over the remaining life of the related item. This is consistent with IAS 16.

(a) and (b) If adopt fair value model, then a change in liability does not affect the valuation but instead it alters the revaluation surplus or deficit on the item which is the difference between its valuation and what would be its carrying amount under the cost model. The effect is treated consistently with other revaluation surpluses/deficits. Any cumulative deficit is taken to profit but cumulative surplus to equity.

(b) Unwinding of discount should be treated in profit or loss as a finance cost as it occurs.

IFRIC 2 *Members Shares in Co-operative Entities and Similar Instruments*

These have some characteristics of equity and they also give the holder the right to request redemption for cash, subject to limitations. IFRIC 2 provides clear guidance on how those redemption terms should be evaluated in determining whether the shares should be classified as financial liabilities or as equity. Under IFRIC 2 they are normally liabilities. However, they are equity if:

- the entity has an unconditional right to refuse redemption or
- local law or charter imposes prohibitions on redemption.

The mere existence of law or charter provisions would not prohibit redemption if conditions are met or, if not met, does not result in members' shares being equity.

IFRIC 4 *Determining whether an Arrangement contains a Lease*

A number of arrangements in recent years do not take up the legal form of a lease but convey rights to use assets in return for a series of payments. Examples include:

- outsourcing;
- telecommunication contracts providing rights to capacity and
- take or pay contracts in which purchasers must make specified payments regardless of taking delivery of the contracted products or services.

IFRIC 4 specifies that an arrangement meeting the following criteria should be accounted for as a lease under IAS 17:

- Fulfilment depends upon a specific asset – need not be explicitly identified by the contractual provisions of the arrangement but may be implicitly specified as it is not

economically feasible nor practicable for the supplier to fulfil the arrangement by providing use of alternative assets.
* The arrangement conveys a right to control the use of the underlying asset as long as the following conditions are met:
    (i)   the purchaser has the ability or right to operate the asset or direct others to operate the asset;
    (ii)   the purchaser has the ability or right to control physical access to the asset;
    (iii) there is only a remote possibility that parties other than the purchaser will take more than an insignificant amount of the output of the asset and the price that the purchaser will pay is neither fixed per unit of output nor equal to current market price at the time of delivery.

Finnish company, Fortum Corporation provides a good example:

Fortum Corporation   Year Ended 31 December 2005

Leasing

The classification criteria when considering whether a lease arrangement is an operating lease or financial lease are different under IFRS than under FRS.

In Fortum this means that some lease arrangements, where Fortum is the lessee are reclassified to be financial leases. The liabilities of these agreements that have previously been reported as contingent liabilities are under FRS included in the balance sheet. The resulting increase in the interest-bearing liabilities at year-end 2004 is €102 million. The main part of this amount relates to Shipping leases.

In some customer contracts Fortum also acts as a lessor. Fortum has evaluated customer contracts against the criteria in IFRIC 4 (leasing). A part of these contracts is classified as financial leases. In the balance sheet the effect will be seen mainly as a reclassification between interest-bearing receivables and tangible assets.

IFRIC 5 *Rights to Interests Arising from Decommissioning, Restoration and Environmental Funds*

Some entities contribute monies to a fund to pay for obligations to decommission assets or perform environmental restoration. It may be done singly or with a group of contributors.

Under IFRIC 5, the entity should apply IAS 27, SIC 12, IAS 28 and IAS 31 to determine whether decommissioning funds should be consolidated, proportionately consolidated or equity accounted. If none of these is carried out and the fund does not relieve the contributor of its obligation to pay decommissioning costs, then the contributor should recognise:

* its obligation to pay decommissioning costs as a liability and
* its rights to receive reimbursement from the fund under IAS 37.

The latter should be measured at the lower of (i) amount of decommissioning obligation recognised and (ii) the contributor's share of the fair value of the net assets of the fund. Changes in the carrying amount of this right should be recognised in profit or loss.

When a contributor has an obligation to make potential additional contributions to the fund, the obligation is a contingent liability within the scope of IAS 37. If it becomes probable that additional contributions will be made then a provision should be recognised.

Finnish electricity generator Fortrum applied IFRIC 5 early to its 2005 Annual Report:

Fortum Corporation   Year Ended 31 December 2005

Fortum owns a nuclear power plant in Finland and accordingly it has a legal liability to fund the decommissioning of the plant and disposal of spent fuel through the Nuclear Waste Fund. The company states that it has adopted early IFRIC 5. Consequently, as it does not have control or joint control over the Nuclear Waste Fund, it measures the fund assets at the lower of its share of the fair value of the net assets of the fund and the value of the related liabilities. As a result, it presents in the balance sheet its part of the Nuclear Waste Fund and the related nuclear liability as non-current assets and provisions which amount to €418 million. Previously, it was presented as a contingent liability.

In addition, the fair value of the provision is calculated by discounting future cash flows whereas previously, calculation of the future liability was on an undiscounted basis.

Assets and liabilities related to decommissioning of nuclear power plants and the disposal of spent fuel

Fortum owns Loviisa nuclear power plant in Finland. Fortum's part of the Nuclear Waste Fund and the related nuclear liability are presented gross as non-current interest-bearing assets and provisions. Fortum's share in the Nuclear Waste Fund has been accounted for according to IFRIC 5, Rights to Interests Arising from Decommissioning. Restoration and Environmental Rehabilitation Funds which states that the fund assets are measured at the lower of fair value or the value of the related liabilities as Fortum does not have control or joint control over the Nuclear Waste Fund.

The fair value of the provisions is calculated by discounting the future cash flows, which are based on estimated future costs and actions already taken. The initial net present value of the provision for decommissioning (at the time of commissioning the nuclear power plant) has been included in the investment cost and it will be adjusted later by the possible changes in the plan. The investment costs due to the decommissioning will be depreciated over the estimated operating time of the nuclear station.

The provision for spent fuel covers the future disposal costs of fuel used until the end of the accounting period. Costs for disposal of spent fuel are expensed during the operating time based on fuel usage. The impact of the possible changes in the plan will be recognised immediately in the income statement based on fuel used until the end of the accounting period.

The timing factor is taken into account by recognising the interest expense related to discounting the nuclear provisions. The interest on the Nuclear Waste Fund assets is presented as financial income.

Fortum's share of the Nuclear Waste Fund, related to Loviisa nuclear power plant, is higher than the adjusted Fund Asset. The nuclear liability, according to the Finnish Nuclear Energy Act, is fully covered in the Nuclear Waste Fund. The nuclear liability is not discounted. Due to the change in the nuclear liability, the share of profit of the Nuclear Waste Fund and incurred costs of taken actions, the annual fee to Nuclear Waste Fund is paid.

Fortum also has minority shareholdings in the associated nuclear power production companies Teollisuuden Voima Oy (TVO) in Finland directly and indirectly OKG AB and Forsmarks Kraftgrupp AB in Sweden. Similar kinds of adjustments have been made through accounting of associates.

30. Nuclear related assets and liabilities

Fortum owns the Loviisa nuclear power plant in Finland. Based on the Nuclear Energy Act in Finland Fortum has a legal liability to fund the decommissioning of the power plant and disposal of spent fuel through the Nuclear Waste Fund. As at 31 December the following carrying values regarding nuclear related assets and liabilities are included in the balance sheet:

€ million	2005	2004
Provisions, Note 29	418	401
Other long-term investments, Note 19	418	401

Provisions

The provisions are related to future obligations for nuclear waste management including decommissioning of the power plant and disposal of spent fuel. The fair value of the provisions is calculated according to IAS 37 based on future cash flows regarding estimated future costs.

Other long-term investments

Other long-term investments include the carrying amount of Fortum's share of the Nuclear Waste Fund. Fortum contributes funds to the Nuclear Waste Fund in Finland to cover future obligations based on the legal liability calculated according to the Nuclear Energy Act. The fund is managed by governmental authorities.

Fortum's legal liability and share of the Nuclear Waste Fund

Fortum's legal liability and share of the Nuclear Waste Fund at year-end are as follows:

€ million	2005	2004
Liability for nuclear waste management according to the Nuclear Energy Act	618	596
Fortum's share of reserves in the Nuclear waste Fund	−610	−581
Difference covered by real estate mortgages	8	15

The legal liability calculated according to the Nuclear Energy Act in Finland and decided by the governmental authorities is €618 (596) million 31 December 2005 (and 2004). The carrying value of the liability in the balance sheet calculated according to IAS 37 is €418 (401) million 31 December 2005. The main reason for the difference in the liability is the fact that the legal liability is not discounted to net present value.

Fortum's share of the Nuclear Waste Fund 31 December 2005 is €610 (581) million. The carrying value in the balance sheet is €418 (401) million. The difference is due to the fact that IFRIC 5 limits the carrying amount of Fortum's share of the Nuclear Waste Fund to the amount of the related liability as Fortum does not have control or joint control over the Fund.

Fortum's share of the legal liability towards the fund is fully funded. The difference between the liability and Fortum's share of the Nuclear Waste Fund at year-end is due to timing of the annual calculation of the liability and will be paid during the first quarter of the following year. Fortum has given real estate mortgages as security, which also covers unexpected events according to the Nuclear Energy Act. The real estate mortgages are included in contingent liabilities.

Fortum uses the right to borrow back from the Nuclear Waste Fund according to certain rules. The loans are included in interest-bearing liabilities (see Note 26).

IFRIC 6 *Liabilities Arising from Participation in a Specific Market – Waste Electrical and Electronic Equipment*

The EU Directive on Waste Electrical and Electronic Equipment (WEEE) prescribes that the cost of waste management for equipment sold to private households before 13 August 2005, should be borne by producers of that type of equipment that are in the market during the period specified by individual states. The contribution is in proportion to the share of market at that time NOT if they produced the equipment.

The liability is triggered by participating in the market during the measurement period. Some of the following examples may help:

- Country A notifies participants in the market in February each year of their market share for immediately preceding year. Waste management costs are allocated on this basis.
- Company Z began operations in September 2005 manufacturing domestic washing machines. Although not responsible for creating historic waste it must contribute to cost of recycling historical WEEE in proportion to its market share during the measurement period.
- Company T ceased to manufacture washing machines in 2004. It has no obligation to fund the collection and recycling of historic waste it produced.

DSG International Plc   Year Ended 29 April 2006

Without referring to IFRIC 6, DSG states that it adopts WEEE within 10 countries of its operations and offers in most stores collection and disposal recycling facilities. It discloses in the corporate responsibility review the date of implementation within the respective countries and what method of disposal is used.

Corporate responsibility statement

To date, we have implemented the WEEE Directive in 10 countries of operation. The Directive introduces new recovery and recycling services for electronic and electrical goods. In many countries, the Group offers in-store facilities for recycling collection and disposal.

International WEEE implementation

More information at www.dsgiplc.com/cr/environment

Country	Chain	Stores	Implemented	Method
Ireland	PC World, Dixons, Currys	21	August 2005	Retail take-back and Membership of the European Recycling Platform (ERP). Collection points also at Local Authority sites.
Hungary	Electro World	6	August 2005	Retail take-back.
Czech Republic	Electro World	8	August 2005	Retail take-back.
Sweden	El Giganten, PC City	59	August 2005	Take-back at stores and upon delivery. 12% of WEEE in the Nordic countries is recovered through our stores.
Finland	Gigantti, Markantalo	43	August 2005	
Iceland	Elko	2	January 2006	
Denmark	El Giganten	29	April 2006	
Norway	Elkjøp, Lefdal Lavpris	96		Operates its own similar non-WEEE national requirements. Take-back at stores and upon delivery.
Spain	PC City	25	January 2006	To local Government or retail collection points and upon delivery.
Greece	Kotsovolos	77	January 2006	Take-back at stores and municipal sites.
France	PC City	11	June 2006	Local authority points, retailer collection points and some installed by manufacturers.
Italy	UniEuro, PC City	117	Underway	Retail take-back.
Poland	Electro World	2	End 2006	Retail take-back and membership of the ERP.
UK	Currys, Currys. digital, PC World. The Link, Dixons	1,013	2007	To local Government collection points or to retail collection points. We plan to continue collecting on delivery for larger items. We currently collect more than 500,000 items a year.

Philips discloses that its activities fall within the scope of the EU Directive. It notes that although EU member states were required to incorporate the Directive's requirements in national law by August 2004, many have not yet enacted it. Consequently, it cannot estimate reliably the effects of the directive for such countries, as the measurement period has not been decided.

It adds that the effects on its income statement are not material for historical waste at the end of 2005, largely because costs are offset by charges to customers. However, future waste disposal costs, not covered by IFRIC 6, may become material over time, and Philips states that provision will be made, insofar as a reliable estimate can be made, based on expected product lives and return rates.

Koninklijke Philips Electronics NV   Year Ended 31 December 2005

Extract from IFRS information: New IFRS Accounting Standards

In September 2005 the IASB's interpretation committee IFRIC issued Interpretation 6 'Liabilities Arising from Participating in a Specific Market – Waste Electrical and Electronic Equipment'. This Interpretation concerns the recognition of liabilities resulting from the European Union's Directive on Waste Electrical and Electronic Equipment (WEEE), which came into effect on February 13, 2003. Member states were required to transform the Directive into national law by August 13, 2004. Under this Directive, costs of disposing of electrical and electronic equipment used by households in an environmentally acceptable manner are borne by producers. The Directive stipulates that the producers of that type of equipment who are in the market in a period specified in the applicable national legislation (the measurement period) must finance costs related to waste management for equipment that was sold to private households before August 13, 2005, the so-called historical waste. For other waste, such as related to equipment sold after August 13, 2005 (future waste) or equipment sold to others than households, the Directive provides that producers are responsible for financing waste management costs. The Directive allows the Member States to allow producers to charge their customers a visible fee for financing waste management.

IFRIC Interpretation 6 is solely related to historical waste and has mandated that no liability shall arise for historical waste held by private households other than for waste costs for equipment in the measurement period.

The Company is a provider of equipment that falls under the EU Directive, particularly in the segments Lighting, Consumer Electronics, Domestic Appliances and Personal Care, and Medical Systems. As at the end of 2005, a number of states including significant EU Member States did not yet have their national legislation in place. Accordingly, the Company was not able to reliably estimate all effects of the WEEE Directive with respect to future waste. In as far as the historical waste is concerned, which is covered by Interpretation 6, the Company concluded that the effects on the income statement are not material as at the end of 2005. This is mainly caused by the fact that the costs are compensated by fees charged to the customers. Also for the coming years the effects are estimated to be limited on the assumption that all Member States will allow visible fees to be charged to the customers. With respect to future waste, however, the effects may become material over time, as we will have to reserve for waste management costs for all products that fall under the Directive and that were or will be sold after the dates of enactment in local laws of the EU Member States. Over the next years when products will be returned and disposed, the estimated cost of future waste management is expected to increase as a function of the expected life of the products and return rates. These expected costs will be charged to the income statement and a provision will be made in the balance sheet as far as amounts can be reliably estimated and represent expected outflows of assets for the Company.

IFRIC 7 *Applying the Restatement Approach under IAS 29 Financial Reporting in Hyperinflationary Economies*

IFRIC 7 is concerned about providing guidance on how an entity would restate its financial statements in the first year it identifies the existence of hyperinflation in the economy of its functional currency.

The restatement approach under IAS 29 distinguishes between monetary and non-monetary items. In practice, there has been uncertainty about how an entity restates deferred tax and comparatives.

IFRIC requires the following:

- In period the entity's functional currency becomes hyperinflationary, should apply IAS 29 as though it had always been hyperinflationary.
- Restatements of non-monetary items carried at historic cost are made from dates at which those items were first recognised, and if revalued, from dates revised values established.
- Deferred tax in opening balance sheet are determined in two stages:
  (a) Remeasured in accordance with IAS 12 after restating the nominal carrying amounts in the opening balance sheet by applying measuring unit at that time.
  (b) Deferred tax items measured in this way are restated for change in measuring unit from date of the opening balance sheet to date of closing balance sheet.

IFRIC 8 *Scope of IFRS 2*

IFRIC 8 clarifies that IFRS 2 applies to arrangements where an entity makes share-based payments for nil or inadequate consideration. If consideration is less than the fair value of equity granted or liability incurred, then this indicates that other consideration has been or will be received. IFRS 2 therefore applies.

Anglo American Plc   Year Ended 31 December 2006

This year, Anglo American discloses that, when it disposes of a portion of a South African based subsidiary or operation to a Black Economic Empowerment (BEE) company at a discount to fair value, this is classed as a share-based payment.

It states that this is in line with the principle of South Africa Interpretation AC 503 'Accounting for Black Economic Empowerment (BEE) Transactions'. The company tells us that the share-based element is not the sole profit or loss involved in a BEE transaction. AC 503 expands on the interpretation of IFRIC 8 'Scope of IFRS 2', which states that, where identifiable consideration received appears to be less than the fair value of equity instruments granted, this typically indicates that other consideration is or will be received. IFRS 2 'Share-Based Payment' requires that, where a company cannot estimate reliably the fair value of goods or services received in a share-based transaction, their value be measured indirectly by reference to the fair value of the equity instruments granted.

There have been two BEE transactions in the year. In the first, the company recognises in the income statement an $84 million loss, which is included below operating profit and disclosed in a note. It discloses that the transaction involved the unbundling of its Kumba operations into two companies, retaining a 64% interest in one and a 23% interest in the other, which the latter accounts for as available for sale financial asset. In the second BEE transaction, there is a transfer of 15% ownership in mining assets to a 'traditional community' and a $52 million loss on part-disposal. Following IFRS 2, the company discloses that the total cost of the share-based element of these BEE transactions in the year is $34 million.

The company adds that, following AC 503, the discount or value provided in BEE transactions is calculated in accordance with IFRS 2 and included in profit or loss on disposal. IFRS 2 also requires that, when the goods or service received in a share-based transaction do not qualify for recognition as assets, they shall be recognised as expenses. The company tells us that AC 503 also states that BEE transactions should not result in recognition of an asset.

These disclosures go some way to indicate the nature of the transactions, though the reason for and legal/commercial context of the transfers are not explained and so the disclosures to some degree lack clarity. In addition, it discloses that $120 million minority interests on the two BEE transactions are valued initially at the fair value of the net assets acquired.

Accounting Policies (Extract)

Black Economic Empowerment (BEE) Transactions Where the Group disposes of a portion of a South African based subsidiary or operation to a BEE Company at a discount to fair value, the transaction is considered to be a share-based payment (in line with the principle contained in South Africa interpretation AC 503 *Accounting for Black Economic Empowerment (BEE) Transactions*). The discount provided or value given is calculated in accordance with IFRS 2 and included in the determination of the profit or loss on disposal.

UPM Kymmene Oyj   Year Ended 31 December 2006

The company adopts early IFRIC 8 and discloses that this results in recognition of a charge of €3 million in the current year. The company recognises €7 million as the cost of share-based payments in the year.

However, there is no narrative explanation of why adoption of IFRIC 8 has led to the additional charge. In this respect, the disclosures fall short of the IFRS 2 requirement to disclose information that allows users to understand the nature and the extent of share-based payment arrangements that existed in the period and thus lack transparency.

IFRIC 9 *Reassessment of Embedded Derivatives*

An embedded derivative is a component of a hybrid instrument that also includes a host contract (e.g. convertible loan). The cash flows of such an instrument often vary in a similar way to standalone derivatives.

IAS 39 requires an entity when first party to such an instrument, to assess whether any embedded derivatives are required to be separated from the host contract and accounted for separately.

IFRIC addresses whether such an assessment can be reconsidered throughout the life of the contract and whether a first time adopter assesses when first party to a contract or when it adopts IFRSs for the first time.

IFRIC 9 concludes that it should be only when first becomes a party to the contract and subsequent reassessment is prohibited unless there is a change in terms of the contract that significantly modifies the cash flows otherwise required under the contract in which case reassessment is required.

A first time adopter must assess when first it becomes a party to the contract unless there has been a subsequent change in terms of contract that significantly modify the cash flows.

IFRIC 10 *Interim Financial Reporting and Impairment*

Addresses the apparent conflict between IAS 34 and other standards on the reversal of impairment of goodwill and certain financial assets. IFRIC concludes:

- Entity shall not reverse an impairment loss recognised in a previous interim period for goodwill or equity or financial asset carried at cost.
- Entity shall not extend this consensus by analogy to other areas of potential conflict.

IFRIC 11 *Group and Treasury Share Transactions*

IFRIC 11 provides guidance on applying IFRS 2 in the following three circumstances:

(1) **Share-based payment involving own equity in which entity chooses or is required to buy its own equity (treasury shares) to settle the obligation – equity or cash settled?**
   Should always be accounted for as equity settled transactions under IFRS 2.

(2)   **A parent grants rights to its equity to employees of its subsidiary**
Assuming treated as equity settled in consolidated accounts, subsidiary must adopt equity settled requirements of IFRS 2 and recognise corresponding increase in equity as a contribution from the parent. Subsidiary has no liability to transfer assets to its employees.

(3)   **A subsidiary grants rights to equity of its parent to its employees**
This is treated as cash settled by the subsidiary as subsidiary has incurred a liability to transfer assets, i.e. the equity instruments of the parent.

IFRIC 12 *Service Concession Arrangements*

Definition

Arrangements whereby a government grants contracts for the supply of public services, e.g. roads, energy distribution, prisons, hospitals, and so on – to private operators. Objective is to clarify how certain aspects of existing IASB literature are to be applied to such arrangements.

Two types of Service Concession Arrangements

Financial asset model
Operator receives a financial asset (right to receive cash from government in return for constructing/upgrading public sector asset).

Intangible asset model
Operator receives an intangible asset (right to charge for use of a public sector asset that it constructs/upgrades – not unconditional right to receive cash, contingent on extent public uses the service).

Accounting treatment

Financial asset model
A financial asset is recognised to the extent to which an entity has an unconditional contractual right to receive cash or another financial asset from or at the discretion of the grantor. Normally, if the grantor contractually guarantees to pay the operator:

(a)   specified or determinable amounts or
(b)   the shortfall between amounts received from users of the public service and specified amounts, even if payment is contingent on the operator ensuring that the infrastructure meets specified quality or efficiency requirements.

The operator measures the financial asset at fair value.

Intangible asset model
Operator recognises an intangible asset to the extent it receives a right (licence) to charge users of the public service. This is not an unconditional right to receive cash because amounts are contingent on the extent the public uses the service.

The operator measures the intangible asset at fair value.

Operating revenue

Revenue is recognised and measured in accordance with IAS 11 and 18 for services it performs.

Accounting by the Government (Grantor)

IFRIC 12 does not address accounting for the government side of service concession arrangements as IFRSs are not designed for not-for-profit activities in the public sector.

IFRIC 13 *Customer Loyalty Agreements*

Background

To provide customers with incentives to buy their products. Entities grant credits (points/ air miles) and these can be redeemed for free or discounted goods/services.

There are different programmes – award credits may be linked to individual purchases, to continued custom. The entity may operate the programme itself or participate in a programme operated by a third party. The awards may include goods/services supplied by the entity or claim goods/services from another vendor.

Scope

Addresses all customer loyalty programmes.

Issues

The issues addressed are:

(a) Whether the entity's obligation to provide free/discounted goods/services should be recognised and measured by allocating some of the consideration received to the award credits and deferring recognition of revenue? or
(b) If consideration allocated, how much and when allocated to revenue?

Consensus

Award credits should be treated as separately identifiable components of sales transactions. The fair value of consideration received should be allocated between the components – i.e. goods/services sold and award credits granted.

Allocation as per relative fair values of the components.

The fair value of the award credits may be estimated by reference to the discount that the customer would obtain when redeeming the award credits for goods/services. The discount would be reduced to account for

(a) any discount offered to customers who have not earned credit awards from an initial sale;
(b) the proportion of award credits expected to be forfeited by customers; and
(c) the time value of money.

If customers can choose from a range of different awards, the fair value of the award credits should reflect the fair values of the range of available discounts weighted in proportion to the frequency with which each is expected to be selected.

The entity should recognise revenue for award credits either:

(a)   in the periods and reflecting the pattern in which award credits are redeemed; or
(b)   if a third party assumes the obligation to supply the awards when it assumes that obligation.

The revenue recognised in (a) is based on the number of award credits that have been redeemed relative to the total number expected to be redeemed.

When a third party takes on the obligation depends on the contract.

If the unavoidable costs of meeting the obligation exceeds the consideration received there is an onerous contract and thus an additional liability should be provided under IAS 37.

Customer loyalty agreements may create or enhance customer relationship intangible assets – these assets are only recognised if the recognition criteria in IAS 38 are met.

Effective date and transition

Effective for annual periods commencing on or after 1st July 2008.

IFRIC 14 IAS 19 – *The Limit on a Defined Benefit Asset, Minimum Funding Requirements and Their Interaction*

Background

Statutory or contractual minimum funding requirements (MFR) exist in many countries to improve the security of the retirement benefits promise made to members of an employee benefit plan. Normally stipulate a minimum level of contributions that must be paid into a plan over a given period.

Normally a statutory or contractual obligation to pay additional contributions to a plan would not affect measurement as, once paid, become plan assets and additional liability would be nil.

IAS 19 limits asset to 'present value of economic benefits available in the form of refunds from the plan or reductions in future contributions to the plan'. Contributions re MFR are not available to entity due to legal restrictions on refunds.

Questions have arisen re interaction between an MFR and limit placed by IAS 19 on measurement of defined benefit (DB) asset/liability.

Scope

IFRIC 14 applies to all long-term and post-employment benefit plans within scope of IAS 19.

Issues

The issues are:

(a)   extent to which the availability of an economic benefit is affected by restrictions on its current realisability;
(b)   the calculation of the amount of economic benefit available as;

   (i)   a refund
   (ii)   a reduction in contributions

(c) when there is an MFR, the effect of an MFR on the measurement of the DB asset or liability.

Consensus

Availability of an economic benefit

Availability of a surplus should be determined in accordance with terms and conditions of the plan and any statutory requirements in the jurisdiction of the plan in question.

An economic benefit is available if realisable during the life of the plan or when liabilities are finally settled.

The economic benefit available as a refund

Measured as the amount that will be refunded to the entity:

(a) during the life of the plan, without assuming that the plan liabilities have to be settled in order to get a refund; or
(b) assuming the gradual settlement of the plan liabilities over time until all members have left the plan; or
(c) assuming the full settlement of the plan liabilities in a single event (i.e. as a plan wind-up).

It should be valued on the basis of most advantageous to the entity – the amount of surplus that would be received by the entity after all associated costs paid (e.g. net of tax).

In wind-ups, a refund should be net of professional fees and costs of insurance premiums to secure the liability on wind-up.

Under IAS 19, surplus is measured at present value thus no further adjustment for the time value of money should be made.

Under IAS 1, key sources of estimation uncertainty could have a material adjustment to the carrying amount of the asset/liability. This may include disclosure of any restrictions on current realisability of the plan assets or disclosure of how to determine the amount of economic benefit available as a refund.

The economic benefit available as a contribution reduction

It should be determined at present value using IAS 19 assumptions at the balance sheet date of:

(a) the service cost to the entity i.e. excluding any part borne by employees, less
(b) any future minimum funding in respect of future accrual of benefits.

Any expected changes in future minimum funding due to paying the minimum contributions due should be reflected in the measurement of available contribution reduction. No allowance should be made for expected changes in the terms and conditions of the minimum funding requirement that are not substantially enacted at the balance sheet date.

Any allowance for expected future changes in the demographic profile of the workforce should be consistent with the assumptions underlying the calculation of the present value of the DB obligation at the balance sheet date.

If the future minimum funding contribution re future accrual of benefits exceeds the future IAS 19 service cost in any year, the present value of that excess reduces the amount of the total asset available as a contribution reduction at the balance sheet date. The asset can never be less than zero.

Effect of a minimum funding requirement on the measurement of the defined benefit asset or liability

If an entity has a statutory or contractual obligation to pay additional contributions into a plan, the entity should determine whether the contributions payable will be available as a refund or reduction in future contributions after paid into the plan.

To extent that the contributions will not be available after paid into plan, an adjustment should be made to reduce the DB asset or increase the DB liability when obligation arises so that no gain/loss results from applying IAS 19 when contributions are paid.

The adjustment to the DB asset or liability re MFR and any subsequent remeasurement of that adjustment should be recognised immediately re IAS 19 policy. In particular:

(a)   an entity that recognises the effect of limit in para 58 of IAS 19 in profit or loss should recognise the adjustment immediately in profit or loss and

(b)   an entity that recognises the effect of the limit in para 58 of IAS 19 should recognise the adjustment immediately in the SORIE.

Effective date

Mandatory for annual periods beginning on or after 1st January 2008.

Transition

To be applied retrospectively in accordance with requirements of IAS 8.

15

Taxation

15.1 IAS 12 *Income Taxes* (revised 2000)

Objective

The objective of IAS 12 is to prescribe the accounting treatment for income taxes, for both current and future tax consequences. These should be accounted for in the same way that it accounts for the transactions and other events themselves, i.e. if transactions are recorded in the income statement then so should any related tax effect.

Scope

IAS 12 applies in accounting for income taxes and this includes all domestic and foreign taxes based on taxable profits. It does not cover government grants. These are covered by IAS 20.

Definitions

- *Accounting profit.* Net profit or loss for a period before deduction of tax.
- *Taxable profit.* Profit for the period determined in accordance with the rules established by the tax authorities upon which income taxes are payable.
- *Tax expense.* The aggregate amount included in net profit for the period for current and deferred tax.
- *Current tax.* The amount of income taxes payable in respect of the taxable profit for the period.
- *Deferred tax liabilities.* The amounts of income taxes payable in future periods in respect of temporary timing differences.

- *Deferred tax assets*. The amounts of income taxes recoverable in future periods in respect of:
  - (a) deductible temporary differences;
  - (b) the carry-forward of unused tax losses; and
  - (c) the carry-forward of unused tax credits.
- *Temporary differences*. These are differences between the carrying amount of an asset or liability in the balance sheet and its tax base. They can be either:
  - (a) taxable temporary differences – these will result in taxable amounts in the future when the carrying amount of the asset or liability is settled or
  - (b) deductible temporary differences – these will result in deductible amounts in determining taxable profit when the carrying amount of the asset or liability is recovered or settled.
- *Tax base*. The amount attributed to that asset or liability for tax purposes.

A number of examples for both assets and liabilities are provided below:

Example – Tax Base of an Asset

(1) Machine costs £10,000. Capital allowances of £3,000 claimed to date. The tax base is now £7,000 as that can be deductible in the future.

(2) Interest receivable has a carrying amount of £1,000. Interest is taxed on a receipt basis thus the tax base is nil.

(3) Trade debtors are £10,000. Revenue has already been included in taxable profits (as sales) thus the tax base is £10,000.

(4) Dividends receivable from a subsidiary have a carrying value of £5,000 but the dividends are not taxable. The tax base is therefore £5,000.

(5) A loan receivable has a carrying value of £1 million but the repayment will have no tax consequences thus the tax base is £1 million.

Example – Tax base of a liability

(1) There are accruals of €1,000 but expense is only allowed for tax when paid. The tax base is therefore nil. However, if it has already been deducted for tax purposes, then the tax base would be €1,000.

(2) There is interest received in advance of €10,000 but it is only taxed when received. The tax base is therefore nil.

(3) There are accruals for disallowed expenditure of €100, e.g. fines, penalties. The tax base is therefore €100.

(4) A loan repayable has a carrying amount of €1 million but the repayment has no tax consequences. The tax base is therefore €1 million.

Where the tax base of an asset/liability is not immediately obvious, the fundamental principle is that a deferred tax liability or asset may only be recognised whenever recovery or settlement of the carrying amount of the asset/liability would make future tax payments larger or smaller than they would have been if such recovery or settlement were to have no tax consequences.

Recognition of current tax liabilities and current tax assets

Current tax for the current and prior periods should be recognised immediately as a liability. If the amount paid exceeds the amount due, then the excess should be recognised as an asset.

The benefit relating to a tax loss that can be carried back to recover current tax of a previous period should be recognised as an asset.

Recognition of deferred tax liabilities and deferred tax assets

Taxable timing differences

A deferred tax liability should be recognised for all taxable timing differences, unless it arises from the following:

(a)   goodwill for which amortisation is not deductible for tax or
(b)   the initial recognition of an asset/liability in a transaction which:
    (i)   is not a business combination and
    (ii) at the time of the transaction does not affect accounting or taxable profit.

However, for taxable timing differences associated with investments in subsidiaries, associates and joint ventures – a deferred tax liability should be recognised.

Example

Asset	Cost		150	Book value	100
	Cumulative tax allowances		90	Tax rate 25%	25%

Tax base   Cost 150 − 90 = 60 − 100 NBV = 40 taxable timing difference
DT liability   40 × 25% = 10

Examples of similar temporary differences:
(a)   Interest revenue and interest received.
(b)   Depreciation and capital allowances.
(c)   Development costs capitalised and amortised, but deducted for tax when incurred.
(d)   Cost of business acquisition is allocated to identifiable assets and liabilities re-fair values but no equivalent adjustment made for tax purposes.
(e)   Assets revalued but no adjustment for tax.
(f)   Goodwill or negative goodwill on consolidation.
(g)   Non-taxable government grants.
(h)   Carrying amount of investments in subsidiaries, associates and so on which becomes different from the tax base of the investment.

Business combinations

In acquisitions when assets are revalued to fair value temporary differences arise when the tax bases are left unaffected. In these cases, a taxable temporary difference arises resulting in a deferred tax liability which also affects the value of goodwill.

Assets carried at fair value

Certain assets may be revalued (e.g. IAS 16 and IAS 25). The process does not affect taxable profit and the tax base remains the same. However, the future recovery of the carrying amount will result in a taxable flow of economic benefits to the enterprise and thus the difference between the carrying amount and the tax base is a temporary difference and should give rise to a deferred tax liability or asset. This is true even if the entity has no intention of disposing of the asset or is able to avail of rollover relief.

Goodwill

Amortisation is not allowable for tax and has a tax base of nil. Any difference between the carrying amount of goodwill and its tax base is a temporary timing difference. IAS 12, however, does not permit a deferred tax liability to be created as goodwill is a residual and any tax would only increase goodwill.

Initial recognition of an asset or liability

A temporary difference may arise on the initial recognition of an asset or liability, e.g. when part of the cost of an asset is not deductible for tax. Its accounting treatment will depend on the nature of the transaction.

(a) Business combination – liability recognised and this will affect the amount of goodwill.
(b) Transaction affects accounting or taxable profit – liability recognised.
(c) If neither of (a) nor (b) – liability or asset is not recognised.

> Example
> Asset cost 100, no residual value, 5 year life, tax rate 40%. Depreciation not allowed for tax and capital gain not taxable nor capital loss deductible.
>   No recognition initially.

Deductible temporary differences

A deferred tax asset should be recognised for all deductible temporary differences to the extent that it is probable that taxable profit will be available against which the deductible temporary difference can be utilised unless the deferred tax asset arises from the following:

(a) Negative goodwill – treated as income as per IFRS 3.
(b) The initial recognition of an asset/liability in a transaction which:
    (i) is not a business combination and
    (ii) at the time of the transaction it affects neither accounting nor taxable profit.

However, for deductible temporary differences associated with investments in subsidiaries, joint ventures and associates a deferred tax asset should be recognised.

> **Example**
> An enterprise recognises a liability of 100 for accrued warranty costs. These are not deductible for tax until paid.
>
> The tax base is nil but the Written down value (WDV) of liability is 100, thus a temporary difference of 100 is created which, at 25%, results in a deferred tax asset of 25 provided. It is probable that there will be sufficient taxable profits in the future to benefit from the costs.

The following are examples of deductible temporary differences which result in deferred tax assets:

(a)   retirement benefit costs;
(b)   research costs;
(c)   cost of acquisition; and
(d)   certain assets revalued to fair value – deductible temporary difference arises if the tax base exceeds its carrying amount.

In all cases, there must be sufficient future taxable profits available against which the deductible temporary differences can be utilised.

It is probable that there will be sufficient taxable profits when there are sufficient taxable temporary differences relating to the same tax authority and same taxable entity which are expected to reverse:

(a)   in the same period as the expected reversal of the deductible temporary difference or
(b)   in periods into which a tax loss can be carried backward or forward.

When there are insufficient taxable temporary differences, the deferred tax asset is recognised to the extent that:

(a)   it is probable there will be sufficient taxable profit to the same tax authority and the same taxable entity in the same period as the reversal or
(b)   tax planning opportunities are available that will create taxable profit in appropriate periods. These might include – electing to have interest income taxed on either a received or receivable basis, deferring the claim for certain taxable deductions, the sale and leaseback of assets, selling an asset that generates non-taxable income, e.g. government bond in order to purchase another investment that generates taxable income.

Negative goodwill

No deferred tax asset is permitted for negative goodwill, as goodwill is a residual figure.

Initial recognition of an asset or liability

Where a non-taxable capital grant is deducted from cost a deductible temporary difference arises but no deferred tax asset should be set up. A similar result occurs for the deferred credit approach.

Unused tax losses and unused tax credits

A deferred tax asset should be recognised for the carry-forward of unused tax losses and unused tax credits to the extent that it is probable that future taxable profit will be available against which the unused tax losses and unused tax credits can be utilised.

The rules are the same as for deductible temporary differences. However, the existence of unused tax losses is strong evidence that future taxable profits may not be available, thus a deferred tax asset may only be recognised to the extent that there is convincing other evidence that sufficient profits will be available. The following criteria should be considered in making that decision:

(a)   Is there sufficient taxable temporary differences relating to the same taxation authority and the same taxable entity to utilise the tax losses or credits?
(b)   Whether it is probable that the enterprise will have taxable profits before the unused tax losses or unused tax credits expire?
(c)   Whether the unused tax losses result from identifiable causes that are unlikely to recur?
(d)   Whether tax planning opportunities are available to create taxable profit in which the unused tax losses or credits can be utilised?

To the extent that it is not probable that taxable profit will be available then the deferred tax asset is not recognised.

Re-assessment of unrecognised deferred tax assets

At each balance sheet date, a company should reassess unrecognised deferred tax assets, e.g. if an improvement in trading occurs, then it may make it more probable that the company will be able to generate sufficient taxable profit in the future for the deferred tax asset to meet the recognition criteria.

Investments in subsidiaries, branches, associates and joint ventures

Temporary differences arise when the carrying amount of investments become different from the tax base (often cost). These differences may arise where:

(a)   there are undistributed profits;
(b)   changes occur in foreign exchange rates when a parent and its subsidiary are based in different countries; and
(c)   there is a reduction in the carrying amount of an investment in an associate to recoverable amount.

A company should recognise a deferred tax liability for all taxable temporary differences associated with these investments except to the extent that both of the following conditions are satisfied:

(a)   The parent can control the timing of the reversal of the temporary difference.
(b)   It is probable that the temporary difference will not reverse in the foreseeable future.

As a parent controls the dividend policy of its subsidiary it controls its timing. It is often impracticable to determine the amount of income taxes payable on reversal, thus if a parent determines that they cannot be distributed, no deferred tax liability should be recognised.

An investor in an associate does not control dividend policy, thus a deferred tax liability should be recognised on temporary taxable differences. If it cannot be precise as to the amount, then a minimum amount should be recognised. Where a joint venturer can control the sharing of profits and it is probable that the profits will not be distributed in the foreseeable future, a deferred tax liability is not recognised.

A company should recognise a deferred tax asset only where it is probable that:

(a) the temporary difference will reverse in the foreseeable future; and
(b) taxable profit will be available against which the temporary difference can be utilised.

Measurement

Current tax liabilities (assets) should be based on tax rates enacted by the balance sheet date. They should be measured at tax rates that are expected to apply to the period when the asset is realised or liability settled.

Where different tax rates apply, average rates should be applied.

The measurement of deferred tax liabilities and assets should reflect the tax consequences that would follow from the manner in which the company expects, at the balance sheet date, to recover or settle the carrying amount of its assets and liabilities.

Example
An asset has a carrying value of 100 and a tax base of 60. A tax rate of 20% applies if asset is sold and 30% is applied to other income.

Solution
A deferred tax liability of 8 (40 × 20%) is recognised if expect to sell the asset, and a liability of 12 (40 × 30%) if expect to retain and recover from use.

Example

Asset			NBV	WDV
	–	Cost	100	100
	–	Depreciation	20	30
	–	Book value	80	70
	–	Revalued	150	150
	–	Capital gain	70	80

Assume capital gains are not taxable.

Solution
Deferred tax   80 × 30% if use = 24 but 30 tax depreciation × 30% = 9 if sell.

Example
Same details as above except assume capital gains are taxable at 40% after deducting an inflation adjusted cost of 110.

Solution
By using the asset
The tax base is 70 but 150 is taxable, thus timing difference is 80 and a tax liability of $80 \times 30\% = 24$.

By selling
The capital gain is 150 proceeds less adjusted cost of $110 = 40 \times 40\% = 16$
The cumulative tax depreciation of $30 \times 30\% = \underline{9}$
Total liability $\underline{\underline{25}}$

Deferred tax assets and liabilities should not be discounted

Discounting requires detailed scheduling of the timing of the reversal of each temporary difference. In many cases, this process is impracticable or highly complex, therefore, it is inappropriate to require discounting. To permit discounting would result in deferred tax assets/liabilities not being comparable between enterprises.

The carrying amount of a deferred tax asset should be reviewed at each balance sheet date. The deferred tax asset should be reduced to the extent that it is no longer probable that sufficient taxable profit will be available to allow the asset to be utilised.

Recognition of current and deferred tax

Income statement

Current and deferred tax should be recognised as income/expense except if it arises from a transaction directly recognised in equity or is a business combination that is an acquisition.

Items credited or charged directly to equity

Current and deferred tax should be charged directly to equity if the tax relates to items that are credited or charged directly to equity.
Examples of such items include:

(a)   A change resulting from a revaluation of property and so on
(b)   The correction of an error under IAS 8.
(c)   Exchange differences arising on the translation of a foreign entity.
(d)   Amounts arising on initial recognition of the equity component of a compound financial instrument.

Exceptionally, it may be difficult to determine the tax that relates to equity, particularly where there are graduated rates of income tax and it is impossible to determine the rate at which a specific component of taxable profit has been taxed. It also occurs if there is a change in tax rate to an item previously charged or credited to equity or where a deferred tax asset relates to an item previously charged or credited to equity. In such cases, the tax should be pro rated on a reasonable basis.

Deferred tax arising from a business combination

Deferred tax assets or liabilities should be recognised on acquisitions at the date of acquisition and these should affect the amount of goodwill calculated.

An acquiror may consider it is probable that it will recover its own deferred tax asset via unused tax losses. In such cases, a deferred tax asset should be recognised and this should be taken into account when determining goodwill.

If a deferred tax asset is not recognised at the date of acquisition, but is done subsequently, then the acquiror should adjust goodwill and related accumulated amortisation and also recognise the reduction in the NBV of goodwill, as an expense. The acquiror, however, does not recognise negative goodwill nor does it increase the amount of negative goodwill in such cases.

> Example
>
> A company acquired a subsidiary with temporary deductible differences of 300. The tax rate was 30%. The deferred tax asset of 90 (300 × 30%) was not recognised in determining goodwill of 500. Goodwill is amortised over 20 years. Two years later, the company assumed that there would be sufficient taxable profits to recover the benefit of the deductible temporary differences.
>
> The company should record a deferred tax asset of 90 and a deferred tax income of 90. It should reduce goodwill by 90 and accumulated amortisation by 9 (2 years). The balance of 81 is expensed in the income statement. Goodwill is now reduced to 410 (500 90) less accumulated amortisation 41 (50 − 9).
>
> If the tax rate increases to 40% a deferred tax asset of 120 (300 × 40%) and deferred tax income of 120 is created. If the tax rate decreases to 20% a deferred tax asset of 60 (300 × 20%) and deferred income of 60 is created. In both cases, goodwill is reduced by 90 and accumulated depreciation by 9.

Presentation

Tax assets and tax liabilities

Tax assets and liabilities should be presented separately from other assets and liabilities on the balance sheet. A distinction should be made between current and non-current assets and liabilities, but it should not classify deferred tax assets as current assets.

Offset

An enterprise should offset current tax assets and current tax liabilities if it has a legally enforceable right of set off and it intends to settle on a net basis. A legally enforceable right to set off normally exists when they relate to income taxes levied by the same taxation authority.

In consolidated accounts, a group offset is only allowed if there is a legally enforceable right to make or receive a single net payment and the enterprises intend to carry that out.

Deferred tax assets and deferred tax liabilities should be offset if the enterprise has a legally enforceable right of set off of current tax assets against current tax liabilities and the deferred tax assets and liabilities relate to income taxes levied by the same taxation authority.

Detailed scheduling may be required to establish reliably, whether the deferred tax liability of one taxable entity will result in increased tax payments in the same period in which a deferred tax asset of another taxable entity will result in decreased payments by that second taxable entity.

Tax expense

The tax expense or income should be presented on the face of the income statement. Where exchange differences on deferred foreign tax liabilities or assets are recognised in the income statement these may be classified as deferred tax expenses or incomes if that presentation is considered to be the most useful to users.

Disclosure

The major components of the tax expense or income should be disclosed separately. This may include the following:

(a)   Current tax expense or income.
(b)   Adjustments for current tax of prior periods.
(c)   The amount of deferred tax expense or income relating to the origination and reversal of temporary differences.
(d)   The amount of deferred tax expense or income caused by changes in tax rates.
(e)   The amount of the benefit arising from a previously unrecognised tax loss, tax credit or temporary difference of a prior period used to reduce current tax expense.
(f)   The amount of the benefit from a previously unrecognised tax loss, tax credit or temporary difference of a prior period used to reduce deferred tax expense.
(g)   Deferred tax expense arising from the write-down or reversal of previous write-down of a deferred tax asset.
(h)   The tax expense or income relating to changes in accounting policies/fundamental errors.

The following should also be disclosed separately:

(a)   The aggregate current and deferred tax charged directly to equity.
(b)   The tax expense or income related to extraordinary items.
(c)   An explanation of the relationship between tax expense and accounting profit via a numerical reconciliation between tax expense and the accounting profit multiplied by the current applicable tax rate or a reconciliation between the average effective tax rate and the applicable tax rate.

(d)   An explanation of changes in applicable tax rates compared to previous years.
(e)   The amount of deductible temporary differences, unused tax losses and so on for which no deferred tax asset is recognised.
(f)   The aggregate amount of temporary differences associated with subsidiaries and so on for which no deferred tax liabilities have not been recognised.
(g)   For each type of temporary difference:

  (i)   the amount of deferred tax assets/liabilities recognised in the balance sheet and
  (ii) the amount of deferred tax income/expense recognised in the income statement.

(h)   For discontinued operations the tax expense relating to:
  (i)   the gain or loss on discontinuance and
  (ii) the profit or loss from ordinary activities of discontinued activities together with corresponding amounts.

The enterprise should disclose the amount of a deferred tax asset and the nature of evidence supporting its recognition when:

(a)   The utilisation of the deferred tax asset is dependent on future taxable profits in excess of profits arising from the reversal of existing taxable temporary differences.
(b)   The enterprise has suffered a loss in either the current or preceding period.
(c)   The tax jurisdiction to which the deferred tax asset relates.

Example

In 19 × 2 an enterprise has an accounting profit of 1,500 in country A (19 × 1: 2,000) and in country B 1,500 (19 × 1: 500). The tax rate is 30% in country A and 20% in country B. In country A, expenses of 100 (19 × 1: 200) are not deductible for tax purposes.

Reconciliation of domestic tax rate:

		19 × 1	19 × 2	
Accounting profit	(2,000 + 500)	2,500	3,000	(1,500 + 1,500)
Tax at domestic rate of 30%		750	900	
Tax effect of expenses that are non-deductible for tax	(200 × 30%)	60	30	(100 × 30%)
Effect of lower tax rates in country B	(500 × 10%)	(50)	(150)	(1500 × 10%)
Tax expense		760	780	

Reconciliation for each national jurisdiction:

		19 × 1	19 × 2	
Accounting profit Tax at domestic rates applicable to profits in the country concerned	(2,000 × 30%)			(1,500 × 30%)
	(500 × 20%)	700	750	(1,500 × 20%)
Tax effect of expenses that are non-deductible for tax		60	30	
Tax expense		760	780	

Effective date

IAS 12 became operable for accounting periods starting on or after 1 January 1998.

Illustrative disclosure

A typical example of good taxation disclosure is provided by Enterprise Inns Plc. It includes a short accounting policy note covering both current and deferred tax policies. In addition, Note 11 backs up the overall charge to the income statement, the amount of tax included in equity, provides a tax reconciliation and backs up the balance sheet deferred tax liability.

Enterprise Inns Plc   Year Ended 30 September 2007

Extracts from notes to the accounts

Accounting Policy

Taxation

The income tax expense comprises both the income tax payable based on taxable profits for the year and deferred tax. Deferred tax is provided using the balance sheet liability method in respect of temporary differences between the carrying value of assets and liabilities for accounting and tax purposes. Deferred tax assets are recognised to the extent that it is probable that future taxable profits will be available against which the asset can be utilised. No deferred tax is recognised if the taxable temporary difference arises from goodwill or the initial recognition of an asset or liability in a transaction that is not a business combination and, at the time of the transaction, affects neither the accounting profit nor taxable profit or loss.

Current tax assets and liabilities are offset where there is a legally enforceable right to set off the recognised amounts and the intention is to either settle on a net basis or realise the asset and liability simultaneously. Deferred tax assets and liabilities are offset where there is a legally enforceable right to offset current tax assets and liabilities and the assets and liabilities relate to taxes levied by the same tax authority which are intended to be settled net or simultaneously.

Both current and deferred tax are recognised in the Income Statement except when it relates to items recognised directly in equity, in which case the corresponding tax is also recognised in equity. Tax is calculated using tax rates enacted or substantively enacted at the balance sheet date.

11. Taxation

(a) Total tax expense recognised in the Group Income Statement

	2007			2006		
	Pre-exceptional items	Exceptional items	Total	Pre-exceptional items	Exceptional items	Total
Current tax	£m	£m	£m	£m	£m	£m
UK corporation tax	79	–	79	82	(1)	81
Adjustments in respect of prior years	4	–	4	(3)	–	(3)
Total current tax	83	–	83	79	(1)	78
Deferred tax						
Origination and reversal of temporary differences (Note 11c)	11	(39)	(28)	16	(4)	12
Adjustments in respect of prior years	(9)	–	(9)	–	–	–
Total deferred tax	2	(39)	(37)	16	(4)	12
Taxation (Note 11b)	85	(39)	46	95	(5)	90

(b) Tax charge reconciliation

	2007			2006		
	Pre-exceptional items	Exceptional items	Total	Pre-exceptional items	Exceptional items	Total
	£m	£m	£m	£m	£m	£m
Profit before tax	301	36	337	315	100	415
Tax at 30% on profit on ordinary activities before taxation (2006: 30%)	90	11	101	94	30	124
Effects of:						
Expenses not deductible for tax purposes	1	1	2	4	–	4

Indexation on property disposals	–	(4)	(4)	–	(14)	(14)
Reduction in deferred tax liability due to indexation	–	(24)	(24)	–	(21)	(21)
Adjustments in respect of prior years	(5)	–	(5)	(3)	–	(3)
Re-statement of deferred tax for change in UK tax rate	–	(23)	(23)	–	–	–
Movement in deferred tax balances during the year at 28%	(1)	–	(1)	–	–	–
Total tax charge in the Income Statement	85	(39)	46	95	(5)	90

(c) Deferred tax recognised in the Group Income Statement

	2007			2006		
	Pre-exceptional items £m	Exceptional items £m	Total £m	Pre-exceptional items £m	Exceptional items £m	Total £m
Accelerated capital allowances	9	–	9	8	–	8
Deferred tax on movement in fair value of interest rates swaps	–	6	6	9	12	21
Utilisation of tax losses	–	–	–	3	–	3
Temporary differences	3	–	3	(4)	–	(4)
Deferred tax on share schemes	(1)	–	(1)	–	–	–
Deferred tax on profit on sale of property	–	6	6	–	18	18
Reduction in deferred tax liability due to indexation	–	(28)	(28)	–	(34)	(34)

Re-statement of deferred tax balances for change in UK tax rate	–	**(23)**	**(23)**	–	–	–

	<u>11</u>	<u>(39)</u>	<u>(28)</u>	<u>16</u>	<u>(4)</u>	<u>12</u>

(d) Tax recognised directly in equity

	2007 £m	2006 £m
Increase in deferred tax liability related to revaluation of property and rolled over gains	**75**	91
Deferred tax relating to share schemes credited to equity	**(3)**	(5)
Movement in deferred tax relating to gains on cash flow hedges	**2**	–
Deferred tax relating to gain on defined benefit pension scheme	**1**	–
Re-statement of deferred tax balances for change in UK tax rate	**(24)**	–
Tax charge in the statement of recognised income and expense	**51**	86

25. Deferred Tax

The deferred tax in the Group Balance Sheet relates to the following:

	2007 £m	2006 £m
Unrealised surplus on revaluation of property	**550**	541
Rolled over gains	**71**	68
Accelerated capital allowances	**102**	98
Fair value of interest rate swaps	**(4)**	(12)
Share-based payments	**(6)**	(8)
Pension scheme	**1**	–
Other temporary differences	**(3)**	5
	711	692

The Group has not provided deferred tax in relation to temporary differences associated with undistributed earnings of subsidiaries on the basis that under current enacted law, no tax is payable on dividends payable and receivable within the Group.

SIC 21 *Income Taxes – Recovery of Revalued Non-Depreciable Assets* (June 2000)

Issue

Under IAS 12, the measurement of deferred tax liabilities and assets should reflect the tax consequences that would follow from the manner in which the entity expects, at the balance sheet date, to recover or settle the carrying amount of those assets and liabilities that give rise to temporary differences.

IAS 20 notes that revaluation does not always affect taxable profit in the period of revaluation and that the tax base of the asset may not be adjusted as a result of the revaluation. If the future recovery of the carrying value will be taxable, any difference between carrying amount of the revalued asset and its tax base is a temporary difference and gives rise to a deferred tax liability or asset.

The issue is how to interpret the term 'recovery' in relation to an asset that is not depreciated and is revalued under IAS 16. It also applies to investment properties.

Consensus

The deferred tax liability or asset that arises from the revaluation of a non-depreciable asset under IAS 16 should be measured based on the tax consequences that would follow from recovery of the carrying amount of that asset through sale. That is, regardless of the basis of measuring the carrying amount of that asset. Thus, if the tax law specifies a tax rate applicable to the taxable amount derived from the sale of an asset that differs from the tax rate applicable to the taxable amount derived from using the asset, the former rate is applied in measuring the deferred tax liability or asset related to a non-depreciable asset.

Effective date

The SIC became effective from 15 July 2000.

SIC 25 Income Taxes – Changes in the Tax Status of an Enterprise or its Shareholders (June 2000)

Issue

A change in tax status of an entity or of its shareholders may have consequences for an entity by increasing or decreasing its tax liabilities or assets. This may occur on the public listing of an entity's equity instruments or upon the restructuring of an entity's equity. It may also occur upon a controlling shareholder's move to a foreign country. As a result of such an event, an entity may be taxed differently; it may, e.g. gain or lose tax incentives or become subject to a different rate of tax in the future.

A change in the tax status of an entity or its shareholders may have an immediate effect on the entity's current tax liabilities or assets. The change may also increase or decrease the deferred tax liabilities and assets recognised by the entity, depending on the effect the change in tax status has on the tax consequences that will arise from recovering or settling the carrying amount of the entity's assets and liabilities.

The issue is how an entity should account for the tax consequences of a change in its tax status or that of its shareholders.

Consensus

A change in tax status does not give rise to increase or decrease in amounts recognised directly in equity. The current and deferred tax consequences of a change in tax status should be included in net profit/loss for the period, unless those consequences relate to transactions and events that result, in the same or a different period, in a direct credit/ charge to equity. Those tax consequences that relate to a change in equity in the same or a different period should be charged or credited directly to equity.

Effective date

The SIC became effective on 15 July 2000.

Index